"Great reading for a tough exam. This book is an excellent introduction to the world of Cisco routers. ... The author's writing style is approachable and light, making the often tough topic easy to learn. ... The plethora of network-activity traces really elucidates certain concepts, especially for those who've dealt with trace analysis before. The questions included at the end of each chapter were very helpful in studying and reviewing the material just read."

From Bookpool.com
Remek Kocz, Network Administrator
Rochester, New York

"This is probably the best (single) source to study from for the CCNA exam. It is easy to follow and covers all the topics."

From Fatbrain.com
phl@cce.org

"A must for professionals wanting to learn about Cisco routers. I have gone through Todd Lammle's book a couple of times before certifying, and countless times afterwards to review and pick up additional detail. It is fantastic. He has put together excellent sections discussing the theory and then shows you how to actually do the work.

"To top if off, I took one of his classes later. He not only knows the information, but knows how to present it for ease of learning. I have never had information given to me in such a smooth manner and retained it so well."

From Bookpool.com
Russell Kaufmann, Ph.D., MCSE+I, MCT, CCNA
Denver, Colorado

"Like talking to a Buddy. This was a very good book and very easy to read. ... [It] gives very good information, and isn't as dry as those 'other' books. Todd Lammle knows exactly when to throw in little analogies and jokes that help the learning process along. I played with routers very little while studying for this exam, but the book does an excellent job teaching the commands and theory behind the networking. The end-of-chapter exercises are very helpful in making sure the concepts are learned, but sometimes do ask for nit picky things (but hey, so does Cisco in those exams!)"

From Amazon.com
Roy Valdez Jr. from Houston, Texas

"[The *CCNA: Cisco Certified Network Associate Study Guide*] is a focused and well-integrated study guide with a strong emphasis on Cisco hardware configuration, troubleshooting, and integration. Each chapter has review questions along with tables and figures that support specific topic discussions."

Fatbrain.com Review

CCNA
Cisco Certified
Network Associate
Study Guide

CCNA™
Cisco® Certified Network Associate
Study Guide
Second Edition

Todd Lammle

San Francisco • Paris • Düsseldorf • Soest • London

SYBEX

Associate Publisher: Neil Edde
Contracts and Licensing Manager: Kristine O'Callaghan
Acquisitions & Developmental Editor: Linda Lee
Editors: Susan Berge, Sally Engelfried, Rebecca Rider, and Marilyn Smith
Production Editor: Lisa Duran
Technical Editors: Patrick Ramseier and Eric Gunnett
Book Designer: Bill Gibson
Graphic Illustrator: Tony Jonick
Electronic Publishing Specialist: Maureen Forys, Happenstance Type-O-Rama
Proofreaders: Molly Glover, Jennifer Campbell, Laurie O'Connell, and Camera Obscura
Indexer: Matthew Spence
CD Coordinator: Kara Schwartz
CD Technician: Keith McNeil
Cover Designer: Archer Design
Cover Photographer: Tony Stone

SYBEX and the SYBEX logo are trademarks of SYBEX Inc. in the USA and other countries.

The CD interface was created using Macromedia Director, COPYRIGHT 1994, 1997-1999 Macromedia Inc. For more information on Macromedia and Macromedia Director, visit http://www.macromedia.com.

This study guide and/or material is not sponsored by, endorsed by or affiliated with Cisco Systems, Inc. Catalyst®, Cisco®, Cisco Systems®, Cisco® IOS, Cisco Systems Networkng Academy™, CCDA™, CCNA™, CCDP™, CCNP™, CCIE™, CCSI™, the Cisco Systems logo and the CCIE logo are trademarks or registered trademarks of Cisco Systems, Inc. in the United States and certain other countries. All other trademarks are trademarks of their respective owners.

TRADEMARKS: SYBEX has attempted throughout this book to distinguish proprietary trademarks from descriptive terms by following the capitalization style used by the manufacturer.

The author and publisher have made their best efforts to prepare this book, and the content is based upon final release software whenever possible. Portions of the manuscript may be based upon pre-release versions supplied by software manufacturer(s). The author and the publisher make no representation or warranties of any kind with regard to the completeness or accuracy of the contents herein and accept no liability of any kind including but not limited to performance, merchantability, fitness for any particular purpose, or any losses or damages of any kind caused or alleged to be caused directly or indirectly from this book.

Library of Congress Card Number: 00-102850

ISBN: 0-7821-2647-2

Manufactured in the United States of America

10 9 8 7 6 5 4 3 2 1

This book is dedicated to all the Cisco Academy instructors, the unsung heroes of the training industry. They work very hard, are extremely dedicated, and make little money teaching. Their reward is the students progressing, learning, and becoming all they can be. I salute you.

Acknowledgments

Creating the Acknowledgments is the most difficult part of the book-writing process. Without the help and support of many different individuals, this book, or any other book for that matter, would never be written. So, how can someone actually take a few paragraphs and thank and acknowledge everyone involved? I will give it a try anyway.

The person I want to thank and acknowledge first is Linda Lee. She is an incredible developmental editor and really helped me develop this book's outline. I am very happy that she was involved in the process. She worked hard on this book, and the reader now gets to reap the rewards of her labor.

Neil Edde is always a shoo-in for appearing in the acknowledgments of all my books. Without Neil, I would not have written the first CCNA book, or even my first Sybex book. He was my first developmental editor, and Linda needs to thank him for working out most of my kinks before he pushed me over to her.

Susan Berge and Lisa Duran did a great job of keeping up with the schedule and worked very hard with me to get this book shipped on time. For that, I thank them. Kudos to Patrick Ramseier and Eric Gunnett, who did a fabulous job of reviewing each chapter for technical accuracy. Thanks also to Sally Engelfried, Marilyn Smith, and Rebecca Rider for assisting with the editing of the chapters, and to Molly Glover, Jennifer Campbell, Laurie O'Connell, and Camera Obscura for proofreading the book. In addition, Maureen Forys deserves a thank you for putting the finishing touches on the book. And I don't want to forget Tony Jonick. He is the artist who had to put up with my changing the figures in this book over and over again. He is very patient and does a fantastic job.

Contents at a Glance

Contents

Introduction

Welcome to the exciting world of Cisco certification! You have picked up this book because you want something better; namely, a better job with more satisfaction. Rest assured that you have made a good decision. Cisco certification can help you get your first networking job, or more money and a promotion if you are already in the field.

Cisco certification can also improve your understanding of the internetworking of more than just Cisco products: You will develop a complete understanding of networking and how different network topologies work together to form a network. This is beneficial to every networking job and is the reason Cisco certification is in such high demand, even at companies with few Cisco devices.

Cisco is the king of routing and switching, the Microsoft of the internetworking world. The new Cisco certifications reach beyond the popular certifications, such as the MCSE and CNE, to provide you with an indispensable factor in understanding today's network—insight into the Cisco world of internetworking. By deciding that you want to become Cisco certified, you are saying that you want to be the best—the best at routing and the best at switching. This book can lead you in that direction.

Cisco—A Brief History

A lot of readers may already be familiar with Cisco and what they do. However, those of you who are new to the field, just coming in fresh from your MCSE, and those of you who maybe have 10 or more years in the field but wish to brush up on the new technology may appreciate a little background on Cisco.

In the early 1980s, Len and Sandy Bosack, a married couple who worked in different computer departments at Stanford University, were having trouble getting their individual systems to communicate (like many married people). So in their living room they created a gateway server that made it easier for their disparate computers in two different departments to communicate using the IP protocol. In 1984, they founded cisco Systems (notice the small *c*) with a small commercial gateway server product that changed networking forever. Some people think the name was intended to be San Francisco Systems but the paper got ripped on the way to the incorporation lawyers—who knows? In 1992, the company name was changed to Cisco Systems, Inc.

The first product the company marketed was called the Advanced Gateway Server (AGS). Then came the Mid-Range Gateway Server (MGS), the Compact Gateway Server (CGS), the Integrated Gateway Server (IGS), and the AGS+. Cisco calls these "the old alphabet soup products."

In 1993, Cisco came out with the amazing 4000 router and then created the even more amazing 7000, 2000, and 3000 series routers. These are still around and evolving (almost daily, it seems).

Cisco has since become an unrivaled worldwide leader in networking for the Internet. Its networking solutions can easily connect users who work from diverse devices on disparate networks. Cisco products make it simple for people to access and transfer information without regard to differences in time, place, or platform.

In the big picture, Cisco provides end-to-end networking solutions that customers can use to build an efficient, unified information infrastructure of their own or to connect to someone else's. This is an important piece in the Internet/networking–industry puzzle because a common architecture that delivers consistent network services to all users is now a functional imperative. Because Cisco Systems offers such a broad range of networking and Internet services and capabilities, users needing regular access to their local network or the Internet can do so unhindered, making Cisco's wares indispensable.

Cisco answers this need with a wide range of hardware products that form information networks using the Cisco Internetwork Operating System (IOS) software. This software provides network services, paving the way for networked technical support and professional services to maintain and optimize all network operations.

Along with the Cisco IOS, one of the services Cisco created to help support the vast amount of hardware it has engineered is the Cisco Certified Internetwork Expert (CCIE) program, which was designed specifically to equip people to effectively manage the vast quantity of installed Cisco networks. The business plan is simple: If you want to sell more Cisco equipment and have more Cisco networks installed, ensure that the networks you install run properly.

However, having a fabulous product line isn't all it takes to guarantee the huge success that Cisco enjoys—lots of companies with great products are now defunct. If you have complicated products designed to solve complicated problems, you need knowledgeable people who are fully capable of installing, managing, and troubleshooting them. That part isn't easy, so Cisco began the CCIE program to equip people to support these complicated networks. This program, known colloquially as the Doctorate of Networking, has also been very successful, primarily due to its extreme difficulty. Cisco continuously monitors the program, changing it as it sees fit, to make sure that it remains pertinent and accurately reflects the demands of today's internetworking business environments.

Building upon the highly successful CCIE program, Cisco Career Certifications permit you to become certified at various levels of technical proficiency, spanning the disciplines of network design and support. So, whether you're beginning a career, changing careers, securing your present position, or seeking to refine and promote your position, this is the book for you!

Cisco's Network Support Certifications

Cisco has created new certifications that will help you get the coveted CCIE, as well as aid prospective employers in measuring skill levels. Before these new certifications, you took only one test and were then faced with the lab, which made it difficult to succeed. With these new certifications, which add a better approach to preparing for that almighty lab, Cisco has opened doors that few were allowed through before. So, what are these new certifications and how do they help you get your CCIE?

Cisco Certified Network Associate (CCNA) 2

The CCNA certification is the first in the new line of Cisco certifications, and it is a precursor to all current Cisco certifications. With the new certification programs, Cisco has created a type of stepping-stone approach to CCIE certification. Now, you can become a Cisco Certified Network Associate for the meager cost of this book, plus $100 for the test. And you don't have to stop there—you can choose to continue with your studies and achieve a higher certification, called the Cisco Certified Network Professional (CCNP). Someone with a CCNP has all the skills and knowledge he or she needs to attempt the CCIE lab. However, because no textbook can take the place of practical experience, we'll discuss what else you need to be ready for the CCIE lab shortly.

Why Become a CCNA?

Cisco, not unlike Microsoft or Novell, has created the certification process to give administrators a set of skills and to equip prospective employers with a way to measure skills or match certain criteria. Becoming a CCNA can be the initial step of a successful journey toward a new, highly rewarding, and sustainable career.

The CCNA program was created to provide a solid introduction not only to the Cisco Internetwork Operating System (IOS) and Cisco hardware, but also to internetworking in general, making it helpful to you in areas that are not exclusively Cisco's. At this point in the certification process, it's not unrealistic to imagine that future network managers—even those without Cisco equipment—could easily require Cisco certifications for their job applicants.

If you make it through the CCNA and are still interested in Cisco and internetworking, you're headed down a path to certain success.

What Skills Do You Need to Become a CCNA?

To meet the CCNA certification skill level, you must be able to understand or do the following:

- Install, configure, and operate simple-routed LAN, routed WAN, and switched LAN and LANE networks.

- Understand and be able to configure IP, IGRP, IPX, serial, AppleTalk, Frame Relay, IP RIP, VLANs, IPX RIP, Ethernet, and access lists.

- Install and/or configure a network.

- Optimize WAN through Internet-access solutions that reduce bandwidth and WAN costs, using features such as filtering with access lists, bandwidth on demand (BOD), and dial-on-demand routing (DDR).

- Provide remote access by integrating dial-up connectivity with traditional, remote LAN-to-LAN access, as well as supporting the higher levels of performance required for new applications such as Internet commerce, multimedia, etc.

How Do You Become a CCNA?

The first step to becoming a CCNA is to pass one little test and—poof!—you're a CCNA. (Don't you wish it were that easy?) True, it's just one test, but you still have to possess enough knowledge to understand (and read between the lines—trust me) what the test writers are saying.

I can't stress this enough—it's critical that you have some hands-on experience with Cisco routers. If you can get ahold of some 2500 routers, you're set. But if you can't, we've worked hard to provide hundreds of configuration examples throughout this book to help network administrators (or people who want to become network administrators) learn what they need to know to pass the CCNA exam.

One way to get the hands-on router experience you'll need in the real world is to attend one of the seminars offered by Globalnet Training Solutions, Inc., which is owned and run by me. The seminars are six days long and will teach you everything you need to become a CCNA and even a CCNP. Each student gets hands-on experience by configuring at least two routers and a switch. See www.lammle.com for more information.

In addition, Cyberstate University provides hands-on Cisco router courses over the Internet using the Sybex Cisco Certification series books. Go to www.cyberstateu.com for more information. And Keystone Learning Systems (www.klscorp.com) offers the popular Cisco video certification series featuring me.

If you are new to networking, you should take a look at *CCNA JumpStart* by Patrick Ciccarelli and Christina Faulkner (Sybex, 1999). This book will give you the background necessary before jumping into more advanced networking with Cisco routers.

Check out this book's CD for a demo of the Sybex *CCNA Virtual Lab e-trainer*, which can give you hands-on experience working with both routers and switches. You can also check out www.routersim.com for another router simulator.

In addition to this book, there are other useful ways to supplement your studies for the CCNA exam. CiscoTests (http://www.networkstudyguides.com) offers an online study guide with sample questions and information about the most current release of the CCNA, CCNP, and CCIE exams.

For the best practice Cisco exam questions on the market, try www.boson.com.

Cisco Certified Network Professional (CCNP)

Cisco Certified Network Professional (CCNP), Cisco's new certification, has opened up many opportunities for those individuals wishing to become Cisco-certified but lacking the training, the expertise, or the bucks to pass the notorious and often failed two-day Cisco torture lab. The new Cisco certifications will truly provide exciting new opportunities for the CNE and MCSE who are unsure of how to advance to a higher level.

So, you're thinking, "Great, what do I do after passing the CCNA exam?" Well, if you want to become a CCIE in Routing and Switching (the most popular certification), understand that there's more than one path to that much-coveted CCIE certification. The first way is to continue studying and become a Cisco Certified Network Professional (CCNP), which means four more tests, in addition to the CCNA certification.

The CCNP program will prepare you to understand and comprehensively tackle the internetworking issues of today and beyond—and it is not limited to the Cisco world. You will undergo an immense metamorphosis, vastly increasing your knowledge and skills through the process of obtaining these certifications.

While you don't need to be a CCNP or even a CCNA to take the CCIE lab, it's extremely helpful if you already have these certifications.

What Skills Do You Need to Become a CCNP?

Cisco demands a certain level of proficiency for its CCNP certification. In addition to mastering the skills required for the CCNA, you should have the following skills for the CCNP:

- Installing, configuring, operating, and troubleshooting complex routed LAN, routed WAN, and switched LAN networks, along with dial-access services

- Understanding complex networks, such as IP, IGRP, IPX, async routing, AppleTalk, extended access lists, IP RIP, route redistribution, IPX RIP, route summarization, OSPF, VLSM, BGP, serial, IGRP, Frame Relay, ISDN, ISL, X.25, DDR, PSTN, PPP, VLANs, Ethernet, ATM LANE–emulation, access lists, 802.10, FDDI, and transparent and translational bridging

To meet the CCNP requirements, you must be able to perform the following:

- Install and/or configure a network to increase bandwidth, quicken network response times, and improve reliability and quality of service.

- Maximize performance through campus LANs, routed WANs, and remote access.

- Improve network security.

- Create a global intranet.

- Provide access security to campus switches and routers.

- Provide increased switching and routing bandwidth—end-to-end resiliency services.

- Provide custom queuing and routed priority services.

How Do You Become a CCNP?

After becoming a CCNA, the four exams you must take to get your CCNP are as follows:

Exam 640-503: Routing   This exam continues to build on the fundamentals learned in the CCNA course. It focuses on large multiprotocol internetworks and how to manage them with access lists, queuing, tunneling, route distribution, route maps, BGP, EIGRP, OSPF, and route summarization.

Exam 640-504: Switching   This exam tests your knowledge of the 1900 and 5000 series of Catalyst switches. The *CCNP: Switching Study Guide* (Sybex, summer 2000) covers all the objectives you need to understand to pass the Switching exam.

Exam 640-506: Support   This tests you on the Cisco troubleshooting skills needed for Ethernet and Token Ring LANs, IP, IPX, and AppleTalk networks, as well as ISDN, PPP, and Frame Relay networks.

Exam 640-505: Remote Access   This exam tests your knowledge of installing, configuring, monitoring, and troubleshooting Cisco ISDN and dial-up access products. You must understand PPP, ISDN, Frame Relay, and authentication. The *CCNP: Remote Access Study Guide* (Sybex, summer 2000) covers all the exam objectives.

If you hate tests, you can take fewer of them by signing up for the CCNA exam and the Support exam and then taking just one more long exam called the Foundation R/S exam (640-509). Doing this also gives you your CCNP—but beware; it's a really long test that fuses all the material listed previously into one exam. Good luck! However, by taking this exam, you get three tests for the price of two, which saves you $100 (if you pass). Some people think it's easier to take the Foundation R/S exam because you can leverage the areas that you would score higher in against the areas in which you wouldn't.

Remember that test objectives and tests can change at any time without notice. Always check the Cisco Web site for the most up-to-date information (www.cisco.com).

Cisco Certified Internetwork Expert (CCIE)

You've become a CCNP, and now you fix your sights on getting your Cisco Certified Internetwork Expert CCIE in Routing and Switching—what do you do next? Cisco recommends that before you take the lab, you take test 640-025: Cisco Internetwork Design (CID) and the Cisco-authorized course called Installing and Maintaining Cisco Routers (IMCR). By the way, no Prometric test for IMCR exists at the time of this writing, and Cisco recommends a *minimum* of two years of on-the-job experience before taking the CCIE lab. After jumping those hurdles, you then have to pass the CCIE-R/S Exam Qualification (exam 350-001) before taking the actual lab.

How Do You Become a CCIE?

To become a CCIE, Cisco recommends you do the following:

1. Attend all the recommended courses at an authorized Cisco training center and pony up around $15,000–$20,000, depending on your corporate discount.

2. Pass the Drake/Prometric exam ($200 per exam—so hopefully, you'll pass it the first time).

3. Pass the two-day, hands-on lab at Cisco. This costs $1,000 per lab, which many people fail two or more times. (Some never make it

through!) Also, because you can take the exam only in San Jose, California; Research Triangle Park, North Carolina; Sydney, Australia; Halifax, Nova Scotia; Tokyo, Japan; or Brussels, Belgium, you might just need to add travel costs to that $1,000. Cisco has added new sites lately for the CCIE lab; it is best to check the Cisco Web site for the most current information.

What Skills Do You Need to Become a CCIE?

The CCIE Routing and Switching exam includes the advanced technical skills that are required to maintain optimum network performance and reliability, as well as advanced skills in supporting diverse networks that use disparate technologies. CCIEs just don't have problems getting jobs; these experts are basically inundated with offers to work for six-figure salaries. But that's because it isn't easy to attain the level of capability that is mandatory for Cisco's CCIE. For example, a CCIE has the following skills down pat:

- Installing, configuring, operating, and troubleshooting complex routed LAN, routed WAN, switched LAN, and ATM LANE networks, and dial-access services

- Diagnosing and resolving network faults

- Using packet/frame analysis and Cisco debugging tools

- Documenting and reporting the problem-solving processes used

- Having general LAN/WAN knowledge, including data encapsulation and layering; windowing and flow control, and their relation to delay; error detection and recovery; link-state, distance vector, and switching algorithms; management, monitoring, and fault isolation

- Having knowledge of a variety of corporate technologies—including major services provided by Desktop, WAN, and Internet groups—as well as the functions; addressing structures; and routing, switching, and bridging implications of each of their protocols

- Having knowledge of Cisco-specific technologies, including router/switch platforms, architectures, and applications; communication servers; protocol translation and applications; configuration commands and system/network impact; and LAN/WAN interfaces, capabilities, and applications

- Designing, configuring, installing, and verifying voice-over-IP and voice-over-ATM networks

Cisco's Network Design Certifications

In addition to the network support certifications, Cisco has created another certification track for network designers. The two certifications within this track are the Cisco Certified Design Associate and Cisco Certified Design Professional certifications. If you're reaching for the CCIE stars, we highly recommend the CCNP and CCDP certifications before attempting the lab (or attempting to advance your career).

This certification will give you the knowledge to design routed LAN, routed WAN, and switched LAN and ATM LANE networks.

Cisco Certified Design Associate (CCDA)

To become a CCDA, you must pass the DCN (Designing Cisco Networks) exam (640-441). To pass this test, you must understand how to do the following:

- Design simple routed LAN, routed WAN, and switched LAN and ATM LANE networks.

- Use Network-layer addressing.

- Filter with access lists.

- Use and propagate VLAN.

- Size networks.

The Sybex *CCDA: Cisco Certified Design Associate Study Guide* (1999) is the most cost-effective way to study for and pass your CCDA exam.

Cisco Certified Design Professional (CCDP)

If you're already a CCNP and want to get your CCDP, you can simply take the CID 640-025 test. If you're not yet a CCNP, however, you must take the CCDA, CCNA, Routing, Switching, Remote Access, and CID exams.

CCDP certification skills include the following:

- Designing complex routed LAN, routed WAN, and switched LAN and ATM LANE networks

- Building upon the base level of the CCDA technical knowledge

CCDPs must also demonstrate proficiency in the following:

- Network-layer addressing in a hierarchical environment

- Traffic management with access lists

- Hierarchical network design

- VLAN use and propagation

- Performance considerations: required hardware and software; switching engines; memory, cost, and minimization

What Does This Book Cover?

This book covers everything you need to know in order to become CCNA certified. However, taking the time to study and practice with routers or a router simulator is the real key to success.

The information you will learn in this book, and need to know for the CCNA exam, is listed in the following bullet points:

- Chapter 1 introduces you to internetworking. You will learn the basics of the Open Systems Interconnection the way Cisco wants you to learn it. Also, the Cisco three-layer hierarchical model will be discussed, along with how to choose Cisco equipment based on this model. Ethernet networking and standards are discussed in detail in this chapter as well.

- Chapter 2 gives you a background on layer-2 switching and how switches perform address learning and make forwarding and filtering decisions. Network loops and how to avoid them with the Spanning-Tree Protocol (STP) will be discussed, as well as the different LAN switch types used by Cisco switches.

- Chapter 3 provides you with the background necessary for success on the exam as well as in the real world by discussing TCP/IP. This in-depth chapter covers the very beginnings of the Internet Protocol stack and then goes all the way to IP addressing and subnetting. If you read this chapter carefully, you will be able to subnet a network in your head!

- Chapter 4 introduces you to the Cisco Internetwork Operating System (IOS). In this chapter you will learn how to turn on a router and configure the basics of the IOS, including setting passwords, banners, and more. IP configuration will be discussed and a hands-on lab will help you gain a firm grasp of the concepts taught in the chapter.

- Chapter 5 teaches you about IP routing. This is a fun chapter, because you will begin to build your network, add IP addresses, and route data between routers. You will also learn about static, default, and dynamic routing in this chapter. Written and hands-on labs will help you understand IP routing to the fullest.

- Chapter 6 covers Virtual LANs and how you can use them in your internetwork. This chapter also covers the nitty-gritty of VLANs and the different concepts and protocols used with VLANs. Written labs and review questions will reinforce the VLAN material.

- Chapter 7 provides you with the management skills needed to run a Cisco ISO network. Backing up and restoring the IOS, as well as router configuration, is covered, as are troubleshooting tools necessary to keep a network up and running.

- Chapter 8 introduces you to the wonderful world of Novell IPX. Since IPX is still around, Cisco thinks it is important to understand IPX routing. Actually, after IP routing, IPX is a breeze. Both written and hands-on labs, along with review questions, will give you the understanding of IPX you need to pass the CCNA exam.

- Chapter 9 covers access lists, which are created on routers to filter the network. Both IP and IPX access lists are covered in detail. Written and hands-on labs, along with review questions, will help you study for the access-list portion of the CCNA exam.

- Chapter 10 concentrates on Cisco Wide Area Network protocols. This chapter covers HDLC, PPP, Frame Relay, and ISDN in depth. You must be proficient in all these protocols to be successful on the CCNA exam.

- Appendix A is a practice exam. If you think you are ready for the CCNA exam, see if you can get by my practice exam. A second practice exam is located on the CD as well.

- Appendix B discusses configuring a Catalyst 1900 switch. The CCNA exam is mostly theory on layer-2 switching; however, reading the appendix, working through the written and hands-on labs, and answering the review questions should prepare you well for the CCNA exam.

- Appendix C lists all the Cisco IOS commands used in this book. It is a great reference if you need to look up what a certain command does and is used for.

- The Glossary is a handy resource for Cisco terms. This is a great tool for understanding some of the more obscure terms used in this book.

Where Do You Take the Exams?

You may take the exams at any of the more than 800 Sylvan Prometric Authorized Testing Centers around the world. For the location of a testing center near you, call (800) 755-3926. Outside the United States and Canada, contact your local Sylvan Prometric Registration Center.

To register for a Cisco Certified Network Professional exam:

1. Determine the number of the exam you want to take. (The CCNA exam number is 640-507.)

2. Register with the nearest Sylvan Prometric Registration Center. At this point, you will be asked to pay in advance for the exam. At the time of this writing, the exams are $100 each and must be taken within one year of payment. You can schedule exams up to six weeks in advance or as soon as one working day prior to the day you wish to take it. If something comes up and you need to cancel or reschedule your exam appointment, contact Sylvan Prometric at least 24 hours in advance. Same-day registration isn't available for the Cisco tests.

3. When you schedule the exam, you'll get instructions regarding all appointment and cancellation procedures, the ID requirements, and information about the testing-center location.

Tips for Taking Your CCNA Exam

The CCNA test contains about 70 questions to be completed in 90 minutes. You must schedule a test at least 24 hours in advance (unlike the Novell or Microsoft exams), and you aren't allowed to take more than one Cisco exam per day.

Many questions on the exam have answer choices that at first glance look identical—especially the syntax questions! Remember to read through the choices carefully because close doesn't cut it. If you get commands in the wrong order or forget one measly character, you'll get the question wrong. So, to practice, do the hands-on exercises at the end of the chapters over and over again until they feel natural to you.

Unlike Microsoft or Novell tests, the exam has answer choices that are syntactically similar—though some syntax is dead wrong, it is usually just *subtly* wrong. Some other choices may be syntactically correct, but they're shown in the wrong order. Cisco does split hairs, and they're not at all averse to giving you classic trick questions. Here's an example:

`access-list 101 deny ip any eq 23` denies Telnet access to all systems.

This question looks correct because most people refer to the port number (23) and think, "Yes, that's the port used for Telnet." The catch is that you can't filter IP on port numbers (only TCP and UDP).

Also, never forget that the right answer is the Cisco answer. In many cases, more than one appropriate answer is presented, but the *correct* answer is the one that Cisco recommends.

Here are some general tips for exam success:

- Arrive early at the exam center, so you can relax and review your study materials.

- Read the questions *carefully*. Don't jump to conclusions. Make sure you're clear about *exactly* what each question asks.

- When answering multiple-choice questions that you're not sure about, use the process of elimination to get rid of the obviously incorrect answers first. Doing this greatly improves your odds if you need to make an educated guess.

- You can no longer move forward and backward through the Cisco exams, so double-check your answer before pressing Next since you can't change your mind.

After you complete an exam, you'll get immediate, online notification of your pass or fail status, a printed Examination Score Report that indicates your pass or fail status, and your exam results by section. (The test administrator will give you the printed score report.) Test scores are automatically forwarded to Cisco within five working days after you take the test, so you don't need to send your score to them. If you pass the exam, you'll receive confirmation from Cisco, typically within two to four weeks.

How to Use This Book

This book can provide a solid foundation for the serious effort of preparing for the Cisco Certified Network Associate (CCNA) exam. To best benefit from this book, use the following study method:

1. Take the assessment test immediately following this introduction. (The answers are at the end of the test.) Carefully read over the explanations for any question you get wrong and note which chapters the material comes from. This information should help you plan your study strategy.

2. Study each chapter carefully, making sure that you fully understand the information and the test topics listed at the beginning of each chapter. Pay extra-close attention to any chapter where you missed questions in the assessment test.

3. Complete all hands-on exercises in the chapter, referring to the chapter so that you understand the reason for each step you take. If you do not have Cisco equipment available, be sure to study the examples carefully. Also, check www.routersim.com for a router simulator.

4. Answer the review questions related to that chapter. (The answers appear at the end of the chapter.) Note the questions that confuse you and study those sections of the book again.

5. Take the practice exam in Appendix A. The answers appear at the end of the exam.

6. Try your hand at the bonus practice exam that is included on the CD that comes with this book. The questions in this exam appear only on the CD. This will give you a complete overview of what you can expect to see on the real thing.

7. Remember to use the products on the CD included with this book. The electronic flashcards, the Boson Software utilities, and the EdgeTest exam preparation software have all been specifically chosen to help you study for and pass your exam. You can also study on the road with the *CCNA Study Guide* electronic book in PDF format.

The electronic flashcards can be used on your Windows computer or on your Palm device.

8. Make sure you read the "Key Terms" and "Commands in This Chapter" lists at the end of the chapters. Appendix C is a copy of all commands used in the book, including explanations for each command.

To learn all the material covered in this book, you'll have to apply yourself regularly and with discipline. Try to set aside the same time period every day to study, and select a comfortable and quiet place to do so. If you work hard, you will be surprised at how quickly you learn this material. All the best!

What's on the CD?

We worked hard to provide some really great tools to help you with your certification process. All of the following tools should be loaded on your workstation when studying for the test.

The EdgeTest Test Preparation Software

The test preparation software, provided by EdgeTek Learning Systems, prepares you to pass the CCNA exam. In this test engine you will find all the questions from the book, plus an additional bonus practice exam that appears exclusively on the CD. You can take the assessment test, test yourself by chapter, take the practice exam that appears in the book or on the CD, or take a randomly generated exam comprising all the questions.

To find more test-simulation software for all Cisco and NT exams, look for the exam link on www.lammle.com and www.boson.com.

Electronic Flashcards for PC and Palm Devices

To prepare for the exam, you can read this book, study the review questions at the end of each chapter, and work through the practice exams included in the book and on the CD. But wait, there's more! Test yourself with the flashcards included on the CD. If you can get through these difficult questions and understand the answers, you'll know you're ready for the CCNA exam.

The flashcards include over 200 questions specifically written to hit you hard and make sure you are ready for the exam. Between the review questions, practice exams, and flashcards, you'll be more than prepared for the exam.

CCNA Study Guide in PDF

Sybex offers the *CCNA Study Guide* in PDF format on the CD so you can read the book on your PC or laptop. This will be helpful to readers who travel and don't want to carry a book, as well as to readers who prefer to read from their computer. (Acrobat Reader 4 is also included on the CD.)

Dictionary of Networking in PDF

As a bonus, you get a second complete book—the *Sybex Dictionary of Networking*, by Peter Dyson—on the CD included with this book. Like the electronic version of the *CCNA Study Guide*, the fully searchable *Dictionary of Networking* is in PDF for ease of use. You will also find Adobe Acrobat 4 with Search on the CD to access the PDF book. This dictionary will help you understand terms found in this book or networking terms found in any book for that matter.

Boson Software Utilities

Boson.com is an impressive company: They provide many free services to help you, the student. Boson.com has the best Cisco exam preparation questions on the market at a very nice price. On this book's CD, they have provided the following:

- Practice exam

- IP Subnetter

- eeSuperPing

- System-Logging

- Wildcard Mask Checker

CCNA Virtual Lab AVI Demo Files

The *CCNA Virtual Lab e-trainer* provides a router and switch simulator to help you gain hands-on experience without having to buy expensive Cisco gear. The AVI demo files on the CD will help you gain an understanding of the product features and the labs that the routers and switches can perform. Read more about the *CCNA Virtual Lab e-trainer* at http://www.sybex .com/cgi-bin/rd_bookpg.pl?2728back.html. You can upgrade this product at www.routersim.com.

How to Contact the Author

You can reach Todd Lammle through Globalnet System Solutions, Inc. (www.lammle.com)—his training and systems integration company in Colorado—or e-mail him at todd@lammle.com.

Assessment Test

1. Where would a router boot from if a configuration register was set to 0x0101?

   A. Flash

   B. ROM

   C. Boot ROM

   D. NVRAM

2. Which of the following is a valid SAP filter 1010 placed on Ethernet 0?

   A. `ip access-group 1010 in`

   B. `ip access-group 1010 out`

   C. `ipx access-group 1010 in`

   D. `ipx input-sap-filter 1010`

   E. `ipx input-sap-filter 1010 in`

3. What is a TE2 device used for in an ISDN connection?

   A. Connecting an NT2 device to a U reference point

   B. Connecting an S/T interface to a U reference point

   C. Connecting a non-ISDN terminal to ISDN through a TA

   D. Connecting to ISDN through a four-wire, twisted-pair digital link

4. What is the correct command to set the router identification to the name Atlanta, which an administrator would see when connecting with Telnet or through the console?

   A. `Description Atlanta Router`

   B. `Banner Motd $`

   C. `Hostname Atlanta`

   D. `Host name Atlanta`

   E. `Set prompt Atlanta`

5. PDUs at the Data Link layer are named what?

   A. Frames ✓

   B. Packets

   C. Datagrams

   D. Transports

   E. Segments

   F. Bits

6. Which of the following is the valid host range for the IP address
   192.168.168.188 255.255.255.192?

   A. 192.168.168.129–190

   B. 192.168.168.129–191 ✓

   C. 192.168.168.128–190

   D. 192.168.168.128–192

7. What are the access list numbers used for IP standard access lists?

   A. 1–10

   B. 1–99

   C. 100–199 ✓

   D. 1000–1999

8. If you type **show interface serial** 0 and receive the following response,
   what could the problem be?

   ```
   RouterA#sh int s0
   Serial0 is up, line protocol is down
   ```

   A. The keepalives could be set wrong between the point-to-point links.

   B. No cable is attached to the interface.

   C. The administrator needs to issue a no shutdown request to the ✓
      interface.

   D. The interface is defective.

9. Which of the following commands will show you the IPX address of an interface? (Choose all that apply.)

   A. `show ipx address int e0`

   B. `show protocol`

   C. `show ipx protocol`

   D. `show ipx interface`

10. How do you create a default route?

   A. By using all 1s in place of the network and mask

   B. By defining a static route and using all 0s in place of the network and mask

   C. By using 255 in place of the network and mask

   D. `Login <name, password>`

11. What is a trunked link?

   A. A link that is only part of one VLAN and is referred to as the native VLAN of the port

   B. A link that can carry multiple VLANs

   C. A switch port connected to the Internet

   D. Data and voice capability on the same interface

12. Which protocol is used to look up an IP address from a known Ethernet address?

   A. IP

   B. ARP

   C. RARP

   D. TCP

13. What is the broadcast address of the subnet address 192.168.99.20 255.255.255.252?

   A. 192.168.99.127 ✓

   B. 192.168.99.63

   C. 192.168.99.23

   D. 192.168.99.31

14. What is the valid host range that the host ID 192.168.10.33 255.255.255.224 is a part of?

   A. 192.168.10.32–63

   B. 192.168.10.33–63 ✓

   C. 192.168.10.33–62

   D. 192.168.10.33–61

15. What does a switch do with a multicast frame received on an interface?

   A. Forwards the switch to the first available link

   B. Drops the frame

   C. Floods the network with the frame looking for the device ✓

   D. Sends back a message to the originating station asking for a name resolution

16. Which command would you use to see the IPX RIP packets being sent and received on an interface?

   A. show ip rip

   B. sh ipx int

   C. debug ipx routing activity

   D. debug ipx interface ✓

17. What is the subnet address of the IP address 192.168.100.30
255.255.255.248?

   A. 192.168.100.32

   B. 192.168.100.24

   C. 192.168.100.0

   D. 192.168.100.16 ✓

18. What is an access link?

   A. A link that is only part of one VLAN and is referred to as the native
   VLAN of the port

   B. A link that can carry multiple VLANs

   C. A switch port connected to the Internet ✓

   D. Data and voice capability on the same interface

19. Which of the following is true? (Choose all that apply.)

   A. PPP can be used with Token Ring.

   B. PPP can be used with synchronous serial links.

   C. PPP can be used with asynchronous serial links.

   D. PPP is proprietary to each vendor's equipment.

20. What command can you use to back up the Cisco router configuration
to a TFTP host?

   A. `copy run tftp`

   B. `copy flash tftp`

   C. `copy nvram startup`

   D. `copy tftp flash`

21. Which of the following are provided by the `show cdp entry *` command? (Choose all that apply.)

A. IP address of the neighbor router

B. Protocol information

C. Platform

D. Capability

E. Time

F. Port ID

G. Holdtime

H. The same information as `show version`

I. Neighbor device ID

J. Local interface

K. Speed of the link

22. Which of the following would you not implement at the distribution layer?

A. Access lists

B. Packet filtering

C. Queuing

D. Breakup of collisions domains

E. Address translation

F. Firewalls

G. Creating of broadcast domains

23. Which LAN switch methods have a fixed latency time? (Choose all that apply.)

A. Cut-through

B. Store and forward

C. FragmentCheck

D. FragmentFree

24. If you were designing a network and needed to break up collision domains, at which Cisco layer would you provide this function?

A. Physical

B. Access

C. Core

D. Network

E. Distribution

F. Data Link

25. If you wanted to find out all the commands that start with "cl" from a certain prompt, what would you type at that particular prompt?

A. Show commands cl

B. Cl ?

C. Cl?

D. Cl ? more

26. What does a VLAN do?

A. Breaks up collision domains

B. Breaks up routing domains

C. Breaks up broadcast domains

D. Provides fragmentation segmentation

27. Which of the following will you find in a routing table? (Choose all that apply.)

A. Network address

B. Routing metric

C. Exit interface for packets

D. Entering interface

28. Which command can you use to see which devices have telnetted into your router?

A. show vty line

B. show vers

C. show users

D. show connections

29. What does an administrative distance of 0 mean?

A. 0 is the default administrative distance for dynamic routing.

B. 0 is the default administrative distance for directly connected routes.

C. There is no routing allowed on this router.

D. There are 0 hops to the next destination.

30. Which of the following is a valid IP extended access list?

A. access-list 110 permit ip any host 1.1.1.1 eq ftp

B. access-list 10 permit tcp ip any any eq 21

C. access-list 99 permit udp any host 2.2.2.2 eq ip

D. access-list 199 permit tcp any 0.0.0.0 255.255.255.255 eq 21

31. What is true regarding the blocking state of an STP switch port? (Choose all that apply.)

  A. Blocking ports do not forward any frames.

  B. Blocking ports listen for BPDUs.

  C. Blocking ports forward all frames.

  D. Blocking ports do not listen for BPDUs.

32. What is the default LAN switch type for the 1900 switch?

  A. FastForward

  B. Cut-through

  C. LAN switch type 1

  D. FragmentFree

  E. Store and forward

33. Which of the following is true about the enable passwords? (Choose all that apply.)

  A. The enable password is encrypted by default.

  B. The enable secret is encrypted by default.

  C. The enable-encrypted password should be set first.

  D. The enable password supersedes the enable secret.

  E. The enable secret password supersedes the enable password.

  F. The enable-encrypted password supersedes all other passwords.

34. What is the default administrative distance of RIP?

  A. 1

  B. 100

  C. 120

  D. 150

35. If you are typing commands and receive the following message, what is wrong and how do you fix it? (Choose all that apply.)

```
Router#clock set 10:30:10
% Incomplete command.
```

A. The IOS doesn't support a clock on this router.

B. The command string is not done.

C. Press the up arrow key and type a question mark.

D. Press the down arrow key and the Tab key.

E. Erase what you typed and reboot the router.

36. In the following command, what does the 175 mean?

```
Ip route 150.150.0.0 255.255.0.0 150.150.150.150 175
```

A. It defines the next hop.

B. It defines the administrative distance.

C. It means that the update is broadcast.

D. Nothing, it is an invalid command.

37. What does a router do with a received packet that is destined for an unknown network?

A. Forwards the packet

B. Drops the packet

C. Holds the packet till the next route update

D. Sends a broadcast for the unknown network

38. Which part is the network and which part is the node of the address 7c8.0001.00c8.1234?

A. network: 7c8.0001, node: 00c8.1234

B. network: 7c8, node: 0001.00c8.1234

C. network: 0001.00c8.1234, node: 7c8

D. network: 7c8.0001.00c8, node: 1234

39. What are the two types of PDUs used at the Network layer?

A. Data

B. Route

C. Static

D. Dynamic

E. Core

F. Segments

40. What type of Cisco encapsulation is used for frame tagging across trunked links?

A. Virtual Trunk Protocol (VTP)

B. 802.1q

C. ISL

D. VLANs

41. What does IPX RIP use to find the best path to a remote network? (Choose all that apply.)

A. Bandwidth of a link

B. Hop count

C. Reliability of a link

D. Amount of delay, counted in 1/18 of a second

42. What are the access list numbers for extended access lists?

A. 1–10

B. 1–99

C. 100–199

D. 1000–1999

43. What does the following command mean? `Access-list 110 permit ip any 0.0.0.0 255.255.255.255`

   A. It is a standard IP access list that permits network 0.0.0.0 only.

   B. It is an extended IP access list that permits network 0.0.0.0 only.

   C. It is an extended list that permits any host or network.

   D. It is invalid.

44. What is a static VLAN?

   A. A VLAN that cannot be renamed or removed

   B. A VLAN created by the administrator

   C. Ports on the switch assigned to a VLAN by an administrator

   D. Ports on the switch assigned to a VLAN by a VTP server

45. Which of the following is true regarding the `isdn switch-type` command?

   A. It can be configured only in global configuration mode.

   B. It can be configured only from interface configuration.

   C. It can be configured from either global or interface configuration mode.

   D. It can be used only when you have a TA.

46. If your Frame Relay network is congested, what mechanism is used to tell the source device to slow down?

   A. HDLC

   B. DLCI

   C. FECN

   D. BECN

47. Which of the following is a method used by Frame Relay for addressing PVCs to IP addresses?

   A. ARP

   B. LMI

   C. SLARP

   D. DLCI

48. What are the two ways to add multiple encapsulations on an Ethernet IPX LAN?

   A. Multiple frame types

   B. Secondaries

   C. Subinterfaces

   D. Virtual secondaries

49. What is the typical time a switch port will go from blocking to forwarding state?

   A. 5 seconds

   B. 50 seconds

   C. 10 seconds

   D. 100 seconds

50. How do you telnet from a 1900 switch CLI?

   A. telnet Atlanta.

   B. telnet 172.16.10.1.

   C. ping 172.16.10.1.

   D. You cannot do this on a 1900 CLI.

51. What command will delete the automatically entered MAC addresses in the MAC filter table?

A. (config)#delete nvram

B. #delete nvram

C. (config)#clear mac-address-table dynamic

D. #clear mac-address-table dynamic

52. If you want to completely clear all configurations on a 1900 switch, what commands must you type in? (Choose all that apply.)

A. Clear config

B. Delete nvram

C. Delete vtp

D. Delete start

E. Erase startup-config

F. Just reboot the switch.

53. If you wanted to view the trunk status on port 27 of a 1900 switch, which command would you use?

A. Show port 27

B. Show trunk

C. Show trunk B

D. Show trunk f0/27

E. Show trunk e0/27

54. What would you type at a 1900 console prompt to see the transmit and receive statistics of VTP?

A. Show vtp stat

B. Show stat

C. Sh vtp domain

D. Sh int e0/9

Answers to the Assessment Test

1. B. The configuration register is used to tell the router how to load the IOS and configuration. The value 0x0101 tells the router to boot from ROM. See Chapter 7 for more information about configuration registers.

2. D. To place a SAP filter on an interface, use the command `ipx input-sap-filter 1010` or `ipx output-sap-filter 1010`. See Chapter 9 for more information on IPX SAP filters.

3. D. This is a hard question. The TE2 is a device that does not understand ISDN standards and uses a four-wire connection. The TE2 must connect into a terminal adapter (TA) and then into an NT1 device to be converted to a two-wire network. See Chapter 10 for more information on ISDN.

4. C. The command `hostname` (one word) is used to set the name of the router. For more information on how to set the hostname of a router, see Chapter 4.

5. A. Protocol Data Units are used to describe the function of the headers used at each layer of the OSI model. At the Data Link layer, framing is used to encapsulate the data packet with control information for transmission on a local network. For more information on PDUs, see Chapter 1.

6. A. Start by using 256, the subnet mask, which is 256–192=64. The first subnet is 64. The next subnet would be 128. This host is in the 128 subnet, the broadcast address is 191, and the valid host range is 129 through 190. See Chapter 3 for more information on IP addressing.

7. B. Standard IP access lists use the numbers 1–99. See Chapter 9 for more information about access lists.

8. A. If you see the line is up, but the protocol is down, you are having a clocking (keepalive) or framing issue. Check the keepalives on both ends to make sure they match; the clock rate is set, if needed; and the encapsulation type is the same on both ends. For more information on interface statistics, see Chapter 4.

9. B, D. The commands `show protocol` and `show ipx interface` will show you the IPX addresses of an interface. See Chapter 8 for more information on IPX networking.

10. B. Default routes are created by using all 0s in place of the network and mask IDs. See Chapter 5 for more information on IP routing.

11. B. Trunked links carry multiple VLANs across the same link. For more information on VLANs, please see Chapter 6.

12. C. The protocol at the Network layer that finds an IP address from a known Ethernet address is Reverse ARP (RARP). See Chapter 3 for more information on IP protocols.

13. C. Start by using 256, the subnet mask, which is 256–25=4. The first subnet is 4. The next subnet would be 8, then 12, 16, 20, and 24. The broadcast address is 23, and the valid host range is 21 and 22. See Chapter 3 for more IP addressing information.

14. C. Start by using 256, the subnet mask, which is 256–224=32. The first subnet is 10.32. The next subnet would be 10.64. This host is in the 10.32 subnet, the broadcast address is 10.63, and the valid host range is 10.33 through 10.62. See Chapter 3 for more IP addressing information.

15. C. The switch will flood the network with the frame looking for the device. For more information on LAN switching, see Chapter 2.

16. B. The command `show ipx interface` will show you the IPX RIP and SAP information being sent and received on an individual interface. See Chapter 8 for more information on IPX.

17. B. Start by using 256, the subnet mask, which is 256–248=8. The first subnet is 8. The next subnet would be 16, then 24, and then 32. This host is in the 24 subnet, the broadcast address is 31, and the valid host range is 25 through 31. See Chapter 3 for more information on IP addressing.

18. A. Access links connect hosts to a switch and are part of only one VLAN. For more information on VLANs, please see Chapter 6.

19. B, C. PPP is used to connect point-to-point links together and uses the ISO's non-proprietary version of HDLC. It can be used on either synchronous or asynchronous links. See Chapter 10 for more information on PPP.

20. A. The command `copy running-config tftp` (`copy run tftp` for short) will copy the router's configuration to a TFTP host for backup purposes. See Chapter 7 for more information about TFTP hosts and Cisco routers.

21. A, B, C, D, F, G, H, I, J. The `show cdp entry *` command is used to gather detailed information about neighbor devices. See Chapter 7 for more information about CDP.

22. D. Cisco recommends that you break up collision domains with layer-2 switches at the access layer, not the distribution layer. For more information on the distribution layer, see Chapter 1.

23. A, D. Cut-through and FragmentFree always read only a fixed amount of a frame. For more information on LAN switch types, see Chapter 2.

24. B. Cisco recommends that you use layer-2 switches, which break up collision domains, at the access layer. For more information on the access layer and collision domains, see Chapter 1.

25. C. You can use a letter, or combination of letters, followed by a question mark without a space to get all the commands starting with those letters from that prompt. For more editing and help information, see Chapter 4.

26. C. VLANs break up broadcast domains in switched networks. For more information on VLANs, please see Chapter 6.

27. A, B, C. Routing tables in a router keep track of where networks in a network are located, not hosts. They also keep track of the distance or cost to that remote network and which interface to exit to get to that remote network. For more information on routing tables, see Chapter 1.

28. C. The `show users` command will show you the virtual connections into your router. See Chapter 7 for more information about using Telnet.

29. B. Directly connected networks have the highest administrative distance, or trustworthiness rating, of zero. See Chapter 5 for more information on IP routing.

30. D. Extended access lists use the numbers 100–199. This eliminates Answers B and C. To filter on an upper-layer protocol, you must use UDP or TCP in the protocol field. This eliminates Answer A. For more information on access lists, see Chapter 9.

31. A, B. When a port is in blocking state, no frames are forwarded. This is used to stop network loops. However, the blocked port will listen for BPDUs received on the port. For more information on STP, see Chapter 2.

32. D. The 1900 defaults to FragmentFree but can be changed to store and forward. For more information on LAN switch types, see Chapter 2.

33. B, E. There is no enable-encrypted password. The enable secret is encrypted by default and supersedes the enable password. To learn how to set the passwords on a router, see Chapter 4.

34. C. RIP has an administrative distance of 120 by default. See Chapter 5 for more information on IP routing.

35. B, C. If you receive an incomplete command, then you know that the command string is not done. Just press the up arrow key to receive the last command entered, and continue with the command by using your question mark. For more information on help and editing, see Chapter 4.

36. B. By default, static routes have an administrative distance of 1. The 175 represents an optional command that changes the default administrative distance. See Chapter 5 for more information on IP routing.

37. B. If a packet is received that is looking for a destination network that is not in the routing table, the router will drop the packet. See Chapter 5 for more information on IP routing.

38. B. The IPX address is 10 bytes (80 bits). The first four bytes are the network number, and the last six bytes are the node address. See Chapter 8 for more information on IPX.

39. A, B. The Network layer uses two different types of packets (called PDUs). The data packets route user data with routed protocols, and the route packets keep and maintain routing tables on routers within the internetwork with routing protocols. Examples of routed protocols are IP and IPX; examples of routing protocols are RIP, IGRP, and OSPF. For more information on PDUs, see Chapter 1.

40. C. Cisco has a proprietary frame tagging method called Inter-Switch Link (ISL), which keeps track of frames across a trunked link. For more information on VLANs, please see Chapter 6.

41. B, D. IPX RIP uses ticks (1/18 of a second) and then hop counts to determine the best way to an internetwork. See Chapter 8 for more information on IPX RIP.

42. C. Extended IP access lists use the numbers 100–199. See Chapter 9 for more information about access lists.

43. C. The command `access-list 110 permit ip any any` (0.0.0.0 255.255.255.255 is the same as the `any` command) is a wildcard allowing any host or network. For more information on access lists, see Chapter 9.

44. C. Static VLANs are VLANs assigned to switch ports by an administrator. For more information on VLANs, please see Chapter 6.

45. C. You can configure the switch type globally and set the switch type for all BRI interfaces, or you can set it at interface level if each BRI is connected to a different type of switch. See Chapter 10 for more information on ISDN.

46. D. Backward-Explicit Congestion Notification (BECN) is used to send information back to an originating router telling it to slow down its transfer rate because the switch is congested. See Chapter 10 for more information on Frame Relay.

47. D. Data Link Connection Identifiers (DLCIs) are used to identify a PVC through a Frame Relay switch. See Chapter 10 for more information on Frame Relay.

48. B, C. You can add multiple encapsulations on an interface either by using the `secondary` command or by creating a subinterface. See Chapter 8 for more information on IPX and multiple encapsulations.

49. B. 50 seconds is the default time for changing from blocking to forwarding state. This is to allow enough time for all switches to update their STP database. For more information on STP, see Chapter 2.

50. D. You can telnet to a 1900, but not from a 1900 switch CLI. See Appendix B for an explanation of the 1900 switch commands.

51. D. To delete the dynamic entries in a MAC address table, use the command `clear mac-address-table dynamic` from privileged mode. See Appendix B for an explanation of the 1900 switch commands.

52. B, C. By typing `delete nvram`, you delete the startup-config. However, this does not delete the VTP configuration on the switch. You must also type `delete vtp`. See Appendix B for more information on the 1900 switch commands.

53. C. The ports 26 and 27 are considered A and B when viewing trunk information. See Appendix B for more on the 1900 switch commands.

54. A. The command `show vtp statistics` will give you the receive and transmit statistics of VTP on a switch. See Appendix B for an explanation of the 1900 switch commands.

Internetworking

THE CCNA EXAM TOPICS COVERED IN THIS CHAPTER INCLUDE THE FOLLOWING:

✓ Describe the benefits of a layered model

✓ Describe the main benefit of the OSI reference model

✓ Understand each of the seven layers of the OSI reference model and what they provide application developers

✓ Describe flow control and how it is used within an internetwork

✓ Understand how the Transport layer flow control mechanism works

✓ Describe how the OSI's Network layer provides routing in an internetwork environment

✓ List the five conversion steps of data encapsulation

Welcome to the exciting world of internetworking. This first chapter will help you understand the basics of internetworking and how to connect networks using Cisco routers and switches.

The Open Systems Interconnection (OSI) model will be discussed in detail in this chapter. The OSI model has seven hierarchical layers that were developed to help different companies communicate between their disparate systems. It is important to understand the OSI model as Cisco sees it, and that is how I will present the seven layers of the OSI model to you.

Cisco has created a three-layer hierarchical network model that can help you build, implement, and maintain networks. By understanding this model, you can effectively build, maintain, and troubleshoot any size network. This chapter will give you both an introduction to the Cisco three-layer model and the details of each layer.

Different types of devices are specified at different layers of the OSI model. It is important to understand the different types of cables and connectors used to connect these devices to a network. Cabling Cisco devices will be discussed with Ethernet LANs, WAN technologies, and even connecting a router or switch with a console connection.

Cisco makes a large range of router, hub, and switch products. By understanding the different products available from Cisco, you can understand which devices can meet the business requirements for your network. The product line for Cisco hubs, routers, and switches is discussed at the end of this chapter.

Internetworking Models

When networks first came into being, computers could typically communicate only with computers from the same manufacturer. For example, companies ran either a complete DECnet solution or an IBM solution—not both together. In the late 1970s, the *OSI (Open Systems Interconnection) model* was created by the International Organization for Standardization (ISO) to break this barrier. The OSI model was meant to help vendors create interoperable network devices. Like world peace, it'll probably never happen completely, but it's still a great goal.

The OSI model is the primary architectural model for networks. It describes how data and network information are communicated from applications on one computer, through the network media, to an application on another computer. The OSI reference model breaks this approach into layers.

Cisco has also created a three-layer model that is used to help design, implement, and maintain any size network. By understanding the three-layer model, you will gain an understanding of how Cisco views internetworking. Also, by having a fundamental understanding of the devices used at each layer of the model, you can effectively design and purchase the correct Cisco equipment to meet your business needs. This chapter will cover both the OSI model and the Cisco three-layer hierarchical model.

The Layered Approach

A *reference model* is a conceptual blueprint of how communications should take place. It addresses all the processes required for effective communication and divides these processes into logical groupings called *layers*. When a communication system is designed in this manner, it's known as *layered architecture*.

Think of it like this: You and some friends want to start a company. One of the first things you'd do is sit down and think through what must be done, who will do them, what order they will be done in, and how they relate to each other. Ultimately, you might group these tasks into departments. Let's say you decide to have an order-taking department, an inventory department, and a shipping department. Each of your departments has its own unique tasks, keeping its staff members busy and requiring them to focus on only their own duties.

In this scenario, departments are a metaphor for the layers in a communication system. For things to run smoothly, the staff of each department will have to both trust and rely heavily on the others to do their jobs and competently handle their unique responsibilities. In your planning sessions, you would probably take notes, recording the entire process to facilitate later discussions about standards of operation that will serve as your business blueprint, or reference model.

Once your business is launched, your department heads, armed with the part of the blueprint relating to their department, will need to develop practical methods to implement their assigned tasks. These practical methods, or protocols, will need to be compiled into a standard operating procedures manual and followed closely. Each of the various procedures in your manual will have been included for different reasons and have varying degrees of importance and implementation. If you form a partnership or acquire another company, it will be imperative for its business protocols—its business blueprint—to match, or be compatible with, yours.

Similarly, software developers can use a reference model to understand computer communication processes and to see what types of functions need to be accomplished on any one layer. If they are developing a protocol for a certain layer, all they need to concern themselves with is the specific layer's functions, not those of any other layer. Another layer and protocol will handle the other functions. The technical term for this idea is *binding*. The communication processes that are related to each other are bound, or grouped together, at a particular layer.

Advantages of Reference Models

The OSI model, like the Cisco three-layer model you will learn about later, is hierarchical, and the same benefits and advantages can apply to any layered model. The primary purpose of all models, and especially the OSI model, is to allow different vendors to interoperate. The benefits of the OSI and Cisco models include, but are not limited to, the following:

- Dividing the complex network operation into more manageable layers

- Changing one layer without having to change all layers. This allows application developers to specialize in design and development.

- Defining the standard interface for the "plug-and-play" multivendor integration

The OSI Reference Model

The OSI reference model was created in the late 1970s to help facilitate data transfer between network nodes. One of the greatest functions of the OSI specifications is to assist in data transfer between disparate hosts. This means you can transfer data between a Unix host and a PC, for example.

The OSI is not physical; rather, it is a set of guidelines that application developers can use to create and implement applications that run on a network. It also provides a framework for creating and implementing networking standards, devices, and internetworking schemes.

The OSI has seven different layers, which are divided into two groups. The top three layers define how the applications within the end stations will communicate with each other and with users. The bottom four layers define how data is transmitted end-to-end. Figure 1.1 shows the three upper layers and their functions, and Figure 1.2 shows the four lower layers and their functions.

FIGURE 1.1   The upper layers

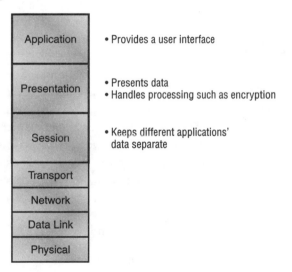

In Figure 1.1, you can see that the user interfaces with the computer at the application layer, and also that the upper layers are responsible for applications communicating between hosts. Remember that none of the upper layers know anything about networking or network addresses. That is the responsibility of the four bottom layers, which are shown in Figure 1.2.

FIGURE 1.2 The lower layers

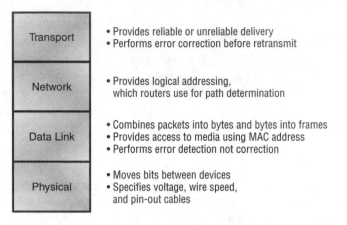

The four bottom layers define how data is transferred through a physical wire or through switches and routers, and how to rebuild a data stream from a transmitting host to a destination host's application.

The OSI Layers

The International Organization for Standardization (ISO) is the Emily Post of the network protocol world. Just like Ms. Post, who wrote the book setting the standards—or protocols—for human social interaction, the ISO developed the OSI reference model as the precedent and guide for an open network protocol set. Defining the etiquette of communication models, it remains today the most popular means of comparison for protocol suites. The OSI reference model has seven layers:

- The Application layer
- The Presentation layer
- The Session layer
- The Transport layer
- The Network layer
- The Data Link layer
- The Physical layer

Figure 1.3 shows the functions defined at each layer of the OSI model. The following pages discuss this in detail.

FIGURE 1.3   Layer functions

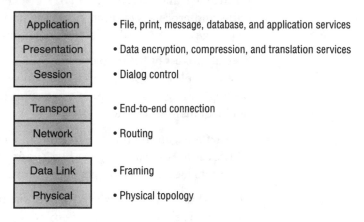

FIGURE 1.3   Layer functions

Application	• File, print, message, database, and application services
Presentation	• Data encryption, compression, and translation services
Session	• Dialog control
Transport	• End-to-end connection
Network	• Routing
Data Link	• Framing
Physical	• Physical topology

The Application Layer

The *Application layer* of the OSI model is where users communicate to the computer. The Application layer is responsible for identifying and establishing the availability of the intended communication partner and determining if sufficient resources for the intended communication exist.

Although computer applications sometimes require only desktop resources, applications may unite communicating components from more than one network application; for example, file transfers, e-mail, remote access, network management activities, client/server processes, and information location. Many network applications provide services for communication over enterprise networks, but for present and future internetworking, the need is fast developing to reach beyond their limits. Today, transactions and information exchanges between organizations are broadening to require internetworking applications like the following:

World Wide Web (WWW)   Connects countless servers (the number seems to grow with each passing day) presenting diverse formats. Most are multimedia and include some or all of the following: graphics, text, video, and even sound. Netscape Navigator, Internet Explorer, and other browsers like Mosaic simplify both accessing and viewing Web sites.

E-mail gateways   Are versatile and can use Simple Mail Transfer Protocol (SMTP) or the X.400 standard to deliver messages between different e-mail applications.

Electronic Data Interchange (EDI)   Is a composite of specialized standards and processes that facilitates the flow of tasks such as accounting, shipping/receiving, and order and inventory tracking between businesses.

Special interest bulletin boards   Include the many Internet chat rooms where people can connect and communicate with each other either by posting messages or by typing a live conversation. They can also share public domain software.

Internet navigation utilities   Include applications like Gopher and WAIS, as well as search engines like Yahoo!, Excite, and Alta Vista, which help users locate the resources and information they need on the Internet.

Financial transaction services   Target the financial community. They gather and sell information pertaining to investments, market trading, commodities, currency exchange rates, and credit data to their subscribers.

The Presentation Layer

The *Presentation layer* gets its name from its purpose: It presents data to the Application layer. It's essentially a translator and provides coding and conversion functions. A successful data transfer technique is to adapt the data into a standard format before transmission. Computers are configured to receive this generically formatted data and then convert the data back into its native format for actual reading (for example, EBCDIC to ASCII). By providing translation services, the Presentation layer ensures that data transferred from the Application layer of one system can be read by the Application layer of another host.

The OSI has protocol standards that define how standard data should be formatted. Tasks like data compression, decompression, encryption, and decryption are associated with this layer. Some Presentation layer standards are involved in multimedia operations. The following serve to direct graphic and visual image presentation:

PICT   This is picture format used by Macintosh or PowerPC programs for transferring QuickDraw graphics.

TIFF   The Tagged Image File Format is a standard graphics format for high-resolution, bitmapped images.

JPEG The Joint Photographic Experts Group brings these photo standards to us.

Other standards guide movies and sound:

MIDI The Musical Instrument Digital Interface is used for digitized music.

MPEG The Moving Picture Experts Group's standard for the compression and coding of motion video for CDs is increasingly popular. It provides digital storage and bit rates up to 1.5Mbps.

QuickTime This is for use with Macintosh or PowerPC programs; it manages audio and video applications.

The Session Layer

The *Session layer* is responsible for setting up, managing, and then tearing down sessions between Presentation layer entities. The Session layer also provides dialog control between devices, or nodes. It coordinates communication between systems and serves to organize their communication by offering three different modes: *simplex*, *half-duplex*, and *full-duplex*. The Session layer basically keeps different applications' data separate from other applications' data.

The following are some examples of Session-layer protocols and interfaces (according to Cisco):

Network File System (NFS) Was developed by Sun Microsystems and used with TCP/IP and Unix workstations to allow transparent access to remote resources.

Structured Query Language (SQL) Was developed by IBM to provide users with a simpler way to define their information requirements on both local and remote systems.

Remote Procedure Call (RPC) Is a broad client/server redirection tool used for disparate service environments. Its procedures are created on clients and performed on servers.

X Window Is widely used by intelligent terminals for communicating with remote Unix computers, allowing them to operate as though they were locally attached monitors.

AppleTalk Session Protocol (ASP)   Is another client/server mechanism, which both establishes and maintains sessions between AppleTalk client and server machines.

Digital Network Architecture Session Control Protocol (DNA SCP)   Is a DECnet Session-layer protocol.

The Transport Layer

Services located in the *Transport layer* both segment and reassemble data from upper-layer applications and unite it onto the same data stream. They provide end-to-end data transport services and can establish a logical connection between the sending host and destination host on an internetwork.

Some of you might already be familiar with TCP and UDP (which you will learn about in Chapter 3) and know that TCP is a reliable service and UDP is not. Application developers have their choice of the two protocols when working with TCP/IP protocols.

The Transport layer is responsible for providing mechanisms for multiplexing upper-layer application, session establishment, and teardown of virtual circuits. It also hides details of any network-dependent information from the higher layers by providing transparent data transfer.

Flow Control

Data integrity is ensured at the Transport layer by maintaining flow control and allowing users the option of requesting reliable data transport between systems. *Flow control* prevents a sending host on one side of the connection from overflowing the buffers in the receiving host—an event that can result in lost data. Reliable data transport employs a connection-oriented communications session between systems, and the protocols involved ensure the following will be achieved:

- The segments delivered are acknowledged back to the sender upon their reception.

- Any segments not acknowledged are retransmitted.

- Segments are sequenced back into their proper order upon arrival at their destination.

- A manageable data flow is maintained in order to avoid congestion, overloading, and data loss.

Connection-Oriented Communication

In reliable transport operation, one device first establishes a connection-oriented session with its peer system. Figure 1.4 portrays a typical reliable session taking place between sending and receiving systems. In it, both hosts' application programs begin by notifying their individual operating systems that a connection is about to be initiated. The two operating systems communicate by sending messages over the network confirming that the transfer is approved and that both sides are ready for it to take place. Once the required synchronization is complete, a connection is fully established and the data transfer begins. Cisco sometimes refers to this as a three-way handshake.

FIGURE 1.4 Establishing a connection-oriented session

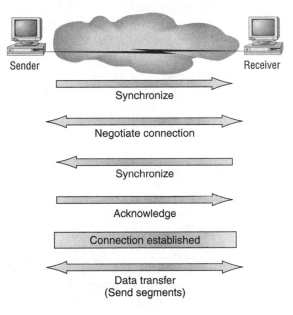

While the information is being transferred between hosts, the two machines periodically check in with each other, communicating through their protocol software to ensure that all is going well and that the data is being received properly.

The following summarizes the steps in the connection-oriented session pictured in Figure 1.4:

- The first "connection agreement" segment is a request for synchronization.

- The second and third segments acknowledge the request and establish connection parameters between hosts.

- The final segment is also an acknowledgment. It notifies the destination host that the connection agreement is accepted and that the actual connection has been established. Data transfer can now begin.

During a transfer, congestion can occur because a high-speed computer is generating data traffic faster than the network can transfer it or because many computers are simultaneously sending datagrams through a single gateway or destination. In the latter case, a gateway or destination can become congested even though no single source caused the problem. In either case, the problem is basically akin to a freeway bottleneck—too much traffic for too small a capacity. Usually, no one car is the problem; there are simply too many cars on that freeway.

When a machine receives a flood of datagrams too quickly for it to process, it stores them in a memory section called a *buffer*. This buffering action solves the problem only if the datagrams are part of a small burst. However, if the datagram deluge continues, a device's memory will eventually be exhausted, its flood capacity will be exceeded, and it will discard any additional datagrams that arrive.

But, no worries—because of the transport function, network flood control systems work quite well. Instead of dumping resources and allowing data to be lost, the transport can issue a "not ready" indicator to the sender, or source, of the flood (as shown in Figure 1.5). This mechanism works kind of like a stoplight, signaling the sending device to stop transmitting segment traffic to its overwhelmed peer. After the peer receiver processes the segments already in its memory reservoir, it sends out a "ready" transport indicator. When the machine waiting to transmit the rest of its datagrams receives this "go" indictor, it then resumes its transmission.

In fundamental, reliable, connection-oriented data transfer, datagrams are delivered to the receiving host in exactly the same sequence they're transmitted; the transmission fails if this order is breached. If any data segments are lost, duplicated, or damaged along the way, a failure will transmit. The answer to the problem is to have the receiving host acknowledge receiving each and every data segment.

FIGURE 1.5   Transmitting segments with flow control

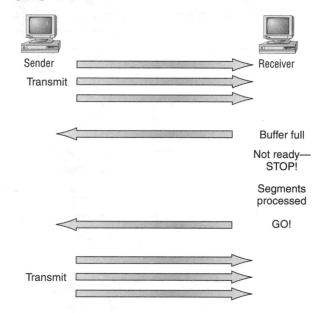

Windowing

Data throughput would be low if the transmitting machine had to wait for an acknowledgment after sending each segment. Because there's time available after the sender transmits the data segment and before it finishes processing acknowledgments from the receiving machine, the sender uses the break to transmit more data. The quantity of data segments the transmitting machine is allowed to send without receiving an acknowledgment for them is called a *window*.

Windowing controls how much information is transferred from one end to the other. While some protocols quantify information by observing the number of packets, TCP/IP measures it by counting the number of bytes. In Figure 1.6, there is a window size of 1 and a window size of 3. When a window size of 1 is configured, the sending machine waits for an acknowledgment for each data segment it transmits before transmitting another.

Configured to a window size of 3, it's allowed to transmit three data segments before an acknowledgment is received. In our simplified example, both the sending and receiving machines are workstations. Reality is rarely that simple, and most often acknowledgments and packets will commingle as they travel over the network and pass through routers. Routing complicates things, but not to worry, you'll learn about applied routing later in the book.

FIGURE 1.6   Windowing

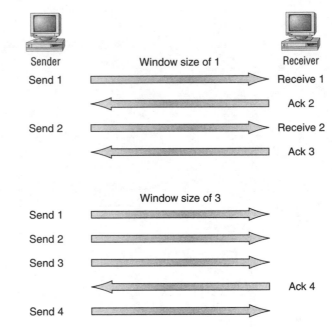

Acknowledgments

Reliable data delivery ensures the integrity of a stream of data sent from one machine to the other through a fully functional data link. It guarantees the data won't be duplicated or lost. The method that achieves this is known as *positive acknowledgment with retransmission.* This technique requires a receiving machine to communicate with the transmitting source by sending an acknowledgment message back to the sender when it receives data. The sender documents each segment it sends and waits for this acknowledgment before sending the next segment. When it sends a segment, the transmitting machine starts a timer and retransmits if it expires before an acknowledgment is returned from the receiving end.

In Figure 1.7, the sending machine transmits segments 1, 2, and 3. The receiving node acknowledges it has received them by requesting segment 4. When it receives the acknowledgment, the sender then transmits segments 4, 5, and 6. If segment 5 doesn't make it to the destination, the receiving node acknowledges that event with a request for the segment to be resent. The sending machine will then resend the lost segment and wait for an acknowledgment, which it must receive in order to move on to the transmission of segment 7.

FIGURE 1.7 Transport layer reliable delivery

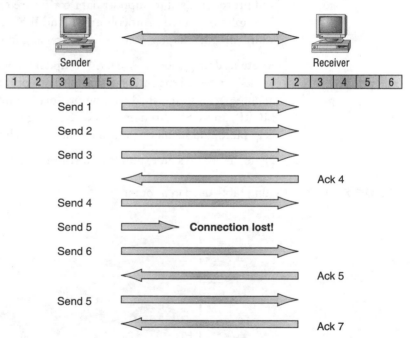

The Network Layer

The *Network layer* is responsible for routing through an internetwork and for network addressing. This means that the Network layer is responsible for transporting traffic between devices that are not locally attached. *Routers*, or other layer-3 devices, are specified at the Network layer and provide the routing services in an internetwork.

When a packet is received on a router interface, the destination IP address is checked. If the packet is not destined for the router, then the router will look up the destination network address in the routing table. Once an exit interface is chosen, the packet will be sent to the interface to be framed and sent out on the local network. If the entry for the destination network is not found in the routing table, the router drops the packet.

Two types of packets are used at the network layer: data and route updates.

Data packets   Are used to transport user data through the internetwork, and protocols used to support data traffic are called routed protocols. Examples of routed protocols are IP and IPX. You'll learn about IP addressing in Chapter 3 and IPX addressing in Chapter 8.

Route update packets   Are used to update neighbor routers about networks connected to routers in the internetwork. Protocols that send route update packets are called routing protocols, and examples are RIP, EIGRP, and OSPF, to name a few. Routing update packets are used to help build and maintain routing tables on each router.

Figure 1.8 shows an example of a routing table.

FIGURE 1.8   Routing table used in a router

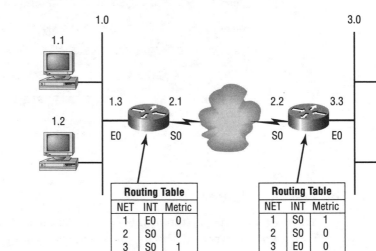

The routing table used in a router includes the following information:

Network addresses Protocol-specific network addresses. A router must maintain a routing table for individual routing protocols because each routing protocol keeps track of a network with a different addressing scheme. Think of it as a street sign in each of the different languages spoken by the residents on a street.

Interface The exit interface a packet will take when destined for a specific network.

Metric The distance to the remote network. Different routing protocols use different methods of computing this distance. Routing protocols are covered in Chapter 5, but you need to understand that some routing protocols use hop count (the number of routers a packet passes through when routing to a remote network), while others use bandwidth, delay of the line, or even tick count (1/18 of a second).

Routers break up *broadcast domains*. This means, by default, that broadcasts are not forwarded through a router. This is good. Routers also break up collision domains, but this can also accomplished through layer-2 switches. Each interface in a router is a separate network and must be assigned unique network identification numbers. Each host on the network connected to that router must use that same network number.

Some points about routers that you must remember:

- Routers, by default, will not forward any broadcast or multicast packets.

- Routers use the logical address in a network layer header to determine the next hop router to forward the packet to.

- Routers can use access lists, created by an administrator, to control security on packets trying to either enter or exit an interface.

- Routers can provide layer-2 bridging functions if needed and can simultaneously route through the same interface.

- Layer-3 devices (routers in this case) provide connections between Virtual LANs (VLANs).

Switching and VLANs and are covered in Chapters 2 and 6, respectively.

- Routers can provide Quality of Service (QoS) for specific types of network traffic.

The Data Link Layer

The *Data Link layer* ensures that messages are delivered to the proper device and translates messages from the Network layer into bits for the Physical layer to transmit. It formats the message into *data frames* and adds a customized header containing the hardware destination and source address. This added information forms a sort of capsule that surrounds the original message in much the same way that engines, navigational devices, and other tools were attached to the lunar modules of the Apollo project. These various pieces of equipment were useful only during certain stages of space flight and were stripped off the module and discarded when their designated stage was complete. Data traveling through networks is similar. Figure 1.9 shows the Data Link layer with the Ethernet and IEEE specifications. Notice in the figure that the IEEE 802.2 standard is used in conjunction with the other IEEE standards, adding functionality to the existing IEEE standards.

FIGURE 1.9   Data Link layer

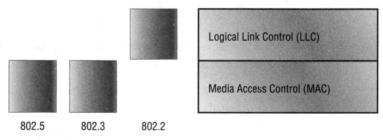

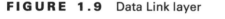

You need to understand that routers, which work at the Network layer, do not care about where a host is located but only where networks are located. They also keep track of the best way to get to a remote network. The Data Link layer is responsible for uniquely identifying each device on a local network.

For a host to send packets to individual hosts and between routers, the Data Link layer uses hardware addressing. Each time a packet is sent between routers, it is framed with control information at the Data Link layer, but that information is stripped off at the receiving router and only the original packet is left completely intact. This framing of the packet continues for each hop until the packet is finally delivered to the receiving host. It is important to understand that the packet was never altered along the route, only encapsulated with the type of control information to be passed on to the different media types.

The IEEE Ethernet Data Link layer has two sublayers:

Media Access Control (MAC) 802.3   This defines how packets are placed on the media. Contention media access is first come, first served access where everyone shares the same bandwidth. Physical addressing is defined here, as well as logical topologies. Logical topology is the signal path through a physical topology. Line discipline, error notification (not correction), ordered delivery of frames, and optional flow control can also be used at this sublayer.

Logical Link Control (LLC) 802.2   This sublayer is responsible for identifying Network layer protocols and then encapsulating them. An LLC header tells the Data Link layer what to do with a packet once a frame is received. For example, a host will receive a frame and then look in the LLC header to understand that the packet is destined for the IP protocol at the Network layer. The LLC can also provide flow control and sequencing of control bits.

Switches and Bridges at the Data Link Layer

Switches and *bridges* both work at the Data link layer and filter the network using hardware (MAC) addresses. Layer-2 switching is considered hardware-based bridging because it uses a specialized hardware called *Application-Specific Integrated Circuits (ASICs)*. ASICs can run up to gigabit speeds with very low latency.

Bridges and switches read each frame as it passes through the network. The layer-2 device then puts the source hardware address in a filter table and keeps track of which port it was received on. This tells the switch where that device is located.

After a filter table is built on the layer-2 device, the device will only forward frames to the segment where the destination hardware address is located. If the destination device is on the same segment as the frame, the layer-2 device will block the frame from going to any other segments. If the destination is on another segment, the frame is only transmitted to that segment. This is called transparent bridging.

When a layer-2 device (switch) interface receives a frame and the destination hardware address is unknown to the device's filter table, it will forward the frame to all connected segments. If the unknown device replies to this forwarding of the frame, the switch updates the filter table on that device's location. However, the destination address of the transmitting frame may be a broadcast address, in which case the switch will forward all broadcasts to every connected segment by default.

All devices that the broadcast is forwarded to are considered to be in the same broadcast domain. Layer-2 devices propagate layer-2 broadcast storms. The only way to stop a broadcast storm from propagating through an internetwork is with a layer-3 device (router).

The biggest benefit of using switches instead of hubs in your internetwork is that each switch port is its own collision domain, whereas a hub creates one large collision domain. However, switches and bridges do not break up broadcast domains, instead forwarding all broadcasts.

Another benefit of LAN switching over hub implementations is that each device on every segment plugged into a switch can transmit simultaneously because each segment is its own collision domain. Hubs allow only one device per network to communicate at a time.

Switches cannot translate between different media types. In other words, each device connected to the switch must use an Ethernet frame type. If you wanted to connect to a Token Ring switch or LAN, you would need a router to provide the translation services.

The Physical Layer

The *Physical layer* has two responsibilities: it sends bits and receives bits. Bits come only in values of 1 or 0—a Morse code with numerical values. The Physical layer communicates directly with the various types of actual communication media. Different kinds of media represent these bit values in different ways. Some use audio tones, while others employ *state transitions*—changes in voltage from high to low and low to high. Specific protocols are needed for each type of media to describe the proper bit patterns to be used, how data is encoded into media signals, and the various qualities of the physical media's attachment interface.

The Physical layer specifications specify the electrical, mechanical, procedural, and functional requirements for activating, maintaining, and deactivating a physical link between end systems.

At the Physical layer, the interface between the Data Terminal Equipment, or DTE, and the Data Circuit-Terminating Equipment, or DCE, is identified. The DCE is usually located at the service provider, while the DTE is the attached device. The services available to the DTE are most often accessed via a modem or Channel Service Unit/Data Service Unit (CSU/DSU).

The Physical layer's connectors and different physical topologies are defined by the OSI as standards, allowing disparate systems to communicate. The CCNA course and exam are only interested in the Ethernet standards.

Hubs at the Physical Layer

Hubs are really multiple port repeaters. A repeater receives a digital signal and reamplifies it or regenerates the digital signal, then forwards the digital signal out all active ports without looking at any data. An Active hub does the same thing. Any digital signal received from a segment on a hub port is regenerated or reamplified and transmitted out all ports on the hub. This means all devices plugged into a hub are in the same collision domain as well as in the same broadcast domain. A broadcast domain is defined as all devices on a network segment that hear all broadcasts sent on that segment.

Hubs, like repeaters, do not look at any traffic as they enter and are transmitted out to the other parts of the physical media. Hubs create a physical star network where the hub is a central device and cables extend in all directions, creating the physical star effect. However, Ethernet networks use a logical bus topology. This means that the signal has to run from end to end of the network. Every device connected to the hub, or hubs, must listen if a device transmits.

Ethernet Networking

E*thernet* is a contention media access method that allows all hosts on a network to share the same bandwidth of a link. Ethernet is popular because it is easy to implement, troubleshoot, and add new technologies, like Fast-Ethernet and Gigabit Ethernet, to existing network infrastructures. Ethernet uses the Data Link and Physical layer specifications, and this section of the chapter will give you both the Data Link and Physical layer information you need to effectively implement, troubleshoot, and maintain an Ethernet network.

Ethernet networking uses what is called *Carrier Sense Multiple Access with Collision Detect (CSMA/CD)*, which helps devices share the bandwidth evenly without having two devices transmit at the same time on the network medium. CSMA/CD was created to overcome the problem of collisions that occur when packets are transmitted simultaneously from different nodes. Good collision management is important, because when a node transmits in a CSMA/CD network, all the other nodes on the network receive and examine that transmission. Only bridges and routers effectively prevent a transmission from propagating through the entire network.

The CSMA/CD protocol works like this: When a host wants to transmit over the network, it first checks for the presence of a digital signal on the wire. If all is clear (no other host is transmitting), the host will then proceed with its transmission. And it doesn't stop there. The transmitting host constantly monitors the wire to make sure no other hosts begin transmitting. If the host detects another signal on the wire, it sends out an extended jam signal that causes all nodes on the segment to stop sending data. The nodes respond to that jam signal by waiting a while before attempting to transmit again. Backoff algorithms determine when the colliding stations retransmit. If after 15 tries collisions keep occurring, the nodes attempting to transmit will then time-out.

Half- and Full-Duplex Ethernet

Half-duplex Ethernet is defined in the original 802.3 Ethernet and uses only one wire pair with a digital signal running in both directions on the wire. It also uses the CSMA/CD protocol to help prevent collisions and retransmit if a collision does occur. If a hub is attached to a switch, it must operate in half-duplex mode because the end stations must be able to detect collisions. Half-duplex Ethernet, typically 10BaseT, is only about 50 to 60 percent efficient, as Cisco sees it. However, you typically will only get 3- to 4Mbps, at most, in a large 10BaseT network.

Full-duplex Ethernet uses two pairs of wires, instead of one wire pair like half duplex. Full duplex uses a point-to-point connection between the transmitter of the transmitting device and the receiver of the receiving device. There are no collisions because it's as if we now have a freeway with multiple lanes instead of the single-lane road associated with half duplex. Full-duplex

Ethernet is supposed to offer 100 percent efficiency in both directions. This means that you can get 20Mbps with a 10Mbps Ethernet running full duplex, or 200Mbps for FastEthernet. This is called an aggregate rate, but it essentially means "you're supposed to get" 100 percent efficiency, though no one is certain.

When a full-duplex Ethernet port is powered on, it connects to the remote end and then negotiates with the other end of the FastEthernet link. This is called an auto-detect mechanism. This mechanism first decides on the exchange capability, which means it checks to see if it can run at 10 or 100Mbps. It then checks to see if it can run full duplex. If it cannot, then it will run half duplex.

Ethernet at the Data Link Layer

Ethernet at the Data Link layer is responsible for Ethernet addressing, which is typically called hardware addressing or MAC addressing. Ethernet is also responsible for framing packets received from the Network layer and preparing them for transmission on the local network through the Ethernet contention media access method. There are four different types of Ethernet frames available:

- Ethernet_II
- IEEE 802.3
- IEEE 802.2
- SNAP

I will discuss all four of the available Ethernet frames in the upcoming sections.

Ethernet Addressing

Ethernet addressing uses the *Media Access Control (MAC) address* burned into each and every Ethernet Network Interface Card (NIC). The MAC address, sometimes referred to as a hardware address, is a 48-bit address written in a canonical format to ensure that addresses are at least written in the same format, even if different LAN technologies are used.

Figure 1.10 shows the 48-bit MAC addresses and how the bits are divided.

FIGURE 1.10   Ethernet addressing using MAC addresses

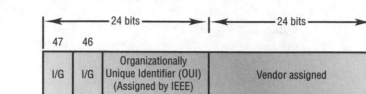

The *Organizationally Unique Identifier (OUI)* is assigned by the IEEE to an organization (24 bits or 3 bytes). The organization, in turn, assigns a globally administered address (24 bits or 3 bytes) that is unique (supposedly) to each and every adapter they manufacturer. Notice bit 46. Bit 46 must be 0 if it is a globally assigned bit from the manufacturer and 1 if it is locally administered from the network administrator.

Ethernet Frames

The Data Link layer is responsible for combining bits into bytes and bytes into *frames*. Frames are used at the Data Link layer to encapsulate packets handed down from the Network layer for transmission on a type of media access. There are three types of media access methods: contention (Ethernet), token passing (Token Ring and FDDI), and polling (IBM Mainframes and 100VGAnylan). This CCNA exam covers primarily Ethernet (contention) media access.

The function of Ethernet stations is to pass data frames between each other using a group of bits known as a MAC frame format. This provides error detection from a cyclic redundancy check (CRC). However, remember that this is error detection, not error correction. The 802.3 frames and Ethernet frame are shown in Figure 1.11.

The following bullet points detail the different fields in the 802.3 and Ethernet frame types.

Preamble   An alternating 1,0 pattern provides a 5MHz clock at the start of each packet, which allows the receiving devices to lock the incoming bit stream. The preamble uses either an SFD or synch field to indicate to the receiving station that the data portion of the message will follow.

Start Frame Delimiter (SFD)/Synch   SFD is 1,0,1,0,1,0, etc., and the synch field is all 1s. The preamble and SFD/synch field are 64 bits long.

FIGURE 1.11 802.3 and Ethernet frame formats

Ethernet_II

Preamble 8 bytes	DA 6 bytes	SA 6 bytes	Type 2 bytes	Data	FCS 4 bytes

802.3_Ethernet

Preamble 8 bytes	DA 6 bytes	SA 6 bytes	Length 2 bytes	Data	FCS

Destination Address (DA)   This transmits a 48-bit value using the Least Significant Bit (LSB) first. DA is used by receiving stations to determine if an incoming packet is addressed to a particular node. The destination address can be an individual address, or a broadcast or multicast MAC address. Remember that a broadcast is all 1s or Fs in hex and is sent to all devices, whereas a multicast is sent to only a similar subset of nodes on a network.

Hex is short for hexadecimal, which is a numbering system that uses the first six letters of the alphabet (A through F) to extend beyond the available 10 digits in the decimal system. Hexadecimal has a total of 16 digits.

Source Address (SA)   SA is a 48-bit MAC address supplied by the transmitting device. It uses the Least Significant Bit (LSB) first. Broadcast and multicast address formats are illegal within the SA field.

Length or Type field   802.3 uses a length field, whereas the Ethernet frame uses a type field to identify the Network layer protocol. 802.3 cannot identify the upper-layer protocol and must be used with a proprietary LAN, for example, IPX.

Data This is a packet sent down to the Data Link layer from the Network layer. The size can vary from 46–1500 bytes.

Frame Check Sequence (FCS) FCS is a field at the end of the frame that is used to store the cyclic redundancy check (CRC).

Let's take a look at some frames caught on our trusty Etherpeek network analyzer. The frame below has only three fields: a destination, source, and type field. This is an Ethernet_II frame. Notice the type field is IP, or 08-00 in hexadecimal.

```
Destination:  00:60:f5:00:1f:27
Source:       00:60:f5:00:1f:2c
Protocol Type:08-00   IP
```

The next frame has the same fields, so it must also be an Ethernet_II frame. We included this one so you could see that the frame can carry more than just IP: It can also carry IPX, or 81-37h. Notice that this frame was a broadcast. You can tell because the destination hardware address is all 1s in binary, or all Fs in hexadecimal.

```
Destination:  ff:ff:ff:ff:ff:ff Ethernet Broadcast
Source:       02:07:01:22:de:a4
Protocol Type:81-37   NetWare
```

Notice the length field in the next frame. This must be an 802.3 frame. Which protocol is this going to be handed to at the Network layer? It doesn't specify in the frame, so it must be IPX. Why? Because when Novell created the 802.3 frame type (before the IEEE did and called it 802.3 Raw), Novell was pretty much the only LAN server out there. So, Novell was assuming that if you're running a LAN, it must be IPX.

```
Flags:         0x80   802.3
Status:        0x00
Packet Length:64
Timestamp:     12:45:45.192000 06/26/1998
Destination:   ff:ff:ff:ff:ff:ff Ethernet Broadcast
Source:        08:00:11:07:57:28
Length:        34
```

802.2 and SNAP

Remember that the 802.3 Ethernet frame cannot by itself identify the upper-layer (Network) protocol; it needs help. The IEEE defined the 802.2 LLC specifications to provide this function and more. Figure 1.12 shows the IEEE 802.3 with LLC (802.2) and the Subnetwork Architecture Protocol (SNAP) frame types.

FIGURE 1.12   802.2 and SNAP

802.2 (SNAP)

1	1	1 or 2	3	2	Variable
Dest SAP AA	Source SAP AA	Ctrl 03	OUI ID	Type	Data

802.2 (SAP)

1	1	1 or 2	Variable
Dest SAP	Source SAP	Ctrl	Data

Figure 1.12 shows how the LLC header information is added to the data portion of the frame.

Now, let's take a look at an 802.2 frame and SNAP captured from our analyzer.

802.2 Frame

The following is an 802.2 frame captured with a protocol analyzer. Notice that the first frame has a length field, so it's probably an 802.3, right? But look again; it also has a DSAP and an SSAP, so it has to be an 802.2 frame. (Remember that an 802.2 frame is an 802.3 frame with the LLC information in the data field of the header, so we know what the upper-layer protocol is.) Here is the frame:

```
Flags:          0x80   802.3
Status:         0x02   Truncated
Packet Length:64
Slice Length:   51
Timestamp:      12:42:00.592000 03/26/1998
Destination:    ff:ff:ff:ff:ff:ff Ethernet Broadcast
Source:         00:80:c7:a8:f0:3d
LLC Length:     37
Dest. SAP:      0xe0   NetWare
Source SAP:     0xe0   NetWare   Individual LLC Sublayer
Management Function
Command:        0x03   Unnumbered Information
```

SNAP Frame

The SNAP frame has its own protocol field to identify the upper-layer protocol. This is really a way to allow an Ethernet_II frame to be used in an 802.3 frame. Even though the following network trace shows a protocol field, it is really an Ethernet_II type (ether-type) field.

```
Flags:          0x80   802.3
Status:         0x00
Packet Length:78
Timestamp:      09:32:48.264000 01/04/2000
802.3 Header
Destination:    09:00:07:FF:FF:FF   AT Ph 2 Broadcast
Source:         00:00:86:10:C1:6F
LLC Length:     60
802.2 Logical Link Control (LLC) Header
Dest. SAP:      0xAA   SNAP
Source SAP:     0xAA   SNAP
Command:        0x03   Unnumbered Information
Protocol:       0x080007809B   AppleTalk
```

You can identify a SNAP frame because the DSAP and SSAP fields are always AA, and the command field is always 3. The reason this frame type was created is because not all protocols worked well with the 802.3 Ethernet frame, which didn't have an ether-type field. To allow the proprietary protocols created by application developers to be used in the LLC frame, the IEEE defined the SNAP format. It is not used that often and is mostly seen only with AppleTalk and proprietary frames. Cisco uses a SNAP frame with their proprietary protocol Cisco Discovery Protocol (CDP), which is covered in Chapter 7.

Ethernet at the Physical Layer

In a shared-hub Ethernet environment, if one station sends a frame, then all devices must synchronize to the digital signal being transmitted and extract the frame from the wire. All devices that use the same physical media and listen to each frame are considered to be in the same collision domain. This means that only one device can transmit at any given time, and any other device on the network segment must synchronize with the signal and extract the frame. If two stations try to transmit at the same time, a collision will occur. In 1984, the IEEE Ethernet committee released the Carrier Sense Multiple Access with Collision Detect (CSMA/CD) protocol. This basically tells all stations to constantly listen for any other device trying to transmit at the same time they are and to stop and wait for a predetermined time if they do sense a collision.

Ethernet uses a bus topology, which means that whenever a device transmits, the signal must run from one end of the segment to the other. Ethernet also defined baseband technology, which means that when a station does transmit, it will use the entire bandwidth on the wire and will not share it. Here are the original IEEE 802.3 standards:

10Base2   10Mbps, baseband technology, up to 185 meters in length. Known as thinnet and can support up to 30 workstations on a single segment.

10Base5   10Mbps, baseband technology, up to 500 meters in length. Known as thicknet.

10BaseT   10Mbps using category-3 twisted-pair wiring. Unlike the 10Base2 and 10Base5 networks, each device must connect into a hub or switch, and you can only have one host per segment or wire.

Each of the 802.3 standards defines an Attachment Unit Interface (AUI), which allows a one-bit-at-a-time transfer to the Physical layer from the Data Link media access method. This allows the MAC to remain constant but means the Physical layer can support any existing and new technologies. The original AUI interface was a 15-pin connector, which allowed a transceiver (transmitter/receiver) that provided a 15-pin–to–twisted-pair conversion. Typically, the AUI has a built-in transceiver, and the connections are now usually just RJ-45 connections.

However, the AUI interface cannot support 100Mbps Ethernet because of the high frequencies involved. 100BaseT needed a new interface, and the 802.3u specifications created one called the Media Independent Interface (MII), which provides 100Mbps throughput. The MII uses a nibble, which is defined as four bits. Gigabit Ethernet uses a Gigabit Media Independent Interface (GMII), which is eight bits at a time.

Data Encapsulation

When a host transmits data across a network to another device, the data is *encapsulated* with protocol information at each layer of the OSI model. Each layer communicates only with its peer layer on the receiving device.

To communicate and exchange information, each layer uses what are called *Protocol Data Units (PDUs)*. These hold the control information attached to the data at each layer of the model, which is typically attached to the header of the data field but can also be in the trailer, or end of the data field.

Each PDU is attached to the data by encapsulating it at each layer of the OSI model. Each PDU has a specific name depending on the information each header has. This PDU information is only read by the peer layer on the receiving device and then is stripped off and the data is handed to the next upper layer.

Figure 1.13 shows the PDUs and how they attach control information to each layer.

This figure shows how the upper-layer user data is converted for transmission on the network. The data stream is then handed down to the Transport layer, which sets up a virtual circuit to the receiving device by sending a synch packet. The data stream is then broken up into smaller pieces, and a Transport layer header (PDU) is created and called a segment. The header control information is attached to the header of the data field. Each segment is sequenced so the data stream can be put back together on the receiving side exactly as transmitted.

FIGURE 1.13 Data encapsulation

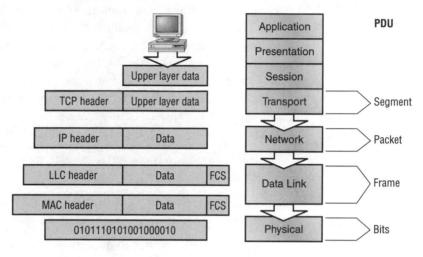

Each segment is then handed to the Network layer for network addressing and routing through an internetwork. Logical addressing, for example, IP, is used to get each segment to the correct network. The Network-layer protocol adds a control header to the segment handed down from the Transport layer, and it is now called a packet or datagram. Remember that the Transport and Network layers work together to rebuild a data stream on a receiving host. However, they have no responsibility for placing their PDUs on a local network segment, which is the only way to get the information to a router or host.

The Data Link layer is responsible for taking packets from the Network layer and placing them on the network medium (cable or wireless). The Data Link layer encapsulates each packet in a frame, and the frame's header carries the hardware address of the source and destination hosts. If the device is on a remote network, then the frame is sent to a router to be routed through an internetwork. Once it gets to the destination network, a new frame is used to get the packet to the destination host.

To put this frame on the network, it must first be put into a digital signal. Since a frame is really a logical group of 1s and 0s, the Physical layer is responsible for encapsulating these digits into a digital signal, which is read by devices on the same local network. The receiving devices will synchronize on the digital signal and extract the 1s and 0s from the digital signal. At this point the devices build the frames, run a cyclic redundancy check (CRC), and then check their answer against the answer in the frame's FCS field. If it matches, the packet is pulled from the frame, and the frame is discarded. This process is called de-encapsulation. The packet is handed to the Network layer, where the address is checked. If the address matches, the segment is pulled from the packet, and the packet is discarded. The segment is processed at the Transport layer, which rebuilds the data stream and acknowledges to the transmitting station that it received each piece. It then happily hands the data stream to the upper-layer application.

At a transmitting device, the data encapsulation method works as follows:

1. User information is converted to data for transmission on the network.

2. Data is converted to segments and a reliable connection is set up between the transmitting and receiving hosts.

3. Segments are converted to packets or datagrams, and a logical address is placed in the header so each packet can be routed through an internetwork.

4. Packets or datagrams are converted to frames for transmission on the local network. Hardware (Ethernet) addresses are used to uniquely identify hosts on a local network segment.

5. Frames are converted to bits, and a digital encoding and clocking scheme is used.

The Cisco Three-Layer Hierarchical Model

Most of us were exposed to hierarchy early in life. Anyone with older siblings learned what it was like to be at the bottom of the hierarchy! Regardless of where you first discovered hierarchy, today most of us experience it in many aspects of our lives. *Hierarchy* helps us understand where things belong, how things fit together, and what functions go where. It brings order and understandability to otherwise complex models. If you want a pay raise, for instance, hierarchy dictates that you ask your boss, not your subordinate. That is the person whose role it is to grant (or deny) your request.

Hierarchy has many of the same benefits in network design that it does in other areas of life. When used properly, it makes networks more predictable. It helps us define at which levels of hierarchy we should perform certain functions. Likewise, you can use tools such as access lists at certain levels in hierarchical networks and avoid them at others.

Let's face it, large networks can be extremely complicated, with multiple protocols, detailed configurations, and diverse technologies. Hierarchy helps us summarize a complex collection of details into an understandable model. Then, as specific configurations are needed, the model dictates the appropriate manner to apply them.

The Cisco hierarchical model can help you design, implement, and maintain a scalable, reliable, cost-effective hierarchical internetwork. Cisco defines three layers of hierarchy, as shown in Figure 1.14, each with specific functions.

FIGURE 1.14   The Cisco hierarchical model

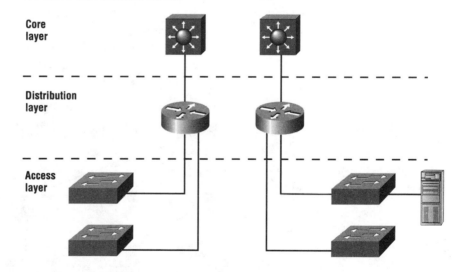

The following are the three layers:

- The Core layer
- The Distribution layer
- The Access layer

Each layer has specific responsibilities. Remember, however, that the three layers are logical and are not necessarily physical devices. Consider the OSI model, another logical hierarchy. The seven layers describe functions but not necessarily protocols, right? Sometimes a protocol maps to more than one layer of the OSI model, and sometimes multiple protocols communicate within a single layer. In the same way, when we build physical implementations of hierarchical networks, we may have many devices in a single layer, or we might have a single device performing functions at two layers. The definition of the layers is logical, not physical.

Before you learn about these layers and their functions, consider a common hierarchical design as shown in Figure 1.15. The phrase "keep local traffic local" has almost become a cliché in the networking world; however, the underlying concept has merit. Hierarchical design lends itself perfectly to fulfilling this concept.

Now, let's take a closer look at each of the layers.

FIGURE 1.15 Hierarchical network design

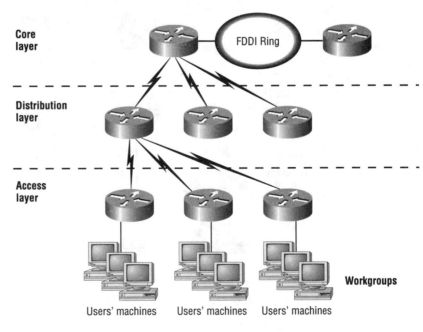

The Core Layer

The *core layer* is literally the core of the network. At the top of the hierarchy, the core layer is responsible for transporting large amounts of traffic both reliably and quickly. The only purpose of the network's core layer is to switch traffic as fast as possible. The traffic transported across the core is common to a majority of users. However, remember that user data is processed at the distribution layer, which forwards the requests to the core if needed.

If there is a failure in the core, *every single user* can be affected. Therefore, fault tolerance at this layer is an issue. The core is likely to see large volumes of traffic, so speed and latency are driving concerns here. Given the function of the core, we can now consider some design specifics. Let's start with some things we don't want to do.

- Don't do anything to slow down traffic. This includes using access lists, routing between virtual local area networks (VLANs), and packet filtering.

- Don't support workgroup access here.

- Avoid expanding the core when the internetwork grows (i.e., adding routers). If performance becomes an issue in the core, give preference to upgrades over expansion.

Now, there are a few things that we want to do as we design the core. They include the following:

- Design the core for high reliability. Consider data-link technologies that facilitate both speed and redundancy, such as FDDI, Fast Ethernet (with redundant links), or even ATM.

- Design with speed in mind. The core should have very little latency.

- Select routing protocols with lower convergence times. Fast and redundant data-link connectivity is no help if your routing tables are shot!

The Distribution Layer

The *distribution layer* is sometimes referred to as the workgroup layer and is the communication point between the access layer and the core. The primary function of the distribution layer is to provide routing, filtering, and WAN access and to determine how packets can access the core, if needed.

The distribution layer must determine the fastest way that network service requests are handled; for example, how a file request is forwarded to a server. After the distribution layer determines the best path, it forwards the request to the core layer. The core layer then quickly transports the request to the correct service.

The distribution layer is the place to implement policies for the network. Here you can exercise considerable flexibility in defining network operation. There are several items that generally should be done at the distribution layer. They include the following:

- Implementation of tools such as access lists, of packet filtering, and of queuing

- Implementation of security and network policies, including address translation and firewalls

- Redistribution between routing protocols, including static routing

- Routing between VLANs and other workgroup support functions

- Definitions of broadcast and multicast domains

Things to avoid at the distribution layer are limited to those functions that exclusively belong to one of the other layers.

The Access Layer

The *access layer* controls user and workgroup access to internetwork resources. The access layer is sometimes referred to as the desktop layer. The network resources most users need will be available locally. The distribution layer handles any traffic for remote services. The following are some of the functions to be included at the access layer:

- Continued (from distribution layer) access control and policies

- Creation of separate collision domains (segmentation)

- Workgroup connectivity into the distribution layer

Technologies such as DDR and Ethernet switching are frequently seen in the access layer. Static routing (instead of dynamic routing protocols) is seen here as well.

As already noted, three separate levels does not imply three separate routers. It could be fewer, or it could be more. Remember, this is a *layered* approach.

Assembling and Cabling Cisco Devices

In this section, I'll address the corporate environment and the different types of cabling required to connect an internetwork. To understand the types of cabling used to assemble and cable Cisco devices, you need to understand the LAN Physical layer implementation of Ethernet.

Ethernet is a media access method that is specified at the Data Link layer and uses specific Physical layer cabling and signaling techniques. It is important to be able to differentiate between the types of connectors that can be used to connect an Ethernet network together. I'll discuss the different unshielded twisted-pair cabling used today in an Ethernet LAN.

Cabling the Ethernet Local Area Network

Ethernet was first implemented by a group called DIX (Digital, Intel, and Xerox). They created and implemented the first Ethernet LAN specification, which the IEEE used to create the IEEE 802.3 committee. This was a 10Mbps network that ran on coax, twisted-pair, and fiber physical media.

The IEEE extended the 802.3 committee to two new committees known as 802.3u (FastEthernet) and 802.3q (Gigabit Ethernet). These are both specified on twisted-pair and fiber physical media. Figure 1.16 shows the IEEE 802.3 and original Ethernet Physical layer specifications.

FIGURE 1.16 Ethernet Physical layer specifications

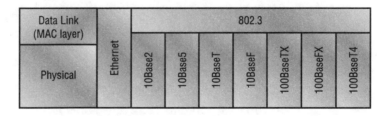

When designing your LAN, it is important to understand the different types of Ethernet media available. It would certainly be great to run Gigabit Ethernet to each desktop and 10Gbps between switches, and although this might happen one day, it is unrealistic to think you can justify the cost of that network today. By mixing and matching the different types of Ethernet media methods today, you can create a cost-effective network that works great.

The following bullet points provide a general understanding of where you can use the different Ethernet media in your hierarchical network:

- Use 10Mbps switches at the access layer to provide good performance at a low price. 100Mbps links can be used for high-bandwidth–consuming clients or servers. No servers should be at 10Mbps if possible.

- Use FastEthernet between access layer and distribution layer switches. 10Mbps links would create a bottleneck.

- Use FastEthernet (or Gigabit if applicable) between distribution layer switches and the core. Also, you should be implementing the fastest media you can afford between the core switches. Dual links between distribution and core switches are recommended for redundancy and load balancing.

Ethernet Media and Connector Requirements

It's important to understand the difference between the media access speeds Ethernet provides. However, it's also important to understand the connector requirements for each implementation before making any decision.

The EIA/TIA (Electronic Industries Association and the newer Telecommunications Industry Association) is the standards body that creates the Physical layer specifications for Ethernet. The EIA/TIA specifies that Ethernet use a *registered jack (RJ) connector* with a 4 5 wiring sequence on *unshielded twisted-pair (UTP)* cabling (RJ-45). The following bullet points outline the different Ethernet media requirements:

10Base2　50-ohm coax, called *thinnet*. Up to 185 meters and 30 hosts per segment. Uses a physical and logical bus with AUI connectors.

10Base5　50-ohm coax called *thicknet*. Up to 500 meters and 208 users per segment. Uses a physical and logical bus with AUI connectors. Up to 2500 meters with repeaters and 1024 users for all segments.

10BaseT　EIA/TIA category 3, 4, or 5, using two-pair unshielded twisted-pair (UTP) wiring. One user per segment; up to 100 meters long. Uses an RJ-45 connector with a physical star topology and a logical bus.

100BaseTX   EIA/TIA category 5, 6, or 7 UTP two-pair wiring. One user per segment; up to 100 meters long. Uses an RJ-45 MII connector with a physical star topology and a logical bus.

100BaseFX   Uses fiber cabling 62.5/125-micron multimode fiber. Point-to-point topology; up to 400 meters long. Uses an ST or SC connector, which are duplex media-interface connectors.

1000BaseCX   Copper shielded twisted-pair that can only run up to 25 meters.

1000BaseT   Category 5, four-pair UTP wiring up to 100 meters long.

1000BaseSX   MMF using 62.5 and 50-micron core; uses a 780-nanometer laser and can go up to 260 meters.

1000BaseLX   Single-mode fiber that uses a 9-micron core, 1300-nanometer laser and can go from 3 km up to 10 km.

100VG-AnyLAN is a twisted-pair technology that was the first 100Mbps LAN. However, since it was incompatible with Ethernet signaling techniques (it used a polling media access method), it was not typically used and is essentially dead.

UTP Connections (RJ-45)

The RJ-45 connector is clear so you can see the eight colored wires that connect to the connector's pins. These wires are twisted into four pairs. Four wires (two pairs) carry the voltage and are considered *tip*. The other four wires are grounded and are called *ring*. The RJ-45 connector is crimped onto the end of the wire, and the pin locations of the connector are numbered from the left, 8 to 1.

Figure 1.17 shows a UTP cable with an RJ-45 connector attached.

The UTP cable has twisted wires inside that eliminate cross talk. Unshielded cable can be used since digital signal protection comes from the twists in the wire. The more twists per inch, the farther the digital signal can supposedly travel without interference. For example, categories 5 and 6 have many more twists per inch than category 3 UTP does.

FIGURE 1.17   UTP wire with an RJ-45 connector attached

Pin	Wire Pair (T Is Tip; R Is Ring)
1	Pair 2 T2
2	Pair 2 R2
3	Pair 3 T3
4	Pair 1 R1
5	Pair 1 T1
6	Pair 3 R3
7	Pair 4 T4
8	Pair 4 R4

RJ-45 connector

Different types of wiring are used when building internetworks. You will need to use either a straight-through or crossover cable.

Straight-Through

In a UTP implementation of a straight-through cable, the wires on both cable ends are in the same order. Figure 1.18 shows the pinouts of the straight-through cable.

FIGURE 1.18   UTP straight-through pinouts

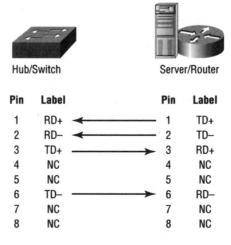

Hub/Switch   Server/Router

Pin	Label		Pin	Label
1	RD+	←	1	TD+
2	RD–	←	2	TD–
3	TD+	→	3	RD+
4	NC		4	NC
5	NC		5	NC
6	TD–	→	6	RD–
7	NC		7	NC
8	NC		8	NC

You can determine that the wiring is a straight-through cable by holding both ends of the UTP cable side by side and seeing that the order of the wires on both ends is identical.

You can use a straight-through cable for the following tasks:

- Connecting a router to a hub or switch

- Connecting a server to a hub or switch

- Connecting workstations to a hub or switch

Crossover

In the implementation of a crossover, the wires on each end of the cable are crossed. Transmit to Receive and Receive to Transmit on each side, for both tip and ring. Figure 1.19 shows the UTP crossover implementation.

FIGURE 1.19 UTP crossover implementation

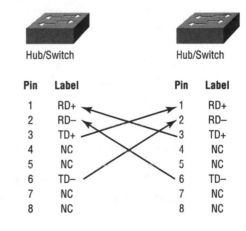

Notice that pin 1 on one side connects to pin 3 on the other side, and pin 2 connects to pin 6 on the opposite end.

You can use a crossover cable for the following tasks:

- Connecting uplinks between switches

- Connecting hubs to switches

- Connecting a hub to another hub

- Connecting a router interface to another router interface
- Connecting two PCs together without a hub or switch

When trying to determine the type of cable needed for a port, look at the port and see if it is marked with an "X." Use a straight-through cable when only one port is designated with an "X." Use a crossover when both ports are designated with an "X" or when neither port has an "X."

Cabling the Wide Area Network

To connect your *wide area network (WAN),* you need to understand the WAN Physical layer implementation provided by Cisco as well as the different WAN serial connectors. In this section, I will give you that information, along with the cabling requirements for ISDN BRI connections.

Cisco serial connections support almost any type of WAN service. The typical WAN connections are dedicated leased lines using High-Level Data Link Control (HDLC), Point-to-Point Protocol (PPP), Integrated Services Digital Network (ISDN), and Frame Relay. Typical speeds are anywhere from 2400bps to 1.544Mbps (T1).

All of these WAN types are discussed in detail in Chapter 10.

HDLC, PPP, and Frame Relay can use the same Physical layer specifications, but ISDN has different pinouts and specifications at the Physical layer.

Serial Transmission

WAN serial connectors use *serial transmission*, which is one bit at a time, over a single channel. *Parallel transmission* can pass at least 8 bits at a time. All WANs use serial transmission.

Cisco routers use a proprietary 60-pin serial connector, which you must buy from Cisco or a provider of Cisco equipment. The type of connector you have on the other end of the cable depends on your service provider or end-device requirements. The different ends available are EIA/TIA-232, EIA/TIA-449, V.35 (used to connect to a CSU/DSU), X.21 (used in X.25), and EIA-530.

Serial links are described in frequency or cycles-per-second (hertz). The amount of data that can be carried within these frequencies is called *bandwidth*. Bandwidth is the amount of data in bits-per-second that the serial channel can carry.

Data Terminal Equipment and Data Communication Equipment

Router interfaces are, by default, *Data Terminal Equipment (DTE)* and connect into *Data Communication Equipment (DCE)*, for example, a *Channel Service Unit/Data Service Unit (CSU/DSU)*. The CSU/DSU then plugs into a demarcation location (demarc) and is the service provider's last responsibility. Typically, the demarc is a jack that has an RJ-45 female connector located close to your equipment. If you report a problem to your service provider, they'll always tell you it tests fine up to the demarc and that the problem must be the CPE, or Customer Premise Equipment, which is your responsibility.

The idea behind a WAN is to be able to connect two DTE networks together through a DCE network. The DCE network includes the CSU/DSU, through the provider's wiring and switches, all the way to the CSU/DSU at the other end. The network's DCE device provides clocking to the DTE-connected interface (the router's serial interface).

Fixed and Modular Interfaces

Some routers Cisco sells have fixed interfaces, while others are modular. The fixed routers, such as the 2500 series, have set interfaces that can't be changed. The 2501 router has two serial connections and one 10BaseT AUI interface. If you need to add a third serial interface, then you need to buy a new router—ouch! However, the 1600, 1700, 2600, 3600, and higher routers have modular interfaces that allow you to buy what you need now and add almost any type of interface you may need later. The 1600 and 1700 are limited and have both fixed and modular ports, but the 2600 and up provide many serials, FastEthernet, and even voice-module availability.

Integrated Services Digital Network (ISDN) Connections

Integrated Services Digital Network (ISDN) Basic Rate Interface (BRI) is two B (Bearer) channels of 64k each and one D (Data) channel of 16k for signaling and clocking.

ISDN BRI routers come with either a U interface or what is known as an S/T interface. The difference between the two is that the U interface is already a two-wire ISDN convention that can plug right into the ISDN local loop. The S/T interface is a four-wire interface and needs a Network Termination type 1 (NT 1) to convert from a four-wire to the two-wire ISDN specification.

ISDN is covered in depth in Chapter 10.

The U interface has a built-in NT 1 device. If your service provider uses an NT 1 device, then you need to buy a router that has an S/T interface. Most Cisco router BRI interfaces are marked with a U or an S/T. When in doubt, ask Cisco or the salesperson you bought it from.

Primary Rate Interface (PRI) provides T1 speeds (1.544Mbps) in the U.S. and E1 speeds (2.048) in Europe. PRI is not discussed further in this course.

The ISDN BRI interface uses an RJ-45, category 5, straight-through cable. It is important to avoid plugging a console cable or other LAN cable into a BRI interface on a router, because it will probably ruin the interface. Cisco says it *will* ruin it, but I have students do it every week and haven't lost one yet (I probably shouldn't have said that…now I will probably lose one next week).

Console Connections

All Cisco devices are shipped with console cables and connectors, which allow you to connect to a device and configure, verify, and monitor it. The cable used to connect between a PC is a rollover cable with RJ-45 connectors.

The pinouts for a rollover cable are as follows:

1–8

2–7

3–6

4–5

5–4

6–3

7–2

8–1

You can see that you just take a straight-through RJ-45 cable, cut the end off, flip it over, and reattach a new connector.

Typically, you will use the DB9 connector to attach to your PC and use a com port to communicate via HyperTerminal. Most Cisco devices now support RJ-45 console connections. However, the Catalyst 5000 series switch still uses a DB25 connector.

Set up the terminal emulation program to run 9600bps, 8 data bits, no parity, 1 stop bit, and no flow control. On some routers, you need to verify that the terminal emulation program is emulating a VT100 dumb-terminal mode, not an auto-sense mode, or it won't work.

Most routers also have an aux port, which is an auxiliary port used to connect a modem. You can then dial this modem and connect the router to the aux port. This will give you console access to a remote router that might be down and that you cannot telnet into. The console port and aux port are considered out-of-band management since you are configuring the router "out of the network." Telnet is considered in-band.

Selecting Cisco Products

You can use the Cisco three-layer model to determine what type of product to buy for your internetwork. By understanding the services required at each layer and what functions the internetworking devices perform, you can then match Cisco products to your business requirements. To select the correct Cisco products for your network, start by gathering information about where devices need to operate in the internetworking hierarchy, and then consider issues like ease of installation, port-capacity requirements, and other features.

If you have remote offices or other WAN needs, you need to first find out what type of service is available. It won't do you any good to design a large Frame Relay network only to discover that Frame Relay is only supported in half the locations you need. After you research and find out about the different options available through your service provider, you can choose the Cisco product that fits your business requirements.

You have a few options, typically: dial-up asynchronous connections, leased lines up to 1.544Mbps, Frame Relay, and ISDN, which are the most popular WAN technologies. However, xDSL is the new front-runner to take over as the fastest, most reliable, cheapest WAN technology. You need to consider your usage before buying and implementing a technology. For example, if your users at a remote branch are connected to the corporate office more than three to four hours a day, then you need either Frame Relay or a leased line. If they connect infrequently, then you might get away with ISDN or dial-up connectivity.

The next sections discuss the different types of Cisco hubs, routers, and switches you can use to build a hierarchical network.

Cisco Hubs

It is hard for me to imagine that you would call Cisco and ask to buy a hub, but I suppose it does happen or they wouldn't be selling them. Cisco actually has an extensive listing of hubs that address an amazing variety of selection issues.

Before you buy any hub, you need to know—not think you know, but actually know—which users can use a shared 10Mbps or shared 100Mbps network. The lower-end model of hubs Cisco offers supports only 10Mbps, while the middle-of-the-road one offers both 10- and 100Mbps auto-sensing ports. The higher-end hubs offer network-management port and console connections. If you are going to spend enough to buy a high-end hub, you should consider just buying a switch. Figure 1.20 shows the different hub products Cisco offers. Any of these hubs can be stacked together to give you more port density.

These are the selection issues you need to know:

- Business requirements for 10- or 100Mbps

- Port density

- Management

- Ease of operation

FIGURE 1.20   Cisco hub products

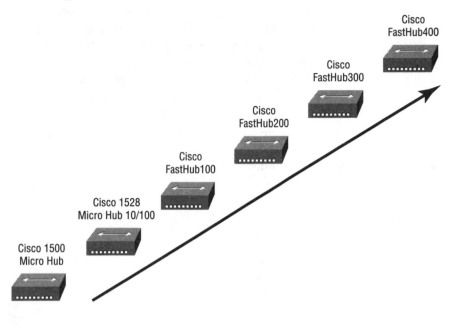

Cisco Routers

When you think of Cisco, what do you think of first? Hubs? I don't think so. You think of routers, of course. Cisco makes the best routers in the world. Everyone knows this, and it is also one of the reasons you are even reading this book.

It seems as though Cisco comes out with a new router almost every month. It is hard to keep up with their new offerings. A key criterion when selecting router products is knowing what feature sets you need to meet your business requirements. For example, do you need IP, Frame Relay, and VPN support? How about IPX, AppleTalk, and DECnet? Cisco has it all.

The other features you need to think about when considering different product-selection criteria are port density and interface speeds. As you get into the higher-end models, you see more ports and faster speeds. For example, the new 12000 series model is Cisco's first gigabit switch and has enormous capability and functionality.

You can tell how much a product is going to cost by looking at the model number. A stripped-down 12000 series switch with no cards or power supplies starts at about $12,000. The price can end up at well over $100,000 for a loaded system. Seems like a loaded 12000 series system would be great for my little home network.

You also need to think about WAN support when buying a router. You can get anything you want in a Cisco router, but you just have to be familiar with the service provided for your area.

Figure 1.21 shows some of the router products Cisco sells.

FIGURE 1.21 Cisco router products

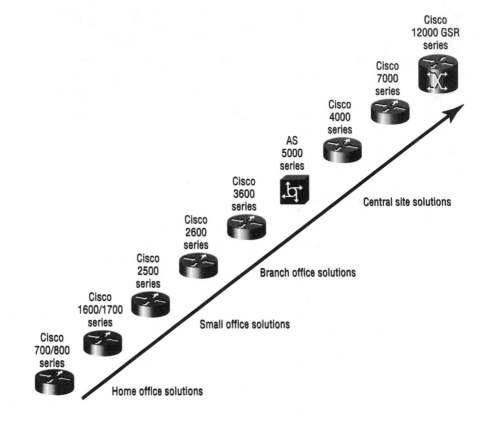

The Cisco 800 series router has mostly replaced the Cisco 700 series because the 700 series does not run the Cisco IOS. In fact, I hope Cisco will soon stop selling the 700 series routers altogether. They are difficult to configure and maintain.

The main selections involved in choosing Cisco routers are listed below:

- Scale of routing features needed

- Port density and variety requirements

- Capacity and performance

- Common user interface

Cisco Switches

It seems like switch prices are dropping almost daily. I just received an e-mail from Cisco announcing that the Catalyst 2900 series switches have dropped in price 30 percent. About four years ago a 12-port 10/100 switch card for the Catalyst 5000 series switch was about $15,000. Now you can buy a complete Catalyst 5000 with a 10/100 card and supervisor module for about $7500 or so. My point is that with switch prices becoming reasonable, it is now easier to install switches in your network. Why buy hubs when you can use switches? I think every closet should have at least one switch.

Cisco has a huge assortment of switches to meet absolutely every business need. You must consider whether you need 10/100 or 1000Mbps for each desktop or to connect between switches. ATM (asynchronous transfer mode) is also a consideration; however, with Gigabit Ethernet out and 10Gbps links just around the corner, who needs ATM? The next criteria to consider are port density. The lower-end models start at 12 ports, and the higher-end models can provide hundreds of switched ports per switch.

Figure 1.22 shows the Cisco-switch product line.

FIGURE 1.22 Cisco Catalyst switch products

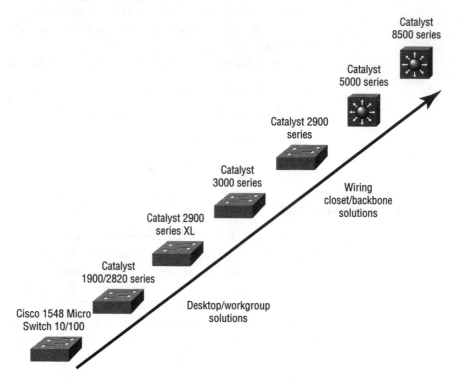

The selection issues you need to know when choosing a Cisco switch are listed below:

- Business requirements for 10,100 or even 1000Mbps

- Need for trunking and interswitch links

- Workgroup segmentation (VLANs)

- Port density needs

- Different user interfaces

Summary

This chapter began with a discussion of the OSI model, which is a seven-layer model used to help application developers design applications that can run on any type of system or network. I provided complete details of each layer and discussed how Cisco views the specifications of the model

Different types of devices are specified at each of the OSI model's layers. This chapter discussed the different types of devices, cables, and connectors used at each layer.

Also, I provided an introduction to the Cisco hierarchical network model, which was created to help administrators design and understand hierarchical networks. By using the Cisco three-layer model, you can effectively design, implement, and maintain any size network.

Cisco makes a large range of router, hub, and switch products. I discussed the different products Cisco creates and sells so that you can make more informed decisions when building your internetwork.

Key Terms

Before taking the exam, be sure you're familiar with the following terms.

access layer	*core layer*
Application layer	*Data Communication Equipment (DCE)*
Application-Specific Integrated Circuits (ASICs)	*data frame*
Basic Rate Interface (BRI)	*Data Link layer*
bridges	*Data Terminal Equipment (DTE)*
broadcast domain	*distribution layer*
buffer	*encapsulation*
Carrier Sense Multiple Access with Collision Detect (CSMA/CD)	*Ethernet*
Channel Service Unit/Data Service Unit (CSU/DSU)	*flow control*

frame	*Protocol Data Units (PDUs)*
full duplex	*registered jack (RJ) connector*
half duplex	*router*
hierarchical addressing	*Session layer*
hubs	*simplex*
Integrated Services Digital Network (ISDN)	*state transitions*
layered architecture	*switch*
Media Access Control (MAC) address	*thicknet*
Network layer	*thinnet*
Organizationally Unique Identifier (OUI)	*Transport layer*
OSI (Open Systems Interconnection) model	*unshielded twisted-pair (UTP)*
Physical layer	*wide area network (WAN)*
Presentation layer	*windowing*

Written Labs

In this section, you will complete the following labs:

- Lab 1.1: OSI Questions
- Lab 1.2: Defining the OSI Layers and Devices
- Lab 1.3: Identifying Collision and Broadcast Domains

Lab 1.1: OSI Questions

Answer the following questions about the OSI model:

1. Which layer chooses and determines the availability of communicating partners, along with the resources necessary to make the connection; coordinates partnering applications; and forms a consensus on procedures for controlling data integrity and error recovery?

2. Which layer is responsible for converting data packets from the Data Link layer into electrical signals?

3. At which layer is routing implemented, enabling connections and path selection between two end systems?

4. Which layer defines how data is formatted, presented, encoded, and converted for use on the network?

5. Which layer is responsible for creating, managing, and terminating sessions between applications?

6. Which layer ensures the trustworthy transmission of data across a physical link and is primarily concerned with physical addressing, line discipline, network topology, error notification, ordered delivery of frames, and flow control?

7. Which layer is used for reliable communication between end nodes over the network and provides mechanisms for establishing, maintaining, and terminating virtual circuits; transport-fault detection and recovery; and controlling the flow of information?

8. Which layer provides logical addressing that routers will use for path determination?

9. Which layer specifies voltage, wire speed, and pin-out cables and moves bits between devices?

10. Which layer combines bits into bytes and bytes into frames, uses MAC addressing, and provides error detection?

11. Which layer is responsible for keeping different applications' data separate on the network?

12. Which layer is represented by frames?

13. Which layer is represented by segments?

14. Which layer is represented by packets?

15. Which layer is represented by bits?

16. Put the following in order of encapsulation:
    - packets
    - frames
    - bits
    - segments

17. Put the following in order of de-encapsulation:
    - packets
    - frames
    - bits
    - segments

Lab 1.2: Defining the OSI Layers and Devices

Fill in the blanks with the appropriate layer of the OSI or hub, switch, or router device.

Description	Device or OSI Layer
Logical port numbers are used at this layer.	
This device sends and receives information about the Network layer.	
This layer creates a virtual circuit before transmitting between two end stations.	
This layer uses service access points.	
This device uses hardware addresses to filter a network.	
Ethernet is defined at these layers.	
This layer supports flow control and sequencing.	
This device can measure the distance to a remote network.	
Logical addressing is used at this layer.	
Hardware addresses are defined at this layer.	
This device creates one big collision domain and one large broadcast domain.	
This device creates many smaller collision domains, but the network is still one large broadcast domain.	
This device breaks up collision domains and broadcast domains.	

Lab 1.3: Identifying Collision and Broadcast Domains

In Figure 1.23, identify the amount of collision domains and broadcast domains in each network.

FIGURE 1.23 Identifying the amount of collision and broadcast domains

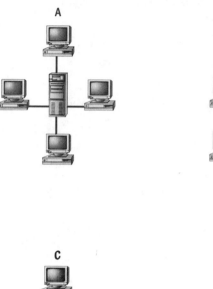

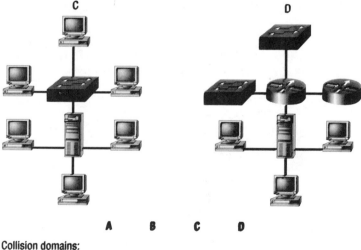

	A	B	C	D
Collision domains:				
Broadcast domains:				

Review Questions

1. Which Cisco layer is responsible for breaking up collision domains?

   A. Physical

   B. Access

   C. Core

   D. Network

   E. Distribution

   F. Data Link

2. PDUs at the Network layer of the OSI are called what?

   A. Core

   B. Frames

   C. Packets

   D. Segments

   E. Access

   F. Distribution

   G. Transport

3. At which Cisco layer would broadcast domains be defined?

   A. Core

   B. Network

   C. Physical

   D. Distribution

   E. Access

   F. Transport

4. PDUs at the Data Link layer are named what?

   A. Frames

   B. Packets

   C. Datagrams

   D. Transports

   E. Segments

   F. Bits

5. Segmentation of a data stream happens at which layer of the OSI model?

   A. Physical

   B. Data Link

   C. Network

   D. Transport

   E. Distribution

   F. Access

6. For which of the following would you not need to provide a crossover cable?

   A. Connecting uplinks between switches

   B. Connecting routers to switches

   C. Connecting hub to hub

   D. Connecting hubs to switches

7. What does the Data Link layer use to find hosts on a local network?

   A. Logical network addresses

   B. Port numbers

   C. Hardware addresses

   D. Default gateways

8. How is a crossover cabled?

   A. The pins 1–8 are completely opposite on the other side.

   B. It has the pins 1–8 cabled the same on the other side.

   C. Pin 1 on one side connects to pin 3 on the other side and pin 2 connects to pin 6 on the other end.

   D. Pin 2 on one side connects to pin 3 on the other side, and pin 1 connects to pin 6 on the other end.

9. Where are routers defined in the OSI model?

   A. Physical

   B. Transport

   C. Data Link

   D. Network

10. At which layer of the OSI are 1s and 0s converted to a digital signal?

    A. Physical

    B. Transport

    C. Data Link

    D. Network

11. Bridges are defined at what layer of the OSI model?

    A. Physical

    B. Transport

    C. Data Link

    D. Network

12. What Cisco layer provides segmentation of contention networks?

   A. Access

   B. Physical

   C. Network

   D. Distribution

   E. Core

   F. Transport

   G. Data Link

13. What is used at the Transport layer to stop a receiving host's buffer from overflowing?

   A. Segmentation

   B. Packets

   C. Acknowledgments

   D. Flow control

   E. PDUs

14. Which layer of the OSI provides translation of data?

   A. Application

   B. Presentation

   C. Session

   D. Transport

   E. Data Link

15. Routers can provide which of the following functions? (Choose all that apply.)

  A. Breakup of collision domains

  B. Breakup of broadcast domains

  C. Logical network addressing

  D. Physical address filtering of the local network

16. Routers are typically used at which layer of the Cisco three-layer model?

  A. Access

  B. Core

  C. Network

  D. Data Link

  E. Distribution

17. How many bits define a hardware address?

  A. 6 bits

  B. 16 bits

  C. 46 bits

  D. 48 bits

18. Which of the following is not an advantage of a layer model?

  A. Dividing the complex network operation into a more manageable layer approach

  B. Allowing changes to occur in one layer without having to change all layers

  C. Allowing changes to occur in all layers without having to change one layer

  D. Defining a standard interface for the "plug-and-play" multivendor integration

19. Which three options use twisted-pair copper wiring?

   A. 100BaseFX

   B. 100BaseTX

   C. 100VG-AnyLAN

   D. 10BaseT

   E. 100BaseSX

20. What does the "Base" indicate in 10BaseT?

   A. Backbone wiring that uses many digital signals at the same time in one wire.

   B. Baseband wiring that uses many digital signals at the same time in one wire.

   C. Backbone wiring that uses only one digital signal at a time in the wire.

   D. Baseband wiring that uses only one digital signal at a time in the wire.

(The answers to the questions begin on the next page.)

Answers to the Written Labs

Answers to Lab 1.1

1. The Application layer is responsible for finding the network resources broadcasted from a server and adding flow control and error control if the application developer chooses.

2. The Physical layer takes frames from the Data Link layer and encodes the 1s and 0s into a digital signal from transmission on the network medium.

3. The Network layer provides routing through an internetwork and logical addressing.

4. The Presentation layer makes sure that data is in a readable format for the Application layer.

5. The Session layer sets up, maintains, and terminates sessions between applications.

6. PDUs at the Data Link layer are called frames. As soon as you see "frame" in a question, you know the answer.

7. The Transport layer uses virtual circuits to create a reliable connection between two hosts.

8. The Network layer provides logical addressing, typically IP addressing and routing.

9. The Physical layer is responsible for the electrical and mechanical connections between devices.

10. The Data Link layer is responsible for the framing of data packets.

11. The Session layer creates sessions between different hosts' applications.

12. The Data Link layer frames packets received from the network layer.

13. The Transport layer segments user data.

14. The Network layer creates packets out of segments handed down from the Transport layer.

15. The Physical layer is responsible for transporting 1s and 0s in a digital signal.

16. segments, packets, frames, bits

17. bits, frames, packets, segments

Answers to Lab 1.2

Description	Device or OSI Layer
Logical port numbers are used at this layer.	Transport
This device sends and receives information about the Network layer.	Router
This layer can create a virtual circuit before transmitting between two end stations.	Transport
This layer uses service access points.	Data Link (LLC sublayer)
This device uses hardware addresses to filter a network.	Bridge or switch
Ethernet is defined at these layers.	Data Link and Physical layers
This layer supports flow control and sequencing.	Transport
This device can measure the distance to a remote network.	Router
Logical addressing is used at this layer.	Network
Hardware addresses are defined at this layer.	Data Link (MAC sublayer)
This device creates one big collision domain and one large broadcast domain.	Hub
This device creates many smaller collision domains but the network is still one large broadcast domain.	Switch or bridge
This device breaks up collision domains and broadcast domains.	Router

Answers to Lab 1.3

FIGURE 1.24   Answers to Lab 1.3

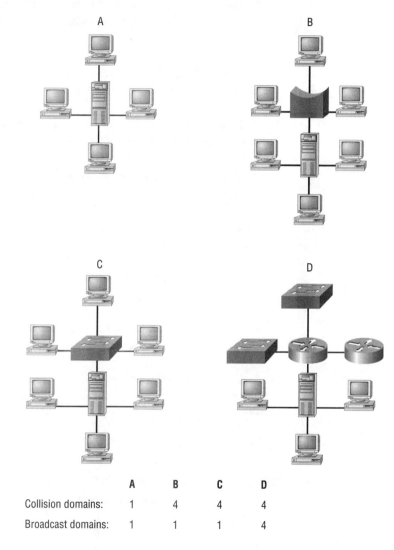

	A	**B**	**C**	**D**
Collision domains:	1	4	4	4
Broadcast domains:	1	1	1	4

Answers to Review Questions

1. B. The access layer is where users gain access to the network and where Cisco recommends users plug into switches, which break up collision domains.

2. C. Protocol Data Units are used to define data at each layer of the OSI model. PDUs at the Network layer are called packets.

3. D. Routers break up broadcast domains. Routers are defined at the distribution layer of the OSI model.

4. A. Data is encapsulated with a media access method at the Data Link layer, and the PDU is called a frame.

5. D. The Transport layer receives large data streams from the upper layers and breaks these up into smaller pieces called segments.

6. B, C. Crossover cables are used to connect switch to switch and hub to switch.

7. C. MAC addresses, also called hardware addresses, are used to uniquely identify hosts on a local network.

8. C. Crossover cables are used to connect hubs to switches, PC to PC, etc. Pin 1 connects to pin 3 on the other end, and pin 2 connects to pin 6.

9. D. Routers are defined at the Network layer of the OSI.

10. A. The Physical layer is used to encode 1s and 0s into a digital signal to be transported over a network medium.

11. C. Bridges break up collision domains and are defined at the Data Link layer.

12. A. The access layer is used to provide access to users and hosts into the internetwork, and switches are used to break up Ethernet (contention) networks at this layer.

13. D. Flow control stops a device from overflowing its buffers. Even though flow control can be used at many layers, the Transport's reliable connection provides the best flow control available in the model.

14. B. The only layer of the OSI that can actually change data is the Presentation layer.

15. A, B, C, D. Bridges provide breaking up of collision domains and filtering of networks with physical addresses, but so can a router. The key word in the question is "can."

16. E. Cisco recommends routers at the distribution layer and layer-2 switches at the other two layers.

17. D. A hardware address is 48 bits long (6 bytes).

18. C. The largest advantage of a layered model is that it can allow application developers to change the aspects of a program in just one layer of the OSI model's specifications.

19. B, C, D. 100BaseTX uses twisted-pair copper wiring, as do 100VG-AnyLAN and 10BaseT. FX and SX are fiber media.

20. D. Baseband signaling is a technique that uses the entire bandwidth of a wire when transmitting. Broadband wiring uses many signals at the same time on a wire.

Chapter

2

Switching Technologies

THE CCNA EXAM TOPICS COVERED IN THIS CHAPTER INCLUDE THE FOLLOWING:

- ✓ Describe layer-2 switching
- ✓ Describe address learning in layer-2 switches
- ✓ Understand when a layer-2 switch will forward or filter a frame
- ✓ Describe network loop problems in layer-2 switched networks
- ✓ Describe the Spanning-Tree Protocol
- ✓ List the LAN switch types and describe how they work with layer-2 switches

This second chapter will teach you the theory you must understand before continuing with the book. Appendix B will cover the Cisco Catalyst 1900 switch configuration, and Chapter 6 will cover Virtual LAN (VLAN) configuration. This chapter will give you the background you need to understand those chapters.

In this chapter you will learn the background behind the following topics:

- Layer-2 switching

- Address learning

- Forward/filtering decisions

- Loop avoidance

- Spanning-Tree Protocol

- LAN switch types

By reading and understanding the information presented in this chapter, you will be ready to configure switches and VLANs in Chapter 6 and Appendix B.

Layer-2 Switching

Layer-2 switching is hardware based, which means it uses the MAC address from the host's NIC cards to filter the network. Switches use Application-Specific Integrated Circuits (ASICs) to build and maintain filter tables. It is OK to think of a layer-2 switch as a multiport bridge. Layer-2 switches are fast because they do not look at the Network layer header information, looking instead at the frame's hardware addresses before deciding to either forward the frame or drop it.

Layer-2 switching provides the following:

- Hardware-based bridging (MAC)
- Wire speed
- Low latency
- Low cost

What makes layer-2 switching so efficient is that there is no modification to the data packet, only to the frame encapsulating the packet. Since no modification of the data packet is performed, the switching process is faster and less error-prone than routing.

Use layer-2 switching for workgroup connectivity and network segmentation (breaking up collision domains). This allows you to create a flatter network design with more network segments than traditional 10BaseT shared networks. Layer-2 switching increases bandwidth for each user because each connection (interface) into the switch is its own collision domain, so you can connect multiple devices to each interface.

Limitations of Layer-2 Switching

Since we think of layer-2 switching as the same as a bridged network, we must also think it has the same problems as a bridged network. Remember that bridges are good if we design the network correctly, meaning we break up the collision domains correctly. The right way to create bridged networks is to make sure that users spend 80 percent of their time on the local segment.

Bridged networks break up collision domains, but the network is still one large broadcast domain. Layer-2 switches (bridges) cannot break up broadcast domains, which can cause performance issues and limit the size of your network. Broadcasts and multicasts, along with the slow convergence of spanning tree, can cause major problems as the network grows. Because of these problems, layer-2 switches cannot completely replace routers (layer-3 devices) in the internetwork.

Bridging versus LAN Switching

Layer-2 switches are really just bridges with more ports. However, there are some important differences you should be aware of:

- Bridges are software based, while switches are hardware based because they use an ASICs chip to help make filtering decisions.

- Bridges can only have one spanning-tree instance per bridge, while switches can have many. (We cover spanning tree later in this chapter.)

- Bridges can only have up to 16 ports, whereas a switch can have hundreds.

Three Switch Functions at Layer 2

There are three distinct functions of layer-2 switching:

Address learning   Layer-2 switches and bridges remember the source hardware address of each frame received on an interface and enter this information into a MAC database.

Forward/filter decisions   When a frame is received on an interface, the switch looks at the destination hardware address and finds the exit interface in the MAC database.

Loop avoidance   If multiple connections between switches are created for redundancy, network loops can occur. The Spanning-Tree Protocol (STP) is used to stop network loops and allow redundancy.

Address learning, forward and filtering decisions, and loop avoidance are discussed in detail in the next sections.

Address Learning

When a switch is powered on, the MAC filtering table is empty. When a device transmits and an interface receives a frame, the switch places the source address in the MAC filtering table, remembering what interface the device is located on. The switch has no choice but to flood the network with this frame because it has no idea where the destination device is located.

If a device answers and sends a frame back, then the switch will take the source address from that frame and place the MAC address in the database, associating this address with the interface that received the frame. Since the switch now has two MAC addresses in the filtering table, the devices can make a point-to-point connection, and the frames will only be forwarded between the two devices. This is what makes layer-2 switches better than hubs. In a hub network, all frames are forwarded out all ports every time.

Figure 2.1 shows the procedures for how a MAC database is built.

FIGURE 2.1 How switches learn hosts' locations

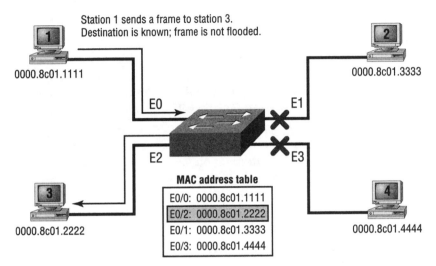

In this figure, there are four hosts attached to a switch. When the switch is powered on, it has nothing in the MAC address table.

1. Host 1 sends a frame to Host 3. Host 1's MAC address is 0000.8c01.1111; Host 3's MAC address is 0000.8c01.2222.

2. The switch receives the frame on the E0/1 interface (interface addressing is covered in Appendix B) and places the source address in the MAC address table.

3. Since the destination address is not in the MAC database, the frame is forwarded out all interfaces.

4. Host 3 receives the frame and responds to Host 1. The switch receives this frame on interface E0/3 and places the source hardware address in the MAC database.

5. Host 1 and Host 3 can now make a point-to-point connection and only the two devices will receive the frames. Hosts 2 and 4 will not see the frames.

If the two devices do not communicate to the switch again within a certain amount of time, the switch will flush the entries from the database to keep it as current as possible.

Forward/Filter Decisions

When a frame arrives at a switch interface, the destination hardware address is compared to the forward/filter MAC database. If the destination hardware address is known and listed in the database, the frame is only sent out the correct exit interface. The switch does not transmit the frame out any interface except for the destination interface. This preserves bandwidth on the other network segments and is called *frame filtering*.

If the destination hardware address is not listed in the MAC database, then the frame is broadcasted out all active interfaces except the interface the frame was received on. If a device answers the broadcast, the MAC database is updated with the device location (interface).

Broadcast and Multicast Frames

Broadcast and multicast frames do not have a destination hardware address specified. The source address will always be the hardware address of the device transmitting the frame, and the destination address will either be all 1s (broadcast), or with the network or subnet address specified and the host address all 1s (multicast). For example, a broadcast and multicast in binary would be as shown in Table 2.1.

TABLE 2.1 Broadcast and Multicast Example

	Binary	Decimal
Broadcast	11111111.11111111.11111111.11111111	255.255.255.255
Multicast	10101100.00010000.11111111.11111111	172.16.255.255

Notice that the broadcast is all 1s, but the multicast is not. They are both a type of broadcast, except that a multicast just sends the frame to a certain network or subnet and all hosts within that network or subnet, and a broadcast of all 1s sends the frame to all networks and hosts.

When a switch receives these types of frames, it is then quickly flooded out all of the switch's active ports by default. To have broadcasts and multicasts only forwarded out a limited amount of administratively assigned ports, you create Virtual LANs (VLANs), which are covered in Chapter 6.

Loop Avoidance

Redundant links are a good idea between switches. They are used to help stop complete network failures if one link fails. Even though redundant links are extremely helpful, they cause more problems than they solve. Because frames can be broadcast down all redundant links simultaneously, network loops can occur, among other problems. Some of the most serious problems are discussed in the following list.

1. If no loop avoidance schemes are put in place, the switches will flood broadcasts endlessly throughout the internetwork. This is sometimes referred to as a *broadcast storm*. Figure 2.2 shows how a broadcast may be propagated throughout the network. Notice in the figure how a frame is continually broadcast through the internetwork Physical network.

FIGURE 2.2 Broadcast storms

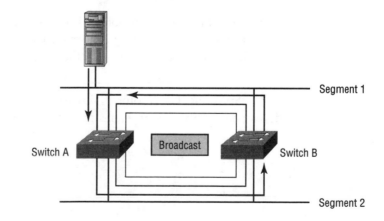

2. A device can receive multiple copies of the same frame since the frame can arrive from different segments at the same time. Figure 2.3 shows how multiple frames can arrive from multiple segments simultaneously.

FIGURE 2.3 Multiple frame copies

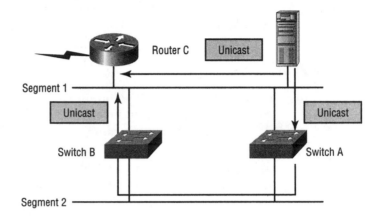

3. The MAC address filter table will be confused about where a device is located since the switch can receive the frame from more than one link. It is possible that the switch can't forward a frame because it is constantly updating the MAC filter table with source hardware address locations. This is called *thrashing* the MAC table.

4. One of the biggest problems is multiple loops generating throughout an internetwork. This means that loops can occur within other loops. If a broadcast storm were to then occur, the network would not be able to perform packet switching.

The Spanning-Tree Protocol, discussed in the following section, was developed to solve the problems presented in this list.

Spanning-Tree Protocol (STP)

Digital Equipment Corporation (DEC), which was purchased and is now called Compaq, was the original creator of Spanning-Tree Protocol (STP). The IEEE created their own version of STP called 802.1d. All Cisco switches run the IEEE 802.1d version of STP, which is not compatible with the DEC version.

STP's main task is to stop network loops from occurring on your layer-2 network (bridges or switches). STP is constantly monitoring the network to find all links and make sure that loops do not occur by shutting down redundant links.

Spanning-Tree Operations

STP finds all links in the network and shuts down redundant links, thereby stopping any network loops from occurring in the network. The way it does this is by electing a root bridge that will decide on the network topology. There can only be one root bridge in any given network. Root-bridge ports are called *designated ports*, which operate in what are called forwarding-state ports. Forwarding-state ports send and receive traffic.

Other switches in your network are called nonroot bridges, as shown in Figure 2.4. However, the port with the lowest cost (as determined by a link's bandwidth) to the root bridge is called a root port and sends and receives traffic.

FIGURE 2.4   Spanning-tree operations

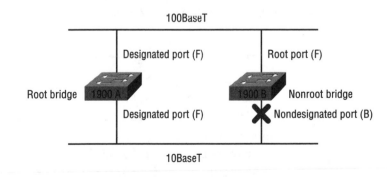

Ports determined to have the lowest-cost path to the root bridge are called designated ports. The other port or ports on the bridge are considered nondesignated and will not send or receive traffic, which is called blocking mode.

Selecting the Root Bridge

Switches or bridges running STP exchange information with what are called Bridge Protocol Data Units (BPDUs). BPDUs send configuration messages using multicast frames. The bridge ID of each device is sent to other devices using BPDUs.

The bridge ID is used to determine the root bridge in the network and to determine the root port. The bridge ID is 8 bytes long and includes the priority and the MAC address of the device. The priority on all devices running the IEEE STP version is 32,768.

To determine the root bridge, the priorities of the bridge and the MAC address are combined. If two switches or bridges have the same priority value, then the MAC address is used to determine which one has the lowest ID. For example, if two switches, which I'll name A and B, both use the default priority of 32,768, then the MAC address will be used. If switch A's MAC address is 0000.0c00.1111.1111 and switch B's MAC address is 0000.0c00.2222.2222, then switch A would become the root bridge.

The following network analyzer output shows a BPDU transmitted from a 1900 switch. BPDUs are sent out every two seconds by default. That may seem like a lot of overhead, but remember that this is only a layer-2 frame, with no layer-3 information in the packet.

From reading Chapter 1 you should be able to look at this frame and notice that it is an 802.2 frame, not only because it tells you so in the frame, but because it uses an 802.3-length field with a DSAP and an SSAP field in the LLC header.

```
Flags:         0x80   802.3
Status:        0x00
Packet Length:64
Timestamp:     19:33:18.726314 02/28/2000
802.3 Header
Destination:   01:80:c2:00:00:00
Source:        00:b0:64:75:6b:c3
LLC Length:    38
```

802.2 Logical Link Control (LLC) Header
   Dest. SAP: 0x42 802.1 Bridge Spanning Tree
   Source SAP: 0x42 802.1 Bridge Spanning Tree
   Command: 0x03 Unnumbered Information
802.1 - Bridge Spanning Tree
   Protocol Identifier: 0
   Protocol Version ID: 0
   Message Type: 0 Configuration Message
   Flags: %00000000
   Root Priority/ID: 0x8000 / 00:b0:64:75:6b:c0
   Cost Of Path To Root: 0x00000000 (0)
   Bridge Priority/ID: 0x8000 / 00:b0:64:75:6b:c0
   Port Priority/ID: 0x80 / 0x03
   Message Age: 0/256 seconds
  (exactly 0seconds)
   Maximum Age: 5120/256 seconds
  (exactly 20seconds)
   Hello Time: 512/256 seconds
  (exactly 2seconds)
   Forward Delay: 3840/256 seconds
  (exactly 15seconds)
  Extra bytes (Padding):
   ....   00 00 00 00 00 00 00 00
Frame Check Sequence: 0x2e006400

Once you get to the actual BPDU data, notice the cost of path to root. It is zero because this switch is actually the root bridge. We discuss path costs more in the following section.

Selecting the Designated Port

To determine the port or ports that will be used to communicate with the root bridge, you must first figure out the path cost. The STP cost is an accumulated total path cost based on the bandwidth of the links. Table 2.2 shows the typical costs associated with the different Ethernet networks.

TABLE 2.2 Typical Costs of Different Ethernet Networks

Speed	New IEEE Cost	Original IEEE Cost
10Gbps	2	1
1Gbps	4	1
100Mbps	19	10
10Mbps	100	100

The IEEE 802.1d specification has recently been revised to handle the new higher-speed links. The 1900 switches use the original IEEE 802.1d specifications.

Spanning-Tree Port States

The ports on a bridge or switch running the STP can transition through four different states:

Blocking   Won't forward frames; listens to BPDUs. All ports are in blocking state by default when the switch is powered up.

Listening   Listens to BPDUs to make sure no loops occur on the network before passing data frames.

Learning   Learns MAC addresses and builds a filter table but does not forward frames.

Forwarding   Sends and receives all data on the bridged port.

Typically, switch ports are in either blocking or forwarding state. A forwarding port has been determined to have the lowest cost to the root bridge. However, if the network has a topology change because of a failed link or even if the administrator adds a new switch to the network, the ports on a switch will be in listening and learning state.

Blocking ports are used to prevent network loops. Once a switch determines the best path to the root bridge, then all other ports will be in blocking state. Blocked ports still receive BPDUs.

If a switch determines that a blocked port should now be the designated port, it will go to listening state. It will check all BPDUs heard to make sure that it won't create a loop once the port goes to forwarding state.

Convergence

Convergence occurs when bridges and switches have transitioned to either the forwarding or blocking states. No data is forwarded during this time. Convergence is important to make sure all devices have the same database.

Before data can be forwarded, all devices must be updated. The problem with convergence is the time it takes for these devices to update. It usually takes 50 seconds to go from blocking to forwarding state. It is not recommended that you change the default STP timers, but the timers can be adjusted if necessary. Forward delay is the time it takes to transition a port from listening to learning state or from learning to forwarding state.

Spanning-Tree Example

It is important to see how spanning tree works in an internetwork, and this section will give you a chance to observe it in a live network. In Figure 2.5, the three switches all have the same priority of 32,768. However, notice the MAC address of each switch. By looking at the priority and MAC addresses of each switch, you should be able to determine the root bridge.

FIGURE 2.5   Spanning-tree example

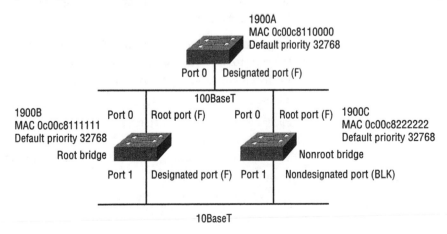

Since 1900A has the lowest MAC address and all three switches use the default priority, then 1900A will be the root bridge.

To determine the root ports on switches 1900B and 1900C, you need to examine the cost of the link connecting the switches. Because the connection from both switches to the root switch is from port 0 using a 100Mbps link and has the best cost, both switches' root ports will be port 0.

To determine the designated ports on the switches, the bridge ID is used. The root bridge always has all ports as designated. However, since both 1900B and 1900C have the same cost to the root bridge, the designated port will be on switch 1900B since it has the lowest bridge ID. Because 1900B has been determined to have the designated port, switch 1900C will put port 1 in blocking state to stop any network loop from occurring.

LAN Switch Types

The latency for packet switching through the switch depends on the chosen switching mode. There are three switching modes:

Store and forward   The complete data frame is received on the switch's buffer, a CRC is run, and then the destination address is looked up in the MAC filter table.

Cut-through   The switch only waits for the destination hardware address to be received and then looks up the destination address in the MAC filter table.

FragmentFree   The default for the Catalyst 1900 switch, it is sometimes referred to as modified cut-through. Checks the first 64 bytes of a frame for fragmentation (because of possible collisions) before forwarding the frame.

Figure 2.6 shows the different points where the switching mode takes place in the frame.

The different switching modes are discussed in detail in the following sections.

FIGURE 2.6 Different switching modes within a frame

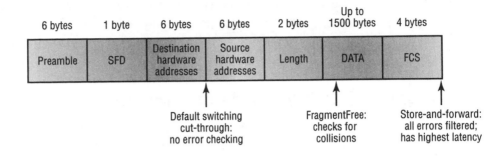

Store and Forward

Store-and-forward switching is one of three primary types of LAN switching. With the store-and-forward switching method, the LAN switch copies the entire frame onto its onboard buffers and computes the cyclic redundancy check (CRC). Because it copies the entire frame, latency through the switch varies with frame length.

The frame is discarded if it contains a CRC error, if it's too short (less than 64 bytes including the CRC), or if it's too long (more than 1518 bytes including the CRC). If the frame doesn't contain any errors, the LAN switch looks up the destination hardware address in its forwarding or switching table and determines the outgoing interface. It then forwards the frame toward its destination. This is the mode used by the Catalyst 5000 series switches and cannot be modified on the switch.

Cut-Through (Real Time)

Cut-through switching is the other main type of LAN switching. With this method, the LAN switch copies only the destination address (the first six bytes following the preamble) onto its onboard buffers. It then looks up the hardware destination address in the MAC switching table, determines the outgoing interface, and forwards the frame toward its destination. A cut-through switch provides reduced latency because it begins to forward the frame as soon as it reads the destination address and determines the outgoing interface.

Some switches can be configured to perform cut-through switching on a per-port basis until a user-defined error threshold is reached. At that point, they automatically change over to store-and-forward mode so they will stop forwarding the errors. When the error rate on the port falls below the threshold, the port automatically changes back to cut-through mode.

FragmentFree (Modified Cut-Through)

FragmentFree is a modified form of cut-through switching, in which the switch waits for the collision window (64 bytes) to pass before forwarding. If a packet has an error, it almost always occurs within the first 64 bytes. FragmentFree mode provides better error checking than the cut-through mode with practically no increase in latency. This is the default switching method for the 1900 switches.

Summary

The information presented in this chapter was designed to give you the background in layer-2 switching that you need before continuing with the rest of this book. Specifically, we covered the following information:

- Layer-2 switching and how switches differ from bridges
- Address learning and how the MAC address filter table was built
- Forward/filtering decisions that layer-2 switches make and how they make them
- Loop avoidance and the problems caused when loop avoidance schemes are not used in the network
- Spanning-Tree Protocol and how it prevents loops
- LAN switch types used on Cisco routers and how they differ

Key Terms

Before taking the exam, be sure you're familiar with the following terms:

address learning

Bridge Protocol Data Units (BPDUs)

cut-through frame switching

designated port

FragmentFree

nondesignated port

root bridge

Spanning-Tree Protocol (STP)

store-and-forward packet switching

Written Lab

Answer the following questions based on the following graphic.

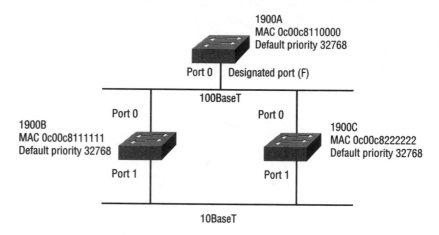

1. Which is the root bridge?

2. What are the designated ports?

3. What are the nondesignated ports?

4. Which ports are blocking?

Review Questions

1. Which LAN switch method runs a CRC on every frame?

   A. Cut-through

   B. Store and forward

   C. FragmentCheck

   D. FragmentFree

2. Which LAN switch type only checks the hardware address before forwarding a frame?

   A. Cut-through

   B. Store and forward

   C. FragmentCheck

   D. FragmentFree

3. What is true regarding the STP blocked state of a port? (Choose all that apply.)

   A. No frames are transmitted or received on the blocked port.

   B. BPDUs are sent and received on the blocked port.

   C. BPDUs are still received on the blocked port.

   D. Frames are sent or received on the block port.

4. Layer-2 switching provides which of the following?

   A. Hardware-based bridging (MAC)

   B. Wire speed

   C. High latency

   D. High cost

5. What is used to determine the root bridge in a network? (Choose all that apply.)

    A. Priority

    B. Cost of the links attached to the switch

    C. MAC address

    D. IP address

6. What is used to determine the designated port on a bridge?

    A. Priority

    B. Cost of the links attached to the switch

    C. MAC address

    D. IP address

7. What are the four port states of an STP switch?

    A. Learning

    B. Learned

    C. Listened

    D. Heard

    E. Listening

    F. Forwarding

    G. Forwarded

    H. Blocking

    I. Gathering

8. What are the three distinct functions of layer-2 switching?

   A. Address learning

   B. Routing

   C. Forwarding and filtering

   D. Creating network loops

   E. Loop avoidance

   F. IP addressing

9. What is true regarding BPDUs?

   A. They are used to send configuration messages using IP packets.

   B. They are used to send configuration messages using multicast frames.

   C. They are used to set the cost of STP links.

   D. They are used to set the bridge ID of a switch.

10. If a switch determines that a blocked port should now be the designated port, what state will the port go into?

   A. Unblocked

   B. Forwarding

   C. Listening

   D. Listened

   E. Learning

   F. Learned

11. What is the difference between a bridge and a layer-2 switch? (Choose all that apply.)

  A. Bridges can only have one spanning-tree instance per bridge.

  B. Switches can have many different spanning-tree instances per switch.

  C. Bridges can have many spanning-tree instances per bridge.

  D. Switches can only have one spanning-tree instance per switch.

12. What is the difference between a bridge and a layer-2 switch? (Choose all that apply.)

  A. Switches are software based.

  B. Bridges are hardware based.

  C. Switches are hardware based.

  D. Bridges are software based.

13. What does a switch do when a frame is received on an interface and the destination hardware address is unknown or not in the filter table?

  A. Forwards the switch to the first available link

  B. Drops the frame

  C. Floods the network with the frame looking for the device

  D. Sends back a message to the originating station asking for a name resolution

14. Which LAN switch type waits for the collision window to pass before looking up the destination hardware address in the MAC filter table and forwarding the frame?

  A. Cut-through

  B. Store and forward

  C. FragmentCheck

  D. FragmentFree

15. What is the default LAN switch type on a 1900 switch?

   A. Cut-through

   B. Store and forward

   C. FragmentCheck

   D. FragmentFree

16. How is the bridge ID of a switch communicated to neighboring switches?

   A. IP Routing

   B. STP

   C. During the four STP states of a switch

   D. Bridge Protocol Data Units

   E. Broadcasts during convergence times

17. How is the root port on a switch determined?

   A. The switch determines the highest cost of a link to the root bridge.

   B. The switch determines the lowest cost of a link to the root bridge.

   C. The fastest BPDU transfer rate is determined by sending and receiving BPDUs between switches, and that interface becomes the root port.

   D. The root bridge will broadcast the bridge ID, and the receiving bridge will determine what interface this broadcast was received on and make this interface the root port.

18. How many root bridges are allowed in a network?

   A. 10

   B. 1

   C. One for each switch

   D. 20

19. What could happen on a network if no loop avoidance schemes are put in place?

   A. Faster convergence times

   B. Broadcast storms

   C. Multiple frame copies

   D. IP routing will cause flapping on a serial link

20. What is the default priority of STP on a switch?

   A. 32,768

   B. 3276

   C. 100

   D. 10

   E. 1

(The answers to the questions begin on the next page.)

Answers to the Written Lab

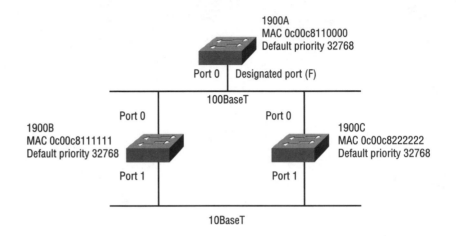

1. 1900A

2. Ports 0 and 1 on the root bridge; port 0 on the 1900B and 1900C switches

3. Port 1 on 1900C

4. Port 1 on 1900C

Answers to Review Questions

1. B. Store-and-forward LAN switching checks every frame for CRC errors. It has the highest latency of any LAN switch type.

2. A. The cut-through method does no error checking and has the lowest latency of the three LAN switch types. Cut-through only checks the hardware destination address before forwarding the frame.

3. A, C. BPDUs are still received on a blocked port, but no forwarding of frames and BPDUs is allowed.

4. A, B. Layer-2 switching uses ASICs to provide frame filtering and is considered hardware based. Layer-2 switching also provides wire-speed frame transfers, with low latency.

5. A, C. Layer-2 devices running STP use the priority and MAC address to determine the root bridge in a network.

6. B. For switches to determine the designated ports, the cost of the links attached to each switch is used.

7. A, E, F, H. The four states are blocking, learning, listening, and forwarding.

8. A, C, E. Layer-2 features include address learning, forwarding and filtering of the network, and loop avoidance.

9. B. Bridge Protocol Data Units are used to send configuration messages to neighboring switches, including the bridge IDs.

10. C. A blocked port will always listen for BPDUs to make sure that when the port is put into forwarding state a loop will not occur.

11. A, B. Unlike a bridge, a switch can have many different spanning-tree instances per switch. Bridges can only have one per bridge.

12. C, D. Bridges are considered software based and switches are considered hardware based.

13. C. Switches forward all frames that have an unknown destination address. If a device answers the frame, the switch will update the MAC address table to reflect the location of the device.

14. D. FragmentFree looks at the first 64 bytes of a frame to make sure a collision has not occurred. It is sometimes referred to as modified cut-through.

15. D. By default, 1900 switches use the FragmentFree LAN switch type. The 1900 can use the store-and-forward method.

16. D. The bridge ID is sent via a multicast frame inside a BPDU update.

17. B. Root ports are determined by using the cost of a link to the root bridge.

18. B. Only one root bridge can be used in any network.

19. B, C. Broadcast storms and multiple frame copies are typically found in a network that has multiple links to remote locations without some type of loop-avoidance scheme.

20. A. The default priorities on all switches are 32,768.

Internet Protocol

THE CCNA EXAM TOPICS COVERED IN THIS CHAPTER INCLUDE THE FOLLOWING:

- ✓ Describe the different classes of IP addresses
- ✓ Perform subnetting for an internetwork
- ✓ Configure IP addresses in an internetwork
- ✓ Verify IP addresses and configuration

The Transmission Control Protocol/Internet Protocol (TCP/IP) suite was created by the Department of Defense (DoD) to ensure and preserve data integrity, as well as maintain communications in the event of catastrophic war. If designed and implemented correctly, a TCP/IP network can be a dependable and resilient one. In this chapter, I'll cover the protocols of TCP/IP, and throughout this book, you'll learn how to create a marvelous TCP/IP network—using Cisco routers, of course.

We'll begin by taking a look at the DoD's version of TCP/IP and then compare this version and protocols with the OSI reference model discussed in Chapter 1. After you have an understanding of the protocols used at the various levels of the DoD model, it will be time to learn about IP addressing. This chapter also covers subnetting an IP network address.

IP addressing and subnetting is not difficult; there is just a lot of material to understand. I will present it in a very detailed manner, which will allow you to read each section over and over again until you feel you have mastered that section of IP addressing.

TCP/IP and the DoD Model

The DoD model is a condensed version of the OSI model. It is comprised of four, instead of seven, layers:

- The Process/Application layer

- The Host-to-Host layer

- The Internet layer

- The Network Access layer

Figure 3.1 shows a comparison of the DoD model and the OSI reference model. As you can see, the two are similar in concept, but each has a different number of layers with different names.

FIGURE 3.1 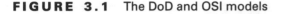 The DoD and OSI models

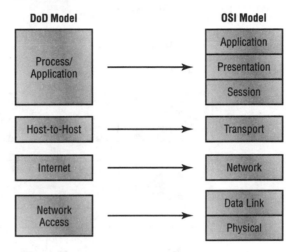

A vast array of protocols combine at the DoD model's *Process/Application layer* to integrate the various activities and duties spanning the focus of the OSI's corresponding top three layers (Application, Presentation, and Session). (We'll be looking closely at those protocols in the next part of this chapter.) The Process/Application layer defines protocols for node-to-node application communication and also controls user-interface specifications.

The *Host-to-Host layer* parallels the functions of the OSI's Transport layer, defining protocols for setting up the level of transmission service for applications. It tackles issues like creating reliable end-to-end communication and ensuring the error-free delivery of data. It handles packet sequencing and maintains data integrity.

The *Internet layer* corresponds to the OSI's Network layer, designating the protocols relating to the logical transmission of packets over the entire network. It takes care of the addressing of hosts by giving them an IP (Internet Protocol) address, and it handles the routing of packets among multiple networks. It also controls the communication flow between two hosts.

At the bottom of the model, the *Network Access layer* monitors the data exchange between the host and the network. The equivalent of the Data Link and Physical layers of the OSI model, the Network Access layer oversees hardware addressing and defines protocols for the physical transmission of data.

While the DoD and OSI models are alike in design and concept and have similar functions in similar places, *how* those functions occur is different. Figure 3.2 shows the TCP/IP protocol suite and how its protocols relate to the DoD model layers.

FIGURE 3.2   The TCP/IP protocol suite

DoD Model

Process/Application				
	Telnet	FTP	LPD	SNMP
	TFTP	SMTP	NFS	X window

Host-to-Host		
	TCP	UDP

Internet				
	ICMP	BootP	ARP	RARP
	IP			

Network Access				
	Ethernet	Fast Ethernet	Token Ring	FDDI

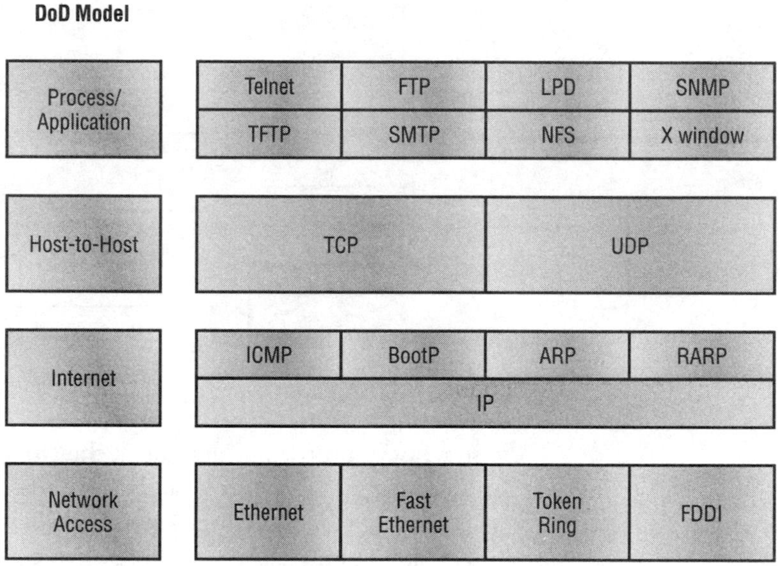

The Process/Application Layer Protocols

In this section, we will describe the different applications and services typically used in IP networks. The different protocols and applications covered in this section include the following:

- Telnet
- FTP
- TFTP
- NFS

- SMTP

- LPD

- X Window

- SNMP

- DNS

- BootP

- DHCP

Telnet

Telnet is the chameleon of protocols—its specialty is terminal emulation. It allows a user on a remote client machine, called the Telnet client, to access the resources of another machine, the Telnet server. Telnet achieves this by pulling a fast one on the Telnet server and making the client machine appear as though it were a terminal directly attached to the local network. This projection is actually a software image, a virtual terminal that can interact with the chosen remote host.

These emulated terminals are of the text-mode type and can execute refined procedures like displaying menus that give users the opportunity to choose options from them and access the applications on the duped server. Users begin a Telnet session by running the Telnet client software and then logging on to the Telnet server.

The name Telnet comes from "telephone network," which is how most Telnet sessions used to occur.

File Transfer Protocol (FTP)

The *File Transfer Protocol (FTP)* is the protocol that actually lets us transfer files; it can facilitate this between any two machines using it. But FTP isn't just a protocol; it's also a program. Operating as a protocol, FTP is used by applications. As a program, it's employed by users to perform file tasks by hand. FTP also allows for access to both directories and files and can accomplish certain types of directory operations, like relocating into different ones. FTP teams up with Telnet to transparently log you in to the FTP server and then provides for the transfer of files.

Accessing a host through FTP is only the first step, though. Users must then be subjected to an authentication login that's probably secured with passwords and usernames implemented by system administrators to restrict access. But you can get around this somewhat by adopting the username "anonymous"—though what you'll gain access to will be limited.

Even when employed by users manually as a program, FTP's functions are limited to listing and manipulating directories, typing file contents, and copying files between hosts. It can't execute remote files as programs.

Trivial File Transfer Protocol (TFTP)

The *Trivial File Transfer Protocol (TFTP)* is the stripped-down, stock version of FTP, but it's the protocol of choice if you know exactly what you want and where to find it. It doesn't give you the abundance of functions that FTP does, though. TFTP has no directory-browsing abilities; it can do nothing but send and receive files. This compact little protocol also skimps in the data department, sending much smaller blocks of data than FTP, and there's no authentication as with FTP, so it's insecure. Few sites support it because of the inherent security risks.

Later in this book, you'll use TFTP to download a new Internetwork Operating System (IOS) to your Cisco router.

Network File System (NFS)

Network File System (NFS) is a jewel of a protocol specializing in file sharing. It allows two different types of file systems to interoperate. It works like this: Suppose the NFS server software is running on an NT server, and the NFS client software is running on a Unix host. NFS allows for a portion of the RAM on the NT server to transparently store Unix files, which can, in turn, be used by Unix users. Even though the NT file system and Unix file system are unlike—they have different case sensitivity, filename lengths, security, and so on—both Unix users and NT users can access that same file with their normal file systems, in their normal way.

Simple Mail Transfer Protocol (SMTP)

Simple Mail Transfer Protocol (SMTP), answering our ubiquitous call to e-mail, uses a spooled, or queued, method of mail delivery. Once a message has been sent to a destination, the message is spooled to a device—usually a disk. The server software at the destination posts a vigil, regularly checking this queue for messages. When it detects them, it proceeds to deliver them to their destination. SMTP is used to send mail; POP3 is used to receive mail.

Line Printer Daemon (LPD)

The *Line Printer Daemon (LPD)* protocol is designed for printer sharing. The LPD, along with the LPR (Line Printer) program, allows print jobs to be spooled and sent to the network's printers using TCP/IP.

X Window

Designed for client-server operations, *X Window* defines a protocol for the writing of graphical user interface–based client/server applications. The idea is to allow a program, called a client, to run on one computer and have it display a program called a window server on another computer.

Simple Network Management Protocol (SNMP)

Simple Network Management Protocol (SNMP) collects and manipulates this valuable network information. It gathers data by polling the devices on the network from a management station at fixed or random intervals, requiring them to disclose certain information. When all is well, SNMP receives something called a *baseline*—a report delimiting the operational traits of a healthy network. This protocol can also stand as a watchdog over the network, quickly notifying managers of any sudden turn of events. These network watchdogs are called *agents,* and when aberrations occur, agents send an alert called a *trap* to the management station.

Domain Name Service (DNS)

Domain Name Service (DNS) resolves host names, specifically Internet names, like www.routersim.com. You don't have to use DNS; you can just type in the *IP address* of any device you want to communicate with. An IP address identifies hosts on a network and the Internet as well. However, DNS was designed to make our lives easier. Also, what would happen if you wanted to move your Web page to a different service provider? The IP address would change and no one would know what the new one was. DNS allows you to use a domain name to specify an IP address. You can change the IP address as often as you want and no one will know the difference.

DNS is used to resolve *Fully Qualified Domain Names* (FQDNs), for example, `www.lammle.com` or `todd.lammle.com`. An FQDN is a hierarchy that can logically locate a system based on its domain identifier.

If you want to resolve the name "todd," you either must type in the FQDN of `todd.lammle.com` or have a device like a PC or router add the suffix for you. For example, on a Cisco router, you can use the command `ip domain-name lammle.com` to append each request with the `lammle.com` domain. If you don't do that, you'll have to type in the FQDN to get the DNS to resolve the name.

Bootstrap Protocol (BootP)

BootP stands for *Bootstrap Protocol*. When a diskless workstation is powered on, it broadcasts a BootP request on the network. A BootP server hears the request and looks up the client's MAC address in its BootP file. If it finds an appropriate entry, it responds by telling the machine its IP address and the file—usually via the TFTP protocol—it should boot from.

BootP is used by a diskless machine to learn the following:

- Its own IP address

- The IP address and host name of a server machine

- The boot filename of a file that is to be loaded into memory and executed at boot-up

BootP is an old program that isn't used anymore, right? Wrong: BootP is still around, but now we just call it the Dynamic Host Configuration Protocol, which you will learn about in the next section.

Dynamic Host Configuration Protocol (DHCP)

The *Dynamic Host Configuration Protocol (DHCP)* gives IP addresses to hosts. It allows easier administration and works well in small–to–even-very-large network environments. All types of hardware can be used as a DHCP server, including a Cisco router.

DHCP differs from BootP in that BootP gives an IP address to a host, but the host's hardware address must be entered manually in a BootP table. You can think of DHCP as a dynamic BootP. However, remember that BootP is also used to send an operating system that a host can boot from. DHCP cannot perform this function.

There is a lot of information a DHCP server can provide to a host when the host is registering for an IP address with the DHCP server. Notice all the information that can be provided by the DHCP server:

- IP address

- Subnet mask

- Domain name

- Default gateway (routers)

- DNS

- WINS information

A DHCP server can provide even more information, but the items in the bulleted list are the most common.

The Host-to-Host Layer Protocols

The Host-to-Host layer's main purpose is to shield the upper-layer applications from the complexities of the network. This layer says to the upper layer, "Just give me your data stream, with any instructions, and I'll begin the process of getting your information ready to send."

The following sections describe the two protocols at this layer:

- Transmission Control Protocol (TCP)

- User Datagram Protocol (UDP)

Transmission Control Protocol (TCP)

The *Transmission Control Protocol (TCP)* takes large blocks of information from an application and breaks them into segments. It numbers and sequences each segment so that the destination's TCP protocol can put the segments back into the order the application intended. After these segments are sent, TCP (on the transmitting host) waits for an acknowledgment of the receiving end's TCP virtual circuit session, retransmitting those that aren't acknowledged.

Before a transmitting host starts to send segments down the model, the sender's TCP protocol contacts the destination's TCP protocol to establish a connection. What is created is known as a *virtual circuit*. This type of communication is called *connection-oriented*. During this initial handshake, the two TCP layers also agree on the amount of information that's going to be sent before the recipient's TCP sends back an acknowledgment. With everything agreed upon in advance, the path is paved for reliable communication to take place.

TCP is a full-duplex, connection-oriented, reliable, accurate protocol, and establishing all these terms and conditions, in addition to error checking, is no small task. TCP is very complicated and, not surprisingly, costly in terms of network overhead. Since today's networks are much more reliable than those of yore, this added reliability is often unnecessary.

TCP Segment Format

Since the upper layers just send a data stream to the protocols in the Transport layers, we'll demonstrate how TCP segments a data stream and prepares it for the Network layer. The Network layer then routes the segments as packets through an internetwork. The packets are handed to the receiving host's Transport layer protocol, which rebuilds the data stream to hand to the upper-layer applications or protocols.

Figure 3.3 shows the TCP segment format. The figure shows the different fields within the TCP header.

FIGURE 3.3 TCP segment format

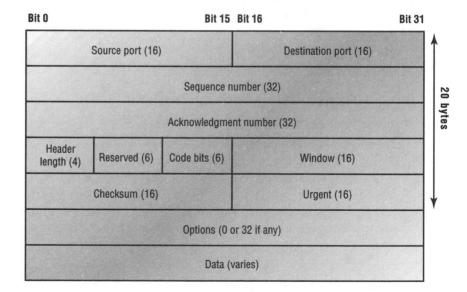

The TCP header is 20 bits long. You need to understand what each field in the TCP segment is. The TCP segment contains the following fields:

Source port Is the port number of the host sending the data. (Port numbers will be explained a little later in this section.)

Destination port Is the port number of the application requested on the destination host.

Sequence number Puts the data back in the correct order or retransmits missing or damaged data, a process called sequencing.

Acknowledgment number Defines which TCP octet is expected next.

HLEN Stands for header length, which defines the number of 32-bit words in the header.

Reserved Is always set to zero.

Code bits Are control functions used to set up and terminate a session.

Window Is the window size the sender is willing to accept, in octets.

Checksum Is the CRC, because TCP doesn't trust the lower layers and checks everything. The Cyclic Redundancy Check (CRC) checks the header and data fields.

Urgent pointer Indicates the end of urgent data.

Option Sets the maximum TCP segment size to either 0 or 32 bits, if any.

Data Is handed down to the TCP protocol at the Transport layer, which includes the upper-layer headers.

Let's take a look at a TCP segment copied from a network analyzer:

```
TCP - Transport Control Protocol
   Source Port:      5973
   Destination Port: 23
   Sequence Number:  1456389907
   Ack Number:       1242056456
   Offset:           5
   Reserved:         %000000
   Code:             %011000
             Ack is valid
             Push Request
```

```
Window:              61320
Checksum:            0x61a6
Urgent Pointer:      0
No TCP Options
TCP Data Area:
vL.5.+.5.+.5.+.5    76 4c 19 35 11 2b 19 35 11 2b 19 35
11 2b 19 35 +. 11 2b 19
Frame Check Sequence:  0x0d00000f
```

Notice that everything I talked about above is in the segment. As you can see from the number of fields in the header, TCP has a lot of overhead. Application developers might not want to use as much reliability as TCP operates with to save overhead, so User Datagram Protocol was also defined at the Transport layer.

User Datagram Protocol (UDP)

Application developers can use the *User Datagram Protocol (UDP)* in place of TCP. UDP is the scaled-down economy model and is considered a *thin protocol*. Like a thin person on a park bench, a thin protocol doesn't take up a lot of room—or in this case, much bandwidth on a network.

UDP also doesn't offer all the bells and whistles of TCP, but it does do a fabulous job of transporting information that doesn't require reliable delivery—and it does so using far fewer network resources. (Please note that UDP is covered thoroughly in RFC 768.)

There are some situations where it would definitely be wise for application developers to opt for UDP rather than TCP. Remember the watchdog SNMP up there at the Process/Application layer? SNMP monitors the network, sending intermittent messages and a fairly steady flow of status updates and alerts, especially when running on a large network. The cost in overhead to establish, maintain, and close a TCP connection for each one of those little messages would reduce what would be an otherwise healthy, efficient network to a dammed-up bog in no time.

Another circumstance calling for UDP over TCP is when the matter of reliability is already accomplished at the Process/Application layer. Network File System (NFS) handles its own reliability issues, making the use of TCP both impractical and redundant. However, the application developer decides whether to use UDP or TCP, not the user who wants to transfer data faster.

UDP receives upper-layer blocks of information, instead of data streams as TCP does, and breaks them into segments. Like TCP, each UDP segment is given a number for reassembly into the intended block at the destination. However, UDP does *not* sequence the segments and does not care in which order the segments arrive at the destination. At least it numbers them, though. But after that, UDP sends the segments off and forgets about them. It doesn't follow through, check up on them, or even allow for an acknowledgment of safe arrival—complete abandonment. Because of this, it's referred to as an *unreliable protocol*. This does not mean that UDP is ineffective, only that it doesn't handle issues of reliability.

Further, UDP doesn't create a virtual circuit, nor does it contact the destination before delivering information to it. It is, therefore, also considered a *connectionless protocol*. Since UDP assumes that the application will use its own reliability method, it doesn't use any. This gives an application developer a choice when running the Internet Protocol stack: TCP for reliability or UDP for faster transfers.

UDP Segment Format

The very low overhead of UDP compared to TCP, which doesn't use windowing or acknowledgments, is shown in Figure 3.4.

FIGURE 3.4 UDP segment

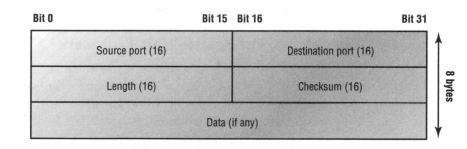

You need to understand what each field in the UDP segment is. The UDP segment contains the following fields:

Source port Port number of the host sending the data

Destination port Port number of the application requested on the destination host

Length of the segment   Length of UDP header and UDP data

CRC   Checksum of both the UDP header and UDP data fields

Data   Upper-layer data

UDP, like TCP, doesn't trust the lower layers and runs its own CRC. Remember that the Frame Check Sequence (FCS) is the field that houses the CRC, which is why you can see the FCS information.

The following shows a UDP segment caught on a network analyzer:

```
UDP - User Datagram Protocol
   Source Port:          1085
   Destination Port:     5136
   Length:               41
   Checksum:             0x7a3c
   UDP Data Area:
   ..Z............     00 01 5a 96 00 01 00 00 00 00 00 11
00 00 00
   ...C..2...._C._C    2e 03 00 43 02 1e 32 0a 00 0a 00 80 43
00 80
Frame Check Sequence:   0x00000000
```

Notice the low overhead! Try to find the sequence number, ack number, and window size. You will notice that these are absent from the UDP segment.

Key Concepts of Host-to-Host Protocols

Since we have seen both a connection-oriented (TCP) and connectionless (UDP) protocol in action, it would be good to summarize the two here. The following list highlights some of the key concepts that you should keep in mind regarding these two protocols.

TCP	UDP
Sequenced	Unsequenced
Reliable	Unreliable
Connection-oriented	Connectionless
Virtual circuit	Low overhead

A telephone analogy might help you understand how TCP works. Most of us know that before you speak to someone on a phone, you must first establish a connection with that other person—wherever they might be. This is like a virtual circuit with the TCP protocol. If you were giving someone important information during your conversation, you might ask, "Did you get that?" A query like that is similar to a TCP acknowledgment. From time to time, for various reasons, people also ask, "Are you still there?" They end their conversations with a "goodbye" of some kind, putting closure on the phone call. TCP also performs these types of functions.

Alternately, using UDP is like sending a postcard. To do that, you don't need to contact the other party first. You simply write your message, address the postcard, and mail it. This is analogous to UDP's connectionless orientation. Since the message on the postcard is probably not a matter of life or death, you don't need an acknowledgment of its receipt. Similarly, UDP does not involve acknowledgments.

Port Numbers

TCP and UDP must use *port numbers* to communicate with the upper layers. Port numbers keep track of different conversations crossing the network simultaneously. Originating-source port numbers are dynamically assigned by the source host, which will be some number starting at 1024. 1023 and below are defined in RFC 1700, which discusses what is called well-known port numbers.

Virtual circuits that do not use an application with a well-known port number are assigned port numbers randomly chosen from within a specific range instead. These port numbers identify the source and destination host in the TCP segment.

Figure 3.5 illustrates how both TCP and UDP use port numbers.

FIGURE 3.5   Port numbers for TCP and UDP

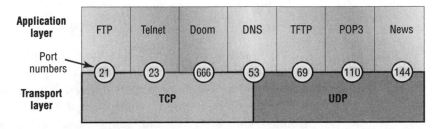

The different port numbers that can be used are explained below:

- Numbers below 1024 are considered well-known port numbers and are defined in RFC 1700.

- Numbers 1024 and above are used by the upper layers to set up sessions with other hosts and by TCP to use as source and destination addresses in the TCP segment.

TCP Session: Source Port

The following listing shows a TCP session captured with the Etherpeek analyzer software. Notice that the source host makes up the source port, which in this case is 5972. The destination port is 23, which is used to tell the receiving host the purpose of the intended connection (Telnet).

```
TCP - Transport Control Protocol
    Source Port:       5973
    Destination Port:  23
    Sequence Number:   1456389907
    Ack Number:        1242056456
    Offset:            5
    Reserved:          %000000
    Code:              %011000
            Ack is valid
            Push Request
    Window:            61320
    Checksum:          0x61a6
    Urgent Pointer:    0
    No TCP Options
    TCP Data Area:
    vL.5.+.5.+.5.+.5    76 4c 19 35 11 2b 19 35 11 2b 19 35
11 2b 19 35 +. 11 2b 19
    Frame Check Sequence:  0x0d00000f
```

As you saw in the above TCP session, the source host makes up the source port. But why is it that the source makes up a port number? The reason is to differentiate between sessions with different hosts. How else would a server know where information is coming from if it didn't have a different number from a sending host? TCP and the upper layers don't use hardware and logical addresses to understand the sending host's address like the Data Link and Network layer protocols do. Instead, they use port numbers. It's easy to imagine the receiving host getting confused if all the hosts used the same port number to get to FTP.

TCP Session: Destination Port

Now, typically you'll look at an analyzer and see that only the source port is above 1024 and the destination port is a well-known port, as shown in the following Etherpeek trace:

```
TCP - Transport Control Protocol
    Source Port:       1144
    Destination Port: 80  World Wide Web HTTP
    Sequence Number:  9356570
    Ack Number:        0
    Offset:            7
    Reserved:          %000000
    Code:              %000010
              Synch Sequence
    Window:            8192
    Checksum:          0x57E7
    Urgent Pointer:    0
    TCP Options:
       Option Type:    2  Maximum Segment Size
          Length:      4
          MSS:         536
       Option Type:    1  No Operation
       Option Type:    1  No Operation
       Option Type:    4
          Length:      2
          Opt Value:
       No More HTTP Data
    Frame Check Sequence:   0x43697363
```

Notice that the source port is over 1024, but the destination port is 80, or HTTP service. The server, or receiving host, will change the destination port if it needs to.

In the preceding trace, a "syn" packet is sent to the destination device. The syn sequence is telling the remote destination device that it wants to create a session.

TCP Session: Syn Packet Acknowledgment

The next trace shows an acknowledgment to the syn packet. Notice the "Ack is valid," which means the source port was accepted and the device agreed to create a virtual circuit with the originating host.

```
TCP - Transport Control Protocol
   Source Port:        80  World Wide Web HTTP
   Destination Port: 1144
   Sequence Number:  2873580788
   Ack Number:       9356571
   Offset:           6
   Reserved:         %000000
   Code:             %010010
              Ack is valid
              Synch Sequence
   Window:           8576
   Checksum:         0x5F85
   Urgent Pointer:   0
   TCP Options:
      Option Type:   2  Maximum Segment Size
          Length:    4
          MSS:       1460
      No More HTTP Data
   Frame Check Sequence:  0x6E203132
```

Notice that the response from the server shows the source is 80 and the destination is the 1144 sent from the originating host.

The Internet Layer Protocols

There are two main reasons for the Internet layer's existence: routing, and providing a single network interface to the upper layers.

None of the upper- or lower-layer protocols have any functions relating to routing. The complex and important task of routing is the job of the Internet layer. The Internet layer's second job is to provide a single network interface to the upper-layer protocols. Without this layer, application programmers would need to write "hooks" into every one of their applications for each different Network Access protocol. This would not only be a pain in the neck, but it would lead to different versions of each application—one for Ethernet, another one for Token Ring, and so on. To prevent this, IP provides one single network interface for the upper-layer protocols. That accomplished, it's then the job of IP and the various Network Access protocols to get along and work together.

All network roads don't lead to Rome—they lead to IP. And all the other protocols at this layer, as well as all those at the upper layers, use it. Never forget that. All paths through the model go through IP. The following sections describe the protocols at the Internet layer.

These are the protocols that work at the Internet layer:

- Internet Protocol (IP)

- Internet Control Message Protocol (ICMP)

- Address Resolution Protocol (ARP)

- Reverse Address Resolution Protocol (RARP)

Internet Protocol (IP)

The *Internet Protocol (IP)* essentially *is* the Internet layer. The other protocols found here merely exist to support it. IP contains the big picture and could be said to "see all," in that it is aware of all the interconnected networks. It can do this because all the machines on the network have a software, or logical, address called an IP address, which we'll cover more thoroughly later in this chapter.

IP looks at each packet's address. Then, using a routing table, it decides where a packet is to be sent next, choosing the best path. The Network Access–layer protocols at the bottom of the model don't possess IP's enlightened scope of the entire network; they deal only with physical links (local networks).

Identifying devices on networks requires answering these two questions: Which network is it on? And what is its ID on that network? The first answer is the *software,* or *logical, address* (the correct street). The second answer is the *hardware address* (the correct mailbox). All hosts on a network have a logical ID called an IP address. This is the software, or logical, address and contains valuable encoded information greatly simplifying the complex task of routing. (Please note that IP is discussed in RFC 791.)

IP receives segments from the Host-to-Host layer and fragments them into datagrams (packets). IP then reassembles datagrams back into segments on the receiving side. Each datagram is assigned the IP address of the sender and of the recipient. Each router (layer-3 device) that receives a datagram makes routing decisions based upon the packet's destination IP address.

Figure 3.6 shows an IP header. This will give you an idea of what the IP protocol has to go through every time user data is sent from the upper layers and wants to be sent to a remote network.

FIGURE 3.6 IP header

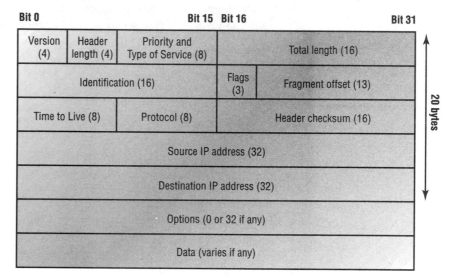

The following fields make up the IP header:

Version   IP version number.

HLEN   Header length in 32-bit words.

Priority or ToS   Type of Service tells how the datagram should be handled. The first three bits are the priority bits.

Total length   Length of the packet including header and data.

Identification   Unique IP-packet value.

Flags   Specifies whether fragmentation should occur.

Frag offset   Provides fragmentation and reassembly if the packet is too large to put in a frame. It also allows different Maximum Transmission Units (MTUs) on the Internet.

TTL   Time to Live is set into a packet when it is originally generated. It gives it a time to live. If it doesn't get to where it wants to go before the TTL expires, boom—it's gone. This stops IP packets from continuously circling the network looking for a home.

Protocol   Port of upper-layer protocol (TCP is port 6 or UDP is port 17 (hex)).

Header checksum   Cyclic Redundancy Check on header only.

Source IP address   32-bit IP address of sending station.

Destination IP address   32-bit IP address of the station this packet is destined for.

IP option   Used for network testing, debugging, security, and more.

Data   Upper-layer data.

Here's a snapshot of an IP packet caught on a network analyzer. Notice that all the information discussed above appears here:

```
IP Header - Internet Protocol Datagram
    Version:              4
    Header Length:        5
    Precedence:           0
    Type of Service:      %000
    Unused:               %00
    Total Length:         187
    Identifier:           22486
    Fragmentation Flags:  %010   Do Not Fragment
    Fragment Offset:      0
    Time To Live:         60
    IP Type:              0x06   TCP
    Header Checksum:      0xd031
    Source IP Address:    10.7.1.30
    Dest. IP Address:     10.7.1.10
    No Internet Datagram Options
```

Notice that there are logical, or IP, addresses in this header.

The type field—it's typically a protocol field, but this analyzer sees it as a type field—is important. If the header didn't carry the protocol information for the next layer, IP wouldn't know what to do with the data carried in the packet.

Figure 3.7 shows how the Network layer sees the protocols at the Transport layer when it needs to hand a packet to the upper-layer protocols.

FIGURE 3.7 The protocol field in an IP header

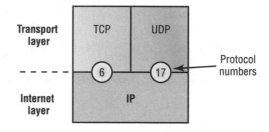

In this example, the protocol field tells IP to send the data to either TCP port 6 or UDP port 17 (both hex addresses). However, it will only be UDP or TCP if the data is part of a data stream headed for an upper-layer service or application. It could just as easily be destined for ICMP (Internet Control Message Protocol), ARP (Address Resolution Protocol), or some other type of Network layer protocol.

Table 3.1 is a list of some other popular protocols that can be specified in the protocol field.

TABLE 3.1 Possible Protocols Found in the Protocol Field of an IP Header

Protocol	Protocol Number
ICMP	1
IGRP	9
IPv6	41
GRE	47

TABLE 3.1 Possible Protocols Found in the Protocol Field of an IP Header *(continued)*

Protocol	Protocol Number
IPX in IP	111
Layer-2 tunnel	115

Internet Control Message Protocol (ICMP)

The *Internet Control Message Protocol (ICMP)* works at the Network layer and is used by IP for many different services. ICMP is a management protocol and messaging service provider for IP. Its messages are carried as IP datagrams. RFC 1256, *ICMP Router Discovery Messages*, is an annex to ICMP, which affords hosts' extended capability in discovering routes to gateways.

Periodically, router advertisements are announced over the network, reporting IP addresses for the router's network interfaces. Hosts listen for these network infomercials to acquire route information. A *router solicitation* is a request for immediate advertisements and may be sent by a host when it starts up. The following are some common events and messages that ICMP relates to:

Destination Unreachable   If a router can't send an IP datagram any further, it uses ICMP to send a message back to the sender, advising it of the situation. For example, if a router receives a packet destined for a network that the router doesn't know about, it will send an ICMP Destination Unreachable message back to the sending station.

Buffer Full   If a router's memory buffer for receiving incoming datagrams is full, it will use ICMP to send out this message.

Hops   Each IP datagram is allotted a certain number of routers, called *hops*, that it may go through. If it reaches its limit of hops before arriving at its destination, the last router to receive that datagram deletes it. The executioner router then uses ICMP to send an obituary message, informing the sending machine of the demise of its datagram.

Ping   Packet Internet Groper uses ICMP echo messages to check the physical connectivity of machines on an internetwork.

Traceroute   Using ICMP timeouts, traceroute is used to find a path a packet takes as it traverses an internetwork.

The following data is from a network analyzer catching an ICMP echo request. Notice that even though ICMP works at the Network layer, it still uses IP to do the Ping request. The type field in the IP header is 0x01h, which specifies the ICMP protocol.

```
    Flags:          0x00
    Status:         0x00
    Packet Length:78
    Timestamp:      14:04:25.967000 05/06/1998
Ethernet Header
    Destination:  00:a0:24:6e:0f:a8
    Source:       00:80:c7:a8:f0:3d
    Ether-Type:08-00   IP
IP Header - Internet Protocol Datagram
    Version:                4
    Header Length:          5
    Precedence:             0
    Type of Service:        %000
    Unused:                 %00
    Total Length:           60
    Identifier:             56325
    Fragmentation Flags:    %000
    Fragment Offset:        0
    Time To Live:           32
    IP Type:                0x01   ICMP
    Header Checksum:        0x2df0
    Source IP Address:      100.100.100.2
    Dest. IP Address:       100.100.100.1
    No Internet Datagram Options
ICMP - Internet Control Messages Protocol
    ICMP Type:              8   Echo Request
    Code:                   0
    Checksum:               0x395c
    Identifier:             0x0300
    Sequence Number:        4352
    ICMP Data Area:
    abcdefghijklmnop   61 62 63 64 65 66 67 68 69 6a 6b 6c 6d
    qrstuvwabcdefghi   71 72 73 74 75 76 77 61 62 63 64 65 66
Frame Check Sequence:   0x00000000
```

If you remember reading about the Data Link layer and the different frame types in Chapter 1, you should be able to look at the above trace and tell me what type of Ethernet frame this is. The only fields are destination hardware address, source hardware address, and Ether-type field. The only frame that uses an Ether-type field is an Ethernet_II frame. (SNAP uses an Ether-type field also, but only within an 802.2 LLC field, which is not present in the frame.)

Address Resolution Protocol (ARP)

The *Address Resolution Protocol (ARP)* finds the hardware address of a host from a known IP address. Here's how it works: When IP has a datagram to send, it must inform a Network Access protocol, such as Ethernet or Token Ring, of the destination's hardware address on the local network. (It has already been informed by upper-layer protocols of the destination's IP address.) If IP doesn't find the destination host's hardware address in the ARP cache, it uses ARP to find this information.

As IP's detective, ARP interrogates the local network by sending out a broadcast asking the machine with the specified IP address to reply with its hardware address. In other words, ARP translates the software (IP) address into a hardware address—for example, the destination machine's Ethernet board address—and from it, deduces its whereabouts. This hardware address is technically referred to as the *media access control (MAC) address* or physical address. Figure 3.8 shows how an ARP might look to a local network.

FIGURE 3.8 Local ARP broadcast

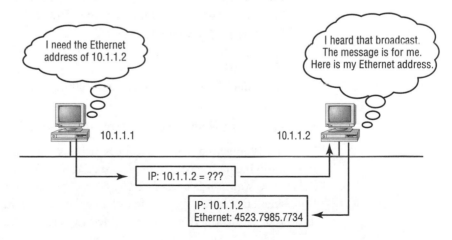

ARP resolves IP addresses to Ethernet addresses.

The following trace shows an ARP broadcast. Notice that the destination hardware address is unknown and is all Fs in hex, which is all 1s in binary, and a hardware address broadcast.

```
Flags:          0x00
  Status:       0x00
  Packet Length:64
  Timestamp:    09:17:29.574000 01/04/2000
Ethernet Header
  Destination:  FF:FF:FF:FF:FF:FF  Ethernet Broadcast
  Source:       00:A0:24:48:60:A5
  Protocol Type:0x0806  IP ARP
ARP - Address Resolution Protocol
  Hardware:                 1  Ethernet (10Mb)
  Protocol:                 0x0800  IP
  Hardware Address Length:  6
  Protocol Address Length:  4
  Operation:                1  ARP Request
  Sender Hardware Address:  00:A0:24:48:60:A5
  Sender Internet Address:  172.16.10.3
  Target Hardware Address:  00:00:00:00:00:00  (ignored)
  Target Internet Address:  172.16.10.10
Extra bytes (Padding):
  ...............  0A 0A 0A 0A 0A 0A 0A 0A 0A 0A 0A 0A 0A
0A 0A 0A 0A 0A
  Frame Check Sequence:  0x00000000
```

Reverse Address Resolution Protocol (RARP)

When an IP machine happens to be a diskless machine, it has no way of initially knowing its IP address, but it does know its MAC address. The *Reverse Address Resolution Protocol (RARP)* discovers the identity of the IP address for diskless machines by sending out a packet that includes its MAC address and a request for the IP address assigned to that MAC address. A designated machine, called a RARP server, responds with the answer, and the identity crisis is over. RARP uses the information it does know about the machine's MAC address to learn its IP address and complete the machine's ID portrait.

NOTE

RARP resolves Ethernet addresses to IP addresses.

Figure 3.9 shows a diskless workstation asking for its IP address with a RARP broadcast.

FIGURE 3.9 RARP broadcast example

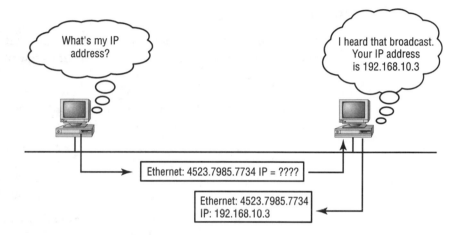

IP Addressing

One of the most important topics in any discussion of TCP/IP is IP addressing. An *IP address* is a numeric identifier assigned to each machine on an IP network. It designates the location of a device on the network. An IP address is a software address, not a hardware address—the latter is hard-coded on a network interface card (NIC) and used for finding hosts on a local network. IP addressing was designed to allow a host on one network to communicate with a host on a different network, regardless of the type of LANs the hosts are participating in.

Before we get into the more complicated aspects of IP addressing, you need to understand some of the basics. In this section you will learn about some of the fundamentals of IP addressing and its terminology. Later on, you will learn about the hierarchical IP addressing scheme and subnetting.

 To understand IP addressing and subnetting, it's important to have already mastered binary-to-decimal conversion and the powers of 2. If you need to review these topics, see the upcoming sidebars covering these issues.

IP Terminology

Throughout this chapter you will learn several terms that are critical to understanding the Internet Protocol. To start, here are a few of the most important:

Bit   One digit; either a 1 or a 0.

Byte   7 or 8 bits, depending on whether parity is used. For the rest of this chapter, always assume a byte is 8 bits.

Octet   Always 8 bits. Base-8 addressing scheme.

Network address   The designation used in routing to send packets to a remote network, for example, 10.0.0.0, 172.16.0.0, and 192.168.10.0.

Broadcast address   Used by applications and hosts to send information to all nodes on a network. Examples include 255.255.255.255, which is all networks, all nodes; 172.16.255.255, which is all subnets and hosts on network 17.16.0.0; and 10.255.255.255, which broadcasts to all subnets and hosts on network 10.0.0.0.

The Hierarchical IP Addressing Scheme

An IP address consists of 32 bits of information. These bits are divided into four sections, referred to as *octets* or *bytes*, each containing 1 byte (8 bits). You can depict an IP address using one of three methods:

- Dotted-decimal, as in 172.16.30.56
- Binary, as in 10101100.00010000.00011110.00111000
- Hexadecimal, as in 82 39 1E 38

All these examples represent the same IP address. Although hexadecimal is not used as often as dotted-decimal or binary when IP addressing is discussed, you still might find an IP address stored in hexadecimal in some programs; for example, the Windows Registry stores a machine's IP address in hex.

The 32-bit IP address is a structured or hierarchical address, as opposed to a flat or nonhierarchical, address. Although either type of addressing scheme could have been used, the hierarchical variety was chosen for a good reason. The advantage of this scheme is that it can handle a large number of addresses, namely 4.3 billion (a 32-bit address space with two possible values for each position—either 0 or 1—gives you 2^{32}, or approximately 4.3 billion). The disadvantage of this scheme, and the reason it's not used for IP addressing, relates to routing. If every address were unique, all routers on the Internet would need to store the address of each and every machine on the Internet. This would make efficient routing impossible, even if only a fraction of the possible addresses were used.

The solution to this dilemma is to use a two- or three-level, hierarchical addressing scheme that is structured by network and host, or network, subnet, and host.

This two- or three-level scheme is comparable to a telephone number. The first section, the area code, designates a very large area. The second section, the prefix, narrows the scope to a local calling area. The final segment, the customer number, zooms in on the specific connection. IP addresses use the same type of layered structure. Rather than all 32 bits being treated as a unique identifier, as in flat addressing, a part of the address is designated as the network address, and the other part is designated as either the subnet and host or just the node address.

Network Addressing

The *network address* uniquely identifies each network. Every machine on the same network shares that network address as part of its IP address. In the IP address 172.16.30.56, for example, 172.16 is the network address.

The *node address* is assigned to, and uniquely identifies, each machine on a network. This part of the address must be unique because it identifies a particular machine—an individual—as opposed to a network, which is a group. This number can also be referred to as a *host address*. In the sample IP address 172.16.30.56, .30.56 is the node address.

The designers of the Internet decided to create classes of networks based on network size. For the small number of networks possessing a very large number of nodes, they created the rank *Class A network*. At the other extreme is the *Class C network*, which is reserved for the numerous networks with a small number of nodes. The class distinction for networks between very large and very small is predictably called the *Class B network*.

Subdividing an IP address into a network and node address is determined by the class designation of one's network. Figure 3.10 summarizes the three classes of networks, which will be described in much more detail throughout this chapter.

FIGURE 3.10 Summary of the three classes of networks

	8 bits	8 bits	8 bits	8 bits
Class A:	Network	Host	Host	Host
Class B:	Network	Network	Host	Host
Class C:	Network	Network	Network	Host
Class D:	Multicast			
Class E:	Research			

To ensure efficient routing, Internet designers defined a mandate for the leading-bits section of the address for each different network class. For example, since a router knows that a Class A network address always starts with a 0, the router might be able to speed a packet on its way after reading only the first bit of its address. This is where the address schemes define the difference between a Class A, Class B, and Class C address.

Network Address Range: Class A

The designers of the IP address scheme said that the first bit of the first byte in a Class A network address must always be off, or 0. This means a Class A address must be between 0 and 127.

Here is how those numbers are defined:

0xxxxxxx: If we turn the other 7 bits all off and then turn them all on, we will find your Class A range of network addresses.

00000000=0
01111111=127

So, a Class A network is defined in the first octet between 0 and 127. It can't be less or more. (We'll talk about illegal addresses in a minute.)

If you are having any difficulty with the binary-to-decimal conversions, please read the "Binary-to-Decimal Conversion Review" sidebar.

Binary-to-Decimal Conversion Review

Prior to learning about IP addressing, you must have a fundamental understanding of binary-to-decimal conversions. Here is how it works: Binary numbers use 8 bits to define a decimal number. These bits are weighted from right to left in an increment that doubles in value.

Here is an example of 8 bits and the value assigned to each bit:

```
128    64    32    16    8    4    2    1
```

Here is an example of binary-to-decimal conversion:

```
128    64    32    16    8    4    2    1    Binary value
0      0     1     0     0    1    1    0    Byte in binary
```

Add the value of the bits that are turned on:

```
32
4
2
=38
```

Any time you find a bit turned on (a one), you add the values of each bit position. Let's practice on a few more:

```
01010101=85
64
16
 4
 1
=85
```

Try a few on your own:

00001111=15
10001100=140
11001100=204

You will need to memorize the binary-to-decimal conversions in the following list. You will use this information when you practice subnetting later in this chapter:

00000000=0
10000000=128
11000000=192
11100000=224
11110000=240
11111000=248
11111100=252
11111110=254
11111111=255

Network Address Range: Class B

In a Class B network, the RFCs state that the first bit of the first byte must always be turned on, but the second bit must always be turned off. If you turn the other six bits all off and then all on, you will find the range for a Class B network:

10000000=128
10111111=191

As you can see, this means that a Class B network can be defined when the first byte is configured from 128 to 191.

Network Address Range: Class C

For Class C networks, the RFCs define the first two bits of the first octet always turned on, but the third bit can never be on. Following the same process as the previous classes, convert from binary to decimal to find the range. Here is the range for a Class C network:

11000000=192
11011111=223

So, if you see an IP address that starts at 192 and goes to 223, you'll know it is a Class C IP address.

Network Address Ranges: Classes D and E

The addresses between 224 and 255 are reserved for Class D and E networks. Class D is used for multicast addresses and Class E for scientific purposes. We will not discuss Class D and E addresses in this book.

Network Addresses: Special Purpose

Some IP addresses are reserved for special purposes, and network administrators shouldn't assign these addresses to nodes. Table 3.2 lists the members of this exclusive little club and why they're included in it.

TABLE 3.2   Reserved IP Addresses

Address	Function
Network address of all 0s	Interpreted to mean "this network or segment."
Network address of all 1s	Interpreted to mean "all networks."
Network 127.0.0.1	Reserved for loopback tests. Designates the local node and allows that node to send a test packet to itself without generating network traffic.
Node address of all 0s	Interpreted to mean "this node."
Node address of all 1s	Interpreted to mean "all nodes" on the specified network; for example, 128.2.255.255 means "all nodes" on network 128.2 (Class B address).
Entire IP address set to all 0s	Used by Cisco routers to designate the default route.
Entire IP address set to all 1s (same as 255.255.255.255)	Broadcast to all nodes on the current network; sometimes called an "all 1s broadcast."

Class A Addresses

In a Class A network address, the first byte is assigned to the network address, and the three remaining bytes are used for the node addresses. The Class A format is

`Network.Node.Node.Node`

For example, in the IP address `49.22.102.70`, 49 is the network address, and 22.102.70 is the node address. Every machine on this particular network would have the distinctive network address of 49.

Class A addresses are one byte long, with the first bit of that byte reserved and the seven remaining bits available for manipulation. As a result, the maximum number of Class A networks that can be created is 128. Why? Because each of the seven bit positions can either be a 0 or a 1, thus 2^7 or 128.

To complicate matters further, the network address of all 0s (0000 0000) is reserved to designate the default route (see Table 3.2 in the previous section). Additionally, the address 127, which is reserved for diagnostics, can't be used either, which means that you can only use the numbers 1 to 126 to designate Class A network addresses. This means the actual number of usable Class A network addresses is 128 minus 2, or 126. Got it?

Each Class A address has three bytes (24-bit positions) for the node address of a machine. Thus, there are 2^{24}—or 16,777,216—unique combinations and, therefore, precisely that many possible unique node addresses for each Class A network. Because addresses with the two patterns of all 0s and all 1s are reserved, the actual maximum usable number of nodes for a Class A network is 2^{24} minus 2, which equals 16,777,214.

Class A Valid Host IDs

Here is an example of how to figure out the valid host IDs in a Class A network address:

`10.0.0.0`   All host bits off is the network address.

`10.255.255.255`   All host bits on is the broadcast address.

The valid hosts are the number in between the network address and the broadcast address: `10.0.0.1` through `10.255.255.254`. Notice that 0s and 255s are valid host IDs. All you need to remember when trying to find valid host addresses is that the host bits cannot all be turned off or on at the same time.

Class B Addresses

In a Class B network address, the first two bytes are assigned to the network address, and the remaining two bytes are used for node addresses. The format is

`Network.Network.Node.Node`

For example, in the IP address `172.16.30.56`, the network address is 172.16, and the node address is 30.56.

With a network address being two bytes (eight bits each), there would be 2^{16} unique combinations. But the Internet designers decided that all Class B network addresses should start with the binary digit 1, then 0. This leaves 14 bit positions to manipulate, therefore 16,384 (2^{14}) unique Class B network addresses.

A Class B address uses two bytes for node addresses. This is 2^{16} minus the two reserved patterns (all 0s and all 1s), for a total of 65,534 possible node addresses for each Class B network.

Class B Valid Host IDs

Here is an example of how to find the valid hosts in a Class B network:

`172.16.0.0`   All host bits turned off is the network address.

`172.16.255.255`   All host bits turned on is the broadcast address.

The valid hosts would be the numbers in between the network address and the broadcast address: `172.16.0.1` through `172.16.255.254`.

Class C Addresses

The first three bytes of a Class C network address are dedicated to the network portion of the address, with only one measly byte remaining for the node address. The format is

`Network.Network.Network.Node`

Using the example IP address `192.168.100.102`, the network address is 192.168.100, and the node address is 102.

In a Class C network address, the first three bit positions are always the binary 110. The calculation is such: 3 bytes, or 24 bits, minus 3 reserved positions, leaves 21 positions. Hence, there are 2^{21}, or 2,097,152, possible Class C networks.

Each unique Class C network has one byte to use for node addresses. This leads to 2^8 or 256, minus the two reserved patterns of all 0s and all 1s, for a total of 254 node addresses for each Class C network.

Class C Valid Host IDs

Here is an example of how to find a valid host ID in a Class C network:

192.168.100.0   All host bits turned off is the network ID.

192.168.100.255   All host bits turned on is the broadcast address.

The valid hosts would be the numbers in between the network address and the broadcast address: 192.168.100.1 through 192.168.100.254.

Subnetting

In the previous section, you learned how to define and find the valid host ranges used in a Class A, Class B, and Class C network address by turning the host bits all off and then all on. However, you were defining only one network. What happens if you wanted to take one network address and create six networks from it? You would have to perform what is called *subnetting*, which allows you to take one larger network and break it into many smaller networks.

There are many reasons to perform subnetting. Some of the benefits of subnetting include the following:

Reduced network traffic   We all appreciate less traffic of any kind. Networks are no different. Without trusty routers, packet traffic could grind the entire network down to a near standstill. With routers, most traffic will stay on the local network; only packets destined for other networks will pass through the router. Routers create broadcast domains. The smaller broadcast domains you create, the less network traffic on that network segment.

Optimized network performance   This is a result of reduced network traffic.

Simplified management   It's easier to identify and isolate network problems in a group of smaller connected networks than within one gigantic network.

Facilitated spanning of large geographical distances   Because WAN links are considerably slower and more expensive than LAN links, a single large network that spans long distances can create problems in every arena listed above. Connecting multiple smaller networks makes the system more efficient.

To create subnetworks, you take bits from the host portion of the IP address and reserve them to define the subnet address. This means fewer bits for hosts, so the more subnets, the fewer bits available for defining hosts.

In this section you will learn how to create subnets, starting with Class C addresses. However, before you implement subnetting, you need to determine your current requirements and plan for future conditions. Follow these steps:

1. Determine the number of required network IDs.

   A. One for each subnet

   B. One for each wide area network connection

2. Determine the number of required host IDs per subnet.

   A. One for each TCP/IP host

   B. One for each router interface

3. Based on the above requirement, create the following:

   A. One subnet mask for your entire network

   B. A unique subnet ID for each physical segment

   C. A range of host IDs for each subnet

Understanding the Powers of 2

Powers of 2 are important to understand and memorize for use with IP subnetting. To review powers of 2, remember that when you see a number with another number to its upper right, this means you should multiply the number by itself as many times as the upper number specifies. For example, 2^3 is 2x2x2, which equals 8. Here is the list of powers of 2 that you should memorize:

$2^1=2$

$2^2=4$

$2^3=8$

$2^4=16$

$2^5=32$

$2^6=64$

$2^7=128$

$2^8=256$

Subnet Masks

For the subnet address scheme to work, every machine on the network must know which part of the host address will be used as the subnet address. This is accomplished by assigning a *subnet mask* to each machine. This is a 32-bit value that allows the recipient of IP packets to distinguish the network ID portion of the IP address from the host ID portion of the IP address.

The network administrator creates a 32-bit subnet mask composed of 1s and 0s. The 1s in the subnet mask represent the positions that refer to the network or subnet addresses.

Not all networks need subnets, meaning they use the default subnet mask. This is basically the same as saying that a network doesn't have a subnet address. Table 3.3 shows the default subnet masks for Classes A, B, and C. These cannot change. In other words, you cannot make a Class B subnet mask read 255.0.0.0. The host will read such an address as invalid and typically won't even let you type it in. For a Class A network, you cannot change the first byte in a subnet mask; it must read 255.0.0.0 at a minimum. Similarly, you cannot assign 255.255.255.255, as this is all 1s and a broadcast address. A Class B address must start with 255.255.0.0, and a Class C must start with 255.255.255.0.

TABLE 3.3 Default Subnet Mask

Class	Format	Default Subnet Mask
A	Net.Node.Node.Node	255.0.0.0
B	Net.Net.Node.Node	255.255.0.0
C	Net.Net.Net.Node	255.255.255.0

Subnetting Class C Addresses

There are many different ways to subnet a network. The right way is the way that works best for you. First you will learn to use the binary method, and then we'll look at an easier way to do the same thing.

In a Class C address, only 8 bits is available for defining the hosts. Remember that subnet bits start at the left and go to the right, without skipping bits. This means that subnet masks can be

```
10000000=128
11000000=192
11100000=224
11110000=240
11111000=248
11111100=252
11111110=254
```

Now, the RFCs state that you cannot have only one bit for subnetting, since that would mean that the bit would always be either off or on, which would be illegal. So, the first subnet mask you can legally use is 192, and the last one is 252, since you need at least two bits for defining hosts.

The Binary Method: Subnetting a Class C Address

In this section you will learn how to subnet a Class C address using the binary method. We will take the first subnet mask available with a Class C address, which borrows two bits from subnetting. For this example, we are using 255.255.255.192.

192=11000000   Two bits for subnetting, 6 bits for defining the hosts in each subnet. What are the subnets? Since the subnet bits can't be both off or on at the same time, the only two valid subnets are

- **01**000000=64 (all host bits off)

or

- **10**000000=128 (all host bits off)

The valid hosts would be defined as the numbers between the subnets, minus the all host bits off and all host bits on.

To find the hosts, first find your subnet by turning all the host bits off, then turn all the host bits on to find your broadcast address for the subnet. The valid hosts must be between those two numbers. Table 3.4 shows the 64 subnet, valid host range, and broadcast address.

TABLE 3.4 Subnet 64

Subnet	Host	Meaning
01	000000=64	The network (do this first)
01	000001=65	The first valid host
01	111110=126	The last valid host
01	111111=127	The broadcast address (do this second)

Table 3.5 shows the 128 subnet, valid host range, and broadcast address.

TABLE 3.5 Subnet 128

Subnet	Host	Meaning
10	000000=128	The subnet address
10	000001=129	The first valid host
10	111110=190	The last valid host
10	111111=191	The broadcast address

That wasn't all that hard. Hopefully you understood what I was trying to show you. However, the example I presented only used two subnet bits. What if you had to subnet using 9, 10, or even 20 subnet bits? Let's learn an alternate method of subnetting that makes it easier to subnet larger numbers.

The Alternate Method: Subnetting a Class C Address

When you have a subnet mask and need to determine the amount of subnets, valid hosts, and broadcast addresses that the mask provides, all you need to do is answer five simple questions:

1. How many subnets does the subnet mask produce?
2. How many valid hosts per subnet?

3. What are the valid subnets?

4. What are the valid hosts in each subnet?

5. What is the broadcast address of each subnet?

It is important at this point that you understand your powers of 2. Please refer to the sidebar earlier in this chapter if you need help. Here is how you determine the answers to the five questions:

1. How many subnets? 2^x-2=amount of subnets. X is the amount of masked bits, or the 1s. For example, 11000000 is 2^2-2. In this example, there are 2 subnets.

2. How many hosts per subnet? 2^x-2=amount of hosts per subnet. X is the amount of unmasked bits, or the 0s. For example, 11000000 is 2^6-2. In this example, there are 62 hosts per subnet.

3. What are the valid subnets? 256–subnet mask=base number. For example, 256–192=64.

4. What are the valid hosts? Valid hosts are the numbers between the subnets, minus all 0s and all 1s.

5. What is the broadcast address for each subnet? Broadcast address is all host bits turned on, which is the number immediately preceding the next subnet.

Now, because this can seem confusing, I need to assure you that it is easier than it looks. Just try a few with me and see for yourself.

Subnetting Practice Examples: Class C Addresses

This section will give you an opportunity to practice subnetting Class C addresses using the method I just described. We're going to start with the first Class C subnet mask and work through every subnet that we can using a Class C address. When we're done, I'll show you how easy this is with Class A and B networks as well.

Practice Example 1: 255.255.255.192

Let's use the Class C subnet address from the preceding example, 255.255.255.192, to see how much simpler this method is than writing out the binary numbers. In this example, you will subnet the network address 192.168.10.0 and subnet mask 255.255.255.192.

> 192.168.10.0=Network address

> 255.255.255.192=Subnet mask

Now, answer the five questions:

1. How many subnets? Since 192 is two bits on (11000000), the answer would be $2^2-2=2$. (The minus 2 is the subnet bits all on or all off, which is not valid by default.)

2. How many hosts per subnet? We have 6 host bits off (11000000), so the equation would be $2^6-2=62$ hosts.

3. What are the valid subnets? 256–192=64, which is the first subnet and our base number or variable. Keep adding the variable to itself until you reach the subnet mask. 64+64=128. 128+64=192, which is invalid because it is the subnet mask (all subnet bits turned on). Our two valid subnets are, then, 64 and 128.

4. What are the valid hosts? These are the numbers between the subnets. The easiest way to find the hosts is to write out the subnet address and the broadcast address. This way the valid hosts are obvious.

5. What is the broadcast address for each subnet? The number right before the next subnet is all host bits turned on and is the broadcast address. Table 3.6 shows the 64 and 128 subnets, the valid host ranges of each, and the broadcast address of both subnets.

TABLE 3.6 The 64 and 128 Subnet Ranges

First Subnet	Second Subnet	Meaning
64	128	The subnets (do this first)
65	129	Our first host (perform host addressing last)
126	190	Our last host
127	191	The broadcast address (do this second)

Notice that we came up with the same answers as when we did it the binary way. This is a much easier way to do it because you never have to do any binary-to-decimal conversions. However, you might be thinking that it is not easier than the first method I showed you. For the first subnet with only two subnet bits, you're right, it isn't that much easier. Remember, we're going for the big one: being able to subnet in your head. You need to practice this approach to be able to perform subnetting in your head.

Practice Example 2: 255.255.255.224

In this example, you will subnet the network address 192.168.10.0 and subnet mask 255.255.255.224.

> 192.168.10.0=Network address
>
> 255.255.255.224=Subnet mask

1. How many subnets? 224 is 11100000, so our equation would be $2^3-2=6$.

2. How many hosts? $2^5-2=30$.

3. What are the valid subnets? 256–224=32. 32+32=64. 64+32=96. 96+32=128. 128+32=160. 160+32=192. 192+64=224, which is invalid because it is our subnet mask (all subnet bits on). Our subnets are 32, 64, 96, 128, 160, and 192.

4. What are the valid hosts?

5. What is the broadcast address for each subnet?

To answer questions 4 and 5, first just write out the subnets, then write out the broadcast addresses, which is the number right before the next subnet. Last, fill in the host addresses. Table 3.7 shows all the subnets for the 255.255.255.224 Class C subnet mask.

TABLE 3.7   The Class C 255.255.255.224 Mask

Subnet 1	Subnet 2	Subnet 3	Subnet 4	Subnet 5	Subnet 6	Meaning
32	64	96	128	160	192	The subnet address
33	65	97	129	161	193	The first valid host
62	94	126	158	190	222	Our last valid host
63	95	127	159	191	223	The broadcast address

Practice Example 3: 255.255.255.240

Let's practice on another one:

> 192.168.10.0=Network number
>
> 255.255.255.240=Subnet mask

1. 240 is 11110000 in binary. $2^4-2=14$ subnets.

2. Four host bits, or $2^4-2=14$.

3. 256–240=16. 16+16=32. 32+16=48. 48+16=64. 64+16=80. 80+16=96. 96+16=112. 112+16=128. 128+16=144. 144+16=160. 160+16=176. 176+16=192. 192+16=208. 208+16=224. 224+16=240, which is our subnet mask and therefore invalid. So, our valid subnets are 16, 32, 48, 64, 80, 96, 112, 128, 144, 160, 176, 192, 208, and 224.

4. What are the valid hosts?

5. What is the broadcast address for each subnet?

To answer questions 4 and 5, view the following table, which shows the subnets, valid hosts, and broadcast addresses for each subnet. First, find the broadcast address of each subnet, then fill in the host addresses.

Subnet	16	32	48	64	80	96	112	128	144	160	176	192	208	224
First Host	17	33	49	65	81	97	113	129	145	161	177	193	209	225
Last Host	30	46	62	78	94	110	126	142	158	174	190	206	222	238
Broadcast	31	47	63	79	95	111	127	143	159	175	191	207	223	239

Practice Example 4: 255.255.255.248

Let's keep practicing:

> 192.168.10.0=Network address
>
> 255.255.255.248=Subnet mask

1. 248 in binary=11111000. $2^5-2=30$ subnets.

   2. $2^3-2=6$ hosts.

   3. 256–248=8, 16, 24, 32, 40, 48, 56, 64, 72, 80, 88, 96, 104, 112, 120, 128, 136, 144, 152, 160, 168, 176, 184, 192, 200, 208, 216, 224, 232, and 240.

   4. First find the broadcast addresses in step 5, then come back and perform step 4 by filling in the host addresses.

   5. Find the broadcast address of each subnet, which is always the number right before the next subnet.

Take a look at the following table, which shows the subnets (first three and last three only), valid hosts, and broadcast addresses for the Class C 255.255.255.248 mask.

Subnet	8	16	24	224	232	240
First Host	9	17	25	225	233	241
Last Host	14	22	30	230	238	246
Broadcast	15	23	31	231	239	247

Practice Example 5: 255.255.255.252

   192.168.10.0=Network number

   255.255.255.252=Subnet mask

   1. 62.

   2. 2.

   3. 4, 8, 12, etc., all the way to 248.

   4. First find the broadcast addresses in step 5, then come back and perform step 4 by filling in the host addresses.

   5. Find the broadcast address of each subnet, which is always the number right before the next subnet.

The following table shows you the subnet, valid host, and broadcast address of the first three and last three subnets in the 255.255.255.252 Class C subnet.

Subnet	4	8	12	240	244	248
First Host	5	9	13	241	245	249
Last Host	6	10	14	242	246	250
Broadcast	7	11	15	243	247	251

Practice Example 6: 255.255.255.128

OK, we told you that using only one subnet bit was illegal and not to use it. But aren't all rules meant to be broken? This mask can be used when you need two subnets, each with 126 hosts. The standard five questions don't work here, and we'll just explain how to use it. First, use the global configuration command `ip subnet-zero` to tell your router to break the rules and use a 1-bit subnet mask.

Since 128 is 1000000 in binary, there is only one bit for subnetting. Since this bit can be either off or on, the two available subnets are 0 and 128. You can determine the subnet value by looking at the decimal value of the fourth octet. The following table will show you the two subnets, valid host range, and broadcast address for the Class C 255.255.255.128 mask.

Subnet	0	128
First Host	1	129
Last Host	126	254
Broadcast	127	255

So, if you have an IP address of 192.168.10.5 using the 255.255.255 .128-subnet mask, you know it is in the range of the 0 subnet and the 128-bit must be off. If you have an IP address of 192.168.10.189, then the 128 must be on, and the host is considered to be in the 128 subnet. You'll see this again in a minute.

Subnetting in Your Head: Class C Addresses

It is possible to perform subnetting in your head. Don't you believe me? I'll show you how; it's relatively easy. Take the following example:

192.168.10.33=Network address

255.255.255.224=Subnet mask

First, determine the subnet and broadcast address of the above IP address. You can do this by answering question 3 in the five-question process. 256–224=32. 32+32=64. Bingo. The address falls between the two subnets and must be part of the 192.168.10.32 subnet. The next subnet is 64, so the broadcast address is 63. (Remember that the broadcast address of a subnet is always the number right before the next subnet.) The valid host range is 10.33–10.62. This is too easy.

Let's try another one. Here, you will subnet another Class C address:

192.168.10.33=Network address

255.255.255.240=Subnet mask

What subnet and broadcast address is the above IP address a member of? 256–240=16. 16+16=32. 32+16=48. Bingo, the host address is between the 32 and 48 subnets. The subnet is 192.168.10.32, and the broadcast address is 47. The valid host range is 33–46.

Now that we have completed all the Class C subnets, what should we do next? Class B subnetting, did you say? Sounds good to me.

Subnetting Class B Addresses

Since we went through all the possible Class C subnets, let's take a look at subnetting a Class B network. First, let's look at all the possible Class B subnet masks. Notice that we have a lot more possible subnets than we do with a Class C network address.

255.255.128.0
255.255.192.0
255.255.224.0
255.255.240.0
255.255.248.0
255.255.252.0

```
255.255.254.0
255.255.255.0
255.255.255.128
255.255.255.192
255.255.255.224
255.255.255.240
255.255.255.248
255.255.255.252
```

The Class B network address has 16 bits available for hosts addressing. This means we can use up to 14 bits for subnetting since we must leave at least two bits for host addressing.

Do you notice a pattern in the subnet values? This is why we had you memorize the binary-to-decimal numbers at the beginning of this section. Since subnet mask bits start on the left, move to the right, and cannot skip bits, the numbers are always the same. Memorize this pattern.

The process of subnetting a Class B network is the same as for a Class C, except you just have more host bits. Use the same subnet numbers you used with Class C, but add a zero to the network portion and a 255 to the broadcast section in the fourth octet. The following table shows you a host range of two subnets used in a Class B subnet.

16.0	32.0
16.255	32.255

Just add the valid hosts between the numbers, and you're set.

Subnetting Practice Examples: Class B Addresses

This section will give you an opportunity to practice subnetting Class B addresses.

Practice Example 1: 255.255.192.0

172.16.0.0=Network address

255.255.192.0=Subnet mask

1. $2^2-2=2$.

2. $2^{14}-2=16,382$.

3. 256–192=64. 64+64=128.

4. First find the broadcast addresses in step 5, then come back and perform step 4 by filling in the host addresses.

5. Find the broadcast address of each subnet, which is always the number right before the next subnet.

The following table shows the two subnets available, the valid host range, and the broadcast address of each.

Subnet	64.0	128.0
First Host	64.1	128.1
Last Host	127.254	191.254
Broadcast	127.255	191.255

Notice we just added the fourth octet's lowest and highest values and came up with the answers. Again, it is the same answer as for a Class C subnet, but we just added the fourth octet.

Practice Example 2: 255.255.240.0

172.16.0.0=Network address

255.255.240.0=Subnet address

1. $2^4-2=14$.

2. $2^{12}-2=4094$.

3. 256–240=16, 32, 48, etc., up to 224. Notice these are the same numbers as a Class C 240 mask.

4. First find the broadcast addresses in step 5, then come back and perform step 4 by filling in the host addresses.

5. Find the broadcast address of each subnet, which is always the number right before the next subnet.

The following table shows the first three subnets, valid hosts, and broadcast addresses in a Class B 255.255.240.0 mask.

Subnet	16.0	32.0	48.0
First Host	16.1	32.1	48.1
Last Host	31.254	47.254	63.254
Broadcast	31.255	47.255	63.255

Practice Example 3: 255.255.254.0

1. $2^7-2=126$.

2. $2^9-2=510$.

3. 256–254=2, 4, 6, 8, etc., up to 252.

4. First find the broadcast addresses in step 5, then come back and perform step 4 by filling in the host addresses.

5. Find the broadcast address of each subnet, which is always the number right before the next subnet.

The following table shows the first four subnets, valid hosts, and broadcast addresses in a Class B 255.255.254.0 mask.

Subnet	2.0	4.0	6.0	8.0
First Host	2.1	4.1	6.1	8.1
Last Host	3.254	4.254	7.254	9.254
Broadcast	3.255	5.255	7.255	9.255

Practice Example 4: 255.255.255.0

Contrary to popular belief, 255.255.255.0 is not a Class C subnet mask. It is amazing how many people see this mask used in a Class B network and think it is a Class C subnet mask. This is a Class B subnet mask with 8 bits of subnetting—it is considerably different from a Class C mask. Subnetting this address is fairly simple:

1. $2^8-2=254$.

2. $2^8-2=254$.

3. 256–255=1, 2, 3, etc. all the way to 254.

4. First find the broadcast addresses in step 5, then come back and perform step 4 by filling in the host addresses.

5. Find the broadcast address of each subnet, which is always the number right before the next subnet.

The following table shows the first three subnets and the last one, valid hosts, and broadcast addresses in a Class B 255.255.255.0 mask.

Subnet	1.0	2.0	3.0	254.0
First Host	1.1	2.1	3.1	254.1
Last Host	1.254	2.254	3.254	254.254
Broadcast	1.255	2.255	3.255	254.255

Practice Example 5: 255.255.255.128

This must be illegal! What type of mask is this? Don't you wish it were illegal? This is one of the hardest subnet masks you can play with. It is actually a good subnet to use in production, as it creates over 500 subnets with 126 hosts for each subnet. That's a nice mixture.

1. $2^9-2=510$.

2. $2^7-2=126$.

3. This is the tricky part. 256–255=1, 2, 3, etc., for the third octet. However, you can't forget the one subnet bit used in the fourth octet. Remember when we showed you how to figure one subnet bit with a Class C mask? You figure this same way. (Now you know why we showed you the 1-bit subnet mask in the Class C section—to make this part easier.) You actually get two subnets for each third octet value, hence the 510 subnets. For example, if the third octet was showing subnet 3, the two subnets would actually be 3.0 and 3.128.

4. First find the broadcast addresses in step 5, then come back and perform step 4 by filling in the host addresses.

5. Find the broadcast address of each subnet, which is always the number right before the next subnet.

The following table shows how you can create subnets, valid hosts, and broadcast addresses using the Class B 255.255.255.128 subnet mask.

Subnet	0.128	1.0	1.128	2.0	2.128	3.0	3.128
First Host	0.129	1.1	1.129	2.1	2.129	3.1	3.129
Last Host	0.254	1.126	1.254	2.126	2.254	3.126	3.254
Broadcast	0.255	1.127	1.255	2.127	2.255	3.127	3.255

Practice Example 6: 255.255.255.192

This one gets just a little tricky. Both the 0 subnet as well as the 192 subnet could be valid in the fourth octet. It just depends on what the third octet is doing.

1. $2^{10}-2=1022$ subnets.

2. $2^6-2=62$ hosts.

3. 256–192=64 and 128. However, as long as all the subnet bits on the third are not all off, then subnet 0 in the fourth octet is valid. Also, as long as all the subnet bits in the third octet are not all on, 192 is valid in the fourth octet as a subnet.

4. First find the broadcast addresses in step 5, then come back and perform step 4 by filling in the host addresses.

5. Find the broadcast address of each subnet, which is always the number right before the next subnet.

The following table shows the first two subnet ranges, valid hosts, and broadcast addresses.

Subnet	0.64	0.128	0.192	1.0	1.64	1.128	1.192
First Host	0.65	0.129	0.193	1.1	1.65	1.129	1.193
Last Host	0.126	0.190	0.254	1.62	1.126	1.190	1.254
Broadcast	0.127	0.191	0.255	1.63	1.127	1.191	1.255

Notice that for each subnet value in the third octet, you get subnets 0, 64, 128, and 192 in the fourth octet. This is true for every subnet in the third octet except 0 and 255. We just demonstrated the 0-subnet value in the third octet.

Notice, however, that for the 1 subnet in the third octet, the fourth octet has four subnets, 0, 64, 128, and 192.

Practice Example 7: 255.255.255.224

This is done the same way as the preceding subnet mask; however, we just have more subnets and fewer hosts per subnet available.

1. $2^{11}-2=2046$ subnets.

2. $2^5-2=30$ hosts.

3. 256–224=32, 64, 96, 128, 160, 192. However, as demonstrated above, both the 0 and 224 subnets can be used as long as the third octet does not show a value of 0 or 255. Here is an example of having no subnet bits in the third octet.

4. First find the broadcast addresses in step 5, then come back and perform step 4 by filling in the host addresses.

5. Find the broadcast address of each subnet, which is always the number right before the next subnet.

The following table shows the first range of subnets.

Subnet	0.32	0.64	0.96	0.128	0.160	0.192	0.224
First Host	0.33	0.65	0.97	0.129	0.161	0.193	0.225
Last Host	0.62	0.94	0.126	0.158	0.190	0.222	0.254
Broadcast	0.63	0.95	0.127	0.159	0.191	0.223	0.255

Let's take a look at a situation where a subnet bit is turned on in the third octet. The following table shows the full range of subnets available in the fourth octet.

Subnet	1.0	1.32	1.64	1.128	1.160	1.192	1.224
First Host	1.1	1.33	1.65	1.129	1.161	1.193	1.225
Last Host	1.30	1.62	1.126	1.158	1.190	1.222	1.254
Broadcast	1.31	1.63	1.127	1.159	1.191	1.223	1.255

This next table shows the last subnet.

Subnet	255.0	255.32	255.64	255.128	255.160	255.192
First Host	255.1	255.33	255.65	255.129	255.161	255.193
Last Host	255.62	255.62	255.126	255.158	255.190	255.222
Broadcast	255.63	255.63	255.127	255.159	255.191	255.223

Subnetting in Your Head: Class B Addresses

Can we subnet Class B addresses in our heads? I know what you are thinking: "Are you nuts?" It's actually easier than writing it out. I'll show you how:

Question: What subnet and broadcast address is the IP address 172.16.10.33 255.255.255.224 a member of?

Answer: 256–224=32. 32+32=64. Bingo—33 is between 32 and 64. However, remember that the third octet is considered part of the subnet, so the answer would be the 10.32 subnet. The broadcast is 10.63, since 10.64 is the next subnet.

Let's try four more:

Question: What subnet and broadcast address is the IP address 172.16.90.66 255.255.255.192 a member of?

Answer: 256–192=64. 64+64=128. The subnet is 172.16.90.64. The broadcast must be 172.16.90.127, since 90.128 is the next subnet.

Question: What subnet and broadcast address is the IP address 172.16.50.97 255.255.255.224 a member of?

Answer: 256–224=32, 64, 96, 128. The subnet is 172.16.50.96, and the broadcast must be 172.16.50.127 since 50.128 is the next subnet.

Question: What subnet and broadcast address is the IP address 172.16.10.10 255.255.255.192 a member of?

Answer: 256–192=64. This address must be in the 172.16.10.0 subnet, and the broadcast must be 172.16.10.63.

Question: What subnet and broadcast address is the IP address 172.16.10.10 255.255.255.224 a member of?

Answer: 256–224=32. The subnet is 172.16.10.0, with a broadcast of 172.16.10.31.

Subnetting Class A Addresses

Class A subnetting is not performed any differently from Classes B and C, though there are 24 bits to play with instead of the 16 in a Class B address and the eight bits in a Class C address.

Let's start by listing all the Class A subnets:

```
255.128.0.0
255.192.0.0
255.224.0.0
255.240.0.0
255.248.0.0
255.252.0.0
255.254.0.0
255.255.0.0
255.255.128.0
255.255.192.0
255.255.224.0
255.255.240.0
255.255.248.0
255.255.252.0
255.255.254.0
255.255.255.0
255.255.255.128
255.255.255.192
255.255.255.224
255.255.255.240
255.255.255.248
255.255.255.252
```

That's it. You must leave at least two bits for defining hosts. We hope you can see the pattern by now. Remember, we're going to do this the same way as a Class B or C subnet, but we just have more host bits.

Subnetting Practice Examples: Class A Addresses

When you look at an IP address and a subnet mask, you must be able to determine the bits used for subnets and the bits used for determining hosts. This is imperative. If you are still struggling with this concept, please reread the preceding "IP Addressing" section, which shows you how to determine the difference between the subnet and host bits.

Practice Example 1: 255.255.0.0

Class A addresses use a default mask of 255.0.0.0, which leaves 22 bits for subnetting since you must leave two bits for host addressing. The 255.255.0.0 mask with a Class A address is using eight subnet bits.

1. $2^8 - 2 = 254$.

2. $2^{16} - 2 = 65,534$.

3. 256−255=1, 2, 3, etc. (all in the second octet). The subnets would be 10.1.0.0, 10.2.0.0, 10.3.0.0, etc., up to 10.254.0.0.

4. First find the broadcast addresses in step 5, then come back and perform step 4 by filling in the host addresses.

5. Find the broadcast address of each subnet, which is always the number right before the next subnet.

Table 3.8 shows the first and last subnet, valid host range, and broadcast addresses.

TABLE 3.8 The First and Last Subnet

	First Subnet	Last Subnet
Subnet	10.1.0.0	10.254.0.0
First Host	10.1.0.1	10.254.0.1
Last Host	10.1.255.254	10.254.255.254
Broadcast	10.1.255.255	10.254.255.255

Practice Example 2: 255.255.240.0

255.255.240.0 gives us 12 bits of subnetting and leaves us 12 bits for host addressing.

1. $2^{12} - 2 = 4094$.

2. $2^{12} - 2 = 4094$.

3. 256–240=16. However, since the second octet is 255, or all subnet bits on, we can start the third octet with 0 as long as a subnet bit is turned on in the second octet. So the subnets become 10.1.0.0, 10.1.16.0, 10.1.32.0, and 10.1.48.0, all the way to 10.1.240.0. The next set of subnets would be 10.2.0.0, 10.2.16.0, 10.2.32.0, 10.2.48.0, all the way to 10.2.240.0. Notice that we can use 240 in the third octet as long as all the subnet bits in the second octet are not on. In other words, 10.255.240.0 is invalid because all subnet bits are turned on. The last valid subnet would be 10.255.224.0.

4. First find the broadcast addresses in step 5, then come back and perform step 4 by filling in the host addresses.

5. Find the broadcast address of each subnet, which is always the number right before the next subnet.

Table 3.9 shows some examples of the host ranges.

TABLE 3.9   Valid Host Ranges for a Class A 255.255.240.0 Mask

	First Subnet	Second Subnet	Last Subnet
Subnet	10.1.0.0	10.1.16.0	10.255.224.0
First Host	10.1.0.1	10.1.16.1	10.255.224.1
Last Host	10.1.15.254	10.1.31.254	10.255.239.254
Broadcast	10.1.15.255	10.1.31.255	10.255.239.255

Practice Example 3: 255.255.255.192

Let's do one more example using the second, third, and fourth octets for subnetting.

1. $2^{18}-2=262,142$ subnets.

2. $2^6-2=62$ hosts.

3. Now, we need to add subnet numbers from the second, third, and fourth octets. In the second and third, they can range from 1 to 255, as long as all subnet bits in the second, third, and fourth octets are not

all on at the same time. For the fourth octet, it will be 256–192=64. However, 0 will be valid as long as at least one other subnet bit is turned on in the second or third octet. Also, 192 will be valid as long as all the bits in the second and third octets are not turned on.

4. First find the broadcast addresses in step 5, then come back and perform step 4 by filling in the host addresses.

5. Find the broadcast address of each subnet, which is always the number right before the next subnet.

The following table will show the first few subnets and find the valid hosts and broadcast addresses in the Class A 255.255.255.192 mask.

Subnet	10.1.0.0	10.1.0.64	10.1.0.128	10.1.0.192
First Host	10.1.0.1	10.1.0.65	10.1.0.129	10.1.0.193
Last Host	10.1.0.62	10.1.0.126	10.1.0.190	10.1.0.254
Broadcast	10.1.0.63	10.1.0.127	10.1.0.192	10.1.0.255

The following table will show the last three subnets and find the valid hosts used in the Class A 255.255.255.192 mask.

Subnet	10.255.255.0	10.255.255.64	10.255.255.128
First Host	10.255.255.1	10.255.255.65	10.255.255.129
Last Host	10.255.255.62	10.255.255.126	10.255.255.190
Broadcast	10.255.255.63	10.255.255.127	10.255.255.191

Summary

Wow, if you made it this far and understood everything the first time through, I am very impressed! We covered a lot of ground in this chapter, and it is the largest chapter in the book. We discussed the Internet Protocol stack, as well as IP addressing and subnetting. This information is important to understand for the CCNA exam, of course, but also in any networking job or production environment you will be building or troubleshooting. It wouldn't hurt to read this chapter more than once and to practice subnetting as much as possible. You can also ask a friend to write out valid IP addresses for which you have to shout out the subnet, broadcast address, and valid host range.

Go through the written and review questions at the end of this chapter and make sure you understand each answer's explanation.

Key Terms

Before taking the exam, be sure you're familiar with the following terms.

Class A network *network address*

Class B network *node address*

Class C network *octet*

host address *subnet mask*

IP address

Written Lab

Write the subnet, broadcast address, and valid host range for the following:

1. 172.16.10.5 255.255.255.128

2. 172.16.10.33 255.255.255.224

3. 172.16.10.65 255.255.255.192

4. 172.16.10.17 255.255.255.252

5. 172.16.10.33 255.255.255.240

6. 192.168.100.25 255.255.255.252

7. 192.168.100.17, with 4 bits of subnetting

8. 192.168.100.66 with 3 bits of subnetting

9. 192.168.100.17 255.255.255.248

10. 10.10.10.5 255.255.255.252

Review Questions

1. Which protocol working at the Transport layer provides a connection-less service between hosts?

   A. IP

   B. ARP

   C. TCP

   D. UDP

2. Which protocol works at the Transport layer and provides virtual circuits between hosts?

   A. IP

   B. ARP

   C. TCP

   D. UDP

3. Which protocol works at the Internet layer and provides a connection service between hosts?

   A. IP

   B. ARP

   C. TCP

   D. UDP

4. If a host broadcasts a frame that includes a source and destination hardware address, and its purpose is to assign IP addresses to itself, which protocol at the Network layer does the host use?

   A. RARP

   B. ARPA

   C. ICMP

   D. TCP

   E. IPX

5. If a router interface is congested, which protocol in the IP suite is used to tell neighbor routers?

   A. RARP

   B. ARP

   C. ICMP

   D. IP

   E. TCP

6. What is the valid host range the IP address `172.16.10.22` `255.255.255.240` is a part of?

   A. 172.16.10.20 through 172.16.10.22

   B. 172.16.10.1 through 172.16.10.255

   C. 172.16.10.16 through 172.16.10.23

   D. 172.16.10.17 through 172.16.10.31

   E. 172.16.10.17 through 172.16.10.30

7. What range of addresses can be used in the first octet of a Class B network address?

   A. 1–126

   B. 1–127

   C. 128–190

   D. 128–191

   E. 129–192

   F. 192–220

8. What range of addresses can be used in the first octet of a Class C address?

   A. 1–127

   B. 129–192

   C. 203–234

   D. 192–223

9. How many bytes is an Ethernet address?

A. 3

B. 4

C. 5

D. 6

E. 7

F. 8

G. 16

10. What protocol is used to find the hardware address of a local device?

A. RARP

B. ARP

C. IP

D. ICMP

E. BootP

11. Which of the following is the broadcast address for a Class B network ID using the default subnet mask?

A. 172.16.10.255

B. 172.16.255.255

C. 172.255.255.255

D. 255.255.255.255

12. Which class of IP address provides a maximum of only 254 host addresses per network ID?

A. A

B. B

C. C

D. D

E. E

13. What is the broadcast address of the subnet address 10.254.255.19 255.255.255.248?

   A. 10.254.255.23

   B. 10.254.255.24

   C. 10.254.255.255

   D. 10.255.255.255

14. What is the broadcast address of the subnet address 172.16.99.99 255.255.192.0?

   A. 172.16.99.255

   B. 172.16.127.255

   C. 172.16.255.255

   D. 172.16.64.127

15. If you wanted to have 12 subnets with a Class C network ID, which subnet mask would you use?

   A. 255.255.255.252

   B. 255.255.255.248

   C. 255.255.255.240

   D. 255.255.255.255

16. What is the port number range that a transmitting host can use to set up a session with another host?

   A. 1–1023

   B. 1024 and above

   C. 1–256

   D. 1–65534

17. Which of the following ranges are considered well-known port numbers?

    A. 1–1023

    B. 1024 and above

    C. 1–256

    D. 1–65534

18. What is the broadcast address of the host subnet address 10.10.10.10 255.255.254.0?

    A. 10.10.10.255

    B. 10.10.11.255

    C. 10.10.255.255

    D. 10.255.255.255

19. What broadcast address will the host 192.168.210.5 255.255.255.252 use?

    A. 192.168.210.255

    B. 192.168.210.254

    C. 192.168.210.7

    D. 192.168.210.15

20. If you need to have a Class B network address subnetted into exactly 510 subnets, what subnet mask would you assign?

    A. 255.255.255.252

    B. 255.255.255.128

    C. 255.255.0.0

    D. 255.255.255.192

(The answers to the questions begin on the next page.)

Answers to the Written Lab

Write the subnet, broadcast address, and valid host range for the following:

1. Subnet is 172.16.10.0, broadcast is 172.16.10.127, and valid host range is 172.16.10.1 through 126. You need to ask yourself, "Is the subnet bit in the fourth octet on or off?" If the host address has a value of less than 128 in the fourth octet, then the subnet bit must be off. If the value of the fourth octet is higher than 128, then the subnet bit must be on. In this case the host address is 10.5, and the bit in the fourth octet must be off. The subnet must be 172.16.10.0.

2. Subnet is 172.16.10.32, broadcast is 172.16.10.63, and valid host range is 172.16.10.33 through 10.62. 256–224=32. 32+32=64—bingo. The subnet is 10.32, and the next subnet is 10.64, so the broadcast address must be 10.63.

3. Subnet is 172.16.10.64, broadcast is 172.16.10.127, and valid host range is 172.16.10.65 through 172.16.10.126. 256–192=64. 64+64=128, so the network address must be 172.16.10.64, with a broadcast of 172.16.10.127.

4. Network is 172.16.10.16, broadcast is 172.16.10.19, and valid host range is 172.16.10.17 through 18. 256–252=4. 4+4=8, plus 4=12, plus 4=16, plus 4=20—bingo. The subnet is 172.16.10.16, and the broadcast must be 10.19.

5. Network is 172.16.10.32, broadcast is 172.16.10.47, and valid host range is 172.16.10.33 through 46. 256–240=16. 16+16=32, plus 16=48. Subnet is 172.16.10.32; broadcast is 172.16.10.47.

6. Subnet is 192.168.100.24, broadcast is 192.168.100.27, and valid hosts are 192.168.100.25 through 26. 256–252=4. 4+4=8, plus 4=12, plus 4=16, plus 4=20, plus 4=24, plus 4=28. Subnet is 100.24; broadcast is 100.27.

7. Subnet is 192.168.100.16, broadcast is 192.168.100.31, and valid host range is 192.168.100.17 through 30. 256–240=16. 16+16=32. Subnet is, then, 100.16, with a broadcast of 100.31 because 32 is the next subnet.

8. Subnet is 192.168.100.64, broadcast is 192.168.100.95, and valid host range is 192.168.100.65 through 94. 256–224=32. 32+32=64, plus 32=96. Subnet is 100.64, and broadcast is 100.95.

9. Subnet is 192.168.100.16, broadcast is 192.168.100.23, and valid host range is 192.168.100.17 through 22. 256–248=8. 8+8=16, plus 8=24. Subnet is 16, and broadcast is 23.

10. Subnet is 10.10.10.4, broadcast is 10.10.10.7, and valid host is 10.10.10.5 through 6. 256–252=4. 4+4=8.

Answers to Review Questions

1. D. User Datagram Protocol is used at the Transport layer to provide a connectionless service.

2. C. Transmission Control Protocol sets up a virtual circuit before transmitting any data. This creates a reliable session and is known as a connection-oriented session.

3. A. Internet Protocol is used to address hosts and route packets through the internetwork. The question does not refer to a connection-oriented service, which is different from a plain connection service.

4. A. Reverse ARP is used to find an IP address from a known hardware address.

5. C. Internet Control Message Protocol (ICMP) is used to send redirects back to an originating router.

6. E. First start by using the 256 mask, which in this case is 256–240=16. The first subnet is 16; the second subnet is 32. This host must be in the 16 subnet; the broadcast address is 31 and the valid host range is 17–30.

7. D. A Class B network is defined in the first octet with the numbers 128–191.

8. D. A Class C network is defined in the first octet with the numbers 192–223.

9. D. An Ethernet (MAC) address is 6 bytes long (48 bits).

10. B. Address Resolution Protocol (ARP) is used to find the hardware address from a known IP address.

11. B. A Class B network address is two bytes long, which means the host bits are two bytes long. The network address must be 172.16.0.0, which is all host bits off. The broadcast address is all bits on, or 172.16.255.255.

12. C. A Class C network address only has 8 bits for defining hosts. $2^8-2=254$.

13. A. First start with 256 mask or in this case, 256–248=8. The first subnet is 8. The second subnet is 16, then 24. This host is in the 16 subnet, the broadcast address is 23, and the valid host range is 17–22.

14. B. First start with 256 mask or in this case, 256–192=64. 64 is the first subnet; 128 is the second subnet. This host is in the 64-subnet range, the broadcast address is 127, and the valid host range is 65–126.

15. C. Take a look at the answers and see which subnet mask will give you what you need for subnetting. 252 gives you 62 subnets, 248 gives you 30 subnets, 240 gives you 14 subnets, and 255 is invalid. Only answer C (240) gives you what you need.

16. B. Source hosts can use any port number starting at 1024.

17. A. The port numbers 1–1023 are defined as and considered well-known port numbers.

18. B. First start with 256–254=2. The first subnet is 2, the second subnet is 4, then 6, 8, 10, and 12. Remember that the fourth octet is host addresses. This host is a part of the subnet 10.0, the broadcast address is 11.255, and the valid host range is 10.1 through 11.254.

19. C. Start with the 256 mask or in this case, 256–252=4. This first subnet is 4. The second subnet is 8. This falls in the 4-subnet range. The broadcast address is 7, and the valid hosts are 5 and 6.

20. B. If you use the mask 255.255.255.0, that only gives you eight subnet bits, or 254 subnets. You are going to have to use one subnet bit from the fourth octet, or 255.255.255.128. This is 9 subnet bits ($2^9-2=510$).

Chapter

4

Configuration and IOS Management Commands

THE CCNA EXAM TOPICS COVERED IN THIS CHAPTER INCLUDE THE FOLLOWING:

- ✓ Use the setup feature on a Cisco router
- ✓ Log into a router in both user and privileged modes
- ✓ Find commands by using the help facilities
- ✓ Use commands on a router by using the editing command
- ✓ Set the router passwords, identification, and banners
- ✓ Configure an interface with IP addresses and subnet masks
- ✓ Copy the configuration to NVRAM

n this chapter, you will be introduced to the Cisco Internetwork Operating System (IOS). The IOS is what runs the Cisco routers and also some Cisco switches, which allows you to configure the devices as well.

You will learn how to configure a Cisco IOS router using both the initial setup mode and the Cisco IOS Command-Line Interface (CLI). Through the IOS interface, you can configure passwords, banners, and more. You will also learn the basics of router configurations in this chapter. The details covered in this chapter include the following:

- Understanding and configuring the Cisco Internetwork Operating System (IOS)

- Connecting to a router

- Bringing up a router

- Logging into a router

- Understanding the router prompts

- Understanding the CLI prompts

- Performing editing and help features

- Gathering basic routing information

- Setting router passwords

- Setting router banners

- Performing interface configurations

- Setting router hostnames

- Setting interface descriptions
- Viewing and saving router configurations
- Verifying routing configurations

It is important to have a firm understanding of the fundamentals taught in this chapter before you go on to the other chapters.

Cisco Router User Interface

The *Cisco Internetwork Operating System (IOS)* is the kernel of Cisco routers and most switches. Cisco has created what they call Cisco Fusion, which is supposed to make all Cisco devices run the same operating system. The reason they don't all run the same OS is because Cisco has acquired more devices than they have designed and built themselves. Almost all Cisco routers run the same IOS, but only about half of the switches currently run the Cisco IOS.

In this section, I'll give you a look at the Cisco IOS and how to configure a Cisco router step-by-step, first using setup mode and then through the Command-Line Interface (CLI).

Cisco Router IOS

The IOS was created to deliver network services and enable networked applications. The Cisco IOS runs on most Cisco routers and on some Cisco Catalyst switches, like the Catalyst 1900 switch (covered in Appendix B).

The Cisco router IOS software is used to complete the following on Cisco hardware:

- Carry network protocols and functions
- Connect high-speed traffic between devices
- Add security to control access and stop unauthorized network use
- Provide scalability for ease of network growth and redundancy
- Supply network reliability for connecting to network resources

You can access the Cisco IOS through the console port of a router, from a modem, or even through Telnet. Access to the IOS command line is called an EXEC session.

Connecting to a Cisco Router

You can connect to a Cisco router to configure the router, verify the configuration, and check statistics. There are different ways to connect to a Cisco router, but the first place you typically would connect to is the console port.

The *console port* is usually a RJ-45 connection on the back of the router. This is used to connect to and configure the router. No password is set on the console port by default.

Another way to connect to a Cisco router is through an *auxiliary port*. This is really the same as a console port and can be used as such. However, it also allows you to configure modem commands to allow a modem connection to the router. This means you can dial up a remote router and attach to the auxiliary port if the router is down and you need to configure it.

The third way to connect to a Cisco router is through the program *Telnet*. Telnet is an emulation program that emulates a dumb-terminal. You can then use Telnet to connect to any active interface on a router like an Ethernet or serial port.

Figure 4.1 shows an illustration of a 2501 Cisco router. Notice the different interfaces and connections.

FIGURE 4.1 2501 router

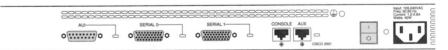

The 2501 router has two serial interfaces for WAN connection and one Attachment Unit Interface (AUI) connection for a 10Mbps Ethernet network connection. The 2501 router also has one console and one auxiliary connection via RJ-45 connectors.

Bringing Up a Router

When you first bring up a Cisco router, it will run a power-on self test (POST), and if that passes, it will look for and load the Cisco IOS from Flash memory if a file is present. Flash memory is an electronically erasable programmable read-only memory (EEPROM). The IOS will load and then look for a valid configuration called startup-config that is stored by default in nonvolatile RAM (NVRAM).

If there is no configuration in NVRAM, then the router will bring up what is called *setup mode*. This is a step-by-step process to help you configure a router. You can also enter setup mode at any time from the command line by typing the command **setup** from global configuration mode. Setup only covers some very global commands, but is helpful if you don't know how to configure certain protocols, like bridging or DECnet, for example.

Setup Mode

You actually have two options when using setup mode: *Basic Management* and *Extended Setup*. Basic Management only gives you enough configurations to allow connectivity to the router, whereas Extended Setup allows you to configure some global parameters as well as interface configuration parameters.

```
        --- System Configuration Dialog ---
Would you like to enter the initial configuration dialog?
[yes/no]: y


At any point you may enter a question mark '?' for help.
Use ctrl-c to abort configuration dialog at any prompt.
Default settings are in square brackets '[]'.
```

Basic Management Setup configures only enough connectivity for management of the system; Extended Setup will ask you to configure each interface on the system.

```
Would you like to enter basic management setup?
[yes/no]: n


First, would you like to see the current interface summary?
[yes]:return
```

```
Any interface listed with OK? value "NO" does not have a
valid configuration

Interface      IP-Address      OK? Method Status  Protocol
FastEthernet0/0    unassigned      NO  unset  up         up
FastEthernet0/1    unassigned      NO  unset  up         up
```

```
Configuring global parameters:
  Enter host name [Router]: Todd

  The enable secret is a password used to protect access to
  privileged EXEC and configuration modes. This password,
  after entered, becomes encrypted in the configuration.
  Enter enable secret: todd

  The enable password is used when you do not specify an
  enable secret password, with some older software
  versions, and some boot images.
  Enter enable password: todd
% Please choose a password that is different from the
  enable secret
  Enter enable password: todd1
```

Let's stop right here for a moment. Notice that setup mode asks you to configure two enable passwords. Passwords are covered later in this chapter, but you should understand that you really only use the enable secret password. The enable password is for pre-10.3 IOS routers. However, you must configure the password in setup mode, and it must be different. It will never be used if the enable secret is configured.

The next password is for setting up Telnet sessions to the router. The reason setup mode has you configure a Telnet (VTY) password is because if a password for the VTY lines is not set, you cannot by default telnet into a router.

```
  The virtual terminal password is used to protect
  access to the router over a network interface.
  Enter virtual terminal password: todd
```

```
Configure SNMP Network Management? [yes]:enter or no
  Community string [public]:enter
Configure DECnet? [no]:enter
Configure AppleTalk? [no]:enter
Configure IP? [yes]:enter
  Configure IGRP routing? [yes]: n
  Configure RIP routing? [no]:enter
Configure bridging? [no]:enter
Configure IPX? [no]:enter
```

The preceding commands can help you configure a protocol if you are not sure which commands you need to do so. However, using the Command-Line Interface (CLI) instead of setup mode gives you much more flexibility.

If you have an Async modem card installed in your router, you can have setup mode configure the modems for you.

```
Async lines accept incoming modems calls. If you will have
users dialing in via modems, configure these lines.


Configure Async lines? [yes]: n
```

If your router has an ISDN BRI interface, you will be prompted for the ISDN switch type to be configured. Here is the router output:

```
BRI interface needs isdn switch-type to be configured
Valid switch types are:
[0]  none..........Only if you don't want to configure
BRI.
[1]  basic-1tr6....1TR6 switch type for Germany
[2]  basic-5ess....AT&T 5ESS switch type for the US/Canada
[3]  basic-dms100..Northern DMS-100 switch type for US/
Canada
[4]  basic-net3....NET3 switch type for UK and Europe
[5]  basic-ni......National ISDN switch type
[6]  basic-ts013...TS013 switch type for Australia
[7]  ntt..........NTT switch type for Japan
[8]  vn3..........VN3 and VN4 switch types for France
Choose ISDN BRI Switch Type [2]: 2
```

After the switch type is configured, you will be prompted for the interface configurations, including IP addresses.

The next section of the Extended Setup is configuring the interfaces. We only have two FastEthernet interfaces on this router, FastEthernet 0/0 and FastEthernet 0/1. The interfaces of a router will be discussed later in this chapter.

```
Configuring interface parameters:

Do you want to configure FastEthernet0/0  interface?
[yes]:return
   Use the 100 Base-TX (RJ-45) connector? [yes]:return
   Operate in full-duplex mode? [no]: y and return
   Configure IP on this interface? [yes]:return
     IP address for this interface: 1.1.1.1
     Subnet mask for this interface [255.0.0.0] :
255.255.0.0
     Class A network is 1.0.0.0, 16 subnet bits; mask is /
16


Do you want to configure FastEthernet0/1  interface?
[yes]:return
   Use the 100 Base-TX (RJ-45) connector? [yes]:return
   Operate in full-duplex mode? [no]:y and return
   Configure IP on this interface? [yes]:return
     IP address for this interface: 2.2.2.2
     Subnet mask for this interface [255.0.0.0] :
255.255.0.0
     Class A network is 2.0.0.0, 16 subnet bits; mask is /
16
```

This configuration is very basic, but it will allow you to get a router up and running quickly. Notice the mask is displayed as /16, which means 16 out of 32 bits are used. See Chapter 3 for more IP subnetting information.

The Extended Setup will now show the running configuration created:

```
The following configuration command script was created:

hostname Todd
```

```
enable secret 5 $1$B0wu$5F0m/EDdtRkQ4vy4a8qwC/
enable password todd1
line vty 0 4
password todd
snmp-server community public
!
no decnet routing
no appletalk routing
ip routing
no bridge 1
no ipx routing
!
interface FastEthernet0/0
media-type 100BaseX
full-duplex
ip address 1.1.1.1 255.255.0.0
no mop enabled
!
interface FastEthernet0/1
media-type 100BaseX
half-duplex
ip address 2.2.2.2 255.255.0.0
no mop enabled
dialer-list 1 protocol ip permit
dialer-list 1 protocol ipx permit
!
end

[0] Go to the IOS command prompt without saving this
config.
[1] Return back to the setup without saving this config.
[2] Save this configuration to nvram and exit.

Enter your selection [2]:0
```

The interesting part of the Extended Setup is the options you get at the end.
You can go to CLI mode and discard the running-config [0]; you can go back

to setup to do it all over again [1]; or you can save this configuration to NVRAM, which is known as startup-config. This file would then be loaded every time the router is rebooted.

I chose "0" to go to the IOS and not save the file we created. This will take us to the CLI.

Command-Line Interface

The *Command-Line Interface (CLI)* is really the best way to configure a router because it gives you the most flexibility. To use the CLI, just say *no* to entering the Initial Configuration Dialog. After you say no, the router will come back with messages stating the status of all the router interfaces.

```
Would you like to enter the initial configuration dialog?
[yes]: n
Would you like to terminate autoinstall? [yes]:return


Press RETURN to get started!


00:00:42: %LINK-3-UPDOWN: Interface Ethernet0, changed
state to up
00:00:42: %LINK-3-UPDOWN: Interface Serial0, changed state
to down
00:00:42: %LINK-3-UPDOWN: Interface Serial1, changed state
to down
00:00:42: %LINEPROTO-5-UPDOWN: Line protocol on Interface
Ethernet0, changed state to up
00:00:42: %LINEPROTO-5-UPDOWN: Line protocol on Interface
Serial0, changed state to down
00:00:42: %LINEPROTO-5-UPDOWN: Line protocol on Interface
Serial1, changed state to down
00:01:30: %LINEPROTO-5-UPDOWN: Line protocol on Interface
Ethernet0, changed state to down
00:01:31: %LINK-5-CHANGED: Interface Serial0, changed
state to administrativelydown
00:01:31: %LINK-5-CHANGED: Interface Ethernet0, changed
state to administratively down
```

```
00:01:31: %LINK-5-CHANGED: Interface Serial1, changed
state to administratively down
00:01:32: %IP-5-WEBINST_KILL: Terminating DNS process
00:01:38: %SYS-5-RESTART: System restarted --
Cisco Internetwork Operating System Software
IOS (tm) 2500 Software (C2500-DS-L), Version 11.3(9),
RELEASE SOFTWARE (fc1)
Copyright (c) 1986-1999 by cisco Systems, Inc.
Compiled Tue 06-Apr-99 19:23 by dschwart
```

Logging into the Router

After the interface status messages appear and you press Return, the
Router> prompt will appear. This is called user mode and is mostly used to
view statistics, though it is also a stepping-stone to logging into privileged
mode. You can only view and change the configuration of a Cisco router in
privileged mode, which you enter with the command enable.

```
Router>
Router>enable
Router#
```

You now end up with a Router#, which indicates you are in privileged
mode. You can both view and change the configuration in privileged mode.
You can go back from privileged mode to user mode by using the disable
command.

```
Router#disable
Router>
```

At this point you can type **logout** to exit the console.

```
Router>logout
```

```
Router con0 is now available
Press RETURN to get started.
```

Or you could just type **logout** or **exit** from the privileged mode prompt to log out.

```
Router>en
```

```
Router#logout

Router con0 is now available
Press RETURN to get started.
```

Overview of Router Modes

To configure from a CLI, you can make global changes to the router by typing **config terminal** (**config t** for short), which puts you in global configuration mode and changes what is known as the running-config. You can type **config** from the privileged mode prompt and then just press Return to take the default of terminal.

```
Router#config
Configuring from terminal, memory, or network
[terminal]?return
Enter configuration commands, one per line.  End with
CNTL/Z.
Router(config)#
```

At this point you make changes that affect the router as a whole, hence the term global configuration mode.

To change the running-config, which is the current configuration running in Dynamic RAM (DRAM), you would use the command `config terminal`, or just `config t`. To change the configuration stored in NVRAM, which is known as startup-config, you would use the command `config memory`, or `config mem` for short. If you wanted to change a router configuration stored on a TFTP host (which is covered in Chapter 7), you would use the command `config network`, or `config net`.

However, understand that for a router to actually make a change to a configuration, it needs to put the configuration in RAM. So, if you actually type `config mem` or `config net`, you will replace the current running-config with the config stored in NVRAM or a configuration stored on a TFTP host.

CLI Prompts

It is important to understand the different prompts you can find when configuring a router so you know where you are at any time within configuration mode. In this section, we will demonstrate the prompts that are used on a Cisco router. Always check your prompts before making any changes to a router's configuration.

This section is not intended to show all the different commands offered but will, instead, describe the different prompts you will see throughout this chapter and the rest of the book.

Interfaces

To make changes to an interface, you use the `interface` command from global configuration mode:

```
Router(config)#interface ?
  Async             Async interface
  BVI               Bridge-Group Virtual Interface
  Dialer            Dialer interface
  FastEthernet      FastEthernet IEEE 802.3
  Group-Async       Async Group interface
  Lex               Lex interface
  Loopback          Loopback interface
  Multilink         Multilink-group interface
  Null              Null interface
  Port-channel      Ethernet Channel of interfaces
  Tunnel            Tunnel interface
  Virtual-Template  Virtual Template interface
  Virtual-TokenRing Virtual TokenRing
Router(config)#interface fastethernet 0/0
Router(config-if)#
```

Notice the prompt changed to `Router(config-if)#` to tell you that you are in interface configuration. It would be nice if it gave you an indication of what interface you were configuring, but it doesn't. This is probably one of the reasons Cisco administrators make more money than Windows administrators.

Subinterfaces

Subinterfaces allow you to create virtual interfaces within the router. The prompt then changes to `Router(config-subif)#`. (You can read more about subinterfaces in Chapter 10 and Appendix B.)

```
Router(config)#int f0/0.?
  <0-4294967295>  FastEthernet interface number
Router(config)#int f0/0.1
Router(config-subif)#
```

Line Commands

To configure user mode passwords, use the `line` command. The prompt then becomes `Router (config-line)#`.

```
Router#config t
Enter configuration commands, one per line.  End with
CNTL/Z.
Router(config)#line ?
  <0-70>   First Line number
  aux      Auxiliary line
  console  Primary terminal line
  tty      Terminal controller
  vty      Virtual terminal

Router(config)#line console 0
Router(config-line)#
```

The `line console 0` command is known as a major, or global, command, and any command typed from the `(config-line)` prompt is known as a subcommand.

Routing Protocol Configurations

To configure routing protocols like RIP and IGRP, use the prompt `(config-router)#`. (We cover routing protocols in Chapter 5.)

```
Router#config t
Enter configuration commands, one per line.  End with
CNTL/Z.
Router(config)#router rip
Router(config-router)#
```

It is not important that you understand what each of these commands does at this time. These will all be explained later in great detail. What you need to understand here is the different prompts available.

Editing and Help Features

You can use the Cisco advanced editing features to help you configure your router. By using a question mark (?) at any prompt, you can see the list of commands available from that prompt.

```
Router#?
Exec commands:
  access-enable     Create a temporary Access-List entry
  access-profile    Apply user-profile to interface
  access-template   Create a temporary Access-List entry
  bfe               For manual emergency modes setting
  clear             Reset functions
  clock             Manage the system clock
  configure         Enter configuration mode
  connect           Open a terminal connection
  copy              Copy configuration or image data
  debug             Debugging functions (see also
'undebug')
  disable           Turn off privileged commands
  disconnect        Disconnect an existing network
connection
  enable            Turn on privileged commands
  erase             Erase flash or configuration memory
  exit              Exit from the EXEC
  help              Description of the interactive help
system
  lock              Lock the terminal
  login             Log in as a particular user
  logout            Exit from the EXEC
mrinfo              Request neighbor and version information
                    from a multicast router
  --More-
```

At this point, you can press the spacebar to get another page of information, or you can press Return to go one command at a time. You can also press any other key to quit and return to the prompt.

To find commands that start with a certain letter, use the letter and the question mark (?) with no space between them.

```
Router#c?
clear  clock  configure  connect  copy

Router#c
```

Notice that by typing "c?", we received a response of all the commands that start with "c". Also notice that the `Router#` prompt appeared with our command still present. This is helpful when you have long commands and need the next possible command. Think about how tiresome it would be if you had to retype the entire command every time you used a question mark!

To find the next command in a string, type the first command and then a question mark.

```
Router#clock ?
  set  Set the time and date

Router#clock set ?
  hh:mm:ss  Current Time

Router#clock set 10:30:10 ?
  <1-31>  Day of the month
  MONTH   Month of the year
Router#clock set 10:30:10 28 ?
  MONTH  Month of the year
Router#clock set 10:30:10 28 may ?
  <1993-2035>  Year
Router#clock set 10:30:10 28 may 2000 ?
  <cr>
Router#
```

By typing the command `clock`, then a space and a question mark, you will get a list of the next possible commands and what they do. Notice that you should just keep typing a command, a space, and then a question mark until `<cr>` (carriage return) is your only option.

If you are typing commands and receive this:

```
Router#clock set 10:30:10
% Incomplete command.
```

then you know that the command string is not done. Just press the up arrow key to receive the last command entered, then continue with the command by using your question mark.

Also, if you receive this error:

```
Router(config)#access-list 110 permit host 1.1.1.1
                                            ^
% Invalid input detected at '^' marker.
```

notice that the ^ marks the point where you have entered the command incorrectly. This is very helpful.

If you receive this error:

```
Router#sh te
% Ambiguous command:  "sh te"
```

it means you did not enter all the keywords or values required by this command. Use the question mark to find the command you need.

```
Router#sh te?
WORD  tech-support  terminal
```

Table 4.1 shows the list of enhanced editing commands available on a Cisco router.

TABLE 4.1   Enhanced Editing Commands

Command	Meaning
Ctrl+A	Moves your cursor to the beginning of the line
Ctrl+E	Moves your cursor to the end of the line
Esc+B	Moves back one word
Ctrl+F	Moves forward one character

TABLE 4.1 Enhanced Editing Commands *(continued)*

Command	Meaning
Esc+F	Moves forward one word
Ctrl+D	Deletes a single character
Backspace	Deletes a single character
Ctrl+R	Redisplays a line
Ctrl+U	Erases a line
Ctrl+W	Erases a word
Ctrl+Z	Ends configuration mode and returns to EXEC
Tab	Finishes typing a command for you

Another editing feature we need to mention is the automatic scrolling of long lines. In the following example, the command typed had reached the right margin and automatically moved ten spaces to the left. The dollar sign ($) indicates that the line has been scrolled to the left.

```
Router#config t
Enter configuration commands, one per line.  End with
CNTL/Z.
Router(config)#$ 110 permit host 171.10.10.10 0.0.0.0 host
```

You can review the router-command history with the commands shown in Table 4.2.

TABLE 4.2 Router-Command History

Command	Meaning
Ctrl+P or up arrow	Shows last command entered
Ctrl+N or down arrow	Shows previous commands entered

TABLE 4.2 Router-Command History *(continued)*

Command	Meaning
Show history	Shows last 10 commands entered by default
Show terminal	Shows terminal configurations and history buffer size
Terminal history size	Changes buffer size (max 256)

Here is an example of the show history command and how to change the history size, as well as how to verify it with the show terminal command.

Use the command show history to see the last 10 commands entered on the router.

```
Router#sh history
  en
  sh history
  show terminal
  sh cdp neig
  sh ver
  sh flash
  sh int e0
  sh history
  sh int s0
  sh int s1
```

We will now use the show terminal command to verify the terminal history size.

```
Router#sh terminal
Line 0, Location: "", Type: ""
[output cut]
History is enabled, history size is 10.
Full user help is disabled
Allowed transports are lat pad v120 telnet mop rlogin
nasi.  Preferred is lat.
```

```
No output characters are padded
No special data dispatching characters
Group codes:    0
```

The command terminal history size, used from privileged mode, can change the size of the history buffer.

```
Router#terminal history size ?
  <0-256>  Size of history buffer
Router#terminal history size 25
```

Verify the change with the show terminal command.

```
Router#sh terminal
Line 0, Location: "", Type: ""
[output cut]
Editing is enabled.
History is enabled, history size is 25.
Full user help is disabled
Allowed transports are lat pad v120 telnet mop rlogin
nasi.  Preferred is lat.
No output characters are padded
No special data dispatching characters
Group codes:    0
```

Gathering Basic Routing Information

The command show version will provide basic configuration for the system hardware as well as the software version, the names and sources of configuration files, and the boot images.

```
Router#sh version
Cisco Internetwork Operating System Software
IOS (tm) 2500 Software (C2500-JS-L), Version 12.0(8),
RELEASE SOFTWARE (fc1)
Copyright (c) 1986-1999 by cisco Systems, Inc.
Compiled Mon 29-Nov-99 14:52 by kpma
Image text-base: 0x03051C3C, data-base: 0x00001000
```

```
ROM: System Bootstrap, Version 11.0(10c), SOFTWARE
BOOTFLASH: 3000 Bootstrap Software (IGS-BOOT-R), Version
11.0(10c), RELEASE SOFTWARE (fc1)

RouterA uptime is 5 minutes
System restarted by power-on
System image file is "flash:c2500-js-l_120-8.bin"

cisco 2522 (68030) processor (revision N) with 14336K/
2048K bytes of memory.
Processor board ID 15662842, with hardware revision
00000003
Bridging software.
X.25 software, Version 3.0.0.
SuperLAT software (copyright 1990 by Meridian Technology
Corp).
TN3270 Emulation software.
Basic Rate ISDN software, Version 1.1.
1 Ethernet/IEEE 802.3 interface(s)
2 Serial network interface(s)
8 Low-speed serial(sync/async) network interface(s)
1 ISDN Basic Rate interface(s)
32K bytes of non-volatile configuration memory.
16384K bytes of processor board System flash (Read ONLY)
Configuration register is 0x2102
```

The show version command lets you know how long the router has been running, how it was restarted, the IOS filename running, the model hardware and processor versions, and the amount of DRAM. Also, the configuration register value is listed last. The configuration register is discussed in Chapter 7.

Setting the Passwords

There are five passwords used to secure your Cisco routers. The first two passwords are used to set your enable password, which is used to secure privileged mode. This will prompt a user for a password when the command enable is used. The other three are used to configure a password when user mode is accessed either through the console port, the auxiliary port, or Telnet.

Enable Passwords

You set the enable passwords from global configuration mode.

```
Router(config)#enable ?
  last-resort  Define enable action if no TACACS servers
               respond
  password     Assign the privileged level password
  secret       Assign the privileged level secret
  use-tacacs   Use TACACS to check enable passwords
```

Last-resort   Is used if you set up authentication through a tacacs server and it is not available. This will allow the administrator to still enter the router. However, it is not used if the tacacs server is working.

Password   Is used to set the enable password on older, pre-10.3 systems. Not used if an enable secret is set.

Secret   Is the newer, encrypted password. Overrides the enable password if set.

Use-tacacs   Tells the router to authenticate through a tacacs server. This is convenient if you have dozens or even hundreds of routers. How would you like to change the password on 200 routers? The tacacs server allows you to only have to change the password once.

```
Router(config)#enable secret todd
Router(config)#enable password todd
The enable password you have chosen is the same as your
enable secret. This is not recommended.  Re-enter the
enable password.
```

If you try and set the enable secret and enable passwords to be the same, it will give you a nice, polite warning the first time, but if you type the same password again it will accept it. However, now neither password will work. If you don't have older legacy routers, don't bother to use the enable password.

User-mode passwords are assigned by using the `line` command.

```
Router(config)#line ?
  <0-4>   First Line number
  aux     Auxiliary line
```

```
console  Primary terminal line
vty      Virtual terminal
```

Aux   Is used to set the user-mode password for the auxiliary port. This is typically used for configuring a modem on the router but can be used as a console as well.

Console   Is used to set a console user-mode password.

Vty   Is used to set a Telnet password on the router. If the password is not set, then Telnet cannot be used by default.

To configure the user-mode passwords, you configure the line you want and use either the login or no login command to tell the router to prompt for authentication.

Auxiliary Password

To configure the auxiliary password, go to global configuration mode and type **line aux ?**. Notice that you only get a choice of 0–0 because there is only one port.

```
Router#config t
Enter configuration commands, one per line.  End with CNTL/Z.
Router(config)#line aux ?
  <0-0>  First Line number
Router(config)#line aux 0
Router(config-line)#login
Router(config-line)#password todd
```

It is important to remember the login command, or the auxiliary port won't prompt for authentication.

Console Password

To set the console password, use the command line console 0. However, notice that when we tried to type line console 0 ? from the aux line configuration, we got an error. You can still type line console 0 and it will accept it; however, the help screens do not work from that prompt. Type "exit" to get back one level.

```
Router(config-line)#line console ?
% Unrecognized command
```

```
Router(config-line)#exit
Router(config)#line console ?
  <0-0>  First Line number
Router(config)#line console 0
Router(config-line)#login
Router(config-line)#password todd1
```

Since there is only one console port, we can only choose line console 0.

Other Console Port Commands

There are a few other important commands to know for the console port.

The exec-timeout 0 0 command sets the timeout for the console EXEC session to zero, or to never time out. To have fun with your friends at work, set it to 0 1, which makes the console time out in 1 second! The way to fix that is to continually press the down arrow key while changing the timeout time with your free hand.

Logging synchronous is a nice command, and it should be a default command, but it is not. What it does is stop console messages from popping up and disrupting input you are trying to type. This makes reading your input messages much easier.

Here is an example of how to configure both commands:

```
Router(config)#line con 0
Router(config-line)#exec-timeout ?
  <0-35791>  Timeout in minutes
Router(config-line)#exec-timeout 0 ?
  <0-2147483>  Timeout in seconds
  <cr>
Router(config-line)#exec-timeout 0 0
Router(config-line)#logging synchronous
```

Telnet Password

To set the user-mode password for Telnet access into the router, use the line vty command. Routers that are not running the Enterprise edition of the Cisco IOS default to five VTY lines, 0 through 4. However, if you have the Enterprise edition, you will have significantly more. The router we are using for this section has 198 (0–197). The best way to find out how many lines you have is to use the question mark.

```
Router(config-line)#line vty 0 ?
<1-197>Last Line Number
<cr>
Router(config-line)#line vty 0 197
Router(config-line)#login
Router(config-line)#password todd2
```

If you try to telnet into a router that does not have a VTY password set, you will receive an error stating that the connection is refused because the password is not set. You can tell the router to allow Telnet connections without a password by using the no login command.

```
Router(config-line)#line vty 0 197
Router(config-line)#no login
```

After your routers are configured with an IP address, you can use the Telnet program to configure and check your routers instead of having to use a console cable. You can use the Telnet program by typing **telnet** from any command prompt (DOS or Cisco). Telnet is covered in more detail in Chapter 7.

Encrypting Your Passwords

Only the enable secret password is encrypted by default. You need to manually configure the user-mode and enable passwords.

Notice that you can see all the passwords except the enable secret when performing a show running-config on a router.

```
Router#sh run
[output cut]
!
enable secret 5 $1$rFbM$8.aXocHg6yHrM/zzeNkAT.
enable password todd1
!
[output cut]
line con 0
 password todd1
```

```
 login
line aux 0
 password todd
 login
line vty 0 4
 password todd2
 login
line vty 5 197
 password todd2
 login
!
end
```

Router#

To manually encrypt your passwords, use the service password-encryption command. Here is an example of how to perform manual password encryption:

```
Router#config t
Enter configuration commands, one per line.  End with
CNTL/Z.
Router(config)#service password-encryption
Router(config)#enable password todd
Router(config)#line vty 0 197
Router(config-line)#login
Router(config-line)#password todd2
Router(config-line)#line con 0
Router(config-line)#login
Router(config-line)#password todd1
Router(config-line)#line aux 0
Router(config-line)#login
Router(config-line)#password todd
Router(config-line)#exit
Router(config)#no service password-encryption
Router(config)#^Z
```

By typing the show running-config command, you can see the enable password and the line passwords are all encrypted.

```
Router#sh run
Building configuration...

[output cut]
!
enable secret 5 $1$rFbM$8.aXocHg6yHrM/zzeNkAT.
enable password 7 0835434A0D
!
[output cut]
!
line con 0
 password 7 111D160113
 login
line aux 0
 password 7 071B2E484A
 login
line vty 0 4
 password 7 0835434A0D
 login
line vty 5 197
 password 7 09463724B
 login
!
end

Router#
```

Banners

You can set a banner on a Cisco router so that when either a user logs into the router or an administrator telnets into the router, for example, a banner will give them the information you want them to have. Another reason for having a banner is to add a security notice to users dialing into your inter-network. There are four different banners available:

```
Router(config)#banner ?
  LINE      c banner-text c, where 'c' is a delimiting
            character
  exec      Set EXEC process creation banner
  incoming  Set incoming terminal line banner
  login     Set login banner
  motd      Set Message of the Day banner
```

The Message of the Day is the most used and gives a message to every person dialing in or connecting to the router via Telnet, auxiliary port, or console port.

```
Router(config)#banner motd ?
  LINE  c banner-text c, where 'c' is a delimiting
character
Router(config)#banner motd #
Enter TEXT message.  End with the character '#'.
$ized to be in Acme.com network, then you must disconnect
immediately.
#
Router(config)#^Z
Router#
00:25:12: %SYS-5-CONFIG_I: Configured from console by
console
Router#exit


Router con0 is now available


Press RETURN to get started.


If you are not authorized to be in Acme.com network, then
you must disconnect immediately.


Router>
```

The above MOTD banner tells anyone connecting to the router that they must either be authorized or they must disconnect. The part to understand is the delimiting character. You can use any character you want, and it is used to tell the router when the message is done. So, you can't use the delimiting character in the message itself. One other thing to note is that once the message is complete, press Return, then the delimiting character, then Return. If you don't do that, it will still work, but if you have more than one banner, for example, it will combine them as one message and put them on one line.

These are the other banners:

Exec banner   You can configure a line-activation (exec) banner to be displayed when an EXEC process (such as a line-activation or incoming connection to a VTY line) is created.

Incoming banner   You can configure a banner to be displayed on terminals connected to reverse Telnet lines. This banner is useful for providing instructions to users who use reverse Telnet.

Login banner   You can configure a login banner to be displayed on all connected terminals. This banner is displayed after the MOTD banner but before the login prompts. The login banner cannot be disabled on a per-line basis. To globally disable the login banner, you must delete the login banner with the `no banner login` command.

Router Interfaces

Interface configuration is one of the most important configurations of the router. Without interfaces, the router is useless. Interface configurations must be exact to communicate with other devices. Some of the configurations used to configure an interface are Network layer addresses, media-type, bandwidth, and other administrator commands.

Different routers use different methods to choose interfaces used on a router. For example, the following command shows a 2522 router with 10 serial interfaces, which are labeled 0 through 9:

```
Router(config)#int serial ?
  <0-9>  Serial interface number
```

At this point you must choose the interface you want to configure. Once you do that, you will be in interface configuration for that interface. The command to choose serial port 5, for example, would be

```
Router(config)#int serial 5
Router(config)-if)#
```

The 2522 router has one Ethernet 10BaseT port. Typing `interface ethernet 0` can configure the interface.

```
Router(config)#int ethernet ?
  <0-0>  Ethernet interface number
Router(config)#int ethernet 0
Router(config-if)#
```

The 2500 router, as previously demonstrated, is a fixed configuration router, which means that when you buy a model of router, you're stuck with that configuration. To configure an interface, you always use the `interface type number` sequence. However, the 2600, 3600, 4000, and 7000 series routers use a physical slot in the router and a port number on the module plugged into that slot. For example, on a 2600 router, the configuration would be `interface type slot/port`:

```
Router(config)#int fastethernet ?
  <0-1>  FastEthernet interface number
Router(config)#int fastethernet 0
% Incomplete command.
Router(config)#int fastethernet 0?
/
Router(config)#int fastethernet 0/?
  <0-1>  FastEthernet interface number
```

Notice that you cannot type `int fastethernet 0`. You must type the full command, which is `type slot/port`, or `int fastethernet 0/0`. You can type `int fa 0/0` as well.

To set the type of connector used, use the command `media-type`. However, this is typically auto-detected.

```
Router(config)#int fa 0/0
Router(config-if)#media-type ?
  100BaseX  Use RJ45 for -TX; SC FO for -FX
  MII       Use MII connector
```

Bringing Up an Interface

You can turn an interface off with the interface command `shutdown` or turn it on with the `no shutdown` command. If an interface is shut down, it will display administratively down when using the `show interface` command,

and the `show running-config` command will show the interface as shut down. All interfaces are shut down by default.

```
Router#sh int e0
Ethernet0 is administratively down, line protocol is down
[output cut]
```

Bring up an interface with the `no shutdown` command.

```
Router#config t
Enter configuration commands, one per line.  End with
CNTL/Z.
Router(config)#int e0
Router(config-if)#no shutdown
Router(config-if)#^Z
00:57:08: %LINK-3-UPDOWN: Interface Ethernet0, changed
state to up
00:57:09: %LINEPROTO-5-UPDOWN: Line protocol on Interface
Ethernet0, changed state to up

Router#sh int e0
Ethernet0 is up, line protocol is up
```

Configuring an IP Address on an Interface

You don't have to use IP on your routers; however, IP is typically used on all routers. To configure IP addresses on an interface, use the `ip address` command from interface configuration mode.

```
Router(config)#int e0
Router(config-if)#ip address 172.16.10.2 255.255.255.0
Router(config-if)#no shut
```

Don't forget to turn on an interface with the `no shut` command. Remember to look at the command `show interface e0`, for example, which will show you if it administratively shut down or not. `Show running-config` will also show you if the interface is shut down.

If you want to add a second subnet address to an interface, then you must use the `secondary` command. If you type another IP address and press Enter, it will replace the existing IP address and mask. To add a secondary IP address, use the secondary command.

```
Router(config-if)#ip address 172.16.20.2 255.255.255.0
secondary
Router(config-if)#^Z
```

You can verify both addresses are configured on the interface with the show running-config command (sh run for short).

```
Router#sh run
Building configuration...
Current configuration:
[output cut]
!
interface Ethernet0
 ip address 172.16.20.2 255.255.255.0 secondary
 ip address 172.16.10.2 255.255.255.0
!
```

VIP Cards

If you have a 7000 or 7500 series router with VIP (Versatile Interface Processor) cards, you define an interface by using the interface type slot/ port adapter/port number. For example

```
7000(config)#interface ethernet 2/0/0
```

Serial Interface Commands

To configure a serial interface, there are a couple of specifics that need to be discussed. Typically, the interface will be attached to a CSU/DSU type of device that provides clocking for the line. However, if you have a back-to-back configuration used in a lab environment, for example, one end must provide clocking. This would be the DCE end of the cable. Cisco routers, by default, are all DTE devices, and you must tell an interface to provide clocking if it is to act as a DCE device. You configure a DCE serial interface with the clock rate command.

```
Router#config t
Enter configuration commands, one per line.  End with
CNTL/Z.
```

```
Router(config)#int s0
Router(config-if)#clock rate ?
        Speed (bits per second)
   1200
   2400
   4800
   9600
   19200
   38400
   56000
   64000
   72000
   125000
   148000
   250000
   500000
   800000
   1000000
   1300000
   2000000
   4000000

   <300-4000000>    Choose clockrate from list above

Router(config-if)#clock rate 64000
%Error: This command applies only to DCE interfaces
Router(config-if)#int s1
Router(config-if)#clock rate 64000
```

It does not hurt anything to try and put a clock rate on an interface. Notice that the clock rate command is in bits per second.

The next command you need to understand is the bandwidth command. Every Cisco router ships with a default serial link bandwidth of a T1, or 1.544Mbps. However, understand that this has nothing to do with how data is transferred over a link. The bandwidth of a serial link is used by routing protocols such as IGRP, EIGRP, and OSPF to calculate the best cost to a remote network. If you are using RIP routing, then the bandwidth setting of a serial link is irrelevant.

```
Router(config-if)#bandwidth ?
  <1-10000000>  Bandwidth in kilobits

Router(config-if)#bandwidth 64
```

Notice that unlike the clock rate command, the bandwidth command is configured in kilobits.

Hostnames

You can set the hostname of the router with the hostname command. This is only locally significant, which means it has no bearing on how the router performs name lookups on the internetwork.

```
Router#config t
Enter configuration commands, one per line.  End with
CNTL/Z.
Router(config)#hostname todd
todd(config)#hostname Atlanta
Atlanta(config)#
```

Even though it is tempting to configure the hostname after your own name, it is better served to name the router something significant to the location.

Descriptions

Setting descriptions on an interface is helpful to the administrator and, like the hostname, only locally significant. This is a helpful command because it can be used to keep track of circuit numbers, for example.

```
Atlanta(config)#int e0
Atlanta(config-if)#description Sales Lan
Atlanta(config-if)#int s0
Atlanta(config-if)#desc Wan to Miami circuit:6fdda4321
```

You can view the description of an interface either with the show running-config command or the show interface command.

```
Atlanta#sh run
[cut]
interface Ethernet0
 description Sales Lan
 ip address 172.16.10.30 255.255.255.0
 no ip directed-broadcast
!
interface Serial0
 description Wan to Miami circuit:6fdda4321
 no ip address
 no ip directed-broadcast
 no ip mroute-cache

Atlanta#sh int e0
Ethernet0 is up, line protocol is up
  Hardware is Lance, address is 0010.7be8.25db (bia
0010.7be8.25db)
  Description: Sales Lan
  [cut]
Atlanta#sh int s0
Serial0 is up, line protocol is up
  Hardware is HD64570
  Description: Wan to Miami circuit:6fdda4321
[cut]
Atlanta#
```

Viewing and Saving Configurations

If you run through setup mode, it will ask you if you want to use the configuration you created. If you say yes, then it will copy the configuration running in DRAM, known as running-config, to NVRAM and name the file startup-config.

You can manually save the file from DRAM to NVRAM by using the copy running-config startup-config command. You can use the shortcut copy run start also.

```
Router#copy run start
Destination filename [startup-config]?return
Warning: Attempting to overwrite an NVRAM configuration
previously written by a different version of the system
image.
Overwrite the previous NVRAM configuration?[confirm]return
Building configuration...
```

Notice that the message stated we were trying to write over the older startup-config. The IOS had been just upgraded to version 12.8, and the last time the file was saved, 11.3 was running.

You can view the files by typing the command show running-config or show startup-config from privileged mode. The sh run command, which is the shortcut for show running-config, tells us that we are viewing the current configuration.

```
Router#sh run
Building configuration...

Current configuration:
!
version 12.0
service timestamps debug uptime
service timestamps log uptime
no service password-encryption
!
hostname Router
ip subnet-zero
frame-relay switching
!
[cut]
```

The sh start command, which is the shortcut for the show startup-config command, shows us the configuration that will be used the next time the router is reloaded and also shows us the amount of NVRAM used to store the startup-config file.

```
Router#sh start
Using 4850 out of 32762 bytes
!
version 12.0
service timestamps debug uptime
service timestamps log uptime
no service password-encryption
!
hostname Router
!
!
ip subnet-zero
frame-relay switching
!
[cut]
```

You can delete the startup-config file by using the command erase startup-config. Once you perform this command, you will receive an error if you try to view the startup-config file.

```
Router#erase startup-config
Erasing the nvram filesystem will remove all files!
Continue? [confirm]
[OK]
Erase of nvram: complete
Router#sh start
%% Non-volatile configuration memory is not present
Router#
```

Verifying Your Configuration

Obviously, the show running-config would be the best way to verify your configuration, and the show startup-config would be the best way to verify the configuration used the next time the router is reloaded.

However, once you take a look at the running-config, and it appears that everything is in order, you can verify your configuration with utilities, like Ping and Telnet.

You can ping with different protocols, and you can see this by typing **ping** ? at the router user-mode or privileged mode prompt.

```
Router#ping ?
  WORD       Ping destination address or hostname
  appletalk  Appletalk echo
  decnet     DECnet echo
  ip         IP echo
  ipx        Novell/IPX echo
  srb        srb echo
  <cr>
```

To find a neighbor's Network layer address, you either need to go to the router or switch, or you can type show cdp nei detail to get the Network layer addresses, which you can use to ping with.

You can also use the trace program to find the path a packet takes as it traverses an internetwork. Trace can also be used with multiple protocols.

```
Router#trace ?
  WORD       Trace route to destination address or
hostname
  appletalk  AppleTalk Trace
  clns       ISO CLNS Trace
  ip         IP Trace
  oldvines   Vines Trace (Cisco)
  vines      Vines Trace (Banyan)
  <cr>
```

Telnet is the best tool, since it uses IP at the Network layer and TCP at the Transport layer to create a session with a remote host. If you can telnet into a device, your IP connectivity must be good. You can only telnet to IP addresses, and you can use Windows hosts or router prompts to telnet from.

```
Router#telnet ?
  WORD  IP address or hostname of a remote system
  <cr>
```

From the router prompt, you do not need to type the command `telnet`. If you just type a hostname or IP address, it will assume you want to telnet.

Verifying with the *Show Interface* Command

Another way to verify your configuration is by typing `show interface` commands. The first command is `show interface ?`, which shows us all the available interfaces to configure. The only interfaces that are not logical are Ethernet and Serial.

```
Router#sh int ?
  Ethernet    IEEE 802.3
  Null        Null interface
  Serial      Serial
  accounting  Show interface accounting
  crb         Show interface routing/bridging info
  irb         Show interface routing/bridging info
  <cr>
```

The next command is `show interface ethernet 0` and shows us the hardware address, logical address, and encapsulation method, as well as statistics on collisions.

```
Router#sh int e0
Ethernet0 is up, line protocol is up
  Hardware is Lance, address is 0010.7b7f.c26c (bia
0010.7b7f.c26c)
Internet address is 172.16.10.1/24
  MTU 1500 bytes, BW 10000 Kbit, DLY 1000 usec,
      reliability 255/255, txload 1/255, rxload 1/255
  Encapsulation ARPA, loopback not set, keepalive set (10
sec)
  ARP type: ARPA, ARP Timeout 04:00:00
  Last input 00:08:23, output 00:08:20, output hang never
  Last clearing of "show interface" counters never
  Queueing strategy: fifo
  Output queue 0/40, 0 drops; input queue 0/75, 0 drops
  5 minute input rate 0 bits/sec, 0 packets/sec
  5 minute output rate 0 bits/sec, 0 packets/sec
```

```
                        25 packets input, 2459 bytes, 0 no buffer
                        Received 25 broadcasts, 0 runts, 0 giants, 0 throttles
                        0 input errors, 0 CRC, 0 frame, 0 overrun, 0 ignored,
                0 abort
                        0 input packets with dribble condition detected
                        33 packets output, 7056 bytes, 0 underruns
                        0 output errors, 0 collisions, 1 interface resets
                        0 babbles, 0 late collision, 0 deferred
                        0 lost carrier, 0 no carrier
                        0 output buffer failures, 0 output buffers swapped out
```

The most important status of the show interface command is the output of the line and data-link protocol status. If Ethernet 0 is up, line protocol is up, and the line is up and running.

```
RouterA#sh int e0
Ethernet0 is up, line protocol is up
```

The first parameter refers to the Physical layer and is up when it receives carrier detect. The second parameter refers to the Data Link layer and looks for keepalives from the connecting end.

```
RouterA#sh int s0
Serial0 is up, line protocol is down
```

If you see the line is up, but the protocol is down, you are having a clocking (keepalive) or framing issue. Check the keepalives on both ends to make sure they match; the clock rate is set, if needed; and the encapsulation type is the same on both ends.

```
RouterA#sh int s0
Serial0 is down, line protocol is down
```

If you see the line interface and protocol down, it is a cable or interface problem. Also, if one end is administratively shut down, then the remote end would show down and down. To turn on the interface, type the command no shutdown in interface configuration.

```
RouterB#sh int s0
Serial0 is administratively down, line protocol is down
```

The next command demonstrates the serial line and the Maximum Transmission Unit (MTU), which is 1500 bytes by default. It also shows the default bandwidth (BW) on all Cisco serial links: 1.544Kbs. This is used to determine the bandwidth of the line for routing protocols such as IGRP, EIGRP, and OSPF. Another important configuration to notice is the keepalive, which is 10 seconds by default. Each router sends a keepalive message to its neighbor every 10 seconds. If both routers are not configured for the same keepalive time, it will not work.

You can clear the counters on the interface by typing the command `clear counters`.

```
Router#sh int s0
Serial0 is up, line protocol is up
  Hardware is HD64570
  MTU 1500 bytes, BW 1544 Kbit, DLY 20000 usec,
      reliability 255/255, txload 1/255, rxload 1/255
  Encapsulation HDLC, loopback not set, keepalive set (10
sec)
  Last input never, output never, output hang never
  Last clearing of "show interface" counters never
  Queueing strategy: fifo
  Output queue 0/40, 0 drops; input queue 0/75, 0 drops
  5 minute input rate 0 bits/sec, 0 packets/sec
  5 minute output rate 0 bits/sec, 0 packets/sec
     0 packets input, 0 bytes, 0 no buffer
     Received 0 broadcasts, 0 runts, 0 giants, 0 throttles
     0 input errors, 0 CRC, 0 frame, 0 overrun, 0 ignored,
0 abort
     0 packets output, 0 bytes, 0 underruns
     0 output errors, 0 collisions, 16 interface resets
     0 output buffer failures, 0 output buffers swapped
out
     0 carrier transitions
     DCD=down  DSR=down  DTR=down  RTS=down  CTS=down
Router#clear counters ?
  Ethernet  IEEE 802.3
  Null      Null interface
  Serial    Serial
```

```
<cr>
Router#clear counters s0
Clear "show interface" counters on this interface
[confirm]return
Router#
00:17:35: %CLEAR-5-COUNTERS: Clear counter on interface
Serial0 by console
Router#
```

Using the *Show Controllers* Command

The show controllers command displays information about the physical interface itself. It will also give you the type of serial cable plugged into a serial port. Typically this will only be a DTE cable, which then plugs into a type of Data Service Unit (DSU).

```
Router#sh controllers s 0
HD unit 0, idb = 0x1229E4, driver structure at 0x127E70
buffer size 1524  HD unit 0, V.35 DTE cable
cpb = 0xE2, eda = 0x4140, cda = 0x4000


Router#sh controllers s 1
HD unit 1, idb = 0x12C174, driver structure at 0x131600
buffer size 1524  HD unit 1, V.35 DCE cable
cpb = 0xE3, eda = 0x2940, cda = 0x2800
```

Notice that serial 0 has a DTE cable, whereas the serial 1 connection has a DCE cable. Serial 1 would have to provide clocking with the clock rate command. Serial 0 would get its clocking from the DSU. Also, understand that this is the only command that needs to have a space after the command serial.

```
Router#sh controllers s1
                       ^
% Invalid input detected at '^' marker.
```

Summary

In this chapter, we introduced you to the Cisco Internetwork Operating System (IOS). It is important that you have a firm understanding of the basics offered in this chapter before you move on to the other chapters in this book. The basics of Cisco routers covered in this chapter include the following:

- Understanding the Cisco Internetwork Operating System (IOS) and how you can use the IOS to run and configure Cisco routers

- Connecting to a router with console connections and LAN connections

- Bringing up a router and entering setup mode

- Logging into a router and understanding the difference between user mode and privileged mode

- Understanding router prompts within router configuration mode

- Understanding editing and help features available from the router CLI

- Gathering basic routing information using the show commands

- Setting router passwords for both usermode and privileged mode access

- Setting router banners for identification

- Performing interface configurations to set the IP address on an interface

- Setting router hostnames for router identification

- Setting interface descriptions to identify each interface on a router

- Viewing and saving router configurations using the show commands and the copy run start command

- Verifying routing configurations using show commands

Key Terms

Before taking the exam, be sure you're familiar with the following terms:

auxiliary port	*console port*
Basic Management Setup	*Extended Setup*
Cisco Internetwork Operating System (IOS)	*setup mode*
Command-Line Interface (CLI)	*Telnet*

Commands in This Chapter

Command	Description
?	Gives you a help screen
Backspace	Deletes a single character
Bandwidth	Sets the bandwidth on a serial interface
Banner	Creates a banner for users who log in to the router
clear counters	Clears the statistics from an interface
Clock rate	Provides clocking on a serial DCE interface
Config memory	Copies the startup-config to running-config
Config network	Copies a configuration stored on a TFTP host to running-config
Config terminal	Puts you in global configuration mode and changes the running-config
Copy run start	Short for copy running-config startup-config. Places a configuration into NVRAM

Command	Description
Ctrl+A	Moves your cursor to the beginning of the line
Ctrl+D	Deletes a single character
Ctrl+E	Moves your cursor to the end of the line
Ctrl+F	Moves forward one character
Ctrl+R	Redisplays a line
Ctrl+U	Erases a line
Ctrl+W	Erases a word
Ctrl+Z	Ends configuration mode and returns to EXEC
Description	Sets a description on an interface
Disable	Takes you from privileged mode back to user mode
Enable	Puts you into privileged mode
Enable password	Sets the unencrypted enable password
Enable secret	Sets the encrypted enable secret password. Supersedes the enable password if set
Erase startup	Deletes the startup-config
Esc+B	Moves back one word
Esc+F	Moves forward one word
Exec-timeout	Sets the timeout in seconds and minutes for the console connection
Hostname	Sets the name of a router

Command	Description
Interface	Puts you in interface configuration mode. Also used with show commands
Interface fastethernet 0/0	Puts you in interface configuration mode for a FastEthernet port. Also used with show commands
Interface fastethernet 0/0.1	Creates a subinterface
Interface serial 5	Puts you in configuration mode for interface serial 5 and can be used for show commands
Ip address	Sets an IP address on an interface
Line	Puts you in configuration mode to change or set your user mode passwords
Line aux	Puts you in the auxiliary interface configuration mode
Line console 0	Puts you in console configuration mode
Line vty	Puts you in VTY (Telnet) interface configuration mode
Logging synchronous	Stops console messages from overwriting your command-line input
Logout	Logs you out of your console session
Media-type	Sets the hardware media type on an interface
No shutdown	Turns on an interface
Ping	Tests IP connectivity

Command	Description
`Router rip`	Puts you in router rip configuration mode
`Service password-encryption`	Encrypts the user mode and enable password
`Show controllers s 0`	Shows the DTE or DCE status of an interface
`Show history`	Shows you the last 10 commands entered by default
`Show interface s0`	Shows the statistics of interface serial 0
`Show run`	Short for `show running-config`. Shows the configuration currently running on the router
`Show start`	Short for `show startup-config`. Shows the backup configuration stored in NVRAM
`Show terminal`	Shows you your configured history size
`Show version`	Shows you statistics of the router
`Shutdown`	Puts an interface in administratively-down mode
`Tab`	Finishes typing a command for you
`Telnet`	Tests IP connectivity and configures a router
`Terminal history size`	Changes your history size from the default of 10 up to 256
`Trace`	Tests IP connectivity

Written Lab

Write out the command or commands for the following questions.

1. What command is used to set a serial interface to provide clocking to another router at 64k?

2. If you were to telnet into a router and you get the response "connection refused, password not set," what would you do to stop receiving this message and not be prompted for a password?

3. If you type show inter et 0 and notice the port is administratively down, what would you do?

4. If you wanted to delete the configuration stored in NVRAM, what would you type?

5. If you wanted to set a user-mode password for the console port, what would you type?

6. If you wanted to set the enable secret password to cisco, what would you type?

7. If you wanted to see if a serial interface needed to provide clocking, what command would you use?

8. What command would you use to see the terminal history size?

9. What old Cisco command will change a configuration stored on a TFTP host?

10. How would you set the name of a router to Chicago?

Hands-on Labs

In this section you will perform commands on a Cisco router that will help you understand what you learned in this chapter. You'll need at least one Cisco router—two would be better, three would be outstanding. The labs in this chapter include the following:

Lab 4.1: Logging into a Router

Lab 4.2: Using the Help and Editing Features

Lab 4.3: Saving a Router Configuration

Lab 4.4: Setting Your Passwords

Lab 4.5: Setting the Hostname, Descriptions, IP Address, and Clock Rate

Lab 4.1: Logging into a Router

1. Press Return to connect to your router. This will put you into user mode.

2. At the `Router>` prompt, type a question mark (?).

3. Notice the –more– at the bottom of the screen.

4. Press the Enter key to view the commands line by line.

5. Press the spacebar to view the commands a full screen at a time.

6. You can type **q** at any time to quit.

7. Type **enable** or **en** and press Enter. This will put you into privileged where you can change and view the router configuration.

8. At the `Router#` prompt, type a question mark (?). Notice how many options are available to you in privileged mode.

9. Type **q** to quit.

10. Type **config** and press Enter.

11. Press Enter to configure your router using your terminal.

12. At the `Router(config)#` prompt, type a question mark (?), then **q** to quit, or hit the spacebar to view the commands.

13. Type **interface e0** or **int e0,** and press Enter. This will allow you to configure interface Ethernet 0.

14. At the `Router(config-if)#` prompt, type a question mark (?).

15. Type **int s0** or **interface s0** (same as the `interface serial 0` command) and press Enter. This will allow you to configure interface serial 0. Notice that you can go from interface to interface easily.

16. Type **encapsulation?**.

17. Type **exit**. Notice how this brings you back one level.

18. Press the Control key and the letter Z at the same time. Notice how this brings you out of configuration mode and places you back into privileged mode.

19. Type **disable**. This will put you into user mode.

20. Type **exit,** which will log you out of the router.

Lab 4.2: Using the Help and Editing Features

1. Log in to the router and go to privileged mode by typing **en** or **enable**.

2. Type a question mark (?).

3. Type **cl?** and then press Enter. Notice that you can see all the commands that start with "cl".

4. Type **clock ?** and press Enter.

Notice the difference between numbers 3 and 4. Number 3 has you type letters with no space and a question mark, which will give you all the commands that start with "cl". Number 4 has you type a command, space, and question mark. By doing this, you will see the next available commands.

5. Set the router's clock by typing **clock ?** and following the help screens; set the router's time and date.

6. Type **clock ?**.

7. Type **clock set ?.**

8. Type **clock set 10:30:30 ?.**

9. Type **clock set 10:30:30 14 March ?.**

10. Type **clock set 10:30:30 14 March 2001.**

11. Press Enter.

12. Type **show clock** to see the time and date.

13. From privileged mode, type **show access-list 10.** *Don't* press Enter.

14. Press Ctrl+A. This takes you to the beginning of the line.

15. Press Ctrl+E. This should take you back to the end of the line.

16. Press Ctrl+A, then Ctrl+F. This should move you forward one character.

17. Press Ctrl+B, which will move you back one character.

18. Press Return, then press Ctrl+P. This will repeat the last command.

19. Press the up arrow on your keyboard. This will also repeat the last command.

20. Type **sh history.** This shows you the last 10 commands entered.

21. Type **terminal history size ?.** This changes the history entry size.

22. Type **show terminal** to gather terminal statistics and history size.

23. Type **terminal no editing.** This turns off advanced editing. Repeat steps 14–18 to see that the shortcut editing keys have no effect until you type **terminal editing.**

24. Type **terminal editing** and press Enter to re-enable advanced editing.

25. Type **sh run,** then press your Tab key. This will finish typing the command for you.

26. Type **sh star,** then press your Tab key. This will finish typing the command for you.

Lab 4.3: Saving a Router Configuration

1. Log into the router and go into privileged mode by typing **en** or **enable**, then press Enter.

2. To see the configuration stored in NVRAM, type **sh start** and press Tab and Enter, or type **show startup-config** and press Enter. However, if no configuration has been saved, you will get an error message.

3. To save a configuration to NVRAM, which is known as startup-config, you can do one of the following:

   - Type **copy run start** and press Enter.
   - Type **copy running**, press Tab, type **start**, press Tab, and press Enter.
   - Type **copy running-config startup-config** and press Enter.

4. Type **sh start**, press tab, then press Enter.

5. Type **sh run**, press tab, then press Enter.

6. Type **erase start**, press Tab, then press Enter.

7. Type **sh start**, press Tab, then press Enter. You should get an error message.

8. Type **reload**, then press Enter. Acknowledge the reload by pressing Enter. Wait for the router to reload.

9. Say no to entering setup mode, or just press Ctrl+C.

Lab 4.4: Setting Your Passwords

1. Log into the router and go into privileged mode by typing **en** or **enable**.

2. Type **config t** and press Enter.

3. Type **enable ?**.

4. Set your enable secret password by typing **enable secret** *password* (the word *password* should be your own personalized password) and pressing Enter. Do not add the command password after the command secret (this would make your password the word *password*). An example would be enable secret todd.

5. Now let's see what happens when you log all the way out of the router and then log in. Log out by pressing Ctrl+Z, and then type **exit** and press Enter. Go to privileged mode. Before you are allowed to enter privileged mode, you will be asked for a password. If you successfully enter the secret password, you can proceed.

6. Remove the secret password. Go to privileged mode, type **config t,** and press Enter. Type **no enable secret** and press Enter. Log out and then in again, and now you should not be asked for a password.

7. One more password used to enter privileged mode is called enable password. It is an older, less secure password and is not used if an enable secret password is set. Here is an example of how to set it:

```
config t
enable password todd1
```

8. Notice that the enable secret and enable passwords are different. They cannot be the same.

9. Type **config t** to be at the right level to set your console and auxiliary passwords, then type **line ?**.

10. Notice the output for the line commands is auxiliary, vty, and console. You will set all three.

11. To set the Telnet or vty password, type **line vty 0 4** and then press Enter. The 0 4 is the five available virtual lines used to connect with Telnet. If you have an enterprise IOS, the number of lines may vary. Use the question mark to determine the last line number available on your router.

12. The next command is used to set the authentication on or off. Type **login** and press Enter to prompt for a user-mode password when telnetting into the router. You will not be able to telnet into a router if the password is not set.

You can use the no login command to disable the user-mode password prompt when using Telnet.

13. One more command you need to set for your vty password is password. Type **password** *password* to set the password. (*Password* is your password.)

14. Here is an example of how to set the VTY passwords:

```
Config t
Line vty 0 4
Login
Password todd
```

15. Set your auxiliary password by first typing **line auxiliary** 0 or **line aux** 0.

16. Type **Login**.

17. Type **password** *password*.

18. Set your console password by first typing **line console** 0 or **line con** 0.

19. Type **login**.

20. Type **password** *password*. Here is an example of the last two commands:

```
Config t
Line con 0
Login
Password todd1
Line aux 0
Login
Password todd
```

21. You can add the command `Exec-timeout 0 0` to the console 0 line. This will stop the console from timing out and logging you out. The command will now look like this:

```
config t
line con 0
login
password todd2
exec-timeout 0 0
```

22. Set the console prompt to not overwrite the command you're typing with console messages by using the command `logging synchronous`.

```
config t
line con 0
logging synchronous
```

Lab 4.5: Setting the Hostname, Descriptions, IP Address, and Clock Rate

1. Log into the router and go into privileged mode by typing **en** or **enable**.

2. Set your hostname on your router by using the hostname command. Notice that it is one word. Here is an example of setting your hostname:

   ```
   Router#config t
   Router(config)#hostname RouterA
   RouterA(config)#
   ```

   Notice that the hostname of the router changed as soon as you pressed Enter.

3. Set a banner that the network administrators will see by using the banner command.

4. Type **config t, banner ?**.

5. Notice that you can set four different banners. In this course we are only interested in the login and Message of the Day (MOTD) banners.

6. Set your MOTD banner, which will be displayed when a console, auxiliary, or Telnet connection is made to the router by typing

   ```
   config t
   banner motd #
   This is an motd banner
   #
   ```

7. The preceding example used a # sign as a delimiting character. This tells the router when the message is done. You cannot use the delimiting character in the message.

8. You can remove the MOTD banner by typing

   ```
   config t
   no banner motd
   ```

9. Set the login banner by typing

   ```
   config t
   banner login #
   This is a login banner
   #
   ```

10. The login banner will display immediately after the MOTD but before the user-mode password prompt. Remember that you set your user-mode passwords by setting the console, auxiliary, and vty line passwords.

11. You can remove the login banner by typing

    ```
    config t
    no banner login
    ```

12. You can add an IP address to an interface with the IP address command. You need to get into interface configuration first; here is an example of how you do that:

    ```
    config t
    int e0 (you can use int Ethernet 0 too)
    ip address 1.1.1.1 255.255.0.0
    no shutdown
    ```

    Notice the IP address (1.1.1.1) and subnet mask (255.255.0.0) are configured on one line. The no shutdown (or no shut for short) command is used to enable the interface. All interfaces are shut down by default.

13. You can add identification to an interface by using the description command. This is useful for adding information about the connection. Administrators only see this, not users. Here is an example:

    ```
    config t
    int s0
    ip address 1.1.1.2 255.255.0.0
    no shut
    description Wan link to Miami
    ```

14. You can add the bandwidth of a serial link as well as the clock rate when simulating a DCE WAN link. Here is an example:

    ```
    config t
    int s0
    bandwidth 64
    clock rate 64000
    ```

Review Questions

1. When a router is first booted, where is the IOS loaded by default?

   A. Boot ROM

   B. NVRAM

   C. Flash

   D. ROM

2. What are the two ways that you can enter setup mode on a router?

   A. By typing the `clear flash` command

   B. By typing the `erase start` command and rebooting the router

   C. By typing the command `setup`

   D. By typing the command `setup mode`

3. If you are in privileged mode and want to return to user mode, what command would you use?

   A. `Exit`

   B. `Quit`

   C. `Disable`

   D. Control+Z

4. What editing command moves your cursor to the beginning of the line?

   A. Ctrl+E

   B. Ctrl+F

   C. Ctrl+B

   D. Ctrl+A

5. Which editing command will move your cursor to the end of the line?

   A. Ctrl+E

   B. Ctrl+F

   C. Esc+B

   D. Ctrl+A

6. Which editing command moves your cursor forward one character?

   A. Ctrl+E

   B. Ctrl+F

   C. Ctrl+B

   D. Ctrl+A

7. Which editing command moves your cursor back one word?

   A. Ctrl+E

   B. Ctrl+F

   C. Esc+B

   D. Ctrl+A

8. Which command will show you the IOS version currently running on your router?

   A. Show flash

   B. Show flash file

   C. Show ip flash

   D. Sh ver

9. Which command will show you the contents of the EEPROM in your router?

   A. Show flash

   B. Show flash file

   C. Show ip flash

   D. Sh ver

10. Which command will show you if a DTE or DCE cable is plugged into serial 0?

A. Sh int s0

B. Sh int serial 0

C. Sho controllers s 0

D. Sho controllers s0

11. What command will stop console messages from writing over the command you are trying to type in?

A. No logging

B. Logging

C. Logging asynchronous

D. Logging synchronous

12. What command will allow users to telnet into a router and not be prompted with a user-mode password?

A. Login

B. No login

C. You can telnet by default, so no command is needed.

D. No password

13. What command will set your console to time out after only one second?

A. Timeout 1 0

B. Timeout 0 1

C. Exec-timeout 1 0

D. Exec-timeout 0 1

14. How do you only set your Telnet line 1 to a password of bob?

A. line vty 0 1
Login
Password bob

B. line vty 0 4
Login
Password bob

C. line vty 1
Login
Password bob

D. line vty 1
Password bob
Login

15. How do you set the password for the auxiliary port?

A. Line aux 1

B. Line aux 0

C. Line aux 0 4

D. Line aux port

16. Which of the following commands will encrypt your Telnet password on a Cisco router?

A. Line telnet 0, encryption on, password todd

B. Line vty 0, password encryption, password todd

C. Service password encryption, line vty 0 4, password todd

D. Password encryption, line vty 0 4, password todd

17. What command do you type to back up your currently running configuration and have it reload if the router is restarted?

A. (Config)#**copy current to starting**

B. Router#**copy starting to running**

C. Router(config)#**copy running-config star**

D. Router#**copy run startup**

18. When using setup mode, what are the two different management setup configurations?

    A. Basic

    B. Advanced

    C. Extended

    D. Expanded

19. Which command will delete the contents of NVRAM on a router?

    A. `Delete NVRAM`

    B. `Delete Startup-config`

    C. `Erase NVRAM`

    D. `Erase start`

20. What is the problem with an interface if you type `show interface serial 0` and receive the following message?

    `Serial0 is administratively down, line protocol is down`

    A. The keepalives are different times.

    B. The administrator has the interface shut down.

    C. The administrator is pinging from the interface.

    D. No cable is attached.

Answers to the Written Lab

1. `clock rate 64000`

2. `config t, line vty 0 4, no login`

3. `config t, int e0, no shut`

4. `erase startup-config`

5. `config t, line console 0, login, password todd`

6. `config t, enable secret cisco`

7. `show controllers s 0`

8. `show terminal`

9. `config net`

10. `config t, hostname Chicago`

Answers to Review Questions

1. C. The Cisco IOS is loaded from Flash memory by default.

2. B, C. Not that you would want to enter setup mode, but if you did, you could erase the contents of NVRAM by using the `erase startup-config` command and then rebooting the router. You can also type `setup` from the privileged mode at any time.

3. C. The command `disable` will take you from privileged mode to user mode.

4. D. The editing command Ctrl+A will take your cursor to the beginning of the line.

5. A. The editing command Ctrl+E will take your cursor to the end of the line.

6. B. The editing command Ctrl+F will take your cursor forward one character.

7. C. The editing command Esc+B will take your cursor back one word.

8. D. `Show version` will give you the IOS version currently running on the router.

9. A. The EEPROM is Flash memory. Flash is where the IOS is stored and loaded from by default. `Show flash` will show you the contents of Flash memory. However, `show version` will show you the version of IOS currently running. If only one IOS is in Flash memory, then `show version` and `show flash` will always be the same.

10. C. The command `show controllers serial 0` will show you if either a DTE or DCE cable is connected to the interface.

11. D. This is a helpful command. The `logging synchronous` under the line `console 0 configuration` stops console messages from overwriting the command you are typing.

12. B. The command `no login` under the `line vty` command sets the VTY ports to not prompt for authentication.

13. D. The `exec-timeout` command sets the console timeout in minutes and seconds.

14. B. The command `line vty 0 4` configures the VTY ports. `Login` tells the VTY ports to authenticate, although that command is on by default for Cisco router VTY ports. The last command is `password bob`.

15. B. You can gain access to the auxiliary port by using the `line auxiliary 0` command. There is only one auxiliary port so it is always aux 0.

16. C. To encrypt your user-mode and enable passwords, use the global configuration command `service password encryption` before setting your passwords.

17. D. To copy the current config to NVRAM so that it will be used if the router is restarted, use the command `copy run start`.

18. A, C. Basic management setup configures only enough connectivity for management of the system; extended setup will ask you to configure each interface on the system.

19. D. The command `erase startup-config` erases the contents of NVRAM and will put you in setup mode if the router is restarted.

20. B. If an interface is shut down, the `show interface` command will show the interface as administratively shut down. (It is possible no cable is attached, but you can't tell that from this message.)

IP Routing

THE CCNA EXAM TOPICS COVERED IN THIS CHAPTER INCLUDE THE FOLLOWING:

✓ **Understand the IP routing process**

✓ **Create and verify static routing**

✓ **Create and verify default routing**

✓ **Resolve network loops in distance-vector routing protocols**

✓ **Configure and verify RIP routing**

✓ **Configure and verify IGRP routing**

This chapter will discuss the IP routing process. This is an important subject to understand as it pertains to all routers and configurations that use IP. IP routing is the process of moving packets from one network to another network and delivering the packets to hosts.

This chapter will give you the background on how to configure and verify IP routing with Cisco routers. I will cover the following:

- Static routing

- Default routing

- Dynamic routing

It is important to be able to configure Cisco routers and then configure and verify IP routing. This chapter will give you this information.

Routing

Routing is used for taking a packet from one device and sending it through the network to another device on a different network. If your network has no routers, then you are not routing. Routers route traffic to all the networks in your internetwork. To be able to route packets, a router must know, at a minimum, the following:

- Destination address

- Neighbor routers from which it can learn about remote networks

- Possible routes to all remote networks

- The best route to each remote network

- How to maintain and verify routing information

The router learns about remote networks from neighbor routers or from an administrator. The router then builds a routing table that describes how to find the remote networks. If the network is directly connected, then the router already knows how to get to the network. If the networks are not attached, the router must learn how to get to the remote network with either static routing, which means that the administrator must hand-type all network locations into the routing table, or use dynamic routing. *Dynamic routing* is the process of routing protocols running on the router communicating with neighbor routers. The routers then update each other about all the networks they know about. If a change occurs in the network, the dynamic routing protocols automatically inform all routers about the change. If static routing is used, the administrator is responsible for updating all changes by hand into all routers.

The IP Routing Process

The IP routing process is fairly simple and doesn't change, regardless of the size of network you have. For an example, we'll use Figure 5.1 to describe step by step what happens when Host A wants to communicate with Host B on a different network.

FIGURE 5.1   IP routing example using two hosts and one router

In our example, a user on Host A pings Host B's IP address. It will not get simpler than this. Let's work through the steps.

1. From a command prompt, the user types **ping 172.16.20.2**. A packet is generated on the Host A machine using the IP and ICMP Network layer protocols.

2. IP works with the ARP protocol to determine what network this packet is destined for by looking at the IP address and the subnet mask of Host A. Since this is a request for a remote host, which means it is not destined to be sent to a host on the local network, the packet must be sent to the router so that it will be routed to the correct remote network.

3. For Host A to send the packet to the router, it must know the hardware address of the router's interface located on the local network. Remember that the Network layer will hand the packet and the destination hardware address to the Data Link layer for framing and transmitting on a local host. To get the hardware address, the host looks in a location in memory called the ARP cache.

4. If the IP address has not already been resolved to a hardware address and is not in the ARP cache, the host sends an ARP broadcast looking, for the hardware address of IP address 172.16.10.1. This is why the first Ping usually times out, and the other four are successful. After the address is cached, no timeouts usually occur.

5. The router responds with the hardware address of the Ethernet interface connected to the local network. The host now has everything it needs to transmit the packet out on the local network to the router. The Network layer hands down the packet it generated with the ICMP echo request (Ping) to the Data Link layer, along with the hardware address of where the host wants to send the packet. The packet includes the IP source address and the destination IP address, as well as the ICMP specified in the Network layer protocol field.

6. The Data Link layer creates a frame, which encapsulates the packet with the control information needed to transmit on the local network. This includes the source and destination hardware addresses and the type field specifying the Network layer protocol (it is a type field since IP uses an Ethernet_II frame by default). Figure 5.2 shows the frame that will be generated by the Data Link layer and sent out on the local media.

FIGURE 5.2 Frame generated from Host A

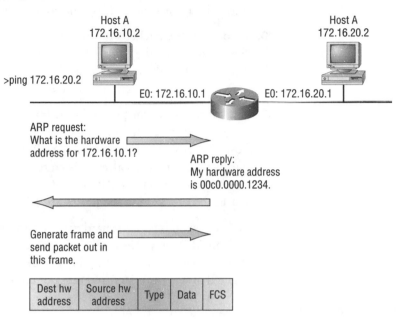

In Figure 5.2, all of the information needed to communicate to the router is shown: the source and destination hardware addresses, the source and destination IP addresses, and finally, the data and the frame's CRC inside the Frame Check Sequence (FCS) field.

7. The Data Link layer of Host A hands the frame to the Physical layer, which encodes the 1s and 0s into a digital signal and transmits this out on the local physical network.

8. The signal is picked up by the router's Ethernet 0 interface, and the interface synchronizes on the digital signal preamble and extracts the frame. The router's interface, after building the frame, runs a CRC and, at the end of the frame, checks the FCS field to make sure that the CRC matches and no fragmentation or collisions occurred.

9. The destination hardware address is checked. Since this will be a match, the type field in the frame will be checked to see what the router should do with the data packet. IP is, of course, in the type field, and the router hands the packet to the IP protocol running on the

router. The frame is discarded, and the original packet that was generated by Host A now sits in the router's buffer.

10. IP looks at the packet's destination IP address to determine if the packet is for the router. Since the destination IP address is 172.16.20.2, the router determines from the routing table that 172.16.20.0 is a directly connected network on interface Ethernet 1.

11. The router places the packet in the buffer of interface Ethernet 1. The router needs to create a frame to send the packet to the destination host. First, the router looks in the ARP cache to determine whether the hardware address has already been resolved from a prior communication. If it is not in the ARP cache, the router sends an ARP broadcast out Ethernet 1 to find the hardware address of 172.16.20.2.

12. Host B responds with the hardware address of its network interface card with an ARP reply. The router's Ethernet 1 interface now has everything it needs to send the packet to the final destination. Figure 5.3 shows the frame that was generated and sent out on the physical network.

FIGURE 5.3 Frame generated from router

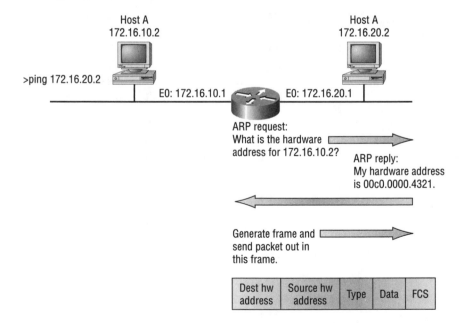

The frame generated from the router's Ethernet 1 interface has the source hardware address of the Ethernet 1 interface and the hardware destination address of Host B's network interface card. However, the most important thing here is that even though the frame's source and destination hardware address changed at every interface of the router it was sent to and from, the IP source and destination addresses never changed. The packet was never modified at all; only the frame changed.

13. Host B receives the frame and runs a CRC. If that checks out, it discards the frame and hands the packet to IP. IP will then check the destination IP address. Since the IP destination address matches the IP configuration of Host B, it looks in the protocol field of the packet to determine what the purpose of the packet is.

14. Since the packet is an ICMP echo request, Host B generates a new ICMP echo-reply packet with a source IP address of Host B and a destination IP address of Host A. The process starts all over again, except that it goes in the opposite direction. However, the hardware address of each device along the path is already known, so each device only needs to look in its ARP cache to determine the hardware address of each interface.

If you had a much larger network, the process would be the same, with the packet simply going through more hops before it finds the destination host.

IP Routing in a Larger Network

In the example given in the previous section, the routing table of the router already has both IP networks in the routing table because the network is directly connected to the router. But what if we add three more routers? Figure 5.4 shows four routers, 2500A, 2500B, 2500C, and 2621A. These routers, by default, only know about their directly connected networks.

FIGURE 5.4   IP routing example 2 with more routers

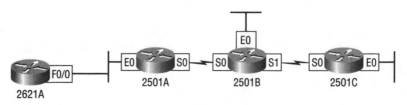

Figure 5.4 shows the three 2500 routers connected via a WAN and the 2621 router connected via the Ethernet network off 2500A. Each router also has an Ethernet network connected.

The first step is to configure each router with the correct configuration. Table 5.1 shows the IP address scheme I used to configure the network. After we go over how the network is configured, I will discuss how to configure IP routing. Each network in the following table has a 24-bit subnet mask (255.255.255.0).

TABLE 5.1   Network Addressing for the IP Network

Router	Network Address	Interface	Address
2621A	172.16.10.0	f0/0	172.16.10.1
2501A	172.16.10.0	e0	172.16.10.2
2501A	172.16.20.0	s0	172.16.20.1
2501B	172.16.20.0	s0	172.16.20.2
2501B	172.16.40.0	s1	172.16.40.1
2501B	172.16.30.0	e0	172.16.30.1
2501C	172.16.40.0	s0	172.16.40.2
2501C	172.16.50.0	e0	172.16.50.1

Router configuration is a fairly simple process, since you just need to add IP addresses to your interfaces and then perform a `no shutdown` on the interfaces. It will get a tad bit more complex in the next section, but first, let's configure the IP addresses in the network.

2621A Configuration

To configure the 2621 router, you just need to add an IP address to interface FastEthernet 0/0. Configuring the hostnames of each router will make identification easier. Here is how I did that:

```
Router> en
Router#config t
```

```
Router (config)#hostname 2621A
2621A(Config)#interface fa0/0
2621A(Config-if)#ip address 172.16.10.1 255.255.255.0
2621A(Config-if)#no shut
```

The configuration is only a few lines. If you have a hard time understanding this process, refer to Chapter 4.

To view the IP routing tables created on a Cisco router, use the privileged mode command show ip route. The command output is shown as follows. Notice that only the configured network is shown in the routing table. This means the router only knows how to get to network 172.16.10.0.

```
2621A#sh ip route
Codes: C - connected, S - static, I - IGRP, R - RIP, M -
mobile, B – BGP D - EIGRP, EX - EIGRP external, O - OSPF,
IA - OSPF inter area N1 - OSPF NSSA external type 1, N2 -
OSPF NSSA external type 2 E1 - OSPF external type 1, E2 -
OSPF external type 2, E – EGP i - IS-IS, L1 - IS-IS level-
1, L2 - IS-IS level-2, * - candidate default U - per-user
static route, o - ODR, P - periodic downloaded static
route T - traffic engineered route
Gateway of last resort is not set

     172.16.0.0/24 is subnetted, 1 subnets
C       172.16.10.0 is directly connected, FastEthernet0/0
2621A#
```

The preceding routing table shows the directly connected network 172.16.10.0. Notice the "C"; this means that the network is directly connected. The codes for each type of connection are listed at the top of the show ip route command with their abbreviations. In the interest of brevity, the codes will be abbreviated in the rest of this chapter.

2501A Configuration

It is now time to configure the next router. To configure 2501A, two interfaces need to be configured: Ethernet 0 and serial 0.

```
Router>en
Router#config t
Router(config)#hostname 2501A
```

```
2501A(config)#int e0
2501A(config-if)#ip address 172.16.10.2 255.255.255.0
2501A(config-if)#no shut
2501A(config-if)#int s0
2501A(config-if)#ip address 172.16.20.1 255.255.255.0
2501A(config-if)#no shut
```

The preceding configuration configured serial 0 into network 172.16.20.0 and Ethernet 0 into network 172.16.10.0. The show ip route command displays the following:

```
2501A#sh ip route
Codes: C - connected, S - static, I - IGRP, R - RIP,
M — [output cut]
Gateway of last resort is not set

     172.16.0.0/24 is subnetted, 2 subnets
C        172.16.20.0 is directly connected, Serial0
C        172.16.10.0 is directly connected, Ethernet0
2501A#
```

Notice that router 2501A knows how to get to networks 172.16.10.0 and 172.16.20.0. Router 2621 and Router A can communicate because they are on the same LAN.

2501B Configuration

The configuration of 2501B is more of the same, except that you also need to add the clock rate command to the DCE interfaces connected to both serial interfaces. For more information on the DCE interfaces and the clock rate command, please see Chapter 4.

```
Router>en
Router#config t
Router(config)#hostname 2501B
2501B(config)#int e0
2501B(config-if)#ip address 172.16.30.1 255.255.255.0
2501B(config-if)#no shut
2501B(config-if)#int s0
```

```
2501B(config-if)#ip address 172.16.20.2 255.255.255.0
2501B(config-if)#clock rate 64000
2501B(config-if)#no shut
2501B(config-if)#int s1
2501B(config-if)#ip address 172.16.40.1 255.255.255.0
2501B(config-if)#clock rate 64000
2501B(config-if)#no shut
```

The above configuration configured the hostname and IP addresses as well as the clock rate on the serial interfaces. The output of the following show ip route command displays the directly connected networks of 172.16.20.0, 172.16.30.0, and 172.16.40.0.

```
2501B#sh ip route
Codes: C - connected, S - static, I - IGRP, R - RIP,
M - [output cut]
Gateway of last resort is not set

      172.16.0.0/24 is subnetted, 3 subnets
C       172.16.40.0 is directly connected, Serial1
C       172.16.30.0 is directly connected, Ethernet0
C       172.16.20.0 is directly connected, Serial0
2501B#
```

Router A and Router B can communicate because they are on the same WAN network. However, Router B cannot communicate with the 2621 router because it does not know about network 172.16.10.0. Router A can ping both the 2621 router and 2501B, but 2501B and 2621 cannot see each other.

2501C Configuration

The configuration of 2501C is the same as 2501A except that it has different network IDs.

```
Router>en
Router#config t
Router(config)#hostname 2501C
2501C(config)#int e0
2501C(config-if)#ip address 172.16.50.1 255.255.255.0
```

```
2501C(config-if)#no shut
2501C(config-if)#int s0
2501C(config-if)#ip address 172.16.40.2 255.255.255.0
2501C(config-if)#no shut
```

Interface Ethernet 0 is configured to participate in the 172.16.50.0 network, and serial 0 is configured into the 172.16.40.0 WAN network. The output of the show ip route command, displayed below, shows the directly connected networks on router 2501C.

```
2501C#sh ip route
Codes: C - connected, S - static, I - IGRP, R - RIP,
M - [output cut]
Gateway of last resort is not set

     172.16.0.0/24 is subnetted, 2 subnets
C       172.16.50.0 is directly connected, Ethernet0
C       172.16.40.0 is directly connected, Serial0
2501C#
```

Router 2501C can communicate with 2501B since they are on the same WAN network. However, by default, 2501C cannot see any other router or network.

IP Routing in Our Network

The network in the previous section has now been configured correctly with IP addressing. However, how does a router send packets to remote networks? The routers can only send packets by looking at the routing table and discovering how to get to the remote networks. But our configured routers only have information containing directly connected networks in each routing table. What happens when a router receives a packet with a network that is not listed in the routing table? It doesn't send a broadcast looking for the remote network—the router just discards it. Period.

There are a few different ways to configure the routing tables to include all the networks in our little internetwork so that packets will be forwarded. However, the best way for one network is not necessarily best for another.

If you understand the different routing types, you will be able to decide what fits best in your business requirements.

The different types of routing you will learn about in this chapter include the following:

- Static routing

- Default routing

- Dynamic routing

We will start off by describing and implementing static routing on our network. Why? Because if you can implement static routing and make it work, it means you have a good understanding of the internetwork.

Static Routing

Static routing is the process of an administrator manually adding routes in each router's routing table. There are benefits and disadvantages to all routing processes.

Static routing has the following benefits:

- No overhead on the router CPU

- No bandwidth usage between routers

- Security (because the administrator only allows routing to certain networks)

Static routing has the following disadvantages:

- The administrator must really understand the internetwork and how each router is connected to configure the routes correctly.

- If one network is added to the internetwork, the administrator must add a route to it on all routers.

- It's not feasible in large networks because it would be a full-time job.

The command used to add a static route to a routing table is

```
ip route [destination_network] [mask] [next_hop_address or
exitinterface] [administrative_distance][permanent]
```

The following list describes each command in the string:

ip route   The command used to create the static route.

destination network   The network you are placing in the routing table.

mask   Indicates the subnet mask being used on the network.

next hop address   The address of the next hop router that will receive the packet and forward it to the remote network. This is a router interface that is on a directly connected network. You must be able to ping the router interface before you add the route.

exit interface   Used in place of the next hop address if desired. Must be on a point-to-point link, such as a WAN. This command does not work on a LAN; for example, Ethernet.

administrative distance   By default, static routes have an administrative distance of 1. You can change the default value by adding an administrative weight at the end of the command.

permanent   If the interface is shut down or the router cannot communicate to the next hop router, the route is automatically discarded from the routing table. Choosing the **permanent** option keeps the entry in the routing table no matter what happens.

To be able to understand how static routes work, I will demonstrate the configuration on my sample internetwork, as shown previously in Figure 5.4.

2621A

Each routing table automatically includes directly connected networks. To be able to route to all networks in the internetwork, the routing table must include information that defines where these other networks are located and how to get there.

The 2621 router is connected only to network 172.16.10.0. For the 2621A router to be able to route to all networks, the following networks must be configured in the routing table:

- 172.16.20.0
- 172.16.30.0
- 172.16.40.0
- 172.16.50.0

The following router output shows the configuration of static routes on the 2621A router and the routing table after the configuration. For the 2621A router to find the remote networks, an entry is placed in the routing table describing the network, the mask, and where to send the packets. Notice that each static route sends the packets to 172.16.10.2, which is the 2621 router's next hop.

```
2621A(Config)#ip route 172.16.20.0 255.255.255.0
172.16.10.2
2621A(Config)#ip route 172.16.30.0 255.255.255.0
172.16.10.2
2621A(Config)#ip route 172.16.40.0 255.255.255.0
172.16.10.2
2621A(Config)#ip route 172.16.50.0 255.255.255.0
172.16.10.2
```

After the router is configured, you can type **show running-config** and **show ip route** to see the static routes. Remember that if the routes don't appear in the routing table, it is because the router cannot communicate to the next hop address you configured. You can use the `permanent` parameter to keep the route in the routing table even if the next hop device cannot be contacted.

```
2621A#sh ip route
Codes: C - connected, S - static, I - IGRP, R - RIP,
M - [output cut]
Gateway of last resort is not set

     172.16.0.0/24 is subnetted, 5 subnets
S       172.16.50.0 [1/0] via 172.16.10.2
S       172.16.40.0 [1/0] via 172.16.10.2
S       172.16.30.0 [1/0] via 172.16.10.2
S       172.16.20.0 [1/0] via 172.16.10.2
C       172.16.10.0 is directly connected, FastEthernet0/0
2621A#
```

The 2621 router now has all the information it needs so that it can communicate to the other remote networks. However, if the 2501A router is not configured with all the same information, the packets will be discarded at 2501A.

2501A

The 2501A router is connected to the networks 172.16.10.0 and 172.16.20.0. The following static routes must be configured on the 2501A router:

- 172.16.30.0

- 172.16.40.0

- 172.16.50.0

Here is the configuration for the 2501A router.

```
2501A(Config)#ip route 172.16.30.0 255.255.255.0
172.16.20.2
2501A(Config)#ip route 172.16.40.0 255.255.255.0
172.16.20.2
2501A(Config)#ip route 172.16.50.0 255.255.255.0
172.16.20.2
```

By looking at the routing table, you can see that the 2501A router now understands how to find each network.

```
2501A#sh ip route
Codes: C - connected, S - static, I - IGRP, R - RIP,
M – [output cut]
Gateway of last resort is not set

     172.16.0.0/24 is subnetted, 5 subnets
S       172.16.50.0 [1/0] via 172.16.20.2
S       172.16.40.0 [1/0] via 172.16.20.2
S       172.16.30.0 [1/0] via 172.16.20.2
C       172.16.20.0 is directly connected, Serial0
C       172.16.10.0 is directly connected, Ethernet0
2501A#
```

The S in the routing table entries means that the network is a static entry. The [1/0] is the administrative distance and hops to the remote network, which is 0.

The 2501A router now has a complete routing table. As long as the other routers in the internetwork have the same routing table, 2501A can communicate to all remote networks.

2501B

The 2501B router is directly connected to networks 172.16.20.0, 172.16.30.0, and 172.16.40.0. Only two routers need to be added: 172.16.10.0 and 172.16.50.0.

```
2501B(Config)#ip route 172.16.10.0 255.255.255.0
172.16.20.1
2501B(Config)#ip route 172.16.50.0 255.255.255.0
172.16.40.2
```

The following output shows the routing table on the 2501B router.

```
2501B#sh ip route
Codes: C - connected, S - static, I - IGRP, R - RIP,
M — [output cut]
Gateway of last resort is not set

     172.16.0.0/24 is subnetted, 5 subnets
S       172.16.50.0 [1/0] via 172.16.40.2
C       172.16.40.0 is directly connected, Serial1
C       172.16.30.0 is directly connected, Ethernet0
C       172.16.20.0 is directly connected, Serial0
S       172.16.10.0 [1/0] via 172.16.20.1
2501B#
```

2501B now shows all the networks in the internetwork and can communicate to all routers and networks, with the exception of the hosts on network 172.16.50.0; this is because 2501C is not configured yet.

2501C

Router 2501C is directly connected to networks 172.16.40.0 and 172.16.50.0. The routing table needs to know about networks 172.16.10.0, 172.16.20.0, and 172.16.30.0. Here is the configuration:

```
2501C(Config)#ip route 172.16.10.0 255.255.255.0
172.16.40.1
```

```
2501C(Config)#ip route 172.16.20.0 255.255.255.0
172.16.40.1
2501C(Config)#ip route 172.16.30.0 255.255.255.0
172.16.40.1
```

Below is the output of the show ip route command as run on the 2501C router.

```
2501C#sh ip route
Codes: C - connected, S - static, I - IGRP, R - RIP,
M - [output cut]
Gateway of last resort is not set

     172.16.0.0/24 is subnetted, 5 subnets
C       172.16.50.0 is directly connected, Ethernet0
C       172.16.40.0 is directly connected, Serial0
S       172.16.30.0 [1/0] via 172.16.40.1
S       172.16.20.0 [1/0] via 172.16.40.1
S       172.16.10.0 [1/0] via 172.16.40.1
2501C#
```

Now all the routers have the correct routing table, and all the routers and hosts should be able to communicate without a problem. However, if you add even one more route or another router to the internetwork, you will have to update all routers' routing tables by hand. This is fine for a small network, but it is too time-consuming a task for a large internetwork.

Verifying Your Configuration

Once all the routers' routing tables are configured, they need to be verified. The best way to do this is with the Ping program. By pinging from routers 2621A and 2501C, the whole internetwork will be tested end-to-end.

Here is the output of a Ping to network 172.16.50.0 from the 2621A router:

```
2621A#ping 172.16.50.1
Type escape sequence to abort.
Sending 5, 100-byte ICMP Echos to 172.16.50.1, timeout is
2 seconds:
.!!!!
```

```
Success rate is 100 percent (5/5), round-trip min/avg/max
= 64/66/68 ms
2621A#
```

Notice that the first response is a period. This is because the first Ping times out waiting for the ARP request and response. Once the ARP has found the hardware address of the default gateway, the IP-to-Ethernet mapping will be in the ARP cache and will stay in the router's cache for four hours. Any other IP connectivity to the next hop router will not time out, as no ARP broadcasts have to be performed.

From router 2501C, a Ping to 172.16.10.0 will test for good IP connectivity. Here is the router output:

```
2501C#ping 172.16.10.1
Type escape sequence to abort.
Sending 5, 100-byte ICMP Echos to 172.16.10.1, timeout is
2 seconds:
!!!!!
Success rate is 80 percent (4/5), round-trip min/avg/max =
64/67/72 ms
```

Notice that the first Ping was not a time-out since the ARP broadcasts are sent only on a LAN, not a WAN. And, since we can ping from end-to-end without a problem, our static route configuration was a success!

Default Routing

Default routing is used to send packets with a remote destination network not in the routing table to the next hop router. You can only use default routing on stub networks, which means that they have only one exit port out of the network.

In the internetworking example used in the previous section, the only routers that are considered to be in a stub network are 2621A and 2501C. If you tried to put a default route on the 2501A and 2501B routers, packets would not be forwarded to the correct networks because they have more than one interface routing to other routers. However, even though the 2501C router has two connections, it does not have a router on the 172.16.50 network that needs packets sent to it. The 2501C router will only send packets to 172.16.40.1, which is the interface of 2501B. The 2621A router will only send packets to the 172.16.10.1 interface of 2501A.

To configure a default route, you use wildcards in the network address and mask locations of a static route. Think of a default route as a static route that uses wildcards instead of network and mask information. In this section, you'll create a default route on the 2501C router.

Router 2501C is directly connected to networks 172.16.40.0 and 172.16.50.0. The routing table needs to know about networks 172.16.10.0, 172.16.20.0, and 172.16.30.0. To configure the router to route to the other three networks, I placed three static routes in the routing table. By using a default route, you can just create one static route entry instead. First, you must delete the existing static routes from the router, then add the default route.

```
2501C(Config)#no ip route 172.16.10.0 255.255.255.0
172.16.40.1
2501C(Config)#no ip route 172.16.20.0 255.255.255.0
172.16.40.1
2501C(Config)#no ip route 172.16.30.0 255.255.255.0
172.16.40.1
2501C(Config)#ip route 0.0.0.0 0.0.0.0 172.16.40.1
```

If you look at the routing table now, you'll see only the two directly connected networks, plus an S*, which indicates that this entry is a candidate for a default route.

```
2501C#sh ip route
Codes: C - connected, S - static, I - IGRP, R - RIP, M -
[output cut]
 - IS-IS level-1, L2 - IS-IS level-2, * - candidate
default U - per-user static route, o - ODR

Gateway of last resort is 172.16.40.1 to network 0.0.0.0
172.16.0.0/24 is subnetted, 5 subnets
C       172.16.50.0 is directly connected, Ethernet0
C       172.16.40.0 is directly connected, Serial0
S*      0.0.0.0/0 [1/0] via 172.16.40.1
2501C#
```

Notice also in the routing table that the gateway of last resort is now set. However, there is one more command you must be aware of when using default routes: the ip classless command. All Cisco routers are classful routers, which means they expect a default subnet mask on each interface of the router. When a router receives a packet for a destination subnet not in the routing table, it will drop the packet by default. If you are using default routing, you must use the `ip classless` command because no remote subnets will be in the routing table.

Since I have version 12.*x* of the IOS on my routers, the `ip classless` command is on by default. If you are using default routing and this command is not in your configuration, you need to add it. The command is shown below:

`2501C(Config)#`**`ip classless`**

Notice that it is a global configuration mode command. The interesting part of the `ip classless` command is that default routing sometimes works without it, but sometimes it doesn't. You should always turn on the `ip classless` command when you use default routing.

Dynamic Routing

Dynamic routing is the process of using protocols to find and update routing tables on routers. This is easier than static or default routing, but you use it at the expense of router CPU processes and bandwidth on the network links. A routing protocol defines the set of rules used by a router when it communicates between neighbor routers.

The two types of routing protocols discussed in this book are Routing Information Protocol (RIP) and Interior Gateway Routing Protocol (IGRP). For information on other types of routing protocols such as Enhanced Interior Gateway Routing Protocol (EIGRP) and Open Shortest Path First (OSPF), read Sybex's *CCNP: Routing Study Guide,* which covers the new Advanced Cisco Router Configuration exam from Cisco.

The CCNA 2 exam covers only RIP and IGRP routing protocols.

There are two types of routing protocols used in internetworks: Interior Gateway Protocol (IGP) and Exterior Gateway Protocol (EGP). IGP routing protocols are used to exchange routing information with routers in the same autonomous system (AS). An AS is a collection of networks under a common administrative domain. EGPs are used to communicate between ASs. An example of an EGP is Border Gateway Protocol (BGP), which is discussed in the *CCNP: Routing Study Guide.*

Administrative Distances

When configuring routing protocols, you need to be aware of *administrative distances* (ADs). These are used to rate the trustworthiness of routing information received on a router from a neighbor router. An administrative distance is an integer from 0 to 255, where 0 is the most trusted and 255 means no traffic will be passed via this route.

Table 5.2 shows the default administrative distances that a Cisco router will use to decide which route to use to a remote network.

TABLE 5.2   Default Administrative Distances

Route Source	Default Distance
Connected interface	0
Static route	1
EIGRP	90
IGRP	100
OSPF	110
RIP	120
External EIGRP	170
Unknown	255 (this route will never be used)

If a network is directly connected, it will always use the interface connected to the network. If an administrator configures a static route, the router will believe that route over any other learned routes. You can change the administrative distance of static routes, but, by default, they have an AD of 1.

Routing Protocols

There are three classes of routing protocols:

Distance vector   The distance-vector routing protocols use a distance to a remote network to find the best path. Each time a packet goes through a router, it's called a hop. The route with the least number of hops to the network is determined to be the best route. The vector is the determination of direction to the remote network. Examples of distance-vector routing protocols are RIP and IGRP.

Link state   Typically called shortest path first, the routers each create three separate tables. One of these tables keeps track of directly attached neighbors, one determines the topology of the entire internetwork, and one is used for the routing table. Link-state routers know more about the internetwork than any distance-vector routing protocol. An example of an IP routing protocol that is completely link state is OSPF.

Hybrid   Uses aspects of distance vector and link state, for example, EIGRP.

There is no set way of configuring routing protocols for use with every business. This is a task that is performed on a case-by-case basis. However, if you understand how the different routing protocols work, you can make good business decisions. This course and equivalent exam only cover distance-vector routing protocols and theory.

Distance-Vector Routing Protocols

The distance-vector routing algorithm passes complete routing tables to neighbor routers. The neighbor routers then combine the received routing table with their own routing tables to complete the internetwork map. This is called routing by rumor, because a router receiving an update from a neighbor router believes the information about remote networks without actually finding out for itself.

It is possible to have a network that has multiple links to the same remote network. If that is the case, the administrative distance is first checked. If the administrative distance is the same, it will have to use other metrics to determine the best path to use to that remote network.

RIP uses only hop count to determine the best path to an internetwork. If RIP finds more than one link to the same remote network with the same hop count, it will automatically perform a round-robin load balance. RIP can perform load balancing for up to six equal-cost links.

However, a problem with this type of routing metric arises when the two links to a remote network are different bandwidths but the same hop count. Figure 5.5, for example, shows two links to remote network 172.16.50.0.

FIGURE 5.5 Pinhole congestion

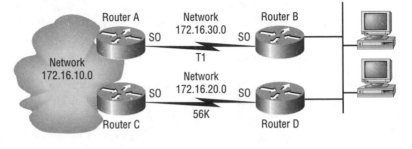

Since network 172.16.30.0 is a T1 link with a bandwidth of 1.544Mbps, and network 172.16.20.0 is a 56K link, you would want the router to choose the T1 over the 56K link. However, since hop count is the only metric used with RIP routing, they would both be seen as equal-cost links. This is called *pinhole congestion*.

It is important to understand what happens when a distance-vector routing protocol does when it starts up. In Figure 5.6, the four routers start off with only their directly connected networks in the routing table. After a distance-vector routing protocol is started on each router, the routing tables are updated with all route information gathered from neighbor routers.

FIGURE 5.6 The internetwork with distance-vector routing

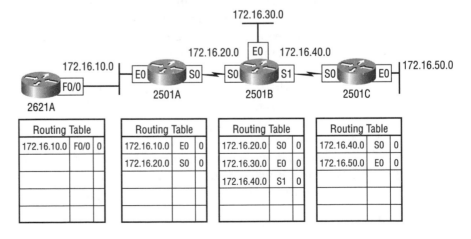

As shown in Figure 5.6, each router has only the directly connected networks in each routing table. Each router sends its complete routing table out to each active interface on the router. The routing table of each router includes the network number, exit interface, and hop count to the network.

In Figure 5.7, the routing tables are complete because they include information about all the networks in the internetwork. They are considered converged. When the routers are converging, no data is passed. That's why fast convergence time is a plus. One of the problems with RIP, in fact, is its slow convergence time.

FIGURE 5.7   Converged routing tables

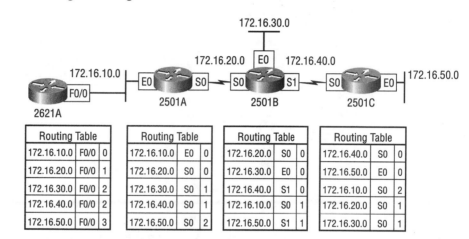

The routing tables in each router keep information regarding the network number, the interface to which the router will send packets out to get to the remote network, and the hop count or metric to the remote network.

Routing Loops

Distance-vector routing protocols keep track of any changes to the internetwork by broadcasting periodic routing updates to all active interfaces. This broadcast includes the complete routing table. This works fine, although it takes up CPU process and link bandwidth. However, if a network outage happens, problems can occur. The slow convergence of distance-vector routing protocols can cause inconsistent routing tables and routing loops.

Routing loops can occur because every router is not updated close to the same time. Let's say that the interface to Network 5 in Figure 5.8 fails. All routers know about Network 5 from Router E. Router A, in its tables, has a path to Network 5 through Routers B, C, and E. When Network 5 fails, Router E tells RouterC. This causes Router C to stop routing to Network 5 through Router E. But Routers A, B, and D don't know about Network 5 yet, so they keep sending out update information. Router C will eventually send out its update and cause B to stop routing to Network 5, but Routers A and D are still not updated. To them, it appears that Network 5 is still available through Router B with a metric of three.

FIGURE 5.8 Routing loop example

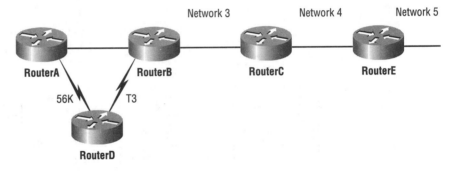

Router A sends out its regular 30-second "Hello, I'm still here—these are the links I know about" message, which includes reachability for Network 5. Routers B and D then receive the wonderful news that Network 5 can be reached from Router A, so they send out the information that Network 5 is available. Any packet destined for Network 5 will go to Router A, to Router B, and then back to Router A. This is a routing loop—how do you stop it?

Maximum Hop Count

The routing loop problem just described is called *counting to infinity,* and it's caused by gossip and wrong information being communicated and propagated throughout the internetwork. Without some form of intervention, the hop count increases indefinitely each time a packet passes through a router.

One way of solving this problem is to define a *maximum hop count.* Distance vector (RIP) permits a hop count of up to 15, so anything that requires

16 hops is deemed unreachable. In other words, after a loop of 15 hops, Network 5 will be considered down. This means that counting to infinity will keep packets from going around the loop forever. Though this is a workable solution, it won't remove the routing loop itself. Packets will still go into the loop, but instead of traveling on unchecked, they'll whirl around for 16 bounces and die.

Split Horizon

Another solution to the routing loop problem is called *split horizon*. This reduces incorrect routing information and routing overhead in a distance-vector network by enforcing the rule that information cannot be sent back in the direction from which it was received. It would have prevented Router A from sending the updated information it received from Router B back to Router B.

Route Poisoning

Another way to avoid problems caused by inconsistent updates is *route poisoning*. For example, when Network 5 goes down, Router E initiates route poisoning by entering a table entry for Network 5 as 16, or unreachable (sometimes referred to as *infinite*). By this poisoning of the route to Network 5, Router C is not susceptible to incorrect updates about the route to Network 5. When Router C receives a router poisoning from Router E, it sends an update, called a *poison reverse*, back to Router E. This makes sure all routes on the segment have received the poisoned route information.

Route poisoning, used with holddowns (discussed next), will speed up convergence time because neighboring routers don't have to wait 30 seconds (an eternity in computer land) before advertising the poisoned route.

Holddowns

And then there are *holddowns*. These prevent regular update messages from reinstating a route that has gone down. Holddowns also help prevent routes from changing too rapidly by allowing time for either the downed route to come back or the network to stabilize somewhat before changing to the next best route. These also tell routers to restrict, for a specific time period, any changes that might affect recently removed routes. This prevents inoperative routers from being prematurely restored to other routers' tables.

When a router receives an update from a neighbor indicating that a previously accessible network is not working and is inaccessible, the holddown timer will start. If a new update arrives from a neighbor with a better metric than the original network entry, the holddown is removed and data is passed. However, if an update is received from a neighbor router before the holddown timer expires and it has a lower metric than the previous route, the update is ignored and the holddown timer keeps ticking. This allows more time for the network to converge.

Holddowns use triggered updates, which reset the holddown timer, to alert the neighbor routers of a change in the network. Unlike update messages from neighbor routers, triggered updates create a new routing table that is sent immediately to neighbor routers because a change was detected in the internetwork.

There are three instances when triggered updates will reset the holddown timer:

1. The holddown timer expires.

2. The router receives a processing task proportional to the number of links in the internetwork.

3. Another update is received indicating the network status has changed.

Routing Information Protocol (RIP)

Routing Information Protocol (RIP) is a true distance-vector routing protocol. It sends the complete routing table out to all active interfaces every 30 seconds. RIP only uses hop count to determine the best way to a remote network, but it has a maximum allowable hop count of 15, meaning that 16 is deemed unreachable. RIP works well in small networks, but it is inefficient on large networks with slow WAN links or on networks with a large number of routers installed.

RIP version 1 uses only classful routing, which means that all devices in the network must use the same subnet mask. This is because RIP version 1 does not send updates with subnet mask information in tow. RIP version 2 provides what is called prefix routing and does send subnet mask information with the route updates. This is called *classless routing*. Only RIP version 1 is discussed further in this book because that is what the CCNA objectives cover.

RIP Timers

RIP uses three different kinds of timers to regulate its performance:

Route update timer   Sets the interval (typically 30 seconds) between periodic routing updates, in which the router sends a complete copy of its routing table out to all neighbors.

Route invalid timer   Determines the length of time that must expire (90 seconds) before a router determines that a route has become invalid. It will come to this conclusion if it hasn't heard any updates about a particular route for that period. When that happens, the router will send out updates to all its neighbors letting them know that the route is invalid.

Route flush timer   Sets the time between a route becoming invalid and its removal from the routing table (240 seconds). Before it is removed from the table, the router notifies its neighbors of that route's impending doom. The value of the route invalid timer must be less than that of the route flush timer. This is to provide the router with enough time to tell its neighbors about the invalid route before the routing table is updated.

Configuring RIP Routing

To configure RIP routing, just turn on the protocol with the `router rip` command and tell the RIP routing protocol which networks to advertise. That's it. As an example, let's configure our four-router internetwork with RIP routing.

2621A

RIP has an administrative distance of 120. Static routes have an administrative distance of 1 by default and, since you currently have static routes configured, the routing tables won't be propagated with RIP information. The first thing you need to do is to delete the static routes off each router. This is done with the `no ip route` command. Notice that in the 2621A router output below you must type the whole `ip route` command to delete the entry.

```
2621A#config t
Enter configuration commands, one per line.  End with
CNTL/Z.
2621A(config)#no ip route 172.16.20.0 255.255.255.0
172.16.10.2
```

```
2621A(config)#no ip route 172.16.30.0 255.255.255.0
172.16.10.2
2621A(config)#no ip route 172.16.40.0 255.255.255.0
172.16.10.2
2621A(config)#no ip route 172.16.50.0 255.255.255.0
172.16.10.2
```

Once the static routes are deleted from the configuration, you can add the RIP routing protocol by using the `router rip` command and the `network` command. The `network` command tells the routing protocol which network to advertise. Notice that in the router configuration below the routing protocol is not told which subnets to advertise; it is told the classful boundary. RIP will find the subnets and advertise them.

```
2621A(config)#router rip
2621A(config-router)#network 172.16.0.0
2621A(config-router)#^Z
2621A#
```

That's it. Two commands, and you're done—sure makes your job a lot easier than when using static routes, doesn't it? However, keep in mind the extra router CPU process and bandwidth that you're consuming.

2501A

To configure RIP on the 2501A router, you need to remove the three static routes you added from the earlier example. Once you make sure no routes are in the routing table with a better administrative distance than 120, you can add RIP. Again, if you do not remove the static routes, RIP routes will never be used on the router.

```
2501A#config t
Enter configuration commands, one per line.  End with
CNTL/Z.
2501A(config)#no ip route 172.16.30.0 255.255.255.0
172.16.20.2
2501A(config)#no ip route 172.16.40.0 255.255.255.0
172.16.20.2
2501A(config)#no ip route 172.16.50.0 255.255.255.0
172.16.20.2
2501A(config)#router rip
```

```
2501A(config-router)#network 172.16.0.0
2501A(config-router)#^Z
2501A#
```

It doesn't get much easier than this.

2501B

The 2501B router had only two static routes. Once you remove those, you can turn on RIP routing.

```
2501B#config t
Enter configuration commands, one per line.  End with
CNTL/Z.
2501B(config)#no ip route 172.16.10.0 255.255.255.0
172.16.20.1
2501B(config)#no ip route 172.16.50.0 255.255.255.0
172.16.40.2
2501B(config)#router rip
2501B(config-router)#network 172.16.0.0
2501B(config-router)#^Z
2501B#
```

There is still one more router to configure RIP routing.

2501C

The 2501C has only a default router because of the default route command. Once you remove the default route, you can add RIP routing.

```
RouterC#config t
Enter configuration commands, one per line.  End with
CNTL/Z.
RouterC(config)#no ip route 0.0.0.0 0.0.0.0 172.16.40.1
RouterC(config)#router rip
RouterC(config-router)#network 172.16.0.0
RouterC(config-router)#^Z
RouterC#
05:10:31: %SYS-5-CONFIG_I: Configured from console by
console
```

It is important to remember why we are doing this. Directly connected routes have an administrative distance of 0, static routes have an administrative distance of 1, and RIP has an administrative distance of 120. I call RIP the gossip protocol because it reminds me of junior high school, where if you hear a rumor, it must be true. That's how RIP behaves on an internetwork— exactly like my 14-year-old son.

Verifying the RIP Routing Tables

Each routing table should now have the routers' directly connected routes as well as RIP-injected routes received from neighbor routers.

The router output below shows the contents of the 2621A routing table.

```
2621A#sh ip route
Codes: C - connected, S - static, I - IGRP, R - RIP, M - [output cut]
Gateway of last resort is not set

     172.16.0.0/24 is subnetted, 5 subnets
R       172.16.50.0 [120/3] via 172.16.10.2, FastEthernet0/0
R       172.16.40.0 [120/2] via 172.16.10.2, FastEthernet0/0
R       172.16.30.0 [120/2] via 172.16.10.2, FastEthernet0/0
R       172.16.20.0 [120/1] via 172.16.10.2, FastEthernet0/0
C       172.16.10.0 is directly connected, FastEthernet0/0
2621A#
```

In this output, notice that the routing table has the same entries that the routing tables had when you were using static routes. However, the R means that the networks were added dynamically using the RIP routing protocol. The [120/3] is the administrative distance of the route (120) along with the number of hops to that remote network (3).

The next router output displays the routing table of the 2501A routers.

```
2501A#sh ip route
Codes: C - connected, S - static, I - IGRP, R - RIP, M - [output cut]
Gateway of last resort is not set

     172.16.0.0/24 is subnetted, 5 subnets
```

```
R        172.16.50.0 [120/2] via 172.16.20.2, 00:00:11, Serial0
R        172.16.40.0 [120/1] via 172.16.20.2, 00:00:11, Serial0
R        172.16.30.0 [120/1] via 172.16.20.2, 00:00:11, Serial0
C        172.16.20.0 is directly connected, Serial0
C        172.16.10.0 is directly connected, Ethernet0
2501A#
```

Notice that in the output above, the same networks are again in the routing table, and you didn't have to put them there manually.

The router output below shows the routing tables for the 2501B and 2501C routers.

```
2501B#sh ip route
Codes: C - connected, S - static, I - IGRP, R - RIP, M – [output cut]
Gateway of last resort is not set

     172.16.0.0/24 is subnetted, 5 subnets
R        172.16.50.0 [120/1] via 172.16.40.2, 00:00:26, Serial1
C        172.16.40.0 is directly connected, Serial1
C        172.16.30.0 is directly connected, Ethernet0
C        172.16.20.0 is directly connected, Serial0
R        172.16.10.0 [120/1] via 172.16.20.1, 00:00:04, Serial0
2501B#
```

```
RouterC#sh ip route
Codes: C - connected, S - static, I - IGRP, R - RIP, M – [output cut]
Gateway of last resort is not set

     172.16.0.0/24 is subnetted, 5 subnets
C        172.16.50.0 is directly connected, Ethernet0
C        172.16.40.0 is directly connected, Serial0
R        172.16.30.0 [120/1] via 172.16.40.1, 00:00:06, Serial0
R        172.16.20.0 [120/1] via 172.16.40.1, 00:00:06, Serial0
R        172.16.10.0 [120/2] via 172.16.40.1, 00:00:06, Serial0
RouterC#
```

RIP has worked well in our little internetwork. However, since this technique has a maximum hop count of only 15 hops (where 16 is deemed unreachable) and performs full routing-table updates every 30 seconds, it can cause havoc on a larger internetwork.

Holding Down RIP Propagations

You may not want your RIP network advertised everywhere on your LAN and WAN. For instance, there is no advantage to advertising your RIP network to the Internet.

There are a few different ways to stop unwanted RIP updates from propagating across your LANs and WANs. The easiest way to do this is through the `passive-interface` command. This command prevents RIP update broadcasts from being sent out a defined interface, but that same interface can still receive RIP updates.

The following is an example of how to configure a `passive-interface` on a router:

```
RouterA#config t
RouterA(config)#router rip
RouterA(config-router)#network 10.0.0.0
RouterA(config-router)#passive-interface serial 0
```

The above command will stop RIP updates from being propagated out serial interface 0, but serial interface 0 can still receive RIP updates.

Interior Gateway Routing Protocol (IGRP)

Interior Gateway Routing Protocol (IGRP) is a Cisco proprietary distance-vector routing protocol. This means that all your routers must be Cisco routers to use IGRP in your network. Cisco created this routing protocol to overcome the problems associated with RIP.

IGRP has a maximum hop count of 255 with a default of 100. This is helpful in larger networks and solves the problem of there being only 15 hops maximum possible in a RIP network. IGRP also uses a different metric from RIP. IGRP uses bandwidth and delay of the line by default as a metric for determining the best route to an internetwork. This is called a *composite metric*. Reliability, load, and Maximum Transmission Unit (MTU) can also be used, although they are not used by default.

IGRP Timers

To control performance, IGRP includes the following timers with default settings:

Update timers   These specify how frequently routing-update messages should be sent. The default is 90 seconds.

Invalid timers   These specify how long a router should wait before declaring a route invalid if it doesn't receive a specific update about it. The default is three times the update period.

Holddown timers   These specify the holddown period. The default is three times the update timer period plus 10 seconds.

Flush timers   These indicate how much time should pass before a route should be flushed from the routing table. The default is seven times the routing update period.

Configuring IGRP Routing

The command used to configure IGRP is the same as the one used to configure RIP routing with one important difference: you use an autonomous system (AS) number. All routers within an autonomous system must use the same AS number, or they will not communicate with routing information. Here is an example of how to turn on IGRP routing:

```
RouterA#config t
RouterA(config)#router igrp 10
RouterA(config-router)#network 172.16.0.0
```

Notice that the configuration in the above router commands is as simple as in RIP routing except that IGRP uses an AS number. This number advertises only to routers you want to share routing information with.

IGRP can load balance up to six unequal links. RIP networks must have the same hop count to load balance, whereas IGRP uses bandwidth to determine how to load balance. To load balance over unequal-cost links, the variance command controls the load balancing between the best metric and the worst acceptable metric.

There are two more commands that are used to help control traffic distribution among IGRP load-sharing routes: `traffic-share balanced` and `traffic-share min`.

The router output below shows the options available under the `router igrp` as command prompt.

```
Router(config-router)#variance ?
  <1-128>  Metric variance multiplier

Router(config-router)#traffic-share ?
  balanced  Share inversely proportional to metric
  min       All traffic shared among min metric paths
```

The router output above shows the `variance` command, which is the available metric multiplier. The `traffic-share` output shows the two options: `balanced` and `min`. The `traffic-share balanced` command tells the IGRP routing protocol to share inversely proportional to the metrics, and the `traffic-share min` command tells the IGRP routing process to use routes that have only minimum costs.

The load balancing and traffic sharing are covered more in depth in Sybex's *CCNP: Routing Study Guide.*

Configuring IGRP in Our Internetwork

Configuring IGRP is pretty straightforward and not much different from configuring RIP. You do need to decide on an AS number before you configure your routers. Remember that all routers in your internetwork must use the same AS number if you want them to share routing information. In our internetwork, we'll use AS 10 to configure the routers.

Okay, let's configure our internetwork with IGRP routing.

2621A

The AS number, as shown in the router output below, can be any number from 1 to 65535. A router can be a member of as many ASs as you need it to be.

```
2621A#config t
Enter configuration commands, one per line.  End with
CNTL/Z.
2621A(config)#router igrp ?
  <1-65535>  Autonomous system number

2621A(config)#router igrp 10
2621A(config-router)#netw 172.16.0.0
2621A(config-router)#^Z
2621A#
```

The `router igrp` command turns IGRP routing on in the router. As with RIP, you still need to add the network number you want to advertise. IGRP uses classful routing, which means that subnet mask information is not sent with the routing protocol updates.

2501A

To configure the 2501A router, all you need to do is turn on IGRP routing using AS 10 and then add the network number, as shown below.

```
2501A#config t
Enter configuration commands, one per line.  End with
CNTL/Z.
2501A(config)#router igrp 10
2501A(config-router)#netw 172.16.0.0
2501A(config-router)#^Z
2501A#
```

2501B

To configure 2501B, you need, once again, to turn on IGRP using AS 10.

```
2501B#config t
Enter configuration commands, one per line.  End with
CNTL/Z.
2501B(config)#router igrp 10
2501B(config-router)#netw 172.16.0.0
2501B(config-router)#^Z
2501B#
```

2501C

The last router is 2501C; you need to use AS 10 as well.

```
2501C#config t
Enter configuration commands, one per line.  End with
CNTL/Z.
2501C(config)#router igrp 10
2501C(config-router)#netw 172.16.0.0
2501C(config-router)#^Z
RouterC#
```

Verifying the IGRP Routing Tables

Once the routers are configured, you need to verify the configuration with the show ip route command.

In all of the following router outputs, notice that the only routes to networks are either directly connected or IGRP-injected routes. Since we did not turn off RIP, it is still running in the background and taking up both router CPU cycles and bandwidth. However, the routing tables will never use a RIP-found route because IGRP has a better administrative distance than RIP does.

The router output below is from the 2621A router. Notice that all routes are in the routing table.

```
2621A#sh ip route
Codes: C - connected, S - static, I - IGRP, R - RIP, M -
[output cut]
      T - traffic engineered route
Gateway of last resort is not set

    172.16.0.0/24 is subnetted, 5 subnets
I     172.16.50.0 [100/160360] via 172.16.10.2, FastEthernet0/0
I     172.16.40.0 [100/160260] via 172.16.10.2, FastEthernet0/0
I     172.16.30.0 [100/158360] via 172.16.10.2, FastEthernet0/0
I     172.16.20.0 [100/158260] via 172.16.10.2, FastEthernet0/0
C     172.16.10.0 is directly connected, FastEthernet0/0
```

The I means IGRP-injected routes. The [100/160360] is the administrative distance of IGRP and the composite metric. The lower the composite metric, the better the route.

The following router output shows the routing table for the 2501A router.

```
2501A#sh ip route
Codes: C - connected, S - static, I - IGRP, R - RIP, M -
[output cut]
      U - per-user static route, o - ODR
Gateway of last resort is not set

    172.16.0.0/24 is subnetted, 5 subnets
I     172.16.50.0 [100/160350] via 172.16.20.2, 00:00:49, Serial0
I     172.16.40.0 [100/160250] via 172.16.20.2, 00:00:49, Serial0
I     172.16.30.0 [100/158350] via 172.16.20.2, 00:00:49, Serial0
C     172.16.20.0 is directly connected, Serial0
C     172.16.10.0 is directly connected, Ethernet0
2501A#
```

The following router output shows the 2501B routing table.

```
2501B#sh ip route
Codes: C - connected, S - static, I - IGRP, R - RIP, M -
[output cut]
      U - per-user static route, o - ODR
Gateway of last resort is not set

     172.16.0.0/24 is subnetted, 5 subnets
I      172.16.50.0 [100/8576] via 172.16.40.2, 00:01:11, Serial1
C      172.16.40.0 is directly connected, Serial1
C      172.16.30.0 is directly connected, Ethernet0
C      172.16.20.0 is directly connected, Serial0
I      172.16.10.0 [100/158350] via 172.16.20.1, 00:00:36, Serial0
2501B#
```

The following router output shows the 2501C routing table.

```
2501C#sh ip route
Codes: C - connected, S - static, I - IGRP, R - RIP, M -
[output cut]
      U - per-user static route, o - ODR
Gateway of last resort is not set

     172.16.0.0/24 is subnetted, 5 subnets
C      172.16.50.0 is directly connected, Ethernet0
C      172.16.40.0 is directly connected, Serial0
I      172.16.30.0 [100/8576] via 172.16.40.1, 00:00:28, Serial0
I      172.16.20.0 [100/160250] via 172.16.40.1, 00:00:28, Serial0
I      172.16.10.0 [100/160350] via 172.16.40.1, 00:00:28, Serial0
2501C#
```

Verifying Your Configurations

It is important to verify your configurations once you have completed them, or at least, once you *think* you have completed them. The following list includes the commands you can use to verify the routed and routing protocols configured on your Cisco routers. The first command is covered in the previous section; the others are covered in upcoming sections.

- show ip route
- show protocols
- show ip protocol
- debug ip rip
- debug ip igrp events
- debug ip igrp transactions

The *Show Protocols* Command

The show protocols command is useful because it shows you the Network layer addresses configured on each interface.

```
2501B#sh protocol
Global values:
   Internet Protocol routing is enabled
Ethernet0 is up, line protocol is up
   Internet address is 172.16.30.1/24
Serial0 is up, line protocol is up
   Internet address is 172.16.20.2/24
Serial1 is up, line protocol is up
   Internet address is 172.16.40.1/24
2501B#
```

The output above shows the IP address of the Ethernet 0, serial 0, and serial 1 interfaces of the 2501B router. If IPX or AppleTalk were configured on the router, those network addresses would have appeared as well.

The *Show IP Protocol* Command

The show ip protocol command shows you the routing protocols that are configured on your router. Notice in the following output that both RIP and IGRP are running on the router, but only IGRP appears in the routing table because of its lower administrative distance.

The show ip protocols command also displays the timers used in the routing protocol. Notice in the output below that RIP is sending updates every 30 seconds, which is the default. Notice further down that RIP is routing for network 172.16.0.0, and the two neighbors it found are 172.16.40.2 and 172.16.20.1.

```
2501B#sh ip protocol
Routing Protocol is "rip"
  Sending updates every 30 seconds, next due in 6 seconds
  Invalid after 180 seconds, hold down 180, flushed after
240
  Outgoing update filter list for all interfaces is
  Incoming update filter list for all interfaces is
  Redistributing: rip
  Default version control: send version 1, receive any
version
    Interface      Send   Recv   Key-chain
    Ethernet0      1      1 2
    Serial0        1      1 2
    Serial1        1      1 2
  Routing for Networks:
    172.16.0.0
  Routing Information Sources:
    Gateway         Distance       Last Update
    172.16.40.2         120        00:00:21
    172.16.20.1         120        00:00:23
  Distance: (default is 120)
```

In the preceding router output, the last entry is the default administrative distance for RIP (120).

The router output below shows the IGRP routing information. The default update timer is 90 seconds by default, and the administrative distance is 100.

```
Routing Protocol is "igrp 10"
  Sending updates every 90 seconds, next due in 42 seconds
  Invalid after 270 seconds, hold down 280, flushed after
630
  Outgoing update filter list for all interfaces is
  Incoming update filter list for all interfaces is
  Default networks flagged in outgoing updates
  Default networks accepted from incoming updates
  IGRP metric weight K1=1, K2=0, K3=1, K4=0, K5=0
  IGRP maximum hopcount 100
  IGRP maximum metric variance 1
  Redistributing: eigrp 10, igrp 10
  Routing for Networks:
    172.16.0.0
  Routing Information Sources:
    Gateway          Distance      Last Update
    172.16.40.2          100       00:00:47
    172.16.20.1          100       00:01:18
  Distance: (default is 100)
```

The information included in the show ip protocols command includes the AS, routing timers, networks being advertised, gateways, and administrative distance (100).

The invalid timer is set at 270 seconds; it is three times the update timer. If a router update is not received in three update periods, the route is considered invalid. The holddown timer is 280, which is around three times the update timer. This is the number of seconds a route is suppressed while waiting for a new update to be received. If a new update is not received before the holddown timer expires, the flush timer will start. When the flush timer expires, the route is removed from the router.

The *Debug IP RIP* Command

The debug ip rip command sends routing updates as they are sent and received on the router to the console session. If you are telnetted into the router, you'll need to type the command terminal monitor to be able to receive the output from the debug commands.

Notice in the following router output that RIP is both sent and received on serial 1, serial 0, and Ethernet 0 interfaces. This is a great troubleshooting tool. The metric is the hop count.

```
2501B#debug ip rip
RIP protocol debugging is on
2501B#
07:12:56: RIP: received v1 update from 172.16.40.2 on
Serial1
07:12:56:        172.16.50.0 in 1 hops
07:12:56: RIP: received v1 update from 172.16.20.1 on
Serial0
07:12:56:        172.16.10.0 in 1 hops
07:12:58: RIP: sending v1 update to 255.255.255.255 via
Ethernet0 (172.16.30.1)
07:12:58:        subnet  172.16.40.0, metric 1
07:12:58:        subnet  172.16.20.0, metric 1
07:12:58: RIP: sending v1 update to 255.255.255.255 via
Serial0 (172.16.20.2)
07:12:58:        subnet  172.16.40.0, metric 1
07:12:58:        subnet  172.16.30.0, metric 1
07:12:58: RIP: sending v1 update to 255.255.255.255 via
Serial1 (172.16.40.1)
07:12:58:        subnet  172.16.30.0, metric 1
07:12:58:        subnet  172.16.20.0, metric 1
2501B#undebug all
All possible debugging has been turned off
2501B#
```

To turn off debugging, use the undebug all or the no debug all command. You can also use the un all shortcut command.

The *Debug IP IGRP* Command

With the debug ip igrp command, there are two options, events and transactions, as shown in the router output below:

```
2501B#debug ip igrp ?
  events       IGRP protocol events
  transactions  IGRP protocol transactions
```

The difference between these commands is explained in the following sections.

The *Debug IP IGRP Events* Command

The debug ip igrp events command is a summary of the IGRP routing information that is running on the network. The following router output shows the source and destination of each update as well as the number of routers in each update. Information about individual routes is not generated with this command.

```
2501B#debug ip igrp events
IGRP event debugging is on
07:13:50: IGRP: received request from 172.16.40.2 on
Serial1
07:13:50: IGRP: sending update to 172.16.40.2 via Serial1
(172.16.40.1)
07:13:51: IGRP: Update contains 3 interior, 0 system, and
0 exterior routes.
07:13:51: IGRP: Total routes in update: 3
07:13:51: IGRP: received update from 172.16.40.2 on
Serial1
07:13:51: IGRP: Update contains 1 interior, 0 system, and
0 exterior routes.
07:13:51: IGRP: Total routes in update: 1
2501B#un
07:13:52: IGRP: received update from 172.16.40.2 on
Serial1
07:13:52: IGRP: Update contains 1 interior, 0 system, and
0 exterior routes.
```

```
07:13:52: IGRP: Total routes in update: 1
2501B#un all
All possible debugging has been turned off
```

You can turn the command off with the undebug all command.

The *Debug IP IGRP Transactions* Command

The debug ip igrp transactions command shows message requests from neighbor routers asking for an update and the broadcasts sent from your router towards that neighbor router.

In the following output, a request was received from a neighbor router on network 172.16.40.2 to serial 1 of 2501B. The 2501B router responded with an update packet.

```
2501B#debug ip igrp transactions
IGRP protocol debugging is on
07:14:05: IGRP: received request from 172.16.40.2 on
Serial1
07:14:05: IGRP: sending update to 172.16.40.2 via Serial1
(172.16.40.1)
07:14:05:          subnet 172.16.30.0, metric=1100
07:14:05:          subnet 172.16.20.0, metric=158250
07:14:05:          subnet 172.16.10.0, metric=158350
07:14:06: IGRP: received update from 172.16.40.2 on
Serial1
07:14:06:          subnet 172.16.50.0, metric 8576 (neighbor
1100)

2501B#un all
All possible debugging has been turned off
2501B#
```

You can turn off the command with the undebug all command (un al for short).

Summary

This chapter covered IP routing in detail. It is important that you understand the basics covered in this chapter because everything that is done on a Cisco router must have some type of IP routing configured and running. This chapter covered the following topics:

- IP routing and how frames are used to transport packets between routers and to the destination host

- Static routing and how an administrator can use it in a Cisco internetwork

- Default routing and how default routing can be used in stub networks

- Dynamic routing and how to solve loops in distance-vector routing protocols

- Configuring and verifying RIP routing

- Configuring and verifying IGRP routing

Key Terms

Before you take the exam, be sure you're familiar with the following terms:

classless routing

composite metric

holddown

hop count

poison reverse updates

route poisoning

split horizon

Commands in This Chapter

Command	Description
show ip route	Displays the IP routing table
IP route	Creates static and default routes on a router
IP classless	Is a global configuration command used to tell a router to forward packets to a default route when the destination network is not in the routing table
router RIP	Turns on IP RIP routing on a router
network	Tells the routing protocol what network to advertise
No IP route	Removes a static or default route
router igrp as	Turns on IP IGRP routing on a router
variance	Controls the load balancing between the best metric and the worst acceptable metric
traffic-share balanced	Tells the IGRP routing protocol to share links inversely proportional to the metrics
traffic-share min	Tells the IGRP routing process to use routes that have only minimum costs
show protocols	Shows the routed protocols and network addresses configured on each interface

Command	Description
show ip protocols	Shows the routing protocols and timers associated with each routing protocol configured on a router
debug ip rip	Sends console messages displaying information about RIP packets being sent and received on a router interface
debug ip igrp events	Provides a summary of the IGRP routing information running on the network
debug ip igrp transactions	Shows message requests from neighbor routers asking for an update and the broadcasts sent from your router to that neighbor router

Written Lab

Write the answers to the following questions.

1. Create a static route to network 172.16.10.0/24 with a next hop gateway of 172.16.20.1 and an administrative distance of 150.

2. Write the commands used to turn RIP routing on in a router and advertise network 10.0.0.0.

3. Write the commands to stop a router from propagating RIP information out serial 1.

4. Write the commands to create an AS 10 with IGRP in your 172.16.0.0 network.

5. Write the commands to configure a default route on a router to go to 172.16.50.3.

6. What works with triggered updates to help stop routing loops in distance-vector networks?

7. What stops routing loops in distance-vector networks by sending out a maximum hop count as soon as a link fails?

8. What stops routing loops in distance-vector networks by not resending information learned on an interface out that same interface?

9. The _____ command controls the load balancing between the best metric and the worst acceptable metric.

10. What command is used to send routing updates as they are sent and received on the router to the console session?

Hands-on Labs

In the following hands-on labs, you will configure a network with three 2501 routers and one 2621 router.

The following labs will be covered:

Lab 5.1: Creating Static Routes

Lab 5.2: Dynamic Routing with RIP

Lab 5.3: Dynamic Routing with IGRP

Figure 5.9 will be used to configure all routers.

FIGURE 5.9 Hands-on lab internetwork

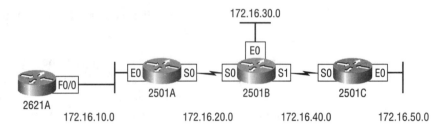

Lab 5.1: Creating Static Routes

In this first lab, you will create a static route in all four routers so that the routers see all networks. Verify with the Ping program when complete.

1. The 2621 router is connected to network 172.16.10.0/24. It does not know about networks 172.16.20.0/24, 172.16.30.0/24, 172.16.40.0/24, and 172.16.50.0/24. Create static routes so that the 2621 router can see all networks, as shown here.

```
2621#config t
2621(config)#ip route 172.16.20.0 255.255.255.0
172.16.10.1
2621(config)#ip route 172.16.30.0 255.255.255.0
172.16.10.1
```

```
2621(config)#ip route 172.16.40.0 255.255.255.0
172.16.10.1
2621(config)#ip route 172.16.50.0 255.255.255.0
172.16.10.1
```

2. Save the current configuration for the 2621 router by going to the enabled mode, typing **copy run start**, and pressing Enter.

3. On Router A, create a static route to see networks 172.16.10.0/24, 172.16.30.0/24, 172.16.40.0/24, and 172.16.50.0/24, as shown here.

```
RouterA#config t
RouterA(config)#ip route 172.16.30.0 255.255.255.0
172.16.20.2
RouterA(config)#ip route 172.16.40.0 255.255.255.0
172.16.20.2
RouterA(config)#ip route 172.16.50.0 255.255.255.0
172.16.20.2
```

These commands told Router A to get to network 172.16.30.0/24 and use either IP address 172.16.20.2, which is the closet neighbor interface connected to network 172.16.30.0/24, or Router B. This is the same interface you will use to get to networks 172.16.40.0/24 and 172.16.50.0/24.

4. Save the current configuration for Router A by going to the enabled mode, typing **copy run start**, and pressing Enter.

5. On Router B, create a static route to see networks 172.16.10.0/24 and 172.16.50.0/24, which are not directly connected. Create static routes so that Router B can see all networks, as shown here.

```
RouterB#config t
RouterB(config)#ip route 172.16.10.0 255.255.255.0
172.16.20.1
RouterB(config)#ip route 172.16.50.0 255.255.255.0
172.16.40.2
```

The first command told Router B that to get to network 172.16.10.0/24, it needs to use 172.16.20.1. The next command told Router B to get to network 172.16.50.0/24 through 172.16.40.2.

Save the current configuration for Router B by going to the enable mode, typing **copy run start**, and pressing Enter.

6. Router C is connected to networks 172.16.50.0/24 and 172.16.40.0/24. It does not know about networks 172.16.30.0/24, 172.16.20.0/24, and 172.16.10.0/24. Create static routes so that Router C can see all networks, as shown here.

```
RouterC#config t
RouterC(config)#ip route 172.16.30.0 255.255.255.0
172.16.40.1
RouterC(config)#ip route 172.16.20.0 255.255.255.0
172.16.40.1
RouterA(config)#ip route 172.16.10.0 255.255.255.0
172.16.40.1
```

Save the current configuration for Router C by going to the enable mode, typing **copy run start**, and pressing Enter.

Now ping from each router to your hosts and from each router to each router. If it is set up correctly, it will work.

Lab 5.2: Dynamic Routing with RIP

In this lab, we will use the dynamic routing protocol RIP instead of static and default routing.

1. Remove any static routes or default routes configured on your routers by using the no ip route command. For example:

```
RouterA#config t
RouterA(config)#no ip route 172.16.10.0
255.255.255.0 172.16.11.2
RouterA(config)#no ip route 172.16.30.0
255.255.255.0 172.16.20.2
RouterA(config)#no ip route 172.16.40.0
255.255.255.0 172.16.20.2
RouterA(config)#no ip route 172.16.50.0
255.255.255.0 172.16.20.2
RouterA(config)#no ip route 172.16.55.0
255.255.255.0 172.16.20.2
```

Do the same thing for Routers B and C and the 2621 router. Type **sh run** and press Enter on each router to verify that all static and default routes are cleared.

2. After your static and default routers are clear, go into configuration mode on Router A by typing **config t.**

3. Tell your router to use RIP routing by typing **router rip** and pressing Enter, as shown here:

```
config t
router rip
```

4. Add the network number you want to advertise by typing **network 172.16.0.0** and pressing Enter.

5. Press Ctrl+Z to get out of configuration mode.

6. Go to Routers B and C and the 2621 router and type the same commands, as shown here:

```
Config t
Router rip
Network 172.16.0.0
```

7. Verify that RIP is running at each router by typing the following commands at each router:

```
show ip protocol
show ip route
show running-config  or show run
```

8. Save your configurations by typing **copy run start** or **copy running-config startup-config** and pressing Enter at each router.

9. Verify the network by pinging all remote networks and hosts.

Lab 5.3: Dynamic Routing with IGRP

In this lab, you will run the IGRP routing protocol simultaneously with RIP routing.

1. Log into your routers and go into privileged mode by typing **en** or **enable.**

2. Keep RIP running on your routers and verify that it is running on each router. If you want to remove RIP, you can use the no `router rip`

global configuration command to remove it from each router. For example,

```
config t
no router rip
```

3. From the configuration mode on Router A, type **router igrp ?**.

4. Notice that it asks for an autonomous system number. This is used to allow only routers with the same AS number to communicate. Type **10** and press Enter. Your router can be configured to be part of as many different ASs as necessary.

5. At the config-router prompt, type **network 172.16.0.0**. Notice that we add the classful network boundary to advertise rather than the subnet numbers.

6. Press Ctrl+Z to get out of configuration mode.

7. Go to Routers B and C and the 2621 router and type the commands shown here:

```
RouterB(config)#router igrp 10
RouterB(config-router)#network 172.16.0.0
```

8. Verify that IGRP is running by typing the following command at each router:

```
show ip protocol
```

Notice that this shows you your RIP and IGRP routing protocols and the update timers.

```
sh ip route
```

This should let you see all eight subnets: 10, 11, 15, 20, 30, 40, 50, and 55. Some will be directly connected, and some will be I routes, which are IGRP-injected routes. RIP is still running, but if you look at the routing table, you'll notice the network entry has a network number (100/23456). The first number (100) is the trustworthiness rating. Since RIP's default trustworthiness rating is 120, the IGRP route is used before a RIP route is used. The second number is the metric, or weight, of the route that is used to determine the best path to a network.

show running-config

This lets you see that RIP and IGRP are configured.

9. To save your configurations, type **copy running-config startup-config** or **copy run start** and press Enter at each router.

10. Verify the network by pinging all routers, switches, and hosts.

Review Questions

1. What is the routing algorithm used by RIP?

   A. Routed information

   B. Link together

   C. Link state

   D. Distance vector

2. What is the routing algorithm used by IGRP?

   A. Routed information

   B. Link together

   C. Link state

   D. Distance vector

3. Which command can you type at the router prompt to verify the broadcast frequency for IGRP?

   A. `sh ip route`

   B. `sh ip protocol`

   C. `sh ip broadcast`

   D. `debug ip igrp`

4. What is the routing metric used by RIP?

   A. Count to infinity

   B. Hop count

   C. TTL

   D. Bandwidth, delay

5. What command is used to stop routing updates from exiting out an interface?

   A. Router(config-if)#**no routing**

   B. Router(config-if)#**passive-interface**

   C. Router(config-router)#**passive-interface s0**

   D. Router(config-router)#**no routing updates**

6. What is the default routing metric used by IGRP? (Choose all that apply.)

   A. Count to infinity

   B. Hop count

   C. TTL

   D. Bandwidth

   E. Delay

7. What does a metric of 16 hops represent in a RIP routing network?

   A. 16ms

   B. Number of routers in the internetwork

   C. Number of hops

   D. 16 hops—unreachable

   E. Last hop available

8. What are holddowns used for?

   A. To hold down the protocol from going to the next hop

   B. To prevent regular update messages from reinstating a route that has gone down

   C. To prevent regular update messages from reinstating a route that has just come up

   D. To prevent irregular update messages from reinstating a route that has gone down

9. What is split horizon?

A. When a router differentiates on which interface a packet arrived and does not advertise that information back out the same interface.

B. When you have a large bus (horizon) physical network, it splits the traffic.

C. It holds the regular updates from broadcasting to a downed link.

D. It prevents regular update messages from reinstating a route that has gone down.

10. What is poison reverse?

A. It sends back the protocol received from a router as a poison pill, which stops the regular updates.

B. It is information received from a router that can't be sent back to the originating router.

C. It prevents regular update messages from reinstating a route that has just come up.

D. It describes when a router sets the metric for a downed link to infinity.

11. What is the default administrative distance for IGRP?

A. 90

B. 100

C. 120

D. 220

12. Which of the following is a correct default route?

A. `route ip 172.0.0.0 255.0.0.0 s0`

B. `ip route 0.0.0.0 0.0.0.0 172.16.20.1`

C. `ip route 0.0.0.0 255.255.255.255 172.16.20.1`

D. `route ip 0.0.0.0 0.0.0.0 172.16.10.1150`

13. Which of the following is an IP link state protocol?

    A. RIP V2

    B. EIGRP

    C. OSPF

    D. IGRP

14. What commands are available for supporting RIP networks? (Choose all that apply.)

    A. `sh ip route`

    B. `sh ip rip`

    C. `sh rip network`

    D. `debug ip rip`

15. Which of the following statements is true about distance-vector-based networks? (Choose the best answer.)

    A. They send out partial updates every 60 seconds.

    B. They send their complete routing table every 60 seconds.

    C. They send their entire routing table every 30 seconds.

    D. They update every 90 seconds.

16. Which Cisco IOS command can you use to see the IP routing table?

    A. `sh ip config`

    B. `sh ip arp`

    C. `sh ip route`

    D. `sh ip table`

17. What is the administrative distance used for in routing?

   A. Determining the network administrator for entering that route

   B. Creating a database

   C. Rating the source's trustworthiness, expressed as a numeric value from 0 to 255

   D. Rating the source's trustworthiness, expressed as a numeric value from 0 to 1023

18. When looking at a routing table, what does the S mean?

   A. Dynamically connected

   B. Directly connected

   C. Statically connected

   D. Sending packets

19. Which of the following is true about IP routing?

   A. The destination IP address changes at each hop.

   B. The source IP address changes at each hop.

   C. The frame does not change at each hop.

   D. The frame changes at each hop.

20. Which of the following is true when creating static routes? (Choose all that apply.)

   A. The mask parameter is optional.

   B. The gateway parameter is required.

   C. The administrative distance is required.

   D. The administrative distance is optional.

   E. None of the above.

Answers to the Written Lab

1. `ip route 172.16.10.0 255.255.255.0 172.16.20.1 150`

2. `config t`
   `router rip`
   `network 10.0.0.0`

3. `config t`
   `router rip`
   `passive-interface serial 1`

4. `config t`
   `router igrp 10`
   `network 172.16.0.0`

5. `config t`
   `ip route 0.0.0.0 0.0.0.0 172.16.50.3`

6. Holddown timers

7. Poison reverse

8. Split horizon

9. `variance`

10. `debug ip rip`

Answers to Review Questions

1. D. RIP uses the distance-vector routing algorithm and uses only hop count as a metric to determine the best path to an internetwork.

2. D. IGRP is Cisco's proprietary distance-vector routing algorithm.

3. B. The command `show ip protocol` will show you the configured routing protocols on your router, which includes the timers.

4. B. RIP only uses hop count to determine the best path to a remote network.

5. C. The config-router `passive-interface` command stops updates from being sent out an interface.

6. D, E. Bandwidth and delay of the line are used by IGRP to determine the best way to a remote network.

7. D. RIP, by default, is only configured to run 15 hops; 16 is deemed unreachable.

8. B. Holddowns prevent regular update messages from reinstating a downed route.

9. A. Split horizon will not advertise a route back to the same router it learned the route from.

10. D. Poison reverse is used to communicate to a router that the router understands the link is down and that the hop count to that network is set to infinity, or unreachable.

11. B. IGRP default administrative distance is 100; RIP's default administrative distance is 120.

12. B. An IP route with a wildcard of all zeroes for the destination network and subnet mask is used to create a default route.

13. C. OSPF (Open Shortest Path First) is a true link state IP routing protocol. It uses only bandwidth as a way to determine the best path to a remote network.

14. A, D. The commands `show ip route` and `debug ip rip` are used to support and verify RIP networks.

15. C. Distance-vector routing protocols send their complete routing table out all active interfaces. RIP is every 30 seconds. The best answer is C, because unlike D, it describes the entire routing table being broadcast.

16. C. The command `show ip route` shows the IP routing table, the metric used, and the interface used to find a remote network.

17. C. The administrative distance is used in routing to decide the trustworthiness of a route. 0 is the highest rating.

18. C. Statically connected routes are identified in the routing table with an S.

19. D. In IP routing, the frame is replaced at each hop as the packet traverses the internetwork.

20. B, D. In static routes, you must enter a destination network and mask and either the next hop router or interface to that router; the administrative distance is optional.

Virtual LANs (VLANs)

THE CCNA EXAM TOPICS COVERED IN THIS CHAPTER INCLUDE THE FOLLOWING:

- ✓ Describe Virtual LANs
- ✓ Describe Frame Tagging
- ✓ Describe Inter-Switch Link Routing
- ✓ Describe Virtual Trunking Protocol

A Virtual Local Area Network (VLAN) is a logical grouping of network users and resources connected to administratively defined ports on a switch. By creating VLANs, you are able to create smaller broadcast domains within a switch by assigning different ports in the switch to different subnetworks. A VLAN is treated like its own subnet or broadcast domain. This means that frames broadcasted onto a network are only switched between ports in the same VLAN.

Using virtual LANs, you're no longer confined to creating workgroups by physical locations. VLANs can be organized by location, function, department, or even the application or protocol used, regardless of where the resources or users are located.

In this chapter, you will learn what a VLAN is and how VLAN memberships are used in a switched internetwork. Also, I'll discuss how Virtual Trunk Protocol (VTP) is used to update switch databases with VLAN information. Trunking FastEthernet links will also be discussed. Trunking allows you to send information about all VLANs across one link.

Virtual LANs

In a layer-2 switched network, the network is flat, as shown in Figure 6.1. Every broadcast packet transmitted is seen by every device on the network, regardless of whether the device needs to receive the data.

FIGURE 6.1 Flat network structure

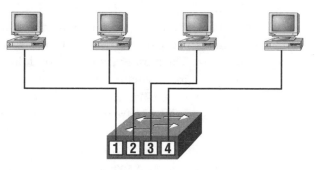

- Each segment has its own collision domain.
- All segments are in the same broadcast domain.

Because layer-2 switching creates individual collision domain segments for each device plugged into the switch, the Ethernet distance constraints are lifted, which means larger networks can be built. The larger the number of users and devices, the more broadcasts and packets each device must handle.

Another problem with a flat layer-2 network is security, as all users can see all devices. You cannot stop devices from broadcasting and users trying to respond to broadcasts. Your security is passwords on the servers and other devices.

By creating VLANs, you can solve many of the problems associated with layer-2 switching, as shown in the upcoming sections.

Broadcast Control

Broadcasts occur in every protocol, but how often they occur depends upon the protocol, the application(s) running on the internetwork, and how these services are used.

Some older applications have been rewritten to reduce their bandwidth needs. However, there is a new generation of applications that are bandwidth-greedy, consuming all they can find. These are multimedia applications that use broadcasts and multicasts extensively. Faulty equipment, inadequate segmentation, and poorly designed firewalls can also add to the problems of broadcast-intensive applications. This has added a new chapter to network design, since broadcasts can propagate through the switched network. Routers, by default, send broadcasts only within the originating network, but switches forward broadcasts to all segments. This is called a *flat network* because it is one broadcast domain.

As an administrator, you must make sure the network is properly segmented to keep one segment's problems from propagating through the internetwork. The most effective way of doing this is through switching and routing. Since switches have become more cost-effective, many companies are replacing the flat network with a pure switched network and VLANs. All devices in a VLAN are members of the same broadcast domain and receive all broadcasts. The broadcasts, by default, are filtered from all ports on a switch that are not members of the same VLAN.

Routers, layer-3 switches, or route switch modules (RSMs) must be used in conjunction with switches to provide connections between networks (VLANs), which can stop broadcasts from propagating through the entire internetwork.

Security

One problem with the flat internetwork is that security was implemented by connecting hubs and switches together with routers. Security was maintained at the router, but anyone connecting to the physical network could access the network resources on that physical LAN. Also, a user could plug a network analyzer into the hub and see all the traffic in that network. Another problem was that users could join a workgroup by just plugging their workstations into the existing hub.

By using VLANs and creating multiple broadcast groups, administrators now have control over each port and user. Users can no longer just plug their workstations into any switch port and have access to network resources. The administrator controls each port and whatever resources it is allowed to use.

Because groups can be created according to the network resources a user requires, switches can be configured to inform a network management station of any unauthorized access to network resources. If inter-VLAN communication needs to take place, restrictions on a router can also be implemented. Restrictions can also be placed on hardware addresses, protocols, and applications.

Flexibility and Scalability

Layer-2 switches only read frames for filtering; they do not look at the Network layer protocol. This can cause a switch to forward all broadcasts. However, by creating VLANs, you are essentially creating broadcast domains. Broadcasts sent out from a node in one VLAN will not be forwarded to ports configured in a different VLAN. By assigning switch ports or users to VLAN groups on a switch or group of connected switches (called a *switch fabric*), you have the flexibility to add only the users you want in the broadcast domain regardless of their physical location. This can stop broadcast storms caused by a faulty network interface card (NIC) or an application from propagating throughout the entire internetwork.

When a VLAN gets too big, you can create more VLANs to keep the broadcasts from consuming too much bandwidth. The fewer users in a VLAN, the fewer users affected by broadcasts.

To understand how a VLAN looks to a switch, it's helpful to begin by first looking at a traditional collapsed backbone. Figure 6.2 shows a collapsed backbone created by connecting physical LANs to a router.

FIGURE 6.2   Physical LANs connected to a router

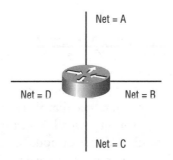

Each network is attached to the router and has its own logical network number. Each node attached to a particular physical network must match that network number to be able to communicate on the internetwork. Now let's look at what a switch accomplishes. Figure 6.3 shows how switches remove the physical boundary.

FIGURE 6.3 Switches removing the physical boundary

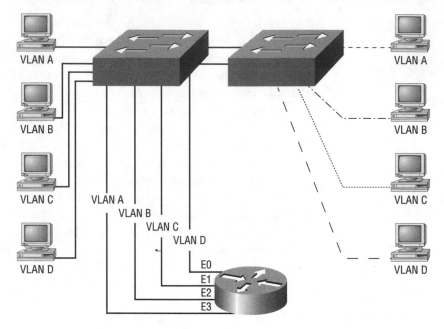

Switches create greater flexibility and scalability than routers can by themselves. You can group users into communities of interest, which are known as VLAN organizations.

Because of switches, we don't need routers anymore, right? Wrong. In Figure 6.3, notice that there are four VLANs or broadcast domains. The nodes within each VLAN can communicate with each other, but not with any other VLAN or node in another VLAN. When configured in a VLAN, the nodes think they are actually in a collapsed backbone as in Figure 6.2. What do the hosts in Figure 6.2 need to do to communicate to a node or host on a different network? They need to go through the router, or other layer-3 device, just like when they are configured for VLAN communication, as shown in Figure 6.3. Communication between VLANs, just as in physical networks, must go through a layer-3 device.

VLAN Memberships

VLANs are typically created by an administrator, who then assigns switch ports to the VLAN. These are called static VLANs. If the administrator wants to do a little more work up front and assign all the host devices' hardware addresses into a database, the switches can be configured to assign VLANs dynamically.

Static VLANs

Static VLANs are the typical way of creating VLANs and the most secure. The switch port that you assign a VLAN association always maintains that association until an administrator changes the port assignment. This type of VLAN configuration is easy to set up and monitor, working well in a network where the movement of users within the network is controlled. Using network management software to configure the ports can be helpful but is not mandatory.

Dynamic VLANs

Dynamic VLANs determine a node's VLAN assignment automatically. Using intelligent management software, you can enable hardware (MAC) addresses, protocols, or even applications to create dynamic VLANs. For example, suppose MAC addresses have been entered into a centralized VLAN management application. If a node is then attached to an unassigned switch port, the VLAN management database can look up the hardware address and assign and configure the switch port to the correct VLAN. This can make management and configuration easier for the administrator. If a user moves, the switch will automatically assign them to the correct VLAN. However, more administration is needed initially to set up the database.

Cisco administrators can use the VLAN Management Policy Server (VMPS) service to set up a database of MAC addresses that can be used for dynamic addressing of VLANs. VMPS is a MAC address–to–VLAN mapping database.

Identifying VLANs

VLANs can span multiple connected switches. Switches in this switch fabric must keep track of frames and which VLAN frames belong to. Frame tagging performs this function. Switches can then direct frames to the appropriate port.

There are two different types of links in a switched environment:

Access links   Links that are only part of one VLAN and are referred to as the native VLAN of the port. Any device attached to an access link is unaware of a VLAN membership. This device just assumes it is part of a broadcast domain, with no understanding of the physical network. Switches remove any VLAN information from the frame before it is set to an access link device. Access link devices cannot communicate with devices outside their VLAN unless the packet is routed through a router.

Trunk links   Trunks can carry multiple VLANs. Originally named after trunks of the telephone system, which carries multiple telephone conversations, trunk links are used to connect switches to other switches, to routers, or even to servers. Trunked links are supported on Fast or Gigabit Ethernet only. To identify the VLAN that a frame belongs to with Ethernet technology, Cisco switches support two different identification techniques: ISL and 802.1q. Trunk links are used to transport VLANs between devices and can be configured to transport all VLANs or just a few. Trunk links still have a native, or default, VLAN that is used if the trunk link fails.

Frame Tagging

The switch in an internetwork needs a way of keeping track of users and frames as they travel the switch fabric and VLANs. A switch fabric is a group of switches sharing the same VLAN information. Frame identification (*frame tagging*) uniquely assigns a user-defined ID to each frame. This is sometimes referred to as a VLAN ID or color.

Cisco created frame tagging to be used when an Ethernet frame traverses a trunked link. The VLAN tag is removed before exiting trunked links. Each switch that the frame reaches must identify the VLAN ID, then determine what to do with the frame based on the filter table. If the frame reaches a switch that has another trunked link, the frame will be forwarded out the trunk link port. Once the frame reaches an exit to an access link, the switch removes the VLAN identifier. The end device will receive the frames without having to understand the VLAN identification.

VLAN Identification Methods

To keep track of frames traversing a switch fabric, VLAN identification is used to identify which frames belong to which VLANs. There are multiple trunking methods:

Inter-Switch Link (ISL) Proprietary to Cisco switches, it is used for FastEthernet and Gigabit Ethernet links only. Can be used on a switch port, router interfaces, and server interface cards to trunk a server. This server trunking is good if you are creating functional VLANs and don't want to break the 80/20 rule. The server that is trunked is part of all VLANs (broadcast domains) simultaneously. The users do not have to cross a layer-3 device to access a company-shared server.

IEEE 802.1q Created by the IEEE as a standard method of frame tagging. It actually inserts a field into the frame to identify the VLAN. If you are trunking between a Cisco switched link and a different brand of switch, you have to use 802.1q for the trunk to work.

LAN emulation (LANE) Used to communicate multiple VLANs over ATM.

802.10 (FDDI) Used to send VLAN information over FDDI. Uses a SAID field in the frame header to identify the VLAN. This is proprietary to Cisco devices.

The CCNA exam covers only the ISL method of VLAN Identification.

Inter-Switch Link (ISL) Protocol

Inter-Switch Link (ISL) is a way of explicitly tagging VLAN information onto an Ethernet frame. This tagging information allows VLANs to be multiplexed over a trunk link through an external encapsulation method. By running ISL, you can interconnect multiple switches and still maintain

VLAN information as traffic travels between switches on trunk links. ISL provides a low-latency, full wire-speed performance over FastEthernet using either half- or full-duplex mode.

Cisco created the ISL protocol, and therefore ISL is proprietary in nature to Cisco devices only. If you need a non-proprietary VLAN protocol, use the 802.1q, which is covered in the *CCNP: Switching Study Guide*.

ISL is an external tagging process, which means the original frame is not altered but instead encapsulated with a new 26-byte ISL header. It also adds a second 4-byte frame check sequence (FCS) field at the end of the frame. Because the frame is encapsulated with information, only ISL-aware devices can read it. Also, the frame can be up to 1522 bytes long. Devices that receive an ISL frame may record this as a giant frame because it is over the maximum of 1518 bytes allowed on an Ethernet segment.

On multi-VLAN (trunk) ports, each frame is tagged as it enters the switch. ISL network interface cards (NICs) allow servers to send and receive frames tagged with multiple VLANs so the frames can traverse multiple VLANs without going through a router, which reduces latency. This technology can also be used with probes and certain network analyzers. It makes it easy for users to attach to servers quickly and efficiently, without going through a router every time they need to communicate with a resource. Administrators can use the ISL technology to include file servers in multiple VLANs simultaneously, for example.

It is important to understand that ISL VLAN information is added to a frame only if the frame is forwarded out a port configured as a trunk link. The ISL encapsulation is removed from the frame if the frame is forwarded out an access link.

Trunking

Trunk links are 100- or 1000Mbps point-to-point links between two switches, between a switch and router, or between a switch and server. Trunked links carry the traffic of multiple VLANs, from 1 to 1005 at a time. You cannot run trunked links on 10Mbps links.

Trunking allows you to make a single port part of multiple VLANs at the same time. The benefit of trunking is that a server, for example, can be in two broadcast domains at the same time. This will stop users from having to cross a layer-3 device (router) to log in and use the server. Also, when connecting switches together, trunk links can carry some or all VLAN information across the link. If you do not trunk these links between switches, then the switches will only send VLAN 1 information by default across the link. All VLANs are configured on a trunked link unless cleared by an administrator by hand.

Cisco switches use the Dynamic Trunking Protocol (DTP) to manage trunk negation in the Catalyst-switch engine software release 4.2 or later, using either ISL or 802.1q. DTP is a point-to-point protocol that was created to send trunk information across 802.1q trunks.

Routing between VLANs

Hosts in a VLAN are within their own broadcast domain and communicate freely. VLANs create network partitioning and traffic separation at layer 2 of the OSI specifications. To have hosts or any device communicate between VLANs, a layer-3 device is absolutely necessary.

You can use a router that has an interface for each VLAN, or a router that supports ISL routing. The least expensive router that supports ISL routing is the 2600 series router. The 1600, 1700, and 2500 series do not support ISL routing.

If you only had a few VLANs (two or three), you could get a router with two or three 10BaseT or FastEthernet connections. 10BaseT is OK, but FastEthernet will work really well.

However, if you have more VLANs available than router interfaces, you can either run ISL routing on one FastEthernet interface or buy a route switch module (RSM) for a 5000 series switch. The RSM can support up to 1005 VLANs and run on the backplane of the switch. If you use one FastEthernet interface and run ISL routing, Cisco calls this a router-on-a-stick.

VLAN Trunk Protocol (VTP)

Cisco created *VLAN Trunk Protocol (VTP)* to manage all the configured VLANs across a switched internetwork and to maintain consistency throughout the network. VTP allows an administrator to add, delete, and rename VLANs, which are then propagated to all switches.

VTP provides the following benefits to a switched network:

- Consistent VLAN configuration across all switches in the network

- Allowing VLANs to be trunked over mixed networks, like Ethernet to ATM LANE or FDDI

- Accurate tracking and monitoring of VLANs

- Dynamic reporting of added VLANs to all switches

- Plug-and-Play VLAN adding

To allow VTP to manage your VLANs across the network, you must first create a VTP server. All servers that need to share VLAN information must use the same domain name, and a switch can only be in one domain at a time. This means that a switch can only share VTP domain information with switches configured in the same VTP domain.

A VTP domain can be used if you have more than one switch connected in a network. If all switches in your network are in only one VLAN, then you don't need to use VTP. VTP information is sent between switches via a trunk port.

Switches advertise VTP-management domain information, as well as a configuration revision number and all known VLANs with any specific parameters. You can configure switches to forward VTP information through trunk ports but not accept information updates, nor update their VTP database. This is called VTP transparent mode.

If you are having problems with users adding switches to your VTP domain, you can add passwords, but remember that every switch must be set up with the same password, which may be difficult.

Switches detect the additional VLANs within a VTP advertisement and then prepare to receive information on their trunk ports with the newly defined VLAN in tow. The information would be VLAN ID, 802.10 SAID fields, or LANE information. Updates are sent out as revision numbers that are the notification plus 1. Anytime a switch sees a higher revision number, it knows the information it is receiving is more current and will overwrite the current database with the new one.

VTP Modes of Operation

There are thee different modes of operation within a VTP domain. Figure 6.4 shows all three.

FIGURE 6.4   VTP modes

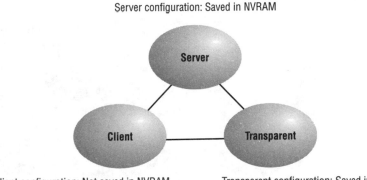

Server configuration: Saved in NVRAM

Client configuration: Not saved in NVRAM   Transparent configuration: Saved in NVRAM

Server   Is the default for all Catalyst switches. You need at least one server in your VTP domain to propagate VLAN information throughout the domain. The switch must be in server mode to be able to create, add, or delete VLANs in a VTP domain. Changing VTP information must also be done in server mode. Any change made to a switch in server mode is advertised to the entire VTP domain.

Client   Receives information from VTP servers and send and receives updates, but cannot make any changes. No ports on a client switch can be added to a new VLAN before the VTP server notifies the client switch of the new VLAN. If you want a switch to become a server, first make it a client so it receives all the correct VLAN information, then change it to a server.

Transparent   Does not participate in the VTP domain but will still forward VTP advertisements through the configured trunk links. VTP transparent switches can add and delete VLANs as the switch keeps its own database and does not share it with other switches. Transparent is considered only locally significant.

Configuration Revision Number

The revision number is the most important piece in the VTP advertisement. Figure 6.5 shows an example of how a revision number is used in an advertisement.

FIGURE 6.5 VTP revision number

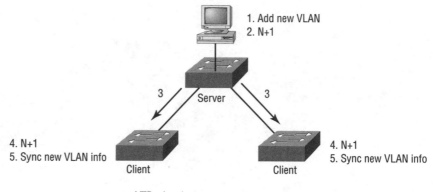

1. Add new VLAN
2. N+1

3   Server   3

4. N+1
5. Sync new VLAN info   Client

4. N+1
5. Sync new VLAN info   Client

VTP advertisements are sent every five minutes or whenever there is a change.

This figure shows a configuration revision number as "N." As a database is modified, the VTP server increments the revision number by 1. The VTP server then advertises the database with the new configuration revision number. When a switch receives an advertisement that has a higher revision number, it overwrites the database in NVRAM with the new database being advertised.

VTP Pruning

You can preserve bandwidth by configuring the VTP to reduce the amount of broadcasts, multicasts, and other unicast packets, which helps preserve bandwidth. This is called pruning. VTP pruning only sends broadcasts to trunk links that must have the information; any trunk link that does not need the broadcasts will not receive them. For example, if a switch does not have any ports configured for VLAN 5, and a broadcast is sent throughout VLAN 5, the broadcast would not traverse the trunk link to this switch. VTP pruning is disabled by default on all switches.

When you enable pruning on a VTP server, you enable it for the entire domain. By default, VLANs 2–1005 are pruning-eligible. VLAN 1 can never prune because it is an administrative VLAN.

Summary

This chapter introduced Virtual LANs and described how Cisco switches can use them. VLANs break up broadcast domains in a switched internetwork. This is important because layer-2 switches only break up collision domains and, by default, all switches make up one large broadcast domain. This chapter also described trunked VLANs across a FastEthernet link. Trunking is important in a network with multiple switches running several VLANs. We also discussed Virtual Trunk Protocol (VTP), which really has nothing to do with trunking. What it does is send VLAN information down a trunked link, but the trunk configuration is not part of VTP.

Key Terms

Be sure you're familiar with the following terms before taking the exam.

access link

broadcast domain

collision domain

dynamic VLAN

flat network

ISL routing

static VLAN

switch fabric

trunk link

Virtual LAN

VLAN Trunk Protocol (VTP)

Written Lab

In this section, write the answers to the following questions.

1. What is the VTP mode that can only accept VLAN information and not change VLAN information?

2. What is the VLAN identification method proprietary to Cisco routers?

3. VLANs break up _____ domains.

4. Switches, by default, only break up _____ domains.

5. What is the default VTP mode?

6. What does trunking provide?

7. What is frame tagging?

8. True/False: The ISL encapsulation is removed from the frame if the frame is forwarded out an access link.

9. What type of link is only part of one VLAN and is referred to as the native VLAN of the port?

10. What type of Cisco tagging information allows VLANs to be multiplexed over a trunk link through an external encapsulation method?

Review Questions

1. Which of the following is a true statement regarding VLANs? (Choose all that apply.)

   A. You must have at least two VLANs defined in every Cisco switched network.

   B. All VLANs are configured at the fastest switch and, by default, propagate this information to all other switches.

   C. You should not have more than 10 switches in the same VTP domain.

   D. VTP is used to send VLAN information to switches in a configured VTP domain.

2. What are the two ways that an administrator can configure VLAN memberships?

   A. Via a DHCP server

   B. Statically

   C. Dynamically

   D. Via a VTP database

3. What size frame is possible with ISL frames?

   A. 1518

   B. 1522

   C. 4202

   D. 8190

4. How are dynamic VLANs configured?

   A. Statically

   B. By an administrator

   C. Via a DHCP server

   D. Via a VLAN Management Policy Server

5. Which of the following protocols is used to configure trunking on a switch? (Choose all that apply.)

   A. Virtual Trunk Protocol

   B. VLAN

   C. Trunk

   D. ISL

6. Which of the following is true regarding VTP? (Choose all that apply.)

   A. VTP pruning is enabled by default on all switches.

   B. VTP pruning is disabled by default on all switches.

   C. You can only run VTP pruning on 5000 or higher switches.

   D. VTP pruning is configured on all switches by default if it is turned on in just one VTP server switch.

7. Which of the following Cisco standards encapsulates a frame and even adds a new FCS field?

   A. ISL

   B. 802.1q

   C. 802.3z

   D. 802.3u

8. What does setting the VTP mode to transparent accomplish?

   A. Transparent mode will only forward messages and advertisements, not add them to their own database.

   B. Transparent mode will both forward messages and advertisements and add them to their own database.

   C. Transparent mode will not forward messages and advertisements.

   D. Transparent mode makes a switch dynamically secure.

9. VTP provides which of the following benefits to a switched network? (Choose all that apply.)

    A. Multiple broadcast domains in VLAN 1

    B. Management of all switches and routers in an internetwork

    C. Consistency of VLAN configuration across all switches in the network

    D. Allowing VLANs to be trunked over mixed networks, like Ethernet to ATM LANE or FDDI

    E. Accurate tracking and monitoring of VLANs

    F. Dynamic reporting of added VLANs to all switches

    G. Plug-and-Play VLAN adding

    H. Plug-and-Play configuration

10. Which of the following is true regarding VTP?

    A. All switches are a VTP server by default.

    B. All switches are VTP transparent by default.

    C. VTP is on by default with a domain name of Cisco on all Cisco switches.

    D. All switches are VTP clients by default.

11. Which of the following is true regarding trunked links?

    A. They are configured by default on all switch ports.

    B. They only work with a type of Ethernet network and not Token Ring, FDDI, or ATM.

    C. You can set trunk links on any 10-, 100-, and 1000Mbps ports.

    D. You must clear the unwanted VLANs by hand.

12. When will a switch update its VTP database?

   A. Every 60 seconds.

   B. When a switch receives an advertisement that has a higher revision number, the switch will overwrite the database in NVRAM with the new database being advertised.

   C. When a switch broadcasts an advertisement that has a lower revision number, the switch will overwrite the database in NVRAM with the new database being advertised.

   D. When a switch receives an advertisement that has the same revision number, the switch will overwrite the database in NVRAM with the new database being advertised.

13. Which of the following is an IEEE standard for frame tagging?

   A. ISL

   B. 802.3z

   C. 802.1q

   D. 802.3u

14. Which of the following statements describes a trunked link?

   A. They can carry multiple VLANs.

   B. Switches remove any VLAN information from the frame before it is sent to an access link device.

   C. Access link devices cannot communicate with devices outside their VLAN unless the packet is routed through a router.

   D. Trunked links are used to transport VLANs between devices and can be configured to transport all VLANs or just a few.

15. Which of the following is true regarding an access link?

A. They can carry multiple VLANs.

B. Switches remove any VLAN information from the frame before it is sent to an access-link device.

C. Access-link devices cannot communicate with devices outside their VLAN unless the packet is routed through a router.

D. Access links are used to transport VLANs between devices and can be configured to transport all VLANs or just a few.

16. Which of the following statements describes access links?

A. They can carry multiple VLANs.

B. They are used to transport VLANs between devices and can be configured to transport all VLANs or just a few.

C. They can only be used with FastEthernet or Gigabit Ethernet.

D. They are only part of one VLAN and are referred to as the native VLAN of the port.

17. What is the IEEE method of frame tagging?

A. ISL

B. LANE

C. SAID field

D. 802.1q

18. What VTP mode does not participate in the VTP domain but will still forward VTP advertisements through the configured trunk links?

A. ISL

B. Client

C. Transparent

D. Server

19. What is the size of an ISL header?

    A. 2 bytes

    B. 6 bytes

    C. 26 bytes

    D. 1522 bytes

20. When is frame tagging used?

    A. When VLANs are traversing an access link

    B. When VLANs are traversing a trunked link

    C. When ISL is used on an access link

    D. When 802.1q is used on an access link

(The answers to the questions begin on the next page.)

Answers to the Written Lab

1. Client

2. ISL

3. broadcast

4. collision

5. Server

6. Trunking allows you to make a single port part of multiple VLANs at the same time.

7. Frame identification (frame tagging) uniquely assigns a user-defined ID to each frame. This is sometimes referred to as a VLAN ID or color.

8. True

9. Access link

10. ISL

Answers to Review Questions

1. D. Switches do not propagate VLAN information by default; you must configure the VTP domain. Virtual Trunk Protocol (VTP) is used to propagate VLAN information across a trunked link.

2. B, C. You can configure VLAN memberships on a port either statically or dynamically.

3. B. An ISL frame can be up to 1522 bytes.

4. D. A VMPS server must be configured with the hardware addresses of all hosts on the internetworks.

5. C, D. VTP is not right because it has nothing to do with trunking, except that it sends VLAN information across a trunked link. Trunk protocol and ISL are used to configure trunking on a port.

6. B, D. Pruning is disabled by default on all switches. However, if you turn on pruning on one VTP server switch, the entire VTP domain is pruning.

7. A. Inter-Switch Link (ISL) encapsulates a frame with new header and CRC information.

8. A. The transparent switch is a stand-alone switch that can be connected to your network for management. It does not add VLAN information to its VLAN database, nor does it share its configured VLAN information. It will pass VLAN-received trunked ports out a different trunked port if configured.

9. B, C, D, E, F, G. VTP is used if you have multiple switches and your network has multiple VLANs configured. VTP can help you have a stable, consistent VLAN database in all your servers.

10. A. All Cisco switches are VTP servers by default. No other VTP information is configured on a Cisco switch by default.

11. D. By default, if you create a trunked link, all VLANs are allowed on that trunked link. You must delete any unwanted VLANs by hand.

12. B. Switches look for a revision number plus 1. If that is found, they will delete their database and update the VLAN database with the new VLAN information.

13. C. 802.1q was created to allow trunked links between disparate switches.

14. A, D. Trunks are used to carry VLAN information between switches.

15. B, C. When a frame traverses a trunked link, it is encapsulated in ISL information. The ISL information is removed before the frame is sent down an access link.

16. D. Access links only carry information about one VLAN.

17. D. 802.1q is the IEEE standard for identifying VLANs as they cross a trunked link.

18. C. Transparent VTP mode passes VTP information through trunked links but does not update the VTP database with VTP information from a VTP server.

19. C. An ISL header is 26 bytes long.

20. B. Cisco created frame tagging to be used when an Ethernet frame traverses a trunked link.

Managing a Cisco Internetwork

THE CCNA EXAM TOPICS COVERED IN THIS CHAPTER INCLUDE THE FOLLOWING:

- ✓ Back up a Cisco IOS to a TFTP server
- ✓ Upgrade or restore a Cisco IOS from a TFTP server
- ✓ Back up and restore a Cisco router configuration using a TFTP server
- ✓ Use the Cisco Discovery Protocol to gather information about neighbor devices
- ✓ Create a host table on a router and resolve host names to IP addresses
- ✓ Verify your IP host table
- ✓ Use the OSI model to test IP

In this chapter, you will learn how to manage Cisco routers on an internetwork. The Internetwork Operating System (IOS) and configuration files reside in different locations in a Cisco device, and it is important to understand where these files are located and how they work.

You will learn about the main components of a router, the router boot sequence, and the configuration register, including how to use the configuration register for password recovery. Then you will learn how to manage routers by performing the following tasks:

- Backing up and restoring the Cisco IOS

- Backing up and restoring the Cisco configuration

- Gathering information about neighbor devices through CDP and Telnet

- Resolving hostnames

- Using the `ping` and `trace` commands to test network connectivity

The Internal Components of a Cisco Router

In order to configure and troubleshoot a Cisco internetwork, you need to know the major components of Cisco routers and understand what these components do. Table 7.1 describes the major Cisco router components.

TABLE 7.1   Cisco Router Components

Component	Description
Bootstrap	Stored in the microcode of the ROM, the bootstrap is used to bring a router up during initialization. It will boot the router and then load the IOS.
POST (power-on self test)	Stored in the microcode of the ROM, the POST is used to check the basic functionality of the router hardware and determines which interfaces are present.
ROM monitor	Stored in the microcode of the ROM, the ROM monitor is used for manufacturing testing and troubleshooting.
Mini-IOS	Called the RXBOOT or bootloader by Cisco, the mini-IOS is a small IOS in ROM that can be used to bring up an interface and load a Cisco IOS into flash memory. The mini-IOS can also perform a few other maintenance operations.
RAM (random access memory)	Used to hold packet buffers, routing tables, and also the software and data structures that allow the router to function. Running-config is stored in RAM, and the IOS can also be run from RAM in some routers.
ROM (read-only memory)	Used to start and maintain the router.

TABLE 7.1 Cisco Router Components *(continued)*

Component	Description
Flash memory	Used on the router to hold the Cisco IOS. Flash memory is not erased when the router is reloaded. It is an EEPROM created by Intel.
NVRAM (nonvolatile RAM)	Used to hold the router and switch configuration. NVRAM is not erased when the router or switch is reloaded.
Configuration register	Used to control how the router boots up. This value can be seen with the show version command and typically is 0x2102, which tells the router to load the IOS from flash memory.

The Router Boot Sequence

When a router boots up, it performs a series of steps, called the boot sequence, to test the hardware and load the necessary software. The boot sequence consists of the following steps:

1. The router performs a POST. The POST tests the hardware to verify that all components of the device are operational and present. For example, the POST checks for the different interfaces on the router. The POST is stored in and run from ROM.

2. The bootstrap looks for and loads the Cisco IOS software. The bootstrap is a program in ROM that is used to execute programs. The bootstrap program is responsible for finding where each IOS program is located and then loading the file. By default, the IOS software is loaded from flash memory in all Cisco routers.

3. The IOS software looks for a valid configuration file stored in NVRAM. This file is called startup-config and is only there if an administrator copies the running-config file into NVRAM.

4. If a `startup-config` file is in NVRAM, the router will load and run this file. The router is now operational. If a `startup-config` file is not in NVRAM, the router will start the setup mode configuration upon bootup.

Managing Configuration Registers

All Cisco routers have a 16-bit software register, which is written into NVRAM. By default, the configuration register is set to load the Cisco IOS from flash memory and to look for and load the `startup-config` file from NVRAM.

Understanding the Configuration Register Bits

The 16 bits of the configuration register are read 15–0, from left to right. The default configuration setting on Cisco routers is 0x2102. This means that bits 13, 8, and 1 are on, as shown in Table 7.2. Notice that each set of four bits is read in binary with a value of 1, 2, 4, and 8, from right to left.

TABLE 7.2 The Configuration Register Bit Numbers

Configuration Register	2	1	0	2
Bit number	15 14 13 12	11 10 9 8	7 6 5 4	3 2 1 0
Binary	0 0 1 0	0 0 0 1	0 0 0 0	0 0 1 0

Add the prefix 0x to the configuration register address. The 0x means that the digits that follow are in hexadecimal.

Table 7.3 lists the software configuration bit meanings. Notice that bit 6 can be used to ignore the NVRAM contents. This bit is used for password recovery, as described in the "Recovering Passwords" section later in this chapter.

TABLE 7.3 Software Configuration Meanings

Bit	Hex	Description
0–3	0x0000–0x000F	Boot field (see Table 7.4).
6	0x0040	Ignore NVRAM contents.
7	0x0080	OEM bit enabled.
8	0x0100	Break disabled.
10	0x0400	IP broadcast with all zeros.
11–12	0x0800–0x1000	Console line speed.
13	0x2000	Boot default ROM software if network boot fails.
14	0x4000	IP broadcasts do not have net numbers.
15	0x8000	Enable diagnostic messages and ignore NVM contents.

The boot field, which consists of bits 0–3 in the configuration register, controls the router boot sequence. Table 7.4 describes the boot field bits.

TABLE 7.4 The Boot Field (Configuration Register Bits 00–03)

Boot Field	Meaning	Use
00	ROM monitor mode	To boot to ROM monitor mode, set the configuration register to 2100. You must manually boot the router with the b command. The router will show the rommon> prompt.
01	Boot image from ROM	To boot an IOS image stored in ROM, set the configuration register to 2101. The router will show the router(boot)> prompt.
02–F	Specifies a default boot filename	Any value from 2102 through 210F tells the router to use the boot commands specified in NVRAM.

Remember that in hex, the scheme is 0–9 and A–F (A=10, B=11, C=12, D=13, E=14, and F=15). This means that a 210F setting for the configuration register is actually 210(15), or 1111 in binary.

Checking the Current Configuration Register Value

You can see the current value of the configuration register by using the show version command (sh version or show ver for short), as in the following example:

```
Router#sh version
Cisco Internetwork Operating System Software
IOS (tm) C2600 Software (C2600-I-M), Version 12.0(3)T3,
RELEASE SOFTWARE (fc1)
[output cut]
Configuration register is 0x2102
```

The last information given from this command is the value of the configuration register. In this example, the value is 0x2102, which is the default setting. Notice the show version command provides the IOS version. In the example above, it shows the IOS version as 12 0(3)T3.

Changing the Configuration Register

You can change the configuration register value to modify how the router boots and runs, as follows:

- Force the system into the ROM monitor mode
- Select a boot source and default boot filename
- Enable or disable the Break function
- Control broadcast addresses
- Set the console terminal baud rate
- Load operating software from ROM
- Enable booting from a TFTP (Trivial File Transfer Protocol) server

NOTE

Before you change the configuration register, make sure you know the current configuration register value. Use the show version command to get this information.

You can change the configuration register by using the config-register command. For example, the following commands tell the router to boot from ROM monitor mode and then show the current configuration register value:

```
Router(config)#config-register 0x0101
Router(config)#^Z
Router#sh ver
[cut]
Configuration register is 0x2102 (will be 0x0101 at next reload)
```

Notice that the show version command shows the current configuration register value, as well as what it will be when the router reboots. Any change to the configuration register will not take effect until the router is reloaded.

Recovering Passwords

If you are locked out of a router because you forgot the password, you can change the configuration register to help you recover. As noted earlier, bit 6 in the configuration register is used to tell the router whether to use the contents of NVRAM to load a router configuration.

The default configuration register value for bit 6 is 0x2102, which means that bit 6 is off. With the default setting, the router will look for and load a router configuration stored in NVRAM (startup-config). To recover a password, you need to turn on bit 6, which will tell the router to ignore the NVRAM contents. The configuration register value to turn on bit 6 is 0x2142.

Here are the main steps to password recovery:

1. Boot the router and interrupt the boot sequence by performing a break.

2. Change the configuration register to turn on bit 6 (with the value 0x2142).

3. Reload the router.

4. Enter privileged mode.

5. Copy the `startup-config` file to `running-config`.

6. Change the password.

7. Reset the configuration register to the default value.

8. Reload the router.

These steps are discussed in more detail in the following sections, showing the commands to restore access to 2600 and 2500 series routers.

Interrupting the Router Boot Sequence

Your first step is to boot the router and perform a break. Typically, you perform a break by pressing the Ctrl+Break key combination when using HyperTerminal.

WARNING Windows NT's default HyperTerminal program will not perform the break. You must upgrade the HyperTerminal program or use Windows 95/98.

You should see something like this:

```
System Bootstrap, Version 11.3(2)XA4, RELEASE SOFTWARE
(fc1)
Copyright (c) 1999 by cisco Systems, Inc.
TAC:Home:SW:IOS:Specials for info
PC = 0xfff0a530, Vector = 0x500, SP = 0x680127b0
C2600 platform with 32768 Kbytes of main memory
PC = 0xfff0a530, Vector = 0x500, SP = 0x80004374
monitor: command "boot" aborted due to user interrupt
rommon 1 >
```

Notice the line `"boot"` aborted due to user interrupt. At this point, you will be at the `rommon 1>` prompt on some routers.

Changing the Configuration Register

As explained earlier, you can change the configuration register by using the config-register command. To turn on bit 6, use the configuration register value 0x2142.

Cisco 2600 Series Commands

To change the bit value on a Cisco 2600 series router, simply enter the command at the rommon 1> prompt:

```
rommon 1 > confreg 0x2142
You must reset or power cycle for new config to take
effect
```

Cisco 2500 Series Commands

To change the configuration register on a 2500 series router, type o after creating a break sequence on the router. This brings up a menu of configuration register option settings. To change the configuration register, enter the command o/r, followed by the new register value. Here is an example of turning on bit 6 on a 2501 router:

```
System Bootstrap, Version 11.0(10c), SOFTWARE
Copyright (c) 1986-1996 by cisco Systems
2500 processor with 14336 Kbytes of main memory
Abort at 0x1098FEC (PC)
>o
Configuration register = 0x2102 at last boot
Bit#    Configuration register option settings:
15      Diagnostic mode disabled
14      IP broadcasts do not have network numbers
13      Boot default ROM software if network boot fails
12-11   Console speed is 9600 baud
10      IP broadcasts with ones
08      Break disabled
07      OEM disabled
06      Ignore configuration disabled
03-00   Boot file is cisco2-2500 (or 'boot system' command)
>o/r 0x2142
```

Reloading the Router and Entering Privileged Mode

At this point, you need to reset the router, as follows:

- From the 2600 series router, type **reset**.

- From the 2500 series router, type **I** (for initialize).

The router will reload and ask if you want to use setup mode (because no `startup-config` is used). Answer No to entering setup mode, press Enter to go into user mode, and then type **enable** to go into privileged mode.

Viewing and Changing the Configuration

Now you are past where you would need to enter the user mode and privileged mode passwords in a router. Copy the `startup-config` file to the `running-config` file:

```
copy running-config startup-config
```

or use the shortcut:

```
copy run start
```

The configuration is now running in RAM, and you are in privileged mode, which means that you can view and change the configuration. Although you cannot view the `enable secret` setting for the password, you can change the password, as follows:

```
config t
enable secret todd
```

Resetting the Configuration Register and Reloading the Router

After you are finished changing passwords, set the configuration register back to the default value with the `config-register` command:

```
config t
config-register 0x2102
```

Finally, reload the router.

Backing Up and Restoring the Cisco IOS

Before you upgrade or restore a Cisco IOS, you should copy the existing file to a TFTP host as a backup in case the new image does not work. You can use any TFTP host to perform this function. By default, the flash memory in a router is used to store the Cisco IOS. The following sections describe how to check the amount of flash memory, copy the Cisco IOS from flash memory to a TFTP host, and then copy the IOS from a TFTP host to flash memory.

Verifying Flash Memory

Before you attempt to upgrade the Cisco IOS on your router with a new IOS file, you should verify that your flash memory has enough room to hold the new image. You can verify the amount of flash memory and the file or files being stored in flash memory by using the show flash command (sh flash for short):

```
Router#sh flash
System flash directory:
File  Length    Name/status
  1   8121000   c2500-js-1.112-18.bin
[8121064 bytes used, 8656152 available, 16777216 total]
16384K bytes of processor board System flash (Read ONLY)
Router#
```

Notice that the filename in this example is c2500-js-1.112-18.bin. The name of the file is platform-specific and is derived as follows:

- c2500 is the platform.

- j indicates that the file is an enterprise image.

- s indicates the file contains extended capabilities.

- 1 indicates that the file can be moved from flash memory if needed and is not compressed.

- 11.2-18 is the revision number.

- .bin indicates that the Cisco IOS is a binary executable file.

The last line in the router output shows that the flash is 16,384KB (or 16MB). So if the new file that you want to use is, say, 10MB in size, you know that there is plenty of room for it. Once you verify that flash memory can hold the IOS you want to copy, you can continue with your backup operation.

Backing Up the Cisco IOS

To back up the Cisco IOS to a TFTP host, you use the command copy flash tftp. This is a straightforward command that requires only the source filename and the IP address of the TFTP host.

The key to success in this backup routine is to make sure that you have good connectivity to the TFTP host. You can check this by pinging the device from the router console prompt, as in the following example:

```
Router#ping 192.168.0.120
Type escape sequence to abort.
Sending 5, 100-byte ICMP Echos to 192.168.0.120, timeout
is 2 seconds:
!!!!!
Success rate is 100 percent (5/5), round-trip min/avg/max
= 4/4/8 ms
```

The Ping (Packet Internet Groper) utility is used to test network connectivity. It is used in some examples in this chapter and discussed in more detail in the "Checking Network Connectivity" section later in this chapter.

After you ping the TFTP host to make sure that IP is working, you can use the copy flash tftp command to copy the IOS to the TFTP host, as shown below. Notice that after you enter the command, the name of the file in flash memory is displayed. This makes it easy for you. You can copy the filename and then paste it when prompted for the source filename.

```
Router#copy flash tftp
System flash directory:
File  Length    Name/status
  1   8121000   c2500-js-1.112-18.bin
[8121064 bytes used, 8656152 available, 16777216 total]
Address or name of remote host [255.255.255.255]?
192.168.0.120
Source file name? c2500-js-1.112-18.bin
Destination file name [c2500-js-1.112-18.bin]? (press
enter)
Verifying checksum for 'c2500-js-1.112-18.bin')file
#1)...OK
Copy '/c2500-js-1.112-18' from Flash to server
  as '/c2500-js-1.112-18'? [yes/no]y
!!!!!!!!!!!!!!!!!!!!!!!!!!!!!!!!!!!!!!!!!!!!!!!!!!!!!!!!!!
!!!!!!!!!!!!!!!!!!!! [output cut]
Upload to server done
Flash copy took 00:02:30 [hh:mm:ss]
Router#
```

In this example, the content of flash memory was copied successfully to the TFTP host. The address of the remote host is the IP address of the TFTP host. The source filename is the file in flash memory.

WARNING   The copy flash tftp command does not prompt you for the location of any file or ask you where to put the file. TFTP is the "grab it and place it" program in this situation. The TFTP host must have a default directory specified, or it won't work.

Restoring or Upgrading the Cisco Router IOS

You may need to restore the Cisco IOS to flash memory to replace an original file that has been damaged or to upgrade the IOS. You can download the file from a TFTP host to flash memory by using the copy tftp flash command. This command requires the IP address of the TFTP host and the name of the file you want to download to flash memory.

Before you begin, make sure that the file you want to place in flash memory is in the default TFTP directory on your host. When you issue the command, TFTP will not ask you where the file is. If the file you want to restore is not in the default directory of the TFTP host, this procedure won't work.

WARNING   Copying the IOS from the TFTP host to flash memory requires a router reboot. So, instead of upgrading or restoring the IOS at 9 A.M. on Monday morning, you should probably wait until lunchtime.

After you enter the `copy tftp flash` command, you will see a message informing you that the router must reboot and run a ROM-based IOS image to perform this operation:

```
Router#copy tftp flash
                         ****  NOTICE  ****
Flash load helper v1.0
This process will accept the copy options and then
terminate
the current system image to use the ROM based image for
the copy.
Routing functionality will not be available during that
time.
If you are logged in via telnet, this connection will
terminate.
Users with console access can see the results of the copy
operation.
                    ---- ******** ----
Proceed? [confirm](press enter)
```

After you press Enter to confirm you understand that the router needs to reboot, the following router output is displayed. Once the router has used the TFTP host, it will remember the address and just prompt you to press Enter.

```
System flash directory:
File  Length    Name/status
   1   8121000  /c2500-js-l.112-18
[8121064 bytes used, 8656152 available, 16777216 total]
Address or name of remote host [192.168.0.120]? (press enter)
```

The next prompt is for the name of the file you want to copy to flash memory. As noted earlier, this file *must* be in your TFTP host's default directory.

```
Source file name? c2500-js56i-l.120-9.bin
Destination file name [c2500-js56i-l.120-9.bin]? (press enter)
Accessing file 'c2500-js56i-l.120-9.bin' on 192.168.0.120...
Loading c2500-js56i-l.120-9.bin from 192.168.0.120 (via
Ethernet0): ! [OK]
```

After you tell the router the filename and where the file is, it asks you to confirm that you understand the contents of flash memory will be erased.

If you do not have enough room in flash memory to store both copies, or if the flash memory is new and no file has been written to flash memory before, the router will ask to erase the contents of flash memory before writing the new file into flash memory.

You are prompted three times, just to make sure that you really want to proceed with erasing flash memory. If you have not issued a copy run start command, you will be prompted to do so, since the router needs to reboot.

```
Erase flash device before writing? [confirm] (press enter)
Flash contains files. Are you sure you want to erase?
[confirm] (press enter)

System configuration has been modified. Save? [yes/no]: y
Building configuration...
[OK]
Copy 'c2500-js56i-l.120-9.bin' from server
   as 'c2500-js56i-l.120-9.bin' into Flash WITH erase?
[yes/no] y
```

After you say "yes" to erasing flash memory, the router must reboot to load a small IOS from ROM memory. You cannot delete the flash file if it is in use.

Then the contents of flash memory are erased, and the file from the TFTP host is accessed and copied to flash memory.

```
%SYS-5-RELOAD: Reload requested
%FLH: c2500-js56i-l.120-9.bin from 192.168.0.120 to flash ...
```

```
System flash directory:
File  Length   Name/status
   1  8121000  /c2500-js-1.112-18
[8121064 bytes used, 8656152 available, 16777216 total]
Accessing file 'c2500-js56i-1.120-9.bin' on 192.168.0.120...
Loading c2500-js56i-1.120-9.bin .from 192.168.0.120 (via
Ethernet0): ! [OK]

Erasing device...
eeeeeeeeeeeeeeeeeeeeeeeeeeeeeeeeeeeeeeeeeeeeeeeeeeeeeeeeeeeeee
Loading c2500-js56i-1.120-9.bin from 192.168.0.120 (via
Ethernet0):
!!!!!!!!!!!!!!!!!!!!!!!!!!!!!!!!!!!!!!!!!!!!!!!!!!!!!!!!!!!!!!!
!!!!!!!!!!!!!!!!!!!!!!!!!!!!!!! [output cut]
```

The row of **e** characters shows the contents of flash memory being erased. Each exclamation point (!) means that one UDP segment has been success- fully transferred.

Once the copy is complete, you should receive this message:

```
[OK - 10935532/16777216 bytes]

Verifying checksum... OK (0x2E3A)
Flash copy took 0:06:14 [hh:mm:ss]
%FLH: Re-booting system after download
```

After the file is loaded into flash memory and a checksum is performed, the router is rebooted to run the new IOS file.

Cisco routers can become a TFTP-server host for a router system image that is run in flash. The global configuration command is tftp-server system *ios-name*.

Backing Up and Restoring the Cisco Configuration

Any changes that you make to the router configuration are stored in the running-config file. If you do not perform a copy run start command after you make a change to running-config, that change will be gone if the router reboots or gets powered down. You may want to make another backup of the configuration information as an extra precaution, in case the router or switch completely dies, or for documentation. The following sections describe how to copy the configuration of a router and switch to a TFTP host and how to restore that configuration.

Backing Up the Cisco Router Configuration

To copy the router's configuration from a router to a TFTP host, you can use either the copy running-config tftp or copy starting-config tftp command. Either command will back up the router configuration that is currently running in DRAM or that is stored in NVRAM.

Verifying the Current Configuration

To verify the configuration in DRAM, use the show running-config command (sh run for short), as follows:

```
Router#sh run
Building configuration...

Current configuration:
!
version 12.0
```

The current configuration information indicates that the router is now running version 12.0 of the IOS.

Verifying the Stored Configuration

Next, you should check the configuration stored in NVRAM. To see this, use the show starting-config command (sh start for short), as follows:

```
Router#sh start
Using 366 out of 32762 bytes
!
version 11.2
```

The second line shows how much room your backup configuration is using. In this example, NVRAM is 32KB and only 366 bytes of it are used. Notice that the version of configuration in NVRAM is 11.2 (because I have not copied running-config to startup-config since upgrading the router).

If you are not sure that the files are the same, and the running-config file is what you want to use, then use the copy running-config startup-config to make sure both files are the same, as described in the next section.

Copying the Current Configuration to NVRAM

By copying running-config to NVRAM as a backup, as shown in the following output, you are assured that your running-config will always be reloaded if the router gets rebooted. In the new IOS version 12.0, you are prompted for the filename you want to use. Also, in this example, since the version of IOS was 11.2 the last time a copy run start was performed, the router will let you know that it is going to replace that file with the new 12.0 version.

```
Router#copy run start
Destination filename [startup-config]? (press enter)
Warning: Attempting to overwrite an NVRAM configuration
previously written by a different version of the system
image.
Overwrite the previous NVRAM configuration?[confirm](press
enter)
Building configuration...
[OK]
```

Now when you run show starting-config, the version shows 12.0:

```
Router#sh start
Using 487 out of 32762 bytes
!
version 12.0
```

Copying the Configuration to a TFTP Host

Once the file is copied to NVRAM, you can make a second backup to a TFTP host by using the copy running-config tftp command (copy run tftp for short), as follows:

```
Router#copy run tftp
Address or name of remote host []? 192.168.0.120
```

```
Destination filename [router-confg]? todd1-confg
!!
487 bytes copied in 12.236 secs (40 bytes/sec)
Router#
```

Notice that this took only two exclamation points (!!), which are two UDP acknowledgments. In this example, I named the file `todd1-confg` because I had not set a hostname for the router. If you have a hostname configured, the command will automatically use the hostname plus the extension –confg as the name of the file.

Restoring the Cisco Router Configuration

If you have changed your router's `running-config` and want to restore the configuration to the version in `startup-config`, the easiest way to do this is to use the `copy startup-config running-config` command (`copy start run` for short). You can also use the older Cisco command, `config mem`, to restore a configuration. Of course, this will work only if you first copied `running-config` into NVRAM before making any changes.

If you copied the router's configuration to a TFTP host as a second backup, you can restore the configuration using the `copy tftp running-config` command (`copy tftp run` for short) or the `copy tftp startup-config` command (`copy tftp start` for short), as shown below. Remember that the old command that provides this function is `config net`.

```
Router#copy tftp run
Address or name of remote host []? 192.168.0.120
Source filename []? todd1-confg
Destination filename [running-config]? (press enter)
Accessing tftp://192.168.0.120/todd1-confg...
Loading todd1-confg from 192.168.0.120 (via Ethernet0):
!!
[OK - 487/4096 bytes]
487 bytes copied in 5.400 secs (97 bytes/sec)
Router#
00:38:31: %SYS-5-CONFIG: Configured from tftp://
192.168.0.120/todd1-confg
Router#
```

The configuration file is an ASCII text file. This means that before you copy the configuration stored on a TFTP host back to a router, you can make changes to the file with any text editor.

Erasing the Configuration

To delete the `startup-config` file on a Cisco router, use the command `erase startup-config`, as follows:

```
Router#erase startup-config
Erasing the nvram filesystem will remove all files!
Continue? [confirm](press enter)
[OK]
Erase of nvram: complete
Router#
```

The preceding command deletes the contents of NVRAM on the router. The next time the router boots, it will run in setup mode.

Using Cisco Discovery Protocol

Cisco Discovery Protocol (CDP) is a proprietary protocol designed by Cisco to help administrators collect information about both locally attached and remote devices. By using CDP, you can gather hardware and protocol information about neighbor devices. This information is useful for troubleshooting and documenting the network.

Getting CDP Timers and Holdtime Information

The `show cdp` command (`sh cdp` for short) shows information about two CDP global parameters that can be configured on Cisco devices:

- CDP timer is how often CDP packets are transmitted to all active interfaces.
- CDP holdtime is the amount of time that the device will hold packets received from neighbor devices.

Both the Cisco routers and the Cisco switches use the same parameters. The output on a router looks like this:

```
Router#sh cdp
Global CDP information:
        Sending CDP packets every 60 seconds
        Sending a holdtime value of 180 seconds
Router#
```

Use the global commands show cdp holdtime and show cdp timer to configure the CDP holdtime and timer on a router.

```
Router#config t
Enter configuration commands, one per line.  End with CNTL/Z.
Router(config)#cdp ?
  holdtime Specify the holdtime (in sec) to be sent in packets
  timer    Specify the rate at which CDP packets are sent(in sec)
  run

Router(config)#cdp timer 90
Router(config)#cdp holdtime 240
Router(config)#^Z
```

You can turn off CDP completely with the no cdp run command from global configuration mode of a router. To turn CDP off or on in a router interface, use the no cdp enable and cdp enable commands, which are discussed in more detail in the "Getting Port and Interface Information" section a bit later in this chapter.

Getting Neighbor Information

The show cdp neighbor command (sh cdp nei for short) shows information about directly connected devices. It is important to remember that CDP packets are not passed through a Cisco switch, and you only see what is directly attached. On a router connected to a switch, you will not see the other devices connected to the switch.

The following output shows the show cdp neighbor command used on a 2509 router.

```
Todd2509#sh cdp nei
Capability Codes: R - Router, T - Trans Bridge, B - Source Route Bridge
                  S - Switch, H - Host, I - IGMP, r - Repeater
Device ID      Local Intrfce   Holdtme   Capability   Platform   Port ID
1900Switch     Eth 0           238          T S        1900        2
2500B          Ser 0           138           R         2500       Ser 0
Todd2501#
```

Table 7.5 summarizes the information displayed by the show cdp neighbor command for each device.

TABLE 7.5   Output of the show cdp neighbor Command

Field	Description
Device ID	The hostname of the device directly connected.
Local Interface	The port or interface on which you are receiving the CDP packet.
Holdtime	The amount of time the router will hold the information before discarding it if no more CDP packets are received.
Capability	The neighbor's capability, such as router, switch, or repeater. The capability codes are listed at the top of the command output.
Platform	The type of Cisco device. In the above output, a Cisco 2509, Cisco 2511, and Catalyst 5000 are attached to the switch. The 2509 only sees the switch and the 2501 router connected through its serial 0 interface.
Port ID	The neighbor device's port or interface on which the CDP packets are broadcast.

Another command that provides neighbor information is the show cdp neighbor detail command (show cdp nei de for short), which also can be run on the router or switch. This command shows detailed information about each device connected to the device, as in the router output below.

```
Todd2509#sh cdp neighbor detail
-------------------------
Device ID: 1900Switch
Entry address(es):
  IP address: 0.0.0.0
Platform: cisco 1900,   Capabilities: Trans-Bridge Switch
Interface: Ethernet0,   Port ID (outgoing port): 2
Holdtime : 166 sec
Version :
V9.00

-------------------------
Device ID: 2501B
Entry address(es):
  IP address: 172.16.10.2
Platform: cisco 2500,   Capabilities: Router
Interface: Serial0,   Port ID (outgoing port): Serial0
Holdtime : 154 sec
Version :
Cisco Internetwork Operating System Software
IOS (tm) 3000 Software (IGS-J-L), Version 11.1(5), RELEASE
SOFTWARE (fc1)Copyright (c) 1986-1996 by cisco Systems,
Inc.Compiled Mon 05-Aug-96 11:48 by mkamson
Todd2509#
```

The output above shows the hostname and IP address of the directly connected devices. In addition to the same information displayed by the show cdp neighbor command (see Table 7.5), the show cdp neighbor detail command shows the IOS version of the neighbor device.

The show cdp entry * command displays the same information as the show cdp neighbor details command. The following is an example of the router output of the show cdp entry * command.

```
Todd2509#sh cdp entry *
-------------------------
Device ID: 1900Switch
```

```
Entry address(es):
   IP address: 0.0.0.0
Platform: cisco 1900,  Capabilities: Trans-Bridge Switch
Interface: Ethernet0,  Port ID (outgoing port): 2
Holdtime : 223 sec
Version :
V9.00

-------------------------
Device ID: 2501B
Entry address(es):
   IP address: 172.16.10.2
Platform: cisco 2500,  Capabilities: Router
Interface: Serial0,  Port ID (outgoing port): Serial0
Holdtime : 151 sec
Version :
Cisco Internetwork Operating System Software
IOS (tm) 3000 Software (IGS-J-L), Version 11.1(5), RELEASE
SOFTWARE (fc1)Copyright (c) 1986-1996 by cisco Systems,
Inc.Compiled Mon 05-Aug-96 11:48 by mkamson
Todd2509#
```

Getting Interface Traffic Information

The show cdp traffic command displays information about interface traffic, including the number of CDP packets sent and received and the errors with CDP.

The following output shows the show cdp traffic command used on a router.

```
Router#sh cdp traffic
CDP counters :
        Packets output: 13, Input: 8
        Hdr syntax: 0, Chksum error: 0, Encaps failed: 0
        No memory: 0, Invalid packet: 0, Fragmented: 0
Router#
```

Getting Port and Interface Information

The show cdp interface command (sh cdp inter for short) shows the CDP status on router interfaces or switch ports.

As explained earlier, you can turn off CDP completely on a router by using the no cdp run command. However, CDP can also be turned off per interface with the no cdp enable command. You can enable a port with the cdp enable command. All ports and interfaces default to cdp enable.

On a router, the show cdp interface command shows information about each interface using CDP, including the encapsulation on the line, the timer, and the holdtime for each interface. Here is an example of this command's output on a router:

```
Router#sh cdp interface
Ethernet0 is up, line protocol is up
  Encapsulation ARPA
  Sending CDP packets every 60 seconds
  Holdtime is 180 seconds
Serial0 is administratively down, line protocol is down
  Encapsulation HDLC
  Sending CDP packets every 60 seconds
  Holdtime is 180 seconds
Serial1 is administratively down, line protocol is down
  Encapsulation HDLC
  Sending CDP packets every 60 seconds
  Holdtime is 180 seconds
```

To turn off CDP on one interface on a router, use the no cdp enable command from interface configuration mode:

```
Router#config t
Enter configuration commands, one per line.  End with CNTL/Z.
Router(config)#int s0
Router(config-if)#no cdp enable
Router(config-if)#^Z
```

Verify the change with the show cdp interface command:

```
Router#sh cdp int
Ethernet0 is up, line protocol is up
```

```
      Encapsulation ARPA
      Sending CDP packets every 60 seconds
      Holdtime is 180 seconds
   Serial1 is administratively down, line protocol is down
      Encapsulation HDLC
      Sending CDP packets every 60 seconds
      Holdtime is 180 seconds
   Router#
```

Notice in the output above that serial 0 does not show up in the router output.

Using Telnet

Telnet is a virtual terminal protocol that is part of the TCP/IP protocol suite. Telnet allows you to make connections to remote devices, gather information, and run programs.

After your routers and switches are configured, you can use the Telnet program to configure and check your routers and switches so that you don't need to use a console cable. You run the Telnet program by typing **telnet** from any command prompt (DOS or Cisco). VTY passwords must be set on the routers for this to work.

You cannot use CDP to gather information about routers and switches that are not directly connected to your device. However, you can use the Telnet application to connect to your neighbor devices and then run CDP on those remote devices to gather CDP information about remote devices.

You can issue the `telnet` command from any router prompt, as in the following example:

```
Todd2509#telnet 172.16.10.2
Trying 172.16.10.2 ... Open

Password required, but none set

[Connection to 172.16.10.2 closed by foreign host]
Todd2509#
```

As you can see, I didn't set my passwords—how embarrassing! Remember that the VTY ports on a router are configured as login, which means you must either set the VTY passwords or use the no login command. (See Chapter 4 for details on setting passwords.)

On a Cisco router, you do not need to use the telnet command. If you just type in an IP address from a command prompt, the router will assume that you want to telnet to the device, as shown below:

```
Todd2509#172.16.10.2
Trying 172.16.10.2 ... Open

Password required, but none set

[Connection to 172.16.10.2 closed by foreign host]
Todd2509#
```

It's time to set VTY passwords on the router I want to telnet into. Here is an example of what I did:

```
2501B#config t
Enter configuration commands, one per line.  End with
CNTL/Z.
2501B(config)#line vty 0 4
2501B(config-line)#login
2501B(config-line)#password todd
2501B(config-line)#^Z
2501B#
%SYS-5-CONFIG_I: Configured from console by console
```

Now, let's try connecting to the router again (from the 2509 router console).

```
Todd2509#172.16.10.2
Trying 172.16.10.2 ... Open

User Access Verification

Password:
2501B>
```

Remember that the VTY password is the user mode password, not the enable mode password. Watch what happens when I try to go into privileged mode after telnetting into router 2501B:

```
2501B>en
% No password set
2501B>
```

This is a good security feature. You don't want anyone telnetting onto your device and then being able to just type the command enable to get into privileged mode. You must set your enable mode password or enable secret password to use Telnet to configure remote devices.

Telnetting into Multiple Devices Simultaneously

If you telnet to a router or switch, you can end the connection by typing exit at any time. However, what if you want to keep your connection to a remote device but still come back to your original router console? To keep the connection, you can press the Ctrl+Shift+6 key combination, release it, and then press X.

Here's an example of connecting to multiple devices from my Todd2509 router console:

```
Todd2509#telnet 172.16.10.2
Trying 172.16.10.2 ... Open

User Access Verification

Password:
2501B>
Todd2509#
```

In the example above, I telnetted to the 2501B router then typed the password to enter user mode. I then pressed Ctrl+Shift+6, then X (this doesn't show on the screen output). Notice my command prompt is now back at the Todd2509 router.

You can also telnet into a 1900 switch. However, you must set the enable mode password level 15 on the switch before you can gain access via the

Telnet application. (See Appendix B for information about how to set the 1900 switch passwords.)

In the following example, I telnet to a 1900 switch, which then gives me the console output of the switch.

```
Todd2509#telnet 192.168.0.148
Trying 192.168.0.148 ... Open

Catalyst 1900 Management Console
Copyright (c) Cisco Systems, Inc.  1993-1999
All rights reserved.
Enterprise Edition Software
Ethernet Address:        00-B0-64-75-6B-C0

PCA Number:              73-3122-04
PCA Serial Number:       FAB040131E2
Model Number:            WS-C1912-A
System Serial Number:    FAB0401U0JQ
Power Supply S/N:        PHI033108SD
PCB Serial Number:       FAB040131E2,73-3122-04
-----------------------------------------------

1 user(s) now active on Management Console.

        User Interface Menu

   [M] Menus
   [K] Command Line

Enter Selection:
```

At this point, I pressed Ctrl+Shift+6, then X, which took me back to my Todd2509 router console.

```
Todd2509#
```

Checking Telnet Connections

To see the connections made from your router to a remote device, use the
show sessions command.

```
Todd2509#sh sessions
Conn Host            Address           Byte  Idle Conn Name
   1 172.16.10.2     172.16.10.2        0     0   172.16.10.2
*  2 192.168.0.148   192.168.0.148      0     0   192.168.0.148
Todd2509#
```

Notice the asterisk (*) next to connection 2. This means that session 2 was
the last session. You can return to your last session by pressing Enter twice.
You can also return to any session by typing the number of the connection
and pressing Enter twice.

Checking Telnet Users

You can list all active consoles and VTY ports in use on your router with the
show users command.

```
Todd2509#sh users
     Line      User       Host(s)              Idle Location
*  0 con 0                172.16.10.2          00:07:52
                          192.168.0.148        00:07:18
```

In the command's output, the con represents the local console. In this
example, the console is connected to two remote IP addresses, or devices.

In the next example, I typed show users on the 2501B router, which the
Todd2509 router had telnetted into.

```
2501B>sh users
     Line      User       Host(s)              Idle Location
   0 con 0                idle                  9
*  2 vty 0
```

This output shows that the console is active and that VTY port 2 is being
used. The asterisk represents the current terminal session user.

Closing Telnet Sessions

You can end Telnet sessions a few different ways. Typing exit or disconnect is probably the easiest and quickest.

To end a session from a remote device, use the exit command.

```
2509# (I pressed enter twice here)
[Resuming connection 2 to 192.168.0.148 ... ]

switch>exit

[Connection to 192.168.0.148 closed by foreign host]
Todd2509#
```

To end a session from a local device, use the disconnect command.

```
Todd2509#disconnect ?
  <1-2>  The number of an active network connection
  WORD   The name of an active network connection
  <cr>


Todd2509#disconnect 1
Closing connection to 172.16.10.2 [confirm]
Todd2509#
```

In this example, I used the session number 1 because that was the connection to the 2501B router that I wanted to end. As explained earlier, you can use the show sessions command to see the connection number.

If you want to end a session of a device attached to your router through Telnet, you might want to first check if any devices are attached to your router. Use the show users command to get that information.

```
2501B#sh users
    Line      User      Host(s)          Idle Location
*   0 con 0             idle             0
    1 aux 0             idle             0
    2 vty 0             idle             0 172.16.10.1
```

This output shows that VTY 2 has IP address 172.16.10.1 connected. That is the Todd2509 router.

To clear the connection, use the `clear line #` command.

```
2501B#clear line 2
[confirm]
 [OK]
```

Verify that the user has been disconnected with the `show users` command.

```
2501B#sh users
    Line      User       Host(s)              Idle Location
*   0 con 0              idle                 0
    1 aux 0              idle                 1


2501B#
```

This output shows that the line has been cleared.

Resolving Hostnames

In order to use a hostname rather than an IP address to connect to a remote device, the device that you are using to make the connection must be able to translate the hostname to an IP address. There are two ways to resolve hostnames to IP addresses: building a host table on each router or building a Domain Name System (DNS) server, which is like a dynamic host table.

Building a Host Table

A host table provides name resolution only on the router on which it was built. The command to build a host table on a router is

```
ip host name tcp_port_number ip_address
```

The default is TCP port number 23. You can create a session using Telnet with a different TCP port number, if needed, and you can assign up to eight IP addresses to a hostname.

Here is an example of configuring a host table with two entries to resolve the names for the 2501B router and the switch:

```
Todd2509#config t
Enter configuration commands, one per line.  End with
CNTL/Z.
Todd2509(config)#ip host ?
  WORD  Name of host

Todd2509(config)#ip host 2501B ?
  <0-65535>  Default telnet port number
  A.B.C.D    Host IP address (maximum of 8)

Todd2509(config)#ip host 2501B 172.16.10.2 ?
  A.B.C.D  Host IP address (maximum of 8)
  <cr>
Todd2509(config)#ip host 2501B 172.16.10.2
Todd2509(config)#ip host switch 192.168.0.148
Todd2509(config)#^Z
```

To see the host table, use the show hosts command.

```
Todd2509#sh hosts
Default domain is not set
Name/address lookup uses domain service
Name servers are 255.255.255.255

Host            Flags      Age Type   Address(es)
2501B           (perm, OK)  0   IP     172.16.10.2
switch          (perm, OK)  0   IP     192.168.0.148
Todd2509#
```

In the preceding router output, you can see the two hostnames and their associated IP addresses. The perm in the Flags column means that the entry is manually configured. If it said temp, it would be an entry resolved by DNS.

To verify that the host table resolves names, try typing the hostnames at a router prompt. Remember that if you don't specify the command, the router assumes you want to telnet. In the following example, I used the hostnames to telnet into the remote devices and then pressed Ctrl+Shift+6, then X to return to the main console of the Todd2509 router.

```
Todd2509#2501b
Trying 2501B (172.16.10.2)... Open

User Access Verification

Password:
2501B>
Todd2509#(control+shift+6,then x)
Todd2509#switch
Trying switch (192.168.0.148)... Open

Catalyst 1900 Management Console
Copyright (c) Cisco Systems, Inc.  1993-1999
All rights reserved.
Enterprise Edition Software
Ethernet Address:        00-B0-64-75-6B-C0

PCA Number:              73-3122-04
PCA Serial Number:       FAB040131E2
Model Number:            WS-C1912-A
System Serial Number:    FAB0401U0JQ
Power Supply S/N:        PHI033108SD
PCB Serial Number:       FAB040131E2,73-3122-04
-----------------------------------------------

1 user(s) now active on Management Console.

        User Interface Menu

    [M] Menus
    [K] Command Line
```

```
Enter Selection: (control+shift+6,then x)
Todd2509#
```

I successfully used the host table to create a session to two devices and used the names to telnet into both devices. Notice in the entries in the show session output below that the hostname now shows up instead of the IP address.

```
Todd2509#sh sess
Conn Host                Address            Byte  Idle Conn Name
   1 switch              192.168.0.148          0     0 switch
*  2 2501b               172.16.10.2            0     0 2501b
Todd2509#
```

You can remove a hostname from the table by using the no ip host command, as in the following example:

```
RouterA(config)#no ip host routerb
```

The problem with the host table method is that you would need to create a host table on each router to be able to resolve names. If you have many routers and want to resolve names, using DNS is a better choice.

Using DNS to Resolve Names

If you have many devices and don't want to create a host table in each device, you can use a DNS server to resolve hostnames.

Anytime a Cisco device receives a command it doesn't understand, it tries to resolve this through DNS by default. Watch what happens when I type the special command todd at a Cisco router prompt.

```
Todd2509#todd
Translating "todd"...domain server (255.255.255.255)
% Unknown command or computer name, or unable to find
computer address
Todd2509#
```

It doesn't know my name, or what command I am trying to type, so it tries to resolve this through DNS. This is annoying for two reasons: first, because it doesn't know my name, and second, because I need to wait for the name lookup to time out. You can prevent the default DNS lookup by using the no ip domain-lookup command on your router from global configuration mode.

If you have a DNS server on your network, you need to add a few commands to make DNS name resolution work:

- The first command is ip domain-lookup, which is turned on by default. It only needs to be entered if you previously turned it off (with the no ip domain-lookup command).

- The second command is ip name-server. This sets the IP address of the DNS server. You can enter the IP addresses of up to six servers.

- The last command is ip domain-name. Although this command is optional, it should be set. It appends the domain name to the hostname you type in. Since DNS uses a Fully Qualified Domain Name (FQDN) system, you must have a full DNS name, in the form domain.com.

Here is an example of using these three commands:

```
Todd2509#config t
Enter configuration commands, one per line.  End with
CNTL/Z.
Todd2509(config)#ip domain-lookup
Todd2509(config)#ip name-server ?
  A.B.C.D  Domain server IP address (maximum of 6)
Todd2509(config)#ip name-server 192.168.0.70
Todd2509(config)#ip domain-name lammle.com
Todd2509(config)#^Z
Todd2509#
```

After the DNS configurations are set, you can test the DNS server by using a hostname to ping or telnet a device, as shown below.

```
Todd2509#ping 2501b
Translating "2501b"...domain server (192.168.0.70) [OK]
Type escape sequence to abort.
Sending 5, 100-byte ICMP Echos to 172.16.10.2, timeout is
2 seconds:
```

```
!!!!!
Success rate is 100 percent (5/5), round-trip min/avg/max
= 28/31/32 ms
```

Notice that the DNS server is used by the router to resolve the name.

After a name is resolved using DNS, use the show hosts command to see that the device cached this information in the host table, as shown below.

```
Todd2509#sh hosts
Default domain is lammle.com
Name/address lookup uses domain service
Name servers are 192.168.0.70


Host                    Flags       Age Type    Address(es)
2501b.lammle.com        (temp, OK)  0    IP     172.16.10.2
switch                  (perm, OK)  0    IP     192.168.0.148
Todd2509#
```

The entry that was resolved is shown as temp, but the switch device is still perm, which means that it is a static entry. Notice that the hostname is a full domain name. If I hadn't used the ip domain-name lammle.com command, I would have needed to type in ping 2501b.lammle.com, which is a pain.

Checking Network Connectivity

You can use the ping and trace commands to test connectivity to remote devices. Both commands can be used with many protocols, not just IP.

Using the *Ping* Command

In this chapter, you've seen many examples of pinging devices to test IP connectivity and name resolution using the DNS server. To see all the different protocols that you can use with ping, use the ping ? command, as shown below.

```
Todd2509#ping ?
  WORD        Ping destination address or hostname
```

```
apollo      Apollo echo
appletalk   Appletalk echo
clns        CLNS echo
decnet      DECnet echo
ip          IP echo
ipx         Novell/IPX echo
srb         srb echo
tag         Tag encapsulated IP echo
vines       Vines echo
xns         XNS echo
<cr>
```

The ping output displays the minimum, average, and maximum times it takes for a Ping packet to find a specified system and return. Here is another example of its use:

```
Todd2509#ping todd2509
Translating "todd2509"...domain server (192.168.0.70) [OK]
Type escape sequence to abort.
Sending 5, 100-byte ICMP Echos to 192.168.0.121, timeout
is 2 seconds:
!!!!!
Success rate is 100 percent (5/5), round-trip min/avg/max
= 32/32/32 ms
Todd2509#
```

You can see that the DNS server was used to resolve the name and the device was pinged in 32 ms (milliseconds).

Using the *Trace* Command

The trace command shows the path a packet takes to get to a remote device. To see the protocols that you can use with trace, use the trace ? command, as shown below.

```
Todd2509#trace ?
  WORD        Trace route to destination address or
hostname
  appletalk  AppleTalk Trace
```

```
clns       ISO CLNS Trace
ip         IP Trace
ipx        IPX Trace
oldvines   Vines Trace (Cisco)
vines      Vines Trace (Banyan)
<cr>
```

If you try to use trace with IPX or AppleTalk, you will receive an error that the command is not supported. These protocols will be supported in the near future.

The trace command shows the hop or hops that a packet traverses on its way to a remote device. Here is an example of its use:

```
Todd2509#trace 2501b
Type escape sequence to abort.
Tracing the route to 2501b.lammle.com (172.16.10.2)

  1 2501b.lammle.com (172.16.10.2) 16 msec *  16 msec
Todd2509#
```

You can see that the packet went through only one hop to find the destination.

Summary

In this chapter, you learned how Cisco routers are configured and how to manage the configuration. The following router internal information was covered in this chapter:

- The internal components of a Cisco router

- The router boot sequence

- The configuration register and how to change it

- Password recovery

Next, you learned how to back up and restore a Cisco IOS, as well as how to back up and restore the configuration of a Cisco router. Then you learned how to use CDP and Telnet to gather information about neighbor devices. Finally, the chapter covered how to resolve hostnames and use the `ping` and `trace` commands to test network connectivity.

Key Terms

Before taking the exam, be sure you're familiar with the following terms:

boot ROM	*ROM*
configuration register	*Telnet*
Flash	*TFTP host*
Ping	*trace*
RAM	

Commands in This Chapter

Command	Description
`cdp enable`	Turns on CDP on an individual interface
`cdp holdtime`	Changes the holdtime of CDP packets
`cdp run`	Turns on CDP on a router
`cdp timer`	Changes the CDP update timer
`clear line`	Clears a connection connected via Telnet to your router
`config-register`	Tells the router how to boot and to change the configuration register setting
`copy flash tftp`	Copies a file from flash memory to a TFTP host

Command	Description
copy run start	Copies the running-config file to the startup-config file
copy run tftp	Copies the running-config file to a TFTP host
copy tftp flash	Copies a file from a TFTP host to flash memory
copy tftp run	Copies a configuration from a TFTP host to the running-config file
Ctrl+Shift+6, then X (keyboard combination)	Returns you to the originating router when you telnet to numerous routers
delete nvram	Deletes the contents of NVRAM on a 1900 switch
disconnect	Disconnects a connection to a remote router from the originating router
erase startup-config	Deletes the contents of NVRAM on a router
exit	Disconnects a connection to a remote router via Telnet
ip domain-lookup	Turns on DNS lookup (which is on by default)
ip domain-name	Appends a domain name to a DNS lookup
ip host	Creates a host table on a router
ip name-server	Sets the IP address of up to six DNS servers
no cdp enable	Turns off CDP on an individual interface

Command	Description
`no cdp run`	Turns off CDP completely on a router
`no ip domain-lookup`	Turns off DNS lookup
`no ip host`	Removes a hostname from a host table
`o/r 0x2142`	Changes a 2501 to boot without using the contents of NVRAM
`ping`	Tests IP connectivity to a remote device
`show cdp`	Displays the CDP timer and holdtime frequencies
`show cdp entry *`	Same as `show cdp neighbor detail`, but does not work on a 1900 switch
`show cdp interface`	Shows the individual interfaces enabled with CDP
`show cdp neighbor`	Shows the directly connected neighbors and the details about them
`show cdp neighbor detail`	Shows the IP address and IOS version and type, and includes all of the information from the `show cdp neighbor` command
`show cdp traffic`	Shows the CDP packets sent and received on a device and any errors
`show flash`	Shows the files in flash memory
`show hosts`	Shows the contents of the host table
`show run`	Displays the `running-config` file

Command	Description
show sessions	Shows your connections via Telnet to remote devices
show start	Displays the startup-config file
show version	Displays the IOS type and version as well as the configuration register
telnet	Connects, views, and runs programs on a remote device
tftp-server system *ios-name*	Creates a TFTP-server host for a router system image that is run in flash.
trace	Tests a connection to a remote device and shows the path it took through the internetwork to find the remote device

Written Lab

Write in the answers to the following questions.

1. What is the command to copy a Cisco IOS to a TFTP host?

2. What is the command to copy a Cisco `startup-config` file to a TFTP host?

3. What is the command to copy the `startup-config` file to DRAM?

4. What is an older command that you can use to copy the `startup-config` file to DRAM?

5. What command can you use to see the neighbor router's IP address from your router prompt?

6. What command can you use to see the hostname, local interface, platform, and remote port of a neighbor router?

7. What keystrokes can you use to telnet into multiple devices simultaneously?

8. What command will show you your active Telnet connections to neighbor and remote devices?

9. What command can you use to upgrade a Cisco IOS?

10. What command can you use to create a host table entry for Bob, using IP addresses 172.16.10.1 and 172.16.20.2?

Hands-on Labs

To complete the labs in this section, you need at least one router (more is better) and at least one PC running as a TFTP host. Here is a list of the labs in this chapter:

Lab 7.1: Backing Up Your Router IOS

Lab 7.2: Upgrading or Restoring Your Router IOS

Lab 7.3: Backing Up the Router Configuration

Lab 7.4: Using the Cisco Discovery Protocol (CDP)

Lab 7.5: Using Telnet

Lab 7.6: Resolving Hostnames

The RouterSim product, available from www.routersim.com, can perform all these labs.

Lab 7.1: Backing Up Your Router IOS

1. Log in to your router and go into privileged mode by typing **en** or **enable**.

2. Make sure you can connect to the TFTP host that is on your network by pinging the IP address from the router console.

3. Type **show flash** to see the contents of flash memory.

4. Type **show version** at the router privileged mode prompt to get the name of the IOS currently running on the router. If there is only one file in flash memory, the show flash and show version commands show the same file. Remember that the show version command shows you the file that is currently running, and the show flash command shows you all of the files in flash memory.

5. Once you know you have good Ethernet connectivity to the TFTP host, and you also know the IOS filename, back up your IOS by typing **copy**

flash tftp. This command tells the router to copy the contents of flash memory (this is where the IOS is stored by default) to a TFTP host.

6. Enter the IP address of the TFTP host and the source IOS filename. The file is now copied and stored in the TFTP host's default directory.

Lab 7.2: Upgrading or Restoring Your Router IOS

1. Log in to your router and go into privileged mode by typing **en** or **enable**.

2. Make sure you can connect to the TFTP host by pinging the IP address of the host from the router console.

3. Once you know you have good Ethernet connectivity to the TFTP host, issue the **copy tftp flash** command.

4. Confirm that the router is not functioning during the restore or upgrade by following the prompts provided on the router console.

5. Enter the IP address of the TFTP host.

6. Enter the IOS filename you want to restore or upgrade.

7. Confirm that you understand that the contents of flash memory will be erased.

8. Watch in amazement as your IOS is deleted out of flash memory, and your new IOS is copied to flash memory.

If the file that was in flash memory is deleted, but the new version wasn't copied to flash memory, the router will boot from ROM monitor mode. You'll need to figure out why the copy operation did not take place.

Lab 7.3: Backing Up the Router Configuration

1. Log in to your router and go into privileged mode by typing **en** or **enable**.

2. Ping the TFTP host to make sure you have IP connectivity.

3. From Router B, type **copy run tftp**.

4. Type the IP address of the TFTP host (for example, 172.16.30.2) and press Enter.

5. The router will prompt you for a filename. The hostname of the router is followed by the prefix –confg (yes, I spelled that correctly). You can use any name you want.

> Name of configuration file to write [RouterB-
> confg)? **Press enter to accept the default name**
> Write file RouterB-confg on host 172.16.30.2?
> [confirm] **Press enter**

The !! are UDP acknowledgments that the file was transferred successfully.

Lab 7.4: Using the Cisco Discovery Protocol (CDP)

1. Log in to your router and go into privileged mode by typing **en** or **enable**.

2. From the router, type **sh cdp** and press Enter. You should see that CDP packets are being sent out to all active interfaces every 60 seconds and the holdtime is 180 seconds (these are the defaults).

3. To change the CDP update frequency to 90 seconds, type **cdp timer 90** in global configuration mode.

> RouterC#**config t**
> Enter configuration commands, one per line.   End
> with CNTL/Z.
> RouterC(config)#**cdp timer ?**
>   <5-900> Rate at which CDP packets are sent (in
> sec)
> RouterC(config)#**cdp timer 90**

4. Verify your CDP timer frequency has changed by using the command **show cdp** in privileged mode.

```
RouteC#sh cdp
Global CDP information:
Sending CDP packets every 90 seconds
Sending a holdtime value of 180 seconds
```

5. Now, use CDP to gather information about neighbor routers. You can get the list of available commands by typing **sh cdp ?**.

```
RouterC#sh cdp ?
  entry      Information for specific neighbor entry
  interface  CDP interface status and configuration
  neighbors  CDP neighbor entries
  traffic    CDP statistics
  <cr>
```

6. Type **sh cdp int** to see the interface information plus the default encapsulation used by the interface. It also shows the CDP timer information.

7. Type **sh cdp entry *** to see the CDP information received from all routers.

8. Type **show cdp neighbor** to gather information about all connected neighbors. (You should know the specific information output by this command.)

9. Type **show cdp neighbor detail**. Notice that it produces the same output as `show cdp entry *`.

Lab 7.5: Using Telnet

1. Log in to your router and go into privileged mode by typing **en** or **enable**.

2. From Router A, telnet into your remote router by typing **telnet ip_ address** from the command prompt.

3. Type in Router B's IP address from Router A's command prompt. Notice that the router automatically tries to telnet to the IP address you specified. You can use the `telnet` command or just type in the IP address.

4. From Router B, press Ctrl+Shift+6, then X to return to Router A's command prompt. Now telnet into your third router, Router C. Press Ctrl+Shift+6, then X to return to Router A.

5. From Router A, type **show sessions**. Notice your two sessions. You can press the number displayed to the left of the session and press Enter twice to return to that session. The asterisk shows this default session. You can press Enter twice to return to that session.

6. Go to the session for your Router B. Type **show user**. This shows the console connection and the remote connection. You can use the `disconnect` command to clear the session, or just type `exit` from the prompt to close your session with Router B.

7. Go to the Router C's console port by typing **show sessions** on the first router and using the connection number to return to Router C. Type **show user** and notice the connection to your first router, Router A.

8. Type **clear line** to disconnect the Telnet session.

Lab 7.6: Resolving Hostnames

1. Log in to your router and go into privileged mode by typing **en** or **enable**.

2. From Router A, type **todd** and press Enter at the command prompt. Notice the error you receive and the delay. The router is trying to resolve the hostname to an IP address by looking for a DNS server. You can turn this feature off by using the `no ip domain-lookup` command from global configuration mode.

3. To build a host table, you use the `ip host` command. From Router A, add a host table entry for Router B and Router C by entering the following commands:

```
ip host routerb ip_address
ip host routerc ip_address
```

Here is an example:

```
ip host routerb 172.16.20.2
ip host routerc 172.16.40.2
```

4. Test your host table by typing **ping routerb** from the command prompt (not the `config` prompt).

> RouterA#**ping routerb**
>
> Type escape sequence to abort.
>
> Sending 5, 100-byte ICMP Echos to 172.16.20.2, timeout is 2 seconds:
>
> !!!!!
>
> Success rate is 100 percent (5/5), round-trip min/ avg/max = 4/4/4 ms

5. Test your host table by typing **ping routerc**.

> RouterA#**ping routerc**
>
> Type escape sequence to abort.
>
> Sending 5, 100-byte ICMP Echos to 172.16.40.2, timeout is 2 seconds:
>
> !!!!!
>
> Success rate is 100 percent (5/5), round-trip min/ avg/max = 4/6/8 ms

6. Keep your session to Router B open, and then return to Router A by pressing Ctrl+Shift+6, then X.

7. Telnet to Router C by typing **routerc** at the command prompt.

8. Return to Router A and keep the session to Router C open by pressing Ctrl+Shift+6, then X.

9. View the host table by typing **show hosts** and pressing Enter.

> Default domain is not set
>
> Name/address lookup uses domain service
>
> Name servers are 255.255.255.255

Host	Flags	Age	Type
Address(es)			
routerb	(perm, OK)	0	IP
172.16.20.2			
routerc	(perm, OK)	0	IP
172.16.40.2			

Review Questions

1. Which command will show you the hostname resolved to the IP address on a router?

   A. sh router

   B. sho hosts

   C. sh ip hosts

   D. sho name resolution

2. Which command will copy the IOS to a backup host on your network?

   A. transfer IOS to 172.16.10.1

   B. copy run start

   C. copy tftp flash

   D. copy start tftp

   E. copy flash tftp

3. Which command will copy a router configuration stored on a TFTP host to the router's NVRAM?

   A. transfer IOS to 172.16.10.1

   B. copy run start

   C. copy tftp startup

   D. copy tftp run

   E. copy flash tftp

4. To copy a configuration from a TFTP host to a Cisco router's DRAM on your network, what two commands can you use?

   A. config netw

   B. config mem

   C. config term

   D. copy tftp run

   E. copy tftp start

5. Which memory in a Cisco router stores packet buffers and routing tables?

   A. Flash

   B. RAM

   C. ROM

   D. NVRAM

6. Which of the following is the correct command to create a host table on a Cisco router?

   A. `bob ip host 172.16.10.1`

   B. `host 172.16.10.1 bob`

   C. `ip host bob 172.16.10.1 172.16.10.2`

   D. `host bob 172.16.10.1`

7. What command will allow you to see the connections made from your router to remote device?

   A. `sh sess`

   B. `sh users`

   C. `disconnect`

   D. `clear line`

8. Which command will show the CDP-enabled interfaces on a router?

   A. `sh cdp`

   B. `sh cdp interface`

   C. `sh interface`

   D. `sh cdp traffic`

9. What is the default update timer and holdtime for CDP?

   A. 240, 90

   B. 90, 240

   C. 180, 60

   D. 60, 180

10. To copy a configuration from the Cisco router's DRAM to a TFTP host on your network, what command can you use?

    A. `config netw`

    B. `config mem`

    C. `config term`

    D. `copy run tftp`

    E. `copy start tftp`

11. If you want to have more than one Telnet session open at the same time, what keystroke combination would you use?

    A. Tab+spacebar

    B. Ctrl+X, then 6

    C. Ctrl+Shift+X, then 6

    D. Ctrl+Shift+6, then X

12. Which of the following commands will give you the same output as the `show cdp neighbors detail` command?

    A. `show cdp`

    B. `show cdp ?`

    C. `sh cdp neigh`

    D. `sh cdp entry *`

13. What does the command `cdp timer 90` do?

    A. Displays the update frequency of CDP packets

    B. Changes the update frequency of CDP packets

    C. Sets the CDP neighbor command to 90 lines

    D. Changes the holdtime of CDP packets

14. Which command disables CDP on an individual interface?

    A. `no cdp run`

    B. `no cdp enable`

    C. `no cdp`

    D. `disable cdp`

15. Which command is used to find the path a packet takes through an internetwork?

    A. `ping`

    B. `trace`

    C. RIP

    D. SAP

16. Which two commands can be used to test IP through your network?

    A. `ping`

    B. `trace`

    C. RIP

    D. SAP

17. Which command will clear a connection to a remote router?

    A. `clear connection`

    B. `clear line`

    C. `disconnect`

    D. `clear user`

18. Which command will clear a VTY connection into your router?

    A. `clear connection`

    B. `clear line #`

    C. `disconnect`

    D. `clear user`

19. The `show cdp neighbor` command, run on a Cisco router, will provide you with which of the following? (Choose all that apply.)

    A. IP address of neighbor

    B. Local port/interface

    C. The same information as `show version`

    D. Capability

    E. The same information as `show cdp entry *`

    F. Remote port ID

    G. Neighbor device ID

    H. Holdtime

    I. Hardware platform

    J. Speed of the link

20. Which command can you use to copy a new IOS into a router?

    A. `copy tftp run`

    B. `copy tftp flash`

    C. `copy tftp start`

    D. `copy flash tftp`

    E. `boot system flash IOS_name`

(The answers to the questions begin on the next page.)

Answers to the Written Lab

1. `copy flash tftp`

2. `copy start tftp`

3. `copy start run`

4. `config mem`

5. `show cdp neighbor detail` or `show cdp entry *`

6. `show cdp neighbor`

7. Ctrl+Shift+6, then X

8. `show sessions`

9. `copy tftp flash`

10. `ip host bob 172.16.10.1 172.16.20.2`

Answers to Review Questions

1. B. The command to see the host table, which resolves hostnames to IP addresses, is `show host` or `show hosts`.

2. E. To copy the IOS to a backup host, which is stored in flash memory by default, use the `copy flash tftp` command.

3. C. To copy a configuration of a router stored on a TFTP host to a router's NVRAM, use the `copy tftp startup-config` command.

4. A, D. To copy a configuration of a router stored on a TFTP host to a router's RAM, you can use the command `copy tftp running-config` or `config net`.

5. B. RAM is used to store packet buffers and routing tables, among other things.

6. C. The command `ip host hostname ip_addresses` is used to create a host table on a Cisco router. The second IP address will only be tried if the first one does not work.

7. A. The `show sessions` command will show you the active connections made from your router.

8. B. The `show cdp interface` command shows the status of interfaces enabled with CDP.

9. D. The update timer for CDP packets is 60 seconds. The amount of time a device will hold CDP information is 180 seconds by default.

10. D. To copy a configuration of a router from DRAM to a TFTP host, use the `copy running-config tftp` command.

11. D. To keep open multiple Telnet sessions, use the Ctrl+Shift+6, then X keystroke combination.

12. D. The `show cdp entry *` command is the same as the `show cdp neighbors detail` command.

13. B. The command `cdp timer 90` changes the update frequency from the default of 60 seconds to 90 seconds.

14. B. The `no cdp enable` command disables CDP on an interface.

15. B. The `trace` command displays the path a packet takes to find a remote destination by using ICMP timeouts.

16. A, B. The `ping` and `trace` commands can both be used to test IP connectivity in an internetwork.

17. C. The `disconnect` command will allow you to disconnect a remote connection from your router.

18. B. The `clear line #` command clears a connection into your router.

19. B, D, F, G, H, I. The `show cdp neighbor` command provides you with a lot of information: the local interface, the name of the device, the remote interface used to send CDP, the hostname of the neighbor device, the amount of time CDP packets are held, and the type of Cisco device.

20. B. To copy a new IOS into a router, use the `copy tftp flash` command.

Chapter 8

Configuring Novell IPX

THE CCNA EXAM TOPICS COVERED IN THIS CHAPTER INCLUDE THE FOLLOWING:

- ✓ Identify the network and host in an IPX address
- ✓ Configure IPX on a Cisco router and configure interfaces
- ✓ Configure multiple encapsulations on an interface by using secondary interfaces and subinterfaces
- ✓ Monitor and verify IPX operation on the router

Most network administrators have, at some point, encountered IPX for two reasons: first, Novell NetWare uses IPX as its default protocol; second, it was the most popular network operating system during the late 1980s and early 1990s. As a result, millions of IPX networks have been installed. But Novell is changing things with the release of NetWare 5. TCP/IP is now the default communications protocol instead of IPX, although Novell still supports IPX. Why do they still bother? Well, considering the multitude of installed IPX clients and servers, it would be pretty impractical to yank the support for it.

There's little doubt that IPX will be around for a while so it's no surprise that the Cisco IOS provides full support for large IPX internetworks. But to really take advantage of Novell IPX's functions and features, we need to review the way it operates and handles addressing because it varies significantly from the TCP/IP method we covered earlier. Armed with a solid grasp of things IPX, we'll then explore the configuration of IPX in the Cisco IOS and, from there, cover the monitoring of IPX traffic.

Introduction to Novell IPX

Novell IPX (Internetwork Packet Exchange) has been in use since its release in the early 1980s. It's quite similar to XNS (Xerox Network Systems), which was developed by Xerox at its Palo Alto Research Center in the 1960s; it even shares a likeness with TCP/IP. IPX is really a family of protocols that coexist and interact to empower sound network communications.

Novell IPX Protocol Stack

IPX doesn't map directly to the OSI model, but its protocols do function in layers. Back when they designed IPX, engineers were more concerned with performance than they were with strict compliance to existing standards or models. Even so, comparisons can be made.

Figure 8.1 illustrates the IPX protocols, layers, and functions relative to those of the OSI model.

FIGURE 8.1   IPX protocol stack and the OSI model

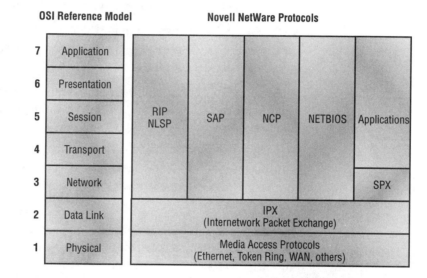

IPX   IPX performs functions at layers 3 and 4 of the OSI model. It controls the assignment of IPX addresses (software addressing) on individual nodes, governs packet delivery across internetworks, and makes routing decisions based on information provided by the routing protocols, RIP or NLSP. IPX is a connectionless protocol (similar to TCP/IP's UDP), so it doesn't require any acknowledgment that packets were received from the destination node. To communicate with the upper-layer protocols, IPX uses *sockets*. These are similar to TCP/IP ports in that they're used to address multiple, independent applications running on the same machine.

SPX SPX (Sequenced Packet Exchange) adds connection-oriented communications to the otherwise connectionless IPX. Through it, upper-layer protocols can ensure data delivery between source and destination nodes. SPX works by creating virtual circuits or connections between machines, with each connection having a specific connection ID included in the SPX header.

RIP RIP (Routing Information Protocol) is a distance-vector routing protocol used to discover IPX routes through internetworks. It employs ticks (1/18 of a second) and *hop counts* (number of routers between nodes) as metrics for determining preferred routes.

SAP SAP (Service Advertising Protocol) is used to advertise and request services. Servers use it to advertise the services they offer, and clients use it to locate network services.

NLSP NLSP (NetWare Link Services Protocol) is an advanced link-state routing protocol developed by Novell. It's intended to replace both RIP and SAP.

NCP NCP (NetWare Core Protocol) provides clients with access to server resources; functions such as file access, printing, synchronization, and security are all handled by NCP.

What does the presence of routing protocols, connection and connectionless transport protocols, and application protocols indicate to you? All of these factors add up to the fact that IPX is capable of supporting large internetworks running many applications. Understanding how Novell uses these protocols clears the way for you to include third-party devices (such as Cisco routers) into an IPX network.

Client-Server Communication

Novell NetWare follows a strict client-server model (there's no overlap): a NetWare node is either a client or a server, and that is that. You won't find peer machines that both provide and consume network resources here. Clients can be workstations running MacOS, DOS, MS Windows, Windows

NT, OS/2, Unix, or VMS. Servers generally run Novell NetWare. NetWare servers provide the following services to clients:

- File

- Print

- Message

- Application

- Database

As you would think, NetWare clients need servers to locate all network resources. Every NetWare server builds an SAP table comprised of all the network resources that it's aware of. (We'll explain how they do this a bit later in the chapter.) When clients require access to a certain resource, they issue an IPX broadcast called a GNS (GetNearestServer) request so they can locate a NetWare server that provides the particular resource the client needs. In turn, the servers receiving the GNS check their SAP tables to locate a NetWare server that matches the specific request; they respond to the client with a GNS reply. The GNS reply points the client to a specific server to contact for the resource it requested. If none of the servers receiving the client's GNS request have or know of another server that has the requested service, they simply don't respond, which leaves the requesting client without the ability to access the requested resource.

Why do we care? Because Cisco routers build SAP tables, too, and because they can respond to client GNS requests just as if they were NetWare servers. This doesn't mean they *offer* the services that NetWare servers do, just that their replies are identical when it comes to locating services. The GNS reply to a client can come from a local NetWare server, a remote NetWare server, or a Cisco router, and generally, if there are local NetWare servers present, they should respond to the client's request.

If there are no local NetWare servers, however, the local Cisco router that connects the client's segment to the IPX internetwork can respond to the client's GNS. This saves the client from having to wait for remote NetWare servers to respond. A second advantage of this arrangement is that precious WAN bandwidth isn't occupied with GNS conversations between clients on a segment with no local NetWare server and remote NetWare servers, as shown in Figure 8.2.

FIGURE 8.2 Remote IPX clients on a serverless network

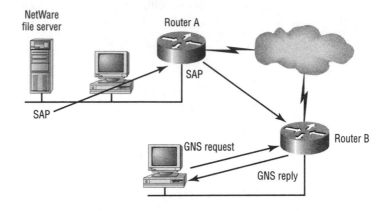

In this figure, you can see client workstations at the remote office site: they require access to server resources at the main office. In this situation, Router B would answer client GNS requests from its SAP table rather than forwarding the request across the WAN to the main office servers. The clients never realize or care that there isn't a NetWare server present on their LAN.

This communication insulates the client from the task of locating and tracking available network resources; it places that burden on the server instead. The client simply broadcasts a GNS and waits for a reply. From the client's perspective, all network resources respond as though they were local, regardless of their physical location in the internetwork.

Server-Server Communication

Communication between two NetWare servers is a bit more complicated than client-server communication. As mentioned earlier, servers are responsible for maintaining tables of all available network resources, regardless of whether those resources are local to the server. Also, keep in mind that each server must be able to locate *any* resource on the internetwork.

Servers exchange two types of information using two separate protocols: SAP (Service Advertising Protocol) and RIP (Routing Information Protocol). As their names suggest, SAP communicates service information, and RIP communicates routing information.

WARNING   Please don't confuse RIP in IPX with RIP in TCP/IP. They're both routing protocols, but they're not the same routing protocol.

Service Advertising Protocol

NetWare servers use SAP to advertise the services they offer by sending out an SAP broadcast every 60 seconds. The broadcast includes all services that the server has learned about from other servers—not just the ones they furnish. All servers receiving the SAP broadcast incorporate the information into their own SAP tables; they then rebroadcast the SAP entries in their own SAP updates. Because SAP information is shared among all servers, all servers eventually become aware of all available services and are thereby equipped to respond to client GNS requests. As new services are introduced, they're added to SAP tables on local servers and are rebroadcast until every server knows they exist and knows where to get them.

So how does a Cisco router fit in here? Well, as far as SAP is concerned, the Cisco router acts just like another NetWare server. By default, an SAP broadcast won't cross a Cisco router. A Cisco router catalogs all SAPs heard on any of its IPX-enabled interfaces into its SAP table; unless you change the settings, the router then broadcasts the whole table from each of those interfaces at 60-second intervals (just as a NetWare server does). This is an important point, especially with WAN links. The router isolates SAP broadcasts to individual segments and passes along only the summarized information to each segment. Let's take a look at an SAP broadcast with the Etherpeek analyzer.

```
Flags:          0x00
  Status:        0x00
  Packet Length:306
  Timestamp:    23:48:36.362000 06/28/1998
Ethernet Header
  Destination:  ff:ff:ff:ff:ff:ff Ethernet Brdcast
  Source:       00:80:5f:ad:14:e4
  Protocol Type:81-37  NetWare
IPX - NetWare Protocol
  Checksum:               0xffff
  Length:                 288
```

```
    Transport Control:
      Reserved:              %0000
      Hop Count:             %0000
    Packet Type:            4  PEP
    Destination Network:   0xcc715b00
    Destination Node:      ff:ff:ff:ff:ff:ff Ethernet Brdcast
    Destination Socket:    0x0452  Service Advertising
Protocol
    Source Network:        0xcc715b00
    Source Node:           00:80:5f:ad:14:e4
    Source Socket:         0x0452  Service Advertising
Protocol
SAP - Service Advertising Protocol
    Operation:             2  NetWare General Service Response
Service Advertising Set #1
    Service Type:          263  NetWare 386
    Service Name:
BORDER3................................
    Network Number:    0x12db8494
    Node Number:       00:00:00:00:00:01
    Socket Number:     0x8104
    Hops to Server:    1
Service Advertising Set #2
    Service Type:      4  File Server
    Service Name:
BORDER3................................
    Network Number:    0x12db8494
    Node Number:       00:00:00:00:00:01
    Socket Number:     0x0451
    Hops to Server:    1
Service Advertising Set #3
    Service Type:      632
    Service Name:      BORDER_____
R.S.I@@@@@D.PJ..
    Network Number:    0x12db8494
    Node Number:       00:00:00:00:00:01
    Socket Number:     0x4006
    Hops to Server:    1
```

This SAP is from a NetWare server named BORDER3. Notice that it is advertising three separate services that it offers. These services—their address and socket information—will be included in the SAP table of all IPX-enabled devices attached to this network (including the routers) and rebroadcast throughout the internetwork.

Routing Information Protocol

RIP information is exchanged between servers much the same way that SAP information is. Servers build routing tables that contain entries for the networks they're directly connected to, they then broadcast this information to all IPX-enabled interfaces. Other servers on those segments receive those updates and broadcast their RIP tables on their IPX interfaces. Just as SAP information travels from server to server until all servers are enlightened, RIP information is spread until all servers and routers know of the internetwork's routes. Like SAP information, RIP information is broadcast at 60-second intervals. Let's take a look at an IPX RIP packet with the Etherpeek analyzer.

```
Flags:          0x80  802.3
  Status:         0x00
  Packet Length:94
  Timestamp:      15:23:05.642000 06/28/1998
802.3 Header
  Destination:  ff:ff:ff:ff:ff:ff Ethernet Brdcast
  Source:       00:00:0c:8d:5c:9d
  LLC Length:   76
802.2 Logical Link Control (LLC) Header
  Dest. SAP:    0xe0  NetWare
  Source SAP:   0xe0  NetWare  Null LSAP
  Command:      0x03  Unnumbered Information
IPX - NetWare Protocol
  Checksum:               0xffff
  Length:                 72
  Transport Control:
    Reserved:             %0000
    Hop Count:            %0000
  Packet Type:            1  RIP
```

```
Destination Network:  0x00002300
Destination Node:     ff:ff:ff:ff:ff:ff Ethernet Brdcast
Destination Socket:   0x0453  Routing Information
Protocol
Source Network:       0x00002300
Source Node:          00:00:0c:8d:5c:9d
Source Socket:        0x0453  Routing Information
Protocol
RIP - Routing Information Protocol
Operation:            2  Response
Network Number Set # 1
  Network Number:   0x00005200
  Number of Hops:   3
  Number of Ticks:  14
Network Number Set # 2
  Network Number:   0x00004100
  Number of Hops:   2
  Number of Ticks:  8
Network Number Set # 3
  Network Number:   0x00003200
  Number of Hops:   1
  Number of Ticks:  2
Network Number Set # 4
  Network Number:   0x00002200
  Number of Hops:   1
  Number of Ticks:  2
Network Number Set # 5
  Network Number:   0x00002100
  Number of Hops:   1
  Number of Ticks:  2
Extra bytes (Padding):
  r                 72
```

See that? It looks a lot like an IP RIP packet, but it's missing the IP addresses. In their place are IPX addresses and network numbers. Also, notice that it has both ticks and hops in the updates. Ticks are how many

1/18 of a second it takes to get to a remote network. This is IPX's way of using link delay to find the best way to a remote network.

There are only three routers in this example, and this packet is sent out every 60 seconds—imagine this happening on a large network with hundreds of routers!

IPX Addressing

After sweating through IP addressing, IPX addressing should seem like a day at the beach. The IPX addressing scheme has several features that make it a lot easier to understand and administer than the TCP/IP scheme is.

IPX addresses use 80 bits, or 10 bytes, of data. As with TCP/IP addresses, they are hierarchical and divided into a network and node portion. The first four bytes always represent the network address, and the last six bytes always represent the node address. There's none of that Class A, Class B, or Class C TCP/IP stuff in IPX addressing—the network and node portions of the address are always the same lengths. After subnet masking, this is sweet indeed!

Just as with IP network addresses, the network portion of the address is assigned by administrators and must be unique on the entire IPX internetwork. Node addresses are automatically assigned to every node. In most cases, the MAC address of the machine is used as the node portion of the address. This offers several notable advantages over TCP/IP addressing. Since client addressing is dynamic (automatic), you don't have to run DHCP or manually configure each individual workstation with an IPX address. Also, since the hardware address (layer 2) is included as part of the software address (layer 3), there's no need for a TCP/IP ARP equivalent in IPX.

As with TCP/IP addresses, IPX addresses can be written in several formats. Most often, though, they're written in hex, such as 00007C80.0000.8609.33E9.

The first eight hex digits (00007C80) represent the network portion of the address. It's a common IPX custom when referring to the IPX network to drop leading 0s. Thus, the above network address would be referred to as IPX network 7C80.

The remaining 12 hex digits (0000.8609.33E9) represent the node portion and are commonly divided into three sections of four hex digits divided by periods. They are the MAC address of the workstation.

Encapsulation

Encapsulation, or *framing*, is the process of taking packets from upper-layer protocols and building frames to transmit them across the network. As you probably recall, frames live at layer 2 of the OSI model. When you're dealing with IPX, encapsulation is the specific process of taking IPX datagrams (layer 3) and building frames (layer 2) for one of the supported media. We'll cover IPX encapsulation on the following physical networks:

- Ethernet
- Token Ring
- FDDI

Why is encapsulation significant? Well, for the very good reason that Net-Ware supports multiple, *incompatible* framing methods, and it does so on the same media. For instance, take Ethernet. NetWare has four different *frame types* to choose from, depending on your needs (see Table 8.1), and each one of those frame types is incompatible with the other ones. It's like this: Say your servers are using Ethernet_802.2 and your clients are configured for Ethernet_II. Does this mean you don't have to worry about anything? Not necessarily. If they're communicating with each other via a router that supports both frame types, you're set. If not—you're cooked—they just won't talk! When configuring any IPX device (including a router) on a network, the frame type has to be consistent for things to work.

TABLE 8.1 Novell Ethernet Encapsulations

NetWare Frame Type	Features
Ethernet_802.3	Default up to NetWare 3.11
Ethernet_802.2	Default since NetWare 3.12
Ethernet_II	Supports both TCP/IP and IPX
Ethernet_SNAP	AppleTalk, IPX, and TCP/IP

Sometimes—and only somctimes—you can intentionally have multiple frame types present on the same network. Typically, you'll start working in an environment that already has all frame types configured—usually because the administrator didn't know what to do and just configured all available frame types on all router and servers, as shown in Figure 8.3.

FIGURE 8.3 Multiple frame types on a single Ethernet segment

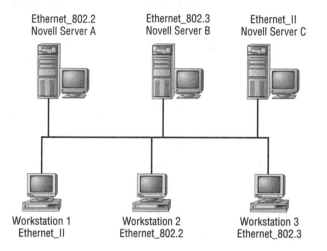

Ethernet_802.2
Novell Server A

Ethernet_802.3
Novell Server B

Ethernet_II
Novell Server C

Workstation 1
Ethernet_II

Workstation 2
Ethernet_802.2

Workstation 3
Ethernet_802.3

Each frame type in Figure 8.3 has a unique IPX network address. Even though there's a single Ethernet segment, there are three *virtual* IPX networks and, therefore, three unique IPX network addresses. Each network will be broadcast across the internetwork every 60 seconds.

In Figure 8.3, Workstation 1 can communicate only with Server C because they're both running Ethernet_II. Workstation 2 can communicate only with Server A, and Workstation 3 can communicate only with Server B. But what if you wanted all the workstations to communicate with all the servers—what would you do? You can add a router that supports all frame types, or you can add more frame types to each server. Adding a router would allow any workstation to communicate with any of the servers, but that router would have to route all packets among all the servers and clients with dissimilar frame types. Adding multiple frame types to servers and routers is not a good solution. It's best to have one frame type, probably 802.2, in your internetwork. However, NetWare 5 runs a native IP, so all this is irrelevant unless you have to support older servers.

When configuring a router, you'll need to know both the frame type and the IPX network address information for each segment that you plan to attach that router to. To find this information, ask the network administrator or go to one of the NetWare servers and type **config** at the server console.

Enabling IPX on Cisco Routers

Cool—with the basics behind you, it's *finally* time to configure IPX on the router! This is easy compared to IP. The only confusing part can be the multiple frame types. But don't worry, I'll show you the configuration in detail.

There are two main tasks to activate IPX across Cisco routers:

- Enabling IPX routing
- Enabling IPX on each individual interface

Enabling IPX Routing

To configure IPX routing, use the `ipx routing` global configuration command. Here is an example:

```
RouterA#config t
RouterA(config)#ipx routing
```

Once you enable IPX routing on the router, RIP and SAP are automatically enabled as well. However, nothing happens until you configure the individual interfaces with IPX addresses.

Enabling IPX on Individual Interfaces

Once you have IPX routing enabled on the router, the next step is to enable IPX on individual interfaces. To enable IPX on an interface, first enter the interface configuration mode, and then issue the following command:

```
ipx network number [encapsulation encapsulation-type]
[secondary]
```

The various parts are defined as follows:

number   The IPX network address.

[encapsulation encapsulation-type]   Optional. Table 8.2 shows the default encapsulation-type on different media.

[secondary]   Indicates a secondary encapsulation (frame type) and network address on the same interface.

Here is an example of configuring IPX on 2501A:

```
2501A#config t
2501A(config)#ipx routing
2501A(config)#int e0
2501A(config-if)#ipx network 10
```

That's all there is to it. Just add the network number, and the rest is done for you. IPX is a very resilient routed protocol because it broadcasts for everything. However, this is also why it causes problems in larger internetworks.

What frame type is now running on Ethernet 0 on 2501A? By default, the frame type is Novell-Ether (802.3). To change the frame type, or to add another frame type, add the encapsulation command to the interface configuration. Table 8.2 shows the different encapsulation (frame types) available with IPX.

TABLE 8.2   Novell IPX Frame Types

Interface Type	Novell Frame Type	Cisco Keyword
Ethernet	Ethernet_802.3	novell-ether (default)
	Ethernet_802.2	sap
	Ethernet_II	arpa
	Ethernet_snap	snap
Token Ring	Token-Ring	sap (default)
	Token-Ring_snap	snap

TABLE 8.2 Novell IPX Frame Types *(continued)*

Interface Type	Novell Frame Type	Cisco Keyword
FDDI	Fddi_snap	snap (default)
	Fddi_802.2	sap
	Fddi_raw	novell-fddi

To change the IPX frame type on Ethernet 0 of 2501A to sap (802.2), use the encapsulation command, as shown below:

```
2501A#config t
2501A(config)#int e0
2501A(config-if)#ipx network 10 encapsulation sap
```

This replaced the existing network number and encapsulation with the 802.2 frame type. If you want to add multiple frame types, you need to either use the secondary command at the end of the network command line, or create subinterfaces. Both the secondary command and subinterfaces are discussed later in this chapter.

To configure a Cisco router into an existing IPX internetwork, you'll need the IPX network address and frame type information from the "config" screen of your NetWare servers for this step. When specifying the encapsulation type on the router, make sure to use the Cisco keyword, *not* the Novell frame type.

Configuring Our Internetwork with IPX

Before you start configuring IPX routing with Cisco routers, let's take another look at our internetwork. Figure 8.4 shows the four routers plus the IP and IPX addressing you'll be using.

Notice that there are IPX network numbers for all network segments in this figure. The IP network numbers are the same as the IP subnet numbers. Remember that IPX addressing has nothing to do with IP, and that you are using the IP subnet numbers as IPX network numbers only for ease of administration.

FIGURE 8.4 Our internetwork

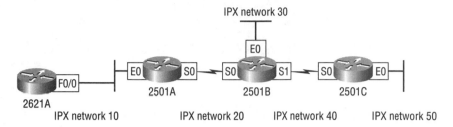

Let's start off by adding the Novell-Ether (802.3) frame type to the internetwork Ethernet networks. Since that is the default encapsulation, the configuration is really simple. The default encapsulation on the serial links is HDLC, and you'll use that as well. HDLC is discussed in Chapter 10.

Configuring IPX on the 2621A Router

To configure IPX on the 2621A router, you just need to start IPX routing on the router with the global configuration command `ipx routing`. Then tell interface FastEthernet 0/0 that it is on IPX network 10.

Here is the configuration for 2621A:

```
2621A(config)#ipx routing
2621A(config)#int f0/0
2621A(config-if)#ipx network 10
```

That's it. The 2621A router will now route IPX traffic through interface FastEthernet 0/0 using IPX network 10.

Configuring IPX on the 2501A Router

The same commands are used on the 2501A router as on the 2621A router. However, the 2501A router has two connections into the internetwork: interface Ethernet 0 is on IPX network 10 and interface serial 0 is on IPX network 20.

Here is the configuration for the 2501A router:

```
2501A(config)#ipx routing
2501A(config)#int e0
```

```
2501A(config-if)#ipx network 10
2501A(config-if)#int s0
2501A(config-if)#ipx network 20
```

That's all you need to do to configure IPX on the 2501A router. Much easier than IP, isn't it?

Configuring IPX on the 2501B Router

To configure IPX routing on the 2501B router, you need to configure three interfaces. Interface Ethernet 0 is on network 30, interface serial 0 is on IPX network 20 and int serial 1 is on network 40.

Here is the configuration for the 2501B router:

```
2501B(config)#ipx routing
2501B(config)#int e0
2501B(config-if)#ipx network 30
2501B(config-if)#int s0
2501B(config-if)#ipx network 20
2501B(config-if)#int s1
2501B(config-if)#ipx network 40
```

That is all you need to do to configure IPX on the 2501B router.

Configuring IPX on the 2501C Router

To configure IPX routing on the 2501C router, you need to configure interface Ethernet 0 into IPX network 50 and interface serial 0 into IPX network 40.

Here is the configuration for the 2501C router:

```
2501C(config)#ipx routing
2501C(config)#int e0
2501C(config-if)#ipx network 50
2501C(config-if)#int s0
2501C(config-if)#ipx network 20
```

All four of the routers are now configured and should be up and working. The best way to verify the configuration is with the show ipx route command.

Verifying the IPX Routing Tables

To view the IPX routing tables, use the command show ipx route. Like IP, IPX routers only know about directly connected networks by default. However, when you turned on IPX routing in the configuration examples above, IPX RIP was automatically started on all routers.

IPX RIP will find all IPX networks in the internetwork and update all routers' routing tables. Let's take a look at all routers in our internetwork and see the IPX routing table.

2621A

The 2621A router is only connected to IPX network 10, so IPX RIP would have to update the routing table of the other four IPX networks in the internetwork.

Here is the routing table on the 2621A router:

```
2621A#sh ipx route
Codes: C - Connected primary network,    c - Connected
secondary network
[output cut]
5 Total IPX routes. Up to 1 parallel paths and 16 hops
allowed.
No default route known.
C        10 (NOVELL-ETHER),  Fa0/0
R        20 [07/01] via      10.0000.0c8d.3a7b,   16s, Fa0/0
R        30 [07/02] via      10.0000.0c8d.3a7c,   17s, Fa0/0
R        40 [07/02] via      10.0000.0c8d.3a7c,   17s, Fa0/0
R        50 [13/03] via      10.0000.0c8d.3a7c,   17s, Fa0/0
2621A#
```

The C means a directly connected IPX network and the Rs are IPX RIP-found networks. The [07/01] is the tick and hops needed to get to the remote network.

2501A

The 2501A router knows only about IPX networks 10 and 20 since that is what is directly connected. IPX RIP will tell router 2501A about networks 30, 40, and 50. Here is the routing table from the 2501A router:

```
2501A#sh ipx route
Codes: C - Connected primary network,    c - Connected
secondary network
[output cut]
5 Total IPX routes. Up to 1 parallel paths and 16 hops
allowed.
No default route known.
C        20 (HDLC),           Se0
C        10 (NOVELL-ETHER),   Et0
R        30 [13/02] via       20.0000.0c8d.2b8c,   16s, Se0
R        40 [07/02] via       20.0000.0c8d.2b8c,   17s, Se0
R        50 [07/03] via       20.0000.0c8d.2b8c,   17s, Se0
2501A#
```

In the routing table above, notice the two directly connected networks and the three RIP-found networks. The IPX address of the neighbor's interface is included in the routing table as well as the interface the router will use to get to the remote network.

2501B

The routes found from IPX RIP in the 2501B router are 10 and 20. Here is the output from the 2501B router:

```
2501B#sh ipx route
Codes: C - Connected primary network,    c - Connected
secondary network
[output cut]
5 Total IPX routes. Up to 1 parallel paths and 16 hops
allowed.
No default route known.
C        20 (HDLC),           Se0
C        40 (HDLC),           Se1
```

```
C          30 (NOVELL-ETHER),   Et0
R          10 [07/01] via       20.0000.0c8d.3d8e,   16s, Se0
R          50 [07/01] via       40.0000.0c8d.5c9d,   17s, Se1
2501B#
```

2501C

In the 2501C router, the routes that are found by IPX RIP are networks 10, 20, and 30. Here is the output from the 2501C router:

```
2501C#sh ipx route
Codes: C - Connected primary network,    c - Connected
secondary network
[output cut]
5 Total IPX routes. Up to 1 parallel paths and 16 hops
allowed.
No default route known.
C          40 (HDLC),           Se0
C          50 (NOVELL-ETHER),   Et0
R          10 [13/02] via       40.0000.0c8d.5c9d,   16s, Se0
R          20 [07/01] via       40.0000.0c8d.5c9d,   17s, Se0
R          30 [07/01] via       40.0000.0c8d.5c9d,   17s, Se0
2501C#
```

Adding Secondary Addresses

What is the Ethernet frame type we are running on our sample internetwork? Novell-Ether (802.3). Since we didn't use the encapsulation command, the default frame type was used.

In this section, I will show you how to configure the other three available frame types on our Ethernet networks. This is not so you can go and do this in production—that would be a bad thing. Rather, this is so that when you see this type of configuration, you know what it is and how to fix it.

To configure multiple frame types on the same LAN network, you can either use the secondary command or create a subinterface. There is absolutely no functional difference on how the secondary or subinterface run on the internetwork. The difference is for administration purposes only.

Configuring Secondary Addresses

To configure a secondary address on an Ethernet LAN to support multiple frame types, use the ipx network command with the secondary parameter at the end of the command.

Here is an example of adding a secondary network to 2501A's Ethernet connection:

```
2501A#config t
Enter configuration commands, one per line.  End with
CNTL/Z.
2501A(config)#int e0
2501A(config-if)#ipx network 10a encap sap sec
```

If you don't use the secondary command at the end of the line, the ipx network command will replace the existing entry. (The shortcut commands encap and sec were used here instead of the whole command encapsulation and secondary.)

The important thing to understand is that each frame type must have a different IPX network number. Notice the 10a in the above example. The 802.3 frame type is using 10 so that you cannot configure the 802.2 frame type with that number.

Subinterfaces

To define IPX network numbers to router interfaces that support multiple networks, you can use a subinterface instead of the secondary command. This allows one physical interface to support multiple logical IPX networks. Each subinterface, like a secondary, must have a unique IPX network number and a unique encapsulation type.

To define subinterfaces, use the `interface ethernet port.number` command. You can use numbers between e0.0 and e0.4292967295—that's a lot of subinterfaces! An example of adding the 802.2 frame type is shown below:

```
2621A(config)#int e0.10
2621A(config-subif)#ipx network 10a encap sap
2621A(config-subif)#^Z
2621A#
```

As I have mentioned before, there is no functional difference between the `secondary` and `subinterface` commands on the IPX internetwork; it is merely an administrative difference. You create subinterfaces instead of a secondary for administrative control because you can place commands under the subinterface that allow more granular control over the subinterface and associated networks. If you use the `secondary` command instead, the network is placed under the physical interface and any change you make to the physical interface affects all networks.

Configuring Our Internetwork with Multiple Ethernet Frame Types

You never really want to do this in a real product network. The only time you would is if you were trying to support clients that just couldn't run the 802.2 frame type and you needed to support 802.3. Remember, the best IPX network is one that uses only one frame type.

However, you should be aware of the different frame types and how they are configured. This section will teach you just that. Let's configure our internetwork to run all possible frame types on the Ethernet LANs. This way, when you see this configuration in a production network, you'll know what is wrong with it and why everyone is complaining that the network is a *not*work.

It is important to understand that this is performed only on the LAN interfaces and that you do not run LAN frames on a WAN interface.

Configuring Multiple Frame Types on the 2621A Router

To configure multiple frame types on the 2621A router, you'll need to add three new IPX network numbers, one for each frame type you want to add. When configuring multiple frame types, I like to use the primary number plus a letter. In this configuration, use 10a for 802.2, 10b for Ethernet_II, and 10c for SNAP.

For the following configuration, you will create one secondary address on each router and two subinterfaces. You can do this any way you want, but this is the way I chose to have you do it.

Here is the configuration for 2621A. Notice that when you use the command `ipx network 10a encap` and a question mark, you can see all the supported encapsulation types and the Cisco keywords.

```
2621A(config)#int f0/0
2621A(config-if)#ipx network 10a encap ?
  arpa         Novell Ethernet_II
  hdlc         HDLC on serial links
  novell-ether Novell Ethernet_802.3
  novell-fddi  Novell FDDI RAW
  sap          IEEE 802.2 on Ethernet, FDDI, Token Ring
  snap     IEEE 802.2 SNAP on Ethernet, Token Ring, and
FDDI
RouterA(config-if)#ipx network 10a encap sap sec
```

After you configure the secondary address, you need to add two subinterfaces. If you were configuring this network for a real production network and needed to support multiple frame types, you would use only subinterfaces and no secondary networks because Cisco will no longer support `secondary` commands in the future. The `secondary` command is only included here so you understand what it is if you see it in a configuration.

The subinterface numbers can be any number, as the help screen (`int f0/0.?`) shows below. The subinterface numbers are only locally significant and have no bearing on how IPX runs on the internetwork.

```
2621A(config)#int f0/0.?
  <0-4294967295>  Ethernet interface number
2621A(config)#int f0/0.10
2621A(config-if)#ipx network 10b encap arpa
```

```
2621A(config)#int f0/0.100
2621A(config-if)#ipx network 10c encap snap
```

All four frame types are now configured on the FastEthernet 0/0 interface of the 2621 router. For any device to communicate with the 2621A router with IPX, they must support the same network numbers configured with each frame type.

Configuring Multiple Frame Types on the 2501A Router

For the 2501A router to communicate to the 2621A router with IPX, it must be configured with the same IPX network numbers for each frame type configured.

Here is the configuration for the 2501A router:

```
2501A(config)#int e0
2501A(config-if)#ipx network 10a encap sap sec
2501A(config-if)#int e0.10
2501A(config-if)#ipx network 10b encap arpa
2501A(config-if)#int e0.100
2501A(config-if)#ipx network 10c encap snap
```

In the above example, the same subinterface numbers were used, but they can be any numbers you want to use. Here is a copy of the running-config after the router is configured with all four IPX Ethernet frame types:

```
hostname RouterA
!
ipx routing 0060.7015.63d6
!
interface Ethernet0
ip address 172.16.10.1 255.255.255.0
ipx network 10
ipx network 10A encapsulation SAP secondary
!
interface Ethernet0.10
ipx network 10B encapsulation ARPA
```

```
!
interface Ethernet0.100
ipx network 10C encapsulation SNAP
!
interface Serial0
ip address 172.16.20.1 255.255.255.0
ipx network 20
```

Notice that under the main Ethernet interface that there are two IPX network numbers, one for the Novell-Ether (802.3) frame type and one for the SAP (802.2) frame type. The Ethernet_II (arpa) frame type and the SNAP frame type have their own subinterfaces, and the secondary command does not need to be used.

Configuring Multiple Frame Types on the 2501B Router

To configure the 2501B router, you need to be concerned with only the Ethernet 0 interface. IPX network 30 is running the 802.3 frame type on the primary interface. I will add the other three possible frame types to Ethernet 0. Here is the configuration for the 2501B router:

```
2501B(config)#int e0
2501B(config-if)#ipx network 30a encap sap sec
2501B(config-if)#int e0.30
2501B(config-subif)#ipx network 30b encap arpa
2501B(config-subif)#int e0.300
2501B(config-subif)#ipx network 30c encap snap
```

The 2501B router now has all four IPX Ethernet frame types configured on the Ethernet 0 interface. Plenty of bandwidth on the Ethernet network is now being wasted.

Configuring Multiple Frame Types on the 2501C Router

The 2501C has only one LAN connection, and that is to IPX network 50. IPX network 50 is running the 802.3 frame type. Let's configure the other three supported IPX network numbers on Ethernet 0.

Here is the configuration for the 2501C router:

```
2501C(config)#int e0
2501C(config-if)#ipx network 50a encap sap sec
2501C(config-if)#int e0.50
2501C(config-subif)#ipx network 50b encap arpa
2501C(config-subif)#int e0.500
2501C(config-subif)#ipx network 50c encap snap
```

All four of the routers are now configured and should be up and working with all four possible IPX Ethernet frame types.

Are you ready to find our why using multiple frame types is so bad for your internetwork? Let's use the show ipx route command and find out.

Verifying the IPX Routing Tables

Remember, when we verified the IPX routing tables earlier, there was one connection for each IPX network in the routing tables of each router. Let's run the command again and see what it shows now. (This is the IPX routing table for the 2621A router only. The other routers will have the same routing table.)

```
2621A#sh ipx route
Codes: C - Connected primary network,    c - Connected
secondary network
[output cut]
14 Total IPX routes. Up to 1 parallel paths and 16 hops
allowed.
No default route known.
C          10 (NOVELL-ETHER),  Fa0/0
C          10A(SAP),           Fa0/0
C          10B(ARPA),          Fa0/0.10
C          10B(SNAP),          Fa0/0.100
R          20 [07/01] via      10.0000.0c8d.3a7b,   16s, Fa0/0
R          30A[07/02] via      10.0000.0c8d.3a7c,   17s, Fa0/0
R          30B[07/02] via      10.0000.0c8d.3a7c,   17s, Fa0/0
R          30C[07/02] via      10.0000.0c8d.3a7c,   17s, Fa0/0
R          30D[07/02] via      10.0000.0c8d.3a7c,   17s, Fa0/0
R          40 [07/02] via      10.0000.0c8d.3a7c,   17s, Fa0/0
```

```
R          50A[13/03] via       10.0000.0c8d.3a7c,   17s, Fa0/0
R          50B[13/03] via       10.0000.0c8d.3a7c,   17s, Fa0/0
R          50C[13/03] via       10.0000.0c8d.3a7c,   17s, Fa0/0
R          50D[13/03] via       10.0000.0c8d.3a7c,   17s, Fa0/0
2621A#
```

Notice that the routing table has 14 IPX routes now instead of the five we had earlier. You did not add any new physical networks, but the new networks are the new encapsulations you added for each network. The three LANs each advertise four IPX networks every 60 seconds out each active interface. Imagine if you had 20 routers and you added all the frame types!

There is one more consideration when adding multiple frame types on a LAN: the SAP activity. Service Advertisement Protocol (SAP) is broadcast over every active interface every 60 seconds. If you have multiple frame types configured on a LAN, the broadcast is sent out in every frame type possible. If you only send one SAP packet, which is unlikely, you would send that same packet out four times. If you have multiple SAP packets, you send each packet out four times every 60 seconds.

Monitoring IPX on Cisco Routers

Once you have IPX configured and running, there are several ways to verify and track that your router is communicating correctly. The following commands will be covered:

- show ipx servers
- show ipx route
- show ipx traffic
- show ipx interface
- show protocol
- debug ipx
- IPX ping

Show IPX Servers

The sho ipx servers command is a lot like the display servers command in NetWare—it displays the contents of the SAP table in the Cisco router, so you should see the names of all SAP services here. Remember that if the router doesn't have entries for remote servers in its own SAP table, local clients will never see those servers. If there are servers missing from this table that shouldn't be, double-check your IPX network addresses and encapsulation settings.

```
2501A#sho ipx servers
Codes: S - Static, P - Periodic, E - EIGRP, N - NLSP,  H - Holddown, + = detail
9 Total IPX Servers
Table ordering is based on routing and server info
```

	Type	Name	Net	Address	Port	Route	Hops	Itf
P	4	BORDER1	350ED6D2.	0000.0000.0001:0451	2/01	1	Et0	
P	4	BORDER3	12DB8494.	0000.0000.0001:0451	2/01	1	Et0	
P	107	BORDER1	350ED6D2.	0000.0000.0001:8104	2/01	1	Et0	
P	107	BORDER3	12DB8494.	0000.0000.0001:8104	2/01	1	Et0	
P	26B	BORDER	350ED6D2.	0000.0000.0001:0005	2/01	1	Et0	
P	278	BORDER	12DB8494.	0000.0000.0001:4006	2/01	1	t0	
P	278	BORDER	350ED6D2.	0000.0000.0001:4006	2/01	1	Et0	
P	3E1	BORDER1	350ED6D2.	0000.0000.0001:9056	2/01	1	Et0	
P	3E1	BORDER3	12DB8494.	0000.0000.0001:9056	2/01	1	Et0	

The output from the router allows you to see all the IPX servers discovered through the SAP advertisements.

The Type field is the type of SAP service being advertised, with 4 being a file service and 7 a print service. The other service numbers listed are specific for that type of application running on the NetWare server. The Net and Address fields are the IPX Internal network numbers configured on each server. The Port field identifies the upper layer application. The socket number for the NetWare Core Protocol (NCP) is 451.

Show IPX Route

The show ipx route command displays the IPX routing table entries that the router knows about. The router reports networks to which it is directly connected, it then reports networks that it has learned of since the router has come online.

```
2501A#sh ipx route
Codes: C - Connected primary network,   c - Connected
secondary network, S - Static, F - Floating static, L -
Local (internal), W - IPXWAN, R - RIP, E - EIGRP, N -
NLSP, X - External, A - Aggregate, s - seconds, u - uses
6 Total IPX routes. Up to 1 parallel paths and 16 hops
allowed.
No default route known.

C       10 (NOVELL-ETHER),  Et0
C       20 (HDLC),          Se0
c       10a (sap),          Et0
C       10b (ARPA),         Et0.10
R       40 [07/01] via      20.00e0.1ea9.c418,    13s, Se0
R       50 [13/02] via      20.00e0.1ea9.c418,    13s, Se0
RouterA#
```

The small c in the routing table tells you that it is a secondary configured IPX network.

Load Balancing with IPX

If you were to set up parallel IPX paths between routers, the Cisco IOS will not learn about these paths by default. The router will learn a single path to a destination and discard information about alternative, parallel, equal-cost paths. Notice in the show ipx route output above the phrase Up to 1 parallel paths and 16 hops allowed. To be able to perform a round-robin load balance over multiple equal-cost paths, you need to add the command ipx maximum-paths [#] (with # being any number up to 64); this will allow the router to accept the possibility that there might be more than one path to the same destination.

The Cisco IOS will perform per-packet load sharing by default over these parallel lines. Packets will be sent on a round-robin basis between all equal-cost lines, without regard to the destination. However, if you want to ensure that all packets sent to a destination or host will always go over the same line, use the IPX per-host-load-share command.

The ipx maximum-paths command is shown below. It tells the IPX RIP protocol to perform a round-robin load balance across two equal costs paths.

```
Router#config t
Router(config)#ipx maximum-paths 2
Router(config)#^Z
Router#sh ipx route
Codes: C - Connected primary network,    c - Connected
[output cut]
5 Total IPX routes. Up to 2 parallel paths and 16 hops
allowed.
[output cut]
```

The show ipx route command shows that two parallel paths are now supported.

Show IPX Traffic

The show ipx traffic command gives you a summary of the number and type of IPX packets received and transmitted by the router. Notice that this command will show you both the IPX RIP and SAP update packets.

```
2501A#sh ipx traffic
System Traffic for 0.0000.0000.0001 System-Name: RouterA
Rcvd:   15 total, 0 format errors, 0 checksum errors, 0
bad hop count, 0 packets pitched, 15 local destination, 0
multicast
Bcast:  10 received, 249 sent
Sent:   255 generated, 0 forwarded
        0 encapsulation failed, 0 no route
SAP:    1 SAP requests, 0 SAP replies, 0 servers
        0 SAP Nearest Name requests, 0 replies
        0 SAP General Name requests, 0 replies
        0 SAP advertisements received, 0 sent
        0 SAP flash updates sent, 0 SAP format errors
```

```
RIP:     1 RIP requests, 0 RIP replies, 6 routes
         8 RIP advertisements received, 230 sent
         12 RIP flash updates sent, 0 RIP format errors
Echo:    Rcvd 0 requests, 5 replies
         Sent 5 requests, 0 replies
         0 unknown: 0 no socket, 0 filtered, 0 no helper
         0 SAPs throttled, freed NDB len 0
Watchdog:
         0 packets received, 0 replies spoofed
Queue lengths:
         IPX input: 0, SAP 0, RIP 0, GNS 0
         SAP throttling length: 0/(no limit), 0 nets
pending lost route reply
 --More–
```

Remember that the show ipx traffic command shows you the statistics for IPX RIP and SAP information received on the router. If you wanted to view the statistics of RIP and SAP information received only on a specific interface, use the next command we discuss: show ipx interface.

Show IPX Interfaces

The show ipx interfaces command gives you the interface status of IPX and the IPX parameters configured on each interface. The show ipx interface e0 command shows you the IPX address and encapsulation type of the interface. If you use the show interface e0 command, remember that it does not provide the IPX address of the interface, only the IP address.

```
2501A#sh ipx int e0
Ethernet0 is up, line protocol is up
  IPX address is 10.0000.0c8d.5c9d, NOVELL-ETHER [up]
  Delay of this IPX network, in ticks is 1 throughput 0
link delay 0
  IPXWAN processing not enabled on this interface.
  IPX SAP update interval is 1 minute(s)
  IPX type 20 propagation packet forwarding is disabled
  Incoming access list is not set
  Outgoing access list is not set
```

```
    IPX helper access list is not set
    SAP GNS processing enabled, delay 0 ms, output filter
list is not set
    SAP Input filter list is not set
    SAP Output filter list is not set
    SAP Router filter list is not set
    Input filter list is not set
    Output filter list is not set
    Router filter list is not set
    Netbios Input host access list is not set
    Netbios Input bytes access list is not set
    Netbios Output host access list is not set
    Netbios Output bytes access list is not set
    Updates each 60 seconds, aging multiples RIP: 3 SAP: 3
    SAP interpacket delay is 55 ms, maximum size is 480
bytes
    RIP interpacket delay is 55 ms, maximum size is 432
bytes
  --More--
```

This command shows you the RIP and SAP information received on a certain interface. The show ipx traffic command shows the RIP and SAP information received on the router in whole.

Show Protocols

There is one more command that shows the IPX address and encapsulation type of an interface: the show protocols command. This command shows the routed protocols configured on your router and the interface addresses.

Here is the show protocol command run on the 2501A router:

```
2501A#sh protocols
Global values:
  Internet Protocol routing is enabled
  IPX routing is enabled
Ethernet0 is up, line protocol is up
  Internet address is 172.16.10.1/24
  IPX address is 10.0060.7015.63d6 (NOVELL-ETHER)
```

```
   IPX address is 10A.0060.7015.63d6 (SAP)
Ethernet0.10 is up, line protocol is up
   IPX address is 10B.0060.7015.63d6
Ethernet0.100 is up, line protocol is up
   IPX address is 10C.0060.7015.63d6
Serial0 is up, line protocol is up
   Internet address is 172.16.20.1/24
   IPX address is 20.0060.7015.63d6
```

Notice that you can see all configured interfaces addresses, even for the subinterfaces. However, although the primary, secondary, and subinterfaces show the interface addresses, the subinterfaces do not show the encapsulation types.

Remember, there are only two commands that show you the IPX address of an interface: show ipx interface and show protocols.

Debug IPX

The debug ipx commands show you IPX as it's running through your internetwork. It's noteworthy that you can see the IPX RIP and SAP updates with this command, but be careful—it can consume your precious CPU if you don't use it wisely.

The two commands that are the most useful with IPX are debug ipx routing activity and debug ipx sap activity, as shown in the router output below:

```
RouterA#debug ipx routing ?
  activity  IPX RIP routing activity
  events    IPX RIP routing events
```

Let's take a look at each command.

Debug IPX Routing Activity

The debug ipx routing activity command shows information about IPX routing updates that are transmitted or received on the router.

```
RouterA#debug ipx routing act
IPX routing debugging is on
RouterA#
```

```
IPXRIP: update from 20.00e0.1ea9.c418
    50 in 2 hops, delay 13
    40 in 1 hops, delay 7
IPXRIP: positing full update to 10.ffff.ffff.ffff via
Ethernet0 (broadcast)
IPXRIP: src=10.0000.0c8d.5c9d, dst=20.ffff.ffff.ffff,
packet sent
    network 50, hops 3,  delay 14
    network 40, hops 2,  delay 8
    network 30, hops 1,  delay 2
    network 20, hops 1,  delay 2
    network 10, hops 1,  delay 2
```

You can turn this command off by using undebug all (un al, for short), or you can type the whole command as demonstrated below:

```
RouterA#undebug ipx routing act
IPX routing debugging is off
RouterA#
```

Debug IPX SAP Activity

The debug ipx sap activity command shows you the IPX SAP packets that are transmitted and received on your router. SAPs are broadcast over every active interface every 60 seconds, just as IPX RIP is. Each SAP packet shows up as multiple lines in the debug output.

In the router output below, the first two lines are IPX SAPs; the other four lines are a packet summary and service detail message.

```
RouterA#debug ipx sap activity
05:31:18: IPXSAP: positing update to 1111.ffff.ffff.ffff
via Ethernet0 (broadcast) (full)
02:31:18: IPXSAP: Update type 0x2 len 288
src:1111.00e0.2f5d.bf2e dest:1111.ffff.ffff.ffff(452)
02:31:18:   type 0x7, " MarketingPrint ",
10.0000.0000.0001(451), 2 hops
02:31:18:   type 0x4, "SalesFS", 30.0000.0000.0001(451),
2 hops
02:31:18:   type 0x4, "MarketingFS",
30.0000.0000.0001(451), 2 hops
```

```
02:31:18:  type 0x7, "SalesFS", 50.0000.0000.0001(451),
2 hops
```

You can turn the debug command off by using undebug all (un al, for short), or you can type the whole command as demonstrated below:

```
RouterA#undebug ipx sap activity
IPX routing debugging is off
```

RouterA#IPX Ping

By either telnetting into a remote router or using the show cdp neighbor detail or show cdp entry * commands, you can find the IPX address of a neighbor router. This will allow you to ping that address with IPX and test your internetwork.

You can ping an IPX address from a router through a regular ping or through an extended ping. The following command was run on Router C and was used to find the IPX network address for Router B.

```
RouterC#sh cdp entry *
-------------------------
Device ID: RouterB
Entry address(es):
  IP address: 172.16.40.1
  Novell address: 40.0000.0c8d.5c9d
Platform: cisco 2500,  Capabilities: Router
Interface: Serial0,  Port ID (outgoing port): Serial1
Holdtime : 155 sec
```

Now that you have the IPX address for Router B, you can ping the router. You can use the ping ipx [address] command from any router prompt, as shown below:

```
RouterC#ping ipx 40.0000.0c8d.5c9d
Sending 5, 100-byte IPX Novell Echoes to 40.0000.0c8d.5c9d
, timeout is 2 seconds:
!!!!!
```

You can also use an extended ping, which has more capabilities than a standard ping.

```
RouterC#ping
Protocol [ip]: ipx
Target IPX address: 40.0000.0c8d.5c9d
Repeat count [5]:
Datagram size [100]:
Timeout in seconds [2]:
Verbose [n]:
Novell Standard Echo [n]: y
Type escape sequence to abort.
Sending 5, 100-byte IPX Novell Echoes to 40.0000.0c8d.5c9d
, timeout is 2 seconds:
!!!!!
Success rate is 100 percent (5/5), round-trip min/avg/max
= 4/7/12 ms
```

Summary

In this chapter, we covered the following points:

- The required IPX address and encapsulation types and the frame types that Cisco routers can use when running IPX.

- How to enable the Novell IPX protocol and configure router interfaces. We talked about and gave examples of how to configure IPX on Cisco routers and its interfaces.

- How to monitor the Novell IPX operation on the router. We covered some basic tools for monitoring IPX on your routers.

- The two parts of network addressing and these parts in specific protocol address examples.

- The IPX host address and the different parts of this address.

Key Terms

Be sure you're familiar with the following terms before taking the exam:

connection ID

encapsulation

framing

socket

virtual circuit

Commands in This Chapter

Command	Description
debug ipx	Shows the RIP and SAP information as it passes through the router.
encapsulation	Sets the frame type used on an interface.
int e0.10	Creates a subinterface.
ipx network	Assigns an IPX network number to an interface.
ipx ping	Is a Packet Internet Groper used to test IPX packet on an internetwork.
ipx routing	Turns on IPX routing.
secondary	Adds a second IPX network on the same physical interface.
show ipx interface	Shows the RIP and SAP information being sent and received on an individual interface. Also shows the IPX address of the interface.
show ipx route	Shows the IPX routing table.

Command	Description
show ipx servers	Shows the SAP table on a Cisco router.
show ipx traffic	Shows the RIP and SAP information sent and received on a Cisco router.
show protocols	Shows the routed protocols and the addresses on each interface.

Written Lab

In this section, you will write out the answers to the following IPX related questions.

1. Write the command that lets you view your configured routed protocols on your router.

2. Write the command to enable the IPX-routed protocol.

3. Write the command that enables IPX on individual interfaces. Configure an Ethernet 0 interface with IPX network 11, Token Ring with IPX network 15, and serial 0 with IPX network 20.

4. Write the command that lets you see the IPX routing table.

5. Write the two commands you can use to see the IPX address of an interface.

6. Write the two commands that will find your neighbor's IPX address.

7. Add the Ethernet_II frame type to an Ethernet 0 interface, but don't use a subinterface to accomplish this. Use IPX network number 11a.

8. Add the 802.2 and SNAP frame types to an Ethernet 0 interface using subinterfaces. Use 11b and 11c IPX network numbers.

9. Write the commands that you can use to verify your IPX configuration.

Hands-on Labs

In this section, you will configure three 2501 routers with IPX routing. There are two labs. The first one configures IPX routing with 802.3 frame types; the second lab configures multiple frame types on the same physical LAN.

Lab 8.1: Configuring Internetworking Packet Exchange (IPX)

Lab 8.2: Adding Secondary Network Addresses and Multiple Frame Types with IPX

Both labs will use Figure 8.5 to configure the network.

FIGURE 8.5 IPX lab figure

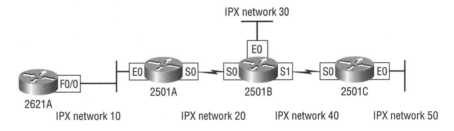

Lab 8.1: Configuring Internetworking Packet Exchange (IPX)

1. Log in a router and go into privileged mode by typing **en** or **enable**.

2. Type **show protocol** or **sh prot** to see your routed protocols configured. Notice that this shows the routed protocol (IP) as well as the configured addresses for each interface.

3. Enable the IPX-routed protocol on your router by using the IPX routing command:

```
RouterA#config t
RouterA(config)#ipx routing
RouterA(config)#^Z
```

4. Check your routed protocols again to see if IPX routing is enabled by typing the commands **sh prot** or **show protocol**. Notice that IPX routing is enabled, but the interfaces don't have IPX addresses, only IP addresses.

5. Enable IPX on the individual interfaces by using the interface command `ipx network`. You can use any number, up to eight characters, hexadecimal (A through F and 0 through 9). Here is an example for router 2501A:

```
2501A#config t
2501A(config)#int e0
2501A(config-if)#ipx network 11
2501A(config-if)#int to0
2501A(config-if)#ipx network 15
2501A(config-if)#int s0
2501A(config-if)#ipx network 20
```

6. Configure the other routers in the lab with IPX networking.

7. Test your configuration. One of the best ways to do this is with the `show ipx route` command.

8. Use the `show protocol` command and `show ipx interface` command to see the IPX addresses of an interface.

9. Once you find the IPX address of your neighbor routers, ping using the IPX protocol. (You can either go to the neighbor routers' console port, use the `show protocol` or `show ipx interface` command, or use the CDP protocol to gather the protocol information, as `sh cdp entry *`.)

10. Use the `ipx maximum-paths` command to tell a Cisco router that it is possible there is more than one link to a remote network. (The IPX protocol, by default, only looks for one route to a remote network. Once it finds a valid route, it will not consider looking for another route, even if a second route exists.)

11. Verify this command with the `show ipx route` command.

Lab 8.2: Adding Secondary Network Addresses and Multiple Frame Types with IPX

In Lab 8.1, you added IPX routing to your routers and IPX network numbers to your interfaces. By default, Cisco routers run the 802.3 Ethernet frame type. To add a second frame type (Ethernet supports four) to your Ethernet, use the `encapsulation` command. However, you need to remember two things: You must use a different network number for each frame type and you cannot add Ethernet frame types to a serial link. Let's configure Router A with a second frame type on the Ethernet LAN.

1. In Ethernet configuration mode, use the `IPX network` command with a different IPX network number and then use the `encapsulation` command. Here is an example on Router A:

   ```
   RouterA#config t
   RouterA(config)#int e0
   RouterA(config-if)#ipx network 11a encapsulation ?
     arpa         Novell Ethernet_II
     hdlc         HDLC on serial links
     novell-ether Novell Ethernet_802.3
     novell-fddi  Novell FDDI RAW
     sap          IEEE 802.2 on Ethernet, FDDI, Token
   Ring
     snap         IEEE 802.2 SNAP on Ethernet, Token
   Ring, and FDDI
   ```

2. Notice the different options available. To use the Ethernet_II frame type, you need to use the `arpa` keyword. You can use `sec` instead of the full command `secondary`. Notice that you are adding the Ethernet_II frame type to your Ethernet LAN off of interface E0 on Router A.

   ```
   RouterA(config-if)#ipx network 11a encapsulation
   arpa ?
   secondary  Make this network a secondary network
     <cr>
   RouterA(config-if)#ipx network 11a encapsulation
   arpa secondary
   ```

3. You can also add a secondary network number and frame type by using subinterfaces. There is not a functional difference between using the secondary command and subinterfaces. However, using subinterfaces will possibly allow you more configuration control over using the secondary command. Use a subinterface command on an Ethernet network:

```
RouterC#config t
RouterC(config)#int e0.?
  <0-4294967295>  Ethernet interface number
RouterC(config)#int e0.1500
RouterC(config-subif)#ipx network 10b encap ?
  arpa          Novell Ethernet_II
  hdlc          HDLC on serial links
  novell-ether  Novell Ethernet_802.3
  novell-fddi   Novell FDDI RAW
  sap           IEEE 802.2 on Ethernet, FDDI, Token
Ring
  snap          IEEE 802.2 SNAP on Ethernet, Token
Ring, and FDDI
RouterC(config-subif)#ipx network 10b encap sap
```

4. Notice that you can create over four billion subinterfaces. In the commands above, I used a number (1500), with no particular significance. I also configured the frame type of 802.2 to run on the LAN. You do not have to use the secondary command when using subinterfaces.

5. There is one more frame type that can be used on Ethernet: SNAP. Create another subinterface on Ethernet 0.

```
RouterC#config t
RouterC(config)#int e0.?
  <0-4294967295>  Ethernet interface number
RouterC(config)#int e0.1600
RouterC(config-subif)#ipx network 10c encap ?
  arpa          Novell Ethernet_II
  hdlc          HDLC on serial links
  novell-ether  Novell Ethernet_802.3
```

```
    novell-fddi    Novell FDDI RAW
    sap            IEEE 802.2 on Ethernet, FDDI, Token
Ring
    snap           IEEE 802.2 SNAP on Ethernet, Token
Ring, and FDDI
RouterC(config-subif)#ipx network 10c encap snap
```

6. Verify your IPX configuration by using the show ipx route, show ipx interface, and show protocol commands.

7. For practice, configure secondary and subinterfaces on all other routers.

Review Questions

1. Which of the following provides connection-oriented transport to upper-layer protocols?

   A. RIP

   B. NLSP

   C. SPX

   D. NCP

2. Which of the following can respond to a client GNS request? (Choose all that apply.)

   A. Local NetWare server

   B. Remote NetWare server

   C. Local client

   D. Cisco router

3. How often do servers exchange RIP and SAP information unless set otherwise?

   A. Every 15 seconds

   B. Every 30 seconds

   C. Every 60 seconds

   D. Every 120 seconds

4. How can you configure a secondary subinterface on your Ethernet interface?

   A. `Config t, int e0.24010`

   B. `Config t, int e100.0`

   C. `config t, 24000 e0`

   D. `config t, 24000 e100`

5. Given the IPX address 71.00A0.2494.E939, which of the following is the associated IPX network and node address?

A. Net 00a0. node 2494 E939

B. Net 71 node 00a0.2494.e939

C. Net 00A0.2494. node E939

D. Net 71 00a0 Node 2494.e939

6. If you bring up a new NetWare server and the Novell clients cannot see the server, what could the problem be?

A. You need to upgrade the client software.

B. You need to load the NetWare patches.

C. You have a frame type mismatch.

D. New NetWare servers do not support IPX.

7. Which of the following are valid methods of including multiple encapsulations on a single interface? (Choose all that apply.)

A. Secondary networks.

B. Subinterfaces.

C. Additional physical interfaces.

D. There is no method to use multiple encapsulations on a single interface.

8. Which command would you use to see if you were receiving SAP and RIP information on an interface?

A. sho ipx route

B. sho ipx traffic

C. sho ipx interface

D. sho ipx servers

9. Which command would you use to check if the router is hearing your server SAPs?

   A. sho ipx route

   B. sho ipx traffic

   C. sho ipx interface

   D. sho ipx servers

10. Which commands will allow you to display the IPX address of an interface? (Choose all that apply.)

    A. sh ipx route

    B. sh int

    C. sh prot

    D. debug ipx int

    E. show ipx inter

11. You want to forward IPX packets over multiple paths. What command do you use?

    A. ipx forward maximum-paths

    B. ipx maximum-paths

    C. ipx forward

    D. ipx forward-paths

12. Which of the following are valid Cisco encapsulation names? (Choose all that apply.)

    A. arpa = IPX Ethernet

    B. hdlc = HDLC on serial links

    C. novell-ether = IPX Ethernet_802.3

    D. novell-fddi = IPX Fddi_Raw

    E. sap = IEEE 802.2 on Ethernet, FDDI, and Token Ring

    F. snap = IEEE 802.2 SNAP on Ethernet, FDDI, and Token Ring

13. Which commands, at a minimum, must be used to enable IPX networking?

    A. `IPX routing, IPX number, network 790`

    B. `IPX routing, int e0, IPX network number 980`

    C. `IPX routing, int e0, IPX network 77790 encapsulation arpa`

    D. `IPX routing, IPX encapsulation SAP, int e0, network 789`

14. What is the default encapsulation on an Ethernet interface when enabling Novell?

    A. SAP

    B. 802.2

    C. SNAP

    D. Token_SNAP

    E. 802.3

    F. Ethernet_II

15. What command will show you the amount of ticks that it takes an IPX packet to reach a remote network?

    A. `show ticks`

    B. `show ip route`

    C. `show ipx route`

    D. `show ipx traffic`

16. If you want to run the 802.2 frame type on your Ethernet interface, which encapsulation type should you choose?

    A. SNAP

    B. 802.2

    C. Ethernet_II

    D. SAP

    E. Novell-Ether

17. If you want to enable the Ethernet_II frame type on your Ethernet interface, which encapsulation should you use?

A. `arpa`

B. `rarpa`

C. `sap`

D. `rip`

E. `snap`

F. `novell-ether`

18. Which of the following commands will show you the routed protocols running on your Cisco router?

A. `show ipx traffic`

B. `show ip route`

C. `show protocols`

D. `show ipx protocols`

19. Which command will show the network servers advertising on your network?

A. `sh novell`

B. `sh ipx sap`

C. `sh ipx servers`

D. `sh servers`

20. Which command will show you the IPX RIP packets being sent and received on your router?

A. `show ip rip`

B. `sh ipx int`

C. `debug ipx routing activity`

D. `debug ipx interface`

(The answers to the questions begin on the next page.)

Answers to the Written Lab

1. show protocol

2. Config tIpx
   routing

3. RouterA#config t
   Enter configuration commands, one per line

   End with CNTL/Z.
   RouterA(config)#**int e0**
   RouterA(config-if)#**ipx network 11**
   RouterA(config-if)#**int to0**
   RouterA(config-if)#**ipx network 15**
   RouterA(config-if)#**int s0**
   RouterA(config-if)#**ipx network 20**

4. show ipx route

5. show proto and show ipx int

6. sh cdp nei detail and show cdp entry *

7. RouterA#config t
   RouterA(config)#**int e0**
   RotuerA(config-if)#ipx network 11a encap arpa sec

8. RouterA#config t
   RouterA(config)#**int e0.10**
   RouterA(config-subif)#**ipx network 11b encap sap**
   RouterA(config-subif)#**int e0.11**
   RouterA(config-subif)#**ipx network 11c encap snap**

9. Sh ipx route
   Sh protocol
   Sh ipx int

Answer to Review Questions

1. C. Sequenced Packet Exchange works with IPX to make a connection-oriented service at the Transport layer.

2. A, D. Only a local NetWare server or a router can respond to a GNS request. A remote server will never see the request.

3. C. IPX RIP and SAP are broadcast every 60 seconds by default by every router and server on the internetwork.

4. A. The only correct answer is A. The command to create a subinterface is `int type int.number` (`int e0.10`, for example).

5. B. The IPX address is four bytes for the network and six bytes for the node address, in hex.

6. C. It is possible that the frame types on a LAN interface are not the same between the server and the clients. This would cause the clients to not see the server.

7. A, B. You can either use the `secondary` command or create subinterfaces on a LAN interface to create multiple virtual IPX networks.

8. C. The command `show ipx traffic` shows all the RIP and SAP information received on the router, but the command `show ipx interface` shows the RIP and SAP information received only on a certain interface.

9. D. `Show ipx servers` lets you see if the router is hearing the server SAPs. Although `show ipx traffic` and `show ipx interface` show SAP information sent and received, they don't show from whom it is received.

10. C, E. The command `show interface` does not show you the IPX address of an interface, it only shows you the IP address. Only the commands `show ipx interface` and `show protocols` show the IPX address of the routers' interfaces.

11. B. The command `ipx maximum-paths` provides round-robin load-balancing between multiple equal-cost links.

12. A, B, C, D, E, F. Each of the answers match to their respective Cisco keyword.

13. C. At a minimum, you must turn on IPX routing and enable one interface with an IPX network address.

14. E. The Cisco default encapsulation on an Ethernet interface is Novell-Ether (802.3).

15. C. The command `show ipx route` will show you the number of ticks and hops that it will take to reach each remote network.

16. D. The Cisco keyword `sap` is used to enable the 802.2 frame type on Ethernet.

17. A. The Cisco keyword `arpa` is used to enable the Ethernet_II frame type on Ethernet.

18. C. The `show protocols` command shows the routed protocols and the configured interfaces and addresses of each routed protocol.

19. C. The `show ipx servers` command shows you all the IPX servers advertising SAPs on your network.

20. C. The `debug ipx routing activity` command will show you the IPX RIP packets being sent and received on your router.

Chapter

9

Managing Traffic with Access Lists

THE CCNA EXAM TOPICS COVERED IN THIS CHAPTER INCLUDE THE FOLLOWING:

✓ Configure IP and IPX standard access lists

✓ Configure IP and IPX extended access lists

✓ Configure IPX SAP filters

✓ Monitor and verify access lists

he proper use and configuration of access lists is a vital part of router configuration because access lists are such vital networking accessories. Contributing mightily to the efficiency and optimization of your network, access lists give network managers a huge amount of control over traffic flow throughout the internetwork. With access lists, managers can gather basic statistics on packet flow and security policies can be implemented. Sensitive devices can also be protected from unauthorized access.

Access lists can be used to permit or deny packets moving through the router, permit or deny Telnet (VTY) access to or from a router, and create dial-on demand (DDR) interesting traffic that triggers dialing to a remote location.

In this chapter, we'll discuss access lists for both TCP/IP and IPX, and we'll cover some of the tools available to test and monitor the functionality of applied access lists.

Access Lists

Access lists are essentially lists of conditions that control access. They're powerful tools that control access both to and from network segments. They can filter unwanted packets and be used to implement security policies. With the right combination of access lists, network managers will be armed with the power to enforce nearly any access policy they can invent.

The IP and IPX access lists work similarly—they're both packet filters that packets are compared with, categorized by, and acted upon. Once the lists are built, they can be applied to either inbound or outbound traffic on any interface. Applying an access list will then cause the router to analyze every packet crossing that interface in the specified direction and take action accordingly.

There are a few important rules a packet follows when it's being compared with an access list:

- It's always compared with each line of the access list in sequential order, i.e., it'll always start with line 1, then go to line 2, then line 3, and so on.

- It's compared with lines of the access list only until a match is made. Once the packet matches a line of the access list, it's acted upon, and no further comparisons take place.

- There is an implicit "deny" at the end of each access list—this means that if a packet doesn't match up to any lines in the access list, it'll be discarded.

Each of these rules has some powerful implications when filtering IP and IPX packets with access lists.

There are two types of access lists used with IP and IPX:

Standard access lists   These use only the source IP address in an IP packet to filter the network. This basically permits or denies an entire suite of protocols. IPX standards can filter on both source and destination IPX address.

Extended access lists   These check for both source and destination IP address, protocol field in the Network layer header, and port number at the Transport layer header. IPX extended access lists use source and destination IPX addresses, Network layer protocol fields, and socket numbers in the Transport layer header.

Once you create an access list, you apply it to an interface with either an inbound or outbound list:

Inbound access lists   Packets are processed through the access list before being routed to the outbound interface.

Outbound access lists   Packets are routed to the outbound interface and then processed through the access list.

There are also some access list guidelines that should be followed when creating and implementing access lists on a router:

- You can only assign one access list per interface, per protocol, or per direction. This means that if you are creating IP access lists, you can only have one inbound access list and one outbound access list per interface.

- Organize your access lists so that the more specific tests are at the top of the access list.

- Anytime a new list is added to the access list, it will be placed at the bottom of the list.

- You cannot remove one line from an access list. If you try to do this, you will remove the entire list. It is best to copy the access list to a text editor before trying to edit the list. The only exception is when using named access lists.

- Unless your access list ends with a `permit any` command, all packets will be discarded if they do not meet any of the lists' tests. Every list should have at least one permit statement, or you might as well shut the interface down.

- Create access lists and then apply them to an interface. Any access list applied to an interface without an access list present will not filter traffic.

- Access lists are designed to filter traffic going through the router. They will not filter traffic originated from the router.

- Place IP standard access lists as close to the destination as possible.

- Place IP extended access lists as close to the source as possible.

Standard IP Access Lists

Standard IP access lists filter the network by using the source IP address in an IP packet. You create a standard IP access list by using the access list numbers 1–99.

Here is an example of the access list numbers that you can use to filter your network. The different protocols that you can use with access lists depend on your IOS version.

```
RouterA(config)#access-list ?
  <1-99>        IP standard access list
```

```
<100-199>    IP extended access list
<1000-1099>  IPX SAP access list
<1100-1199>  Extended 48-bit MAC address access list
<1200-1299>  IPX summary address access list
<200-299>    Protocol type-code access list
<300-399>    DECnet access list
<400-499>    XNS standard access list
<500-599>    XNS extended access list
<600-699>    Appletalk access list
<700-799>    48-bit MAC address access list
<800-899>    IPX standard access list
<900-999>    IPX extended access list
```

By using the access list numbers between 1–99, you tell the router that you want to create a standard IP access list.

```
RouterA(config)#access-list 10 ?
  deny    Specify packets to reject
  permit  Specify packets to forward
```

After you choose the access list number, you need to decide if you are creating a permit or deny list. For this example, you will create a deny statement:

```
RouterA(config)#access-list 10 deny ?
  Hostname or A.B.C.D  Address to match
  any                  Any source host
  host                 A single host address
```

The next step requires a more detailed explanation. There are three options available. You can use the any command to permit or deny any host or network, you can use an IP address to specify or match a specific network or IP host, or you can use the host command to specify a specific host only.

Here is an example of using the host command:

```
RouterA(config)#access-list 10 deny host 172.16.30.2
```

This tells the list to deny any packets from host 172.16.30.2. The default command is host. In other words, if you type **access-list 10 deny 172.16.30.2,** the router assumes you mean host 172.16.30.2.

However, there is another way to specify a specific host: you can use wildcards. In fact, to specify a network or a subnet, you have no option but to use wildcards in the access list.

Wildcards

Wildcards are used with access lists to specify a host, network, or part of a network. To understand wildcards, you need to understand block sizes. Block sizes are used to specify a range of addresses. The following list shows some of the different block sizes available.

Block Sizes

64

32

16

8

4

When you need to specify a range of addresses, you choose the closest block size for your needs. For example, if you need to specify 34 networks, you need a block size of 64. If you want to specify 18 hosts, you need a block size of 32. If you only specify two networks, then a block size of 4 would work.

Wildcards are used with the host or network address to tell the router a range of available addresses to filter. To specify a host, the address would look like this:

```
172.16.30.5 0.0.0.0
```

The four zeros represent each octet of the address. Whenever a zero is present, it means that octet in the address must match exactly. To specify that an octet can be any value, the value of 255 is used. As an example, here is how a full subnet is specified with a wildcard:

```
172.16.30.0 0.0.0.255
```

This tells the router to match up the first three octets exactly, but the fourth octet can be any value.

Now, that was the easy part. What if you want to specify only a small range of subnets? This is where the block sizes come in. You have to specify the range of values in a block size. In other words, you can't choose to specify 20 networks. You can only specify the exact amount as the block size value. For example, the range would either have to be 16 or 32, but not 20.

Let's say that you want to block access to part of network that is in the range from 172.16.8.0 through 172.16.15.0. That is a block size of 8. Your network number would be 172.16.8.0, and the wildcard would be 0.0.7.255. Whoa! What is that? The 7.255 is what the router uses to determine the block size. The network and wildcard tell the router to start at 172.16.8.0 and go up a block size of eight addresses to network 172.16.15.0.

It is actually easier than it looks. I could certainly go through the binary math for you, but actually all you have to do is remember that the wildcard is always one number less than the block size. So, in our example, the wildcard would be 7 since our block size is 8. If you used a block size of 16, the wildcard would be 15. Easy, huh?

We'll go through some examples to help you really understand it. The following example tells the router to match the first three octets exactly but that the fourth octet can be anything.

```
RouterA(config)#access-list 10 deny 172.16.10.0 0.0.0.255
```

The next example tells the router to match the first two octets and that the last two octets can be any value.

```
RouterA(config)#access-list 10 deny 172.16.0.0 0.0.255.255
```

Try to figure out this next line:

```
RouterA(config)#access-list 10 deny 172.16.16.0 0.0.3.255
```

The above configuration tells the router to start at network 172.16.16.0 and use a block size of 4. The range would then be 172.16.16.0 through 172.16.19.0.

The example below shows an access list starting at 172.16.16.0 and going up a block size of 8 to 172.16.23.0.

```
RouterA(config)#access-list 10 deny 172.16.16.0 0.0.7.255
```

The next example starts at network 172.16.32.0 and goes up a block size of 32 to 172.16.63.0.

```
RouterA(config)#access-list 10 deny 172.16.32.0 0.0.31.255
```

The last example starts at network 172.16.64.0 and goes up a block size of 64 to 172.16.127.0.

RouterA(config)#**access-list 10 deny 172.16.64.0 0.0.63.255**

Here are two more things to keep in mind when working with block sizes and wildcards:

- Each block size must start at 0. For example, you can't say that you want a block size of 8 and start at 12. You must use 0–7, 8–15, 16–23, etc. For a block size of 32, the ranges are 0–31, 32–63, 64–95, etc.

- The command any is the same thing as writing out the wildcard 0.0.0.0 255.255.255.255.

Standard IP Access List Example

In this section, you'll learn how to use a standard IP access list to stop certain users from gaining access to the finance-department LAN.

In Figure 9.1, a router has three LAN connections and one WAN connection to the Internet. Users on the Sales LAN should not have access to the Finance LAN, but they should be able to access the Internet and the marketing department. The Marketing LAN needs to access the Finance LAN for application services.

FIGURE 9.1 IP access list example with three LANs and a WAN connection

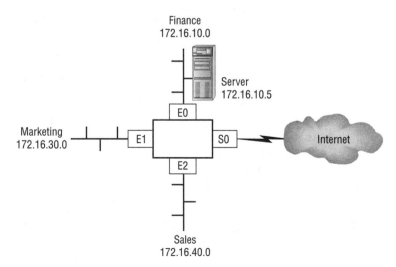

On the Acme router, the following standard IP access list is applied:

```
Acme#config t
Acme(config)#access-list 10 deny 172.16.40.0 0.0.0.255
Acme(config)#access-list 10 permit any
```

It is very important to understand that the any command is the same thing as saying this:

```
Acme(config)#access-list 10 permit 0.0.0.0 255.255.255.255
```

At this point, the access list is denying the Sales LAN and allowing everyone else. But where should this access list be placed? If you place it as an incoming access list on E2, you might as well shut down the Ethernet interface because all of the Sales LAN devices are denied access to all networks attached to the router. The best place to put this router is the E0 interface as an outbound list.

```
Acme(config)#int e0
Acme(config-if)#ip access-group 10 out
```

This completely stops network 172.16.40.0 from getting out Ethernet 0, but it can still access the Marketing LAN and the Internet.

Controlling VTY (Telnet) Access

You will have a difficult time trying to stop users from telnetting into a router because any active port on a router is fair game for VTY access. However, you can use a standard IP access list to control access by placing the access list on the VTY lines themselves.

To perform this function:

1. Create a standard IP access list that permits only the host or hosts you want to be able to telnet into the routers.

2. Apply the access list to the VTY line with the access-class command.

Here is an example of allowing only host 172.16.10.3 to telnet into a router:

```
RouterA(config)#access-list 50 permit 172.16.10.3
RouterA(config)#line vty 0 4
RouterA(config-line)#access-class 50 in
```

Because of the implied deny any at the end of the list, the access list stops any host from telnetting into the router except the host 172.16.10.3.

Extended IP Access Lists

In the standard IP access list example, notice how you had to block the whole subnet from getting to the finance department. What if you wanted them to gain access to only a certain server on the Finance LAN, but not to other network services, for obvious security reasons? With a standard IP access list, you can't allow users to get to one network service and not another. However, extended IP access lists allow you to do this. Extended IP access lists allow you to choose your IP source and destination address as well as the protocol and port number, which identify the upper-layer protocol or application. By using extended IP access lists, you can effectively allow users access to a physical LAN and stop them from using certain services.

Here is an example of an extended IP access list. The first command shows the access list numbers available. You'll use the extended access list range from 100 to 199.

```
RouterA(config)#access-list ?
  <1-99>        IP standard access list
  <100-199>     IP extended access list
  <1000-1099>   IPX SAP access list
  <1100-1199>   Extended 48-bit MAC address access list
  <1200-1299>   IPX summary address access list
  <200-299>     Protocol type-code access list
  <300-399>     DECnet access list
  <400-499>     XNS standard access list
  <500-599>     XNS extended access list
  <600-699>     Appletalk access list
  <700-799>     48-bit MAC address access list
  <800-899>     IPX standard access list
  <900-999>     IPX extended access list
```

At this point, you need to decide what type of list entry you are making. For this example, you'll choose a deny list entry.

```
RouterA(config)#access-list 110 ?
  deny      Specify packet
  dynamic   Specify a DYNAMIC list of PERMITs or DENYs
  permit    Specify packets to forward
```

Once you choose the access list type, you must choose a Network layer protocol field entry. It is important to understand that if you want to filter the network by Application layer, you must choose an entry here that allows you to go up through the OSI model. For example, to filter by Telnet or FTP, you must choose TCP here. If you were to choose IP, you would never leave the Network layer, and you would not be allowed to filter by upper-layer applications.

```
RouterA(config)#access-list 110 deny ?
  <0-255>  An IP protocol number
  eigrp    Cisco's EIGRP routing protocol
  gre      Cisco's GRE tunneling
  icmp     Internet Control Message Protocol
  igmp     Internet Gateway Message Protocol
  igrp     Cisco's IGRP routing protocol
  ip       Any Internet Protocol
  ipinip   IP in IP tunneling
  nos      KA9Q NOS compatible IP over IP tunneling
  ospf     OSPF routing protocol
  tcp      Transmission Control Protocol
  udp      User Datagram Protocol
```

Once you choose to go up to the Application layer through TCP, you will be prompted for the source IP address of the host or network. You can choose the any command to allow any source address.

```
RouterA(config)#access-list 110 deny tcp ?
  A.B.C.D  Source address
  any      Any source host
  host     A single source host
```

After the source address is selected, the destination address is chosen.

```
RouterA(config)#access-list 110 deny tcp any ?
  A.B.C.D  Destination address
  any      Any destination host
  eq       Match only packets on a given port number
  gt       Match only packets with a greater port number
  host     A single destination host
```

lt	Match only packets with a lower port number
neq	Match only packets not on a given port number
range	Match only packets in the range of port numbers

In the example below, any source IP address that has a destination IP address of 172.16.30.2 has been denied.

```
RouterA(config)#access-list 110 deny tcp any host
172.16.30.2 ?
```

eq	Match only packets on a given port number
established	Match established connections
fragments	Check fragments
gt	Match only packets with a greater port number
log	Log matches against this entry
log-input	Log matches against this entry,including inputinterface
lt	Match only packets with a lower port number
neq	Match only packets not on a given port number
precedence	Match packets with given precedence value
range	Match only packets in the range of port numbers
tos	Match packets with given TOS value
<cr>	

Now, you can press Enter here and leave the access list as is. However, you can be even more specific: once you have the host addresses in place, you can specify the type of service you are denying. The following help screen gives you the options. You can choose a port number or use the application or even the program name.

```
RouterA(config)#access-list 110 deny tcp any host
172.16.30.2 eq ?
```

<0-65535>	Port number
bgp	Border Gateway Protocol (179)
chargen	Character generator (19)
cmd	Remote commands (rcmd, 514)
daytime	Daytime (13)

```
discard    Discard (9)
domain     Domain Name Service (53)
echo       Echo (7)
exec       Exec (rsh, 512)
finger     Finger (79)
ftp        File Transfer Protocol (21)
ftp        File Transfer Protocol (21)
gopher     Gopher (70)
hostname   NIC hostname server (101)
ident      Ident Protocol (113)
irc        Internet Relay Chat (194)
klogin     Kerberos login (543)
kshell     Kerberos shell (544)
login      Login (rlogin, 513)
lpd        Printer service (515)
nntp       Network News Transport Protocol (119)
pop2       Post Office Protocol v2 (109)
pop3       Post Office Protocol v3 (110)
smtp       Simple Mail Transport Protocol (25)
sunrpc     Sun Remote Procedure Call (111)
syslog     Syslog (514)
tacacs     TAC Access Control System (49)
talk       Talk (517)
telnet     Telnet (23)
time       Time (37)
uucp       Unix-to-Unix Copy Program (540)
whois      Nicname (43)
www        World Wide Web (HTTP, 80)
```

At this point, let's block Telnet (port 23) to host 172.16.30.2 only. If the users want to FTP, that is allowed. The log command is used to send messages to the console every time the access list is hit. This would not be a good thing to do in a busy environment, but it is great when used in a class or in a home network.

```
RouterA(config)#access-list 110 deny tcp any host
172.16.30.2 eq 23 log
```

You need to keep in mind that the next line is an implicit deny any by default. If you apply this access list to an interface, you might as well just shut the interface down, since by default there is an implicit deny all at the end of every access list. You must follow up the access list with the following command:

```
RouterA(config)#access-list 110 permit ip any 0.0.0.0
255.255.255.255
```

Remember, the 0.0.0.0 255.255.255.255 is the same command as any.

Once the access list is created, you need to apply it to an interface. It is the same command as the IP standard list:

```
RouterA(config-if)#ip access-group 110 in
```

or

```
RouterA(config-if)#ip access-group 110 out
```

Extended IP Access List Example

Using Figure 9.1 from the IP standard access list example again, let's use the same network and deny access to a server on the finance-department LAN for both Telnet and FTP services on server 172.16.10.5. All other services on the LAN are acceptable for the sales and marketing departments to access.

The following access list should be created:

```
Acme#config t
Acme(config)#access-list 110 deny tcp any host 172.16.10.5 eq 21
Acme(config)#access-list 110 deny tcp any host 172.16.10.5 eq 23
Acme(config)#access-list 110 permit ip any any
```

It is important to understand why the denies were placed first in the list. This is because if you had configured the permits first and the denies second, the Finance LAN would have not been able to go to any other LAN or to the Internet because of the implicit deny at the end of the list. It would be difficult to configure the list any other way than the preceding example.

After the lists are created, they need to be applied to the Ethernet 0 port. This is because the other three interfaces on the router need access to the

LAN. However, if this list were created to only block Sales, then we would have wanted to put this list closest to the source, or on Ethernet interface 2.

```
Acme(config-if)#ip access-group 110 out
```

Monitoring IP Access Lists

It is important to be able to verify the configuration on a router. The following commands can be used to verify the configuration:

show access-list   Displays all access lists and their parameters configured on the router. This command does not show you which interface the list is set on.

show access-list 110   Shows only the parameters for the access list 110. This command does not show you the interface the list is set on.

show ip access-list   Shows only the IP access lists configured on the router.

show ip interface   Shows which interfaces have access lists set.

show running-config   Shows the access lists and which interfaces have access lists set.

IPX Access Lists

IPX access lists are configured the same way as any other list. You use the `access-list` command to create your access list of packet tests and then apply the list to an interface with the `access-group` command.

I will discuss the following IPX access lists:

IPX standard   These access lists filter on IPX source and destination host or network number. They use the access-list numbers 800–899. IPX standard access lists are similar to IP standard access lists, except that IP standards only filter on source IP addresses, whereas IPX standards filter on source and destination IPX addresses.

IPX extended   These access lists filter on IPX source and destination host or network number, IPX protocol field in the Network layer header, and socket number in the Transport layer header. They use the access list numbers 900–999.

IPX SAP filter   These filters are used to control SAP traffic on LANs and WANs. IPX SAP filters use the access list numbers 1000–1099. Network administrators can set up IPX access lists to control the amount of IPX traffic, including IPX SAPs across low WAN links.

Standard IPX Access Lists

Standard IPX access lists use the source or destination IPX host or network address to filter the network. This is configured much the same way IP standard access lists are. The parameter to configure IPX standard access lists is

```
access-list 800-899 deny or permit source_Address
destination_address
```

Wildcards can be used for the source and destination IPX addresses; however, the wildcard is –1, which means it is equal to any host and network.

Figure 9.2 shows an example of an IPX network and how IPX standard access lists can be configured.

FIGURE 9.2   IPX access list example

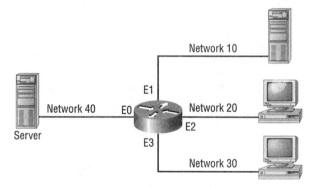

The following configuration is used with Figure 9.2. Interface Ethernet 0 is on Network 40; interface Ethernet 1 is on Network 10; interface Ethernet 2 is on Network 20; interface Ethernet 3 is on Network 30.

The access list is configured and applied as shown. This IPX access list permits packets generated from IPX Network 20 out interface Ethernet 0 to Network 40.

```
Router(config)#access-list 810 permit 20 40
Router(config)#int e0
Router(config-if)#ipx access-group 810 out
```

Think about what this configuration accomplishes. First and most obvious, any IPX devices on IPX Network 20 off interface Ethernet 2 can communicate to the server on Network 40, which is connected to interface Ethernet 0. However, notice what else this configuration accomplishes with only one line (remember that there is an implicit deny all at the end of the list):

- Hosts on Network 10 cannot communicate to the server on Network 40.

- Hosts on Network 40 can get to Network 10, but the packets cannot get back.

- Hosts on Network 30 can communicate to Network 10, and Network 10 can communicate to Network 30.

- Hosts on Network 30 cannot communicate to the server on Network 40.

- Hosts on Network 40 can get to hosts on Network 30, but the packets can't come back from Network 30 in response.

- Hosts on Network 20 can communicate to all devices in the internetwork.

Extended IPX Access Lists

Extended IPX access lists can filter based on any of the following:

- Source network/node

- Destination network/node

- IPX protocol (SAP, SPX, etc.)

- IPX socket

These are access lists in the range of 900–999 and are configured just like standard access lists, with the addition of protocol and socket information.

Let's take a look at a template for building lines in an IPX extended access list.

```
access-list {number} {permit/deny} {protocol} {source}
{socket} {destination} {socket}
```

Again, when you move from standard to extended access lists, you're simply adding the ability to filter based on protocol and socket (port for IP).

IPX SAP Filters

IPX SAP filters are implemented using the same tools we've been discussing all along in this chapter. They have an important place in controlling IPX SAP traffic. Why is this important? Because if you can control the SAPs, you can control the access to IPX devices. IPX SAP filters use access lists in the 1000–1099 range. IPX SAP filters should be placed as close as possible to the source of the SAP broadcasts; this is to stop unwanted SAP traffic from crossing a network because it will only be discarded.

Two types of access list filters control SAP traffic:

IPX input SAP filter   This is used to stop certain SAP entries from entering a router and updating the SAP table.

IPX output SAP filter   This stops certain SAP updates from being sent in the regular 60-second SAP updates.

Here's the template for each line of an IPX SAP filter:

```
access-list {number} {permit/deny} {source} {service type}
```

Here is an example of an IPX SAP filter that allows service type 4 (file services) from a NetWare service named Sales.

```
Router(config)#access-list 1010 permit ?
  -1          Any IPX net
  <0-FFFFFFFF>  Source net
  N.H.H.H       Source net.host address
Router(config)#access-list 1010 permit -1 ?
  <0-FFFF>  Service type-code (0 matches all services)
  N.H.H.H   Source net.host mask
  <cr>
```

```
Router(config)#access-list 1010 permit -1 4 ?
  WORD  A SAP server name
  <cr>
Router(config)#access-list 1010 permit -1 4 Sales
```

The −1 in the access list is a wildcard that says any node, any network. After the list is created, apply it to an interface with either of the two following commands:

```
RouterA(config-if)#ipx input-sap-filter
RouterA(config-if)#ipx output-sap-filter
```

The input-sap-filter is used to stop SAP entries from being added to the SAP table on the router, and the output-sap-filter is used to stop SAP entries from being propagated out of the router.

Verifying IPX Access Lists

To verify the IPX access lists and their placement on a router, use the commands show ipx interface and show ipx access-list.

Notice in the output of the show ipx interface command that the IPX address is shown, the outgoing access list is set with list 810, and the SAP input filter is 1010.

```
Router#sh ipx int
Ethernet0 is up, line protocol is up
  IPX address is 10.0060.7015.63d6, NOVELL-ETHER [up]
  Delay of this IPX network, in ticks is 1 throughput 0
link delay 0
  IPXWAN processing not enabled on this interface.
  IPX SAP update interval is 1 minute(s)
  IPX type 20 propagation packet forwarding is disabled
  Incoming access list is not set
  Outgoing access list is 810
  IPX helper access list is not set
  SAP GNS processing enabled, delay 0 ms, output filter
list is not set
  SAP Input filter list is 1010
  SAP Output filter list is not set
```

```
    SAP Router filter list is not set
    Input filter list is not set
    Output filter list is not set
    Router filter list is not set
    Netbios Input host access list is not set
    Netbios Input bytes access list is not set
    Netbios Output host access list is not set
    Netbios Output bytes access list is not set
    Updates each 60 seconds, aging multiples RIP: 3 SAP: 3
    SAP interpacket delay is 55 ms, maximum size is 480
bytes
    RIP interpacket delay is 55 ms, maximum size is 432
bytes
  --More-
```

The show ipx access-list shows the two IPX lists set on the router.

```
Router#sh ipx access-list
IPX access list 810
    permit FFFFFFFF 30
IPX SAP access list 1010
    permit FFFFFFFF 4 Sales
Router#
```

The Fs are hexadecimal and are the same as all 1s or permit any. Since you used the –1 in the IPX commands, the running-config shows them as all Fs.

Summary

In this chapter, we covered the following points:

- How to configure standard access lists to filter IP traffic. We learned what a standard access list is and how to apply it to a Cisco router to add security to our network.

- How to configure extended access lists to filter IP traffic. We learned the difference between a standard and an extended access list and how to apply these lists to Cisco routers.

- How to configure IPX access lists and SAP filters to control basic Novell traffic. We learned the difference between a standard and extended IPX access list and how to apply the lists to a Cisco router.

- How to monitor and verify selected access list operations on the router. We went over some basic monitoring commands to verify and test IP and IPX access lists.

Key Terms

Before you take the exam, be sure you're familiar with the following terms:

access list

extended IP access list

extended IPX access list

standard IP access list

standard IPX access list

wildcard

Commands in This Chapter

Command	Description
`0.0.0.0 255.255.255.255`	Is a wildcard command; same as the any command
`access-class`	Applies a standard IP access list to a VTY line
`Access-list`	Creates a list of tests to filter the networks
`Any`	Specifies any host or any network; same as the `0.0.0.0 255.255.255.255` command

Command	Description
Host	Specifies a single host address
ip access-group	Applies an IP access list to an interface
ipx access-group	Applies an IPX access list to an interface
ipx input-sap-filter	Applies an inbound IPX SAP filter to an interface
ipx output-sap-filter	Applies an outbound IPX SAP filter to an interface
show access-list	Shows all the access lists configured on the router
show access-list 110	Shows only access-list 110
show ip access-list	Shows only the IP access lists
show ip interface	Shows which interfaces have IP access lists applied
show ipx access-list	Shows the IPX access lists configured on a router
show ipx interface	Shows which interfaces have IPX access lists applied

Written Lab

In this section, write the answers to the following questions:

1. Configure a standard IP access list to prevent all machines on network 172.16.0.0 from accessing your Ethernet network.

2. Apply the access list to your Ethernet interface.

3. Create an access list that denies host 196.22.15.5 access to your Ethernet network.

4. Write the command to verify that you've entered the access list correctly.

5. Write the two commands that verify the access list was properly applied to the Ethernet interface.

6. Create an extended access list that stops host 172.16.10.1 on Ethernet 0 from telnetting to host 172.16.30.5 on Ethernet 1.

7. Apply the access list to the correct interface.

8. Configure an IPX SAP access list that prevents any file service SAP messages other than those from IPX address 45.0000.0000.0001 from leaving the Ethernet 0 network.

9. Apply the IPX SAP access list to the Ethernet interface.

Hands-on Labs

In this section, you will complete three labs. To complete these labs, you will need at least three 2500 series routers, or the RouterSim product.

Lab 9.1: Standard IP Access Lists

Lab 9.2: Extended IP Access Lists

Lab 9.3: Standard IPX Access Lists

All of the labs will use Figure 9.3 for configuring the routers.

FIGURE 9.3 Access list lab figure

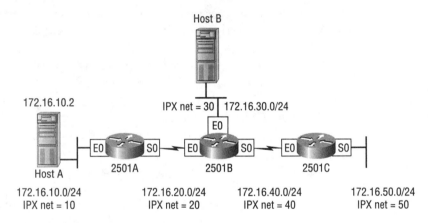

Lab 9.1: Standard IP Access Lists

In this lab, you will allow only Host B from network 172.16.30.0 to enter network 172.16.10.0.

1. Go to 2501A and enter global configuration mode by typing **config t**.

2. From global configuration mode, type **access-list ?** to get a list of all the different access lists available.

3. Choose an access list number that will allow you to create an IP standard access list. This is a number between 1 and 99.

4. Choose to permit host 172.16.30.2:

```
2501A(config)#access-list 10 permit 172.16.30.2 ?
A.B.C.D  Wildcard bits
<cr>
```

To specify only host 172.16.30.2, use the wildcards 0.0.0.0:

```
RouterA(config)#access-list 10 permit 172.16.30.2
0.0.0.0
```

5. Now that the access list is created, you must apply it to an interface to make it work:

```
2501A(config)#int e0
2501A(config-if)#ip access-group 10 out
```

6. Verify your access lists with the following commands:

```
RouterA#sh access-list
Standard IP access list 10
    permit 172.16.30.2
RouterA#sh run

-cut-

interface Ethernet0
 ip address 172.16.10.1 255.255.255.0
 ip access-group 10 out
 ipx network 10A
```

7. Test your access list by pinging from Host B (172.16.30.2) to Host A (172.16.10.2).

8. Ping from 2501B and 2501C to Host A (172.16.10.2); this should fail if your access list is correct.

Lab 9.2: Extended IP Access Lists

In this lab, you will use an extended IP access list to stop host 172.16.10.2 from creating a Telnet session to router 2501B (172.16.20.2). However, the host still should be able to ping the 2501B router. IP extended lists should be placed closest to the source, so add the extended list on router 2501A.

1. Remove any access lists on 2501A and add an extended list to 2501A.

2. Choose a number to create an extended IP list. The IP extended lists use 100–199.

3. Use a deny statement (you'll add a permit statement in step 7 to allow other traffic to still work).

```
2501A(config)#access-list 110 deny ?
  <0-255>  An IP protocol number
  ahp      Authentication Header Protocol
  eigrp    Cisco's EIGRP routing protocol
  esp      Encapsulation Security Payload
  gre      Cisco's GRE tunneling
  icmp     Internet Control Message Protocol
  igmp     Internet Gateway Message Protocol
  igrp     Cisco's IGRP routing protocol
  ip       Any Internet Protocol
  ipinip   IP in IP tunneling
  nos      KA9Q NOS compatible IP over IP tunneling
  ospf     OSPF routing protocol
  pcp      Payload Compression Protocol
  tcp      Transmission Control Protocol
  udp      User Datagram Protocol
```

4. Since you are going to deny Telnet, you must choose TCP as a Transport layer protocol:

```
2501A(config)#access-list 110 deny tcp ?
  A.B.C.D  Source address
  any      Any source host
  host     A single source host
```

5. Add the source IP address you want to filter on, then add the destination host IP address. Use the host command instead of wildcard bits.

```
2501A(config)#access-list 110 deny tcp host
172.16.10.2 host 172.16.20.2 ?
  ack          Match on the ACK bit
  eq           Match only packets on a given port
               number
  established  Match established connections
  fin          Match on the FIN bit
  fragments    Check fragments
  gt           Match only packets with a greater
               port number
  log          Log matches against this entry
  log-input    Log matches against this entry,
               including input interface
  lt           Match only packets with a lower port
               number
  neq          Match only packets not on a given
               port number
  precedence   Match packets with given precedence
               value
  psh          Match on the PSH bit
  range        Match only packets in the range of
               port numbers
  rst          Match on the RST bit
  syn          Match on the SYN bit
  tos          Match packets with given TOS value
  urg          Match on the URG bit
  <cr>
```

6. At this point, you can add the eq telnet command. The log command can also be used at the end of the command so that whenever the access-list line is hit, a log will be generated on the console.

```
2501A(config)#access-list 110 deny tcp host
172.16.10.2 host 172.16.20.2 eq telnet log
```

7. It is important to add this line next to create a permit statement.

   2501A(config)#**access-list 110 permit ip any 0.0.0.0**
   255.255.255.255

8. You must create a permit statement; if you just add a deny statement, nothing will be permitted at all. Please see the sections earlier in this chapter for more detailed information on the permit command.

9. Apply the access list to the Ethernet 0 on 2501A to stop the Telnet traffic as soon as it hits the first router interface.

   RouterB(config)#**int e0**
   RouterB(config-if)#**ip access-group 110 in**
   RouterB(config-if)#**^Z**

10. Try telnetting from host 172.16.10.2 to Router B using the destination IP address of 172.16.20.2. The following messages should be generated on 2501A's console. However, the ping command should work.

    From host 172.16.10.2: >telnet 172.16.20.2

    On Router B's console, this should appear as follows:

    01:11:48: %SEC-6-IPACCESSLOGP: list 110 denied tcp
    172.16.10.2(1030) -> 172.16.20.2(23), 1 packet
    01:13:04: %SEC-6-IPACCESSLOGP: list 110 denied tcp
    172.16.10.2(1030) -> 172.16.20.2(23), 3 packets

Lab 9.3: Standard IPX Access Lists

In this lab, you will configure IPX to allow only IPX traffic from IPX Network 30 and not from IPX Network 50.

1. Remove any existing access lists on the 2501A router. Because this is an IPX standard access list, the filtering can be placed anywhere on the network since it can filter based on IPX source and destination IP addresses.

2. Verify that you have the IPX network working as shown in Figure 9.3. Use the show ipx route command to see all networks on your routers.

3. Configure an access list on 2501A to allow only IPX traffic from Network 30 and to deny IPX Network 50. IPX standard lists use the access list numbers 800–899.

```
2501A#config t
RouterC(config)#access-list 810 ?
  deny    Specify packets to reject
  permit  Specify packets to permit
```

4. First, deny IPX Network 50, then permit everything else. The −1 is a wildcard in IPX.

```
2501A(config)#access-list 810 deny ?
  -1           Any IPX net
  <0-FFFFFFFF> Source net
  N.H.H.H      Source net.host address
```

5. Choose Network 30 as a source address:

```
2501A(config)#access-list 810 deny 50
  -1           Any IPX net
  <0-FFFFFFFF> Destination net
  N.H.H.H      Destination net.host address
  <cr>
```

6. Choose Network 10 as the destination network:

```
2501A(config)#access-list 810 permit 50 10
```

7. Permit everything else with an IPX wildcard:

```
2501A(config)#access-list 810 permit -1 -1
```

8. Apply the list to the serial interface of 2501A to stop the packets as they reach the router:

```
2501A(config)#int s0
2501A(config-if)#ipx access-group 810 in
2501A(config-if)#^Z
```

9. Verify the list by looking at the IPX routing table. Network 50 should not be in the 2501A IPX routing table. Also, use the show access-list and show ipx access-list commands to vary the list.

Review Questions

1. IP standard access lists use which of the following as a basis for permitting or denying packets?

   A. Source address

   B. Destination address

   C. Protocol

   D. Port

2. IP extended access lists use which of the following as a basis for permitting or denying packets?

   A. Source address

   B. Destination address

   C. Protocol

   D. Port

   E. All of the above

3. To specify all hosts in the Class B IP network 172.16.0.0, which wildcard access list mask would you use?

   A. 255.255.0.0

   B. 255.255.255.0

   C. 0.0.255.255

   D. 0.255.255.255

   E. 0.0.0.255

4. Which of the following are valid ways to refer only to host 172.16.30.55 in an IP access list?

   A. `172.16.30.55 0.0.0.255`

   B. `172.16.30.55 0.0.0.0`

   C. `any 172.16.30.55`

   D. `host 172.16.30.55`

   E. `0.0.0.0 172.16.30.55`

   F. `ip any 172.16.30.55`

5. Which of the following access lists will allow only WWW traffic into network 196.15.7.0?

   A. `access-list 100 permit tcp any 196.15.7.0 0.0.0.255 eq www`

   B. `access-list 10 deny tcp any 196.15.7.0 eq www`

   C. `access-list 100 permit 196.15.7.0 0.0.0.255 eq www`

   D. `access-list 110 permit ip any 196.15.7.0 0.0.0.255`

   E. `access-list 110 permit www 196.15.7.0 0.0.0.255`

6. Which of the following commands will show the ports that have IP access lists applied?

   A. `show ip port`

   B. `show access-list`

   C. `show ip interface`

   D. `show access-list interface`

   E. `show running-config`

7. What wildcard would you use to filter networks 172.16.16.0 through 172.16.23.0?

   A. 172.16.16.0 0.0.0.255

   B. 172.16.255.255 255.255.0.0

   C. 172.16.0.0 0.0.255.255

   D. 172.16.16.0 0.0.8.255

   E. 172.16.16.0 0.0.7.255

   F. 172.16.16.0 0.0.15.255

8. Which of the following is a valid IPX standard access list?

   A. `access-list 800 permit 30 50`

   B. `access-list 900 permit 30 50`

   C. `access-list permit all 30 50`

   D. `access-list 800 permit 30 50 eq SAP`

   E. `access-list 900 permit -1 50`

9. What wildcard would you use for the following networks? 172.16.32.0 through 172.16.63.0

   A. 172.16.0.0 0.0.0.255

   B. 172.16.255.255 0.0.0.0

   C. 0.0.0.0 255.255.255.255

   D. 172.16.32.0 0.0.0.255

   E. 172.16.32.0 0.0.0.31

   F. 172.16.32.0 0.0.31.255

   G. 172.16.32.0 0.31.255.255

   H. 172.16.32.0 0.0.63.255

10. Which of the following commands will apply IPX SAP access list 1050 for incoming traffic, assuming you're already at interface configuration?

   A. `ipx access-group 1050 in`

   B. `ipx input-sap-filter 1050`

   C. `ipx access-list 1050 in`

   D. `ipx input-sap-filter 1050 in`

   E. `ipx access-group 1050`

11. Which of the following commands will show extended access list 187?

   A. `sh ip int`

   B. `sh ip access-list`

   C. `sh access-list 187`

   D. `sh access-list 187 extended`

12. What is the IP extended access list range?

   A. 1–99

   B. 200–299

   C. 1000–1999

   D. 100–199

13. Which of the following commands is valid for creating an extended IP access list?

   A. `access-list 101 permit ip host 172.16.30.0 any eq 21`

   B. `access-list 101 permit tcp host 172.16.30.0 any eq 21 log`

   C. `access-list 101 permit icmp  host 172.16.30.0 any ftp log`

   D. `access-list 101 permit ip any eq 172.16.30.0 21 log`

14. What is the extended IPX access list range?

   A. 100–199

   B. 900–999

   C. 1000–1999

   D. 700–799

15. What does the –1 mean in an extended IPX access list?

   A. Deny this host

   B. Deny any network or host

   C. Local network only, no hops

   D. Any host or any network

16. What are three commands you can use to monitor IP access lists?

   A. `sh int`

   B. `sh ip interface`

   C. `sh run`

   D. `sh access-list`

17. Which of the following commands should follow this command?
`access-list 110 deny tfp any any eq ftp`

   A. `access-list 110 deny ip any any`

   B. `access-list 110 permit tcp any any`

   C. `access-list 110 permit ip any`

   D. `access-list 110 permit ip any 0.0.0.0 255.255.255.255`

18. Which access configuration allows only traffic from network 172.16.0.0 to enter int s0?

    A. Access-list 10 permit 172.16.0.0 0.0.255.255, int s0, ip access-list 10 in

    B. Access-group 10 permit 172.16.0.0 0.0.255.255, int s0, ip access-list 10 out

    C. Access-list 10 permit 172.16.0.0 0.0.255.255, int s0, ip access-group 10 in

    D. Access-list 10 permit 172.16.0.0 0.0.255.255, int s0, ip access-group 10 out

19. Where should you place standard access lists in a network?

    A. On the closest switch

    B. Closest to the source

    C. Closest to the destination

    D. On the Internet

20. Where should you place extended access lists in a network?

    A. On the closest switch

    B. Closest to the source

    C. Closest to the destination

    D. On the Internet

Answers to the Written Lab

1. access-list 10 deny 172.16.0.0 0.0.255.255
   access-list 10 permit ip any

2. ip access-group 10 out

3. access-list 10 deny host 196.22.15.5
   access-list 10 permit any

4. show access-list

5. show running-config
   sh ip interface

6. access-list 110 deny host 172.16.10.1 host 172.16.30.5 eq 23
   access-list 110 permit ip any any

7. Int e0
   IP Access-group 110 in

8. Access-list 1010 permit 45.0000.0000.0001 4

9. Int e0
   input-sap-filter 1010

Answers to Review Questions

1. A. Only the source IP address is used to filter the network.

2. E. IP extended lists use source and destination IP addresses, Network layer protocol files, and port fields in the Transport layer header.

3. C. The mask 0.0.255.255 tells the router to match the first two octets and that the last two octets can be any value.

4. B, D. The wildcard 0.0.0.0 tells the router to match all four octets. The wildcard command can be replaced with the host command.

5. A. The first thing to check in a question like this is the access list number. Right away, you can see that Answer B is wrong because it is using a standard IP access list number. The second thing to check is the protocol. If you are filtering by upper-layer protocol, then you must be using either UDP or TCP. This eliminates Answer D. Answers C and E have the wrong syntax.

6. C, E. Only the commands `show ip interface` and `show run` will tell you which ports have access lists applied.

7. E. Networks 172.16.16.0 through 172.16.23.0 have a block size of 8. The wildcard is always one less than the block size; in this example, 7.

8. A. Only Answers A and D are in the right access list number range for standard IPX access lists. Answer D is wrong, though, because standard IPX access lists cannot filter on upper-layer applications or services.

9. F. Networks 172.16.32.0 through 172.16.63.0 have a block size of 32. The wildcard would be 0.0.31.255.

10. B. You don't add the in or out parameters at the end of the list with SAP access lists.

11. B, C. You can see the access lists with the `show ip access-list` command or the `show access-list #` command.

12. D. IP extended lists use the range from 100 to 199.

13. B. Remember to first look for the access list numbers. Since all of the access lists are using 101, they are all set for IP extended access lists. The second thing to look for is the protocol. Only one list is using TCP, which is needed to access the FTP protocol.

14. B. Standard IPX uses the range 800–899 and extended IPX lists use the range 900–999.

15. D. –1 is a wildcard in the IPX access lists.

16. B, C, D. The command `show interface` is wrong because it will not give you any access list information. `Show ip interface`, `show run`, and `show access-list` will give you monitoring information about access lists.

17. D. The command `access-list 110 permit ip any any` is used to specify and permit all traffic. The command `0.0.0.0 255.255.255 .255` is the same as the `any` command.

18. C. This is a standard IP access list that only filters on source IP addresses. The number range for IP access list is 1–99. The command to place an IP access list on an interface is `ip access-group`. Since the question specified incoming traffic, only Answer C works.

19. B. Cisco's rule of thumb states that standard lists should be placed closest to the source, and extended lists should be placed closest to the destination.

20. C. Cisco's rule of thumb states that standard lists should be placed closest to the source and extended lists should be placed closest to the destination.

Chapter

10

Wide Area Networking Protocols

THE CCNA EXAM TOPICS COVERED IN THIS CHAPTER INCLUDE THE FOLLOWING:

- ✓ Identify PPP operations to encapsulate WAN data on Cisco routers

- ✓ Configure authentication with PPP

- ✓ Understand how Frame Relay works on a large WAN network

- ✓ Configure Frame Relay LMIs, maps, and subinterfaces

- ✓ Monitor Frame Relay operation in the router

- ✓ Understand the ISDN protocols, function groups, and reference points

- ✓ Describe how Cisco implements ISDN BRI

he Cisco IOS WAN can support many different WAN protocols that can help you extend your LANs to other LANs at remote sites. Connecting company sites together so information can be exchanged is imperative in this economy. However, it would take a truckload of money to put in your own cable or connections to connect all of your company's remote locations. Service providers allow you to lease or share connections that the service provider already has installed, which can save money and time.

It is important to understand the different types of WAN support provided by Cisco. Although this chapter does not cover every type of Cisco WAN support, it does cover the HDLC, PPP, Frame Relay, and ISDN protocols.

Wide Area Networks

To understand WAN technologies, you need to understand the different WAN terms and connection types that can be used to connect your networks together. This section will discuss the different WAN terms and connection types typically used by service providers.

Defining WAN Terms

Before you order a WAN service type, it is important to understand the terms that the service providers use.

Customer premises equipment (CPE)   Equipment that is owned and located at the subscriber's premises.

Demarcation (demarc) The last responsibility of the service provider, usually an RJ-45 jack located close to the CPE. The CPE at this point would be a CSU/DSU or ISDN interface that plugs into the demarc.

Local loop Connects the demarc to the closest switching office, called a central office.

Central office (CO) Connects the customers to the provider's switching network. A CO is sometimes referred to as a point of presence (POP).

Toll network Trunk lines inside a WAN provider's network. It is a collection of switches and facilities.

It is important to familiarize yourself with these terms, as they are crucial to understanding WAN technologies.

WAN Connection Types

Figure 10.1 shows the different WAN connection types that can be used to connect your LANs together over a DCE network.

FIGURE 10.1 WAN connection types

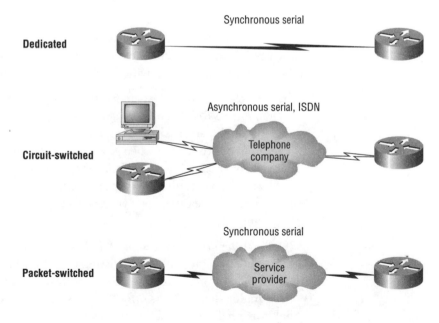

The following list explains the WAN connection types:

Leased lines   Typically referred to as a point-to-point or dedicated connection. It is a pre-established WAN communications path from the CPE, through the DCE switch, to the CPE of the remote site, allowing DTE networks to communicate at any time with no setup procedures before transmitting data. It uses synchronous serial lines up to 45Mbps.

Circuit switching   Sets up line like a phone call. No data can transfer before the end-to-end connection is established. Uses dial-up modems and ISDN. It is used for low-bandwidth data transfers.

Packet switching   WAN switching method that allows you to share bandwidth with other companies to save money. Think of packet switching networks as a party line. As long as you are not constantly transmitting data and are instead using bursty data transfers, packet switching can save you a lot of money. However, if you have constant data transfers, then you will need to get a leased line. Frame Relay and X.25 are packet-switching technologies. Speeds can range from 56Kbps to 2.048Mbps.

WAN Support

In this section, we will define the most prominent WAN protocols used today. These are Frame Relay, ISDN, LAPB, HDLC, and PPP. The rest of the chapter will be dedicated to explaining in depth how WAN protocols work and how to configure them with Cisco routers.

Frame Relay   A packet-switched technology that emerged in the early 1990s. *Frame Relay* is a Data Link and Physical layer specification that provides high performance. Frame Relay assumes that the facilities used are less error prone than when X.25 was used and that they transmit data with less overhead. Frame Relay is more cost-effective than point-to-point links and can typically run at speeds of 64Kbps to 1.544Mbps. Frame Relay provides features for dynamic-bandwidth allocation and congestion control.

ISDN   *Integrated Services Digital Network* is a set of digital services that transmit voice and data over existing phone lines. ISDN can offer a cost-effective solution for remote users who need a higher-speed connection than analog dial-up links offer. ISDN is also a good choice as a backup link for other types of links such as Frame Relay or a T-1 connection.

LAPB *Link Access Procedure, Balanced* was created to be used as a connection-oriented protocol at the Data Link layer for use with X.25. It can also be used as a simple Data Link transport. LAPB has a tremendous amount of overhead because of its strict timeout and windowing techniques. You can use LAPB instead of the lower-overhead HDLC if your link is very error prone. However, that typically is not a problem any longer.

HDLC *High-Level Data Link Control* was derived from Synchronous Data Link Control (SDLC), which was created by IBM as a Data Link connection protocol. HDLC is a connection-oriented protocol at the Data Link layer, but it has very little overhead compared to LAPB. HDLC was not intended to encapsulate multiple Network layer protocols across the same link. The HDLC header carries no identification of the type of protocol being carried inside the HDLC encapsulation. Because of this, each vendor that uses HDLC has their own way of identifying the Network layer protocol, which means that each vendor's HDLC is proprietary for their equipment.

PPP *Point-to-Point Protocol* is an industry-standard protocol. Because many versions of HDLC are proprietary, PPP can be used to create point-to-point links between different vendors' equipment. It uses a Network Control Protocol field in the Data Link header to identify the Network layer protocol. It allows authentication and multilink connections and can be run over asynchronous and synchronous links.

High-Level Data-Link Control Protocol (HDLC)

The High-Level Data-Link Control protocol (HDLC) is a popular ISO-standard, bit-oriented Data Link layer protocol. It specifies an encapsulation method for data on synchronous serial data links using frame characters and checksums. HDLC is a point-to-point protocol used on leased lines. No authentication can be used with HDLC.

In byte-oriented protocols, control information is encoded using entire bytes. Bit-oriented protocols, on the other hand, may use single bits to represent control information. Bit-oriented protocols include SDLC, LLC, HDLC, TCP, IP, etc.

HDLC is the default encapsulation used by Cisco routers over synchronous serial links. Cisco's HDLC is proprietary—it won't communicate with any other vendor's HDLC implementation—but don't give Cisco grief for it; everyone's HDLC implementation is proprietary. Figure 10.2 shows the Cisco HDLC format.

FIGURE 10.2   Cisco HDLC frame format

• Each vendor's HDLC has a proprietary data field to support multiprotocol environments.

• Supports only single-protocol environments.

As shown in the figure, the reason that every vendor has a proprietary HDLC encapsulation method is that each vendor has a different way for the HDLC protocol to communicate with the Network layer protocols. If the vendors didn't have a way for HDLC to communicate with the different layer-3 protocols, then HDLC would only be able to carry one protocol. This propriety header is placed in the data field of the HDLC encapsulation.

If you had only one Cisco router and you needed to connect to, say, a Bay router because you had your other Cisco router on order, then you couldn't use the default HDLC serial encapsulation. You would use something like PPP, which is an ISO standard way of identifying the upper-layer protocols.

Point-to-Point Protocol (PPP)

PPP (Point-to-Point Protocol) is a data-link protocol that can be used over either asynchronous serial (dial-up) or synchronous serial (ISDN) media and that uses the LCP (Link Control Protocol) to build and maintain data-link connections.

The basic purpose of PPP is to transport layer-3 packets across a Data Link layer point-to-point link. Figure 10.3 shows the protocol stack compared to the OSI reference model.

FIGURE 10.3   Point-to-point protocol stack

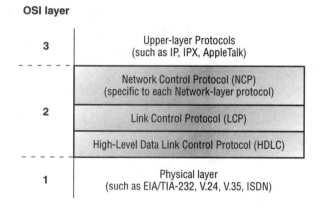

PPP contains four main components:

EIA/TIA-232-C   A Physical-layer international standard for serial communication.

HDLC   A method for encapsulating datagrams over serial links.

LCP   A method of establishing, configuring, maintaining, and terminating the point-to-point connection.

NCP   A method of establishing and configuring different Network layer protocols. PPP is designed to allow the simultaneous use of multiple Network layer protocols. Some examples of protocols here are IPCP (Internet Protocol Control Protocol) and IPXCP (Internetwork Packet Exchange Control Protocol).

It is important to understand that the PPP protocol stack is specified at the Physical and Data Link layers only. NCP is used to allow communication of multiple Network layer protocols by encapsulating the protocols across a PPP data link.

You must know your PPP protocols!

Link Control Protocol (LCP) Configuration Options

Link Control Protocol offers PPP encapsulation different options, including the following:

Authentication   This option tells the calling side of the link to send information that can identify the user. The two methods discussed in this course are PAP and CHAP.

Compression   This is used to increase the throughput of PPP connections. PPP decompresses the data frame on the receiving end. Cisco uses the Stacker and Predictor compression methods, discussed in the Advanced Cisco Router Configuration course.

Error detection   PPP uses Quality and Magic Number options to ensure a reliable, loop-free data link.

Multilink   Starting in IOS version 11.1, multilink is supported on PPP links with Cisco routers. This splits the load for PPP over two or more parallel circuits and is called a bundle.

PPP Session Establishment

PPP can be used with authentication. This means that communicating routers must provide information to identify the link as a valid communication link. When PPP connections are started, the links go through three phases of session establishment:

Link-establishment phase   LCP packets are sent by each PPP device to configure and test the link. The LCP packets contain a field called the Configuration Option that allows each device to see the size of the data, compression, and authentication. If no Configuration Option field is present, then the default configurations are used.

Authentication phase   If configured, either CHAP or PAP can be used to authenticate a link. Authentication takes place before Network-layer protocol information is read.

Network-layer protocol phase   PPP uses the Network Control Protocol to allow multiple Network-layer protocols to be encapsulated and sent over a PPP data link.

PPP Authentication Methods

There are two methods of authentication that can be used with PPP links, either Password Authentication Protocol (PAP) or Challenge Authentication Protocol (CHAP).

Password Authentication Protocol (PAP)

The *Password Authentication Protocol (PAP)* is the less secure of the two methods. Passwords are sent in clear text, and PAP is only performed upon the initial link establishment. When the PPP link is first established, the remote node sends back to the sending router the username and password until authentication is acknowledged. That's it.

Challenge Authentication Protocol (CHAP)

The *Challenge Authentication Protocol (CHAP)* is used at the initial startup of a link and at periodic checkups on the link to make sure the router is still communicating with the same host.

After PPP finishes its initial phase, the local router sends a challenge request to the remote device. The remote device sends a value calculated using a one-way hash function called MD5. The local router checks this hash value to make sure it matches. If the values don't match, the link is immediately terminated.

Configuring PPP on Cisco Routers

Configuring PPP encapsulation on an interface is a fairly straightforward process. To configure it, follow these router commands:

```
Router#config t
Enter configuration commands, one per line. End with CNTL/Z.
Router(config)#int s0
```

```
Router(config-if)#encapsulation ppp
Router(config-if)#^Z
Router#
```

Of course, PPP encapsulation must be enabled on both interfaces connected to a serial line to work, and there are several additional configuration options available by using the help command.

Configuring PPP Authentication

After you configure your serial interface to support PPP encapsulation, you can then configure authentication using PPP between routers. First set the hostname of the router if it is not already set. Then set the username and password for the remote router connecting to your router.

```
Router#config t
Enter configuration commands, one per line. End with CNTL/Z.
Router(config)# hostname RouterA
RouterA(config)#username todd password cisco
```

When using the hostname command, remember that the username is the hostname of the remote router connecting to your router. It is case-sensitive. Also, the password on both routers must be the same. It is a plain-text password and can be seen with a show run command. You can configure the password to be encrypted by using the command service password-config before you set the username and password. You must have a username and password configured for each remote system you are going to connect to. The remote routers must also be configured with usernames and passwords.

After you set the hostname, usernames, and passwords, choose the authentication type, either CHAP or PAP.

```
RouterA#config t
Enter configuration commands, one per line. End with CNTL/Z.
RouterA(config)#int s0
RouterA(config-if)#ppp authentication chap
RouterA(config-if)#ppp autherntication pap
RouterA(config-if)#^Z
RouterA#
```

If both methods are configured, as shown in the preceding configuration example, then only the first method is used during link negotiation. If the first method fails, then the second method will be used.

Verifying PPP Encapsulation

Now that we have PPP encapsulation enabled, let's take a look to verify that it's up and running. You can verify the configuration with the show interface command:

```
RouterA#show int s0
Serial0 is up, line protocol is up
 Hardware is HD64570
 Internet address is 172.16.20.1/24
 MTU 1500 bytes, BW 1544 Kbit, DLY 20000 usec, rely
255/255, load 1/255
 Encapsulation PPP, loopback not set, keepalive set
(10 sec)
 LCP Open
 Listen: IPXCP
 Open: IPCP, CDPCP, ATCP
 Last input 00:00:05, output 00:00:05, output hang never
 Last clearing of "show interface" counters never
 Input queue: 0/75/0 (size/max/drops); Total output drops:
0
 Queueing strategy: weighted fair
 Output queue: 0/1000/64/0 (size/max total/threshold/
drops)
    Conversations 0/2/256 (active/max active/max total)
    Reserved Conversations 0/0 (allocated/max allocated)
 5 minute input rate 0 bits/sec, 0 packets/sec
 5 minute output rate 0 bits/sec, 0 packets/sec
    670 packets input, 31845 bytes, 0 no buffer
    Received 596 broadcasts, 0 runts, 0 giants, 0 throttles
    0 input errors, 0 CRC, 0 frame, 0 overrun, 0 ignored, 0
abort
    707 packets output, 31553 bytes, 0 underruns
    0 output errors, 0 collisions, 18 interface resets
```

```
    0 output buffer failures, 0 output buffers swapped out
21 carrier transitions
    DCD=up DSR=up DTR=up RTS=up CTS=up
RouterA#
```

Notice that the fifth line lists encapsulation as PPP, and the sixth line tells us that LCP is open. Remember that LCP's job is to build and maintain connections. The eighth line tells us that IPCP, CDPCP, and ATCP are open. This shows the IP, CDP, and AppleTalk support from NCP. The seventh line reports that we are listening for IPXCP.

You can verify the PPP authentication configuration by using the debug ppp authentication command.

Frame Relay

Recently, the high-performance WAN encapsulation method known as Frame Relay has become one of the most popular technologies in use. It operates at the Physical and Data Link layers of the OSI reference model and was originally designed for use across Integrated Services Digital Network (ISDN) interfaces. But today, Frame Relay is used over a variety of other network interfaces.

Cisco Frame Relay supports the following protocols:

- IP
- DECnet
- AppleTalk
- Xerox Network Service (XNS)
- Novell IPX
- Connectionless Network Service (CLNS)
- International Organization for Standards (ISO)
- Banyan Vines
- Transparent bridging

Frame Relay provides a communications interface between DTE (Data Terminal Equipment) and DCE (Data Circuit-Terminating Equipment, such as packet switches) devices. DTE consists of terminals, PCs, routers, and bridges—customer-owned end-node and internetworking devices. DCE consists of carrier-owned internetworking devices.

Popular opinion maintains that Frame Relay is more efficient and faster than X.25 because it assumes error checking will be done through higher-layer protocols and application services.

Frame Relay provides connection-oriented, Data Link layer communication via virtual circuits just as X.25 does. These virtual circuits are logical connections created between two DTEs across a packet-switched network, which is identified by a DLCI, or *Data Link Connection Identifier*. (We'll get to DLCIs in a bit.) Also, like X.25, Frame Relay uses both PVCs (Permanent Virtual Circuits) and SVCs (Switched Virtual Circuits), although most Frame Relay networks use only PVCs. This virtual circuit provides the complete path to the destination network prior to the sending of the first frame.

Frame Relay Terminology

To understand the terminology used in Frame Relay networks, first you need to know how the technology works. Figure 10.4 is labeled with the various terms used to describe different parts of a Frame Relay network.

FIGURE 10.4 Frame Relay technology and terms

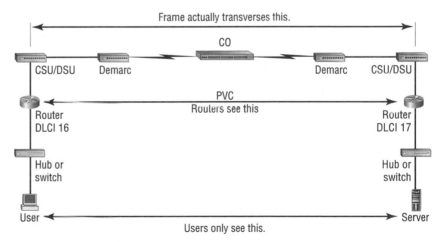

The basic idea behind Frame Relay networks is to allow users to communicate between two DTE devices through DCE devices. The users should not see the difference between connecting to and gathering resources from a local server and a server at a remote site connected with Frame Relay. Chances are this connection will be slower than a 10Mbps Ethernet LAN, but the physical difference in the connection should be transparent to the user.

Figure 10.4 illustrates everything that must happen in order for two DTE devices to communicate. Here is how the process works:

1. The user's network device sends a frame out on the local network. The hardware address of the router (default gateway) will be in the header of the frame.

2. The router picks up the frame, extracts the packet, and discards the frame. It then looks at the destination IP address within the packet and checks to see whether it knows how to get to the destination network by looking in the routing table.

3. The router then forwards the data out the interface that it thinks can find the remote network. (If it can't find the network in its routing table, it will discard the packet.) Because this will be a serial interface encapsulated with Frame Relay, the router puts the packet onto the Frame Relay network encapsulated within a Frame Relay frame. It will add the DLCI number associated with the serial interface. DLCIs identify the virtual circuit (PVC or SVC) to the routers and provider's switches participating in the Frame Relay network.

4. The channel service unit/data service unit (CSU/DSU) receives the digital signal and encodes it into the type of digital signaling that the switch at the Packet Switch Exchange (PSE) can understand. The PSE receives the digital signal and extracts the 1s and 0s from the line.

5. The CSU/DSU is connected to a demarcation (demarc) installed by the service provider, and its location is the service provider's first point of responsibility (last point on the receiving end). The demarc is typically just an RJ-45 jack installed close to the router and CSU/DSU.

6. The demarc is typically a twisted-pair cable that connects to the local loop. The local loop connects to the closest central office (CO), sometimes called a point of presence (POP). The local loop can connect using various physical mediums, but twisted-pair or fiber is very common.

7. The CO receives the frame and sends it through the Frame Relay "cloud" to its destination. This cloud can be dozens of switching offices—or more! It looks for the destination IP address and DLCI number. It typically can find the DLCI number of the remote device or router by looking up an IP-to-DLCI mapping. Frame Relay mappings are usually created statically by the service provider, but they can be created dynamically using the Inverse ARP (IARP) protocol. Remember that before data is sent through the cloud, the virtual circuit is created from end to end.

8. Once the frame reaches the switching office closest to the destination office, it is sent through the local loop. The frame is received at the demarc and then is sent to the CSU/DSU. Finally, the router extracts the packet, or datagram, from the frame and puts the packet in a new LAN frame to be delivered to the destination host. The frame on the LAN will have the final destination hardware address in the header. This was found in the router's ARP cache, or an ARP broadcast was performed. Whew!

The user and server do not need to know, nor should they know, everything that happens as the frame makes its way across the Frame Relay network. The remote server should be as easy to use as a locally connected resource.

Frame Relay Encapsulation

When configuring Frame Relay on Cisco routers, you need to specify it as an encapsulation on serial interfaces. There are only two encapsulation types: *Cisco* and *IETF (Internet Engineering Task Force)*. The following router output shows the two different encapsulation methods when choosing Frame Relay on your Cisco router:

```
RouterA(config)#int s0
RouterA(config-if)#encapsulation frame-relay ?
  ietf  Use RFC1490 encapsulation
  <cr>
```

The default encapsulation is Cisco unless you manually type in IETF, and Cisco is the type used when connecting two Cisco devices. You'd opt for the IETF-type encapsulation if you needed to connect a Cisco device to a non-Cisco device with Frame Relay. So before choosing an encapsulation type, check with your ISP and find out which one they use. (If they don't know, hook up with a different ISP!)

Data Link Connection Identifiers (DLCIs)

Frame Relay virtual circuits (PVCs) are identified by DLCIs. A Frame Relay service provider, such as the telephone company, typically assigns DLCI values, which are used by Frame Relay to distinguish between different virtual circuits on the network. Because many virtual circuits can be terminated on one multipoint Frame Relay interface, many DLCIs are often affiliated with it.

For the IP devices at each end of a virtual circuit to communicate, their IP addresses need to be mapped to DLCIs. This mapping can function as a multipoint device—one that can identify to the Frame Relay network the appropriate destination virtual circuit for each packet that is sent over the single physical interface. The mappings can be done dynamically through IARP or manually through the Frame Relay map command.

Frame Relay uses DLCIs the same way that X.25 uses X.121 addresses, and every DLCI number can be given either global or local meaning everywhere within the Frame Relay network.

Sometimes a provider can give a site a DLCI that is advertised to all remote sites as the same PVC. This PVC is said to have a global significance. For example, a corporate office might have a DLCI of 20. All remote sites would know that the corporate office is DLCI 20 and use this PVC to communicate to the corporate office. However, the customary implementation is to give each DLCI local meaning. What does this mean? It means that DLCI numbers do not necessarily need to be unique. Two DLCI numbers can be the same on different sides of a link because Frame Relay maps a local DLCI number to a virtual circuit on each interface of the switch. Each remote office can have its own DLCI number and communicate with the corporate office using unique DLCI numbers.

DLCI numbers, used to identify a PVC, are typically assigned by the provider and start at 16. Configuring a DLCI number to be applied to an interface is shown below:

```
RouterA(config-if)#frame-relay interface-dlci ?
  <16-1007> Define a DLCI as part of the current
subinterface
RouterA(config-if)#frame-relay interface-dlci 16
```

Local Management Interface (LMI)

The *Local Management Interface (LMI)* was developed in 1990 by Cisco Systems, StrataCom, Northern Telecom, and Digital Equipment Corporation and became known as the Gang-of-Four LMI or Cisco LMI. This gang took the basic Frame Relay protocol from the CCIT and added extensions onto the protocol features that allow internetworking devices to communicate easily with a Frame Relay network.

The LMI is a signaling standard between a CPE device (router) and a frame switch. The LMI is responsible for managing and maintaining status between these devices. LMI messages provide information about the following:

Keepalives   Verify data is flowing

Multicasting   Provides a local DLCI PVC

Multicast addressing   Provides global significance

Status of virtual circuits   Provides DLCI status

Beginning with IOS version 11.2, the LMI type is auto-sensed. This enables the interface to determine the LMI type supported by the switch.

If you're not going to use the auto-sense feature, you'll need to check with your Frame Relay provider to find out which type to use instead. The default type is Cisco, but you may need to change to ANSI or Q.933A. The three different LMI types are depicted in the router output below.

```
RouterA(config-if)#frame-relay lmi-type ?
  cisco
  ansi
  q933a
```

As seen in the output, all three standard LMI signaling formats are supported:

Cisco   LMI defined by the Gang of Four (default)

ANSI   Annex D defined by ANSI standard T1.617

ITU-T (q933a)   Annex A defined by Q.933

Routers receive LMI information on a frame-encapsulated interface and update the virtual circuit status to one of three different states:

Active state   Everything is up and routers can exchange information.

Inactive state   The router's interface is up and working with a connection to the switching office, but the remote router is not working.

Deleted state   This means that no LMI information is being received on the interface from the switch. It could be a mapping problem or a line failure.

Subinterfaces

You can have multiple virtual circuits on a single serial interface and yet treat each as a separate interface. These are known as *subinterfaces*. Think of a subinterface as a hardware interface defined by the IOS software. An advantage gained through using subinterfaces is the ability to assign different Network layer characteristics to each subinterface and virtual circuit, such as IP routing on one virtual circuit and IPX on another.

Partial Meshed Networks

You can use subinterfaces to mitigate partial meshed Frame Relay networks and split horizon protocols. For example, say you were running the IP protocol on a LAN network. If, on the same physical network, Router A can talk to Router B, and Router B to Router C, you can usually assume that Router A can talk to Router C. Though this is true with a LAN, it's not true with a Frame Relay network, unless Router A has a PVC to Router C.

In Figure 10.5, Network 1 is configured with five locations. To be able to make this network function, you would have to create a meshed network as shown in Network 2. However, even though Network 2's example works, it's an expensive solution—configuring subinterfaces as shown in the Network 3 solution is much more cost-effective.

In Network 3, configuring subinterfaces actually works to subdivide the Frame Relay network into smaller subnetworks—each with its own network number. So locations A, B, and C connect to a fully meshed network, while locations C and D, and D and E, are connected via point-to-point connections. Locations C and D connect to two subinterfaces and forward packets.

Subinterfaces also solve the problem with routing protocols that use split horizon. As you may recall, split horizon protocols do not advertise routes out the same interface they received the route update on. This can cause a problem on a meshed Frame Relay network. However, by using subinterfaces, routing protocols that receive route updates on one subinterface can send out the same route update on another subinterface.

FIGURE 10.5   Partial meshed network examples

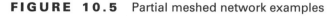

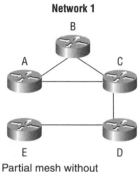

Network 1

Partial mesh without full connectivity and without subinterfaces

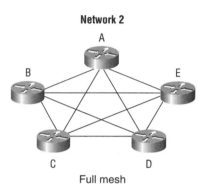

Network 2

Full mesh

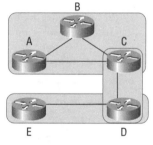

Network 3

Partial mesh with full connectivity using subinterfaces

Creating Subinterfaces

You define subinterfaces with the int s0.subinterface number command as shown below. You first set the encapsulation on the serial interface, then you can define the subinterfaces.

```
RouterA(config)#int s0
RouterA(config)#encapsulation frame-relay
```

```
RouterA(config)#int s0.?
  <0-4294967295>  Serial interface number
RouterA(config)#int s0.16 ?
  multipoint       Treat as a multipoint link
  point-to-point  Treat as a point-to-point link
```

You can define an almost limitless number of subinterfaces on a given physical interface (keeping router memory in mind). In the above example, we chose to use subinterface 16 because that represents the DLCI number assigned to that interface. However, you can choose any number between 0 and 4,292,967,295.

There are two types of subinterfaces:

Point-to-point   Used when a single virtual circuit connects one router to another. Each point-to-point subinterface requires its own subnet.

Multipoint   Used when the router is the center of a star of virtual circuits. Uses a single subnet for all routers' serial interfaces connected to the frame switch.

An example of a production router running multiple subinterfaces is shown below. Notice that the subinterface number matches the DLCI number. This is not a requirement but helps in the administration of the interfaces. Also notice that there is no LMI type defined, which means they are running either the default of Cisco or using autodetect if running Cisco IOS version 11.2 or newer. This configuration was taken from one of my customers' production routers (used by permission). Notice that each interface is defined as a separate subnet, separate IPX network, and separate Apple-Talk cable range (AppleTalk is beyond the scope of this course):

```
interface Serial0
 no ip address
 no ip directed-broadcast
 encapsulation frame-relay
!
interface Serial0.102 point-to-point
 ip address 10.1.12.1 255.255.255.0
 no ip directed-broadcast
 appletalk cable-range 12-12 12.65
 appletalk zone wan2
```

```
 appletalk protocol eigrp
 no appletalk protocol rtmp
 ipx network 12
 frame-relay interface-dlci 102
!
interface Serial0.103 point-to-point
 ip address 10.1.13.1 255.255.255.0
 no ip directed-broadcast
 appletalk cable-range 13-13 13.174
 appletalk zone wan3
 appletalk protocol eigrp
 no appletalk protocol rtmp
 ipx network 13
 frame-relay interface-dlci 103
!
interface Serial0.104 point-to-point
 ip address 10.1.14.1 255.255.255.0
 no ip directed-broadcast
 appletalk cable-range 14-14 14.131
 appletalk zone wan4
 appletalk protocol eigrp
 no appletalk protocol rtmp
 ipx network 14
 frame-relay interface-dlci 104
!
interface Serial0.105 point-to-point
 ip address 10.1.15.1 255.255.255.0
 no ip directed-broadcast
 appletalk cable-range 15-15 15.184
 appletalk zone wan5
 appletalk protocol eigrp
 no appletalk protocol rtmp
 ipx network 15
 frame-relay interface-dlci 105
!
interface Serial0.106 point-to-point
```

```
       ip address 10.1.16.1 255.255.255.0
       no ip directed-broadcast
       appletalk cable-range 16-16 16.28
       appletalk zone wan6
       appletalk protocol eigrp
       no appletalk protocol rtmp
       ipx network 16
       frame-relay interface-dlci 106
      !
      interface Serial0.107 point-to-point
       ip address 10.1.17.1 255.255.255.0
       no ip directed-broadcast
       appletalk cable-range 17-17 17.223
       appletalk zone wan7
       appletalk protocol eigrp
       no appletalk protocol rtmp
       ipx network 17
       frame-relay interface-dlci 107
      !
      interface Serial0.108 point-to-point
       ip address 10.1.18.1 255.255.255.0
       no ip directed-broadcast
       appletalk cable-range 18-18 18.43
       appletalk zone wan8
       appletalk protocol eigrp
       no appletalk protocol rtmp
       ipx network 18
       frame-relay interface-dlci 108
```

Mapping Frame Relay

As we explained earlier, in order for IP devices at the ends of virtual circuits to communicate, their addresses must be mapped to the DLCIs. There are two ways to make this mapping happen:

- Use the Frame Relay map command.

- Use the inverse-arp function.

Here's an example using the Frame Relay map command:

```
RouterA(config)#int s0
RouterA(config-if)#encap frame
RouterA(config-if)#int s0.16 point-to-point
RouterA(config-if)#no inverse-arp
RouterA(config-if)#ip address 172.16.30.1 255.255.255.0
RouterA(config-if)#frame-relay map ip 172.16.30.17 16 ietf
broadcast
RouterA(config-if)#frame-relay map ip 172.16.30.18 17
broadcast
RouterA(config-if)#frame-relay map ip 172.16.30.19 18
```

Here's what we did: First, we chose configured interface serial 0 to use the encapsulation type of Cisco (default), then we created our subinterface. We then turned off inverse arp and mapped three virtual circuits and their corresponding DLCI numbers.

Notice that we changed the encapsulation type for the first mapping. The frame map command is the only way to configure multiple frame encapsulation types on an interface.

The broadcast keyword at the end of the map command tells the router to forward broadcasts for this interface to this specific virtual circuit. Remember that Frame Relay is a nonbroadcast multiaccess (NBMA) encapsulation method, which will not broadcast routing protocols. You can either use the map command with the broadcast keyword or the neighbor command within the routing process.

Instead of putting in map commands for each virtual circuit, you can use the inverse-arp function to perform dynamic mapping of the IP address to the DLCI number. This makes our configuration look like this:

```
RouterA(config)#int s0.16 point-to-point
RouterA(config-if)#encap frame-relay ietf
RouterA(config-if)#ip address 172.16.30.1 255.255.255.0
```

Yes, this configuration is a whole lot easier to do, but it's not as stable as using the map command. Why? Sometimes, when using the inverse-arp function, configuration errors occur because virtual circuits can be insidiously and dynamically mapped to unknown devices.

Frame Relay Congestion Control

In this section we will define how the Frame Relay switch handles congestion problems.

DE (Discard Eligibility)   When a Frame Relay router detects congestion on the Frame Relay network, it will turn the DE bit on in a Frame Relay packet header. If the switch is congested, the Frame Relay switch will discard the packets with the DE bit set first. If your bandwidth is configured with a CIR of zero, the DE will always be on.

FECN (Forward-Explicit Congestion Notification)   When the Frame Relay network recognizes congestion in the cloud, the switch will set the FECN bit to 1 in a Frame Relay packet header. This will indicate to the destination DCE that the path just traversed is congested.

BECN (Backward-Explicit Congestion Notification)   When the switch detects congestion in the Frame Relay network, it will set the BECN bit in a Frame Relay packet and send it to the source router, telling it to slow down the rate at which it is transmitting packets.

Committed Information Rate (CIR)

Frame Relay provides a packet-switched network to many different customers at the same time. This is a great idea because it spreads the cost of the switches among many customers. However, Frame Relay is based on the assumption that not all customers need to transmit constant data all at the same time. Frame Relay works best with bursty traffic.

Think of Frame Relay as a party line. Remember party lines? That is when many people on your block had to share the same phone number. Okay, I am showing my age here, but understand that party lines were created on the assumption that few people needed to use the phone each day. If you needed to talk excessively, you had to pay for the more expensive dedicated circuit. Frame Relay works somewhat on the same principle, except many devices can transmit at the same time. However, if you need a constant data-stream connection, then Frame Relay is not for you. Buy a dedicated, point-to-point T-1 instead.

Frame Relay works by providing a dedicated bandwidth to each user, who is committed to that bandwidth at any given time. Frame Relay providers allow customers to buy a lower amount of bandwidth than what they really might need. This is called the *Committed Information Rate (CIR)*. What this means is that the customer can buy bandwidth of, for example, 256k, but it is possible to burst up to T-1 speeds. The CIR specifies that as long as the data input by a device to the Frame Relay network is below or equal to the CIR, then the network will continue to forward data for the PVC. However, if data rates exceed the CIR, it is not guaranteed.

It is sometimes possible to also purchase a Bc (Committed Burst), which allows customers to exceed their CIR for a specified amount of time. In this situation, the DE bit will always be set.

Choose a CIR based on realistic, anticipated traffic rates. Some Frame Relay providers allow you to purchase a CIR of zero. You can use a zero CIR to save money if retransmission of packets is acceptable. However, understand that the DE bit will always be turned on in every frame.

Monitoring Frame Relay

There are several ways to check the status of your interfaces and PVCs once you have Frame Relay encapsulation set up and running:

```
RouterA>sho frame ?
 ip     show frame relay IP statistics
 lmi    show frame relay lmi statistics
 map    Frame-Relay map table
 pvc    show frame relay pvc statistics
 route  show frame relay route
 traffic Frame-Relay protocol statistics
```

Show Frame-Relay Lmi

The show frame-relay lmi command will give you the LMI traffic statistics exchanged between the local router and the Frame Relay switch.

```
Router#sh frame lmi

LMI Statistics for interface Serial0 (Frame Relay DTE) LMI TYPE
= CISCO
    Invalid Unnumbered info 0        Invalid Prot Disc 0
    Invalid dummy Call Ref 0         Invalid Msg Type 0
    Invalid Status Message 0         Invalid Lock Shift 0
```

Invalid Information ID 0   Invalid Report IE Len 0
Invalid Report Request 0   Invalid Keep IE Len 0
Num Status Enq. Sent 0   Num Status msgs Rcvd 0
Num Update Status Rcvd 0   Num Status Timeouts 0
Router#

The router output from the show frame-relay lmi command shows you LMI errors as well as the LMI type.

Show Frame-Relay Pvc

The show frame pvc command will list all configured PVCs and DLCI numbers. It provides the status of each PVC connection and traffic statistics. It will also give you the number of BECN and FECN packets received on the router.

RouterA#**sho frame pvc**

PVC Statistics for interface Serial0 (Frame Relay DTE)

DLCI = 16,DLCI USAGE = LOCAL,PVC STATUS =ACTIVE,INTERFACE
= Serial0.1
  input pkts 50977876   output pkts 41822892   in bytes
3137403144
 out bytes 3408047602   dropped pkts 5   in FECN pkts 0
 in BECN pkts 0   out FECN pkts 0   out BECN pkts 0
 in DE pkts 9393   out DE pkts 0
 pvc create time 7w3d, last time pvc status changed 7w3d

DLCI = 18,DLCI USAGE =LOCAL,PVC STATUS =ACTIVE,INTERFACE =
Serial0.3
  input pkts 30572401   output pkts 31139837   in bytes
1797291100
 out bytes 3227181474   dropped pkts 5   in FECN pkts 0
 in BECN pkts 0   out FECN pkts 0   out BECN pkts 0
 in DE pkts 28   out DE pkts 0
 pvc create time 7w3d, last time pvc status changed 7w3d

To see information about only PVC 16, you can type the command show frame-relay pvc 16.

Show Interface

We can also use the show interface command to check for LMI traffic. The show interface command displays information about the encapsulation as well as layer-2 and layer-3 information.

The LMI DLCI, as bolded in the command, is used to define the type of LMI being used. If it is 1023, it is the default LMI type of Cisco. If the LMI DLCI is zero, then it is the ANSI LMI type.

```
RouterA#sho int s0
Serial0 is up, line protocol is up
 Hardware is HD64570
 MTU 1500 bytes, BW 1544 Kbit, DLY 20000 usec, rely 255/
255, load 2/255
 Encapsulation FRAME-RELAY, loopback not set, keepalive
set (10 sec)
 LMI enq sent 451751,LMI stat recvd 451750,LMI upd recvd
164,DTE LMI up
 LMI enq recvd 0, LMI stat sent 0, LMI upd sent 0
 LMI DLCI 1023 LMI type is CISCO frame relay DTE
 Broadcast queue 0/64, broadcasts sent/dropped 0/0,
interface broadcasts 839294
```

The show interface command displays line, protocol, DLCI, and LMI information.

Show Frame Map

The show frame map command will show you the Network layer–to–DLCI mappings.

```
RouterB#show frame map
 Serial0 (up): ipx 20.0007.7842.3575 dlci 16(0x10,0x400),
dynamic, broadcast,, status defined, active
 Serial0 (up): ip 172.16.20.1 dlci 16(0x10,0x400),
dynamic,
             broadcast,, status defined, active
```

```
    Serial1 (up): ipx 40.0007.7842.153a dlci 17(0x11,0x410),
dynamic, broadcast,, status defined, active
    Serial1 (up): ip 172.16.40.2 dlci 17(0x11,0x410),
dynamic,
                    broadcast,, status defined, active
```

Notice that the search interface has two mappings, one for IP and one for IPX. Also, notice that the Network layer addresses were resolved with the dynamic protocol Inverse ARP (IARP). If an administrator mapped the addresses, the output would say "static."

After the DLCI number is listed, you can see some numbers in parentheses. Notice the first number is 0x10, which is the hex equivalent for the DLCI number 16 used on serial 0, and the 0x11 is the hex for DLCI 17 used on serial 1. The second numbers, 0x400 and 0x410, are the DLCI numbers configured in the Frame Relay frame. They are different because of the way the bits are spread out in the frame.

To clear the dynamic mappings, you can use the command clear frame-relay-inarp.

Debug Frame Lmi

The debug frame lmi command will show output on the router consoles by default. The information from this command will allow you to verify and troubleshoot the Frame Relay connection by helping you to determine whether the router and switch are exchanging the correct LMI information.

```
Router#debug frame-relay lmi
Serial3/1(in): Status, myseq 214
RT IE 1, length 1, type 0
KA IE 3, length 2, yourseq 214, myseq 214
PVC IE 0x7 , length 0x6 , dlci 130, status 0x2 , bw 0
Serial3/1(out): StEnq, myseq 215, yourseen 214, DTE up
datagramstart = 0x1959DF4, datagramsize = 13
FR encap = 0xFCF10309
00 75 01 01 01 03 02 D7 D6
```

```
Serial3/1(in): Status, myseq 215
RT IE 1, length 1, type 1
KA IE 3, length 2, yourseq 215, myseq 215
Serial3/1(out): StEnq, myseq 216, yourseen 215, DTE up
datagramstart = 0x1959DF4, datagramsize = 13
FR encap = 0xFCF10309
00 75 01 01 01 03 02 D8 D7
```

Integrated Services Digital Network (ISDN)

Integrated Services Digital Network (ISDN) is a digital service designed to run over existing telephone networks. ISDN can support both data and voice—a telecommuter's dream. But ISDN applications require bandwidth. Typical ISDN applications and implementations include high-speed image applications (such as Group IV facsimile), high-speed file transfer, videoconferencing, and multiple links into homes of telecommuters.

ISDN is actually a set of communication protocols proposed by telephone companies that allows them to carry a group of digital services that simultaneously convey data, text, voice, music, graphics, and video to end users, and it was designed to achieve this over the telephone systems already in place. ISDN is referenced by a suite of ITU-T standards that encompass the OSI model's Physical, Data Link, and Network layers. The ISDN standards define the hardware and call-setup schemes for end-to-end digital connectivity.

PPP is typically used with ISDN to provide data encapsulation, link integrity, and authentication. These are the benefits of ISDN:

- Can carry voice, video, and data simultaneously

- Has faster call setup than a modem

- Has faster data rates than a modem connection

ISDN Components

The components used with ISDN include functions and reference points. Figure 10.6 shows how the different types of terminal and reference points can be used in an ISDN network.

FIGURE 10.6  ISDN functions and reference points

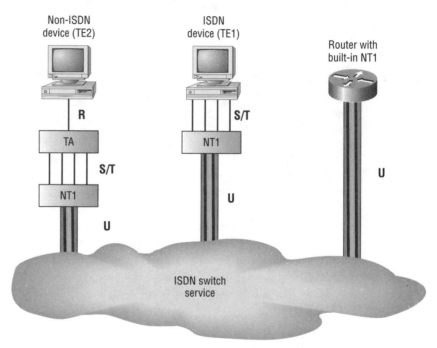

In North America, ISDN uses a two-wire connection into a home or office. That is called a "U" reference point. The NT1 device is used to convert the two-wire connection to a four-wire connection that is used by ISDN phones and terminal adapters (TAs). Most routers can now be purchased with a built-in NT1 (U) interface.

Figure 10.7 shows the different reference points and terminal equipment that can be used with Cisco ISDN BRI interfaces.

FIGURE 10.7   ISDN BRI reference points and terminal equipment

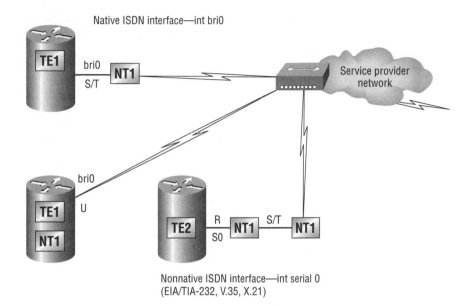

ISDN Terminals

Devices connecting to the ISDN network are known as terminal equipment (TE) and network termination (NT) equipment. There are two types of each:

TE1   Terminal equipment type 1 refers to those terminals that understand ISDN standards and can plug right into an ISDN network.

TE2   Terminal equipment type 2 refers to those that predate ISDN standards. To use a TE2, you have to use a terminal adapter (TA) to be able to plug into an ISDN network.

NT1   Network termination 1 implements the ISDN Physical layer specifications and connects the user devices to the ISDN network.

NT2   Network termination 2 is typically a provider's equipment, such as a switch or PBX. It also provides Data Link and Network layer implementation. It's very rare at a customer premises.

TA   Terminal adapter converts TE2 wiring to TE1 wiring that then connects into an NT1 device for conversion into a two-wire ISDN network.

ISDN Reference Points

Reference points are a series of specifications that define the connection between the various equipment used in an ISDN network. ISDN has four reference points that define logical interfaces:

R reference point   Defines the reference point between non-ISDN equipment (TE2) and a TA.

S reference point   Defines the reference point between the customer router and an NT2. Enables calls between the different customer equipment.

T reference point   Defines the reference point between NT1 and NT2 devices. S and T reference points are electrically the same and can perform the same function. Therefore, they are sometimes referred to as an S/T reference point.

U reference point   Defines the reference point between NT1 devices and line-termination equipment in a carrier network. (This is only in North America where the NT1 function isn't provided by the carrier network.)

ISDN Protocols

ISDN protocols are defined by the ITU, and there are several series of protocols dealing with diverse issues:

- Protocols beginning with the letter *E* deal with using ISDN on the existing telephone network.

- Protocols beginning with the letter *I* deal with concepts, aspects, and services.

- Protocols beginning with the letter *Q* cover switching and signaling.

ISDN Switch Types

We can credit AT&T and Nortel for the majority of the ISDN switches in place today, but additional companies also make them. In Table 10.1 under "Keyword," you'll find the right keyword to use along with the `isdn switch-type` command to configure a router for the variety of switches it's going to connect to. If you don't know which switch your provider is using at their central office, simply call them to find out.

TABLE 10.1 ISDN Switch Types

Switch Type	Keyword
AT&T basic rate switch	Basic-5ess
Nortel DMS-100 basic rate switch	Basic-dms100
National ISDN-1 switch	Basic-ni1
AT&T 4ESS (ISDN PRI only)	Primary-4ess
AT&T 5ESS (ISDN PRI only)	Primary-5ess
Nortel DMS-100 (ISDN PRI only)	Primary-dms100

Basic Rate Interface (BRI)

ISDN Basic Rate Interface (BRI, also known as 2B+1D) service provides two B channels and one D channel. The BRI B-channel service operates at 64Kbps and carries data, while the BRI D-channel service operates at 16Kbps and usually carries control and signaling information.

The D-channel signaling protocol spans the OSI reference model's Physical, Data Link, and Network layers. The D channel carries signaling information to set up and control calls. The D channel can also be used for other functions like an alarm system for a building, or anything that doesn't need much bandwidth, since it is only a whopping 16k. D channels work with LAPD at the Data Link layer.

When configuring ISDN BRI, you will need to obtain SPIDs (Service Profile Identifiers), and you should have one SPID for each B channel. SPIDs can be thought of as the telephone number of each B channel. The ISDN device gives the SPID to the ISDN switch, which then allows the device to access the network for BRI or PRI service. Without a SPID, many ISDN switches don't allow an ISDN device to place a call on the network.

To set up a BRI call, four events must take place:

1. The D channel between the router and the local ISDN switch comes up.

2. The ISDN switch uses the SS7 signaling technique to set up a path to a remote switch.

3. The remote switch sets up the D-channel link to the remote router.

4. The B channels are then connected end-to-end.

Primary Rate Interface (PRI)

In North America and Japan, the ISDN *Primary Rate Interface* (PRI, also known as 23B+D1) service delivers 23 64Kbps B channels and one 64Kbps D channel for a total bit rate of up to 1.544Mbps.

In Europe, Australia, and other parts of the world, ISDN provides 30 64Kbps B channels and one 64Kbps D channel for a total bit rate of up to 2.048Mbps.

ISDN with Cisco Routers

Accessing ISDN with a Cisco router means that you will need to purchase either a router with a built-in NT1 (U reference point) or an ISDN modem (called a TA). If your router has a BRI interface, you're ready to rock. Otherwise, you can use one of your router's serial interfaces if you can get ahold of a TA. A router with a BRI interface is called a TE1 (terminal endpoint 1), and one that requires a TA is called a TE2 (terminal endpoint 2).

ISDN supports virtually every upper-layer network protocol (IP, IPX, AppleTalk, you name it), and you can choose PPP, HDLC, or LAPD as your encapsulation protocol.

When configuring ISDN, you'll need to know the type of switch that your service provider is using. To see which switches your router will support, use the `isdn switch-type ?` command in global configuration mode or interface configuration mode. You need to do this because each manufacturer has a proprietary protocol for signaling.

For each ISDN BRI interface, you need to specify the SPIDs that are using the `isdn spid1` and `isdn spid2` interface subcommands. These are provided by the ISDN provider and identify you on the switch, sort of like a telephone number. However, some providers no longer require SPIDs to be configured on the router. Check with your provider to be sure.

The second part of the SPID configuration is the local dial number for that SPID. It is optional, but some switches need to have those set on the router in order to use both B channels simultaneously.

An example is shown below:

```
RouterA#config t
Enter configuration commands, one per line. End with CNTL/Z.
RouterA(config)#isdn switch-type basic-ne1
RouterA(config)#int bri0
RouterA(config-if)#encap ppp (optional)
RouterA(config-if)#isdn spid1 086506610100 8650661
RouterA(config-if)#isdn spid2 086506620100 8650662
```

The `isdn switch-type` command can be configured in either global configuration or interface configuration mode. Configuring the switch type global will set the switch type for all BRI interfaces in the router. If you only have one interface, it doesn't matter where you use the `isdn switch-type` command.

Dial-on-Demand Routing (DDR)

Dial-on-demand routing (DDR) is used to allow two or more Cisco routers to dial an ISDN dial-up connection on an as-needed basis. DDR is only used for low-volume, periodic network connections using either a Public Switched Telephone Network (PSTN) or ISDN. This was designed to reduce WAN costs if you have to pay on a per-minute or per-packet basis.

DDR works when a packet received on an interface meets the requirements of an access list defined by an administrator, which defines interesting traffic. The following five steps give a basic description of how DDR works when an interesting packet is received in a router interface:

1. Route to the destination network is determined.

2. Interesting packets dictate a DDR call.

3. Dialer information is looked up.

4. Traffic is transmitted.

5. Call is terminated when no more traffic is being transmitted over a link and the idle-timeout period ends.

Configuring DDR

To configure legacy DDR, you need to perform three tasks:

1. Define static routes, which define how to get to the remote networks and what interface to use to get there.

2. Specify the traffic that is considered interesting to the router.

3. Configure the dialer information that will be used to dial the interface to get to the remote network.

Configuring Static Routes

To forward traffic across the ISDN link, you configure static routes in each of the routers. You certainly can configure dynamic routing protocols to run on your ISDN link, but then the link will never drop. The suggested routing method is static routes. Keep the following in mind when creating static routes:

- All participating routers must have static routes defining all routes of known networks.

- Default routing can be used if the network is a stub network.

An example of static routing with ISDN is shown below:

```
RouterA(config)#ip route 172.16.50.0 255.255.255.0
172.16.60.2
RouterA(config)#ip route 172.16.60.2 255.255.255.255 bri0
```

What this does is tell the router how to get to network 172.16.50.0, which is through 172.16.60.2. The second line tells the router how to get to 172.16.60.2.

Specifying Interesting Traffic

After setting the route tables in each router, you need to configure the router to determine what brings up the ISDN line. An administrator using the `dialer-list` global configuration command defines interesting packets.

The command to turn on all IP traffic is shown as follows:

```
804A(config)#dialer-list 1 protocol ip permit
804A(config)#int bri0
804A(config-if)#dialer-group 1
```

The `dialer-group` command sets the access list on the BRI interface. Extended access lists can be used with the `dialer-list` command to define interesting traffic to just certain applications. We'll cover that in a minute.

Configuring the Dialer Information

There are five steps in the configuration of the dialer information.

1. Choose the interface.

2. Set the IP address.

3. Configure the encapsulation type.

4. Link interesting traffic to the interface.

5. Configure the number or numbers to dial.

Here is an example of how to configure the five steps:

```
804A#config t
804A(config)#int bri0
804A(config-if)#ip address 172.16.60.1 255.255.255.0
804A(config-if)#no shut
804A(config-if)#encapsulation ppp
804A(config-if)#dialer-group 1
804A(config-if)#dialer-string 8350661
```

Instead of the `dialer-string` command, you can use a dialer map, which provides more security.

```
804A(config-if)#dialer map ip 172.16.60.2 name 804B
8350661
```

The `dialer map` command can be used with the `dialer-group` command and its associated access list to initiate dialing. The `dialer map` command uses the IP address of the next hop router, the hostname of the remote router for authentication, and then the number to dial to get there.

Take a look at the following configuration of an 804 router:

```
804B#sh run
Building configuration...
Current configuration:
!
version 12.0
no service pad
service timestamps debug uptime
service timestamps log uptime
no service password-encryption
!
hostname 804B
!
ip subnet-zero
!
isdn switch-type basic-ni
!
interface Ethernet0
 ip address 172.16.50.10 255.255.255.0
 no ip directed-broadcast
!
interface BRI0
 ip address 172.16.60.2 255.255.255.0
 no ip directed-broadcast
 encapsulation ppp
 dialer idle-timeout 300
 dialer string 8358661
 dialer load-threshold 2 either
 dialer-group 1
 isdn switch-type basic-ni
 isdn spid1 0835866201 8358662
 isdn spid2 0835866401 8358664
 hold-queue 75 in
!
ip classless
```

```
ip route 172.16.30.0 255.255.255.0 172.16.60.1
ip route 172.16.60.1 255.255.255.255 BRI0
!
dialer-list 1 protocol ip permit
!
```

The BRI interface is running the PPP encapsulation and has a timeout value of 300 seconds. The `load-threshold` command makes both BRI interfaces come up immediately (Okay, I feel that if I am paying for both I want them both up all the time). The one thing you really want to notice is the `dialer-group 1` command. That number must match the dialer-list number. The `hold-queue 75 in` command tells the router that when it receives an interesting packet, it should queue up to 75 packets while it is waiting for the BRI to come up. If there are more than 75 packets queued before the link comes up, the packets will be dropped.

Optional Commands

There are two other commands that you should configure on your BRI interface: the `dialer load-threshold` command and the `dialer idle-timeout` command.

The `dialer load-threshold` command tells the BRI interface when to bring up the second B channel. The option is from 1–255, where 255 tells the BRI to bring up the second B channel only when the first channel is 100 percent loaded. The second option for that command is in, out, or either. This calculates the actual load on the interface either on outbound traffic, inbound traffic, or combined. The default is outbound.

The `dialer idle-timeout` command specifies the number of seconds before a call is disconnected after the last interesting traffic is sent. The default is 120 seconds.

```
RouterA(config-if)#dialer load-threshold 125 either
RouterA(config-if)#dialer idle-timeout 180
```

The `dialer load-threshold 125` tells the BRI interface to bring up the second B channel if either the inbound or outbound traffic load is 50 percent. The `dialer idle-timeout 180` changes the default disconnect time from 120 to 180 seconds.

DDR with Access Lists

You can use access lists to be more specific about what is interesting traffic. In the preceding example we just set the dialer list to allow any IP traffic to bring up the line. That is great if you are testing, but it can defeat the purpose of why you use a DDR line in the first place. You can use extended access lists to set the restriction, for example, to only e-mail or Telnet.

Here is an example of how you define the dialer list to use an access list:

```
804A(config)#dialer-list 1 list 110
804A(config)#access-list 110 permit tcp any any eq smtp
804A(config)#access-list 110 permit tcp any any eq telnet
804A(config)#int bri0
804A(config-if)#dialer-group 1
```

In the preceding example, you configure the dialer-list command to look at an access list. This doesn't have to be IP; it can be used with any protocol. Create your list, then apply it to the BRI interface with the dialer-group command.

Verifying the ISDN Operation

The following commands can be used to verify legacy DDR and ISDN:

Ping and Telnet   Are great IP tools for any network. However, your interesting traffic must dictate that Ping and Telnet are acceptable as interesting traffic to bring up a link. Once a link is up, you can ping or telnet to your remote router regardless of your interesting traffic lists.

Show dialer   Gives good information about your dialer diagnostic information and shows the number of times the dialer string has been reached, the idle-timeout values of each B channel, the length of cal, and the name of the router to which the interface is connected.

Show isdn active   Shows the number called and whether a call is in progress.

Show isdn status   Is a good command to use before trying to dial. Shows if your SPIDs are valid and if you are connected and communicating with layers 1 through 3 information to the provider's switch.

Sho ip route Shows all routes the router knows about.

Debug isdn q921 Is used to see layer-2 information only.

Debug isdn q931 Is used to see layer-3 information, including call setup and teardown.

Debug dialer Gives you call-setup and teardown activity.

Isdn disconnect int bri0 Clears the interface and drops the connection. Performing a shutdown on the interface can give you the same results.

Summary

In this chapter, we covered the following key points:

- The difference between the following WAN services: X.25/LAPB, Frame Relay, ISDN/LAPD, SDLC, HDLC, and PPP

- Important Frame Relay and X.25 terms and features

- The commands to configure Frame Relay LMIs, maps, and subinterfaces

- The commands to monitor Frame Relay operation in the router

- How to identify PPP operations to encapsulate WAN data on Cisco routers

- How to state a relevant use and context for ISDN networking

- How to identify ISDN protocols, function groups, reference points, and channels

- How to describe Cisco's implementation of ISDN BRI

Key Terms

Be sure you are familiar with these terms before you take the exam.

Basic Rate Interface	*Local Management Interface (LMI)*
BECN (Backward-Explicit Congestion Notification)	*NT1*
central office (CO)	*NT2*
Challenge Authentication Protocol (CHAP)	*packet switching*
circuit switching	*Password Authentication Protocol (PAP)*
customer premises equipment (CPE)	*PPP*
DE (Discard Eligibility)	*NT1*
demarcation (demarc)	*R reference point*
FECN (Forward-Explicit Congestion Notification)	*S reference point*
Frame Relay	*T reference point*
HDLC	*TA*
ISDN	*TE1*
LAPB	*TE2*
local loop	*toll network*
leased lines	*U reference point*

Commands in This Chapter

Command	Description
`debug dialer`	Shows you the call setup and teardown procedures
`debug frame-relay lmi`	Shows the lmi exchanges between the router and the Frame Relay switch
`debug isdn q921`	Shows layer-2 processes
`debug isdn q931`	Shows layer-3 processes
`dialer idle-timeout number`	Tells the BRI line when to drop if no interesting traffic is found
`dialer list number protocol protocol permit/deny`	Specifies interesting traffic for a DDR link
`dialer load-threshold number inbound/outbound/either`	Sets the parameters that describe when the second BRI comes up on a ISDN link
`dialer map protocol address name hostname number`	Used instead of a dialer string to provide more security in an ISDN network
`dialer-string`	Sets the phone number to dial for a BRI interface
`encapsulation frame-relay`	Changes the encapsulation to Frame Relay on a serial link
`encapsulation frame-relay ietf`	Sets the encapsulation type to the Internet Engineering Task Force (IETF). Connects Cisco routers to off-brand routers.
`encapsulation hdlc`	Restores the default encapsulation of HDLC on a serial link
`encapsulation ppp`	Changes the encapsulation on a serial link to PPP

Command	Description
`frame-relay interface-dlci`	Configures the PVC address on a serial interface or subinterface
`frame-relay lmi-type`	Configures the LMI type on a serial link
`frame-relay map protocol address`	Creates a static mapping for use with a Frame Relay network
`interface s0.16 multipoint`	Creates a multipoint subinterface on a serial link that can be used with Frame Relay networks
`interface s0.16 point-to-point`	Creates a point-to-point subinterface on a serial link that can be used with Frame Relay
`isdn spid1`	Sets the number that identifies the first DS0 to the ISDN switch
`isdn spid2`	Sets the number that identifies the second DS0 to the ISDN switch
`isdn switch-type`	Sets the type of ISDN switch that the router will communicate with. Can be set at interface level or global configuration mode.
`no inverse-arp`	Turns off the dynamic IARP used with Frame Relay. Static mappings must be configured.
`ppp authentication chap`	Tells PPP to use CHAP authentication
`ppp authentication pap`	Tells PPP to use PAP authentication

Command	Description
`show dialer`	shows the number of times the dialer string has been reached, the idle-timeout values of each B channel, the length of call, and the name of the router to which the interface is connected
`show frame-relay lmi`	Sets the LMI type on a serial interface
`show frame-relay map`	Shows the static and dynamic Network layer–to–PVC mappings
`show frame-relay pvc`	Shows the configured PVCs and DLCI numbers configured on a router
`show ip route`	Shows the IP routing table
`show isdn active`	Shows the number called and whether a call is in progress
`show isdn status`	Shows if your SPIDs are valid and if you are connected and communicating with the provider's switch.
`username name password password`	Creates usernames and passwords for authentication on a Cisco router

Written Lab

1. Write the command to see the encapsulation method on serial 0 of a Cisco router.

2. Write the commands to configure s0 to PPP encapsulation.

3. Write the commands to configure a username of todd and password of cisco that is used on a Cisco router.

4. Write the commands to enable CHAP authentication on a Cisco BRI interface.

5. Write the commands to configure the DLCI numbers for two serial interfaces, 0 and 1. Use 16 for s0 and 17 for s1.

6. Write the commands to configure a remote office using a point-to-point subinterface. Use dlci 16 and IP address 172.16.60.1/24. The IPX network is 16.

7. Write the commands to set the switch type of basic-ni on a Cisco router BRI interface.

8. Set the switch type on a Cisco router at the interface level.

9. Write the command that will specify interesting traffic to bring up the ISDN link. Choose all IP traffic.

10. Write the commands necessary to apply the command that you specified in question 9 to a Cisco router.

11. Write the commands to configure the dialer information on a Cisco router.

12. Write the commands to set the dialer load-threshold and the idle-time percentage.

13. Write the commands that will set the queue for packets at 75 when they are found interesting and need a place to wait for the ISDN link to come up.

14. Write out the five steps in the configuration of the dialer information.

15. Write out the five steps that give a basic description of how DDR works when an interesting packet is received in a router interface.

Hands-on Labs

In this section, you will configure Cisco routers in four different WAN labs using the figure supplied in each lab.

Lab 10.1: Configuring PPP Encapsulation and Authentication

Lab 10.2: Configuring and Monitoring HDLC

Lab 10.3: Configuring Frame Relay and Subinterfaces

Lab 10.4: Configuring ISDN and BRI Interfaces

Lab 10.1: Configuring PPP Encapsulation and Authentication

By default, Cisco routers use High-Level Data Link Control (HDLC) as a point-to-point encapsulation method on serial links. If you are connecting to non-Cisco equipment, then you can use the PPP encapsulation method to communicate.

The lab you will configure is shown in Figure 10.8.

FIGURE 10.8 PPP lab

1. Type **sh int s0** on Routers A and B to see the encapsulation method.

2. Make sure that each router has the hostname assigned:

```
RouterA#config t
RouterA(config)#hostname RouterA

RouterB#config t
RouterB(config)#hostname RouterB
```

3. To change the default HDLC encapsulation method to PPP on both routers, use the encapsulation command at interface configuration. Both ends of the link must run the same encapsulation method.

```
RouterA#Config t
RouterA(config)#Int s0
RouterA(config)#Encap ppp
```

4. Now go to Router B and set serial 0 to PPP encapsulation.

```
RouterB#config t
RouterB(config)#int s0
RouterB(config)#encap ppp
```

5. Verify the configuration by typing **sh int s0** on both routers.

6. Notice the IPCP, IPXCP, and CDPCP. This is the information used to transmit the upper-layer (Network layer) information across the ISO HDLC at the MAC sublayer.

7. Define a username and password on each router. Notice that the username is the name of the remote router. Also, the password MUST be the same.

```
RouterA#config t
RouterA(config)#username RouterB password todd

RouterB#config t
RouterB(config)#username RouterA password todd
```

8. Enable CHAP or PAP authentication on each interface.

```
RouterA(config)#int s0
RouterA(config-if)#ppp authentication chap

RouterB(config)#int s0
RouterB(config-if)#ppp authentication chap
```

9. Verify the PPP configuration on each router by using these two commands:

```
sh int s0
debug PPP authentication
```

Lab 10.2: Configuring and Monitoring HDLC

There is no configuration for HDLC, but if you completed Lab 10.1, then the PPP encapsulation would be set on both routers. This is why I put the PPP lab first. This allows you to actually configure HDLC encapsulation on a router.

This second lab will use the same Figure 10.8 as Lab 10.1 used.

1. Set the encapsulation for each serial interface by using the encapsulation hdlc command.

   RouterA#**config t**
   RouterA(config)#**int s0**
   RouterA(config-if)#**encapsulation hdlc**

   RouterB#**config t**
   RouterB(config)#**int s0**
   RouterB(config-if)#**encapsulation hdlc**

2. Verify the HDLC encapsulation by using the show interface s0 command on each router.

Lab 10.3: Configuring Frame Relay and Subinterfaces

This lab will use Figure 10.9 to describe and configure Frame Relay configurations.

FIGURE 10.9 Frame Relay lab

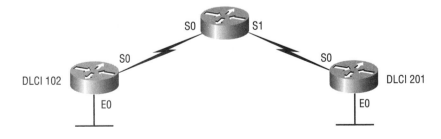

In my seminars I usually use a 2522 router as a frame switch, which provides 10 serial connections. But, since it is possible you may only have some 2501s, I have written this lab to work with three 2501 routers.

1. Set the hostname, `frame-relay switching` command, and the encapsulation of each serial interface on the Frame Relay switch.

```
Router#config t
Router(config)#hostname RouterB
RouterB(config)#frame-relay switching
RouterB(config)#int s0
RouterB(config-if)#encapsulation frame-relay
RouterB(config-if)#int s1
RouterB(config-if)#encapsulation frame-relay
```

2. Configure the Frame Relay mappings on each interface. You do not have to have IP addresses on these interfaces, as they are only switching one interface to another with Frame Relay frames.

```
RouterB(config-if)#int s0
RouterB(config-if)#frame-relay route 102 interface
Serial1 201
RouterB(config-if)#frame intf-type dce
RouterB(config-if)#int s1
RouterB(config-if)#frame-relay route 201 interface
Serial0 102
RouterB(config-if)#frame intf-type dce
```

This is not as hard as it looks. The route command just says that if you receive frames from PVC 102, send them out int s1 using PVC 201. The second mapping on serial 1 is just the opposite. Anything that comes in int s1 is routed out serial 0 using PVC 102.

3. Configure your Router A with a point-to-point subinterface.

```
Router#config t
Router(config)#hostname RouterA
RouterA(config)#int s0
RouterA(config-if)#encapsulation frame-relay
RouterA(config-if)#int s0.102 point-to-point
RouterA(config-if)#ip address 172.16.10.1
```

```
                      255.255.255.0
                      RouterC(config-if)#ipx network 10
                      RouterA(config-if)#frame-relay interface-dlci 102
```

4. Configure Router C with a point-to-point subinterface.

```
            Router#config t
            Router(config)#hostname RouterC
            RouterC(config)#int s0
            RouterC(config-if)#encapsulation frame-relay
            RouterC(config-if)#int s0.102 point-to-point
            RouterC(config-if)#ip address 172.16.10.2
            255.255.255.0
            RouterC(config-if)#ipx network 10
            RouterC(config-if)#frame-relay interface-dlci 201
```

5. Verify your configurations with the following commands:

```
            RouterA>sho frame ?
             ip        show frame relay IP statistics
             lmi       show frame relay lmi statistics
             map       Frame-Relay map table
             pvc       show frame relay pvc statistics
             route     show frame relay route
             traffic   Frame-Relay protocol statistics
```

6. Also, use Ping and Telnet to verify connectivity.

Lab 10.4: Configuring ISDN and BRI Interfaces

This lab will use Figure 10.10 as a reference for configuring and monitoring ISDN on Cisco routers. In this lab, you will configure routers 804A and 804B to dial ISDN between the networks 172.16.30.0 and 172.16.50.0, using network 172.16.60.0 on the ISDN BRI interfaces.

FIGURE 10.10 ISDN lab

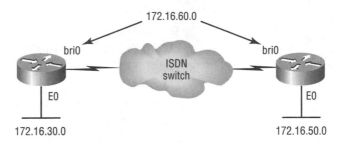

1. Go to 804B and set the hostname and ISDN switch type.

   ```
   Router#Config t
   Router(config)#hostname 804B
   804B(config)#isdn switch-type basic-ni
   ```

2. Set the hostname and switch type on 804A at the interface level. The point of steps 1 and 2 is to show you that you can configure the switch type either through global configuration mode or interface level.

   ```
   Router#Config t
   Router(config)#hostname 804A
   804A(config)#int bri0
   804B(config-if)#isdn switch-type basic-ni
   ```

3. On 804A, set the SPID numbers on BRI 0 and make the IP address 171.16.60.1/24. If you have either a real connection into an ISDN network or an ISDN simulator, put your SPID numbers in.

   ```
   804a#config t
   804A(config)#int bri0
   804A(config-if)#isdn spid 1 0835866101 ldn 8358661
   804A(config-if)#isdn spid 2 0835866301 ldn 8358663
   804A(config-if)#ip address 172.16.60.1
   255.255.255.0
   804A(config-if)#no shut
   ```

4. Set the SPIDs on 804B and make the IP address of the interface
   172.16.60.2/24.

   ```
   804A#config t
   804A(config)#int bri0
   804A(config-if)#isdn spid 1 0835866201 ldn 8358662
   804A(config-if)#isdn spid 2 0835866401 ldn 8358664
   804A(config-if)#ip address 172.16.60.2
   255.255.255.0
   804A(config-if)#no shut
   ```

5. Create static routes on the routers to use the remote ISDN interface.
   Dynamic routing will create two problems: (1) the ISDN line will
   always stay up, and (2) a network loop will occur because of multiple
   links between the same location. The CCNA exam only discusses dis-
   tant vector routing protocols (RIP and IGRP). Static routes are recommended with ISDN.

   ```
   804A(config)#ip route 172.16.50.0 255.255.255.0
   172.16.60.2
   804A(config)#ip route 172.16.60.2 255.255.255.255
   bri0


   804B(config)#ip route 172.16.30.0 255.255.255.0
   172.16.60.1
   804B(config)#ip route 172.16.60.1 255.255.255.255
   bri0
   ```

6. Specify interesting traffic to bring up the ISDN link. Let's choose all IP
   traffic. This is a global configuration mode command.

   ```
   804A(config)#dialer-list 1 protocol ip permit


   804B(config)#dialer-list 1 protocol ip permit
   ```

7. Under the BRI interface of both routers, add the command `dialer-group 1`, which matches the dialer-list number.

   ```
   804B(config)#config t
   804B(config)#int bri0
   804B(config)#dialer-group 1
   ```

8. Configure the dialer information on both routers.

```
804A#Config t
804A(config)#Int bri0
804A(config-if)#Dialer string 8358662

804B#Config t
804B(config)#Int bri0
804B(config-if)#Dialer string 8358661
```

9. Set the `dialer load-threshold` and `multilink` commands, as well as the idle-time percentage on both 804 routers.

```
804A#Config t
804A(config)#int bri0
804B(config-if)#Dialer load-threshold 125 either
804B(config-if)#Dialer idle-timeout 180

804B#Config t
804B(config)#int bri0
804B(config-if)#Dialer load-threshold 125 either
804B(config-if)#Dialer idle-timeout 180
```

10. Set the hold queue for packets when they are found interesting and need a place to wait for the ISDN link to come up.

```
804A#Config t
804A(config)#int bri0
804B(config-if)#hold-queue 75 in

804B#Config t
804B(config)#int bri0
804B(config-if)#hold-queue 75 in
```

11. Verify the ISDN connection.

```
Ping
Telnet
Show dialer
Show isdn status
Sh ip route
```

Review Questions

1. Which of the following protocols support PPP?

   A. HDLC

   B. LCP

   C. SDLC

   D. NCP

   E. LAPB

2. When would you use ISDN?

   A. To connect IBM mainframes

   B. To connect local area networks (LANs) using digital service with dissimilar media

   C. To support applications requiring high-speed voice, video, and data communications

   D. When you need both a consistent and very high rate of data speed and transfer

3. How many Frame Relay encapsulation types are available with Cisco routers?

   A. Two

   B. Three

   C. Four

   D. Five

4. How many LMI types are available?

   A. Two

   B. Three

   C. Four

   D. Five

5. Regarding Frame Relay, which of the following statements is true?

   A. You must use Cisco encapsulation if connecting to non-Cisco equipment.

   B. You must use ANSI encapsulation if connecting to non-Cisco equipment.

   C. You must use IETF encapsulation if connecting to non-Cisco equipment.

   D. You must use Q.933A encapsulation if connecting to non-Cisco equipment.

6. What is the default LMI type?

   A. Q.933A

   B. ANSI

   C. IETF

   D. Cisco

7. Which of the following uses a PVC at layer 2?

   A. X.25

   B. ISDN

   C. Frame Relay

   D. HDLC

8. Which ISDN protocol prefix specifies switching?

   A. I

   B. E

   C. S

   D. Q

9. If you wanted to view the DLCI numbers configured for your Frame Relay network, which command would you use? (Choose all that apply.)

    A. `sh frame-relay`

    B. `show running`

    C. `sh int s0`

    D. `sh frame-relay dlci`

    E. `sh frame-relay pvc`

10. What is IARP used for?

    A. Mapping X.121 addresses to X.25 addresses

    B. Mapping DLCIs to network protocol addresses

    C. SMDS addressing

    D. Mapping ATM addresses to virtual addresses

11. What does the ISDN Basic Rate Interface (BRI) provide?

    A. 23 B channels and one 64Kbps D channel

    B. Total bit rate of up to 1.544Mbps

    C. Two 56Kbps B channels and one 64Kbps D channel

    D. Two 64Kbps B channels and one 16Kbps D channel

12. What is true about Frame Relay DLCI?

    A. DLCI is optional in a Frame Relay network.

    B. DLCI represents a single physical circuit.

    C. DLCI identifies a logical connection between DTE devices.

    D. DLCI is used to tag the beginning of a frame when using LAN switching.

13. Which command will list all configured PVCs and DLCIs?

A. `sh frame pvc`

B. `sh frame`

C. `sh frame lmi`

D. `sh pvc`

14. What is the default encapsulation on point-to-point links between two Cisco routers?

A. SDLC

B. HDLC

C. Cisco

D. ANSI

15. What information is provided by the Local Management Interface? (Choose all that apply.)

A. The status of virtual circuits

B. The current DLCI values

C. The global or local significance of the DLCI values

D. LMI encapsulation type

16. Which protocol used in PPP allows multiple Network-layer protocols to be used during a connection?

A. LCP

B. NCP

C. HDLC

D. X.25

17. Which protocol is used with PPP to establish, configure, and authenticate a data-link connection?

    A. LCP

    B. NCP

    C. HDLC

    D. X.25

18. In Frame Relay, what identifies the PVC?

    A. NCP

    B. LMI

    C. IARP

    D. DLCI

19. Which of the following is true about LMIs?

    A. LMIs map DLCI numbers to virtual circuits.

    B. LMIs map X.121 addresses to virtual circuits.

    C. LMIs report the status of virtual circuits.

    D. LMI messages provide information about the current DLCI values.

20. Which of the following contains Frame Relay control information?

    A. DLCI

    B. IARP

    C. LMI

    D. BECN

(The answers to the questions begin on the next page.)

Answers to the Written Lab

1. sh int s0

2. Config t
   Int s0
   Encap ppp

3. Config t
   username todd password cisco

4. Config t
   int s0
   ppp authentication chap

5. Config t
   Int s0
   Frame interface-dlci 16
   Int s1
   Frame interface-dlci 17

6. config t
   int s0
   encap frame
   int s0.16 point-to-point
   ip address 172.16.60.1 255.255.255.0
   ipx netw 16
   frame interface-dlci 16

7. Config t
   Isdn switch-type basic-ni

8. Config t
   Interface bri 0
   Isdn switch-type basic-ni

9. **Router(config)#dialer-list 1 protocol ip permit**

10. config t
    int bri0
    dialer-group 1

11. Config t
Int bri0
Dialer string 8358662

12. Config t
Int bri0
Dialer load-threshold 125 either
Dialer idle-timeout 180

13. Config t
Int bri0
Hold-queue 75 in

14.   **1.** Choose the interface.

   2. Set the IP address.

   3. Configure the encapsulation type.

   4. Link interesting traffic to the interface.

   5. Configure the number or numbers to dial.

15.   **1.** Route to the destination network is determined.

   2. Interesting packets dictate a DDR call.

   3. Dialer information is looked up.

   4. Traffic is transmitted.

   5. Call is terminated when no more traffic is being transmitted over
a link and the idle-timeout period ends.

Answers to Review Questions

1. A, B, and D. The PPP protocols are HDLC and LCP at the MAC sublayer of the Data Link layer, and NCP at the LLC sublayer of the Data Link layer.

2. C. ISDN can support voice, video, and data.

3. A. Cisco routers support two Frame Relay encapsulation types: Cisco and IETF.

4. B. Cisco routers support three LMI types: Cisco, ANSI, and Q.933A.

5. C. Internet Engineering Task Force (IETF) is the encapsulation method used when connecting Frame Relay to non-Cisco routers.

6. D . The default LMI type is Cisco.

7. C. Frame Relay uses a PVC at the Data Link layer.

8. D. The ISDN specification that is used for switching and signaling is the Q specification.

9. B, E. You can use the commands `show running-config` and `show frame-relay pvc` to see the DLCI numbers configured on your router.

10. B. Inverse ARP is used to map Network-layer protocol addresses to DLCI numbers.

11. D. BRI is two DS0s, which are 64Kbps each. It also has one Data channel of 16Kbps to provide clocking.

12. C. DLCI is required to be used on each circuit with Frame Relay. The DLCI number identifies the PVC of each circuit. PVCs are logical links between two DTE devices.

13. A. The `show frame-relay pvc` command will show the PVCs configured and the associated DLCI numbers.

14. B. Cisco uses a proprietary HDLC as the default encapsulation on all their serial interfaces.

15. A, B, C. The Local Management Interface provides PVC status messaging, the DLCI values associated with a PV, and global or local significance of the DLCI values.

16. B. Network Control Protocol works at the LLC sublayer of the Data Link layer and is responsible for allowing multiple Network-layer protocols to be used with PPP.

17. A. Link Control Protocol works at the MAC sublayer of the Data Link layer to establish, maintain, and authenticate a data-link connection.

18. D. Data Link Connection Identifiers (DLCIs) are used to identify a PVC.

19. C, D. The Local Management Interface provides PVC status messaging, the DLCI values associated with a VC, and global or local significance of the DLCI values.

20. D. Backward-Explicit Congestion Notification (BECN) is used to send information back to an originating router telling it to slow down its transfer rate because the switch is congested.

A

Practice Exam

Questions to the Practice Exam

1. What protocol does PPP use to identify the Network layer protocol?

   A. NCP

   B. ISDN

   C. HDLC

   D. LCP

2. You work in a large application-development company providing MIS services. This company has four 10Mbps shared hubs providing network services to an NT server. To meet the business requirements, you must provide many different types of hosts to allow the application developers to test the different applications they create. These hosts must be able to share data between each host and also send data to and from an enterprise server. The hosts run at 10Mbps and the server at 100Mbps. Some applications only need 3Mbps of bandwidth to run at any given time. What network recommendation would you give this company if money were an issue?

   A. Replace the 10Mbps hubs with 100Mbps hubs.

   B. Install a router and connect all the hubs into separate collision domains and one large broadcast domain.

   C. Install a layer-2 switch and run a 10Mbps connection to the hosts and a 100Mbps connection to the server.

   D. Uses bridges to break up the collision domains and create one large broadcast domain.

3. Write the command to configure IPX routing on a Cisco router with two interfaces. The first interface is an Ethernet LAN and must support 802.3 and 802.2. The second interface is a WAN interface and uses HDLC encapsulation. Use any IPX network numbers that you wish.

4. What does the command routerA(config)#**line cons 0** allow you to perform next?

   A. Set the Telnet password.

   B. Shut down the router.

   C. Set your console password.

   D. Disable console connections.

5. What ISDN command will bring up the second BRI at 50 percent load?

   A. load balance 50

   B. load share 50

   C. dialer load-threshold 125

   D. dialer idle-timeout 125

6. What PPP protocol provides dynamic addressing, authentication, and multilink?

   A. NCP

   B. HDLC

   C. LCP

   D. X.25

7. What command will display the line, protocol, DLCI, and LMI information of an interface?

   A. sh pvc

   B. show interface

   C. show frame-rely pvc

   D. sho runn

8. What type of access list uses the numbers 1–99?

    A. IP standard

    B. IPX standard

    C. IP extended

    D. IPX extended

    E. IPX SAP filter

9. What does the `passive` command provide to dynamic routing protocols?

    A. Stops an interface from sending or receiving periodic dynamic updates

    B. Stops an interface from sending periodic dynamic updates but still receives updates

    C. Stops the router from receiving any dynamic updates

    D. Stops the router from sending any dynamic updates

10. Which protocol does Ping use?

    A. TCP

    B. ARP

    C. ICMP

    D. BootP

11. Write the command that will show the IPX RIP and SAP information sent and received on a router.

12. Which of the following commands will set your Telnet password on a Cisco router?

    A. `Line telnet 0 4`

    B. `Line aux 0 4`

    C. `Line vty 0 4`

    D. `Line con 0`

13. Which of the following commands will create VLAN 5 with an ID of Marketing on a 1900 switch?

    A. 1900A#vlan 5 name Marketing

    B. 1900A(config)#vlan name Marketing 5

    C. 1900A(config)#vlan 5 name Marketing

    D. 1900A(config)# Marketing vlan 5

14. Which port on a bridge is the root port?

    A. The port with the lowest cost to the root bridge

    B. The port with the highest cost to the root bridge

    C. Any active port

    D. Any 100Mbps port

15. If you wanted to delete the configuration stored in NVRAM, what would you type?

    A. Erase startup

    B. Erase nvram

    C. Delete nvram

    D. Erase running

16. Write the command to create a second IPX network running the SNAP frame type on Ethernet 0.

17. Which class of IP address has the most host addresses available by default?

    A. A

    B. B

    C. C

    D. A and B

18. How often are BPDU sent from a layer-2 device?

   A. Never

   B. Every two seconds

   C. Every 10 minutes

   D. Every 30 seconds

19. Which of the following is true regarding VLANs? (Choose all that apply.)

   A. Two VLANs are configured by default on all Cisco switches.

   B. VLANs only work if you have a complete Cisco switched internetwork. No off-brand switches are allowed.

   C. You should not have more than 10 switches in the same VTP domain.

   D. VTP is used to send VLAN information to switches in a configured VTP domain.

20. What LAN switch mode keeps CRC errors to a minimum but still has a fixed latency rate?

   A. STP

   B. Store and forward

   C. Cut-through

   D. FragmentFree

21. How many broadcast domains are created when you segment a network with a 12-port switch?

   A. One

   B. Two

   C. Five

   D. 12

22. What PDU is at the Transport layer?

   A. User data

   B. Session

   C. Segment

   D. Frame

23. What protocols are used to configure trunking on a switch? (Choose all that apply.)

   A. Virtual Trunk Protocol

   B. VLAN

   C. Trunk

   D. ISL

24. What is a stub network?

   A. A network with more than one exit point

   B. A network with more than one exit and entry point

   C. A network with only one entry and no exit point

   D. A network that has only one entry and exit

25. Where is a hub specified in the OSI model?

   A. Session layer

   B. Physical layer

   C. Data Link layer

   D. Application layer

26. If you wanted to configure ports on a Cisco switch, what are the different ways available to configure VLAN memberships? (Choose all that apply.)

    A. Via a DHCP server

    B. Statically

    C. Dynamically

    D. Via a VTP database

27. What does the command `show controllers s 0` provide?

    A. The type of serial port connection (e.g., Ethernet or Token Ring)

    B. The type of connection (e.g., DTE or DCE)

    C. The configuration of the interface including the IP address and clock rate

    D. The controlling processor of that interface

28. What is a pre-10.3 IOS command that copies the contents of NVRAM to DRAM?

    A. `config t`

    B. `config net`

    C. `config mem`

    D. `wr mem`

29. What is the main reason the OSI model was created?

    A. To create a layered model larger than the DoD model

    B. So application developers can change only one layer's protocols at a time

    C. So different vendors' equipment can work together

    D. So Cisco could use the model

30. Which layer of the OSI model creates a virtual circuit between hosts before transmitting data?

A. Application

B. Session

C. Transport

D. Network

E. Data Link

31. Which protocol does DHCP use at the Transport layer?

A. IP

B. TCP

C. UDP

D. ARP

32. How do you copy a router IOS to a TFTP host?

A. `copy run starting`

B. `copy start running`

C. `copy running tftp`

D. `copy flash tftp`

33. If your router is facilitating a CSU/DSU, which of the following commands do you need to use to provide the router with a 64000bps serial link?

A. RouterA(config)#**bandwidth 64**

B. RouterA(config-if)#**bandwidth 64000**

C. RouterA(config)#**clockrate 64000**

D. RouterA(config-if)**clock rate 64**

E. RouterA(config-if)**clock rate 64000**

34. Which of the following is provided by the distribution layer? (Choose all that apply.)

A. Breaking up of collision domains

B. Routing

C. Access lists

D. VLANs

35. Which of the following commands will set your Telnet password on a Cisco router?

A. Line telnet 0 4

B. Line aux 0 4

C. Line vty 0 4

D. Line con 0

36. What command do you use to set the enable secret password on a Cisco router?

A. RouterA(config)#**enable password todd**

B. RouterA(config)#**enable secret todd**

C. RouterA(config)#**enable secret password todd**

D. RouterA(config-if)#**enable secret todd**

37. Which protocol is used to find an Ethernet address from a known IP address?

A. IP

B. ARP

C. RARP

D. BootP

38. Which command is used to upgrade an IOS on a Cisco router?

   A. `copy tftp run`

   B. `copy tftp start`

   C. `config net`

   D. `copy tftp flash`

39. If you want to copy a configuration from the router's DRAM to NVRAM, which command do you use?

   A. `copy run start`

   B. `copy start run`

   C. `config net`

   D. `config mem`

   E. `copy flash nvram`

40. If an interface is administratively down, what is the problem?

   A. The interface is bad.

   B. The interface is not connected to another device.

   C. There is no problem.

   D. The interface is looped.

41. If you are looking at an Ethernet analyzer and notice that the ISL frames are larger than a normal Ethernet frame, what size should you be seeing on the analyzer?

   A. 1518

   B. 1522

   C. 4202

   D. 8190

42. How many collision domains are created when you segment a network with a 12-port switch?

A. One

B. Two

C. Five

D. 12

43. What is the administrative distance of static routes by default?

A. 0

B. 1

C. 10

D. 100

44. What was the first solution for counting to infinity?

A. Holddowns

B. Triggered updates

C. Setting a maximum hop count

D. Reverse poison

45. Which protocol is used to send a Destination Network Unknown message back to originating hosts?

A. TCP

B. ARP

C. ICMP

D. BootP

46. What is the distance of a 1000BaseSX MMF using a 62.5- and 50-micron core and a 780-nanometer laser?

A. 100 meters

B. 260 meters

C. 400 meters

D. 1000 feet

47. At which layer do packets occur?

    A. Session

    B. Transport

    C. Network

    D. Data Link

48. Which of the following is not one of the advantages of using static routes over dynamic routing?

    A. Fast convergence

    B. No CPU usage

    C. No bandwidth usage

    D. Security

49. How do you copy a configuration stored on a TFTP host to DRAM?

    A. `copy run start`

    B. `copy start run`

    C. `copy tftp flash`

    D. `copy tftp running`

50. If you wanted to create dynamic VLANs, how would you do it?

    A. Use statical memberships

    B. Hire a junior administrator

    C. Via a DHCP server

    D. Via a VLAN Management Policy Server

51. What type of access list uses the numbers 100–199?

    A. IP standard

    B. IPX standard

    C. IP extended

    D. IPX extended

    E. IPX SAP filter

52. Write the command to add a subinterface to Ethernet 0 with the 802.3 frame type.

53. Which of the following routing protocols uses bandwidth and delay of the line when making routing decisions?

A. RIP

B. Static

C. IGRP

D. OSPF

54. What type of access list uses the numbers 1000–1099?

A. IP standard

B. IPX standard

C. IP extended

D. IPX extended

E. IPX SAP filter

55. What is a pre-10.3 IOS command that lets you copy a configuration from a TFTP host to DRAM?

A. config t

B. config net

C. config mem

D. wr mem

56. Which of the following commands is a way of turning on RIP routing?

A. RouterA#**routing rip**

B. Router(config)#**routing rip**

C. RouterA#**router rip**

D. Router(config)#**router rip**

E. router(config-router)#**router rip**

57. What type of access list uses the numbers 800–899?

   A. IP standard

   B. IPX standard

   C. IP extended

   D. IPX extended

   E. IPX SAP filter

58. What two commands will show you all your configured PVCs?

   A. `sh pvc`

   B. `show interface`

   C. `show frame-rely pvc`

   D. `sho runn`

59. If you connect a Cisco router and a 3Com router through a T-1, why won't they work by default?

   A. Cisco and 3Com are not compatible.

   B. 3Com was purchased by Cisco and scrapped.

   C. The serial encapsulations are not compatible by default.

   D. The Ethernet frame types are not compatible by default.

60. You have a large Ethernet network in your office. Which of the following is true regarding this network?

   A. You can use a FastEthernet full-duplex connection using 10Base2.

   B. You can use full duplex when connecting a point-to-point connection between two nodes.

   C. You can use store and forward with a full-duplex connection.

   D. You can use cut-through with half duplex.

61. You have large files that you need to transfer from your home to your remote corporate office. You need to do this periodically and quickly. What technology would be best suited for your situation?

    A. Frame Relay

    B. Ethernet

    C. ISDN

    D. Token Ring

    E. ATM

62. Write the command to see the NetWare servers running on your network.

63. What protocol is used at layer 2 to help stop network loops?

    A. BPDU

    B. STP

    C. VLANs

    D. Switches

64. Write the command to create a subinterface on Ethernet 0 that allows the Ethernet_II frame type.

65. What command would you use to verify your VLAN configuration on a 1900 switch?

    A. `Show config`

    B. `Show vlan`

    C. `Show vlan info`

    D. `Sh startup-config`

66. BECN is used for what?

    A. PPP authentication

    B. ISDN BRI load balancing

    C. Frame Relay congestion control

    D. HDLC protocol identification of the Network layer

67. Write the command to see the IPX routing table.

68. Which of the following is the valid host range for the IP address
192.168.168.188 255.255.255.192?

   A. 192.168.168.129–190

   B. 192.168.168.129–191

   C. 192.168.168.128–190

   D. 192.168.168.128–192

69. What type of access list uses the numbers 900–999?

   A. IP standard

   B. IPX standard

   C. IP extended

   D. IPX extended

   E. IPX SAP filter

70. In a network with dozens of switches, how many root bridges would
you have?

   A. One

   B. Two

   C. Five

   D. 12

Answers to the Practice Exam

1. A. Network Control Protocol identifies the Network layer protocol used in the packet. See Chapter 10 for more information.

2. C. The best answer is to use a layer-2 switch and provide collision domains to each device. This will provide the most bang for the buck in terms of network equipment.

3.  ```
    Config t
    Ipx routing
    Int e0
    Ipx network 10
    Int e0.10
    Ipx network 10a encap sap
    Int s0
    Ipx network 20
    ```

    The global command to configure IPX is `ipx routing`. To configure an interface, you must be in interface configuration. `Sap` is the Cisco keyword for 802.2; 802.3 is the default if no encapsulation is specified. See Chapter 8 for more information.

4. C. The command `line console` 0 places you at a prompt where you can then set your console user-mode password. See Chapter 4 for more information.

5. C. The `dialer load-threshold 125` command tells the router to bring up the second BRI at 50 percent load. See Chapter 10 for more information.

6. C. Link Control Protocol in the PPP stack provides dynamic addressing, authentication, and multilink. See Chapter 10 for more information.

7. B. The `show interface` command shows the line, protocol, DLCI, and LMI information of an interface. See Chapter 10 for more information.
    ```

8. A. IP standard access lists use the numbers 1–99. See Chapter 9 for more information.

9. B. The `passive` command, short for `passive-interface`, stops regular updates from being sent out an interface. However, the interface can still receive updates. See Chapter 5 for more information.

10. C. ICMP is the protocol at the Network layer that is used to send echo requests and replies. See Chapter 3 for more information.

11. `show ipx traffic`. The command `show ipx traffic` shows the RIP and SAP information being sent and received on a router. The command `show ipx interface` shows the IPX RIP and SAP information being sent and received on a specific interface. See Chapter 8 for more information.

12. C. The command `line vty 0 4` places you in a prompt that will allow you to set or change your Telnet password. See Chapter 4 for more information.

13. C. To create a VLAN on a 1900 switch, use the global configuration command `vlan [#] name [name]`. For more information on how to create VLANs, see Appendix B.

14. A. The port with the lowest cost to the root bridge is the root port of the bridge. See Chapter 2 for more information.

15. A. The command `erase-startup-config` deletes the configuration stored in NVRAM. See Chapter 4 for more information.

16. `Config t`
`Ipx network 10c encap snap secondary`

The keyword for SNAP is `snap`. See Chapter 8 for more information.

17. A. Class A addressing provides 24 bits for hosts addressing. See Chapter 3 for more information.

18. B. Every two seconds, BPDUs are sent out from all active bridge ports by default. See Chapter 2 for more information.

19. D. Switches do not propagate VLAN information by default; you must configure the VTP domain. Virtual Trunk Protocol (VTP) is used to propagate VLAN information across a trunked link. See Chapter 6 for more information.

20. D. FragmentFree LAN switching checks into the data portion of the frame to make sure no fragmentation has occurred. See Chapter 2 for more information.

21. A. By default, switches break up collision domains but are one large broadcast domain. See Chapter 2 for more information.

22. C. Segmentation happens at the Transport layer. See Chapter 1 for more information.

23. C, D. VTP is not right because it has nothing to do with trunking, except that it sends VLAN information across a trunked link. Trunk protocol and ISL are used to configure trunking on a port. See Chapter 6 for more information.

24. D. Stub networks have only one connection to an internetwork. Default routes can only be set on a stub network, or network loops may occur. See Chapter 5 for more information.

25. B. Hubs regenerate electrical signals, which are specified at the Physical layer. See Chapter 1 for more information.

26. B, C. You can configure VLAN memberships on a port either statically or dynamically. See Chapter 6 for more information.

27. B. The command `show controllers s 0` tells you what type of serial connection you have. If it is a DCE, you need to provide the clock rate. See Chapter 4 for more information.

28. C. The old command `config mem` was used to copy the configuration stored in NVRAM to RAM and append the file in DRAM, not replace it. The new command is `copy start run`. See Chapter 7 for more information.

29. C. The primary reason the OSI model was created was so that different vendors' equipment could interoperate. See Chapter 1 for more information.

30. C. The Transport layer creates virtual circuits between hosts before transmitting any data. See Chapter 1 for more information.

31. C. User Datagram Protocol is a connection network service at the Transport layer, and DHCP uses this connectionless service. See Chapter 3 for more information.

32. C. The command used to copy a configuration from a router to a TFTP host is `copy running-config tftp`, or `copy startup-config tftp`, depending on which file you want to use. See Chapter 7 for more information.

33. E. The clock rate command is two words, and the speed of the line is in bps. See Chapter 4 for more information.

34. B, C, D. The distribution layer is where routers are defined. Access lists and VLANs can be created at this layer as well. See Chapter 1 for more information.

35. C. The command `line vty 0 4` places you in a prompt that will allow you to set or change your Telnet password. See Chapter 4 for more information.

36. B. The command `enable secret todd` sets the enable secret password to todd. See Chapter 4 for more information.

37. B. If a device knows the IP address of where it wants to send a packet, but doesn't know the hardware address, it will send an ARP broadcast looking for the hardware or, in this case, Ethernet address. See Chapter 3 for more information.

38. D. The `copy tftp flash` command places a new file in flash memory, which is the default location for the Cisco IOS in Cisco routers. See Chapter 7 for more information.

39. A. The command to copy `running-config`, which is the file in DRAM, to NVRAM is `copy running-config startup-config`. See Chapter 7 for more information.

40. C. If an interface is administratively shut down, it just means the administrator needs to perform a `no shutdown` on the interface. See Chapter 4 for more information.

41. B. An ISL frame can be up to 1522 bytes. See Chapter 6 for more information.

42. D. Layer-2 switching creates individual collision domains. See Chapter 2 for more information.

43. B. Static routes have an administrative distance of one by default. See Chapter 5 for more information.

44. C. Before a maximum hop count was used in distance-vector networks, the only way to solve network loops was to reboot all the routers in the network. See Chapter 5 for more information.

45. C. ICMP is the protocol at the Network layer that is used to send messages back to an originating router. See Chapter 3 for more information.

46. B. Gigabit Ethernet, using multimode fiber, can run up to 260 meters. See Chapter 1 for more information.

47. C. PDUs at the Network layer are called packets. See Chapter 1 for more information.

48. A. Static routes do not converge and must be updated by hand. See Chapter 5 for more information.

49. D. The `copy tftp running-config` command copies the running-config file to DRAM. See Chapter 7 for more information.

50. D. A VMPS server must be configured with the hardware addresses of all hosts on the internetworks. See Chapter 6 for more information.

51. C. IP extended access lists use the numbers 100–199. See Chapter 9 for more information.

52. Config t
Int e0.100
Ipx network 10a encap novell-ether

The command int e0. followed by a number creates a subinterface. 802.3 is the Cisco keyword novell-ether. See Chapter 8 for more information.

53. C. IGRP, as well as EIGRP. Use bandwidth and delay of the line, by default, when making routing decisions. See Chapter 5 for more information.

54. E. IPX SAP filters use the access list numbers 1000–1099. See Chapter 9 for more information.

55. B. The old command to copy a file from a TFTP host to DRAM is config net. See Chapter 7 for more information.

56. D. The global command router rip will turn RIP routing on in the router. You then need to tell the RIP routing protocol which network to advertise. See Chapter 5 for more information.

57. B. IPX standard access lists use the numbers 800–899. See Chapter 9 for more information.

58. C, D. The commands show running-config and show frame pvc will show you the configured PVC for each interface or subinterface. See Chapter 10 for more information.

59. C. Each vendor uses HDLC by default on the serial links. They are both proprietary. To communicate between vendors, you must use something like PPP or Frame Relay. See Chapter 10 for more information.

60. B. Full-duplex Ethernet creates a point-to-point connection between the transmitter circuitry of the transmitting station and the receiving circuitry of the receiving station.

61. C. Even though newer technologies are probably a better choice at this point for home–to–corporate office connections, Cisco's answer to this question is ISDN because of the period connection that is needed.

62. `show ipx servers`. The command `show ipx servers` shows from which NetWare servers the routers have received SAP packets. See Chapter 8 for more information.

63. B. To stop network loops from occurring with redundant links, layer-2 devices implement the Spanning-Tree Protocol. See Chapter 2 for more information.

64. `Config t`
`Int e0.10`
`Ipx network 10b encap arpa`

The keyword for Ethernet_II is `arpa`. See Chapter 8 for more information.

65. B. The command `show vlan` will show you all configured VLANs on the switch. For more information on how to verify VLAN configurations, see Appendix B.

66. C. Backward-Explicit Congestion Notification is used to tell the transmitting device to slow down because the Frame Relay switch is congested. See Chapter 10 for more information.

67. `show ipx route`. The command `show ipx route` will show you the IPX routing table on a Cisco router. See Chapter 8 for more information.

68. A. 256–192=64. 64+64=128. 128+64=192. The subnet is 128, the broadcast address is 191, and the valid host range is the numbers in between, or 129–190. See Chapter 3 for more information.

69. D. IPX extended access lists use the numbers 900–999. See Chapter 9 for more information.

70. A. You should only have one root bridge per network. See Chapter 2 for more information.

Configuring the Catalyst 1900 Switch

THE CCNA EXAM TOPICS COVERED IN THIS APPENDIX INCLUDE THE FOLLOWING:

- ✓ Configure the Catalyst 1900 Switch CLI
- ✓ Configure the Catalyst 1900 Switch hostname and passwords
- ✓ Configure the Catalyst 1900 Switch security
- ✓ Configure Virtual LANs
- ✓ Configure ISL Routing

The CCNA courseware for the new CCNA exam covers the Cisco Catalyst 1900 switch. You need to have a good understanding of how this switch works.

The 1900 switch is a low-end model in the Cisco Catalyst switch family. You can buy two different models in the Catalyst 1900 switch family: the 1912 and the 1924. The 1912 switches have 12 10BaseT ports and the 1924 switches have 24 10BaseT ports. Each has two 100Mbps uplinks—either twisted-pair or fiber.

Since the 1900 switch can now run a version of the Cisco IOS, you can use it to thoroughly understand switching through all Cisco switching products. Not all Cisco switches run a version of the IOS, but they will eventually.

In this appendix, you will learn how to start up and configure a Cisco Catalyst 1900 switch using the Command-Line Interface (CLI). I will begin by explaining how to connect a console cable, and then I will discuss what happens when a 1900 switch is powered up. After you learn how to connect a console cable to the switch and get the switch working, I will teach you the basic configuration commands that you can use on the 1900 switch.

After you learn the basic commands, I will show you how to configure Virtual LANs (VLANs) on the switch as well as ISL routing and Virtual Trunk Protocol (VTP).

The basic commands covered in this appendix include the following:

- Setting the passwords

- Setting the hostname

- Configuring the IP address and subnet mask

- Identifying the interfaces

- Setting a description on the interfaces

- Defining the port duplex of a port
- Verifying the configuration
- Managing the MAC address table
- Setting permanent and static MAC addresses
- Configuring port security
- Describing the `show version` command
- Changing the LAN switch type
- Configuring VLANs
- Adding VLAN memberships to switch ports
- Creating a VTP domain
- Configuring trunking
- Configuring pruning

The end of the appendix includes both written and hands-on labs as well as review questions to make sure you have a firm understanding of the 1900 switch configuration.

Features of the 1900 Switch

The Catalyst 1900 switch can now use a CLI to configure the Cisco Internetworking Operating System (IOS) on the switch. Before the CLI was available, the 1900 switch could only be configured through a menu system.

The CLI makes configuring the switch really close to how you would configure a router. The Cisco Catalyst 5000 series, which is one of Cisco's higher-end models, is still *set-based*, which means you use the `set` command to configure the router. This book only covers the Catalyst 1900 switch configuration commands.

There are two types of operating systems that run on Cisco switches:

IOS-based   In this system, you can configure the switch from a CLI that is similar to Cisco routers. Catalyst 1900, 2820, and 2900 switches can be used with an IOS-based CLI, although they can be set with a menu system as well.

Set-based This system uses older, set-based CLI configuration commands. The Cisco switches that use the set-based CLI are the 2926, 1948G, 4000, 5000, and 6000 series.

It's time to be introduced to the 1900 series of Catalyst switches. Why the 1900? Because that is what Cisco uses on the CCNA exam, of course, and also because it allows you to run a CLI with IOS-based commands on a less expensive switch than the 5000 series. The 1900 switches are great for home offices or other small offices where you can get 10Mbps switched ports with 100Mbps uplinks at a decent price.

The Three Configuration Options

The Catalyst switch uses a CLI, which is more like the router configuration I showed you in Chapter 4. However, you can configure the switch with a Web-based method using the Visual Switch Manager (VSM). To configure the switch through the VSM, you just have to type in the IP address of the switch at a Web browser. You will learn how to add an IP address to the switch later in this appendix.

The 1900 switches also have the original menu system that allows you to configure the switch through a series of menu-based options. To configure the switch with Telnet or VSM, an IP address must be configured on the switch.

Connecting to the Console Port

The 1900 switch has a console port on the back of the switch, just like the 2500 routers I showed you in Chapter 4. It is an RJ-45 port, and it uses a rolled cable to connect to a terminal.

1924 switches use a null-modem cable for the console port.

At this point, you need to start a terminal emulation program like Hyper-Term in Windows. The settings for this program are as follows:

- 9600Bps
- 8 Data Bits
- Parity None

- Stop Bits 1
- Flow Control None

WARNING Do not connect an Ethernet cable, ISDN, or live telephone line into the console port. These can damage the electronics of the switch.

1900 Switch Startup

Before you power on the switch for the first time, check to make sure you have completed the following:

- You have plugged in all the network cables securely.
- You have connected a terminal to the console port.
- You have configured your terminal software correctly.

Once you have checked everything in this list, plug the power cable into the switch and watch the light sequence. Then check the output on the console. Figure B.1 shows the 1900 switch and the Light Emitting Diode (LED) locations.

FIGURE B.1 Catalyst 1900 switch

A green system light appears if the switch is operational. It will be amber if a system malfunction has occurred. The RPS is a redundant power supply light that is on if an RPS is detected in the switch.

The only button on the 1900 switch is the mode button. By pressing the mode button, you can see three different status lights on the switch:

Stat This light shows the status of the ports. If it is green, this indicates a device is plugged into the switch. Green is active, and a green blinking light is activity on the port. If the port is amber, there has been a link fault.

UTL This light indicates the bandwidth of the switch. When you press the mode button on a 1912 switch, and the LEDs for ports 1 through 4 come on, this means the bandwidth utilization of the switch is somewhere between 0.1 and1.5Mbps. If lights 5 through 8 come on, this indicates that the utilization is between 1.5 and 20Mbps, and lights 9 through 12 indicate bandwidth between 20 and 120Mbps.

FDUP This light will show you which ports are configured at full duplex.

When the 1900 switch is first powered on, it runs through a power-on self test (POST). At the start, all port LEDs are green. These LEDs turn off after the POST completes. If a port is determined failed by the POST, both the System LED and the port LED turn amber. If no failures occur during the POST, all LEDs blink and turn off.

After the POST runs and you have a console cable connected to the switch, the following menu shows up. By pressing K, you can use the Command-Line Interface, and when you press M, you will be allowed to configure the switch through a menu system. Pressing I allows you to configure the IP configuration of the switch; however, this can also be accomplished through the menu or CLI at any time. Once the IP configuration is set, the I selection no longer appears.

The switch output below is the output on the console screen after the switch is powered up.

```
1 user(s) now active on Management Console.


        User Interface Menu


    [M] Menus
    [K] Command Line
    [I] IP Configuration


Enter Selection:  K


        CLI session with the switch is open.
        To end the CLI session, enter [Exit].
    >
```

Connecting to an Ethernet Port

The Catalyst 1900 series of switches have fixed port types. They are not modular like the 5000 series switches. The 1900 switches use only 10BaseT ports for workstations and 100BaseT or FX for uplinks. Each switch has either 12 (model 1912) or 24 (model 1924) 10BaseT switch ports, each having one or two FastEthernet uplinks. The 100BaseX ports are referred to as ports A and B. To connect the ports to another switch as an uplink, you must use a crossover cable. It would be nice if they had a button for this function, but they don't.

When connecting devices like workstations, servers, printers, and routers to the switch, you must use a straight-through cable. Connecting between switches uses a crossover cable.

When a device is connected to a port, the port-status LED light comes on and stays on. If the light does not come on, the other end might be off, or there might be a cable problem. Also, if a light goes on and off, there is a possible auto-speed and duplex problem. I'll show you how to check that in the next section. If you do not have a device connected to the switch, the port light will come on when booted, and then it will turn off.

Cisco 1900 IOS Configuration Commands

In this section, I will show you how to configure the basics on the 1900 Catalyst switch. I will show you how to

- Set the passwords
- Set the hostname
- Configure the IP address and subnet mask
- Identify the interfaces
- Set a description on the interfaces
- Define the duplex of a port
- Verify the configuration

- Manage the MAC address table

- Set permanent and static MAC address

- Configure port security

- Use the show version command

- Change the LAN switch type

This list is important to know for your CCNA. Without the above information under your belt, you will not be able to go on to more advanced configurations.

Setting the Passwords

The first thing that you should configure on a switch is the passwords. You don't want unauthorized users connecting to the switch. You can set both the user mode and privileged mode passwords, just like a router. However, it is mostly done with different commands than for a router.

The login (user mode) password can be used to verify authorization of the switch, including accessing any line and the console. The enable password is used to allow access to the switch so the configuration can be viewed or changed. This is the same as any Cisco router.

The passwords cannot be less than four characters or more than eight. They are not case sensitive.

Even though the 1900 switch uses a CLI running an IOS, the commands for the user mode and enable mode passwords are different than for a router. You use the command enable password, which is the same, but you choose different access levels, which are optional on a Cisco router but not on the 1900 switch.

Setting the User Mode and Enable Mode Passwords

You use the same command to set the user mode password and enable mode password on the 1900 switch. However, you do use different level commands to control the type of access each password provides.

To configure the user mode and enable mode password, press K at the router console output. Enter enable mode by using the enable command

and then enter global configuration mode by using the `config t` command. The following output shows an example of how to get into enable mode and then into global configuration mode.

```
1 user(s) now active on Management Console.


        User Interface Menu

    [M] Menus
    [K] Command Line
    [I] IP Configuration

Enter Selection:  K

    CLI session with the switch is open.
    To end the CLI session, enter [Exit].

>enable
#config t
Enter configuration commands, one per line.  End with CNTL/Z
(config)#
```

Once you are in global configuration mode, you can set the user mode and enable mode passwords by using the `enable password` command. The following output shows the configuration of both the user mode and enable mode passwords.

```
(config)#enable password ?
   level  Set exec level password
(config)#enable password level ?
   <1-15>  Level number
```

To enter the user mode password, use level number 1. To enter the enable mode password, use level mode 15. Remember the password must be at least four characters, but not longer than eight characters. The switch output below shows the user mode password being set and denied because it is more than eight characters.

```
(config)#enable password level 1 toddlammle
Error: Invalid password length.
Password must be between 4 and 8 characters
```

The following output is an example of how to set both the user mode and enable mode passwords on the 1900 switch.

```
(config)#enable password level 1 todd
(config)#enable password level 15 todd1
(config)#exit
#exit
CLI session with the switch is now closed.
Press any key to continue.
```

At this point, you can press Enter and test your passwords. You will be prompted for a user mode password after you press K and then an enable mode password after you type **enable**.

After I exited configuration mode and then the privileged mode, the following console screen appeared. Notice that when I pressed K this time, the switch prompted me for a user mode password.

```
Catalyst 1900 Management Console
Copyright (c) Cisco Systems, Inc.   1993-1998
All rights reserved.
Enterprise Edition Software
Ethernet Address:        00-30-80-CC-7D-00
PCA Number:              73-3122-04
PCA Serial Number:       FAB033725XG
Model Number:            WS-C1912-A
System Serial Number:    FAB0339T01M
Power Supply S/N:        PHI031801CF
PCB Serial Number:       FAB033725XG,73-3122-04

-------------------------------------------------
1 user(s) now active on Management Console.
        User Interface Menu
    [M] Menus
    [K] Command Line
Enter Selection:  K
Enter password:  ****
        CLI session with the switch is open.
        To end the CLI session, enter [Exit].
>en
Enter password:  ****
#
```

After I entered user mode, I typed **en**, which is a shortcut for the `enable` command, and was prompted for the enable password.

WARNING   You need to remember your passwords because there is no password recovery for the 1900 switch. If you forget the password on a 1900 switch, you can only call Cisco for help.

You have now set the user mode and enable mode passwords, but there still is one more password on a 1900 switch: the enable secret.

Setting the Enable Secret Password

The enable secret password is a more secure password and supersedes the enable password if set. You set this password the same way you set the enable secret password on a router. If you have an enable secret set, you don't even need to bother setting the enable mode password.

```
(config)#enable secret todd2
```

You can make the `enable password` and `enable secret` commands the same on the 1900 switch, but on a router you are not allowed to do this. You can use the command `show running-config` (`show run` for short) to see the current configuration on the switch.

```
#sh run
Building configuration...
Current configuration:

enable secret 5 $1$FMFQ$wFVYVLYn2aXscfB3J95.w.
enable password level 1 "TODD"
enable password level 15 "TODD1"
```

Notice the enable mode passwords are not encrypted by default, but the enable secret is. This is the same password configuration technique that you will find on a router.

One more thing to notice is that even though I typed the passwords as lowercase, the running-config shows the passwords as uppercase. It doesn't matter how you type them or how they appear in the configuration because the passwords are not case sensitive.

Setting the Hostname

The hostname on a switch, as well as on a router, is only locally significant. This means that it doesn't have any function on the network or name resolution whatsoever. However, it is helpful to set a hostname on a switch so that you can identify the switch when connecting to it. A good rule of thumb is to name the switch after the location it is serving.

The 1900 switch command to set the hostname is exactly like any router: you use the hostname command. Remember, it is one word. The switch output below shows the console screen. Press K to go into user mode, enter the password, use the enable command, and enter the enable secret password. From global configuration mode, type the command hostname **hostname**.

```
1 user(s) now active on Management Console.


             User Interface Menu


        [M] Menus
        [K] Command Line
        [I] IP Configuration
Enter Selection:  K
Enter password:  ****
        CLI session with the switch is open.
        To end the CLI session, enter [Exit].
>en
Enter password:  ****
#config t
Enter configuration commands, one per line.  End with
CNTL/Z
(config)#hostname Todd1900EN
Todd1900EN(config)#
```

Notice that as soon as I pressed Enter, the hostname of the switch appeared. Remember that from global configuration mode, which you enter by using the config t command, the running-config is changed. Any changes you make in this mode take effect immediately.

Setting IP Information

You do not have to set any IP configuration on the switch to make it work. You can just plug in devices and they should start working, just like they would on a hub. There are two reasons why you would set the IP address information on the switch: so you can manage the switch via Telnet or other management software, or if you wanted to configure the switch with different VLANs and other network functions. VLANs are discussed in Chapter 6.

The Catalyst 1900 switch has some default settings already configured on the switch from the factory. The default settings on the switch are as follows:

IP address and default gateway: 0.0.0.0

CDP: Enabled

Switching Mode: FragmentFree

100BaseT ports: Auto-negotiate duplex mode

10BaseT ports: Half duplex

Spanning Tree: Enabled

Console password: Not set

By default, no IP address or default-gateway information is set. You would set both the IP address and the default gateway on a layer-2 switch, just like any host. By typing the command show ip (or sh ip), you can see the default IP configuration of the switch.

```
Todd1900EN#sh ip
IP Address: 0.0.0.0
Subnet Mask: 0.0.0.0
Default Gateway: 0.0.0.0
Management VLAN:  1
Domain name:
Name server 1: 0.0.0.0
Name server 2: 0.0.0.0
HTTP server : Enabled
HTTP port :  80
RIP : Enabled
```

Notice in the above switch output that no IP address, default gateway, or other IP parameters are configured. To set the IP configuration on a 1900 switch, use the command `ip address`. The default gateway should also be set using the `ip default-gateway` command.

The switch output below shows an example of how to set the IP address and default gateway on a 1900 switch.

```
Todd1900EN#config t
Enter configuration commands, one per line.  End with
CNTL/Z
Todd1900EN(config)#ip address 172.16.10.16 255.255.255.0
Todd1900EN(config)#ip default-gateway 172.16.10.1
Todd1900EN(config)#
```

Once you have your IP information set, use the `show ip` command to verify your changes.

```
Todd1900EN#sh ip
IP Address: 172.16.10.16
Subnet Mask: 255.255.255.0
Default Gateway: 172.16.10.1
Management VLAN:  1
Domain name:
Name server 1: 0.0.0.0
Name server 2: 0.0.0.0
HTTP server : Enabled
HTTP port :   80
RIP : Enabled
Todd1900EN#
```

To change the IP address and default gateway on the switch, you can either type in new addresses or remove the IP information with the `no ip address` and `no ip default-gateway` commands.

Configuring Switch Interfaces

It is important to understand how to access switch ports. The 1900 switch uses the `type slot/port` command. For example, Ethernet 0/3 is 10BaseT port 3. Another example would be FastEthernet 0/26. This is the first of the two FastEthernet ports available on the 1900 switch.

The 1900 switch `type slot/port` command can be used with either the `interface` command or the `show` command. The `interface` command allows you to set interface-specific configurations. The 1900 switch has only one slot: zero (0).

The help screens, for configuring interfaces, are only moderately helpful. The help screens will show you that the ports are 1–25 for Ethernet, and ports 26 and 27 are available for FastEthernet only. Since this is a 1912, it really only has ports 1–12. However, there is a port 25 on the back of the switch. This is an Attachment Unit Interface (AUI) adapter for connecting switches together, or even for connecting the 1900 switch to a coax Ethernet network.

Configuring the 10BaseT Interfaces

To configure an interface on a 1900 switch, go to global configuration mode and use the `interface` command. The following help screens describe the `type slot/port` configuration method. From global configuration, use the `interface` command and the type, either Ethernet or FastEthernet interface. I am going to demonstrate the Ethernet interface configuration first.

```
Todd1900EN#config t
Enter configuration commands, one per line.  End with
CNTL/Z
Todd1900EN(config)#int ethernet ?
  <0-0>  IEEE 802.3
```

The previous output asks for the slot. Since the 1900 switch is not modular, there is only one slot. The next output gives us a slash (/) to separate the slot/port configuration.

```
Todd1900EN(config)#int ethernet 0?
  /
Todd1900EN(config)#int ethernet 0/?
  <1-25>  IEEE 802.3
```

After the 0/ configuration command, the above output shows the amount of ports you can configure. However, if you only have a 1912 switch, you really only have ports 1–12, 25 on the back of the switch, and 26 and 27 as the 100Mbps uplinks. The FastEthernet ports did not show up on the above output because we chose the Ethernet interface as our type and the ports are FastEthernet.

The output below shows the completed command.

```
Todd1900EN(config)#int ethernet 0/1
```

Once you are in interface configuration, the prompt changes to (config-if). After you are at the interface prompt, you can use the help commands to see the available commands.

```
Todd1900EN(config-if)#?
Interface configuration commands:
  cdp                Cdp interface subcommands
  description        Interface specific description
  duplex             Configure duplex operation
  exit               Exit from interface configuration mode
  help               Description of the interactive help
                     system
  no                 Negate a command or set its defaults
  port               Perform switch port configuration
  shutdown           Shutdown the selected interface
  spantree           Spanning tree subsystem
  vlan-membership    VLAN membership configuration
```

You can switch between interface configuration by using the int e 0/# command at any time from global configuration mode.

FastEthernet Interface Configuration

To configure the two FastEthernet ports, the command is still type slot/port, but the type is FastEthernet instead of Ethernet. An example would be interface fastethernet 0\#.

The switch output below shows the configuration of a FastEthernet port on the 1900 switch. Notice that the command is interface fastethernet, but the slot is still 0. The only ports available are 26 and 27.

```
Todd1900EN(config)#int fastEthernet ?
  <0-0>  FastEthernet IEEE 802.3
Todd1900EN(config)#int fastEthernet 0/?
  <26-27>  FastEthernet IEEE 802.3
Todd1900EN(config)#int fastEthernet 0/26
Todd1900EN(config-if)#int fast 0/27
Todd1900EN(config-if)# [control+Z]
```

After you make any changes you want to the interfaces, you can view the different interfaces with the show interface command.

The switch output below shows the command used to view a 10BaseT interface and the command to view a FastEthernet interface.

```
Todd1900EN#sh int e0/1
Ethernet 0/1 is Suspended-no-linkbeat
Hardware is Built-in 10Base-T
Address is 0030.80CC.7D01
MTU 1500 bytes, BW 10000 Kbits
802.1d STP State:  Forwarding    Forward Transitions:  1
[output cut]
 Todd1900EN#sh int f0/26
FastEthernet 0/26 is Suspended-no-linkbeat
Hardware is Built-in 100Base-TX
Address is 0030.80CC.7D1A
MTU 1500 bytes, BW 100000 Kbits
802.1d STP State:  Blocking    Forward Transitions:  0
[output cut]
```

Configuring Interface Descriptions

You can administratively set a name for each interface on the 1900 switch. Like the hostname, the descriptions are only locally significant.

For the 1900 series switch, use the description command. You cannot use spaces with the description command, but you can use underscores if you need to.

Setting Descriptions

To set the descriptions, you need to be in interface configuration mode. From interface configuration mode, use the description command to describe each interface. You can make the descriptions more than one word, but you can't use spaces. You'll have to use the underscore as shown below:

```
Todd1900EN#config t
Enter configuration commands, one per line.  End with CNTL/Z
Todd1900EN(config)#int e0/1
Todd1900EN(config-if)#description Finance_VLAN
Todd1900EN(config-if)#int f0/26
Todd1900EN(config-if)#description trunk_to_Building_4
Todd1900EN(config-if)#
```

In the configuration example above, I set the description on both a 10Mbps port and a 100Mbps port.

Viewing Descriptions

Once you have configured the descriptions you want on each interface, you can then view the descriptions with either the show interface command or the show running-config command.

```
Todd1900EN#sh int e0/1
Ethernet 0/1 is Suspended-no-linkbeat
Hardware is Built-in 10Base-T
Address is 0030.80CC.7D01
MTU 1500 bytes, BW 10000 Kbits
802.1d STP State:  Forwarding      Forward Transitions:  1
Port monitoring: Disabled
Unknown unicast flooding: Enabled
Unregistered multicast flooding: Enabled
Description: Finance_VLAN
Duplex setting: Half duplex
Back pressure: Disabled

Todd1900EN#sh run
Building configuration...

Current configuration:
hostname "Todd1900EN"
!
ip address 172.16.10.16 255.255.255.0
ip default-gateway 172.16.10.1
!
interface Ethernet 0/1

   description "Finance_VLAN"
!
[output cut]
```

Notice in the above switch output that the sh int e0/1 command and the show run command both show the description command set on an interface.

Configuring the Port Duplex

The 1900 switch has only 12 or 24 10BaseT ports and comes with one or two FastEthernet ports. You can only set the duplex on the 1900 switch, as the ports are all fixed speeds. Use the duplex command in interface configuration.

In the switch output below, notice the options available on the Fast-Ethernet ports.

```
Todd1900EN(config)#int f0/26
Todd1900EN(config-if)#duplex ?
   auto                Enable auto duplex configuration
   full                Force full duplex operation
   full-flow-control   Force full duplex with flow control
   half                Force half duplex operation
Todd1900EN(config-if)#duplex full
```

Table B.1 shows the different duplex options available on the 1900 switches. The 1900 FastEthernet ports default to *auto duplex*, which means they will try to auto detect the duplex the other end is running. This may or may not work. It is a good rule of thumb to set the duplex to half on a Fast-Ethernet port.

TABLE B.1 Duplex Options

Parameter	Definition
Auto	Set the port into auto-negotiation mode. Default for all 100BaseTX ports.
Full	Forces the 10 or 100Mbps ports into full-duplex mode.
Full-flow-control	Works only with 100BaseTX ports, uses flow control so buffers won't overflow.
Half	Default for 10BaseT ports, forces the ports to work only in half-duplex mode.

Once you have the duplex set, you can use the show interface command to view the duplex configuration.

```
Todd1900EN#sh int f0/26
FastEthernet 0/26 is Suspended-no-linkbeat
Hardware is Built-in 100Base-TX
Address is 0030.80CC.7D1A
MTU 1500 bytes, BW 100000 Kbits
802.1d STP State:  Blocking     Forward Transitions:  0
Port monitoring: Disabled
Unknown unicast flooding: Enabled
Unregistered multicast flooding: Enabled
Description: trunk_to_Building_4
Duplex setting: Full duplex
Back pressure: Disabled
```

In the output above, the duplex setting shows full duplex.

Verifying IP Connectivity

It is important to test the switch IP configuration. You can use the Ping program, and you can telnet into the 1900 switch. However, you cannot telnet from the 1900 switch or use traceroute.

In the following example, I pinged a host on the network from the 1900 CLI. Notice the output on a successful ping: exclamation point (!). If you receive periods (.) instead of exclamation points, that signifies a timeout.

```
Todd1900EN#ping 172.16.10.10
Sending 5, 100-byte ICMP Echos to 172.16.10.10, time out
is 2 seconds:
!!!!!
Success rate is 100 percent (5/5), round-trip min/avg/max
0/2/10/ ms
Todd1900EN#telnet 172.16.10.10
             ^
% Invalid input detected at '^' marker.
```

In the Telnet example above, notice the error when I tried to telnet from the 1900 switch. The command is not available on the 1900 switch. However, remember that you can telnet into a switch at any time, as long as IP is configured correctly.

Erasing the Switch Configuration

The switch configuration is stored in NVRAM, just as any router. You cannot view the startup-config, or contents of NVRAM. You can only view the running-config. When you make a change to the switches' running-config, the switches automatically copy the configuration on the switch to NVRAM. This is a big difference from a router where you have to type `copy running-config startup-config`. That option is not available on the 1900 switch.

You can delete the configuration in NVRAM on the 1900 switch if you want to start over on the switches' configuration. To delete the contents of NVRAM on a 1900 switch, use the `delete nvram` command.

Notice in the switch output below that there are two options: `nvram` and `vtp`. I want to delete the contents of NVRAM to the factory default settings.

```
Todd1900EN#delete ?
  nvram   NVRAM configuration
  vtp     Reset VTP configuration to defaults
Todd1900EN#delete nvram
This command resets the switch with factory defaults.  All
system parameters will revert to their default factory
settings.  All static and dynamic addresses will be
removed.
Reset system with factory defaults, [Y]es or [N]o?  Yes
```

Notice the message received from the switch when the command `delete nvram` is used. Once you say yes, the configuration is gone.

Managing the MAC Address Table

Do you remember how bridges and switches filter a network? They use MAC (hardware) addresses burned into a host's network interface card (NIC) to make forwarding decisions. The switches create a MAC table that includes dynamic, permanent, and static addresses. This filter table is created by hosts sending a frame and by the switch learning the source MAC address and from which segment and port it was received.

The switch keeps adding new MAC addresses that are sent on the network into the MAC filter table. As hosts are added or removed, the switch dynamically updates the MAC filter table. If a device is removed, or if it is not connected to the switch for a period of time, the switch will age out the entry.

You can see the switch's filter table by using the command show mac-address-table. The following output shows the information received when using the show mac-address-table command.

```
Todd1900EN#sh mac-address-table
Number of permanent addresses : 0
Number of restricted static addresses : 0
Number of dynamic addresses : 4

Address           Dest Interface    Type       Source
Interface List
00A0.246E.0FA8    Ethernet 0/2      Dynamic    All
0000.8147.4E11    Ethernet 0/5      Dynamic    All
0000.8610.C16F    Ethernet 0/1      Dynamic    All
00A0.2448.60A5    Ethernet 0/4      Dynamic    All
```

The addresses in the table above are from the four hosts connected to my 1900 switch. They are all *dynamic entries*, which means the switch looked at the source address of a frame as it entered the switch interface, and it placed that address in the filter table. Notice that I have hosts in interfaces 1, 2, 4, and 5.

The Catalyst 1900 switch can store up to 1024 MAC addresses in the filter table. If the MAC filter table gets full, the switch will flood all new addresses until one of the existing entries gets aged out.

You can also clear the MAC filter table by using the clear mac-address-table command. You can clear dynamic, permanent, and restricted static addresses.

The switch output below shows the different options available when using the clear mac-address-table command.

```
#clear mac-address-table ?
  dynamic      Clear 802.1d dynamic address
  permanent    Clear 802.1d permanent addresses
  restricted   Clear 802.1d restricted static address
  <cr>
```

Setting Permanent and Static MAC Addresses

Administrators can specifically assign permanent addresses to a switch port. These addresses are never aged out. You can do this to provide security to a port, which means that unless you specifically configure a hardware address to a switch port, it won't work. Administrators can also create static entries in the switch; these entries actually create a path for a source hardware address. This can be really restrictive, and you need to be careful when setting static entries because you can basically shut your switch down if you do not plan the configuration carefully.

Setting Permanent MAC Address Entries

You can configure a permanent MAC address to a switch port by using the global configuration command mac-address-table permanent [mac-address] [interface].

In the example below, the options are as follows:

Aging-time   This can be used to change the age a MAC address is allowed to stay in the filter table before being cleared.

Permanent   This sets a permanent address to an interface. If the user changes the host NIC card, then the host will not work until you change the permanent entry address.

Restricted   This is used with the static command to set a path for source hardware addresses. Very restrictive for where a host can send a frame.

To configure a permanent hardware address to an interface, use the command mac-address-table permanent from global configuration mode, as shown below:

```
Todd1900EN#config t
Enter configuration commands, one per line.  End with CNTL/Z
Todd1900EN(config)#mac-address-table ?
   aging-time  Aging time of dynamic addresses
   permanent   Configure a permanent address
   restricted  Configure a restricted static address
```

After you choose the mac-address-table permanent command, add the hardware address and the interface it is associated with. This will restrict the interface to only accept frames from this source hardware address.

```
Todd1900EN(config)#mac-address-table permanent ?
   H.H.H  48 bit hardware address
Todd1900EN(config)#mac-address-table permanent
00A0.2448.60A5 e0/4
```

Once you have configured the entry, you can verify this entry by using the show mac-address-table command.

```
Todd1900EN#sh mac-address-table
Number of permanent addresses : 1
Number of restricted static addresses : 0
Number of dynamic addresses : 3
```

Address Interface List	Dest Interface	Type	Source
00A0.2448.60A5	Ethernet 0/4	Permanent	All
00A0.246E.0FA8	Ethernet 0/2	Dynamic	All
0000.8147.4E11	Ethernet 0/5	Dynamic	All
0000.8610.C16F	Ethernet 0/1	Dynamic	All

```
Todd1900EN#
```

In the switch output above, notice that interface 4 now has a permanent entry with hardware address 00A0.2448.60A5. No other device can connect into interface 4 without updating the permanent entry in the MAC filter table.

Setting Static MAC Address Entries

You can take this security thing one step further. You can now tell a source interface that it is only allowed to send frames out of a defined interface. You do this with the restricted static command. Seems that it could cause some real havoc at work; you may only want to use this command on your friends if it is a slow day at work. That'll liven things up a bit.

The command mac-address-table restricted static is looking for two options: The first one is the hardware address of the destination interface. The second option will be the source interface that is allowed to communicate with this destination interface.

After entering the command mac-address-table restricted static from global configuration mode, enter the hardware address of the destination device:

```
Todd1900EN(config)#mac-address-table restricted static ?
   H.H.H  48 bit hardware address
Todd1900EN(config)#mac-address-table restricted static
00A0.246E.0FA8 ?
```

```
Ethernet       IEEE 802.3
FastEthernet  FastEthernet IEEE 802.3
```

Once you add the hardware address of the destination device, add the interface address this destination hardware address is associated with.

```
Todd1900EN(config)#mac-address-table restricted static
00A0.246E.0FA8 e0/2 ?
Ethernet       IEEE 802.3
FastEthernet  FastEthernet IEEE 802.3
<cr>
```

Now that you have entered the destination information, enter the source interface that is allowed to communicate with the destination address.

```
Todd1900EN(config)#$-table restricted static
00A0.246E.0FA8  e0/2 e0/5
```

Once you have finished your command string, you can see the three different types of entries we now have in the MAC filter table by using the show mac-address-table command (use sh mac for a shortcut).

```
Todd1900EN#sh mac
Number of permanent addresses : 1
Number of restricted static addresses : 1
Number of dynamic addresses : 2

Address          Dest Interface    Type        Source Interface List
-----------------------------------------------------------------
00A0.2448.60A5   Ethernet 0/4      Permanent   All
00A0.246E.0FA8   Ethernet 0/2      Static      Et0/5
0000.8147.4E11   Ethernet 0/5      Dynamic     All
0000.8610.C16F   Ethernet 0/1      Dynamic     All
Todd1900EN#
```

The command I just entered has restricted interface 0/5 to only send frames to interface 0/2 using the destination hardware address 00A0.246E.0FA8.

Remember that you can clear the entries with the clear mac-address-table [dynamic/permanent/restricted] [int dest] [int source] command.

Configuring Port Security

Port security is a way of stopping users from plugging a hub into their jack in their office or cubicle and adding a bunch of hosts without your knowledge. By default, 132 hardware addresses can be allowed on a single switch interface. To change this, use the interface command `port secure max-mac-count`.

The following switch output shows the command `port secure max-mac-count` being set on interface 0/2 to allow only one entry.

```
Todd1900EN#config t
Enter configuration commands, one per line.  End with
CNTL/Z
Todd1900EN(config)#int e0/2
Todd1900EN(config-if)#port secure ?
  max-mac-count  Maximum number of addresses allowed on
the port
  <cr>

Todd1900EN(config-if)#port secure max-mac-count ?
  <1-132>  Maximum mac address count for this secure port

Todd1900EN(config-if)#port secure max-mac-count 1
```

The secured port or ports you create can use either static or sticky-learned hardware addresses. If the hardware addresses on a secured port are not statically assigned, the port sticky-learns the source address of incoming frames and automatically assigns them as permanent addresses. *Sticky-learns* is a term Cisco uses for a port dynamically finding a source hardware address and creating a permanent entry in the MAC filter table.

Using the *Show Version* Command

You can use the `show version` command to view basic information about the switch. This includes how long the switch has been running, the IOS version, and the base MAC address of the switch.

This MAC address is important because if you lose your password, there is no password recovery on the 1900 switch. You need to send Cisco this MAC address, and they'll send you a password that will allow you to get into your switch.

The switch output below shows you the configuration of the system hardware, the software version, and the names and sources of the configuration and boot files.

```
Todd1900EN#sh ver
Cisco Catalyst 1900/2820 Enterprise Edition Software
Version V9.00.00
Copyright (c) Cisco Systems, Inc.  1993-1999
Todd1900EN uptime is 0day(s) 03hour(s) 37minute(s)
15second(s)
cisco Catalyst 1900 (486sxl) processor with 2048K/1024K
bytes of memory
Hardware board revision is 5
Upgrade Status: No upgrade currently in progress.
Config File Status: No configuration upload/download is in
progress
15 Fixed Ethernet/IEEE 802.3 interface(s)
Base Ethernet Address: 00-B0-64-75-6A-C0
Todd1900EN#
```

Notice that the output shows 15 fixed Ethernet 802.3 interfaces, which will tell you this is a 1912 switch. The 1912 has 12 10BaseT ports, 1 AUI port, and 2 FastEthernet ports: 15 ports in all. The 1924 has 24 10BaseT, 1 AUI, and 2 FastEthernet ports: 27 ports in all.

Changing the LAN Switch Type

You can see the LAN switch version running on a 1900 switch by using the show port system command. You can change it from global configuration mode with the switching-mode command. You can only use store-and-forward or FragmentFree.

The command show port system will show you the default LAN switch type of FragmentFree. The command switching-mode from global configuration mode allows you to change the LAN switch type to store-and-forward.

```
1900EN#sh port system
Switching mode: FragmentFree
Use of store and forward for multicast: Disabled
Network port: None
```

```
Half duplex backpressure (10 Mbps ports): Disabled
Enhanced Congestion Control (10 Mbps ports): Disabled
Default port LED display mode: Port Status

1900EN(config)#switching-mode ?
  fragment-free      Fragment Free mode
  store-and-forward  Store-and-Forward mode
```

If you change the LAN switch type, you change it for all ports on the switch.

Configuring VLANs

Configuring VLANs is the easy part of the job. It is trying to understand which users you want in each VLAN that is time consuming. Once you have decided the number of VLANs you want to create and the users that will be members of each VLAN, you can create your VLAN. You can create up to 64 VLANs on a 1900 switch. A separate spanning-tree instance can be configured per VLAN.

To configure VLANs on the 1900 series switch, choose K from the initial user interface menu to get into IOS configuration. Even though you can create VLANs with the Menu system available with the 1900 switch, I will only show you how to configure VLANs with the 1900 switch CLI. This is because it is the Cisco IOS and also because the CCNA exam objectives only cover the CLI method of configuration on the 1900 switch.

The following switch output is the console display when connecting to a 1900 switch. Press K to enter the CLI mode, and enter global configuration mode using the enable command and then config t.

```
1 user(s) now active on Management Console.


            User Interface Menu

    [M] Menus
    [K] Command Line
    [I] IP Configuration
```

```
Enter Selection:  K

     CLI session with the switch is open.
     To end the CLI session, enter [Exit].
```

To configure VLANs on an IOS-based switch, use the `vlan [vlan#]` name `[vlan name]` command. I am going to demonstrate how to configure VLANs on the switch by creating three VLANs for three different departments.

```
>en
#config t
Enter configuration commands, one per line.  End with
CNTL/Z
(config)#hostname 1900EN
1900EN(config)#vlan 2 name sales
1900EN(config)#vlan 3 name marketing
1900EN(config)#vlan 4 name mis
1900EN(config)#exit
```

After you create the VLANs that you want, you can use the `show vlan` command to see the configured VLANs. However, notice that by default all ports on the switch are in VLAN 1. To change the VLAN associated with a port, you need to go to each interface and tell it what VLAN to be a part of.

Remember that a created VLAN is unused until it is mapped to a switch port or ports and that all ports are always in VLAN 1 unless set otherwise.

Once the VLANs are created, verify your configuration with the `show vlan` command (`sh vlan` for short).

```
1900EN#sh vlan
```

VLAN	Name	Status	Ports
1	default	Enabled	1-12, AUI, A, B
2	sales	Enabled	
3	marketing	Enabled	
4	mis	Enabled	

```
1002 fddi-default      Suspended
1003 token-ring-defau  Suspended
1004 fddinet-default   Suspended
1005 trnet-default     Suspended
-------------------------------------
```

[output cut]

Now that we can see the three VLANs created, we can assign switch ports to a single VLAN. Each port can only be part of one VLAN. Trunking, which I will cover in a minute, makes a port available to more than one VLAN at a time.

Assigning Switch Ports to VLANs

You can configure each port to be in a VLAN by using the vlan-membership command. You can only configure VLANs one port at a time. There is no command to assign more than one port to a VLAN at a time with the 1900 switch.

Remember that you can configure either static memberships or dynamic memberships on a port. This book and the CCNA exam objectives only cover the static VLAN memberships.

In the following example, I configure interface 2 to VLAN 2, interface 4 to VLAN 3, and interface 5 to VLAN 4.

```
1900EN#config t
Enter configuration commands, one per line.  End with
CNTL/Z
1900EN(config)#int e0/2
1900EN(config-if)#vlan-membership ?
  dynamic  Set VLAN membership type as dynamic
  static   Set VLAN membership type as static
1900EN(config-if)#vlan-membership static ?
  <1-1005>  ISL VLAN index
1900EN(config-if)#vlan-membership static 2
1900EN(config-if)#int e0/4
1900EN(config-if)#vlan-membership static 3
1900EN(config-if)#int e0/5
1900EN(config-if)#vlan-membership static 4
```

```
1900EN(config-if)#exit
1900EN(config)#exit
```

Now, type **show vlan** again to see the ports assigned to each VLAN.

```
1900EN#sh vlan
```

VLAN	Name	Status	Ports
1	default	Enabled	1, 3, 6-12, AUI, A, B
2	sales	Enabled	2
3	marketing	Enabled	4
4	mis	Enabled	5
1002	fddi-default	Suspended	
1003	token-ring-defau	Suspended	
1004	fddinet-default	Suspended	
1005	trnet-default	Suspended	

```
[ouput cut]
```

You could also just type **show vlan #** to gather information about only one VLAN at a time.

```
1900EN#sh vlan 2
```

VLAN	Name	Status	Ports
2	sales	Enabled	2

VLAN	Type	SAID	MTU	Parent	RingNo	BridgeNo	Stp	Trans1	Trans2
2	Ethernet	100002	1500	0	1	1	Unkn	0	0

```
1900EN#
```

Another command you can use to see the ports assigned to a VLAN is show vlan-membership. Notice that this command shows each port on the switch, which VLAN the port is a member of, and the membership type (static or dynamic).

```
1900A#sh vlan-membership
  Port   VLAN     Membership
  1       1         Static
  2       2         Static
  3       1         Static
  4       4         Static
  5       5         Static
  6       1         Static
  7       1         Static
  8       1         Static
  9       1         Static
  10      1         Static
  11      1         Static
  12      1         Static

  AUI     1         Static
  A       1         Static
  B       1         Static

1900A#
```

Configuring Trunk Ports

The 1900 switch only runs the Dynamic Inter-Switch Link (DISL) encapsulation method. To configure trunking on a FastEthernet port, use the interface command trunk [parameter].

The following switch output shows the trunk configuration on interface 26 to trunk on.

```
1900EN#config t
Enter configuration commands, one per line.  End with
CNTL/Z
1900EN(config)#int f0/26
1900EN(config-if)#trunk ?
  auto         Set DISL state to AUTO
  desirable    Set DISL state to DESIRABLE
  nonegotiate  Set DISL state to NONEGOTIATE
```

```
    off         Set DISL state to OFF
    on          Set DISL state to ON
1900EN(config-if)#trunk on
```

The following list describes the different options available when setting a trunk interface.

Auto   The interface will become trunked only if the connected device is set to on or desirable.

Desirable   If a connected device is either on, desirable, or auto, it will negotiate to become a trunk port.

Nonegotiate   The interface becomes a permanent ISL trunk port and will not negotiate with any attached device.

Off   The interface is disabled from running trunking and tries to convert any attached device to be on-trunk as well.

On   The interface becomes a permanent ISL trunk port. It can negotiate with a connected device to convert the link to trunk mode.

Which VLANs are now on the trunked port? All of them by default. You cannot configure the trunked port to only allow certain VLANs by default. In the next section, I will show you how to clear VLANs from a trunked port.

Clearing VLANs from Trunk Links

As previously discussed, all VLANs are configured on a trunked link unless cleared by an administrator. Use the clear trunk command if you don't want a trunked link to carry VLAN information for two reasons: because you want to stop broadcasts on a certain VLAN from traversing the trunk link, or because you want to stop topology-change information from being sent across a link where a VLAN is not supported.

To delete VLANs from a trunk port on a 1900, use the interface command no trunk-vlan. In the following example, I clear VLAN 5 from being communicated across the trunked link.

```
1900EN(config-if)#no trunk-vlan ?
  <1-1005>  ISL VLAN index
1900EN(config-if)#no trunk-vlan 5
1900EN(config-if)#
```

Unfortunately, there is no command to clear more than one VLAN at a time on the 1900. You would not typically clear more than a few VLANs anyway because, functionally, it makes no difference if they are turned on. If you had security, broadcast, or routing update issues, then you would need to consider it.

Verifying Trunk Links

To verify your trunk ports, use the show trunk command. If you have more than one port trunking and want to see statistics on only one trunk port, you can use the show trunk [port_number] command.

For the 1900 switch, the FastEthernet port 0/26 is identified by trunk A, and port 0/27 is identified by trunk B. Below, I demonstrate how to view the trunk port on interface 26:

```
1900EN#sh trunk ?
 A   Trunk A
 B   Trunk B
1900EN#sh trunk a
DISL state: Auto, Trunking: On, Encapsulation type: ISL
```

Notice in this output that DISL is auto, trunking is on, and ISL is the VLAN-encapsulation type on trunk links.

To see which VLANs are allowed on a trunked link, use the show trunk [A or B] allowed-vlans command. The following example shows the VLANs allowed on the trunked interface 26.

```
1900EN#sh trunk ?
 A   Trunk A
 B   Trunk B
1900EN#sh trunk a ?
 allowed-vlans   Display allowed vlans
 joined-vlans    Display joined vlans
 joining-vlans   Display joining vlans
 prune-eligible  Display pruning eligible vlans
 <cr>
1900EN#sh trunk a allowed-vlans
1-4, 6-1004
1900EN#
```

We cleared VLAN 5 in the preceding section, and the output now states that VLAN 5 is not being included on the trunked link.

Configuring ISL Routing

To support ISL routing on one FastEthernet interface, the router's interface is divided into logical interfaces, one for each VLAN. These are called *subinterfaces*. Since we have four VLANs, we need four subinterfaces. Each one of the VLANs is a separate subnet, so here is the addressing I want to use:

VLAN 1   default   172.16.10.0/24

VLAN 2   sales   172.16.20.0.24

VLAN 3   marketing   172.16.30.0.24

VLAN 4   mis   172.16.40.0/24

Each of the hosts in their VLAN must use the same subnet addressing. To configure the router-on-a-stick for inter-VLAN routing, you need to complete three steps:

1. Enable ISL trunking on the switch port the router connects to.

2. Enable ISL encapsulation on the router's subinterface.

3. Assign an IP address to the subinterface and other logical addressing if applicable (IPX, for example).

To create a subinterface from global configuration mode, choose the FastEthernet interface, a period, and then a number. You will now be in the (`config-subif`) prompt for the interface.

To configure ISL routing on a subinterface, use the `encapsulation isl` [`vlan-number`] command. You can then assign an IP address, IPX address, AppleTalk address, etc., to the subinterface. This is a unique subnet and all the hosts on that VLAN should be in that same subnet. It is not required but is highly recommended.

Here is how to configure the 2621 router to support ISL routing with our four VLANs. First, I'll configure a subinterface with the same number as the VLAN I want to route. This is locally significant only, which means it doesn't matter at all what the subinterface numbers are on the network . Notice that you need to set the encapsulation next, or you will receive an error when trying to set the subinterface's IP address. VLAN 1 is in the

172.16.10.0 network. I need to assign a subinterface a valid host address from within that subnet.

```
2621#config t
2621(config) int f0/0.1
2621(config-subif)# encapsulation isl 1
2621(config-subif)# ip address 172.16.10.1 255.255.255.0
2621(config-subif)# int f0/0.2
2621(config-subif)# encapsulation isl 2
2621(config-subif)# ip address 172.16.20.1 255.255.255.0
2621(config-subif)# int f0/0.3
2621(config-subif)# encapsulation isl 3
2621(config-subif)# ip address 172.16.30.1 255.255.255.0
2621(config-subif)# int f0/0.4
2621(config-subif)# encapsulation isl 4
2621(config-subif)# ip address 172.16.40.1 255.255.255.0
2621(config-subif)# exit
2621(config)#int f0/0
2621(config-if) no shutdown
```

After setting the encapsulation and IP address for VLAN 1, I did the same configurations for VLANs 2, 3, and 4. Notice, however, that each subinterface is in a separate subnet.

Configuring VTP

A Catalyst 1900 switch is configured by default to be a VTP server, as are all switches. To configure VTP, first configure the domain name you want to use, as discussed in the next section. Once you configure the VTP information on a switch, you need to verify the configuration.

Configuring the Domain

When you create the VTP domain, you have the option to set the domain name, password, operating mode, and pruning capabilities of the switch (we discuss pruning in a minute). Use the vtp global configuration mode

command to set this information. In the following example, I set the switch
to a vtp server, the vtp domain to Lammle, and the vtp password to todd.

```
Todd1900EN(config)#vtp ?
   client       VTP client
   domain       Set VTP domain name
   password     Set VTP password
   pruning      VTP pruning
   server       VTP server
   transparent  VTP transparent
   trap         VTP trap
Todd1900EN(config)#vtp server
Todd1900EN(config)#vtp domain lammle
Todd1900EN(config)#vtp password todd
```

After you configure the VTP information, you can verify it with the show
vtp command.

```
Todd1900EN#sh vtp
     VTP version: 1
     Configuration revision: 0
     Maximum VLANs supported locally: 1005
     Number of existing VLANs: 5
     VTP domain name        : lammle
     VTP password           : todd
     VTP operating mode     : Server
     VTP pruning mode       : Disabled
     VTP traps generation   : Enabled
     Configuration last modified by: 0.0.0.0 at 00-00-0000
00:00:00
Todd1900EN#
```

The preceding switch output shows the VTP domain, the VTP password,
and the switch's mode.

Adding to a VTP Domain

You need to be careful when adding a new switch into an existing domain.
If a switch is inserted into the domain and has incorrect VLAN information,
the result could be a VTP database propagated throughout the internetwork

with false information. Cisco recommends that you delete the VTP database before adding a switch to a VTP domain.

In this appendix, I showed you how to delete the NVRAM on the 1900 switch. However, this does not delete the VTP configuration on the switch, because VTP information has its own NVRAM. To delete the VTP information configured on a 1900 switch, you must use the **delete vtp** command. The following switch output shows how to delete the VTP NVRAM database.

```
Todd1900EN#delete ?
  nvram  NVRAM configuration
  vtp    Reset VTP configuration to defaults
Todd1900EN#delete vtp
This command resets the switch with VTP parameters set to
factory defaults.
All other parameters will be unchanged.


Reset system with VTP parameters set to factory defaults,
[Y]es or [N]o? Yes
```

Once you type in the command, you will be prompted to set the VTP information back to the factory default configuration.

VTP Pruning

The following example shows how to turn on pruning in a 1900 switch. There is not a lot to it. Remember that if you turn VTP pruning on in a VTP server, you turn it on for the whole domain as well.

```
Todd1900EN(config)#vtp ?
  client       VTP client
  domain       Set VTP domain name
  password     Set VTP password
  pruning      VTP pruning
  server       VTP server
  transparent  VTP transparent
  trap         VTP trap
Todd1900EN(config)#vtp pruning ?
  disable  Disable VTP pruning
  enable   Enable VTP pruning
Todd1900EN(config)#vtp pruning enable
Todd1900EN(config)#
```

Notice that you turn VTP pruning on for the whole switch. This will not send VTP broadcasts down a trunked link if no VLANs configured on this switch are present down the link.

Restoring or Upgrading the Catalyst 1900 IOS

You can upgrade or restore the IOS on Cisco Catalyst 1900 switches, although there is no command to back up the IOS image from the Catalyst 1900 switch to a TFTP host.

The command to upgrade or restore the IOS to a 1900 switch is

```
copy tftp://tftp_host_address/IOS_filename opcode
```

where:

- `copy tftp` tells the switch to copy an IOS from a TFTP host.

- `//tftp_host_address` is the address of the TFTP host.

- *IOS_filename* is the IOS file stored in your TFTP default directory (for example, `cat1900EN_9_00.bin` is my enterprise edition).

- `opcode` is the command that tells the router to download the file to flash memory.

Here is an example of the command being used:

```
1900B#copy tftp://192.168.0.120/cat1900EN_9_00.bin opcode
TFTP operation succeeded
1900B#
```

Backing Up and Restoring the Catalyst 1900 Configuration

The configuration file for a Cisco Catalyst 1900 switch is just called `nvram` on the 1900 switch. The command to copy the file to a TFTP host is

```
copy nvram tftp://tftp_host_address/config_name
```

Before you make a backup, it's a good idea to ping the TFTP host from the console of the device to make sure you have good LAN connectivity:

```
1900B#ping 192.168.0.120
```

Sending 5, 100-byte ICMP Echos to 192.168.0.120, time out
is 2 seconds:

!!!!!

Success rate is 100 percent (5/5), round-trip min/avg/max
0/2/10/ ms

After checking the connectivity, you can issue the copy nvram tftp:
command to make a backup copy of the configuration, as in the following
example.

1900B#**copy nvram tftp://192.168.0.120/1900en**

Configuration upload is successfully completed

And here's an example of the output from the console of a TFTP host.

Wed June 01 14:16:10 2000: Receiving '1900en' file from
192.168.0.120 in ASCII mode

##

Wed Mar 01 14:16:11 2000: Successful.

Notice the TFTP host copied two UDP packets, which are represented by
pound signs (#) in ASCII mode.

You can restore a configuration back to a Catalyst 1900 switch from a
TFTP host by using the following command:

copy tftp://tftp_host_address/config_name nvram

You need to know the filename as well as the IP address of the TFTP host
to run this command, as in this example:

1900B#**copy tftp://192.168.0.120/1900en nvram**

TFTP successfully downloaded configuration file

The command at the end of the string tells the TFTP host where to copy
the file to—in this case, nvram.

To delete the startup-config file, or what is just called nvram, on the
1900 switch, use the delete nvram command, as follows:

1900B#**delete nvram**

This command resets the switch with factory defaults. All
system parameters will revert to their default factory
settings. All static and dynamic addresses will be
removed.

Reset system with factory defaults, [Y]es or [N]o? **Yes**

The above command does not affect the switch too much unless you have VLANs set. The switch will work fine without a configuration. However, adding an IP address for management is recommended.

CDP with the 1900 Switch

CDP works with all Cisco devices, including the Catalyst 1900 switch. The output on the 1900 switch looks like this:

```
switch#sh cdp
Global CDP information :
CDP version: 2
Sending CDP packets every 60 seconds
Sending a holdtime value of 180 seconds
#
```

Notice that both the router and the switch have a CDP timer of 60 seconds and a holdtime of 180 seconds. (See Chapter 7 for a refresher on CDP with Cisco routers). This means that CDP information received from neighbor routers will be kept for 180 seconds. If the router or switch does not hear from the neighbor again before the holdtime expires, the information will be discarded.

The 1900 switch has an option to advertise CDP version 2, which is a newer version of CDP running on some new Cisco devices. The 1900 switch can send both version CDP 1 and 2 and receive version 1 of CDP. CDP version 2 is not discussed in this appendix.

You can change the timers on both devices with the cdp timer and cdp holdtime commands from global configuration mode:

```
switch#config t
Enter configuration commands, one per line.  End with
CNTL/Z
switch(config)#cdp ?
  advertise-v2  CDP sends version-2 advertisements
```

```
    holdtime Specify the holdtime (in sec) to be sent in
packets
    timer    Specify the rate at which CDP packets are
sent(in sec)
```

At this point, you can change the timer and holdtime on the 1900 switch, as follows:

```
switch(config)#cdp timer 90
switch(config)#cdp holdtime 240
```

Summary

This appendix introduced you to the Catalyst 1900 switch. You also learned how to do the following:

- Set the passwords. Three passwords were discussed: two enable passwords and the enable secret password.

- Set the hostname and configure a name for the switch.

- Configure the IP address and subnet mask.

- Identify the interfaces with either a `show interface` or `configuration` command.

- Set a description on the interfaces by using the `description` command.

- Define the port duplex of a port, with full or half duplex.

- Verify the configuration with the `show running-config` command.

- Manage the MAC address table with the `show mac-address-table` command.

- Set permanent and static MAC addresses with the `mac-address-table` command.

- Configure port security with the `port secure` command.

Key Terms

Be sure you're familiar with the following terms before taking the exam.

auto duplex

dynamic entries

port security

set-based

Commands in This Appendix

Here is a list of commands used in this appendix.

Command	Description
K	Used at the startup of the 1900 switch and puts the switch into CLI mode
Config t	Puts the switch into global configuration mode
Enable password level 1	Sets the user mode password
Enable password level 15	Sets the enable mode password
Enable secret	Sets the enable secret password
Show run	Shows the running-config
Hostname	Sets the name of the switch
Show ip	Shows the IP configuration of the switch
Ip address	Sets the IP address of the switch
Ip default-gateway	Sets the default gateway of the switch
Interface ethernet 0/1	Configures interface e0/1
Interface fastethernet 0/26	Configures interface f0/26
Show inter e0/1	Shows the statistics of interface e0/1

Command	Description
Show int f0/26	Shows the statistics of f0/26
Description	Sets a description on an interface
Duplex	Sets the duplex of an interface
Ping	Tests the IP configuration
Delete nvram	Deletes the configuration of the switch
Show mac-address-table	Shows the filter table created dynamically by the switch
Clear mac-address-table	Clears the filter table created dynamically by the switch
mac-address-table permanent	Makes a permanent MAC address entry in the filter database
mac-address-table restricted static	Sets a restricted address in the MAC filter database to allow only the configured interfaces to communicate with the restricted address
port secure max-mac-count	Allows only the configured amount of devices to attach and work on an interface
show version	Gives the IOS information of the switch, as well as the uptime and base Ethernet address
Show vlan	Shows all configured VLANs
Interface e0/5	Configures Ethernet interface 5
Interface f0/26	Configures FastEthernet interface 26
Vlan 2 name Sales	Creates a VLAN 2 named Sales
Vlan-membership static 2	Assigns a static VLAN to a port

Command	Description
Show vlan-membership	Shows all port VLAN assignments
Trunk on	Sets a port to permanent trunking mode
Trunk auto	Sets the port to auto trunking mode
Show trunk A	Shows the trunking status of port 26
Show trunk B	Shows the trunking status of port 27
Vtp domain	Sets the domain name for the VTP configuration
Vtp server	Sets the switch to be a VTP server
Vtp client	Sets the switch to be a VTP client
Vtp password	Sets a password on the VTP domain
Show vtp	Shows the VTP configuration of a switch
vtp pruning enable	Makes the switch a pruning switch
Delete vtp	Deletes VTP configurations from a switch
Int f0/0.1	Creates a subinterface
encapsulation isl 2	Sets ISL routing for VLAN 2

Written Lab

In this lab, you will write out the commands to answer the questions.

1. Write the command to display the configuration of the switch.

2. Write the command to see the IP configuration of the switch.

3. Write the command to see the MAC filter table.

4. Write the command to set port e0/2 to a secure table size of 1.

5. Write the command to assign MAC address 1234.4567.8912 to port e0/1 as a permanent address.

6. Write the command to remove the permanent address you just added to port e0/1.

7. Write the command to view the statistics of port e0/5.

8. Write the commands to create three VLANs: Purchasing, Sales, and MIS.

9. Write the command to assign ports 2 and 3 to Sales, 4 and 5 to Purchasing, and 6 and 7 to MIS. Use only static assignments.

10. Write the command to make your switch a VTP client.

11. Write the command to set your switch to be a transparent switch.

12. Write the command that will show the VTP status of your switch.

13. Write the command that will put interface B into auto trunk mode.

14. Write the command to view all VLAN information on a switch.

15. Write the command to set interface 5 to VLAN 2.

Hands-on Labs

There are seven hands-on labs in this section. You need to have access to a 1900 switch. However, you can use the Sybex CCNA e-trainer for the first two labs, or the RouterSim version 2.0 product found at www.routersim.com to complete all of these labs.

Lab B.1: Managing the 1900 Switch

Lab B.2: 1900 Switch Operations

Lab B.3: Creating VLANs

Lab B.4: Assigning VLANs to Switch Ports

Lab B.5: Configuring Trunking

Lab B.6: Configuring VTP

Lab B.7: Configuring Inter-VLAN Routing with ISL

Lab B.1: Managing the 1900 Switch

In this lab, you will connect to the Cisco Catalyst 1900 switch and manage the switch features.

1. From your 1900 switch, type **K** to enter into CLI mode.

2. From the 1900 CLI, press Enter and then from the user mode prompt (>), type **enable**.

3. Type **show running-config** to view the current configuration. Notice the default settings.

4. Type **show version** to view the IOS version running on the switch.

5. Set the name of the router by using the hostname command:

   config t
   hostname 1900A

6. Type **show ip** to see the default IP address, subnet mask, and default gateway settings.

7. Set the IP address, subnet mask, and default gateway of the switch by typing the following:

```
config t
ip address 172.16.10.3 255.255.255.0
ip default-gateway 172.16.10.1
```

8. Type **show ip** to see the new configuration.

9. Ping Router A by typing **ping [ip address]** at the CLI.

10. Type **show mac-address-table** to view the filter table used in the switch to make forwarding decisions.

11. Type **show interfaces** to gather statistics on all interfaces.

12. Type **show int ?** to see the available Ethernet and FastEthernet commands.

13. Type **sho int Ethernet ?** to choose the card 0. <0-0> means only one card with 12 or 24 ports.

14. Type **sh int e 0/?** to see all available interfaces.

15. Type **sh int e 0/2** to see statistics for interface Ethernet 2.

16. Type **delete nvram** to delete the startup-config.

You cannot view the startup-config, only the running-config. Also, the running-config is saved automatically to NVRAM.

Lab B.2: 1900 Switch Operations

This second lab will have you set the passwords, IP addresses, and port security available on a 1900 switch.

1. Type **K** from the 1900A or 1900B switch console to enter CLI mode.

2. Type **en** or **enable** to enter privileged mode.

3. Set the three passwords by typing the following:

   ```
   config t
   enable password level 1 todd
   enable password level 15 todd1
   enable secret todd2
   ```

4. Type **sh run** to see the password. Notice that the enable passwords are not encrypted.

5. Go to int Ethernet 0/5 and set the duplex to full.

   ```
   config t
   int e0/5
   duplex full
   ```

6. Go to interface Ethernet 0/6 and set the duplex to half.

   ```
   config t
   int e0/6
   duplex half
   ```

7. Verify the setting by typing **sh interface** or **sh int e0/5** and **sh int e0/6**.

8. Type the command to remove any IP configuration from the switch:

   ```
   Config t
   no ip address
   ```

9. Verify that the switch is IP-less by typing **show ip**.

10. Set the IP address, subnet mask, and default gateway of the switch:

    ```
    config t
    ip address 172.16.10.100 255.255.255.0
    ip default-gateway 172.16.10.1
    ```

11. Verify the configuration by typing **show ip**.

12. Type **show mac-address-table** to see the forwarding table. Notice that all MAC addresses have been found dynamically.

13. Add a static entry into the filter table by using the command **permanent**:

    ```
    config t
    mac-address-table permanent 083c.0000.0001 e0/9
    ```

14. Type **show mac-address-table**, and notice the permanent entry for interface e0/9.

15. Use the `mac-address-table restricted static` global configuration command to associate a restricted static address with a particular switched-port interface:

```
Config t
Mac-address-table restricted static 083c.0000.0002
e0/3 e0/4
```

The above command only allows traffic to the restricted static address 083c.0000.0002 on interface e0/3 from interface e0/4.

16. Go to interface e0/1 and use the `port secure max-mac-count 1` command to enable addressing security and allow only one MAC address in the filter table on that port. By default, up to 132 MAC addresses can be associated with a single port. By using this command, we will allow only one workstation.

```
Config t
Int e0/1
Port secure max-mac-count 1
```

17. Verify which ports have port security on them by typing **show mac-address-table security**. Notice that port e0/1 security is enabled.

Lab B.3: Creating VLANs

In this lab, you will create multiple VLANs on only one switch. Lab B.4 will have you create VTP configurations that will allow this VLAN information to be propagated to the second switch.

1. Telnet or connect to the first 1900 switch. Set the hostname of the switch to 1900A.

```
#config t
(config)#hostname 1900A
1900A#
```

2. Create four VLANs (2–5) and name them according to the following list:

VLAN2=Sales

VLAN3=Management

VLAN4=Engineering

VLAN5=Marketing

```
1900A#config t
Enter configuration commands, one per line.  End
with CNTL/Z
1900A(config)#vlan 2 name Sales
1900A(config)#vlan 3 name Management
1900A(config)#vlan 4 name Engineering
1900A(config)#vlan 5 name Marketing
1900A(config)#exit
```

Verify your VLANs with the show vlan command.

```
1900A#sh vlan

VLAN Name                 Status     Ports
--------------------------------------
1    default              Enabled    1-12, AUI, A, B
2    Sales                Enabled
3    Management           Enabled
4    Engineering          Enabled
5    Marketing            Enabled
1002 fddi-default         Suspended
1003 token-ring-defau     Suspended
1004 fddinet-default      Suspended
1005 trnet-default        Suspended
--------------------------------------
# [output cut]
```

Lab B.4: Assigning VLANs to Switch Ports

In this lab, you will configure two ports of the switch to be a member of each VLAN.

1. Configure ports 1 and 2 to be in VLAN 2. Remember that all ports are in VLAN 1 unless set differently.

```
1900A#config t
Enter configuration commands, one per line.  End
with CNTL/Z
1900A(config)#int e0/1
1900A(config-if)#vlan-membership static 2
1900A(config-if)#int e0/2
1900A(config-if)#vlan-membership static 2
```

2. Assign ports 3 and 4 to be in VLAN 3.

```
1900A(config-if)#int e0/3
1900A(config-if)#vlan-membership static 3
1900A(config-if)#int e0/4
1900A(config-if)#vlan-membership static 3
```

Assign ports 5 and 6 to be in VLAN 4.

```
1900A(config-if)#int e0/5
1900A(config-if)#vlan-membership static 4
1900A(config-if)#int e0/6
1900A(config-if)#vlan-membership static 4
```

Assign ports 7 and 8 to be in VLAN 5.

```
1900A(config-if)#int e0/7
1900A(config-if)#vlan-membership static 5
1900A(config-if)#int e0/8
1900A(config-if)#vlan-membership static 5
1900A(config-if)#exit
1900A(config)#exit
```

3. Verify your configuration with the show vlan command.

1900A#**sh vlan**

```
VLAN Name             Status        Ports
----------------------------------------
1    default          Enabled       8-12, AUI, A, B
2    Sales            Enabled       1-2
3    Management       Enabled       3-4
4    Engineering      Enabled       5-6
5    Marketing        Enabled       7-8
1002 fddi-default     Suspended
1003 token-ring-defau Suspended
1004 fddinet-default  Suspended
1005 trnet-default    Suspended
```

4. Verify your VLAN memberships with the show vlan-membership command.

1900A#**sh vlan-membership**

```
Port  VLAN   Membership
-----------------------
1     2      Static
2     2      Static
3     3      Static
4     3      Static
5     4      Static
6     4      Static
7     5      Static
8     5      Static
9     1      Static
10    1      Static
11    1      Static
12    1      Static

AUI   1      Static
A     1      Static
B     1      Static
```

1900A#

Lab B.5: Configuring Trunking

Before we can share information with our second switch, we need to configure the link between the switches. We don't necessarily have to configure a trunked link, but then only VLAN 1 information would be transferred between switches, and we want to configure all VLANs' information to be transferred between switches.

1. On 1900A, configure port 26 to be in auto trunk mode. This will allow the link to become trunked as soon as we set the second switch's trunk port to on.

```
1900A#config t
Enter configuration commands, one per line.  End
with CNTL/Z
1900A(config)#int f0/26
1900A(config-if)#trunk ?
   auto        Set DISL state to AUTO
   desirable   Set DISL state to DESIRABLE
   nonegotiate Set DISL state to NONEGOTIATE
   off         Set DISL state to OFF
   on          Set DISL state to ON
1900EN(config-if)#trunk auto
```

2. Attach to the second 1900 switch and name the switch 1900B. Create port 26 as a permanent trunk port.

```
#config t
Enter configuration commands, one per line.  End
with CNTL/Z
(config)#hostname 1900B
1900B(config)#int f0/26
1900B(config-if)#trunk ?
   auto        Set DISL state to AUTO
   desirable   Set DISL state to DESIRABLE
   nonegotiate Set DISL state to NONEGOTIATE
   off         Set DISL state to OFF
   on          Set DISL state to ON
1900B(config-if)#trunk on
```

Lab B.6: Configuring VTP

In this lab, you will configure the 1900A switches with a VTP domain name, configure the second switch as a client, and verify that VTP information is updated from the server to the client.

1. Telnet or connect a console to the 1900A switch. Set the switch to be a server VTP switch. (This is the default, but type it in anyway for practice.)

   ```
   1900A#config t
   1900A(config)#vtp server
   ```

2. Set the VTP domain name to Classroom1.

   ```
   1900A#config t
   1900A(config)#vtp domain Classroom1
   ```

3. Verify that the VTP information is configured correctly.

   ```
   1900A#show vtp
   ```

4. Telnet or connect to 1900B, set the VTP domain name, and set the VTP mode to client.

   ```
   1900B#config t
   1900B(config)#vtp domain Classroom1
   1900B(config)#vtp client
   ```

5. Verify both switches' VTP configuration by using the show vtp command. Also verify that the VLAN information is propagated from the server switch to the client by using the show vlan command.

6. From 1900B, type **show vlan** to see if the VLAN information was propagated from the 1900A switch.

1900B#**sh vlan**

```
VLAN Name            Status     Ports
-------------------------------------------
1    default         Enabled    1-12, AUI, A, B
2    Sales           Enabled
3    Management      Enabled
4    Engineering     Enabled
5    Marketing       Enabled
1002 fddi-default    Suspended
1003 token-ring-defau Suspended
1004 fddinet-default Suspended
1005 trnet-default   Suspended
-------------------------------------------
```

Notice that it found all the VLANs, but that all of 1900B's switch ports are in VLAN 1. Unless you tell it differently, all ports are always in VLANs. You have to set the ports at each switch. (VTP sends VLAN information, not port information.)

Lab B.7: Configuring Inter-VLAN Routing with ISL

Now that we have configured our VLANs and set up VTP domain information so both switches have the same VLAN configurations, we need to configure the 2600 router to support inter-VLAN routing.

1. Plug the 2600 into one of the FastEthernet ports on either switch. It doesn't matter where you plug the router into the switch fabric.

2. Configure the switch port as a trunk port.

1900A#**config t**
1900A(config)**int f0/027**
1900A(config-if)# **trunk on**

3. Configure the 2600 router FastEthernet port to route between all VLANs.

```
2621#config t
2621(config)int f0/0.1
2621(config-if)no shutdown
2621(config-subif)# encapsulation isl 1
2621(config-subif)# ip address 172.16.10.1
255.255.255.0
2621(config-subif)# int f0/0.2
2621(config-subif)# encapsulation isl 2
2621(config-subif)# ip address 172.16.20.1
255.255.255.0
2621(config-subif)# int f0/0.3
2621(config-subif)# encapsulation isl 3
2621(config-subif)# ip address 172.16.30.1
255.255.255.0
2621(config-subif)# int f0/0.4
2621(config-subif)# encapsulation isl 4
2621(config-subif)# ip address 172.16.40.1
255.255.255.0
2621(config-subif)# encapsulation isl 5
2621(config-subif)# ip address 172.16.50.1
255.255.255.0
2621(config-subif)# exit
2621(config)#int f0/0
```

Remember that each host in their configured VLAN should have the same subnet information.

Review Questions

1. Which of the following is *not* true regarding the 1900 switch?

   A. You can ping from a 1900 switch if configured.

   B. You can ping to a 1900 switch if configured.

   C. You can telnet to a 1900 switch if configured.

   D. You can telnet from a 1900 switch if configured.

2. What command sets interface e0/10 on a 1900 switch to run full-duplex Ethernet?

   A. `full duplex on`

   B. `duplex on`

   C. `duplex full`

   D. `full-duplex`

   E. `set duplex on full`

3. Which command sets a 1900 switch interface to communicate so its buffers will not overflow on a congested link?

   A. `flow on`

   B. `duplex flow control`

   C. `duplex full-flow-control`

   D. `full duplex-flow`

4. If you wanted to verify the duplex on a 1900 switch, port 26, what command should you use?

   A. `show port 26`

   B. `show int 26`

   C. `show int e0/26`

   D. `show int f0/26`

   E. `show int g0/26`

   F. `show int h0/26`

5. Which of the following is true regarding a port status light on a switch?

   A. It is used to see if a loop has occurred on the network.

   B. It is used to identify RTS signaling.

   C. When a device is connected to a port, the port status LED light comes on and stays on.

   D. When a device is connected to a port, the port status LED light comes on and then goes off.

6. If you want to delete the startup-config on a 1900 switch, what command do you use?

   A. `erase startup-config`

   B. `delete startup-config`

   C. `delete nvram`

   D. `delete startup`

7. What command would you use to identify port 3 on a 1900 switch to be Finance Server?

   A. `int e0/3, description Finance Server`

   B. `int e0/3, description Finance_Server`

   C. `set port name e0/3 Finance Server`

   D. `set port name e0/3 Finance_Server`

8. What type of cable must you use to connect between two switch uplink ports?

   A. Straight

   B. Rolled

   C. Crossover

   D. Fiber

9. How do you set the user mode password on a 1900 switch?

    A. `usermode password todd`

    B. `enable password todd`

    C. `enable password level 1 todd`

    D. `enable password level 15 todd`

10. What command will set the enable mode password on a 1900 switch?

    A. 1900EN(config)#**enable password level 1 todd**

    B. 1900EN(config)#**enable password level 15 todd**

    C. 1900EN#**set enable password todd**

    D. 1900EN(Config)#**enable password todd**

11. What command will show you the IP configuration on a 1900 switch?

    A. `sh ip config`

    B. `sh ip`

    C. `sh int config`

    D. `sh int`

12. What commands should you use to set the IP address and default gateway on a 1900 switch? (Choose all that apply.)

    A. `ip address 172.16.10.16 255.255.255.0`

    B. `ip default-gateway 172.16.10.1`

    C. `ip address 172.16.10.1 mask 255.255.255.0`

    D. `default-gateway 172.16.10.10`

13. What is true regarding passwords on a Catalyst 1900 switch?

    A. They must by a minimum of eight characters.

    B. They are case sensitive.

    C. The passwords cannot be less than four characters or more than eight.

    D. They are not case sensitive.

14. What is true about the enable secret password?

    A. It is case sensitive.

    B. It is not used on the 1900 switch.

    C. It is used instead of the enable password if both are set.

    D. It is not used instead of the enable password if both are set.

15. Which command will show you the permanent MAC addresses stored in the filter table?

    A. Todd1900EN#`sh mac-filter-table`

    B. Todd1900EN#`sh mac-address-table`

    C. Todd1900EN(config)#`sh mac-address-table`

    D. Todd1900EN#`sh filter-address-table`

16. What are the three ways to configure a 1900 switch?

    A. VSM

    B. VLSM

    C. Menu

    D. CLI

    E. CLIM

17. Which command will allow you to set the name of the switch?

    A. `Switch name Cisco1900`

    B. `Description 1900switch`

    C. `host name 1900`

    D. `hostname 1900ethernet`

18. Which of the following is part of the default configuration of the 1900 switch?

    A. CDP: Enabled

    B. IP address: 192.168.10.2

    C. Default gateway: 0.0.0.0

    D. Switching mode: FragmentFree

    E. 10BaseT ports: Auto-negotiate duplex mode

    F. 100BaseT ports: Half duplex

    G. Spanning Tree: Enabled

    H. Console password: Cisco

19. What command will allow you to view the switch statistics for port 2?

    A. show int 2

    B. show int eth 0/2

    C. sh int e/2

    D. show inter f0/2

20. Which command will show you the statistics for port 27?

    A. show int 27

    B. show int eth 0/27

    C. sh int f/27

    D. sh inter f0/27

21. Which of the following will allow only one MAC address to be associated with a port?

    A. Todd1900EN(config-if)#**port secure max-mac-count 1**

    B. Todd1900EN(config-if)#**port max-mac-count secure 1**

    C. Todd1900EN(config)#**mac-address-table restricted static 00A0.246E.0FA8 e0/2**

    D. Todd1900EN(config)#**mac-address-table permanent 00A0.2448.60A5 e0/4**

22. Which of the following ports will set a hardware address on port e0/4 to only MAC address 00A0.2448.60A5?

    A. `int e0/4 set MAC  00A0.2448.60A5`

    B. Todd1900EN(config)#**mac-address-table restricted static 00A0.2448.60A5 e0/2**

    C. Todd1900EN(config)#**mac-address-table permanent 00A0.2448.60A5 e0/4**

    D. Todd1900EN(config-if)#**port secure max-mac-count 00A0.2448.60A5**

23. Which of the following commands allows only port e0/5 on a 1900 switch to communicate with hardware address 00A0.246E.0FA8?

    A. `int e0/5 out 00A0.246E.0FA8`

    B. Todd1900EN(config)#**mac-address-table permanent 00A0.246E.0FA8 e0/4**

    C. Todd1900EN(config-if)#**port secure max-mac-count 00A0.246E.0FA8**

    D. Todd1900EN(config)#**mac-address-table restricted static 00A0.246E.0FA8 e0/2 e0/5**

Answers to the Written Lab

1. `show running-config`

2. `sh ip`

3. `show mac-address-table`

4. `port secure max-mac-count 1`

5. `mac-address-table permanent 1234.4567.8912 e0/1`

6. `clear mac-address-table permanent 1234.4567.8912 e0/1`

7. `show int e0/5`

8. **config t**
   vlan 2 Purchasing
   vlan 3 Sales
   vlan 4 MIS

9. **int e0/2**
   vlan-membership static 3
   int e0/3
   vlan-membership static 3
   int e0/4
   vlan-membership static 2
   int e0/5
   vlan-membership static 2
   int e0/6
   vlan-membership static 4
   int e0/7
   vlan-membership static 4

10. `config t, vtp client`

11. `config t, vtp transparent`

12. `show vtp`

13. `int f0/27, trunk auto`

14. `show vlan`

15. `config t, int e0/5, vlan-membership static 2`

Answers to Review Questions

1. D. You cannot telnet from the 1900 switch CLI or Menu.

2. C. The interface command `duplex full` sets the interface to full-duplex communication.

3. C. By using the `duplex full-flow-control`, the interface will use flow-control to stop the switch buffers from filling up and dropping packets.

4. D. The 1900 switch uses the `show type slot/port` command to verify the duplex on a 1900 switch.

5. C. If a device is connected to a switch port, the light comes on and then stays on. If a device is not connected, then when the switch is powered on, the light comes on and then goes off.

6. C. The command `delete nvram` clears the configuration and restores the factory default configuration of the switch.

7. B. The 1900 switch must use an underscore if you want to use two words.

8. C. Crossover cables are used to connect switch to switch, or hub to switch.

9. C. By using the command `enable password` and the level command set to 1, the user mode password will be set on the switch.

10. B. To set the enable password, use the level command set to 15.

11. B. The command `show ip` will give you the current IP configuration on the switch.

12. A, B. The commands `IP address` and `IP default-gateway` will set the IP address and default gateway of the switch.

13. C, D. The passwords cannot be less than four characters or more than eight. They are also not case sensitive.

14. C. If you have both an enable password and an enable secret password set, the enable secret takes precedence over the enable password and the enable password will not be used.

15. B. The command `show mac-address-table` will show you all the addresses in the filter table including dynamic, static, and permanent.

16. A, C, D. The three ways to configure a port on the 1900 switch are through the Virtual Switch Manager, the Menu system, and the Command-Line Interface.

17. D. The command to set the switch name is `hostname`, one word.

18. A, C, D, G. CDP is enabled, no IP address or default gateway is set, the switching mode is FragmentFree, the 10BaseT ports are half duplex, the FastEthernet ports are auto-negotiate duplex mode, Spanning Tree is enabled, and no console password is set.

19. B. The switch uses the `type slot/port` command. The first 24 ports are Ethernet, and ports 26 and 27 are FastEthernet.

20. D. The switch uses the `type slot/port` command. The first 24 ports are Ethernet, and ports 26 and 27 are FastEthernet.

21. A. To allow only a certain amount of MAC address to be assigned to a port, use the `port secure max-mac-count [count]` command. The default is 132.

22. C. To set a permanent MAC address on an interface, use the `mac-address-table permanent [mac-address] [interface]` command.

23. D. To allow only port e0/5 to communicate via the hardware address attached to port e0/2, use the `mac-address-table restricted static [mac-address] [destination interface] [source interface]` command.

Commands in This
Study Guide

This appendix is a compilation of the "Commands in This Chapter" sections at the end of the chapters.

Command	Description	Chapter
?	Gives you a help screen	4
0.0.0.0 255.255.255.255	Is a wildcard command; same as the any command	9
access-class	Applies a standard IP access list to a VTY line	9
access-list	Creates a list of tests to filter the networks	9
any	Specifies any host or any network; same as the 0.0.0.0 255.255.255.255 command	9
Backspace	Deletes a single character	4
bandwidth	Sets the bandwidth on a serial interface	4
banner	Creates a banner for users who log in to the router	4
cdp enable	Turns on CDP on an individual interface	7
cdp holdtime	Changes the holdtime of CDP packets	7
cdp run	Turns on CDP on a router	7
cdp timer	Changes the CDP update timer	7
clear counters	Clears the statistics from an interface	4
clear line	Clears a connection connected via Telnet to your router	7

Command	Description	Chapter
`clear mac-address-table`	Clears the filter table created dynamically by the switch	App. B
`clock rate`	Provides clocking on a serial DCE interface	4
`config memory`	Copies the `startup-config` to `running-config`	4
`config network`	Copies a configuration stored on a TFTP host to `running-config`	4
`config terminal`	Puts you in global configuration mode and changes the running-config	4
`config-register`	Tells the router how to boot and to change the configuration register setting	7
`copy flash tftp`	Copies a file from flash memory to a TFTP host	7
`copy run start`	Short for `copy running-config startup-config`. Places a configuration into NVRAM	4, 7
`copy run tftp`	Copies the `running-config` file to a TFTP host	7
`copy tftp flash`	Copies a file from a TFTP host to flash memory	7
`copy tftp run`	Copies a configuration from a TFTP host to the `running-config` file	7
Ctrl+A	Moves your cursor to the beginning of the line	4
Ctrl+D	Deletes a single character	4

Command	Description	Chapter
Ctrl+E	Moves your cursor to the end of the line	4
Ctrl+F	Moves forward one character	4
Ctrl+R	Redisplays a line	4
Ctrl+Shift+6, then X (keyboard combination)	Returns you to the originating router when you telnet to numerous routers	7
Ctrl+U	Erases a line	4
Ctrl+W	Erases a word	4
Ctrl+Z	Ends configuration mode and returns to EXEC	4
`debug dialer`	Shows you the call setup and teardown procedures	10
`debug frame-relay lmi`	Shows the lmi exchanges between the router and the Frame Relay switch	10
`debug ip igrp events`	Provides a summary of the IGRP routing information running on the network	5
`debug ip igrp transactions`	Shows message requests from neighbor routers asking for an update and the broadcasts sent from your router to that neighbor router	5
`debug ip rip`	Sends console messages displaying information about RIP packets being sent and received on a router interface	5

Command	Description	Chapter
debug ipx	Shows the RIP and SAP information as it passes through the router	8
debug isdn q921	Shows layer-2 processes	10
debug isdn q931	Shows layer-3 processes	10
delete nvram	Deletes the contents of NVRAM on a 1900 switch	7, App. B
delete vtp	Deletes VTP configurations from a switch	App. B
description	Sets a description on an interface	4, App. B
dialer idle-timeout number	Tells the BRI line when to drop if no interesting traffic is found	10
dialer list number protocol protocol permit/deny	Specifies interesting traffic for a DDR link	10
dialer load-threshold number inbound/ outbound/either	Sets the parameters that describe when the second BRI comes up on a ISDN link	10
dialer map protocol address name hostname number	Used instead of a dialer string to provide more security in an ISDN network	10
dialer-string	Sets the phone number to dial for a BRI interface	10
disable	Takes you from privileged mode back to user mode	4
disconnect	Disconnects a connection to a remote router from the originating router	7

Command	Description	Chapter
`duplex`	Sets the duplex of an interface	App. B
`enable`	Puts you into privileged mode	4
`enable password`	Sets the unencrypted enable password	4
`enable password level 1`	Sets the user mode password	App. B
`enable password level 15`	Sets the enable mode password	App. B
`enable secret`	Sets the encrypted enable secret password. Supersedes the enable password if set	4, App. B
`encapsulation`	Sets the frame type used on an interface	8
`encapsulation frame-relay`	Changes the encapsulation to Frame Relay on a serial link	10
`encapsulation frame-relay ietf`	Sets the encapsulation type to the Internet Engineering Task Force (IETF). Connects Cisco routers to off-brand routers	10
`encapsulation hdlc`	Restores the default encapsulation of HDLC on a serial link	10
`encapsulation isl 2`	Sets ISL routing for VLAN 2	App. B
`encapsulation ppp`	Changes the encapsulation on a serial link to PPP	10
`erase startup`	Deletes the `startup-config`	4
`erase startup-config`	Deletes the contents of NVRAM on a router	7
Esc+B	Moves back one word	4
Esc+F	Moves forward one word	4

Command	Description	Chapter
`exec-timeout`	Sets the timeout in seconds and minutes for the console connection	4
`exit`	Disconnects a connection to a remote router via Telnet	7
`frame-relay interface-dlci`	Configures the PVC address on a serial interface or subinterface	10
`frame-relay lmi-type`	Configures the LMI type on a serial link	10
`frame-relay map protocol address`	Creates a static mapping for use with a Frame Relay network	10
`Host`	Specifies a single host address	9
`hostname`	Sets the name of a router or a switch	4, App. B
`int e0.10`	Creates a subinterface	8
`int f0/0.1`	Creates a subinterface	App. B
`interface`	Puts you in interface configuration mode. Also used with **show** commands	4
`interface e0/5`	Configures Ethernet interface 5	App. B
`interface ethernet 0/1`	Configures interface e0/1	App. B
`interface f0/26`	Configures FastEthernet interface 26	App. B
`interface fastethernet 0/0`	Puts you in interface configuration mode for a FastEthernet port. Also used with show commands	4

Command	Description	Chapter
`interface fastethernet 0/0.1`	Creates a subinterface	4
`interface fastethernet 0/26`	Configures interface f0/26	App. B
`interface s0.16 multipoint`	Creates a multipoint subinterface on a serial link that can be used with Frame Relay networks	10
`interface s0.16 point-to-point`	Creates a point-to-point subinterface on a serial link that can be used with Frame Relay	10
`interface serial 5`	Puts you in configuration mode for interface serial 5 and can be used for show commands	4
`ip access-group`	Applies an IP access list to an interface	9
`ip address`	Sets an IP address on an interface or a switch	4, App. B
`ip classless`	Is a global configuration command used to tell a router to forward packets to a default route when the destination network is not in the routing table	5
`ip default-gateway`	Sets the default gateway of the switch	App. B
`ip domain-lookup`	Turns on DNS lookup (which is on by default)	7
`ip domain-name`	Appends a domain name to a DNS lookup	7

Command	Description	Chapter
`ip host`	Creates a host table on a router	7
`ip name-server`	Sets the IP address of up to six DNS servers	7
`IP route`	Creates static and default routes on a router	5
`ipx access-group`	Applies an IPX access list to an interface	9
`ipx input-sap-filter`	Applies an inbound IPX SAP filter to an interface	9
`ipx network`	Assigns an IPX network number to an interface	8
`ipx output-sap-filter`	Applies an outbound IPX SAP filter to an interface	9
`ipx ping`	Is a Packet Internet Groper used to test IPX packet on an internetwork	8
`ipx routing`	Turns on IPX routing	8
`isdn spid1`	Sets the number that identifies the first DS0 to the ISDN switch	10
`isdn spid2`	Sets the number that identifies the second DS0 to the ISDN switch	10
`isdn switch-type`	Sets the type of ISDN switch that the router will communicate with. Can be set at interface level or global configuration mode	10
`K`	Used at the startup of the 1900 switch and puts the switch into CLI mode	App. B

Command	Description	Chapter
`line`	Puts you in configuration mode to change or set your user mode passwords	4
`line aux`	Puts you in the auxiliary interface configuration mode	4
`line console 0`	Puts you in console configuration mode	4
`line vty`	Puts you in VTY (Telnet) interface configuration mode	4
`logging synchronous`	Stops console messages from overwriting your command-line input	4
`logout`	Logs you out of your console session	4
`mac-address-table permanent`	Makes a permanent MAC address entry in the filter database	App. B
`mac-address-table restricted static`	Sets a restricted address in the MAC filter database to allow only the configured interfaces to communicate with the restricted address	App. B
`media-type`	Sets the hardware media type on an interface	4
`network`	Tells the routing protocol what network to advertise	5
`no cdp enable`	Turns off CDP on an individual interface	7
`no cdp run`	Turns off CDP completely on a router	7

Command	Description	Chapter
`no inverse-arp`	Turns off the dynamic IARP used with Frame Relay. Static mappings must be configured	10
`no ip domain-lookup`	Turns off DNS lookup	7
`no ip host`	Removes a hostname from a host table	7
`No IP route`	Removes a static or default route	5
`no shutdown`	Turns on an interface	4
`o/r 0x2142`	Changes a 2501 to boot without using the contents of NVRAM	7
`ping`	Tests IP connectivity to a remote device	4, 7, App. B
`port secure max-mac-count`	Allows only the configured amount of devices to attach and work on an interface	App. B
`ppp authentication chap`	Tells PPP to use CHAP authentication	10
`ppp authentication pap`	Tells PPP to use PAP authentication	10
`router igrp as`	Turns on IP IGRP routing on a router	5
`router rip`	Puts you in router rip configuration mode	4, 5
`secondary`	Adds a second IPX network on the same physical interface	8

Command	Description	Chapter
Service password-encryption	Encrypts the user mode and enable password	4
show access-list	Shows all the access lists configured on the router	9
show access-list 110	Shows only access list 110	9
show cdp	Displays the CDP timer and holdtime frequencies	7
show cdp entry *	Same as show cdp neighbor detail, but does not work on a 1900 switch	7
show cdp interface	Shows the individual interfaces enabled with CDP	7
show cdp neighbor	Shows the directly connected neighbors and the details about them	7
show cdp neighbor detail	Shows the IP address and IOS version and type, and includes all of the information from the show cdp neighbor command	7
show cdp traffic	Shows the CDP packets sent and received on a device and any errors	7
Show controllers s 0	Shows the DTE or DCE status of an interface	4
show dialer	Shows the number of times the dialer string has been reached, the idle-timeout values of each B channel, the length of call, and the name of the router to which the interface is connected	10

Command	Description	Chapter
show flash	Shows the files in flash memory	7
show frame-relay lmi	Sets the LMI type on a serial interface	10
show frame-relay map	Shows the static and dynamic Network layer–to–PVC mappings	10
show frame-relay pvc	Shows the configured PVCs and DLCI numbers configured on a router	10
Show history	Shows you the last 10 commands entered by default	4
show hosts	Shows the contents of the host table	7
show int f0/26	Shows the statistics of f0/26	App. B
show inter e0/1	Shows the statistics of interface e0/1	App. B
Show interface s0	Shows the statistics of interface serial 0	4
show ip	Shows the IP configuration of the switch	App. B
show ip access-list	Shows only the IP access lists	9
show ip interface	Shows which interfaces have IP access lists applied	9
show ip protocols	Shows the routing protocols and timers associated with each routing protocol configured on a router	5
show ip route	Displays the IP routing table	5, 10

Command	Description	Chapter
`show ipx access-list`	Shows the IPX access lists configured on a router	9
`show ipx interface`	Shows the RIP and SAP information being sent and received on an individual interface. Also shows the IPX address of the interface	8, 9
`show ipx route`	Shows the IPX routing table	8
`show ipx servers`	Shows the SAP table on a Cisco router	8
`show ipx traffic`	Shows the RIP and SAP information sent and received on a Cisco router	8
`show isdn active`	Shows the number called and whether a call is in progress	10
`show isdn status`	Shows if your SPIDs are valid and if you are connected and communicating with the provider's switch	10
`show mac-address-table`	Shows the filter table created dynamically by the switch	App. B
`show protocols`	Shows the routed protocols and network addresses configured on each interface	5, 8
`show run`	Short for `show running-config`. Shows the configuration currently running on the router	4, 7, App. B
`show sessions`	Shows your connections via Telnet to remote devices	7

Command	Description	Chapter
`show start`	Short for `show startup-config`. Shows the backup configuration stored in NVRAM	4, 7
`Show terminal`	Shows you your configured history size	4
`show trunk A`	Shows the trunking status of port 26	App. B
`show trunk B`	Shows the trunking status of port 27	App. B
`show version`	Gives the IOS information of the switch, as well as the uptime and base Ethernet address	4, 7, App. B
`show vlan`	Shows all configured VLANs	App. B
`show vlan-membership`	Shows all port VLAN assignments	App. B
`show vtp`	Shows the VTP configuration of a switch	App. B
`shutdown`	Puts an interface in administratively down mode	4
Tab	Finishes typing a command for you	4
`telnet`	Connects, views, and runs programs on a remote device	4, 7
`Terminal history size`	Changes your history size from the default of 10 up to 256	
`trace`	Tests a connection to a remote device and shows the path it took through the internetwork to find the remote device	4, 7

Command	Description	Chapter
`traffic-share balanced`	Tells the IGRP routing protocol to share links inversely proportional to the metrics	5
`traffic-share min`	Tells the IGRP routing process to use routes that have only minimum costs	5
`trunk auto`	Sets the port to auto trunking mode	App. B
`trunk on`	Sets a port to permanent trunking mode	App. B
`username name password password`	Creates usernames and passwords for authentication on a Cisco router	10
`variance`	Controls the load balancing between the best metric and the worst acceptable metric	5
`vlan 2 name Sales`	Creates a VLAN 2 named Sales	App. B
`vlan-membership static 2`	Assigns a static VLAN to a port	App. B
`vtp client`	Sets the switch to be a VTP client	App. B
`vtp domain`	Sets the domain name for the VTP configuration	App. B
`vtp password`	Sets a password on the VTP domain	App. B
`vtp pruning enable`	Makes the switch a pruning switch	App. B
`vtp server`	Sets the switch to be a VTP server	App. B

Glossary

A&B bit signaling   Used in T1 transmission facilities and sometimes called "24th channel signaling." Each of the 24 T1 subchannels in this procedure uses one bit of every sixth frame to send supervisory signaling information.

AAL   ATM Adaptation Layer: A service-dependent sublayer of the Data Link layer, which accepts data from other applications and brings it to the ATM layer in 48-byte ATM payload segments. CS and SAR are the two sublayers that form AALs. Currently, the four types of AAL recommended by the ITU-T are AAL1, AAL2, AAL3/4, and AAL5. AALs are differentiated by the source-destination timing they use, whether they are CBR or VBR, and whether they are used for connection-oriented or connectionless mode data transmission. *See also: AAL1, AAL2, AAL3/4, AAL5, ATM,* and *ATM layer.*

AAL1   ATM Adaptation Layer 1: One of four AALs recommended by the ITU-T, it is used for connection-oriented, time-sensitive services that need constant bit rates, such as isochronous traffic and uncompressed video. *See also: AAL.*

AAL2   ATM Adaptation Layer 2: One of four AALs recommended by the ITU-T, it is used for connection-oriented services that support a variable bit rate, such as voice traffic. *See also: AAL.*

AAL3/4   ATM Adaptation Layer 3/4: One of four AALs (a product of two initially distinct layers) recommended by the ITU-T, supporting both connectionless and connection-oriented links. Its primary use is in sending SMDS packets over ATM networks. *See also: AAL.*

AAL5   ATM Adaptation Layer 5: One of four AALs recommended by the ITU-T, it is used to support connection-oriented VBR services primarily to transfer classical IP over ATM and LANE traffic. This least complex of the AAL recommendations uses SEAL, offering lower bandwidth costs and simpler processing requirements but also providing reduced bandwidth and error-recovery capacities. *See also: AAL.*

AARP   AppleTalk Address Resolution Protocol: The protocol in an AppleTalk stack that maps data-link addresses to network addresses.

AARP probe packets   Packets sent by the AARP to determine whether a given node ID is being used by another node in a nonextended AppleTalk network. If the node ID is not in use, the sending node appropriates that node's ID. If the node ID is in use, the sending node will select a different ID and then send out more AARP probe packets. *See also: AARP.*

ABM Asynchronous Balanced Mode: When two stations can initiate a transmission, ABM is an HDLC (or one of its derived protocols) communication technology that supports peer-oriented, point-to-point communications between both stations.

ABR Area Border Router: An OSPF router that is located on the border of one or more OSPF areas. ABRs are used to connect OSPF areas to the OSPF backbone area.

access layer One of the layers in Cisco's three-layer hierarchical model. The access layer provides users with access to the internetwork.

access link Is a link used with switches and is only part of one Virtual LAN (VLAN). Trunk links carry information from multiple VLANs.

access list A set of test conditions kept by routers that determines "interesting traffic" to and from the router for various services on the network.

access method The manner in which network devices approach gaining access to the network itself.

access server Also known as a "network access server," it is a communications process connecting asynchronous devices to a LAN or WAN through network and terminal emulation software, providing synchronous or asynchronous routing of supported protocols.

acknowledgment Verification sent from one network device to another signifying that an event has occurred. May be abbreviated as ACK. *Contrast with: NAK.*

ACR allowed cell rate: A designation defined by the ATM Forum for managing ATM traffic. Dynamically controlled using congestion control measures, the ACR varies between the minimum cell rate (MCR) and the peak cell rate (PCR). *See also: MCR and PCR.*

active monitor The mechanism used to manage a Token Ring. The network node with the highest MAC address on the ring becomes the active monitor and is responsible for management tasks such as preventing loops and ensuring tokens are not lost.

address learning   Used with transparent bridges to learn the hardware addresses of all devices on an internetwork. The switch then filters the network with the known hardware (MAC) addresses.

address mapping   By translating network addresses from one format to another, this methodology permits different protocols to operate interchangeably.

address mask   A bit combination descriptor identifying which portion of an address refers to the network or subnet and which part refers to the host. Sometimes simply called the mask. *See also: subnet mask.*

address resolution   The process used for resolving differences between computer addressing schemes. Address resolution typically defines a method for tracing Network layer (Layer 3) addresses to Data-Link layer (Layer 2) addresses. *See also: address mapping.*

adjacency   The relationship made between defined neighboring routers and end nodes, using a common media segment, to exchange routing information.

administrative distance   A number between 0 and 225 that expresses the value of trustworthiness of a routing information source. The lower the number, the higher the integrity rating.

administrative weight   A value designated by a network administrator to rate the preference given to a network link. It is one of four link metrics exchanged by PTSPs to test ATM network resource availability.

ADSU   ATM Data Service Unit: The terminal adapter used to connect to an ATM network through an HSSI-compatible mechanism. *See also: DSU.*

advertising   The process whereby routing or service updates are transmitted at given intervals, allowing other routers on the network to maintain a record of viable routes.

AEP   AppleTalk Echo Protocol: A test for connectivity between two AppleTalk nodes where one node sends a packet to another and receives an echo, or copy, in response.

AFI   Authority and Format Identifier: The part of an NSAP ATM address that delineates the type and format of the IDI section of an ATM address.

AFP AppleTalk Filing Protocol: A Presentation-layer protocol, supporting AppleShare and Mac OS File Sharing, that permits users to share files and applications on a server.

AIP ATM Interface Processor: Supporting AAL3/4 and AAL5, this interface for Cisco 7000 series routers minimizes performance bottlenecks at the UNI. *See also: AAL3/4* and *AAL5.*

algorithm A set of rules or process used to solve a problem. In networking, algorithms are typically used for finding the best route for traffic from a source to its destination.

alignment error An error occurring in Ethernet networks, in which a received frame has extra bits; that is, a number not divisible by eight. Alignment errors are generally the result of frame damage caused by collisions.

all-routes explorer packet An explorer packet that can move across an entire SRB network, tracing all possible paths to a given destination. Also known as an all-rings explorer packet. *See also: explorer packet, local explorer packet,* and *spanning explorer packet.*

AM Amplitude Modulation: A modulation method that represents information by varying the amplitude of the carrier signal. *See also: modulation.*

AMI Alternate Mark Inversion: A line-code type on T1 and E1 circuits that shows zeros as "01" during each bit cell, and ones as "11" or "00," alternately, during each bit cell. The sending device must maintain ones density in AMI but not independently of the data stream. Also known as binary-coded, alternate mark inversion. *Contrast with: B8ZS. See also: ones density.*

amplitude An analog or digital waveform's highest value.

analog transmission Signal messaging whereby information is represented by various combinations of signal amplitude, frequency, and phase.

ANSI American National Standards Institute: The organization of corporate, government, and other volunteer members that coordinates standards-related activities, approves U.S. national standards, and develops U.S. positions in international standards organizations. ANSI assists in the creation of international and U.S. standards in disciplines such as communications, networking, and a variety of technical fields. It publishes over 13,000 standards, for engineered products and technologies ranging from screw threads to networking protocols. ANSI is a member of the IEC and ISO.

anycast An ATM address that can be shared by more than one end system, allowing requests to be routed to a node that provides a particular service.

AppleTalk Currently in two versions, the group of communication protocols designed by Apple Computer for use in Macintosh environments. The earlier Phase 1 protocols supports one physical network with only one network number that resides in one zone. The later Phase 2 protocols support more than one logical network on a single physical network, allowing networks to exist in more than one zone. *See also: zone.*

Application layer Layer 7 of the OSI reference network model, supplying services to application procedures (such as electronic mail or file transfer) that are outside the OSI model. This layer chooses and determines the availability of communicating partners along with the resources necessary to make the connection, coordinates partnering applications, and forms a consensus on procedures for controlling data integrity and error recovery.

ARA AppleTalk Remote Access: A protocol for Macintosh users establishing their access to resources and data from a remote AppleTalk location.

area A logical, rather than physical, set of segments (based on either CLNS, DECnet, or OSPF) along with their attached devices. Areas are commonly connected to others using routers to create a single autonomous system. *See also: autonomous system.*

ARM Asynchronous Response Mode: An HDLC communication mode using one primary station and at least one additional station, in which transmission can be initiated from either the primary or one of the secondary units.

ARP Address Resolution Protocol: Defined in RFC 826, the protocol that traces IP addresses to MAC addresses. *See also: RARP.*

ASBR Autonomous System Boundary Router: An area border router placed between an OSPF autonomous system and a non-OSPF network that operates both OSPF and an additional routing protocol, such as RIP. ASBRs must be located in a non-stub OSPF area. *See also: ABR, non-stub area,* and *OSPF.*

ASCII American Standard Code for Information Interchange: An 8-bit code for representing characters, consisting of seven data bits plus one parity bit.

ASICs Application-Specific Integrated Circuits: Used in layer-2 switches to make filtering decisions. The ASIC looks in the filter table of MAC addresses and determines which port the destination hardware address of a received hardware address is destined for. The frame will be allowed to traverse only that one segment. If the hardware address is unknown, the frame is forwarded out all ports.

ASN.1 Abstract Syntax Notation One: An OSI language used to describe types of data that is independent of computer structures and depicting methods. Described by ISO International Standard 8824.

ASP AppleTalk Session Protocol: A protocol employing ATP to establish, maintain, and tear down sessions, as well as sequence requests. *See also: ATP.*

AST Automatic Spanning Tree: A function that supplies one path for spanning explorer frames traveling from one node in the network to another, supporting the automatic resolution of spanning trees in SRB networks. AST is based on the IEEE 802.1 standard. *See also: IEEE 802.1 and SRB.*

asynchronous transmission Digital signals sent without precise timing, usually with different frequencies and phase relationships. Asynchronous transmissions generally enclose individual characters in control bits (called start and stop bits) that show the beginning and end of each character. *Contrast with: isochronous transmission and synchronous transmission.*

ATCP AppleTalk Control Program: The protocol for establishing and configuring AppleTalk over PPP, defined in RFC 1378. *See also: PPP.*

ATDM Asynchronous Time-Division Multiplexing: A technique for sending information, it differs from normal TDM in that the time slots are assigned when necessary rather than preassigned to certain transmitters. *Contrast with: FDM, statistical multiplexing, and TDM.*

ATG Address Translation Gateway: The mechanism within Cisco DECnet routing software that enables routers to route multiple, independent DECnet networks and to establish a user-designated address translation for chosen nodes between networks.

ATM   Asynchronous Transfer Mode: The international standard, identified by fixed-length 53-byte cells, for transmitting cells in multiple service systems, such as voice, video, or data. Transit delays are reduced because the fixed-length cells permit processing to occur in the hardware. ATM is designed to maximize the benefits of high-speed transmission media, such as SONET, E3, and T3.

ATM ARP server   A device that supplies logical subnets running classical IP over ATM with address-resolution services.

ATM endpoint   The initiating or terminating connection in an ATM network. ATM endpoints include servers, workstations, ATM-to-LAN switches, and ATM routers.

ATM Forum   The international organization founded jointly by Northern Telecom, Sprint, Cisco Systems, and NET/ADAPTIVE in 1991 to develop and promote standards-based implementation agreements for ATM technology. The ATM Forum broadens official standards developed by ANSI and ITU-T and creates implementation agreements before official standards are published.

ATM layer   A sublayer of the Data Link layer in an ATM network that is service independent. To create standard 53-byte ATM cells, the ATM layer receives 48-byte segments from the AAL and attaches a 5-byte header to each. These cells are then sent to the Physical layer for transmission across the physical medium. *See also: AAL.*

ATMM   ATM Management: A procedure that runs on ATM switches, managing rate enforcement and VCI translation. *See also: ATM.*

ATM user-user connection   A connection made by the ATM layer to supply communication between at least two ATM service users, such as ATMM processes. These communications can be uni- or bidirectional, using one or two VCCs, respectively. *See also: ATM layer and ATMM.*

ATP   AppleTalk Transaction Protocol: A transport-level protocol that enables reliable transactions between two sockets, where one requests the other to perform a given task and to report the results. ATP fastens the request and response together, assuring a loss-free exchange of request-response pairs.

attenuation   In communication, weakening or loss of signal energy, typically caused by distance.

AURP   AppleTalk Update-based Routing Protocol: A technique for encapsulating AppleTalk traffic in the header of a foreign protocol that allows the connection of at least two noncontiguous AppleTalk internetworks through a foreign network (such as TCP/IP) to create an AppleTalk WAN. The connection made is called an AURP tunnel. By exchanging routing information between exterior routers, the AURP maintains routing tables for the complete AppleTalk WAN. *See also: AURP tunnel.*

AURP tunnel   A connection made in an AURP WAN that acts as a single, virtual link between AppleTalk internetworks separated physically by a foreign network such as a TCP/IP network. *See also: AURP.*

authority zone   A portion of the domain-name tree associated with DNS for which one name server is the authority. *See also: DNS.*

auto duplex   A setting on layer-1 and -2 devices that sets the duplex of a switch or hub port automatically.

automatic call reconnect   A function that enables automatic call rerouting away from a failed trunk line.

autonomous confederation   A collection of self-governed systems that depend more on their own network accessibility and routing information than on information received from other systems or groups.

autonomous switching   The ability of Cisco routers to process packets more quickly by using the ciscoBus to switch packets independently of the system processor.

autonomous system (AS)   A group of networks under mutual administration that share the same routing methodology. Autonomous systems are subdivided by areas and must be assigned an individual 16-bit number by the IANA. *See also: area.*

autoreconfiguration   A procedure executed by nodes within the failure domain of a Token Ring, wherein nodes automatically perform diagnostics, trying to reconfigure the network around failed areas.

auxiliary port   The console port on the back of Cisco routers that allows you to dial the router and make console configuration settings.

B8ZS   Binary 8-Zero Substitution: A line-code type, interpreted at the remote end of the connection, that uses a special code substitution whenever eight consecutive zeros are transmitted over the link on T1 and E1 circuits. This technique assures ones density independent of the data stream. Also known as bipolar 8-zero substitution. *Contrast with: AMI. See also: ones density.*

backbone   The basic portion of the network that provides the primary path for traffic sent to and initiated from other networks.

back end   A node or software program supplying services to a front end. *See also: server.*

bandwidth   The gap between the highest and lowest frequencies employed by network signals. More commonly, it refers to the rated throughput capacity of a network protocol or medium.

baseband   A feature of a network technology that uses only one carrier frequency, for example Ethernet. Also named "narrowband." *Compare with: broadband.*

Basic Management Setup   Used with Cisco routers when in setup mode. Only provides enough management and configuration to get the router working so someone can telnet into the router and configure it.

baud   Synonymous with bits per second (bps), if each signal element represents one bit. It is a unit of signaling speed equivalent to the number of separate signal elements transmitted per second.

B channel   Bearer channel: A full-duplex, 64Kbps channel in ISDN that transmits user data. *Compare with: D channel, E channel,* and *H channel.*

beacon   An FDDI device or Token Ring frame that points to a serious problem with the ring, such as a broken cable. The beacon frame carries the address of the station thought to be down. *See also: failure domain.*

BECN   Backward Explicit Congestion Notification: BECN is the bit set by a Frame Relay network in frames moving away from frames headed into a congested path. A DTE that receives frames with the BECN may ask higher-level protocols to take necessary flow control measures. *Compare with: FECN.*

BGP4 BGP Version 4: Version 4 of the interdomain routing protocol most commonly used on the Internet. BGP4 supports CIDR and uses route-counting mechanisms to decrease the size of routing tables. *See also: CIDR.*

binary A two-character numbering method that uses ones and zeros. The binary numbering system underlies all digital representation of information.

BIP Bit Interleaved Parity: A method used in ATM to monitor errors on a link, sending a check bit or word in the link overhead for the previous block or frame. This allows bit errors in transmissions to be found and delivered as maintenance information.

BISDN Broadband ISDN: ITU-T standards created to manage high-bandwidth technologies such as video. BISDN presently employs ATM technology along SONET-based transmission circuits, supplying data rates between 155Mbps and 622Mbps and beyond. Contrast with N-ISDN. *See also: BRI, ISDN,* and *PRI.*

bit-oriented protocol Regardless of frame content, the class of Data-Link layer communication protocols that transmits frames. Bit-oriented protocols, as compared with byte-oriented, supply more efficient and trustworthy, full-duplex operation. *Compare with: byte-oriented protocol.*

Boot ROM Used in routers to put the router into bootstrap mode. Bootstrap mode then boots the device with an operating system. The ROM can also hold a small Cisco IOS.

border gateway A router that facilitates communication with routers in different autonomous systems.

BPDU Bridge Protocol Data Unit: A Spanning-Tree Protocol initializing packet that is sent at definable intervals for the purpose of exchanging information among bridges in networks.

BRI Basic Rate Interface: The ISDN interface that facilitates circuit-switched communication between video, data, and voice; it is made up of two B channels (64Kbps each) and one D channel (16Kbps). *Compare with: PRI. See also: BISDN.*

bridge   A device for connecting two segments of a network and transmitting packets between them. Both segments must use identical protocols to communicate. Bridges function at the Data Link layer, Layer 2 of the OSI reference model. The purpose of a bridge is to filter, send, or flood any incoming frame, based on the MAC address of that particular frame.

broadband   A transmission methodology for multiplexing several independent signals onto one cable. In telecommunications, broadband is classified as any channel with bandwidth greater than 4kHz (typical voice grade). In LAN terminology, it is classified as a coaxial cable on which analog signaling is employed. Also known as wideband. *Contrast with: baseband.*

broadcast   A data frame or packet that is transmitted to every node on the local network segment (as defined by the broadcast domain). Broadcasts are known by their broadcast address, which is a destination network and host address with all the bits turned on. Also called "local broadcast." *Compare with: directed broadcast.*

broadcast domain   A group of devices receiving broadcast frames initiating from any device within the group. Because they do not forward broadcast frames, broadcast domains are generally surrounded by routers.

broadcast storm   An undesired event on the network caused by the simultaneous transmission of any number of broadcasts across the network segment. Such an occurrence can overwhelm network bandwidth, resulting in time-outs.

buffer   A storage area dedicated to handling data while in transit. Buffers are used to receive/store sporadic deliveries of data bursts, usually received from faster devices, compensating for the variations in processing speed. Incoming information is stored until everything is received prior to sending data on. Also known as an information buffer.

bus topology   A linear LAN architecture in which transmissions from various stations on the network are reproduced over the length of the medium and are accepted by all other stations. *Compare with: ring and star.*

bus   Any physical path, typically wires or copper, through which a digital signal can be used to send data from one part of a computer to another.

BUS broadcast and unknown servers: In LAN emulation, the hardware or software responsible for resolving all broadcasts and packets with unknown (unregistered) addresses into the point-to-point virtual circuits required by ATM. *See also: LANE, LEC, LECS,* and *LES.*

BX.25 AT&T's use of X.25. *See also: X.25.*

bypass mode An FDDI and Token Ring network operation that deletes an interface.

bypass relay A device that enables a particular interface in the Token Ring to be closed down and effectively taken off the ring.

byte-oriented protocol Any type of data-link communication protocol that, in order to mark the boundaries of frames, uses a specific character from the user character set. These protocols have generally been superseded by bit-oriented protocols. *Compare with: bit-oriented protocol.*

cable range In an extended AppleTalk network, the range of numbers allotted for use by existing nodes on the network. The value of the cable range can be anywhere from a single to a sequence of several touching network numbers. Node addresses are determined by their cable range value.

CAC Connection Admission Control: The sequence of actions executed by every ATM switch while connection setup is performed in order to determine if a request for connection is violating the guarantees of QoS for established connections. Also, CAC is used to route a connection request through an ATM network.

call admission control A device for managing of traffic in ATM networks, determining the possibility of a path containing adequate bandwidth for a requested VCC.

call priority In circuit-switched systems, the defining priority given to each originating port; it specifies in which order calls will be reconnected. Additionally, call priority identifies which calls are allowed during a bandwidth reservation.

call set-up time The length of time necessary to effect a switched call between DTE devices.

CBR   Constant Bit Rate: An ATM Forum QoS class created for use in ATM networks. CBR is used for connections that rely on precision clocking to guarantee trustworthy delivery. *Compare with: ABR and VBR.*

CD   Carrier Detect: A signal indicating that an interface is active or that a connection generated by a modem has been established.

CDP   Cisco Discovery Protocol: Cisco's proprietary protocol that is used to tell a neighbor Cisco device about the type of hardware, software version, and active interfaces that the Cisco device is using. It uses a SNAP frame between devices and is not routable.

CDVT   Cell Delay Variation Tolerance: A QoS parameter for traffic management in ATM networks specified when a connection is established. The allowable fluctuation levels for data samples taken by the PCR in CBR transmissions are determined by the CDVT. *See also: CBR and PCR.*

cell   In ATM networking, the basic unit of data for switching and multiplexing. Cells have a defined length of 53 bytes, including a 5-byte header that identifies the cell's data stream and 48 bytes of payload. *See also: cell relay.*

cell payload scrambling   The method by which an ATM switch maintains framing on some medium-speed edge and trunk interfaces (T3 or E3 circuits). Cell payload scrambling rearranges the data portion of a cell to maintain the line synchronization with certain common bit patterns.

cell relay   A technology that uses small packets of fixed size, known as cells. Their fixed length enables cells to be processed and switched in hardware at high speeds, making this technology the foundation for ATM and other high-speed network protocols. *See also: cell.*

Centrex   A local exchange carrier service, providing local switching that resembles that of an on-site PBX. Centrex has no on-site switching capability. Therefore, all customer connections return to the CO. *See also: CO.*

CER   Cell Error Ratio: The ratio in ATM of transmitted cells having errors to the total number of cells sent in a transmission within a certain span of time.

channelized E1   Operating at 2.048Mpbs, an access link that is sectioned into 29 B-channels and one D-channel, supporting DDR, Frame Relay, and X.25. *Compare with: channelized T1.*

channelized T1   Operating at 1.544Mbps, an access link that is sectioned into 23 B-channels and 1 D-channel of 64Kbps each, where individual channels or groups of channels connect to various destinations, supporting DDR, Frame Relay, and X.25. *Compare with: channelized E1.*

CHAP   Challenge Handshake Authentication Protocol: Supported on lines using PPP encapsulation, it is a security feature that identifies the remote end, helping keep out unauthorized users. After CHAP is performed, the router or access server determines whether a given user is permitted access. It is a newer, more secure protocol than PAP. *Compare with: PAP.*

checksum   A test for ensuring the integrity of sent data. It is a number calculated from a series of values taken through a sequence of mathematical functions, typically placed at the end of the data from which it is calculated, and then recalculated at the receiving end for verification. *Compare with: CRC.*

choke packet   When congestion exists, it is a packet sent to inform a transmitter that it should decrease its sending rate.

CIDR   Classless Interdomain Routing: A method supported by classless routing protocols, such as OSPF and BGP4, based on the concept of ignoring the IP class of address, permitting route aggregation and VLSM that enable routers to combine routes in order to minimize the routing information that needs to be conveyed by the primary routers. It allows a group of IP networks to appear to other networks as a unified, larger entity. In CIDR, IP addresses and their subnet masks are written as four dotted octets, followed by a forward slash and the numbering of masking bits (a form of subnet notation shorthand). *See also: BGP4.*

CIP   Channel Interface Processor: A channel attachment interface for use in Cisco 7000 series routers that connects a host mainframe to a control unit. This device eliminates the need for an FBP to attach channels.

CIR   Committed Information Rate: Averaged over a minimum span of time and measured in bps, a Frame Relay network's agreed-upon minimum rate of transferring information.

circuit switching   Used with dial-up networks such as PPP and ISDN. Passes data, but needs to set up the connection first—just like making a phone call.

Cisco FRAD   Cisco Frame-Relay Access Device: A Cisco product that supports Cisco IPS Frame Relay SNA services, connecting SDLC devices to Frame Relay without requiring an existing LAN. May be upgraded to a fully functioning multiprotocol router. Can activate conversion from SDLC to Ethernet and Token Ring, but does not support attached LANs. *See also: FRAD.*

CiscoFusion   Cisco's name for the internetworking architecture under which its Cisco IOS operates. It is designed to "fuse" together the capabilities of its disparate collection of acquired routers and switches.

Cisco IOS software   Cisco Internet Operating System software. The kernel of the Cisco line of routers and switches that supplies shared functionality, scalability, and security for all products under its CiscoFusion architecture. *See also: CiscoFusion.*

CiscoView   GUI-based management software for Cisco networking devices, enabling dynamic status, statistics, and comprehensive configuration information. Displays a physical view of the Cisco device chassis and provides device-monitoring functions and fundamental troubleshooting capabilities. May be integrated with a number of SNMP-based network management platforms.

Class A network   Part of the Internet Protocol hierarchical addressing scheme. Class A networks have only 8 bits for defining networks and 24 bits for defining hosts on each network.

Class B network   Part of the Internet Protocol hierarchical addressing scheme. Class B networks have 16 bits for defining networks and 16 bits for defining hosts on each network.

Class C network   Part of the Internet Protocol hierarchical addressing scheme. Class C networks have 24 bits for defining networks and only 8 bits for defining hosts on each network.

classical IP over ATM   Defined in RFC 1577, the specification for running IP over ATM that maximizes ATM features. Also known as CIA.

classless routing   Routing that sends subnet mask information in the routing updates. Classless routing allows Variable-Length Subnet Mask (VLSM) and supernetting. Routing protocols that support classless routing are RIP version 2, EIGRP, and OSPF.

CLI   Command-Line Interface: Allows you to configure Cisco routers and switches with maximum flexibility.

CLP   Cell Loss Priority: The area in the ATM cell header that determines the likelihood of a cell being dropped during network congestion. Cells with CLP = 0 are considered insured traffic and are not apt to be dropped. Cells with CLP = 1 are considered best-effort traffic that may be dropped during congested episodes, delivering more resources to handle insured traffic.

CLR   Cell Loss Ratio: The ratio of discarded cells to successfully delivered cells in ATM. CLR can be designated a QoS parameter when establishing a connection.

CO   Central Office: The local telephone company office where all loops in a certain area connect and where circuit switching of subscriber lines occurs.

collapsed backbone   A nondistributed backbone where all network segments are connected to each other through an internetworking device. A collapsed backbone can be a virtual network segment at work in a device such as a router, hub, or switch.

collision   The effect of two nodes sending transmissions simultaneously in Ethernet. When they meet on the physical media, the frames from each node collide and are damaged. *See also: collision domain.*

collision domain   The network area in Ethernet over which frames that have collided will spread. Collisions are propagated by hubs and repeaters, but not by LAN switches, routers, or bridges. *See also: collision.*

composite metric   Used with routing protocols, such as IGRP and EIGRP, that use more than one metric to find the best path to a remote network. IGRP and EIGRP both use bandwidth and delay of the line by default. However, Maximum Transmission Unit (MTU), load, and reliability of a link can be used as well.

configuration register   A 16-bit configurable value stored in hardware or software that determines how Cisco routers function during initialization. In hardware, the bit position is set using a jumper. In software, it is set by specifying specific bit patterns used to set startup options, configured using a hexadecimal value with configuration commands.

congestion   Traffic that exceeds the network's ability to handle it.

congestion avoidance   To minimize delays, the method an ATM network uses to control traffic entering the system. Lower-priority traffic is discarded at the edge of the network when indicators signal it cannot be delivered, thus using resources efficiently.

congestion collapse   The situation that results from the retransmission of packets in ATM networks where little or no traffic successfully arrives at destination points. It usually happens in networks made of switches with ineffective or inadequate buffering capabilities combined with poor packet discard or ABR congestion feedback mechanisms.

connection ID   Identifications given to each Telnet session into a router. The `show sessions` command will give you the connections a local router will have to a remote router. The `show users` command will show the connection IDs of users telnetted into your local router.

connectionless   Data transfer that occurs without the creating of a virtual circuit. No overhead, best-effort delivery, not reliable. *Contrast with: connection-oriented. See also: virtual circuit.*

connection-oriented   Data transfer method that sets up a virtual circuit before any data is transferred. Uses acknowledgments and flow control for reliable data transfer. *Contrast with: connectionless. See also: virtual circuit.*

console port   Typically an RJ-45 port on a Cisco router and switch that allows Command-Line Interface capability.

control direct VCC   One of three control connections defined by Phase I LAN Emulation; a bi-directional virtual control connection (VCC) established in ATM by an LEC to an LES. *See also: control distribute VCC.*

control distribute VCC   One of three control connections defined by Phase 1 LAN Emulation; a unidirectional virtual control connection (VCC) set up in ATM from an LES to an LEC. Usually, the VCC is a point-to-multipoint connection. *See also: control direct VCC.*

convergence   The process required for all routers in an internetwork to update their routing tables and create a consistent view of the network, using the best possible paths. No user data is passed during a convergence time.

core layer   Top layer in the Cisco three-layer hierarchical model, which helps you design, build, and maintain Cisco hierarchical networks. The core layer passes packets quickly to distribution-layer devices only. No packet filtering should take place at this layer.

cost   Also known as path cost, an arbitrary value, based on hop count, bandwidth, or other calculation, that is typically assigned by a network administrator and used by the routing protocol to compare different routes through an internetwork. Routing protocols use cost values to select the best path to a certain destination: the lowest cost identifies the best path. Also known as path cost. *See also: routing metric.*

count to infinity   A problem occurring in routing algorithms that are slow to converge where routers keep increasing the hop count to particular networks. To avoid this problem, various solutions have been implemented into each of the different routing protocols. Some of those solutions include defining a maximum hop count (defining infinity), route poising, poison reverse, and split horizon.

CPCS   Common Part Convergence Sublayer: One of two AAL sublayers that is service-dependent, it is further segmented into the CS and SAR sublayers. The CPCS prepares data for transmission across the ATM network; it creates the 48-byte payload cells that are sent to the ATM layer. *See also: AAL and ATM layer.*

CPE   Customer Premises Equipment: Items such as telephones, modems, and terminals installed at customer locations and connected to the telephone company network.

crankback   In ATM, a correction technique used when a node somewhere on a chosen path cannot accept a connection setup request, blocking the request. The path is rolled back to an intermediate node, which then uses GCAC to attempt to find an alternate path to the final destination.

CRC   Cyclical Redundancy Check: A methodology that detects errors, whereby the frame recipient makes a calculation by dividing frame contents with a prime binary divisor and compares the remainder to a value stored in the frame by the sending node. *Contrast with: checksum.*

CSMA/CD   Carrier Sense Multiple Access Collision Detect: A technology defined by the Ethernet IEEE 802.3 committee. Each device senses the cable for a digital signal before transmitting. Also, CSMA/CD allows all devices on the network to share the same cable, but one at a time. If two devices transmit at the same time, a frame collision will occur and a jamming pattern will be sent; the devices will stop transmitting, wait a predetermined amount of time, and then try to transmit again.

CSU   Channel Service Unit: A digital mechanism that connects end-user equipment to the local digital telephone loop. Frequently referred to along with the data service unit as CSU/DSU. *See also: DSU.*

CTD   Cell Transfer Delay: For a given connection in ATM, the time period between a cell exit event at the source user-network interface (UNI) and the corresponding cell entry event at the destination. The CTD between these points is the sum of the total inter-ATM transmission delay and the total ATM processing delay.

cut-through frame switching   A frame-switching technique that flows data through a switch so that the leading edge exits the switch at the output port before the packet finishes entering the input port. Frames will be read, processed, and forwarded by devices that use cut-through switching as soon as the destination address of the frame is confirmed and the outgoing port is identified.

data direct VCC   A bidirectional point-to-point virtual control connection (VCC) set up between two LECs in ATM and one of three data connections defined by Phase 1 LAN Emulation. Because data direct VCCs do not guarantee QoS, they are generally reserved for UBR and ABR connections. *Compare with: control distribute VCC and control direct VCC.*

data frame   Protocol Data Unit encapsulation at the Data Link layer of the OSI reference model. Encapsulates packets from the Network layer and prepares the data for transmission on a network medium.

datagram   A logical collection of information transmitted as a Network layer unit over a medium without a previously established virtual circuit. IP datagrams have become the primary information unit of the Internet. At various layers of the OSI reference model, the terms *cell, frame, message, packet,* and *segment* also define these logical information groupings.

Data Link control layer   Layer 2 of the SNA architectural model, it is responsible for the transmission of data over a given physical link and compares somewhat to the Data Link layer of the OSI model.

Data Link layer   Layer 2 of the OSI reference model, it ensures the trustworthy transmission of data across a physical link and is primarily concerned with physical addressing, line discipline, network topology, error notification, ordered delivery of frames, and flow control. The IEEE has further segmented this layer into the MAC sublayer and the LLC sublayer. Also known as the Link layer. Can be compared somewhat to the Data Link control layer of the SNA model. *See also: Application layer, LLC, MAC, Network layer, Physical layer, Presentation layer, Session layer,* and *Transport layer.*

DCC   Data Country Code: Developed by the ATM Forum, one of two ATM address formats designed for use by private networks. *Compare with: ICD.*

DCE   data communications equipment (as defined by the EIA) or data circuit-terminating equipment (as defined by the ITU-T): The mechanisms and links of a communications network that make up the network portion of the user-to-network interface, such as modems. The DCE supplies the physical connection to the network, forwards traffic, and provides a clocking signal to synchronize data transmission between DTE and DCE devices. *Compare with: DTE.*

D channel   1) Data channel: A full-duplex, 16Kbps (BRI) or 64Kbps (PRI) ISDN channel. *Compare with: B channel, E channel,* and *H channel.* 2) In SNA, anything that provides a connection between the processor and main storage with any peripherals.

DDP   Datagram Delivery Protocol: Used in the AppleTalk suite of protocols as a connectionless protocol that is responsible for sending datagrams through an internetwork.

DDR   dial-on-demand routing: A technique that allows a router to automatically initiate and end a circuit-switched session per the requirements of the sending station. By mimicking keepalives, the router fools the end station into treating the session as active. DDR permits routing over ISDN or telephone lines via a modem or external ISDN terminal adapter.

DE   Discard Eligibility: Used in Frame Relay networks to tell a switch that a frame can be discarded if the switch is too busy. The DE is a field in the frame that is turned on by transmitting routers if the Committed Information Rate (CIR) is oversubscribed or set to 0.

default route   The static routing table entry used to direct frames whose next hop is not spelled out in the dynamic routing table.

delay   The time elapsed between a sender's initiation of a transaction and the first response they receive. Also, the time needed to move a packet from its source to its destination over a path. *See also: latency.*

demarc   The demarcation point between the customer premises equipment (CPE) and the telco's carrier equipment.

demodulation   A series of steps that return a modulated signal to its original form. When receiving, a modem demodulates an analog signal to its original digital form (and, conversely, modulates the digital data it sends into an analog signal). *See also: modulation.*

demultiplexing   The process of converting a single multiplex signal, comprising more than one input stream, back into separate output streams. *See also: multiplexing.*

designated bridge   In the process of forwarding a frame from a segment to the route bridge, the bridge with the lowest path cost.

designated port   Used with the Spanning-Tree Protocol (STP) to designate forwarding ports. If there are multiple links to the same network, STP will shut a port down to stop network loops.

designated router   An OSPF router that creates LSAs for a multiaccess network and is required to perform other special tasks in OSPF operations. Multiaccess OSPF networks that maintain a minimum of two attached routers identify one router that is chosen by the OSPF Hello protocol, which makes possible a decrease in the number of adjacencies necessary on a multiaccess network. This in turn reduces the quantity of routing protocol traffic and the physical size of the database.

destination address   The address for the network devices that will receive a packet.

directed broadcast   A data frame or packet that is transmitted to a specific group of nodes on a remote network segment. Directed broadcasts are known by their broadcast address, which is a destination subnet address with all the bits turned on.

discovery mode   Also known as dynamic configuration, this technique is used by an AppleTalk interface to gain information from a working node about an attached network. The information is subsequently used by the interface for self-configuration.

distance-vector routing algorithm   In order to find the shortest path, this group of routing algorithms repeats on the number of hops in a given route, requiring each router to send its complete routing table with each update, but only to its neighbors. Routing algorithms of this type tend to generate loops, but they are fundamentally simpler than their link-state counterparts. *See also: link-state routing algorithm* and *SPF.*

distribution layer   Middle layer of the Cisco three-layer hierarchical model, which helps you design, install, and maintain Cisco hierarchical networks. The distribution layer is the point where access layer devices connect. Routing is performed at this layer.

DLCI   Data-Link Connection Identifier: Used to identify virtual circuits in a Frame Relay network.

DNS   Domain Name System: Used to resolve host names to IP addresses.

DSAP   Destination Service Access Point: The service access point of a network node, specified in the destination field of a packet. *See also: SSAP* and *SAP.*

DSR Data Set Ready: When a DCE is powered up and ready to run, this EIA/TIA-232 interface circuit is also engaged.

DSU Data Service Unit: This device is used to adapt the physical interface on a data terminal equipment (DTE) mechanism to a transmission facility such as T1 or E1 and is also responsible for signal timing. It is commonly grouped with the channel service unit and referred to as the CSU/DSU. *See also: CSU.*

DTE data terminal equipment: Any device located at the user end of a user-network interface serving as a destination, a source, or both. DTE includes devices such as multiplexers, protocol translators, and computers. The connection to a data network is made through data channel equipment (DCE) such as a modem, using the clocking signals generated by that device. *See also: DCE.*

DTR data terminal ready: An activated EIA/TIA-232 circuit communicating to the DCE the state of preparedness of the DTE to transmit or receive data.

DUAL Diffusing Update Algorithm: Used in Enhanced IGRP, this convergence algorithm provides loop-free operation throughout an entire route's computation. DUAL grants routers involved in a topology revision the ability to synchronize simultaneously, while routers unaffected by this change are not involved. *See also: Enhanced IGRP.*

DVMRP Distance Vector Multicast Routing Protocol: Based primarily on the Routing Information Protocol (RIP), this Internet gateway protocol implements a common, condensed-mode IP multicast scheme, using IGMP to transfer routing datagrams between its neighbors. *See also: IGMP.*

DXI Data Exchange Interface: Described in RFC 1482, DXI defines the effectiveness of a network device such as a router, bridge, or hub to act as an FEP to an ATM network by using a special DSU that accomplishes packet encapsulation.

dynamic entries Used in layer-2 and -3 devices to create a table of either hardware addresses or logical addresses dynamically.

dynamic routing Also known as adaptive routing, this technique automatically adapts to traffic or physical network revisions.

dynamic VLAN   An administrator will create an entry in a special server with the hardware addresses of all devices on the internetwork. The server will then assign dynamically used VLANs.

E1   Generally used in Europe, a wide-area digital transmission scheme carrying data at 2.048Mbps. E1 transmission lines are available for lease from common carriers for private use.

E.164   1) Evolved from standard telephone numbering system, the standard recommended by ITU-T for international telecommunication numbering, particularly in ISDN, SMDS, and BISDN. 2) Label of field in an ATM address containing numbers in E.164 format.

E channel   Echo channel: A 64Kbps ISDN control channel used for circuit switching. Specific description of this channel can be found in the 1984 ITU-T ISDN specification, but was dropped from the 1988 version. *See also: B, D,* and *H channels.*

edge device   A device that enables packets to be forwarded between legacy interfaces (such as Ethernet and Token Ring) and ATM interfaces based on information in the data link and Network layers. An edge device does not take part in the running of any Network layer routing protocol; it merely uses the route description protocol in order to get the forwarding information required.

EEPROM   Electronically Erasable Programmable Read-Only Memory: Programmed after their manufacture, these nonvolatile memory chips can be erased if necessary using electric power and reprogrammed. *See also: EPROM, PROM.*

EFCI   Explicit Forward Congestion Indication: A congestion feedback mode permitted by ABR service in an ATM network. The EFCI may be set by any network element that is in a state of immediate or certain congestion. The destination end-system is able to carry out a protocol that adjusts and lowers the cell rate of the connection based on value of the EFCI. *See also: ABR.*

EIGRP   *See: Enhanced IGRP.*

EIP   Ethernet Interface Processor: A Cisco 7000 series router interface processor card, supplying 10Mbps AUI ports to support Ethernet Version 1 and Ethernet Version 2 or IEEE 802.3 interfaces with a high-spced data path to other interface processors.

ELAN   Emulated LAN: An ATM network configured using a client/server model in order to emulate either an Ethernet or Token Ring LAN. Multiple ELANs can exist at the same time on a single ATM network and are made up of an LAN emulation client (LEC), an LAN Emulation Server (LES), a Broadcast and Unknown Server (BUS), and an LAN Emulation Configuration Server (LECS). ELANs are defined by the LANE specification. *See also: LANE, LEC, LECS,* and *LES.*

ELAP   EtherTalk Link Access Protocol: In an EtherTalk network, the link-access protocol constructed above the standard Ethernet Data Link layer.

encapsulation   The technique used by layered protocols in which a layer adds header information to the protocol data unit (PDU) from the layer above. As an example, in Internet terminology, a packet would contain a header from the Physical layer, followed by a header from the Network layer (IP), followed by a header from the Transport layer (TCP), followed by the application protocol data.

encryption   The conversion of information into a scrambled form that effectively disguises it to prevent unauthorized access. Every encryption scheme uses some well-defined algorithm, which is reversed at the receiving end by an opposite algorithm in a process known as decryption.

Enhanced IGRP   Enhanced Interior Gateway Routing Protocol: An advanced routing protocol created by Cisco, combining the advantages of link-state and distance-vector protocols. Enhanced IGRP has superior convergence attributes, including high operating efficiency. *See also: IGP, OSPF,* and *RIP.*

enterprise network   A privately owned and operated network that joins most major locations in a large company or organization.

EPROM   Erasable Programmable Read-Only Memory: Programmed after their manufacture, these nonvolatile memory chips can be erased if necessary using high-power light and reprogrammed. *See also: EEPROM, PROM.*

ESF   Extended Superframe: Made up of 24 frames with 192 bits each, with the 193rd bit providing other functions including timing. This is an enhanced version of SF. *See also: SF.*

Ethernet   A baseband LAN specification created by the Xerox Corporation and then improved through joint efforts of Xerox, Digital Equipment Corporation, and Intel. Ethernet is similar to the IEEE 802.3 series standard and, using CSMA/CD, operates over various types of cables at 10Mbps. *Also called: DIX (Digital/Intel/Xerox) Ethernet. See also: 10BaseT, Fast Ethernet, and IEEE.*

EtherTalk   A data-link product from Apple Computer that permits Apple-Talk networks to be connected by Ethernet.

excess rate   In ATM networking, traffic exceeding a connection's insured rate. The excess rate is the maximum rate less the insured rate. Depending on the availability of network resources, excess traffic can be discarded during congestion episodes. *Compare with: maximum rate.*

expansion   The procedure of directing compressed data through an algorithm, restoring information to its original size.

expedited delivery   An option that can be specified by one protocol layer, communicating either with other layers or with the identical protocol layer in a different network device, requiring that identified data be processed faster.

explorer packet   An SNA packet transmitted by a source Token Ring device to find the path through a source-route-bridged network.

extended IP access list   IP access list that filters the network by logical address, protocol field in the Network layer header, and even the port field in the Transport layer header.

extended IPX access list   IPX access list that filters the network by logical IPX address, protocol field in the Network layer header, or even socket number in the Transport layer header.

Extended Setup   Used in setup mode to configure the router with more detail than Basic Setup mode. Allows multiple-protocol support and interface configuration.

failure domain   The region in which a failure has occurred in a Token Ring. When a station gains information that a serious problem, such as a cable break, has occurred with the network, it sends a beacon frame that includes the station reporting the failure, its NAUN, and everything between. This defines the failure domain. Beaconing then initiates the procedure known as autoreconfiguration. *See also: autoreconfiguration* and *beacon.*

fallback   In ATM networks, this mechanism is used for scouting a path if it isn't possible to locate one using customary methods. The device relaxes requirements for certain characteristics, such as delay, in an attempt to find a path that meets a certain set of the most important requirements.

Fast Ethernet   Any Ethernet specification with a speed of 100Mbps. Fast Ethernet is ten times faster than 10BaseT, while retaining qualities like MAC mechanisms, MTU, and frame format. These similarities make it possible for existing 10BaseT applications and management tools to be used on Fast Ethernet networks. Fast Ethernet is based on an extension of IEEE 802.3 specification (IEEE 802.3u). *Compare with: Ethernet. See also: 100BaseT, 100BaseTX,* and *IEEE.*

fast switching   A Cisco feature that uses a route cache to speed packet switching through a router. *Contrast with: process switching.*

FDM   Frequency-Division Multiplexing: A technique that permits information from several channels to be assigned bandwidth on one wire based on frequency. *See also: TDM, ATDM,* and *statistical multiplexing.*

FDDI   Fiber Distributed Data Interface: An LAN standard, defined by ANSI X3T9.5 that can run at speeds up to 200Mbps and uses token-passing media access on fiber-optic cable. For redundancy, FDDI can use a dual-ring architecture.

FECN   Forward Explicit Congestion Notification: A bit set by a Frame Relay network that informs the DTE receptor that congestion was encountered along the path from source to destination. A device receiving frames with the FECN bit set can ask higher-priority protocols to take flow-control action as needed. *See also: BECN.*

FEIP   Fast Ethernet Interface Processor: An interface processor employed on Cisco 7000 series routers, supporting up to two 100Mbps 100BaseT ports.

firewall   A barrier purposefully erected between any connected public networks and a private network, made up of a router or access server or several routers or access servers, that uses access lists and other methods to ensure the security of the private network.

Flash   Electronically Erasable Programmable Read-Only Memory (EEPROM). Used to hold the Cisco IOS in a router by default.

flash memory   Developed by Intel and licensed to other semiconductor manufacturers, it is nonvolatile storage that can be erased electronically and reprogrammed, physically located on an EEPROM chip. Flash memory permits software images to be stored, booted, and rewritten as needed. Cisco routers and switches use flash memory to hold the IOS by default. *See also: EPROM, EEPROM.*

flat network   Network that is one large collision domain and one large broadcast domain.

flooding   When traffic is received on an interface, it is then transmitted to every interface connected to that device with exception of the interface from which the traffic originated. This technique can be used for traffic transfer by bridges and switches throughout the network.

flow control   A methodology used to ensure that receiving units are not overwhelmed with data from sending devices. Pacing, as it is called in IBM networks, means that when buffers at a receiving unit are full, a message is transmitted to the sending unit to temporarily halt transmissions until all the data in the receiving buffer has been processed and the buffer is again ready for action.

FRAD   Frame Relay Access Device: Any device affording a connection between a LAN and a Frame Relay WAN. *See also: Cisco FRAD, FRAS.*

fragment   Any portion of a larger packet that has been intentionally segmented into smaller pieces. A packet fragment does not necessarily indicate an error and can be intentional. *See also: fragmentation.*

fragmentation   The process of intentionally segmenting a packet into smaller pieces when sending data over an intermediate network medium that cannot support the larger packet size.

FragmentFree LAN switch type that reads into the data section of a frame to make sure fragmentation did not occur. Sometimes called modified cut-through.

frame A logical unit of information sent by the Data Link layer over a transmission medium. The term often refers to the header and trailer, employed for synchronization and error control, that surround the data contained in the unit.

Frame Relay A more efficient replacement of the X.25 protocol (an unrelated packet relay technology that guarantees data delivery). Frame Relay is an industry-standard, shared-access, best-effort, switched Data-Link layer encapsulation that services multiple virtual circuits and protocols between connected mechanisms.

Frame Relay bridging Defined in RFC 1490, this bridging method uses the identical spanning–tree algorithm as other bridging operations but permits packets to be encapsulated for transmission across a Frame Relay network.

framing Encapsulation at the Data Link layer of the OSI model. It is called framing because the packet is encapsulated with both a header and a trailer.

FRAS Frame Relay Access Support: A feature of Cisco IOS software that enables SDLC, Ethernet, Token Ring, and Frame Relay-attached IBM devices to be linked with other IBM mechanisms on a Frame Relay network. *See also: FRAD.*

frequency The number of cycles of an alternating current signal per time unit, measured in hertz (cycles per second).

FSIP Fast Serial Interface Processor: The Cisco 7000 routers' default serial interface processor, it provides four or eight high-speed serial ports.

FTP File Transfer Protocol: The TCP/IP protocol used for transmitting files between network nodes, it supports a broad range of file types and is defined in RFC 959. *See also: TFTP.*

full duplex The capacity to transmit information between a sending station and a receiving unit at the same time. *See also: half duplex.*

full mesh   A type of network topology where every node has either a physical or a virtual circuit linking it to every other network node. A full mesh supplies a great deal of redundancy but is typically reserved for network backbones because of its expense. *See also: partial mesh.*

GNS   Get Nearest Server: On an IPX network, a request packet sent by a customer for determining the location of the nearest active server of a given type. An IPX network client launches a GNS request to get either a direct answer from a connected server or a response from a router disclosing the location of the service on the internetwork to the GNS. GNS is part of IPX and SAP. *See also: IPX and SAP.*

GRE   Generic Routing Encapsulation: A tunneling protocol created by Cisco with the capacity for encapsulating a wide variety of protocol packet types inside IP tunnels, thereby generating a virtual point-to-point connection to Cisco routers across an IP network at remote points. IP tunneling using GRE permits network expansion across a single-protocol backbone environment by linking multiprotocol subnetworks in a single-protocol backbone environment.

guard band   The unused frequency area found between two communications channels, furnishing the space necessary to avoid interference between the two.

half duplex   The capacity to transfer data in only one direction at a time between a sending unit and receiving unit. *See also: full duplex.*

handshake   Any series of transmissions exchanged between two or more devices on a network to ensure synchronized operations.

H channel   High-speed channel: A full-duplex, ISDN primary rate channel operating at a speed of 384Kbps. *See also: B, D, and E channels.*

HDLC   High-Level Data Link Control: Using frame characters, including checksums, HDLC designates a method for data encapsulation on synchronous serial links and is the default encapsulation for Cisco routers. HDLC is a bit-oriented synchronous Data-Link layer protocol created by ISO and derived from SDLC. However, most HDLC vendor implementations (including Cisco's) are proprietary. *See also: SDLC.*

helper address   The unicast address specified, which instructs the Cisco router to change the client's local broadcast request for a service into a directed unicast to the server.

hierarchical addressing   Any addressing plan employing a logical chain of commands to determine location. IP addresses are made up of a hierarchy of network numbers, subnet numbers, and host numbers to direct packets to the appropriate destination.

HIP   HSSI Interface Processor: An interface processor used on Cisco 7000 series routers, providing one HSSI port that supports connections to ATM, SMDS, Frame Relay, or private lines at speeds up to T3 or E3.

holddown   The state a route is placed in so that routers can neither advertise the route nor accept advertisements about it for a defined time period. Holddown is used to surface bad information about a route from all routers in the network. A route is generally placed in holddown when one of its links fails.

hop   The movement of a packet between any two network nodes. *See also: hop count.*

hop count   A routing metric that calculates the distance between a source and a destination. RIP employs hop count as its sole metric. *See also: hop* and *RIP.*

host address   Logical address configured by an administrator or server on a device. Logically identifies this device on an internetwork.

HSCI   High-Speed Communication Interface: Developed by Cisco, a single-port interface that provides full-duplex synchronous serial communications capability at speeds up to 52Mbps.

HSRP   Hot Standby Router Protocol: A protocol that provides high network availability and provides nearly instantaneous hardware fail-over without administrator intervention. It generates a Hot Standby router group, including a lead router that lends its services to any packet being transferred to the Hot Standby address. If the lead router fails, it will be replaced by any of the other routers—the standby routers—that monitor it.

HSSI   High-Speed Serial Interface: A network standard physical connector for high-speed serial linking over a WAN at speeds of up to 52Mbps.

hubs Physical-layer devices that are really just multiple port repeaters. When an electronic digital signal is received on a port, the signal is reamplified or regenerated and forwarded out all segments except the segment from which the signal was received.

ICD International Code Designator: Adapted from the subnetwork model of addressing, this assigns the mapping of Network layer addresses to ATM addresses. HSSI is one of two ATM formats for addressing created by the ATM Forum to be utilized with private networks. *See also: DCC.*

ICMP Internet Control Message Protocol: Documented in RFC 792, it is a Network layer Internet protocol for the purpose of reporting errors and providing information pertinent to IP packet procedures.

IEEE Institute of Electrical and Electronics Engineers: A professional organization that, among other activities, defines standards in a number of fields within computing and electronics, including networking and communications. IEEE standards are the predominant LAN standards used today throughout the industry. Many protocols are commonly known by the reference number of the corresponding IEEE standard.

IEEE 802.1 The IEEE committee specification that defines the bridging group. The specification for STP (Spanning-Tree Protocol) is IEEE 802.1d. The STP uses SPA (spanning-tree algorithm) to find and prevent network loops in bridged networks. The specification for VLAN trunking is IEEE 802.1q.

IEEE 802.3 The IEEE committee specification that defines the Ethernet group, specifically the original 10Mbps standard. Ethernet is a LAN protocol that specifies Physical layer and MAC sublayer media access. IEEE 802.3 uses CSMA/CD to provide access for many devices on the same network. FastEthernet is defined as 802.3u, and Gigabit Ethernet is defined as 802.3q. *See also: CSMA/CD.*

IEEE 802.5 IEEE committee that defines Token Ring media access.

IGMP Internet Group Management Protocol: Employed by IP hosts, the protocol that reports their multicast group memberships to an adjacent multicast router.

IGP   Interior Gateway Protocol: Any protocol used by the Internet to exchange routing data within an independent system. Examples include RIP, IGRP, and OSPF.

ILMI   Integrated (or Interim) Local Management Interface. A specification created by the ATM Forum, designated for the incorporation of network-management capability into the ATM UNI. Integrated Local Management Interface cells provide for automatic configuration between ATM systems. In LAN emulation, ILMI can provide sufficient information for the ATM end station to find an LECS. In addition, ILMI provides the ATM NSAP (Network Service Access Point) prefix information to the end station.

in-band management   In-band management is the management of a network device "through" the network. Examples include using Simple Network Management Protocol (SNMP) or Telnet directly via the local LAN. *Compare with: out-of-band management.*

insured burst   In an ATM network, it is the largest, temporarily permitted data burst exceeding the insured rate on a PVC and not tagged by the traffic policing function for being dropped if network congestion occurs. This insured burst is designated in bytes or cells.

interarea routing   Routing between two or more logical areas. *Contrast with: intra-area routing. See also: area.*

interface processor   Any of several processor modules used with Cisco 7000 series routers. *See also: AIP, CIP, EIP, FEIP, HIP, MIP, and TRIP.*

Internet   The global "network of networks," whose popularity has exploded in the last few years. Originally a tool for collaborative academic research, it has become a medium for exchanging and distributing information of all kinds. The Internet's need to link disparate computer platforms and technologies has led to the development of uniform protocols and standards that have also found widespread use within corporate LANs. *See also: TCP/IP and MBONE.*

internet   Before the rise of the Internet, this lowercase form was shorthand for "internetwork" in the generic sense. Now rarely used. *See also: internetwork.*

Internet protocol   Any protocol belonging to the TCP/IP protocol stack. *See also: TCP/IP.*

internetwork   Any group of private networks interconnected by routers and other mechanisms, typically operating as a single entity.

internetworking   Broadly, anything associated with the general task of linking networks to each other. The term encompasses technologies, procedures, and products. When you connect networks to a router, you are creating an internetwork.

intra-area routing   Routing that occurs within a logical area. *Contrast with: interarea routing.*

Inverse ARP   Inverse Address Resolution Protocol: A technique by which dynamic mappings are constructed in a network, allowing a device such as a router to locate the logical network address and associate it with a permanent virtual circuit (PVC). Commonly used in Frame Relay to determine the far-end node's TCP/IP address by sending the Inverse ARP request to the local DLCI.

IP   Internet Protocol: Defined in RFC 791, it is a Network layer protocol that is part of the TCP/IP stack and allows connectionless service. IP furnishes an array of features for addressing, type-of-service specification, fragmentation and reassembly, and security.

IP address   Often called an Internet address, this is an address uniquely identifying any device (host) on the Internet (or any TCP/IP network). Each address consists of four octets (32 bits), represented as decimal numbers separated by periods (a format known as "dotted-decimal"). Every address is made up of a network number, an optional subnetwork number, and a host number. The network and subnetwork numbers together are used for routing, while the host number addresses an individual host within the network or subnetwork. The network and subnetwork information is extracted from the IP address using the subnet mask. There are five classes of IP addresses (A–E), which allocate different numbers of bits to the network, subnetwork, and host portions of the address. *See also: CIDR, IP,* and *subnet mask.*

IPCP   IP Control Program: The protocol used to establish and configure IP over PPP. *See also: IP* and *PPP.*

IP multicast   A technique for routing that enables IP traffic to be reproduced from one source to several endpoints or from multiple sources to many destinations. Instead of transmitting only one packet to each individual point of destination, one packet is sent to a multicast group specified by only one IP endpoint address for the group.

IPX   Internetwork Packet Exchange: Network layer protocol (Layer 3) used in Novell NetWare networks for transferring information from servers to workstations. Similar to IP and XNS.

IPXCP   IPX Control Program: The protocol used to establish and configure IPX over PPP. *See also: IPX and PPP.*

IPXWAN   Protocol used for new WAN links to provide and negotiate line options on the link using IPX. After the link is up and the options have been agreed upon by the two end-to-end links, normal IPX transmission begins.

ISDN   Integrated Services Digital Network: Offered as a service by telephone companies, a communication protocol that allows telephone networks to carry data, voice, and other digital traffic. *See also: BISDN, BRI, and PRI.*

ISL routing   Inter-Switch Link routing is a Cisco proprietary method of frame tagging in a switched internetwork. Frame tagging is a way to identify the VLAN membership of a frame as it traverses a switched internetwork.

isochronous transmission   Asynchronous data transfer over a synchronous data link, requiring a constant bit rate for reliable transport. *Compare with: asynchronous transmission and synchronous transmission.*

ITU-T   International Telecommunication Union Telecommunication Standardization Sector: This is a group of engineers that develops worldwide standards for telecommunications technologies.

LAN   Local Area Network: Broadly, any network linking two or more computers and related devices within a limited geographical area (up to a few kilometers). LANs are typically high-speed, low-error networks within a company. Cabling and signaling at the Physical and Data Link layers of the OSI are dictated by LAN standards. Ethernet, FDDI, and Token Ring are among the most popular LAN technologies. *Compare with: MAN.*

LANE LAN emulation: The technology that allows an ATM network to operate as a LAN backbone. To do so, the ATM network is required to provide multicast and broadcast support, address mapping (MAC-to-ATM), SVC management, in addition to an operable packet format. Additionally, LANE defines Ethernet and Token Ring ELANs. *See also: ELAN.*

LAN switch A high-speed, multiple-interface transparent bridging mechanism, transmitting packets between segments of data links, usually referred to specifically as an Ethernet switch. LAN switches transfer traffic based on MAC addresses. Multilayer switches are a type of high-speed, special-purpose, hardware-based router. *See also: multilayer switch,* and *store-and-forward packet switching.*

LAPB Link Accessed Procedure, Balanced: A bit-oriented Data-Link layer protocol that is part of the X.25 stack and has its origin in SDLC. *See also: SDLC* and *X.25.*

LAPD Link Access Procedure on the D channel. The ISDN Data-Link layer protocol used specifically for the D channel and defined by ITU-T Recommendations Q.920 and Q.921. LAPD evolved from LAPB and is created to comply with the signaling requirements of ISDN basic access.

latency Broadly, the time it takes a data packet to get from one location to another. In specific networking contexts, it can mean either 1) the time elapsed (delay) between the execution of a request for access to a network by a device and the time the mechanism actually is permitted transmission, or 2) the time elapsed between when a mechanism receives a frame and the time that frame is forwarded out of the destination port.

Layer-3 switch *See also: multilayer switch.*

layered architecture Industry standard way of creating applications to work on a network. Layered architecture allows the application developer to make changes in only one layer instead of the whole program.

LCP Link Control Protocol: The protocol designed to establish, configure, and test data link connections for use by PPP. *See also: PPP.*

leaky bucket An analogy for the basic cell rate algorithm (GCRA) used in ATM networks for checking the conformance of cell flows from a user or network. The bucket's "hole" is understood to be the prolonged rate at which cells can be accommodated, and the "depth" is the tolerance for cell bursts over a certain time period.

learning bridge A bridge that transparently builds a dynamic database of MAC addresses and the interfaces associated with each address. Transparent bridges help to reduce traffic congestion on the network.

LE ARP LAN Emulation Address Resolution Protocol: The protocol providing the ATM address that corresponds to a MAC address.

leased lines Permanent connections between two points leased from the telephone companies.

LEC LAN Emulation Client: Software providing the emulation of the Link layer interface that allows the operation and communication of all higher-level protocols and applications to continue. The LEC client runs in all ATM devices, which include hosts, servers, bridges, and routers. The LANE client is responsible for address resolution, data transfer, address caching, interfacing to the emulated LAN, and driver support for higher-level services. *See also: ELAN and LES.*

LECS LAN Emulation Configuration Server: An important part of emulated LAN services, providing the configuration data that is furnished upon request from the LES. These services include address registration for Integrated Local Management Interface (ILMI) support, configuration support for the LES addresses and their corresponding emulated LAN identifiers, and an interface to the emulated LAN. *See also: LES and ELAN.*

LES LAN Emulation Server: The central LANE component that provides the initial configuration data for each connecting LEC. The LES typically is located on either an ATM-integrated router or a switch. Responsibilities of the LES include configuration and support for the LEC, address registration for the LEC, database storage and response concerning ATM addresses, and interfacing to the emulated LAN *See also: ELAN, LEC,* and *LECS.*

link-state routing algorithm A routing algorithm that allows each router to broadcast or multicast information regarding the cost of reaching all its neighbors to every node in the internetwork. Link-state algorithms provide a consistent view of the network and are therefore not vulnerable to routing loops. However, this is achieved at the cost of somewhat greater difficulty in computation and more widespread traffic (compared with distance-vector routing algorithms). *See also: distance-vector routing algorithm.*

LLAP LocalTalk Link Access Protocol: In a LocalTalk environment, the data link-level protocol that manages node-to-node delivery of data. This protocol provides node addressing and management of bus access, and it also controls data sending and receiving to assure packet length and integrity.

LLC Logical Link Control: Defined by the IEEE, the higher of two Data-Link layer sublayers. LLC is responsible for error detection (but not correction), flow control, framing, and software-sublayer addressing. The predominant LLC protocol, IEEE 802.2, defines both connectionless and connection-oriented operations. *See also: Data Link layer* and *MAC.*

LMI An enhancement to the original Frame Relay specification. Among the features it provides are a keepalive mechanism, a multicast mechanism, global addressing, and a status mechanism.

LNNI LAN Emulation Network-to-Network Interface: In the Phase 2 LANE specification, an interface that supports communication between the server components within one ELAN.

local explorer packet In a Token Ring SRB network, a packet generated by an end system to find a host linked to the local ring. If no local host can be found, the end system will produce one of two solutions: a spanning explorer packet or an all-routes explorer packet.

local loop Connection from a demarcation point to the closest switching office.

LocalTalk Utilizing CSMA/CD, in addition to supporting data transmission at speeds of 230.4Kbps, LocalTalk is Apple Computer's proprietary baseband protocol, operating at the Data Link and Physical layers of the OSI reference model.

LSA link-state advertisement: Contained inside of link-state packets (LSPs), these advertisements are usually multicast packets, containing information about neighbors and path costs, that are employed by link-state protocols. Receiving routers use LSAs to maintain their link-state databases and, ultimately, routing tables.

LUNI LAN Emulation User-to-Network Interface: Defining the interface between the LAN Emulation Client (LEC) and the LAN Emulation Server, LUNI is the ATM Forum's standard for LAN Emulation on ATM networks. *See also: LES* and *LECS.*

MAC   Media Access Control: The lower sublayer in the Data Link layer, it is responsible for hardware addressing, media access, and error detection of frames. *See also: Data Link layer and LLC.*

MAC address   A Data-Link layer hardware address that every port or device needs in order to connect to a LAN segment. These addresses are used by various devices in the network for accurate location of logical addresses. MAC addresses are defined by the IEEE standard and their length is six characters, typically using the burned-in address (BIA) of the local LAN interface. Variously called hardware address, physical address, burned-in address, or MAC-layer address.

MacIP   In AppleTalk, the Network layer protocol encapsulating IP packets in Datagram Delivery Protocol (DDP) packets. MacIP also supplies substitute ARP services.

MAN   Metropolitan-Area Network: Any network that encompasses a metropolitan area; that is, an area typically larger than a LAN but smaller than a WAN. *See also: LAN.*

Manchester encoding   A method for digital coding in which a mid-bit–time transition is employed for clocking, and a 1 (one) is denoted by a high voltage level during the first half of the bit time. This scheme is used by Ethernet and IEEE 802.3.

maximum burst   Specified in bytes or cells, the largest burst of information exceeding the insured rate that will be permitted on an ATM permanent virtual connection for a short time and will not be dropped even if it goes over the specified maximum rate. *Compare with: insured burst. See also: maximum rate.*

maximum rate   The maximum permitted data throughput on a particular virtual circuit, equal to the total of insured and uninsured traffic from the traffic source. Should traffic congestion occur, uninsured information may be deleted from the path. Measured in bits or cells per second, the maximum rate represents the highest throughput of data the virtual circuit is ever able to deliver and cannot exceed the media rate. *Compare with: excess rate. See also: maximum burst.*

MBS   Maximum Burst Size: In an ATM signaling message, this metric, coded as a number of cells, is used to convey the burst tolerance.

MBONE   multicast backbone: The multicast backbone of the Internet, it is a virtual multicast network made up of multicast LANs, including point-to-point tunnels interconnecting them.

MCDV   Maximum Cell Delay Variation: The maximum two-point CDV objective across a link or node for the identified service category in an ATM network. The MCDV is one of four link metrics that are exchanged using PTSPs to verify the available resources of an ATM network. Only one MCDV value is assigned to each traffic class.

MCLR   Maximum Cell Loss Ratio: The maximum ratio of cells in an ATM network that fail to transit a link or node compared with the total number of cells that arrive at the link or node. MCDV is one of four link metrics that are exchanged using PTSPs to verify the available resources of an ATM network. The MCLR applies to cells in VBR and CBR traffic classes whose CLP bit is set to zero. *See also: CBR, CLP,* and *VBR.*

MCR   Minimum Cell Rate: A parameter determined by the ATM Forum for traffic management of the ATM networks. MCR is specifically defined for ABR transmissions and specifies the minimum value for the allowed cell rate (ACR). *See also: ACR* and *PCR.*

MCTD   Maximum Cell Transfer Delay: In an ATM network, the total of the maximum cell delay variation and the fixed delay across the link or node. MCTD is one of four link metrics that are exchanged using PNNI topology state packets to verify the available resources of an ATM network. There is one MCTD value assigned to each traffic class. *See also: MCDV.*

MIB   Management Information Base: Used with SNMP management software to gather information from remote devices. The management station can poll the remote device for information, or the MIB running on the remote station can be programmed to send information on a regular basis.

MIP   Multichannel Interface Processor: The resident interface processor on Cisco 7000 series routers, providing up to two channelized T1 or E1 connections by serial cables connected to a CSU. The two controllers are capable of providing 24 T1 or 30 E1 channel groups, with each group being introduced to the system as a serial interface that can be configured individually.

mips   millions of instructions per second: A measure of processor speed.

MLP   Multilink PPP: A technique used to split, recombine, and sequence datagrams across numerous logical data links.

MMP   Multichassis Multilink PPP: A protocol that supplies MLP support across multiple routers and access servers. MMP enables several routers and access servers to work as a single, large dial-up pool with one network address and ISDN access number. MMP successfully supports packet fragmenting and reassembly when the user connection is split between two physical access devices.

modem   modulator-demodulator: A device that converts digital signals to analog and vice-versa so that digital information can be transmitted over analog communication facilities, such as voice-grade telephone lines. This is achieved by converting digital signals at the source to analog for transmission and reconverting the analog signals back into digital form at the destination. *See also: modulation* and *demodulation.*

modem eliminator   A mechanism that makes possible a connection between two DTE devices without modems by simulating the commands and physical signaling required.

modulation   The process of modifying some characteristic of an electrical signal, such as amplitude (AM) or frequency (FM), in order to represent digital or analog information. *See also: AM.*

MOSPF   Multicast OSPF: An extension of the OSPF unicast protocol that enables IP multicast routing within the domain. *See also: OSPF.*

MPOA   Multiprotocol over ATM: An effort by the ATM Forum to standardize how existing and future Network-layer protocols such as IP, Ipv6, AppleTalk, and IPX run over an ATM network with directly attached hosts, routers, and multilayer LAN switches.

MTU   maximum transmission unit: The largest packet size, measured in bytes, that an interface can handle.

multicast   Broadly, any communication between a single sender and multiple receivers. Unlike broadcast messages, which are sent to all addresses on a network, multicast messages are sent to a defined subset of the network addresses; this subset has a group multicast address, which is specified in the packet's destination address field. *See also: broadcast, directed broadcast.*

multicast address   A single address that points to more than one device on the network by specifying a special non-existent MAC address specified in that particular multicast protocol. Identical to group address. *See also: multicast.*

multicast send VCC   A two-directional point-to-point virtual control connection (VCC) arranged by an LEC to a BUS, it is one of the three types of informational link specified by phase 1 LANE. *See also: control distribute VCC and control direct VCC.*

multilayer switch   A highly specialized, high-speed, hardware-based type of LAN router, the device filters and forwards packets based on their Layer 2 MAC addresses and Layer 3 network addresses. It's possible that even Layer 4 can be read. Sometimes called a Layer 3 switch. *See also: LAN switch.*

multiplexing   The process of converting several logical signals into a single physical signal for transmission across one physical channel. *Contrast with: demultiplexing.*

NAK   negative acknowledgment: A response sent from a receiver, telling the sender that the information was not received or contained errors. *Compare with: acknowledgment.*

NAT   Network Address Translation: An algorithm instrumental in minimizing the requirement for globally unique IP addresses, permitting an organization whose addresses are not all globally unique to connect to the Internet, regardless, by translating those addresses into globally routable address space.

NBP   Name Binding Protocol: In AppleTalk, the transport-level protocol that interprets a socket client's name, entered as a character string, into the corresponding DDP address. NBP gives AppleTalk protocols the capacity to discern user-defined zones and names of mechanisms by showing and keeping translation tables that map names to their corresponding socket addresses.

neighboring routers   Two routers in OSPF that have interfaces to a common network. On networks with multiaccess, these neighboring routers are dynamically discovered using the Hello protocol of OSPF.

NetBEUI NetBIOS Extended User Interface: An improved version of the NetBIOS protocol used in a number of network operating systems including LAN Manager, Windows NT, LAN Server, and Windows for Workgroups, implementing the OSI LLC2 protocol. NetBEUI formalizes the transport frame not standardized in NetBIOS and adds more functions. *See also: OSI.*

NetBIOS Network Basic Input/Output System: The API employed by applications residing on an IBM LAN to ask for services, such as session termination or information transfer, from lower-level network processes.

NetView A mainframe network product from IBM, used for monitoring SNA (Systems Network Architecture) networks. It runs as a VTAM (Virtual Telecommunications Access Method) application.

NetWare A widely used NOS created by Novell, providing a number of distributed network services and remote file access.

network address Used with the logical network addresses to identify the network segment in an internetwork. Logical addresses are hierarchical in nature and have at least two parts: network and host. An example of a hierarchical address is 172.16.10.5, where 172.16 is the network and 10.5 is the host address.

Network layer In the OSI reference model, it is Layer 3—the layer in which routing is implemented, enabling connections and path selection between two end systems. *See also: Application layer, Data Link layer, Physical layer, Presentation layer, Session layer,* and *Transport layer.*

NFS Network File System: One of the protocols in Sun Microsystems' widely used file system protocol suite, allowing remote file access across a network. The name is loosely used to refer to the entire Sun protocol suite, which also includes RPC, XDR (External Data Representation), and other protocols.

NHRP Next Hop Resolution Protocol: In a nonbroadcast multiaccess (NBMA) network, the protocol employed by routers in order to dynamically locate MAC addresses of various hosts and routers. It enables systems to communicate directly without requiring an intermediate hop, thus facilitating increased performance in ATM, Frame Relay, X.25, and SMDS systems.

NHS Next Hop Server: Defined by the NHRP protocol, this server maintains the next-hop resolution cache tables, listing IP-to-ATM address maps of related nodes and nodes that can be reached through routers served by the NHS.

NIC network interface card: An electronic circuit board placed in a computer. The NIC provides network communication to a LAN.

NLSP NetWare Link Services Protocol: Novell's link-state routing protocol, based on the IS-IS model.

NMP Network Management Processor: A Catalyst 5000 switch processor module used to control and monitor the switch.

node address Used to identify a specific device in an internetwork. Can be a hardware address, which is burned into the network interface card or a logical network address, which an administrator or server assigns to the node.

nondesignated port The Spanning-Tree Protocol tells a port on a layer-2 switch to stop transmitting and creating a network loop. Only designated ports can send frames.

non-stub area In OSPF, a resource-consuming area carrying a default route, intra-area routes, interarea routes, static routes, and external routes. Non-stub areas are the only areas that can have virtual links configured across them and exclusively contain an anonymous system boundary router (ASBR). *Compare with: stub area. See also: ASBR and OSPF.*

NRZ Nonreturn to Zero: One of several encoding schemes for transmitting digital data. NRZ signals sustain constant levels of voltage with no signal shifting (no return to zero-voltage level) during a bit interval. If there is a series of bits with the same value (1 or 0), there will be no state change. The signal is not self-clocking. *See also: NRZI.*

NRZI Nonreturn to Zero Inverted: One of several encoding schemes for transmitting digital data. A transition in voltage level (either from high to low or vice-versa) at the beginning of a bit interval is interpreted as a value of 1; the absence of a transition is interpreted as a 0. Thus, the voltage assigned to each value is continually inverted. NRZI signals are not self-clocking. *See also: NRZ.*

NT1   network termination 1: Is an ISDN designation to devices that understand ISDN standards.

NT2   network termination 2: Is an ISDN designation to devices that do not understand ISDN standards. To use an NT2, you must use a terminal adapter (TA).

NVRAM   Non-Volatile RAM: Random-access memory that keeps its contents intact while power is turned off.

OC   Optical Carrier: A series of physical protocols, designated as OC-1, OC-2, OC-3, and so on, for SONET optical signal transmissions. OC signal levels place STS frames on a multimode fiber-optic line at various speeds, of which 51.84Mbps is the lowest (OC-1). Each subsequent protocol runs at a speed divisible by 51.84. *See also: SONET.*

octet   Base-8 numbering system used to identify a section of a dotted decimal IP address. Also referred to as a byte.

100BaseT   Based on the IEEE 802.3u standard, 100BaseT is the Fast Ethernet specification of 100Mbps baseband that uses UTP wiring. 100BaseT sends link pulses (containing more information than those used in 10BaseT) over the network when no traffic is present. *See also: 10BaseT, Fast Ethernet,* and *IEEE 802.3.*

100BaseTX   Based on the IEEE 802.3u standard, 100BaseTX is the 100Mbps baseband Fast Ethernet specification that uses two pairs of UTP or STP wiring. The first pair of wires receives data; the second pair sends data. To ensure correct signal timing, a 100BaseTX segment cannot be longer than 100 meters.

ones density   Also known as pulse density, this is a method of signal clocking. The CSU/DSU retrieves the clocking information from data that passes through it. For this scheme to work, the data needs to be encoded to contain at least one binary 1 for each eight bits transmitted. *See also: CSU* and *DSU.*

OSI   Open System Interconnection: International standardization program designed by ISO and ITU-T for the development of data networking standards that make multivendor equipment interoperability a reality.

OSI reference model   Open System Interconnection reference model: A conceptual model defined by the International Organization for Standardization (ISO), describing how any combination of devices can be connected for the purpose of communication. The OSI model divides the task into seven functional layers, forming a hierarchy with the applications at the top and the physical medium at the bottom, and it defines the functions each layer must provide. *See also: Application layer, Data Link layer, Network layer, Physical layer, Presentation layer, Session layer,* and *Transport layer.*

OSPF   Open Shortest Path First: A link-state, hierarchical IGP routing algorithm derived from an earlier version of the IS-IS protocol, whose features include multipath routing, load balancing, and least-cost routing. OSPF is the suggested successor to RIP in the Internet environment. *See also: Enhanced IGRP, IGP,* and *IP.*

OUI   Organizationally Unique Identifier: Is assigned by the IEEE to an organization that makes network interface cards. The organization then puts this OUI on each and every card they manufacture. The OUI is 3 bytes (24 bits) long. The manufacturer then adds a 3-byte identifier to uniquely identify the host on an internetwork. The total length of the address is 48 bits (6 bytes) and is called a hardware address or MAC address.

out-of-band management   Management "outside" of the network's physical channels. For example, using a console connection not directly interfaced through the local LAN or WAN or a dial-in modem. *Compare to: in-band management.*

out-of-band signaling   Within a network, any transmission that uses physical channels or frequencies separate from those ordinarily used for data transfer. For example, the initial configuration of a Cisco Catalyst switch requires an out-of-band connection via a console port.

packet   In data communications, the basic logical unit of information transferred. A packet consists of a certain number of data bytes, wrapped or encapsulated in headers and/or trailers that contain information about where the packet came from, where it's going, and so on. The various protocols involved in sending a transmission add their own layers of header information, which the corresponding protocols in receiving devices then interpret.

packet switch   A physical device that makes it possible for a communication channel to share several connections, its functions include finding the most efficient transmission path for packets.

packet switching   A networking technology based on the transmission of data in packets. Dividing a continuous stream of data into small units—packets—enables data from multiple devices on a network to share the same communication channel simultaneously but also requires the use of precise routing information.

PAP   Password Authentication Protocol: In Point-to-Point Protocol (PPP) networks, a method of validating connection requests. The requesting (remote) device must send an authentication request, containing a password and ID, to the local router when attempting to connect. Unlike the more secure CHAP (Challenge Handshake Authentication Protocol), PAP sends the password unencrypted and does not attempt to verify whether the user is authorized to access the requested resource; it merely identifies the remote end. *See also: CHAP.*

parity checking   A method of error-checking in data transmissions. An extra bit (the parity bit) is added to each character or data word so that the sum of the bits will be either an odd number (in odd parity) or an even number (even parity).

partial mesh   A type of network topology in which some network nodes form a full mesh (where every node has either a physical or a virtual circuit linking it to every other network node), but others are attached to only one or two nodes in the network. A typical use of partial-mesh topology is in peripheral networks linked to a fully meshed backbone. *See also: full mesh.*

PCR   Peak Cell Rate: As defined by the ATM Forum, the parameter specifying, in cells per second, the maximum rate at which a source may transmit.

PDN   Public Data Network: Generally for a fee, a PDN offers the public access to computer communication network operated by private concerns or government agencies. Small organizations can take advantage of PDNs, aiding them creating WANs without investing in long-distance equipment and circuitry.

PGP   Pretty Good Privacy: A popular public-key/private-key encryption application offering protected transfer of files and messages.

Physical layer   The lowest layer—Layer 1—in the OSI reference model, it is responsible for converting data packets from the Data Link layer (Layer 2) into electrical signals. Physical-layer protocols and standards define, for example, the type of cable and connectors to be used, including their pin assignments and the encoding scheme for signaling 0 and 1 values. *See also: Application layer, Data Link layer, Network layer, Presentation layer, Session layer,* and *Transport layer.*

ping   packet Internet groper: A Unix-based Internet diagnostic tool, consisting of a message sent to test the accessibility of a particular device on the IP network. The acronym (from which the "full name" was formed) reflects the underlying metaphor of submarine sonar. Just as the sonar operator sends out a signal and waits to hear it echo ("ping") back from a submerged object, the network user can ping another node on the network and wait to see if it responds.

pleisochronous   Nearly synchronous, except that clocking comes from an outside source instead of being embedded within the signal as in synchronous transmissions.

PLP   Packet Level Protocol: Occasionally called X.25 Level 3 or X.25 Protocol, a Network-layer protocol that is part of the X.25 stack.

PNNI   Private Network-Network Interface: An ATM Forum specification for offering topology data used for the calculation of paths through the network, among switches and groups of switches. It is based on well-known link-state routing procedures and allows for automatic configuration in networks whose addressing scheme is determined by the topology.

point-to-multipoint connection   In ATM, a communication path going only one way, connecting a single system at the starting point, called the "root node," to systems at multiple points of destination, called "leaves." *See also: point-to-point connection.*

point-to-point connection   In ATM, a channel of communication that can be directed either one way or two ways between two ATM end systems. *See also: point-to-multipoint connection.*

poison reverse updates   These update messages are transmitted by a router back to the originator (thus ignoring the split-horizon rule) after route poisoning has occurred. Typically used with DV routing protocols in order to overcome large routing loops and offer explicit information when a subnet or network is not accessible (instead of merely suggesting that the network is unreachable by not including it in updates). *See also: route poisoning.*

polling   The procedure of orderly inquiry, used by a primary network mechanism, to determine if secondary devices have data to transmit. A message is sent to each secondary, granting the secondary the right to transmit.

POP   1) Point Of Presence: The physical location where an interexchange carrier has placed equipment to interconnect with a local exchange carrier. 2) Post Office Protocol (currently at version 3): A protocol used by client e-mail applications for recovery of mail from a mail server.

port security   Used with layer-2 switches to provide some security. Not typically used in production because it is difficult to manage. Allows only certain frames to traverse administrator-assigned segments.

PDU   Protocol Data Unit: Is the name of the processes at each layer of the OSI model. PDUs at the Transport layer are called segments; PDUs at the Network layer are called packets or datagrams; and PDUs at the Data Link layer are called frames. The Physical layer uses bits.

PPP   Point-to-Point Protocol: The protocol most commonly used for dial-up Internet access, superseding the earlier SLIP. Its features include address notification, authentication via CHAP or PAP, support for multiple protocols, and link monitoring. PPP has two layers: the Link Control Protocol (LCP) establishes, configures, and tests a link; and then any of various Network Control Programs (NCPs) transport traffic for a specific protocol suite, such as IPX. *See also: CHAP, PAP,* and *SLIP.*

Presentation layer   Layer 6 of the OSI reference model, it defines how data is formatted, presented, encoded, and converted for use by software at the Application layer. *See also: Application layer, Data Link layer, Network layer, Physical layer, Session layer,* and *Transport layer.*

PRI   Primary Rate Interface: A type of ISDN connection between a PBX and a long-distance carrier, which is made up of a single 64Kbps D channel in addition to 23 (T1) or 30 (E1) B channels. *See also: ISDN.*

priority queueing   A routing function in which frames temporarily placed in an interface output queue are assigned priorities based on traits such as packet size or type of interface.

process switching   As a packet arrives on a router to be forwarded, it's copied to the router's process buffer, and the router performs a lookup on the Layer 3 address. Using the route table, an exit interface is associated with the destination address. The processor forwards the packet with the added new information to the exit interface, while the router initializes the fast-switching cache. Subsequent packets bound for the same destination address follow the same path as the first packet.

PROM   programmable read-only memory: ROM that is programmable only once, using special equipment. *Compare with: EPROM.*

propagation delay   The time it takes data to traverse a network from its source to its destination.

protocol   In networking, the specification of a set of rules for a particular type of communication. The term is also used to refer to the software that implements a protocol.

protocol stack   A collection of related protocols.

PSE   Packet Switch Exchange: The X.25 term for a switch.

PSN   packet-switched network: Any network that uses packet-switching technology. Also known as packet-switched data network (PSDN). *See also: packet switching.*

PSTN   Public Switched Telephone Network: Colloquially referred to as "plain old telephone service" (POTS). A term that describes the assortment of telephone networks and services available globally.

PVC   permanent virtual circuit: In a Frame-Relay network, a logical connection, defined in software, that is maintained permanently. *Compare with: SVC. See also: virtual circuit.*

PVP   permanent virtual path: A virtual path made up of PVCs. *See also: PVC.*

PVP tunneling   permanent virtual path tunneling: A technique that links two private ATM networks across a public network using a virtual path; wherein the public network transparently trunks the complete collection of virtual channels in the virtual path between the two private networks.

QoS   Quality of Service: A set of metrics used to measure the quality of transmission and service availability of any given transmission system.

queue   Broadly, any list of elements arranged in an orderly fashion and ready for processing, such as a line of people waiting to enter a movie theater. In routing, it refers to a backlog of information packets waiting in line to be transmitted over a router interface.

R reference point   Used with ISDN networks to identify the connection between an NT1 and an S/T device. The S/T device converts the 4-wire network to the two-wire ISDN standard network.

RAM   random access memory: Used by all computers to store information. Cisco routers use RAM to store packet buffers and routing tables, along with the hardware addresses cache.

RARP   Reverse Address Resolution Protocol: The protocol within the TCP/IP stack that maps MAC addresses to IP addresses. *See also: ARP.*

rate queue   A value, assigned to one or more virtual circuits, that specifies the speed at which an individual virtual circuit will transmit data to the remote end. Every rate queue identifies a segment of the total bandwidth available on an ATM link. The sum of all rate queues should not exceed the total available bandwidth.

RCP   Remote Copy Protocol: A protocol for copying files to or from a file system that resides on a remote server on a network, using TCP to guarantee reliable data delivery.

redistribution   Command used in Cisco routers to inject the paths found from one type of routing protocol into another type of routing protocol. For example, networks found by RIP can be inserted into an IGRP network.

redundancy   In internetworking, the duplication of connections, devices, or services that can be used as a backup in the event that the primary connections, devices, or services fail.

RJ connector   registered jack connector: Is used with twisted-pair wiring to connect the copper wire to network interface cards, switches, and hubs.

reload   An event or command that causes Cisco routers to reboot.

RIF   Routing Information Field: In source-route bridging, a header field that defines the path direction of the frame or token. If the Route Information Indicator (RII) bit is not set, the RIF is read from source to destination (left to right). If the RII bit is set, the RIF is read from the destination back to the source, so the RIF is read right to left. It is defined as part of the Token Ring frame header for source-routed frames, which contains path information.

ring   Two or more stations connected in a logical circular topology. In this topology, which is the basis for Token Ring, FDDI, and CDDI, information is transferred from station to station in sequence.

ring topology   A network logical topology comprising a series of repeaters that form one closed loop by connecting unidirectional transmission links. Individual stations on the network are connected to the network at a repeater. Physically, ring topologies are generally organized in a closed-loop star. *Compare with: bus topology* and *star topology.*

RIP   Routing Information Protocol: The most commonly used interior gateway protocol in the Internet. RIP employs hop count as a routing metric. *See also: Enhanced IGRP, IGP, OSPF,* and *hop count.*

ROM   read-only memory: Chip used in computers to help boot the device. Cisco routers use a ROM chip to load the bootstrap, which runs a power-on self test, and then find and load the IOS in flash memory by default.

root bridge   Used with the Spanning-Tree Protocol to stop network loops from occurring. The root bridge is elected by having the lowest bridge ID. The bridge ID is determined by the priority (32,768 by default on all bridges and switches) and the main hardware address of the device. The root bridge determines which of the neighboring layer-2 devices' interfaces become the designated and nondesignated ports.

routed protocol   Routed protocols (such as IP and IPX) are used to transmit user data through an internetwork. By contrast, routing protocols (such as RIP, IGRP, and OSPF) are used to update routing tables between routers.

route poisoning   Used by various DV routing protocols in order to overcome large routing loops and offer explicit information about when a subnet or network is not accessible (instead of merely suggesting that the network is unreachable by not including it in updates). Typically, this is accomplished by setting the hop count to one more than maximum. *See also: poison reverse updates.*

route summarization   In various routing protocols, such as OSPF, EIGRP, and IS-IS, the consolidation of publicized subnetwork addresses so that a single summary route is advertised to other areas by an area border router.

router   A Network-layer mechanism, either software or hardware, using one or more metrics to decide on the best path to use for transmission of network traffic. Sending packets between networks by routers is based on the information provided on Network layers. Historically, this device has sometimes been called a gateway.

routing   The process of forwarding logically addressed packets from their local subnetwork toward their ultimate destination. In large networks, the numerous intermediary destinations a packet might travel before reaching its destination can make routing very complex.

routing domain   Any collection of end systems and intermediate systems that operate under an identical set of administrative rules. Every routing domain contains one or several areas, all individually given a certain area address.

routing metric   Any value that is used by routing algorithms to determine whether one route is superior to another. Metrics include such information as bandwidth, delay, hop count, path cost, load, MTU, reliability, and communication cost. Only the best possible routes are stored in the routing table, while all other information may be stored in link-state or topological databases. *See also: cost.*

routing protocol   Any protocol that defines algorithms to be used for updating routing tables between routers. Examples include IGRP, RIP, and OSPF.

routing table A table kept in a router or other internetworking mechanism that maintains a record of only the best possible routes to certain network destinations and the metrics associated with those routes.

RP Route Processor: Also known as a supervisory processor, a module on Cisco 7000 series routers that holds the CPU, system software, and most of the memory components used in the router.

RSP Route/Switch Processor: A processor module combining the functions of RP and SP used in Cisco 7500 series routers. *See also: RP and SP.*

RTS Request To Send: An EIA/TIA-232 control signal requesting permission to transmit data on a communication line.

S reference point ISDN reference point that works with a T reference point to convert a 4-wire ISDN network to the 2-wire ISDN network needed to communicate with the ISDN switches at the network provider.

sampling rate The rate at which samples of a specific waveform amplitude are collected within a specified period of time.

SAP 1) Service Access Point: A field specified by IEEE 802.2 that is part of an address specification. 2) Service Advertising Protocol: The Novell NetWare protocol that supplies a way to inform network clients of resources and services availability on network, using routers and servers. *See also: IPX.*

SCR Sustainable Cell Rate: An ATM Forum parameter used for traffic management, it is the long-term average cell rate for VBR connections that can be transmitted.

SDLC Synchronous Data Link Control: A protocol used in SNA Data-Link layer communications. SDLC is a bit-oriented, full-duplex serial protocol that is the basis for several similar protocols, including HDLC and LAPB. *See also: HDLC and LAPB.*

seed router In an AppleTalk network, the router that is equipped with the network number or cable range in its port descriptor. The seed router specifies the network number or cable range for other routers in that network section and answers to configuration requests from nonseed routers on its connected AppleTalk network, permitting those routers to affirm or modify their configurations accordingly. Every AppleTalk network needs at least one seed router physically connected to each network segment.

server   Hardware and software that provide network services to clients.

set-based   Set-based routers and switches use the `set` command to configure devices. Cisco is moving away from set-based commands and is using the Command-Line Interface (CLI) on all new devices.

Session layer   Layer 5 of the OSI reference model, responsible for creating, managing, and terminating sessions between applications and overseeing data exchange between Presentation layer entities. *See also: Application layer, Data Link layer, Network layer, Physical layer, Presentation layer,* and *Transport layer.*

setup mode   Mode that a router will enter if no configuration is found in nonvolatile RAM when the router boots. Allows the administrator to configure a router step-by-step. Not as robust or flexible as the Command-Line Interface.

SF   super frame: A super frame (also called a D4 frame) consists of 12 frames with 192 bits each, and the 193rd bit providing other functions including error checking. SF is frequently used on T1 circuits. A newer version of the technology is Extended Super Frame (ESF), which uses 24 frames. *See also: ESF.*

signaling packet   An informational packet created by an ATM-connected mechanism that wants to establish connection with another such mechanism. The packet contains the QoS parameters needed for connection and the ATM NSAP address of the endpoint. The endpoint responds with a message of acceptance if it is able to support the desired QoS, and the connection is established. *See also: QoS.*

silicon switching   A type of high-speed switching used in Cisco 7000 series routers, based on the use of a separate processor (the Silicon Switch Processor, or SSP). *See also: SSE.*

simplex   The mode at which data or a digital signal is transmitted. Simplex is a way of transmitting in only one direction. Half duplex transmits in two directions but only one direction at a time. Full duplex transmits both directions simultaneously.

sliding window   The method of flow control used by TCP, as well as several Data-Link layer protocols. This method places a buffer between the receiving application and the network data flow. The "window" available for accepting data is the size of the buffer minus the amount of data already there. This window increases in size as the application reads data from it and decreases as new data is sent. The receiver sends the transmitter announcements of the current window size, and it may stop accepting data until the window increases above a certain threshold.

SLIP   Serial Line Internet Protocol: An industry standard serial encapsulation for point-to-point connections that supports only a single routed protocol, TCP/IP. SLIP is the predecessor to PPP. *See also: PPP.*

SMDS   Switched Multimegabit Data Service: A packet-switched, datagram-based WAN networking technology offered by telephone companies that provides high speed.

SMTP   Simple Mail Transfer Protocol: A protocol used on the Internet to provide electronic mail services.

SNA   System Network Architecture: A complex, feature-rich, network architecture similar to the OSI reference model but with several variations; created by IBM in the 1970s and essentially composed of seven layers.

SNAP   Subnetwork Access Protocol: SNAP is a frame used in Ethernet, Token Ring, and FDDI LANs. Data transfer, connection management, and QoS selection are three primary functions executed by the SNAP frame.

socket   1) A software structure that operates within a network device as a destination point for communications. 2) In AppleTalk networks, an entity at a specific location within a node; AppleTalk sockets are conceptually similar to TCP/IP ports.

SONET   Synchronous Optical Network: The ANSI standard for synchronous transmission on fiber-optic media, developed at Bell Labs. It specifies a base signal rate of 51.84Mbps and a set of multiples of that rate, known as Optical Carrier levels, up to 2.5Gbps.

SP   Switch Processor: Also known as a ciscoBus controller, it is a Cisco 7000 series processor module acting as governing agent for all CxBus activities.

span A full-duplex digital transmission line connecting two facilities.

SPAN Switched Port Analyzer: A feature of the Catalyst 5000 switch, offering freedom to manipulate within a switched Ethernet environment by extending the monitoring ability of the existing network analyzers into the environment. At one switched segment, the SPAN mirrors traffic onto a predetermined SPAN port, while a network analyzer connected to the SPAN port is able to monitor traffic from any other Catalyst switched port.

spanning explorer packet Sometimes called limited-route or single-route explorer packet, it pursues a statically configured spanning tree when searching for paths in a source-route bridging network. *See also: all-routes explorer packet, explorer packet,* and *local explorer packet.*

spanning tree A subset of a network topology, within which no loops exist. When bridges are interconnected into a loop, the bridge, or switch, cannot identify a frame that has been forwarded previously, so there is no mechanism for removing a frame as it passes the interface numerous times. Without a method of removing these frames, the bridges continuously forward them—consuming bandwidth and adding overhead to the network. Spanning trees prune the network to provide only one path for any packet. *See also: Spanning-Tree Protocol and spanning tree algorithm.*

spanning-tree algorithm (STA) An algorithm that creates a spanning tree using the Spanning-Tree Protocol (STP). *See also: spanning-tree* and *Spanning-Tree Protocol.*

Spanning-Tree Protocol (STP) The bridge protocol (IEEE 802.1d) that enables a learning bridge to dynamically avoid loops in the network topology by creating a spanning tree using the spanning-tree algorithm. Spanning-tree frames called bridge protocol data units (BPDUs) are sent and received by all switches in the network at regular intervals. The switches participating in the spanning tree don't forward the frames; instead, they're processed to determine the spanning-tree topology itself. Cisco Catalyst series switches use STP 802.1d to perform this function. *See also: BPDU, learning bridge, MAC address, spanning tree,* and *spanning-tree algorithm.*

SPF Shortest Path First algorithm: A routing algorithm used to decide on the shortest-path spanning tree. Sometimes called Dijkstra's algorithm and frequently used in link-state routing algorithms. *See also: link-state routing algorithm.*

SPID Service Profile Identifier: A number assigned by service providers or local telephone companies and assigned by administrators to a BRI port. SPIDs are used to determine subscription services of a device connected via ISDN. ISDN devices use SPID when accessing the telephone company switch that initializes the link to a service provider.

split horizon Useful for preventing routing loops, a type of distance-vector routing rule where information about routes is prevented from leaving the router interface through which that information was received.

spoofing 1) In dial-on-demand routing (DDR), where a circuit-switched link is taken down to save toll charges when there is no traffic to be sent, spoofing is a scheme used by routers that causes a host to treat an interface as if it were functioning and supporting a session. The router pretends to send "spoof" replies to keepalive messages from the host in an effort to convince the host that the session is up and running. *See also: DDR.* 2) The illegal act of sending a packet labeled with a false address, in order to deceive network security mechanisms such as filters and access lists.

spooler A management application that processes requests submitted to it for execution in a sequential fashion from a queue. A good example is a print spooler.

SPX Sequenced Packet Exchange: A Novell NetWare transport protocol that augments the datagram service provided by Network layer (Layer 3) protocols, it was derived from the Switch-to-Switch Protocol of the XNS protocol suite.

SQE Signal Quality Error: In an Ethernet network, a message sent from a transceiver to an attached machine that the collision-detection circuitry is working.

SRB Source-Route Bridging: Created by IBM, the bridging method used in Token-Ring networks. The source determines the entire route to a destination before sending the data and includes that information in route information fields (RIF) within each packet. *Contrast with: transparent bridging.*

SRT source-route transparent bridging: A bridging scheme developed by IBM, merging source-route and transparent bridging. SRT takes advantage of both technologies in one device, fulfilling the needs of all end nodes. Translation between bridging protocols is not necessary. *Compare with: SR/TLB.*

SR/TLB source-route translational bridging: A bridging method that allows source-route stations to communicate with transparent bridge stations aided by an intermediate bridge that translates between the two bridge protocols. Used for bridging between Token Ring and Ethernet. *Compare with: SRT.*

SSAP Source Service Access Point: The SAP of the network node identified in the Source field of the packet. *See also: DSAP and SAP.*

SSE Silicon Switching Engine: The software component of Cisco's silicon switching technology, hard-coded into the Silicon Switch Processor (SSP). Silicon switching is available only on the Cisco 7000 with an SSP. Silicon-switched packets are compared to the silicon-switching cache on the SSE. The SSP is a dedicated switch processor that offloads the switching process from the route processor, providing a fast-switching solution, but packets must still traverse the backplane of the router to get to the SSP and then back to the exit interface.

standard IP access list IP access list that uses only the source IP addresses to filter a network.

standard IPX access list IPX access list that uses only the source and destination IPX address to filter a network.

star topology A LAN physical topology with endpoints on the network converging at a common central switch (known as a hub) using point-to-point links. A logical ring topology can be configured as a physical star topology using a unidirectional closed-loop star rather than point-to-point links. That is, connections within the hub are arranged in an internal ring. *See also: bus topology and ring topology.*

startup range If an AppleTalk node does not have a number saved from the last time it was booted, then the node selects from the range of values from 65280 to 65534.

state transitions Digital signaling scheme that reads the "state" of the digital signal in the middle of the bit cell. If it is five volts, the cell is read as a one. If the state of the digital signal is zero volts, the bit cell is read as a zero.

static route A route whose information is purposefully entered into the routing table and takes priority over those chosen by dynamic routing protocols.

static VLANs   Static VLANs are manually configured port-by-port. This is the method typically used in production networks.

statistical multiplexing   Multiplexing in general is a technique that allows data from multiple logical channels to be sent across a single physical channel. Statistical multiplexing dynamically assigns bandwidth only to input channels that are active, optimizing available bandwidth so that more devices can be connected than with other multiplexing techniques. Also known as statistical time-division multiplexing or stat mux.

STM-1   Synchronous Transport Module Level 1. In the European SDH standard, one of many formats identifying the frame structure for the 155.52Mbps lines that are used to carry ATM cells.

store-and-forward packet switching   A technique in which the switch first copies each packet into its buffer and performs a cyclical redundancy check (CRC). If the packet is error-free, the switch then looks up the destination address in its filter table, determines the appropriate exit port, and sends the packet.

STP   1) Shielded Twisted Pair: A two-pair wiring scheme, used in many network implementations, that has a layer of shielded insulation to reduce EMI. 2) Spanning-Tree Protocol.

stub area   An OSPF area carrying a default route, intra-area routes, and interarea routes, but no external routes. Configuration of virtual links cannot be achieved across a stub area, and stub areas are not allowed to contain an ASBR. *See also: non-stub area, ASBR,* and *OSPF.*

stub network   A network having only one connection to a router.

STUN   Serial Tunnel: A technology used to connect an HDLC link to an SDLC link over a serial link.

subarea   A portion of an SNA network made up of a subarea node and its attached links and peripheral nodes.

subarea node   An SNA communications host or controller that handles entire network addresses.

subchannel   A frequency-based subdivision that creates a separate broadband communications channel.

subinterface   One of many virtual interfaces available on a single physical interface.

subnet   *See: subnetwork.*

subnet address   The portion of an IP address that is specifically identified by the subnet mask as the subnetwork. *See also: IP address, subnetwork,* and *subnet mask.*

subnet mask   Also simply known as mask, a 32-bit address mask used in IP to identify the bits of an IP address that are used for the subnet address. Using a mask, the router does not need to examine all 32 bits, only those selected by the mask. *See also: address mask* and *IP address.*

subnetwork   1) Any network that is part of a larger IP network and is identified by a subnet address. A network administrator segments a network into subnetworks in order to provide a hierarchical, multilevel routing structure, and at the same time protect the subnetwork from the addressing complexity of networks that are attached. Also known as a subnet. *See also: IP address, subnet mask,* and *subnet address.* 2) In OSI networks, the term specifically refers to a collection of ESs and ISs controlled by only one administrative domain, using a solitary network connection protocol.

SVC   switched virtual circuit: A dynamically established virtual circuit, created on demand and dissolved as soon as transmission is over and the circuit is no longer needed. In ATM terminology, it is referred to as a switched virtual connection. *See also: PVC.*

switch   1) In networking, a device responsible for multiple functions such as filtering, flooding, and sending frames. It works using the destination address of individual frames. Switches operate at the Data Link layer of the OSI model. 2) Broadly, any electronic/mechanical device allowing connections to be established as needed and terminated if no longer necessary.

switch fabric   Term used to identify a layer-2 switched internetwork with many switches.

switched LAN   Any LAN implemented using LAN switches. *See also: LAN switch.*

synchronous transmission   Signals transmitted digitally with precision clocking. These signals have identical frequencies and contain individual characters encapsulated in control bits (called start/stop bits) that designate the beginning and ending of each character. *See also: asynchronous transmission* and *isochronous transmission.*

T reference point   Used with an S reference point to change a 4-wire ISDN network to a 2-wire ISDN network.

T1   Digital WAN that uses 24 DS0s at 64K each to create a bandwidth of 1.536Mbps, minus clocking overhead, providing 1.544Mbps of usable bandwidth.

T3   Digital WAN that can provide bandwidth of 44.763Mbps.

tag switching   Based on the concept of label swapping, where packets or cells are designated to defined-length labels that control the manner in which data is to be sent, tag switching is a high-performance technology used for forwarding packets. It incorporates Data-Link layer (Layer 2) switching and Network layer (Layer 3) routing and supplies scalable, high-speed switching in the network core.

tagged traffic   ATM cells with their cell loss priority (CLP) bit set to 1. Also referred to as discard-eligible (DE) traffic. Tagged traffic can be eliminated in order to ensure trouble-free delivery of higher priority traffic, if the network is congested. *See also: CLP.*

TCP   Transmission Control Protocol: A connection-oriented protocol that is defined at the Transport layer of the OSI reference model. Provides reliable delivery of data.

TCP/IP   Transmission Control Protocol/Internet Protocol. The suite of protocols underlying the Internet. TCP and IP are the most widely known protocols in that suite. *See also: IP* and *TCP.*

TDM   time division multiplexing: A technique for assigning bandwidth on a single wire, based on preassigned time slots, to data from several channels. Bandwidth is allotted to each channel regardless of a station's ability to send data. *See also: ATDM, FDM,* and *multiplexing.*

TE terminal equipment: Any peripheral device that is ISDN-compatible and attached to a network, such as a telephone or computer. TE1s are devices that are ISDN-ready and understand ISDN signaling techniques. TE2s are devices that are not ISDN-ready and do not understand ISDN signaling techniques. A terminal adapter must be used with a TE2.

TE1 A device with a four-wire, twisted-pair digital interface is referred to as terminal equipment type 1. Most modern ISDN devices are of this type.

TE2 Devices known as terminal equipment type 2 do not understand ISDN signaling techniques, and a terminal adapter must be used to convert the signaling.

telco A common abbreviation for the telephone company.

Telnet The standard terminal emulation protocol within the TCP/IP protocol stack. Method of remote terminal connection, enabling users to log in on remote networks and use those resources as if they were locally connected. Telnet is defined in RFC 854.

10BaseT Part of the original IEEE 802.3 standard, 10BaseT is the Ethernet specification of 10Mbps baseband that uses two pairs of twisted-pair, Category 3, 4, or 5 cabling—using one pair to send data and the other to receive. 10BaseT has a distance limit of about 100 meters per segment. *See also: Ethernet* and *IEEE 802.3*.

terminal adapter A hardware interface between a computer without a native ISDN interface and an ISDN line. In effect, a device to connect a standard async interface to a non-native ISDN device, emulating a modem.

terminal emulation The use of software, installed on a PC or LAN server, that allows the PC to function as if it were a "dumb" terminal directly attached to a particular type of mainframe.

TFTP Conceptually, a stripped-down version of FTP, it's the protocol of choice if you know exactly what you want and where it's to be found. TFTP doesn't provide the abundance of functions that FTP does. In particular, it has no directory browsing abilities; it can do nothing but send and receive files.

thicknet Also called 10Base5. Bus network that uses a thick cable and runs Ethernet up to 500 meters.

thinnet   Also called 10Base2. Bus network that uses a thin coax cable and runs Ethernet media access up to 185 meters.

token   A frame containing only control information. Possessing this control information gives a network device permission to transmit data onto the network. *See also: token passing.*

token bus   LAN architecture that is the basis for the IEEE 802.4 LAN specification and employs token passing access over a bus topology. *See also: IEEE.*

token passing   A method used by network devices to access the physical medium in a systematic way based on possession of a small frame called a token. *See also: token.*

Token Ring   IBM's token-passing LAN technology. It runs at 4Mbps or 16Mbps over a ring topology. Defined formally by IEEE 802.5. *See also: ring topology* and *token passing.*

toll network   WAN network that uses the Public Switched Telephone Network (PSTN) to send packets.

trace   IP command used to trace the path a packet takes through an internetwork.

transparent bridging   The bridging scheme used in Ethernet and IEEE 802.3 networks, it passes frames along one hop at a time, using bridging information stored in tables that associate end-node MAC addresses within bridge ports. This type of bridging is considered transparent because the source node does not know it has been bridged, because the destination frames are sent directly to the end node. *Contrast with: SRB.*

Transport layer   Layer 4 of the OSI reference model, used for reliable communication between end nodes over the network. The Transport layer provides mechanisms used for establishing, maintaining, and terminating virtual circuits, transport fault detection and recovery, and controlling the flow of information. *See also: Application layer, Data Link layer, Network layer, Physical layer, Presentation layer,* and *Session layer.*

TRIP Token Ring Interface Processor: A high-speed interface processor used on Cisco 7000 series routers. The TRIP provides two or four ports for interconnection with IEEE 802.5 and IBM media with ports set to speeds of either 4Mbps or 16Mbps set independently of each other.

trunk link Link used between switches and from some servers to the switches. Trunk links carry information about many VLANs. Access links are used to connect host devices to a switch and carry only VLAN information that the device is a member of.

TTL Time To Live: A field in an IP header, indicating the length of time a packet is valid.

TUD Trunk Up-Down: A protocol used in ATM networks for the monitoring of trunks. Should a trunk miss a given number of test messages being sent by ATM switches to ensure trunk line quality, TUD declares the trunk down. When a trunk reverses direction and comes back up, TUD recognizes that the trunk is up and returns the trunk to service.

tunneling A method of avoiding protocol restrictions by wrapping packets from one protocol in another protocol's packet and transmitting this encapsulated packet over a network that supports the wrapper protocol. *See also: encapsulation.*

U reference point Reference point between a TE1 and an ISDN network. The U reference point understands ISDN signaling techniques and uses a 2-wire connection.

UDP User Datagram Protocol: A connectionless Transport layer protocol in the TCP/IP protocol stack that simply allows datagrams to be exchanged without acknowledgements or delivery guarantees, requiring other protocols to handle error processing and retransmission. UDP is defined in RFC 768.

unnumbered frames HDLC frames used for control-management purposes, such as link startup and shutdown or mode specification.

UTP unshielded twisted-pair: Copper wiring used in small-to-large networks to connect host devices to hubs and switches. Also used to connect switch to switch or hub to hub.

VBR   Variable Bit Rate: A QoS class, as defined by the ATM Forum, for use in ATM networks that is subdivided into real time (RT) class and non-real time (NRT) class. RT is employed when connections have a fixed-time relationship between samples. Conversely, NRT is employed when connections do not have a fixed-time relationship between samples, but still need an assured QoS.

VCC   Virtual Channel Connection: A logical circuit that is created by VCLs. VCCs carry data between two endpoints in an ATM network. Sometimes called a virtual circuit connection.

VIP   1) Versatile Interface Processor: An interface card for Cisco 7000 and 7500 series routers, providing multilayer switching and running the Cisco IOS software. The most recent version of VIP is VIP2. 2) Virtual IP: A function making it possible for logically separated switched IP workgroups to run Virtual Networking Services across the switch ports of a Catalyst 5000.

virtual circuit   Abbreviated VC, a logical circuit devised to assure reliable communication between two devices on a network. Defined by a virtual path connection (VPC)/virtual path identifier (VCI) pair, a virtual circuit can be permanent (PVC) or switched (SVC). Virtual circuits are used in Frame Relay and X.25. Known as virtual channel in ATM. *See also: PVC and SVC.*

virtual ring   In an SRB network, a logical connection between physical rings, either local or remote.

VLAN   Virtual LAN: A group of devices on one or more logically segmented LANs (configured by use of management software), enabling devices to communicate as if attached to the same physical medium, when they are actually located on numerous different LAN segments. VLANs are based on logical instead of physical connections and thus are tremendously flexible.

VLSM   variable-length subnet mask: Helps optimize available address space and specify a different subnet mask for the same network number on various subnets. Also commonly referred to as "subnetting a subnet."

VTP   VLAN Trunk Protocol: Used to update switches in a switch fabric about VLANs configured on a VTP server. VTP devices can be a VTP server, client, or transparent device. Servers update clients. Transparent devices are only local devices and do not share information with VTP clients. VTPs send VLAN information down trunked links only.

WAN   wide area network: Is a designation used to connect LANs together across a DCE (data communications equipment) network. Typically, a WAN is a leased line or dial-up connection across a PSTN network. Examples of WAN protocols include Frame Relay, PPP, ISDN, and HDLC.

wildcard   Used with access-list, supernetting, and OSPF configurations. Wildcards are designations used to identify a range of subnets.

windowing   Flow-control method used with TCP at the Transport layer of the OSI model.

WinSock   Windows Socket Interface: A software interface that makes it possible for an assortment of applications to use and share an Internet connection. The WinSock software consists of a Dynamic Link Library (DLL) with supporting programs such as a dialer program that initiates the connection.

workgroup switching   A switching method that supplies high-speed (100Mbps) transparent bridging between Ethernet networks as well as high-speed translational bridging between Ethernet and CDDI or FDDI.

X.25   An ITU-T packet-relay standard that defines communication between DTE and DCE network devices. X.25 uses a reliable Data-Link layer protocol called LAPB. X.25 also uses PLP at the Network layer. X.25 has mostly been replaced by Frame Relay.

ZIP   Zone Information Protocol: A Session-layer protocol used by Apple-Talk to map network numbers to zone names. NBP uses ZIP in the determination of networks containing nodes that belong to a zone. *See also: ZIP storm and zone.*

ZIP storm   A broadcast storm occurring when a router running AppleTalk reproduces or transmits a route for which there is no corresponding zone name at the time of execution. The route is then forwarded by other routers downstream, thus causing a ZIP storm. *See also: broadcast storm and ZIP.*

zone   A logical grouping of network devices in AppleTalk. *See also: ZIP.*

Index

Note to the Reader: Page numbers in **bold** indicate the principal discussion of a topic or the definition of a term. Page numbers in *italic* indicate illustrations.

D

J

K

L

M

S

T

X

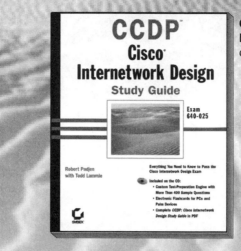

SYBEX BOOKS ON THE WEB

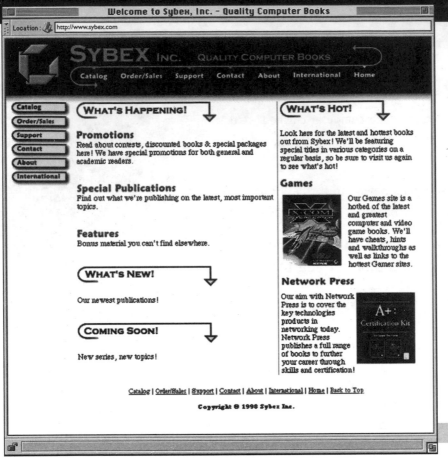
At the dynamic and informative Sybex Web site, you can:

- view our complete online catalog
- preview a book you're interested in
- access special book content

- order books online at special discount prices
- learn about Sybex

www.sybex.com

SYBEX Inc. • 1151 Marina Village Parkway, Alameda, CA 94501 • 510-523-8233

SYBEX